Aristophanes in Performance 421 BC–AD 2007
Peace, Birds and *Frogs*

LEGENDA

LEGENDA, founded in 1995 by the European Humanities Research Centre of the University of Oxford, is now a joint imprint of the Modern Humanities Research Association and Maney Publishing. Titles range from medieval texts to contemporary cinema and form a widely comparative view of the modern humanities, including works on Arabic, Catalan, English, French, German, Greek, Italian, Portuguese, Russian, Spanish, and Yiddish literature. An Editorial Board of distinguished academic specialists works in collaboration with leading scholarly bodies such as the Society for French Studies and the British Comparative Literature Association.

MHRA

The Modern Humanities Research Association (MHRA) encourages and promotes advanced study and research in the field of the modern humanities, especially modern European languages and literature, including English, and also cinema. It also aims to break down the barriers between scholars working in different disciplines and to maintain the unity of humanistic scholarship in the face of increasing specialization. The Association fulfils this purpose primarily through the publication of journals, bibliographies, monographs and other aids to research.

MANEY
publishing

Maney Publishing is one of the few remaining independent British academic publishers. Founded in 1900 the company has offices both in the UK, in Leeds and London, and in North America, in Boston. Since 1945 Maney Publishing has worked closely with learned societies, their editors, authors, and members, in publishing academic books and journals to the highest traditional standards of materials and production.

Design by Abd' Elkader Farrah for *The Burdies*, 1966

Aristophanes in Performance
421 BC–AD 2007

Peace, *Birds* and *Frogs*

❖

EDITED BY EDITH HALL AND AMANDA WRIGLEY

l

LEGENDA

Modern Humanities Research Association and Maney Publishing
2007

Published by the
Modern Humanities Research Association and Maney Publishing
1 Carlton House Terrace
London SW1Y 5DB
United Kingdom

LEGENDA is an imprint of the
Modern Humanities Research Association and Maney Publishing

Maney Publishing is the trading name of W. S. Maney & Son Ltd,
whose registered office is at Suite 1C, Joseph's Well, Hanover Walk, Leeds LS3 1AB

ISBN 9-781-904350-61-3

First published 2007

Printed in Great Britain

Cover: 875 Design

Copy-Editor: Dr Leofranc Holford-Strevens

CONTENTS

❖

ACKNOWLEDGEMENTS

❖

We are most grateful to the Arts and Humanties Research Council and the Leverhulme Trust, both of whom have supported the personnel of the Archive of Performances of Greek and Roman Drama (APGRD) at the University of Oxford in different ways from its inception in 1996.

This book arises out of a conference on 'Aristophanes Upstairs and Downstairs: *Peace*, *Birds* and *Frogs* in Ancient and Modern Performance', held at Magdalen College, Oxford, 16–18 September 2004. We thank the following bodies whose generous support made the conference possible: the British Academy; the Classical Association; the Society for the Promotion of Hellenic Studies; and, at the University of Oxford, the Craven Committee, the Faculty of Classics, and the Passmore Edwards Fund.

We thank all those who attended the conference, especially the speakers, many of whose papers form the basis of this volume. It is with great sadness that we record the deaths of two exceptional people associated with this conference: Margot Schmidt of Basel, who had agreed to deliver the opening paper but died earlier in 2004; and the theatre designer Abd' Elkader Farrah, who generously allowed us to use his original design for the 1966 Edinburgh production of *The Burdies* as the conference logo. We are grateful to his daughter Leylah Farrah for permitting us to reproduce it as the frontispiece to this volume. We especially wish to thank the following people for their help and support in various ways with the conference and the book: Eugenia Arsenis, James Baughan, Olympia Bobou, Piero Bordin, Erica Clarke, Elina Dagonaki, Catherine Hughes, Eleftheria Ioannidou, James Kilvington, Neil Leeder, Mike Poulton, Richard Poynder, Ghislaine Rowe, Barrie Rutter, Maggie Sasanow, Masaru Sekine, Gerry Wardle, and Chris Weaver.

The conference included a concert of five Aristophanic suites arranged by Benjamin Wardhaugh from music by Leonard Bernstein (*Birds*, 1939), Manos Hatzidakis (*Birds*, 1959), Dudley Moore (*Birds*, 1959), J. R. Planché (*Birds*, 1846), and Stephen Sondheim (*Frogs*, 1974). We are grateful to Boosey & Hawkes, Josef Weinberger Ltd, the Leonard Bernstein Office Inc., and the estate of Manos Hatzidakis for granting permission for the performance of extracts from these works on that occasion. For their hard work on this concert we are grateful to Ellen Wiles (producer), Benjamin Wardhaugh (arranger; bassoon), Peter Brown (voice), Helen Clarke (flute), Benjamin Skipp (oboe), Edward Littleton (clarinet), and Richard Ashby (sound engineer).

At Legenda Press we thank Graham Nelson for his enthusiasm for the project; without Leofranc Holford-Strevens's brilliant copy-editing it would have been much less accurate in every respect.

Last but no means least we offer warm thanks to our current colleagues at the APGRD, Peter Brown, Fiona Macintosh, Pantelis Michelakis, Scott Scullion, and Oliver Taplin, for their help and support with the conference and this volume.

LIST OF ILLUSTRATIONS

❖

Cover. Erich Heckel (1883–1970), 'Schüleraufführung "Die Vögel" des Aristophanes', 1932. Water and opaque colours on crayon, 55 × 69 cm. Gift of Siddi Heckel to the Brücke-Museum Berlin, 1970. © DACS (Design and Artists Copyright Society), London 2006. Reproduced by courtesy of the Erich Heckel Estate, Hemmenhofen.

Frontispiece. Design by Abd' Elkader Farrah (1926–2005) for a production of *The Burdies*, a Scots adaptation of *Birds* by Douglas Young, directed by Tom Fleming at the Edinburgh Festival, 1966. Reproduced by kind permission of Leila and Safi Farrah.

1.1. A Herakles figure approaches a door with his club, accompanied by a baggage-laden figure on a donkey, quite possibly reflecting the opening scene of *Frogs*. The 'Berlin Herakles' Apulian bell-krater (375–350 BC); formerly Berlin, Staatliche Museen F3046, destroyed or plundered. Photograph originally from Bieber (1920), pl. 80; reproduced from Taplin (1993), pl. 13.7.

1.2. Line-drawing of the 'Berlin Herakles'. Drawing from Panofka (1849), 17–20; reproduced from Taplin (1993), 46.

1.3. Frontispiece and title page from the 1692 edition of Anne Le Fèvre (by marriage Madame Dacier), *Comedies grecques d'Aristophane*. Reproduced by courtesy of the Bodleian Library, Oxford.

1.4. 'Goethe in Weimar', etching by Wilhelm von Kaulbach (1804–74), showing Goethe in Greek costume before the dowager duchess Anna Amalia (centre). Reproduced from Lewes (1867) by courtesy of the Bodleian Library, Oxford.

1.5. Etching of Fleeming Jenkin in his laboratory by William Hole, with comic and tragic masks hanging on the wall (by his right elbow), above acting editions of Sophocles and Aeschylus. Reproduced from Hole (1884), 107.

1.6. Etching by Henry Gillard Glindoni (1852–1913) of the 1883 *Birds* at the University of Cambridge, reproduced by courtesy of the Wellcome Library, London (image no. 32433i).

1.7. Sketch of the boys of Blackheath Proprietary School in *Acharnians*, 1883, reproduced by courtesy of the APGRD.

1.8. Trygaios (Simon Rhodes) and the chorus sing and dance (to music by Jamie Masters and John White) around Harvest (Annette Ross) and Festival (Gillian Forshaw) (standing l–r before Peace), as Hermes (Lawrence McGrandles Jr) looks on. Thiasos Theatre Company's *Peace* (2001) was translated by Douglass Parker, directed by Yana Zarifi and designed by Abd' Elkader Farrah. Reproduced by courtesy of Yana Zarifi and the Thiasos Theatre Company.

1.9. Aristophanes in Detroit: Mosaic Youth Theatre adapts *Peace* as a battle between love and hate in their eclectic musical piece *HeartBEAT*, 2002.

3.1. Euripides and Aristophanes: detail from the title page woodcut of Erasmus, *Adagiorum chiliades* (Basel: Froben, 1515), reproduced from *The Correspondence of Erasmus*, trans. R. A.

left) goad the Sausage-Seller (Augusto Masiello, second from right) to beat the Paphlagonian (Enzo Toma, right) in a verbal contest which is peppered with angry words and colourful expressions in Puglian slang. Photographed by Giacomo Gorini, and reproduced by courtesy of the photographer and Teatro delle Albe.

15.3. The *agōn* scene from *Wealth* in Marco Martinelli's production of *All'inferno!*: Moussa (Mandiaye N'Diaye; Chremylus in *Wealth*), pictured centre, is surprized to discover that his jenny-ass Farì (Ermanna Montanari) is actually the Goddess of Poverty — his worst enemy! — in disguise. Ironically, the poor man has to plead the cause of Wealth as a boxer, fighting with Poverty. After winning the match he celebrates with the musician/Dionysus (El Hadji Niang, left) and his servant Dara (Mor Awa Niang, right), but the victory is ambiguous and the worst is yet to come . . . Photographed by Maurizio Montanari, and reproduced by courtesy of the photographer and Teatro delle Albe.

16.1. One of the panels, showing a caricature of Umberto Bossi's face, which were to appear as part of the backdrop set of Luca Ronconi's *Frogs* (2002). Reproduced by courtesy of the Archivio Fotografico, Piccolo Teatro di Milano.

16.2. The Underworld as 'car-cemetery': car-wrecks lie before two of the four panels which were to appear on the set of Ronconi's *Frogs* (2002). The panels show caricatures of Silvio Berlusconi and Gianfranco Fini (l–r). Reproduced by courtesy of the Archivio Fotografico, Piccolo Teatro di Milano.

17.1. The chorus of *The Birds* 'in flight', in the translation by Sean O'Brien and directed by Kathryn Hunter (Royal National Theatre/Mamaloucos Circus, 2002). Photograph kindly supplied by the Royal National Theatre, and reproduced by courtesy of Stephen Vaughan.

17.2. *The Birds* as circus theatre; translated by Sean O'Brien and directed by Kathryn Hunter (Royal National Theatre/Mamaloucos Circus, 2002). Photograph kindly supplied by the Royal National Theatre, and reproduced by courtesy of Stephen Vaughan.

17.3. The descent of the Nightingale (Matilda Leyser) in *The Birds*, translated by Sean O'Brien and directed by Kathryn Hunter (Royal National Theatre/Mamaloucos Circus, 2002). Photograph kindly supplied by Mamaloucos, and reproduced by courtesy of Stephen Vaughan.

17.4. Eck (Mark Cronfield) and Pez (Leslie Simpson) struggle to interpret the birds' directions in threeovereden's 2006 production of Sean O'Brien's *The Birds*, directed by Bill Martin (Act 1, pp. 5–6). Photograph reproduced by courtesy of the theatre company and the photographer Holly Eve Watson.

17.5. Pez (Leslie Simpson) detains Iris (Sophie Scott) in threeovereden's 2006 production of Sean O'Brien's *The Birds*, directed by Bill Martin (Act 2, pp. 66–69). Photograph reproduced by courtesy of the theatre company and the photographer Holly Eve Watson.

18.1. The programme cover for the 1988 US tour of the King's College London production of *Frogs*. Reproduced by courtesy of Michael Silk.

18.2. Aeschylus (Jim Evans) *à la* Jolson and bemused frog chorus in front of Deco backcloth in the King's College London production of *Frogs* on its 1988 US tour. Reproduced by courtesy of Michael Silk.

19.1. The 1498 'Aldine Aristophanes', reproduced by courtesy of L. Tom Perry Special Collections, Harold B. Lee Library, Brigham Young University (classmark: Aldine Collection 1130 HBLL).

LIST OF CONTRIBUTORS

❖

Malika Bastin-Hammou is Maître de conférences at the University of Toulouse II — Le Mirail. She has published numerous articles on ancient drama and its reception, and has translated four ancient plays for the stage (Sophocles' *Antigone*, Euripides' *Iphigeneia among the Taurians*, Aristophanes' *Acharnians* and *Peace*). She is currently working on a book on ancient theories about comedy.

Ewen Bowie has taught Greek language and literature at Corpus Christi College, Oxford, as E. P. Warren Praelector in Classics since 1965. From 1968 to 1996 he was a University Lecturer, from 1996 to 2004 a Reader, and since 2004 a Professor of Classical Languages and Literature. Of his work more than half (some forty articles or chapters in collective works) has been on the Greek literature and culture of the Roman empire; he has also published substantially on the Greek poetry of the archaic period, especially elegiac and iambic, and ten or so articles on Old Comedy and on Hellenistic poetry. He is currently completing a commentary on Longus' *Daphnis and Chloe*.

Mary-Kay Gamel is Professor of Classics, Comparative Literature, and Theater Arts at the University of California, Santa Cruz. She has staged seventeen productions of Greek and Roman drama, often in her own translations or versions, and has directed works by O'Neill, Orff, Ayckbourn, and new scripts. She is the author of many articles and reviews on ancient drama in performance, Roman poetry, film, and the representation of the ancient Mediterranean in contemporary popular culture. She is co-author of *Women on the Edge: Four Plays by Euripides* (1999), and editor of a special issue of *American Journal of Philology*, 'Performing/Transforming Aristophanes' *Thesmophoriazousai*' (2002). She is currently working on concepts of authenticity in staging ancient Mediterranean drama.

Vasiliki Giannopoulou is currently a full-time mother. She has taught at the University of Oxford, where she studied for her D.Phil. at Somerville College and worked for the Archive of Performances of Greek and Roman Drama as a special researcher. Besides publishing articles on Euripides, she has written a book *Tyche: Fortune and Chance in Fifth-Century Tragedy and Historiography* forthcoming in the Oxford Classical Monographs series at Oxford University Press.

Edith Hall After holding appointments at the universities of Cambridge, Reading, Oxford and Durham, in 2006 Edith Hall was appointed Professor jointly in Classics and Drama at Royal Holloway, University of London. She is also co-founder and co-director of the Archive of Performances of Greek and Roman Drama at the University of Oxford. Her books include *Inventing the Barbarian* (1989), *Greek and Roman Actors* (2002, co-edited with Pat Easterling), *Greek Tragedy and the British*

Theatre (2005, with Fiona Macintosh), *The Theatrical Cast of Athens* (2006), and *The Return of Ulysses: A Cultural History of the Odyssey* (2007). She is working on a book entitled *Classics and Class*.

Sean O'Brien is a poet who lives in Newcastle. His *Cousin Coat: Selected Poems 1976–2001* (Picador) appeared in 2002. His essays *The Deregulated Muse* (Bloodaxe) and anthology *The Firebox: Poetry in Britain and Ireland after 1945* (Picador) were published in 1998. His plays have been staged by the National Theatre and Live Theatre / Royal Shakespeare Company. His version of Dante's *Inferno* was published by Picador in 2006. A new collection follows in 2007. Awards include the Forward Prize (twice) and the E. M. Forster Award. He writes for *The Independent*, *The Sunday Times* and *The Times Literary Supplement*. Formerly Professor of Poetry at Sheffield Hallam University, he is now Professor of Creative Writing at the University of Newcastle. Agent: Gerry Wardle, Triple PA (triplepa@blueyonder.co.uk).

Charalampos Orfanos has been Maître de conférences of Greek language and literature at the University of Toulouse II — Le Mirail since 1996. He is the author of *Les Sauvageons d'Athènes ou la didactique du rire chez Aristophane* (2006). He has also published a brief commentary on Aristophanes' *Wasps* (1998) and several articles.

Francesca Schironi is Assistant Professor of Classics at Harvard University, Cambridge, Massachusetts. Her main research area is ancient scholarship, in particular Aristarchus of Samothrace and the Hellenistic editions and commentaries of Homer and Greek classical authors. In addition to studying grammar and exegesis in the Hellenistic and Imperial periods, she is also interested in reception and performance studies, especially concerning Aristophanes, Greek drama, opera and Renaissance Italian theatre.

Bernd Seidensticker is Professor of Classics at the Freie Universität Berlin. His research centres on Greek and Roman Drama and on the reception of classical antiquity in contemporary literature. His publications include: *Die Gesprächsverdichtung in den Tragödien Senecas* (1969), *Palintonos Harmonia: Studien zu komischen Elementen in der griechischen Tragödie* (1982), *'Erinnern wird sich wohl mancher an uns … '*, *Studien zur Antikerezeption nach 1945* (2003), *Über das Vergnügen an tragischen Gegenständen. Studien zum antiken Drama* (2005). He has also coedited the following volumes: *Das griechische Satyrspiel* (1999, with Ralf Krumeich and Nikolaus Pechstein), *Mythen in nachmythischer Zeit: Die Antike in der deutschsprachigen Literatur der Gegenwart* (2002a, with Martin Vöhler), *Urgeschichten der Moderne: Die Antike im 20. Jahrhundert* (2002b, with Martin Vöhler), and *Mythenkorrekturen: Zu einer paradoxalen Form der Mythenrezeption* (2005, with Martin Vöhler and Wolfgang Emmerich).

Michael Silk was Professor of Greek Language and Literature at King's College London from 1991 to 2006, and is now Professor of Classical and Comparative Literature there; in recent years he has also been Visiting Professor at Boston University. Recent publications include: *Aristophanes and the Definition of Comedy* (2000/2002), *Homer, The Iliad* (2nd edn, 2004), *Alexandria, Real and Imagined* (ed. with Anthony Hirst, 2004). Research interests: poetry, tragedy, comedy, in theory and practice; Greek poetry and drama; literary theory, ancient and modern; the classical tradition.

Matthew Steggle is Senior Lecturer in English at Sheffield Hallam University. His research is in early modern English literature, including the early modern reception of classical drama. Publications include *Wars of the Theatres: The Poetics of Personation in the Age of Jonson* (1998); *Richard Brome: Place and Politics on the Caroline Stage* (2004); and articles on Milton's use of Greek tragedy in *A Masque at Ludlow Castle*.

Martina Treu teaches ancient theatre and works as a researcher at the IULM University in Milan (Libera Università di Lingue e Comunicazione). She is co-founder of the Centro di Ricerca Interdipartimentale Multimediale sul Teatro Antico at the University of Pavia (http://crimta.unipv.it) and has been Visiting Assistant Professor of Ancient Drama at the University of Venice for six years. She has worked with many theatre companies (e.g. Teatro Olimpico, Vicenza; Istituto Nazionale del Dramma Antico, Syracuse; Piccolo Teatro, Milan) and acted as dramaturge for several adaptations of classical texts on the Italian stage (*Appunti per un'Orestiade italiana*, 1999–2000; *Iliade-Troiane*, 2004–2005; *Repubblica da Platone*, 2003–2004). She has published on Aristophanes' chorus and satire (*Undici cori comici*, 1999), and on modern performance and reception of Greek drama (*Cosmopolitico: Il teatro greco sulla scena italiana contemporanea*, 2005).

Gonda Van Steen earned a BA degree in Classics in her native Belgium and a PhD degree in Classics and Hellenic Studies from Princeton University. As an Associate Professor in Classics and Modern Greek at the University of Arizona, she teaches courses in ancient and modern Greek language and literature. Her first book, *Venom in Verse: Aristophanes in Modern Greece*, published by Princeton University Press in 2000, was awarded the John D. Criticos Prize from the London Hellenic Society. She has also published articles on ancient Greek and late antique literature, on the reception of Greek tragedy, on Greek coinage, and on postwar Greek feminism. She is currently researching a book on theatre and censorship under the Greek military dictatorship of 1967–74.

Betine van Zyl Smit was appointed as a Senior Lecturer in the Classics Department of the University of Nottingham in 2006, having previously taught at the University of the Western Cape, the Rand Afrikaans University, and Stellenbosch University in South Africa for more than thirty years. One of her main research interests is the reception of Greek and Roman literature in South Africa on which she has published a number of articles and chapters, including 'The Reception of Greek Tragedy in the "Old" and the "New" South Africa' (2003); '*Antigone* in South Africa' (2006); '*Medea* in Afrikaans' (forthcoming); and 'Multicultural Reception: Greek Drama in South Africa in the Late 20th and Early 21st Centuries' (forthcoming).

Angeliki Varakis holds a PhD in Theatre from Royal Holloway, University of London and is a permanent Lecturer in the Department of Drama, Film and Visual Arts at the University of Kent at Canterbury. She has contributed an article to the electronic journal *Didaskalia* titled 'Research on the Ancient Mask' (2004); has written the commentary and notes for the Methuen Student Editions of *Antigone* (2006) and *Oedipus the King* (forthcoming); and is contributing a chapter to the forthcoming Blackwell *Companion to Classical Reception*. She has actively participated in a series of practice-based research projects involving the mask. In 2002 she was appointed key organiser of the international conference 'The Greek Theatre Mask in Ancient and Modern Performance', organized by Royal Holloway, University of London in collaboration with the University of Glasgow.

Phiroze Vasunia is Reader in the Department of Classics at the University of Reading. He is the author of *The Gift of the Nile: Hellenizing Egypt from Aeschylus to Alexander* (2001) and a forthcoming book on the religion of ancient Persia. He is currently investigating the relationship between Classics and the British empire in the nineteenth and twentieth centuries and has written numerous essays on the subject.

Amanda Wrigley is Researcher at the APGRD at the University of Oxford, where she is also Research Associate of the Faculty of Classics. She is a Classics graduate and qualified librarian who specializes in the archival investigation of theatre history. At the APGRD she is editor of the APGRD Database of Modern Performances of Ancient Drama (www.apgrd.ox.ac.uk/database). She is co-editor of *Dionysus Since 69: Greek Tragedy at the Dawn of the Third Millennium* (2004, with Edith Hall and Fiona Macintosh). Her research focuses on the popular reception of ancient Greek tragedy — as an educational subject, cultural phenomenon, and dramatic entertainment — in Britain in roughly the first half of the twentieth century, especially via BBC Radio. She is also writing a book on the performance history of Greek plays in Oxford and by the touring Balliol Players (forthcoming).

Rosie Wyles, after reading Classics at St Anne's College, Oxford, was awarded an Arts and Humanities Research Council-funded postgraduate studentship to pursue doctoral research on the ancient reception of Euripides, with special reference to costume, at the Archive of Performances of Greek and Roman Drama at Oxford, where she is a Graduate Associate. Her supervisor is Edith Hall, with whom she moved from Durham University to Royal Holloway, University of London in 2006. She is currently editing *New Directions in Ancient Pantomime* with Edith Hall (forthcoming with Oxford University Press).

CHAPTER 1

❖

Introduction:
Aristophanic Laughter across the Centuries

Edith Hall

Distant Quests

In all cultural history, few figures are as hard to avoid as Aristophanes. There can be no satisfactory cultural history that ignores comedy, and from Aristotle onwards no worthwhile discussion of comedy, jokes, or humour has been able to ignore Aristophanes.[1] Indeed, there is so much self-conscious scrutiny of the nature and function of comic theatre in Aristophanes' plays themselves that he can legitimately be described as the founding father not only of comedy but of the theory of the Comic.[2] Intercultural comparisons of forms of comic humour usually juxtapose non-European models — Japanese Kyogen, contemporary Japanese comic fiction, the masked Yuyachkani festive drama of Peru — first and foremost with Aristophanes.[3] Arab playwrights and dramatic theorists stress that the pagan ancient Greeks contributed to the cultural base of both the eastern and western Mediterranean, and use Aristophanes as inspiration and point of comparison in discussions of comic dialects and the role of laughter in public life.[4] Precedents for every single tradition of comic theatre and humour in the West have also, with justification, been identified in Aristophanes: personal satire, philosophical satire, mimicry, parody, puns, *double entendre*, Saturnalian role inversion, Rabelaisian and Bakhtinian carnival, drag acts and cross-dressing, stand-up, bawd and scatology, slapstick, farce and knockabout.[5]

In addition, Aristophanes is routinely invoked as ancestor in discussions of Shakespearean comedy and romance, W. S. Gilbert's operettas, the grotesque Absurdist theatre of Alfred Jarry (especially *Ubu Roi* of 1896), the anti-war comedy of Bernard Shaw, Brecht's distancing and self-conscious narrative modes, the Theatre of the Absurd of Beckett and Ionesco, the plays of Friedrich Dürrenmatt, the surrealism of Spike Milligan and Monty Python, and the political puppets in the satirical series *Spitting Image*, broadcast on BBC television from the mid-1980s to mid-1990s.[6] Although some have tried to deny any continuity between Old Comedy and Menander, proposing instead that it is the latter's Hellenistic New Comedy that heads the family tree leading to domestic sitcom via the genteel comedy of the eighteenth century,[7] shrewder analysts have always seen that even this species of comedy is ultimately descended from the confrontations between father and son, slave and master, already to be found at war in the households at the centre of several Aristophanic plays.[8]

Not that the acknowledged influence of Aristophanes on later culture has been confined to texts and forms of entertainment that have advertised themselves as 'comic theatre': Aristophanes has been identified behind the birth of Western Literary Criticism, the Western notion of Freedom of Speech, the transformation of folktale into narrative fiction, Platonic irony, Menippean satire, Juvenalian vituperation, Swift's satire, Sterne's novels, eighteenth-century German classicism, humorous journalism, and the tradition of the political cartoon.[9] Historians of Science Fiction claim a genealogy reaching back to the supernatural journeys to Other Worlds undertaken by Aristophanic heroes; Marcel Duchamp traced the roots of Dada's farcical spirit directly to Aristophanic scenarios; Albert Cook argued from the combined cases of Aristophanes, Molière, W. S. Gilbert, and Chaplin that great comedy always happens in the social milieu of an imperialist society with a rapidly expanding middle class; *Birds, Frogs,* and *Wasps* are routinely invoked in connection with fables of zoomorphism from Aesop and Apuleius to Kafka and Orwell; *Acharnians* and *Peace* are often mentioned in connection with the radically politicized, populist revue theatre of Joan Littlewood; more than one feminist novel about women taking over the reins of power in the modern world has been inspired by *Lysistrata.*[10]

Such has been the impact of the eleven surviving plays of Aristophanes (out of a total of forty-four), both on Graeco-Roman antiquity and the post-Renaissance world, that the near-absence of sustained previous research into the history of Aristophanic reception, let alone Aristophanic performance, seems almost unfathomable.[11] The implications of the realisation that the texts of Greek tragedy and comedy were composed as playscripts designed for performance seem only to have dawned gradually since the academic stage revivals of the late nineteenth century. Moreover, although a few individual twentieth-century scholars, such as Karl Reinhardt, had stressed the importance of reconstructing gesture and movement alongside the texts of plays, the great difference between theatrical poetry and other genres does not seem to have been defined until as late as the first years of the 1960s. This was the period when the Greek director Alexis Solomos and the Italian scholar Carlo Ferdinando Russo published, a year apart, two very different books which were nevertheless united in articulating what then seemed like a radically new, performance-based approach to the dramatic texts of antiquity.[12] It took more than another decade and a half for their approach to be fully integrated into classical scholarship, partly as a result of the translation of Solomos into English in 1974, but more importantly as a result of the performance-based philological perspective of Oliver Taplin's reappraisal not of comedy but tragedy in his *Stagecraft of Aeschylus* (1977).

The performance *history* of the ancient plays did not, however, inch gradually towards the centre of the radar operated by the Classics academy until a couple of decades later. The progress resulted partly from the increasing acceptance of Reception as a legitimate avenue to the understanding of Mediterranean antiquity. At the same time, the greater appreciation of the cultural importance even in antiquity of genres and performance media that were enjoyed across a wide social spectrum (e.g. the novel, mime, and pantomime) encouraged Classical scholars to be more open to studies of the presence of the ancient Greeks and Romans in contemporary popular culture, above all cinema and television. But a more important factor in the invention of the sub-discipline of the performance reception of ancient playscripts has been connected with the new economies of the Academy.[13] An awareness has dawned that the very survival of Classics may depend upon the continuing vigour of the presence of the ancient Greeks and Romans in the wider community: the renaissance of ancient drama upon the commercial as well as the pedagogical stage over the last three decades is a remarkable cultural phenomenon, now increasingly manifested on a global scale.[14] This phenomenon alone will ensure that the ancient Greeks remain in the public eye, at least for the time being, and it demands attempts at excavation, analysis, and explanation.

Most of the essays included in this collection, the goal of which is the exploration of the history of the relationship between live performance and the texts of the Athenian comic poet Aristophanes, were delivered as papers in September 2004 at the third triennial conference of the Archive of Performances of Greek and Roman Drama (APGRD). This is a research centre founded at the University of Oxford in 1996 in order to attempt a documentation and investigation of the afterlife of ancient dramatists in their natural habitats — theatres, cinemas, concert halls. The first two conferences held by the APGRD had been devoted to two tragedies with particularly important histories in terms of performance reception, Euripides' *Medea* and Aeschylus' *Agamemnon*; the papers delivered at these meetings have been published by Legenda and Oxford University Press respectively.[15] For the third conference it was decided to concentrate on the comedies of Aristophanes, but, rather than isolate the performance history of a single comedy, it was preferred to compare the *Nachleben* in performance of three of his most imaginative, utopian, influential, and spectacular plays — the three that might be described as the 'distant quest' plays, those that provided staged journeys of an 'upstairs' (anabatic) or 'downstairs' (katabatic) nature. All three journeys, however surreal or supernatural, are inseparable from political issues. In *Peace* the Athenian hero Trygaeus flies to Olympus in order to ask the gods to end a decade-old war; in *Birds* two disenchanted Athenians leave home to join the birds, and found Cloudcuckooland with them in the sky; in *Frogs* the god of drama, Dionysus, travels to the Underworld and retrieves a great tragedian who can save the very soul of the city of Athens, symbolized by its traditions of theatre, choral dancing and poetry.

One reason behind this choice of comedies was that we did not want to make gender relations our primary focus after two consecutive projects devoted to plays treating famously dysfunctional mythical marriages, and the performance reception of which was intimately connected with the history of struggles for women's equality. But a more important argument was that the three comedies featuring *anabasis* or *katabasis* were known to have enjoyed longer and certainly more *varied* afterlives in performance since the Renaissance than Aristophanes' other plays, including the early Humanist favourites *Plutus* and *Clouds*, and the now popular 'women' plays, *Lysistrata*, *Ecclesiazusae*, and *Thesmophoriazusae*. *Peace* was performed in the English Renaissance; *Frogs* was adapted by Henry Fielding in *The Author's Farce*, produced in 1730, and fifty years later, in 1780, Goethe staged his own adaptation of *Birds* at Weimar.

The intellectual core of this volume consists of its third section, 'From Revival to Repertoire', which covers the period from the revival of Aristophanes as a performable playwright in academic Greek-language productions in the late nineteenth century to the establishment of his *Birds*, *Peace*, and *Frogs*, in modern-language versions, within the mid-twentieth century repertoire by such mainstream theatre professionals as Karolos Koun in Greece, Peter Hacks in East Germany, and Stephen Sondheim in North America. But we were also aware that these three plays, with their imaginative scenarios, had in antiquity exerted more intangible influences on the development of other comic traditions, such as the satirical prose of Lucian, and that researching their cultural presences diachronically might illuminate more general cultural trends. From this perspective, the type of performance history that is most important is not so much the academic revival of ancient playscripts. It is rather, for example, the type of influence that Holtermann has shown was exerted by ideas about Aristophanes in topical *Lustspiele* in the early decades of the nineteenth century, and the uses made of Aristophanes by German poets longing for an acerbic political comedy, such as the extraordinary trilogy *Napoleon* by Friedrich Rückert (1815–18).[16]

There have been only a few books entirely devoted to the performance reception of ancient Greek drama, and only a tiny handful of these have spared some thought for Aristophanes alongside the more popular texts of Greek tragedy.[17] There have also been a very few important studies of the reception of Aristophanes, especially in Germany, including one or two that have devoted some space to Aristophanic performance.[18] Van Steen's prize-winning *Venom in Verse* (2000) demonstrated the possibilities for tracing the history of Aristophanic performance in individual countries and theatrical traditions (Greece, in her case). The recent collection of essays on Aristophanes' *Thesmophoriazusae* edited by Mary-Kay Gamel has illustrated the value that classical scholars can find in excavating performances of their Old Comic canon.[19] Yet the essays collected here represent the first attempt known to us to document phases in the relationship between performance history and a selection of Aristophanic dramas, from antiquity until the third millennium.

The collection makes no attempt to provide comprehensive coverage of every era and event in Aristophanic theatrical reception. The same applies to major topics in comic theatre, although some of these are certainly addressed, including on the one hand the textually based issues of the translatability of jokes and comic verse forms, and on the other the performance conventions of the mask (especially in Varakis' chapter), the chorus (especially in Treu's), and music (especially in the studies by Van Steen, Seidensticker, Gamel and Silk). Nor does the volume represent in any sense a work of reference. It is hoped that the papers do, however, offer a series of mutually illuminating insights into key issues and occasions in the performance reception of this playwright, and thus fill a significant gap in our understanding of Aristophanes' importance not only in élite scholarly circles but also to cultural history; this includes his continuing subterranean presence as well as his repeated rediscovery in arenas of entertainment. The essays have been grouped in approximate chronological order under four headings which reflect our understanding of the origins and evolution of the relationship between Aristophanic comedy and third-millennial theatre.

I. Precedents: Aristophanes and the Stage before the Twentieth Century

The type of theatre of which Aristophanes was the most famous exponent reached its zenith in the fifth century BC in democratic Athens. It has been called, since later antiquity, 'Old Comedy', in order to distinguish it from the more domestic and genteel 'New Comedy' identified with Menander, which arose at Athens towards the end of the fourth century. It also demarcates it from the lost comic plays of the interim, which are (controversially) labelled 'Middle Comedy'. Aristophanes was by no means the only great author of Old Comedy: indeed, two of his plays bear titles that had earlier been used by a comic poet named Magnes (*Birds* and *Frogs*), and he seems to have had quite a struggle to make his name in competition with his slightly older colleagues and rivals, especially Cratinus and Eupolis.[20]

At the conference which gave rise to this volume it had been planned that the crucial opening paper, on representations of Old Comedy in Greek vase-painting, would be delivered by Margot Schmidt, Assistant Director of the Antikenmuseum in Basel, where she had worked devotedly since 1966. In 1982 she had also been appointed Professor at the University of Basel. Margot accepted our invitation, but on the night of 24 March 2004, just a few months before the conference, she tragically died of the cancer against which she had struggled for some time. Her outstanding work on the relationship between ancient Greek iconography and its stage practices, which began with her 1960 study of the Dareios painter, can only underline what our investigation into the performance history of Aristophanes lost by her death. In 1998 she published in the journal *Antike Kunst* an article reviewing almost all the important evidence for Old Comedy that has been identified — rightly or wrongly — in images painted on late fifth- and fourth-century vases, especially from the Greek cities in southern Italy. These include the so-called 'Getty Birds' vase,[21] a krater in Würzburg illustrating a scene from *Thesmophoriazusae*, the mysterious 'Chorēgoi vase' in the Fleischman collection in New York, and the 'New York Goose Play' vase. She also discussed two scenes which have been associated with *Frogs*. One is the scene on the krater once in Berlin (Inv. F 3046), most unfortunately lost as a result of World War II and therefore only to be studied via an old photograph (see fig. 1.1, and also the sketch at fig. 1.2, which is reproduced for the sake of clarity since no new photograph can be taken), which many scholars think portrayed the entrance scene of *Frogs*: one figure dressed as Heracles approaches a door, followed by another riding an ass and carrying baggage over his shoulder. The other is a fragment in Museo Nazionale di Taranto (inv. no. 121613) which may well portray the competition in Hades between Aeschylus and Euripides, adjudicated by a *thyrsos*-wielding Dionysus. In this article by Schmidt the reader will not only discover engagement with all the significant scholarship on the subject that preceded it — especially Oliver Taplin's study *Comic Angels* (1993), which has excellent photographic reproductions — but an extraordinarily perceptive eye for detail and for the visual language into which the vase-painters transposed the impact of the live performances of comedy by Aristophanes and his colleagues.

The discussions of these vases by scholars like Schmidt, Taplin, Green, and Csapo have done much to advance our understanding of the revival of Old Comedies, including those by Aristophanes, in the theatre-mad Greek cities of fourth-century southern Italy.[22] The 'New York Goose Play Vase' suggests that the original Attic dialect of Athenian comedy was retained even in communities where Doric Greek was spoken; moreover, the audiences were clearly experienced watchers of productions of Athenian tragedy, and the 'Chorēgoi vase' proves incontrovertibly that they enjoyed plays which, like Aristophanes' Frogs, developed jokes and whole episodes that contrasted these two types of drama.[23] Indeed, the vase in Würzburg illustrates a scene from Thesmophoriazusae where the audience needed to know a famous tragedy by Euripides — his Telephus — if they were to enjoy either the vase-painting or the comic production which inspired it.[24] In Italy the conditions of production will however have been rather different from those at major Athenian festivals, to judge from the way in which actual stage construction is depicted on the vases.[25] It is also likely that indigenous theatrical traditions coexisted with the revival of exported Athenian comedy, and affected the ways in which it was altered for reperformance.[26] But there remains a great deal that we do not know about the early days of the medium, and the conditions in which it was performed, especially before the earliest surviving play by Aristophanes, his Acharnians of 425 BC.

The performance context in which the plays premièred seems almost invariably to have been drama competitions held at Athenian festivals of the wine-god Dionysus, where the comic poets competed annually against each other with new plays.[27] Peace was first performed in 421, Birds in 414, and Frogs in 405. Yet even the statement that Athenian poets competed annually with a new play needs modification. It is not just that it seems to have been possible — although extremely unusual — for a play that achieved such immediate success as Frogs to have been performed again soon after its première, as the ancient records apparently stated;[28] most scholars have assumed that it must have been repeated at a Dionysiac festival in the following year.[29] It may also be relevant that certain kinds of title — as in the case of Magnes' Birds and Frogs — seem to have become traditional in Old Comedy; Aristophanes may have adapted his famous predecessor's works in his own plays of the same name. There is also a certain amount of frustratingly recalcitrant evidence that any script could be revised by its original author — with varying degrees of radicalism — and updated for a second performance. There were certainly two versions of Aristophanes' Clouds, and two apparently rather different plays by him called Peace. But the picture is even further complicated by the fact that the same title could be bestowed by an author on two plays with completely dissimilar plots, as in the case of Thesmophoriazusae.[30]

Plays by poets of Old Comedy as well as tragedy could be performed in the local theatres of individual Attic demes: an inscription found near the deme of Halai Aixonides commemorates the performances of plays directed by dramatic poets including the comic poet Cratinus and the tragedian Sophocles.[31] It is unfortunate that we are unable to consult the treatise On Old Comedy written in the second century BC by the North African scientist and scholar Eratosthenes, since this might have included material that corrected our impression that there were no performed

FIG. 1.1. Scene from the 'Berlin Herakles' Apulian bell-krater (375–350 BC)

FIG. 1.2. Line-drawing of the 'Berlin Herakles'

stage revivals of Aristophanes or his rivals beyond the end of the fourth century BC. The only serious piece of evidence to the contrary is Suetonius' statement that the emperor Augustus 'relished old comedy and often put it on at public spectacles' (*Vita Augusti* 89.1). This is possible, but perhaps unlikely given that 'Old Comedy' by this date often meant Greek New Comedy, and also given the vehemence with which Aristophanic coarseness is derogated in the ancient text attributed to Plutarch that compares Aristophanes with Menander.[32] On the other hand, Aristophanes certainly continued to be recited in academies where rhetoric was studied, to judge from the praise lavished upon him by Quintilian (10.1.65):

> The Old Comedy is almost alone in preserving the true charm (*sinceram gratiam*) of Attic speech; at the same time it has the most expressive freedom of speech (*facundissimae libertatis*), especially in denouncing vice, though it is full of strength all through. It is grand, elegant and charming (*grandis, elegans, venusta*), and — Homer always excepted, like Achilles — I doubt if any other literature is more akin to oratory or more suitable for making orators. [33]

Nor was oratorical practice the only way in which famous passages might be reperformed: a tantalising suggestion that Aristophanic songs might be sung — perhaps at symposia — all over the Greek-speaking Mediterranean world of later antiquity has been made by the discovery in Upper Egypt of a fascinating ostrakon. Musical notation to some words of the hoopoe's song from *Birds* seems to have been inscribed upon it, and this will soon be published by Annie Bélis, Director of Research at the Centre National de la Recherche Scientifique, Paris.[34]

Aristophanes indeed continued to be read across the Roman Empire, and enjoyed something of a revival, since a striking number of papyrus scraps show consistent interest in Old Comedy, especially *Clouds*, *Birds*, *Frogs* and *Wasps*, and evidence for individual scribes being paid for making copies of his plays.[35] This may have been partly a result of the strong interest in Aristophanes shown during the revival of interest in classical Greek literature that characterized the so-called Second Sophistic, which is the topic considered by Ewen Bowie in the first essay in this volume. When Lucian's character Menippus flies to heaven in order to discover which philosopher had the correct answer concerning the gods in his *Icaromenippus* (10), his fantastic journey follows directly in the path carved out by Trygaeus' dung-beetle in *Peace*; it is to the descent of Dionysus to the Underworld in *Frogs* that Lucian's discussion in *Sailing Down, or the Tyrant* (7, 14, 18) of the correct order of embarkation in Charon's boat on the banks of the Styx must ultimately be traced.[36] The travel plot of *Birds* also influenced Diogenes Laertius, the author of biographies of philosophers. Since his interest in fantastic travel seems itself to have underlain the famous ancient Greek novels of Achilles Tatius, Heliodorus and Iamblichus, the *ultimate* impact of Aristophanic 'distant quest' plays on European fiction — mediated through the Greek prose authors of imperial times and their Renaissance rediscovery — is likely to have been considerable. It is interesting that from time to time editions have been published that pair Aristophanic and Lucianic texts, explicitly underlining their perceived affinities. The earliest is Adrianus Chilius' Latin translations of *Plutus* along with Lucian's *Podagra*, published at Antwerp in 1533.[37]

The printed *editio princeps* of nine of the eleven surviving plays of Aristophanes was published in 1498 (see fig. 19.1), and our book is concluded by a fascinating catalogue of translations of Aristophanes that were published between his discovery at that moment and 1920. By the end of World War I every single one of his surviving plays had been staged, and translations became so numerous that a full account would require a volume in itself. The catalogue published here is part of a larger piece of research conducted by Vasiliki Giannopoulou, documenting editions of Aristophanes in addition to translations, which can be consulted at the APGRD. Her work has confirmed the intimacy with which the history of performance of Aristophanes is bound up with the history of translation and of adaptation.

The play that was translated earliest in the Renaissance — into easy Latin — was also the play that was first performed: *Plutus* (an adaptation of which was staged in Florence as early as 1512), followed not long after by *Clouds*.[38] The third play to receive individual attention, in the form of a separate scholarly edition, was *Frogs*, issued with a Latin preface at Basel in 1524. Scholars passably competent in Latin could read all of Aristophanes' works in Andreas Divus' Venice translation as early as 1538; what is far more remarkable is that the plays were all published in Italian translation only seven years later. Literary theorists at the time were well aware of the significance of this feat, and envisaged the impact that it might have on contemporary comedy.[39] But it was Divus' Latin translation that was reprinted several times within only a few years, and it was his book that probably explains the speed at which knowledge of Aristophanes spread all over Europe: *Peace* was performed in Cambridge, for example, in 1546 (see below, Steggle, p. 54).

Indeed, despite the early Italian translation, it was in England that Aristophanes seems first to have been taken seriously as an ancestor of Early Modern comedy, an author whose scripts offered a wealth of ideas and scenes that could be developed by contemporary playwrights. Matthew Steggle's chapter takes up the story in the English Renaissance, asking the question: what was it in Aristophanes that Ben Jonson and his contemporaries found so consistently stimulating? Part of the answer is that the Renaissance and Early Modern Aristophanes was seen from the perspective of the Roman poet Horace, whose allusions to Greek Old Comedy reveal a belief that it was fundamentally a vehicle not for fantasy or politics, but for personal satire. Another part of the answer is that Aristophanes became familiar to many through the hundreds of quotations and excerpts included in Erasmus' monumental and highly influential *Adagia* (1500). But Steggle's argument proceeds to a reappraisal of the forms of Aristophanic influence that can be inferred from Jonson's plays, especially the neglected *The Staple of News*; while Aristophanic precedent certainly informs the type of personal satire to be found in this play, it also reveals fascinating aesthetic debts in terms of setting, concept, character and an entire episode (it includes a trial of dogs transparently borrowed from *Wasps*).

In the case of *Birds*, a long tradition of adaptation into modern languages, in addition to translation, can be traced as far back as 1579, and the publication of the Rabelaisian adaptation by Pierre Le Loyer under the title *La Néphélococugie, ou la nuée des cocus*, which has recently been reissued with a modern commentary.[40] *La Néphélococugie* is an updated adaptation; the heroes are two brothers from Toulouse.

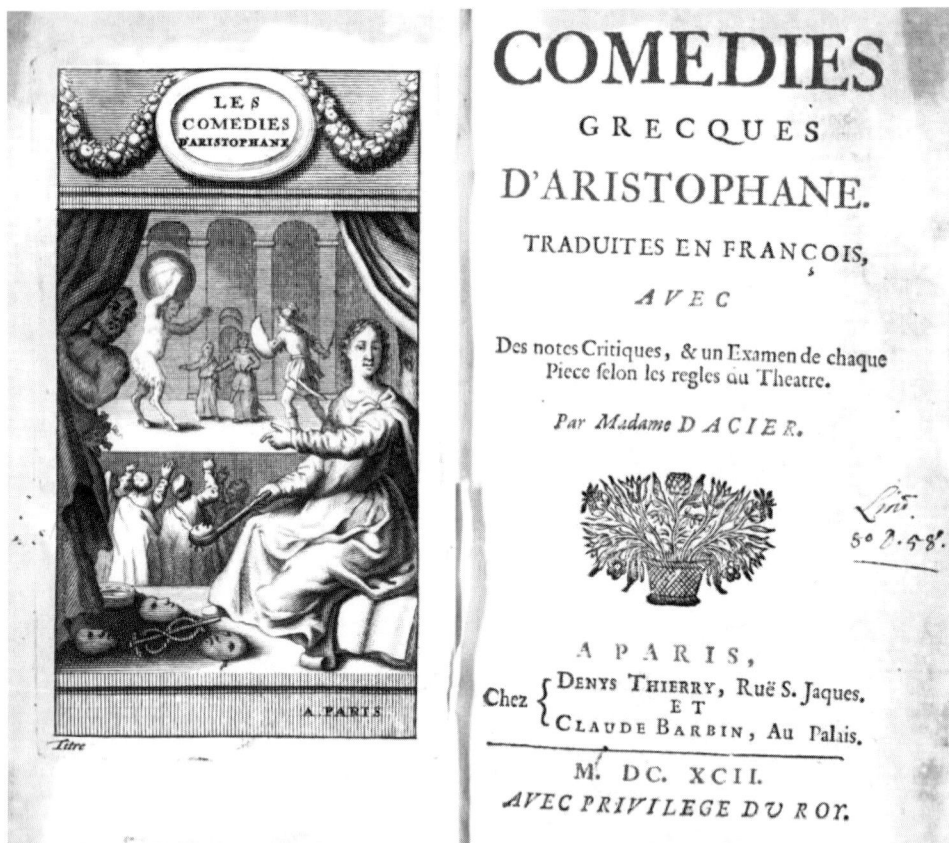

FIG. 1.3. Frontispiece and title page from *Comedies grecques d'Aristophane*

But it is a fascinating example of the sixteenth-century French taste for literary imitations of classical archetypes, through which authors sought to impress their readers by being the first to introduce them to an ancient text in new, French guise.[41] The French also recognized early that Aristophanic texts themselves had the potential, at least, for being translated into contemporary tongues and performed on the contemporary stage. Racine drew on *Wasps* for his comedy *Les Plaideurs* in 1668, and the performance potential of Aristophanes seems to inform the presentation of the excellent French version of *Le Plutus et les Nuées d'Aristophane*, translated with notes by Anne Le Fèvre (by marriage Madame Dacier) and first published in 1684. The figure reproduced here is from the 1692 edition (see fig. 1.3).

   This remarkable woman was the daughter of Tannegui Le Fèvre (Tanaquil Faber), Professor of Greek at the famous Protestant Academy at Saumur in the Loire valley, who had ensured that his daughter received the same education as any clever boy. It seems appropriate that amongst his numerous editions of Greek and Roman authors, when it came to Aristophanes it was the play featuring the articulate woman Praxagora, *Ecclesiazusae*, that he had himself edited and translated into Latin.[42] His articulate daughter's French prose translation of *Plutus* and *Clouds* is the earliest Aristophanic translation to divide the plays into acts and scenes, and to add notes discussing them from the perspective of the neoclassical 'rules' of theatre, suggesting that she was visualising the texts in performance as she translated them. This certainly seems to be the promise held out by the frontispiece reproduced here, in which the translator is represented literally ladling out roles in the form of masks to actors in a live theatre. The structure looks more seventeenth-century than ancient Greek; it is complete with raised platform, curtains, painted backdrop, and responsive groundlings. It is not certain what scene is being enacted: the best guess is that it is the confrontation in *Plutus* between the boulder-carrying Cyclops (despite the inappropriate hooves) and Odysseus, as enacted after the opening scene by Cario and the chorus respectively. The actor peering from behind the curtain on the left may be about to dress for the role of Hermes/Mercury, who enters later in the play: this may be implied by the caduceus lying amidst the masks at Madame Dacier's feet.

Dacier's translation proved very popular, was much reprinted, and inspired similar ventures in other modern languages, including Lewis Theobald's English translations of the same two plays in 1715, published separately with attractive frontispiece engravings (see below, Hall, pp. 71–72 and fig. 4.1). Although echoes of Aristophanic plots are to be heard in several comedies of the Restoration, it is in the first third of the eighteenth century that Aristophanes finds his way into the English commercial theatre, with the adaptation of *Frogs* included in Henry Fielding's *The Author's Farce* (see pp. 72–73). Fifty years later Goethe staged his own German-language adaptation of *Birds* at Weimar. Greek studies had preoccupied Goethe for several years when he was made responsible in 1775 for the direction of the Court Amateur Theatre in the duchy of Weimar. He had made use of Pierre Brumoy's *Théâtre des Grecs* (1730), which had summarized all the plays of Aristophanes alongside those of the tragedians (on this publication see further, below, pp. 74–75).[43] During the winter of 1787–88 Goethe read a good deal of Aristophanes.[44] Father Brumoy had also recommended Jean Boivon's 1729 translation of *Birds*, published as a pair with a translation of Sophocles' *Oedipus*, which had made Aristophanes' Cloudcuckooland by this time as well known in literary circles as *Plutus* and *Clouds*.

Die Vögel was one of several short plays that Goethe wrote and produced for his Weimar patrons.[45] Several of them are satires on literary movements and the publishing industry, and indeed *Die Vögel*, which was completed at a time when Goethe was reassessing his ambitions, and heralded a pause of several years in his creative output, is all about the poet's relations with publishers and his readership: Goethe's most recent biographer concluded that 'the play as a whole seems the work of an author who is shaking from his feet the dust of a public literary career'.[46]

Die Vögel was staged at the Ettersburg summer palace, recently built for the duchess Anna Amalia, which was then an hour's drive north-west of Weimar itself, and is now better known for the grim reason that Buchenwald concentration camp was built adjacent to it. The production took place on 18 August, against a set designed by Adam Oeser, the Director of the Leipzig Academy of Painting.[47]

A precious source comes in the form of some notes made by Karl von Lyncker, who was a page-boy at the Weimar Court and sometimes participated in Goethe's theatricals. At the time of *Die Vögel* he would have been about thirteen years old, and his analysis is not sophisticated. But it gives an indication of the exuberance and spectacular effects entailed by the production:

> The birds appeared in papier-mâché coats of feathers, very naturally painted; the people dressed as birds, of whom I was one, could turn their heads freely and move their tails to and fro by means of a string; the horned owl and the owl could even make their eyes roll; the voices were clearly to be heard. These scenes had to be frequently rehearsed, of course, and the whole troop was generally driven over to Ettersburg once or twice a week in the afternoons.[48]

Although no visual records of the production seem to have survived, an idea of what the set and costumes may have looked like can be gleaned from illustrations of other productions directed by Goethe at Weimar, especially the painting by Georg Melchior Kraus of the actors dressing in the costumes of birds and animals for Goethe's production of Mozart's *Magic Flute* in 1794, and Goethe's own sketch of a design for the set — complete with Doric columns — of a scene from the same production.[49]

The adaptation of *Birds* played a role in the evolution of Goethe's troubled relationship with the Greeks, even if the results of this lone direct encounter with an Aristophanic text were not to affect the more general tone of his poetry until several years later, when the theatre at Weimar became a much more serious enterprise and Goethe's role in it was celebrated all over German-speaking Europe (fig. 1.4).[50]

He seems initially to have gone to Aristophanes in search of a comic spirit that offered something warmer, more vivid, and more real — that had more to say to a poet recently emerged from his *Sturm und Drang* period — than Plautus or Terence. The Greek is indeed transformed into the light-hearted and idiomatic German usually associated with the fashionable farces then popular in Frankfurt,[51] as is clear from the rendering of the names of the friends Peisthetairos and Euelpides as Treufreund and Hoffegut; there is extensive parody of botanical and zoological Latin and an attractively obtuse music-loving bird named Papagei (Parrot). There is also a certain charm to the mountainside setting (inspired by Goethe's recent vacation in the Alps). The central conceit is that Goethe (who took the leading role of Treufreund) finds his reading public as daft, fickle, and easily led as the cynical Peisthetairos finds the birds that haunt the skies beyond Athens. But it was not until three years later, when J. G. Schlosser published his version of *Frogs*, that a German-language translator first treated Aristophanes as a political author rather than a moralist,[52] and *Birds* needs more political substance to work well; the dissatisfaction with the community abandoned by Goethe's hero needed to be grounded in something more than the temporary writer's block with which the poet seems to have been struggling.

The final chorus sung by Goethe's birds includes the lines 'To get from Athens to Ettersburg you need to make a mortal leap',[53] and that hazardous transcultural leap into their own world is one that has proved challenging to every author discussed

FIG. 1.4. Wilhelm von Kaulbach's etching 'Goethe in Weimar'

in this volume. My own chapter, for example, traces the distinctive experience of authors who tried to make the leap from classical Athens to the English-speaking world between the mid-seventeenth century and the end of the nineteenth. It argues that it was precisely the problem of bridging the gap between the comic conventions of classical Athens and the contemporary environment that made it so difficult to revive Aristophanes. Although the cavalier dramatists reinstated at the Restoration had seen Aristophanes as the very emblem and mouthpiece of the theatrical entertainments that the Puritans had opposed, once Henry Fielding's theatrical experiments had been curtailed in the 1730s, Aristophanes remained consistently identified as a poet with a reactionary political outlook combined with unpalatable sexual coarseness. The latter attitude towards him is well exemplified in the defensive remarks with which Charles Dunster, a pious Worcestershire clergyman, prefaced his translation of *Frogs* in 1785; he reassured his reader that the 'offensive parts are either omitted, or qualified'. The very few attempts to adapt him for production in Britain, notably J. R. Planché's lyrical *The Birds of Aristophanes* in 1846, found little more commercial success than they did anywhere else (for example, a rather mysterious production of *Frogs* in Berlin in 1843–44).[54] But the foundations were nevertheless laid during this period for the revival of Aristophanic drama in performance that is such a feature of the late nineteenth and early twentieth centuries. One block was laid by the late Georgian diplomat and poet John Hookham Frere when he produced the first translations in idiomatic and potentially performable English verse forms, which eventually led to the first known British performance of Aristophanes, unadapted, in English translation. This was *Frogs* in the private theatre run in Edinburgh of the 1870s by the engineer Henry Fleeming Jenkin (fig. 1.5). Matthew Arnold and George Meredith developed new ways of understanding Aristophanic humour as social critique; W.S. Gilbert's librettos reveal a deep appreciation of Aristophanic poetry.

II. Excursus: Publication as Performance

There is a missing piece in the historical puzzle constituted by Aristophanes. Initially it may seem surprising that in a book that focuses on theatrical performances of *Peace*, *Birds*, and *Frogs* there is a section concerned with the publication, for reading purposes, of other plays. Moreover, these three essays were not delivered at the original conference, but were instead commissioned after it in order to clarify its overall argument. The reason is that once the performance history of the three focal plays had been reconstructed in outline, it became apparent that there was a 'missing link' in the historical chain of evolution.

The plays of Aristophanes were eventually rediscovered as scripts that could be directly realized in physical performance in the wholly apolitical context of the late nineteenth-century private and academic Greek play, the primary interest of which was to excavate authentic ancient theatre conventions, acting styles, and costume designs, as part of an élite, or at least professional-class education. Yet by the turn of the twentieth century, the political dimension of Aristophanes began to be appropriated in other types of performance venues — whether feminist, socialist,

FIG. 1.5. Fleeming Jenkin: etching by William Hole, 1884

or anti-war. Politically motivated or engaged *stagings* of Aristophanes had, however, almost no historical precedent. Moreover, in many countries Aristophanes had remained a figure appropriated almost exclusively by establishment and conservative forces. So where did the oppositional, critical, performed Aristophanes of the early twentieth century come from? The answer, we discovered, lay in published modern-language translations or adaptations that had — because for one reason or another performance was impossible — taken the form of political statements or interventions in themselves. Robert Prutz's 'Aristophanic' comedy *Die politische Wochenstube* (1845), for example, was published as an attack on the regime of Friedrich Wilhelm IV, and resulted in the author's prosecution.[55] It was to this tradition, the voice of Aristophanes issuing through suppressed critical voices from the printing press, that the ancestry of Laurence Housman's suffragette Edwardian *Lysistrata* must be traced, as well as Karolos Koun's anti-clerical *Birds* and the utopian thrust of Hacks's East German *Peace*.

The play that sparked the most divergent political readings, by the end of the nineteenth century, was undoubtedly *Ecclesiazusae*, whose fantastic rubric for a communist utopia that empowered women became, in Germany, bitterly contested. Social Democratic revolutionaries used it to illustrate their own vision — a tradition that fed into the adoption of Aristophanes by the earlier phase of revolutionary Russia, where the brilliant Anatoly Lunacharsky, appointed the first Commissar of Enlightenment in 1917, announced that Aristophanes would take a permanent place in the proletarian theatre.[56] Yet Prussian conservatives launched a massive anti-communist propaganda war in which Aristophanes was construed as a satirical *opponent* of social reform.

Something of a precedent for these contests over the possession of Aristophanic cultural property had been set more than a century before by versions that were published in the wake of the French revolution. Christoph Martin Wieland saw the recent experiences in France as the ultimate key to understanding Aristophanes; he felt that his own critique of the demagogic excesses on the Parisian political scene had been almost miraculously foreshadowed by Aristophanes' *Knights* and *Acharnians*. He was indeed the earliest German translator of these plays, and his versions, which set the seal on the longstanding identification of the French revolutionary leaders with the Athenian demagogue Cleon, made a great impact on authors of the period, including Goethe.[57]

In France itself there was one remarkable attempt to make Aristophanes speak to the times, and that was the version of *Lysistrata* discussed by Charalampos Orfanos in this volume, François-Benoît Hoffman's *Lisistrata ou les Athéniennes*, performed in the Théâtre Feydeau in January 1802 — or rather in Nivôse of the 10th year of the Revolution. It was written during the final negotiations for the ephemeral peace treaty of Amiens. According to its subtitle, *Lisistrata* is a *Comedy in one act and in prose, fused with vaudeville and imitating Aristophanes' play*. Although the adaptation doctored its Aristophanic model both politically and morally, the Consulat's censorship did not tolerate it: its fourth performance was the last one. In his different editions, the author added a preface and footnotes defending himself against his censors and critics. It had shocked Napoleon because of its irreverent manner of treating the war, apparently too serious a subject for laughter, even on the eve of a truce.

In England, meanwhile, it was *Plutus* that Francis Wrangham had adapted in his publication *Reform: A Farce, Modernised from Aristophanes* (1792), an assault on the revolutionary ideas of the British radical Tom Paine (see Hall, below, p. 75); historically speaking, *Plutus* was indeed the play that had from as early as the seventeenth century most often been used for making political statements in the form of a publication. Perhaps the example by the most significant author is the translation of *Plutus* on which Henry Fielding collaborated in order to protest against the first British Prime Minister Robert Walpole's censorship of the theatre (see below Hall, p. 74). But Fielding could look to a precedent in the earliest complete English-language translation (rather than adaptation) of Aristophanes, *The World's Idol; or, Plutus the God of Wealth, a translation from Aristophanes* by H. H. B. (1659). As Rosie Wyles explains in her chapter, this publication represents a landmark in the reception history of Aristophanes because it offered a fresh approach to the way in which dramatic material might be used to make a political statement, even in an era when theatrical activity had been almost completely curtailed. Moreover, it holds a fascinating place in the debates surrounding the colonisation of Ireland, and presents an individual's critical view of the English colonial ventures of the time.

The presence of Aristophanes in debates about colonial rule can also be seen at a far earlier stage than politicized theatrical productions of his plays in *Lakshmi* (1850), a Gujarati version of *Plutus* published in the colonial world of mercantile Ahmedabad. It was the work of Dalpatram, a prominent local intellectual and poet, with some assistance from Alexander Forbes, a civil servant and judge who had gone much further than most British imperial administrators in immersing himself, with great enthusiasm, in the language and culture of the area of India he had been employed to run. In his essay Phiroze Vasunia unravels the ideological complexities underlying Dalpatram's version.

Although Dalpatram's initial interest in Aristophanes' play resulted from coming into contact with the western classical syllabus studied by his colonial masters, *Lakshmi* is little interested in either Britain or classical Athens; instead, the village in which the action unfolds is largely set in a timeless past and is the home of several stock characters derived from Indian, and specifically Gujarati, folk theatre. Dalpatram's play also frames the intruders of the play in terms suggestive of the colonial atmosphere of Ahmedabad, producing a complex fusion which stresses the concept of moneyed Ahmedabad as a potential breeding ground of the hybrid; it blends Europeans and Indians, writers and kings, the old and the new. The publication of this fascinating play represents an important step in the globalisation of the ancient Greek theatrical canon, expressing power relations and incipient identities as well as anticipating by many decades the attraction of postcolonial dramatists in Africa and the Caribbean to explorations of cultural hybridity through their own appropriations of the 'European' classical repertoire.[58]

III. Revival to Repertoire

It was therefore through the publication of loaded modern-language adaptations that Aristophanes had, by the last three decades of the nineteenth century, already long been established in roles with which he was to be closely associated on the twentieth-century stage — as a potential mouthpiece for radical protest, social critique, and the forging of hybrid identities created during the age of empires. But before he was to enter the live theatre in any such adversarial or adventurous role, he first needed to enter it as an aesthetically interesting writer of performable stage plays. This is where the late nineteenth-century academic revival performances become, historically speaking, so important. Politically and ideologically anodyne they might have been, but they were crucial in creating a sense that Aristophanic comedy was pleasurable and intellectually rewarding for not only actors but spectators, and that it might even be funny. Once Henry Fleeming Jenkin (see above) had staged an English translation of *Frogs* in the early 1870s, Cambridge University scored an immense hit with its spectacular costumes and memorable music for *Birds* in Greek in 1883 (see fig. 1.6), in the same year that the boys of the Blackheath Proprietary School dazzled the audience with their varied costumes in the British première of *Acharnians* (see fig. 1.7). Amanda Wrigley's chapter explains the choice of plays in the early academic productions, and their interest in recreating, from an antiquarian point of view, the visual impact of the original productions. The late nineteenth century not only saw a newly consistent wave of revivals, but a spin-off industry that included original plays in the style of Aristophanes, or even allegedly rediscovered 'lost' plays and fragments.[59]

A series of adaptations and productions of *Lysistrata* can also be traced that was crucially important to the struggle for women's equality in the early twentieth century, as well as aesthetically significant for using this play as a charter text of theatrical Modernism in ways that have been well discussed by other scholars.[60] But the 'distant quest' plays became important once again during in the central decades of the twentieth century, when three productions proved stimulating to writers and directors exploring the potential of ancient Greek literature to inform progressive contemporary art or to form the basis of musical entertainment.

In the summer of 1959, Karolos Koun's Art Theatre brought to Athens a première of Aristophanes' *Birds* that subverted all the conventions that had previously governed modern Greek productions of ancient comedy. Branded anti-clerical, anti-American, and dangerously left-leaning, the production was closed down by the government of Karamanlis and sparked off a far-reaching controversy that was to reverberate throughout Europe and North America during the ensuing two decades of unrest. Gonda Van Steen's essay shows how the production's dissident content and the unforeseen protests it spurred became critical public issues in stage politics until after the fall of the Greek dictatorship of 1967–74. Koun's self-conscious populism, which not only drew on longstanding Greek folk traditions of comedy and festival, but was intended to make Aristophanes more approachable and demotic in spirit, directly led to Greek audiences, especially the lower and middle classes, growing familiar with Attic comedy. This development is ultimately connected with the performance of choruses from *Birds* and *Frogs* at the incomparably populist venue of the Athens-based Eurovision Song Contest in 2006 (discussed below, p. 26).

It can be argued that the new theatrical aesthetic that Koun forged within his productions of Aristophanes ultimately had even more impact than his political stance, and fundamental to the development of that aesthetic were his experimental masks. Angeliki Varakis argues that the mask was crucial to Koun's wider project, because it was inspired by the surreal and primitive mask used in popular festivities, and thus became the perfect means for fulfilling his vision of a sensual and ritual Aristophanes. She identifies the origins of Koun's interests in folk culture as the particular forms taken by Modernism in Greece of the 1930s, and the contested notions of Greek identity and the 'popular' sensibility. This led to a rejection of the archaeological classicism marking earlier Aristophanic theatre designs in Greece, but the aesthetic form and signifying function of the masks Koun used in his different productions, which included important performances of *Frogs* and *Peace* as well as *Birds*, nevertheless varied widely.

FIG. 1.6. *Birds* at Cambridge in 1883: etching by Henry Gillard Glindoni (1852–1913)

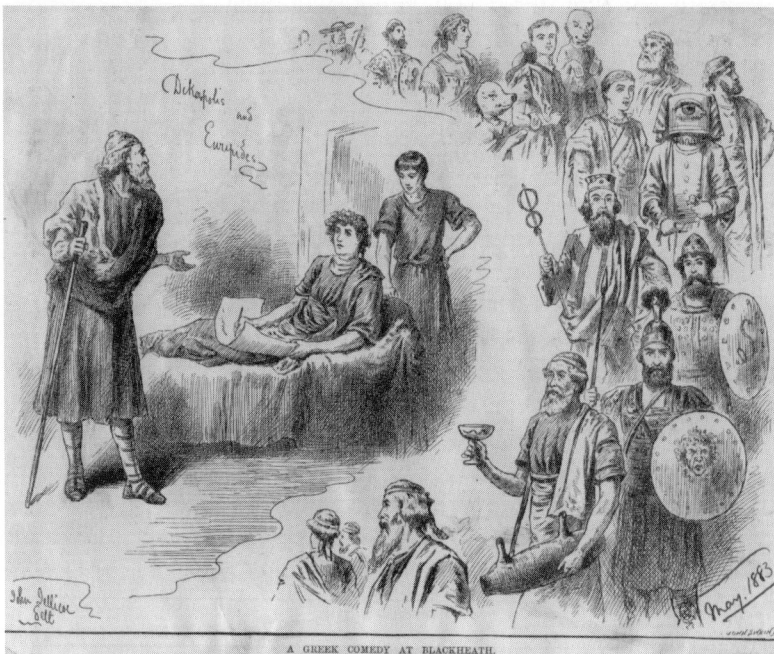

A GREEK COMEDY AT BLACKHEATH.

FIG. 1.7. Boys of Blackheath Proprietary School in *Acharnians*, 1883

The combination of aesthetic and political innovation was shared by the second of our central case studies, Peter Hacks's *Peace*, which in 1962 premièred under the direction of Benno Besson at the Deutsches Theater, in what was then East Berlin. This production was not only the most significant post-war German-language staging of any ancient play until Peter Stein's *Oresteia* nearly twenty years later, but it heralded — and some critics maintain precipitated — the flowering of adaptations of classical myth and literature in the German Democratic Republic over the following two and a half decades.[61] As a student of Brecht, Hacks was working both in and against the (by then) canonical model of a Marxist 'People's Theatre', a tradition which suffered from ambivalence towards 'classical' texts which had been composed under societal conditions other than recent revolutionary socialism. Hacks himself likened the plays of Shakespeare and Aristophanes to the 'elephants' of the classical repertoire, but his own production, as Bernd Seidensticker's essay reveals, itself expressed some extreme tensions in terms of the contradiction between its radical, utopian ardour (reflected in its avant-garde stage aesthetics) and the need to conform to the orthodox ideological imperatives dictated by the state government of the time. These tensions became even more apparent in the exploration of the notion of 'freedom' in Hacks's subsequent Aristophanic effort, his 'Comic Opera, after Aristophanes', as he described his *Birds* of 1973.[62]

If in Greece Aristophanes emerged as a democratic champion of popular Eastern Mediterranean peasant culture in opposition to US-backed conservatism, and in the GDR he was a neo-Brechtian advocate of utopian people's theatre enacted in the name of peace, in North America one manifestation of Aristophanes was as a tuneful Broadway songster suited to light entertainment. In 1974 a version of *Frogs* that Burt Shevelove had written and directed at Yale in 1941, where it had been performed at a swimming pool, acquired music and songs by Stephen Sondheim after the two men had worked together on *A Funny Thing Happened on the Way to the Forum* (1962). Mary-Kay Gamel's essay argues that Sondheim, as a lyricist, is one of very few able to equal Aristophanes' linguistic and poetic brilliance, and that the Shevelove/Sondheim *Frogs* enables the audience to experience the play in one way very much as it was intended — as a show including dazzling musical turns. But it also substitutes Shakespeare and Bernard Shaw for Aeschylus and Euripides, and when Dionysus chooses Shakespeare he chooses poetry over politics, thus in effect reversing the decision he takes in the Aristophanic play. When Nathan Lane rewrote the collaborative script for a new two-act musical performed at the Lincoln Centre in New York City in 2004, under the supervision of the prominent Broadway director Susan Stroman, a certain new political acuity was added with awareness of the post 9/11 crisis, George Bush, and the occupation of Iraq. Yet the production suffered from a tension between the commercially motivated desire to please and entertain and its more serious political undertow. It tried, but ultimately failed to satisfy the goal the chorus of initiates set themselves in *Frogs*, which is 'to say many serious things' as well as jocular ones (*Frogs* 391–92).

IV. Close Encounters

The final group of essays in the volume looks at some instances of Aristophanic performances in recent decades, as they have taken shape in diverse theatrical and political contexts. Although Aristophanes has still not attained the same importance in the global repertoire as Greek tragedy, which is performed with some regularity in every continent, nowhere has he been such contested cultural property as in later twentieth-century South Africa. Originally introduced as part of the syllabus read by the colonial master classes, both British and Dutch, in their schools and universities, by the 1970s productions of Aristophanes were beginning — with greater or less explicitness — to address the terrible problem of apartheid. In an Afrikaans adaptation by André P. Brink of *Birds* entitled *Die hand vol vere* (*The hand full of feathers*), staged by the Performing Arts Council of the Transvaal's Youth Theatre in 1971, the birds created a new flag for the new kingdom out of yellow, green and black feathers, the colours of the African National Congress, at that time a banned organization. In her study of the reception of Aristophanes in the South African theatre, Betine van Zyl Smit argues that its evolution parallels the political changes in the country.

Back in Europe, a recent study by Pantelis Michelakis has shown how *Peace* was staged not only by Peter Hacks in East Berlin as the Cold War grew coldest, but at other painfully appropriate moments in twentieth-century history: in Greece in 1919, Switzerland in 1945, and in a Parisian adaptation during the Algerian war (1961).[63] Indeed, Trygaeus, the hero of *Peace*, has always enjoyed a certain popularity in France, where audiences find it easy to identify with a pastoral idyll based on viticulture. Traditionally called 'Lavendange', Trygaeus has been identified as the ancestor of famous French roles including Molière's con-man Scapin, and the valet Sganarelle in *Don Juan*; this has been related to the French tendency to see Aristophanes as a forerunner of indigenous French writers — Rabelais, Voltaire, and Giraudoux — in having advocated peace in a comic medium.[64]

Malika Hammou is an academic who has translated Greek drama for the French stage, and her essay explores the reasons why twentieth-century French directors were strikingly attracted to *Peace*. She concludes that the explanation goes beyond the requirements of the political contexts of the rise of fascism in the 1930s, the Algerian war in the 1960s, and the Gulf War in the 1990s. *Peace* has also proved *aesthetically* fascinating to French directors on account of its potential for theatrical and mechanical innovation in the flight of Trygaeus' dung-beetle and the different levels — divine and human, domestic, Olympic and cavernous — on which the action takes place. French directors have also been demonstrably excited by the potential offered by the chorus in the famous 'hauling scene' in which Peace is dragged from her bunker; this has proved an opportunity for ambitious experiments with spectator integration and participation, especially in the production of Jean Vilar in 1961.

Along with Hammou in France, the Italian scholars Martina Treu and Francesca Schironi represent the new wave of young Classicists on the European Continent who are currently forging links between traditional Philology and Theatre Studies.

Although they agree that Italian directors outside the conventional state-sponsored productions in Sicily have come very late to the Aristophanic repertoire, they have different perspectives on the theatrical success achieved in some recent performances. Treu argues that the failure of most Italian productions to engage with the collective, civic dimension of Aristophanes instantiated in his choruses means that the only true heir to his theatre practising in contemporary Italian theatre is Marco Martinelli. The production she analyses is his *All'inferno!*, which adapts the scripts of Aristophanes in order to discover acerbic political statements, performed by groups of disadvantaged youths, about the exploitation of immigrants and the plight of the urban poor. But Schironi's commentary takes as its starting-point the notorious production by Luca Ronconi of *Frogs* in 2002, which was allegedly censored by the government of Silvio Berlusconi. In a valuable documentary study of the rumours and press reports that circulated at the time, Schironi argues that while Ronconi's postmodern set and decadent, proletarian Roman Dionysus made Aristophanes intelligible to third-millennial Italian audiences, there inevitably remains a fundamental problem with staging Aristophanes in a country where he has long been synonymous with the élite and conservative comic canon. In Italy, Schironi argues, the very requirement that productions of ancient comedy be discernibly hilarious presents an almost insuperable obstacle to the discovery of a truly political Aristophanes.

The final two essays return the argument to the UK, where Sean O'Brien (an internationally acclaimed poet and playwright) and Michael Silk (an Aristophanes scholar with considerable experience of translating comedy and of stage direction) come from different angles to discuss the challenges involved in translating Aristophanes either linguistically or culturally from classical Athens to Postmodernity. Sean O'Brien's essay describes his experiences after being invited to write a new verse version of *Birds* for the National Theatre's Transformation season, staged in 2002. The idea for the production had come from Mamaloucos Theatre, a circus theatre company, which planned to use performers with aerial skills in order to exploit the potential of the avian theme, and after opening at the Lyttleton Theatre to tour in Mamaloucos's big top. Yet the conjunction of O'Brien's text with this physical approach produced serious tensions that were never resolved in performance. O'Brien's tactic had been to cast the two heroes of *Birds* as Geordies (inhabitants of the north-eastern English city of Newcastle upon Tyne where O'Brien lives), a creative process which his essay illuminates. But the cuts imposed on the performance text radically diminished the power and coherence of his translocated script. Its potency was only realized when it was staged subsequently by a group of performers more respectful of his text — threeovereden, a local theatre company based in the North East.

If the tension in performances of O'Brien's version was between physical performer and poetic script, Michael Silk's essay explores the relationship between inherited words and modern melody. Silk begins with a discussion of the relative *density* of Aristophanes' texts, in that they involve several clusters of effects within short passages, and this requires that a translator into a different language — especially for a performance — establish a mode that facilitates the creation of new clusters entirely.

But for 'transposing' a play into a modern performance that retains the ancient language, another solution is required. In an illuminating example, for 'transposing' the particular features of Aristophanic verbal and rhythmic idiom, Silk explores the potential of the combination of sophistication and demotic immediacy of the American song tradition of the early 1920s to the 1940s (the tradition from which Sondheim's musical style, discussed by Gamel earlier in the volume, is descended). To elucidate this, Silk discusses the music and songs used in the 'Art Deco' production of *Frogs* that he directed at King's College, London in 1988, and subsequently took on tour in the USA. Here ancient Greek lyrics were performed to the pre-existing music constituted by American standard songs of the appropriate period, including Tin Pan Alley and big-band jazz arrangements, Dixie and Ira Gershwin.

Conclusion: The Songs of Aristophanes

Michael Silk's essay certainly offers an appropriate finale to this essay collection, on account of his innovative approach, as a director, to identifying persuasive musical vehicles for the contemporary performance of Aristophanic poetry. Yet Silk has also been closely involved, as a scholar, in one of the more important debates about the nature of Aristophanes' status as a poet. As this Introduction has indicated, Aristophanes has been configured over the last five centuries, by people whom the reader will meet in the course of this volume, as a realist and a surrealist, proto-Brechtian and proto-Absurdist, philosopher and philistine, amoral satirist and moral sage, revolutionary and counter-revolutionary, sexist and feminist, forerunner of Christianity, and as a boorish anti-clerical loudmouth. But there is another, more aesthetically oriented and poetic Aristophanes with an important place in the story. 'The person who wants to learn about metre should begin with Aristophanes', announced the incomparable German scholar Ulrich von Wilamowitz-Moellendorff eighty years ago,[65] in response to the remarkable variety and vigour of the verse forms to be found in all the comedies. In *Birds*, especially, Aristophanes seems to have exploited the idea of a community of natural songsters in order to thrill his audience with an exhibition of metrical virtuosity.

Scholars are in no doubt about Aristophanes' mastery of contemporary forms of song, from the epinician odes sung for victors at the Olympic and Pythian competitions to the more recherché and avant-garde experiments in freeform metrical flow that were being conducted by advocates of the New Music such as Timotheus. He could not otherwise have written the metrical section of the debate in *Frogs* (1201–1363), nor used every single type of metre found in Attic drama.[66] But in some of the lyric episodes in his plays it is impossible to be clear whether Aristophanes was aiming at aesthetic beauty to rival the lyrics of Stesichorus, Pindar, or Sophocles, or at an irreverent parodic tone that reduced the conventions of lyric to a familiar — and possibly exaggerated, distorted, or simplified — level, the aim of which was *always* comic (the answer to this question, of course, could be sometimes the former and sometimes the latter).[67]

The superb analysis of Aristophanes' songs by L. P. E. Parker (1997) is, however, surely correct to stress that Aristophanes' lyrics belong firmly to musical theatre, and need to be assessed as such. Musical theatre can accommodate a huge diversity of lyric performance, from work or drinking songs familiar from everyday contexts (to which the audience can sing along), to passages from the most elevated and solemn genres, to exquisite showcase arias (for example, the song of the hoopoe in *Birds*), to the class of song that Parker calls 'light verse', to be appreciated 'as well-turned verse, designed to join with spectacle and music to produce a complete theatrical experience, not to be subjected to close analysis as lyric poetry.'[68]

Such Aristophanic light theatrical verse has enticed an impressive range of composers into creating musical scores. *Lysistrata* has inspired many musical versions, including Franz Schubert's Viennese *Singspiel* entitled *The Conspirators* (*Die Verschworenen*, published in 1823),[69] a Berlin operetta by Paul Lincke,[70] and a more experimental operatic score (1961) by Milhaud's student Paul Kont. The theme of *Peace* has tended to produce rather solemn works, such as V. W. Popham's *Hymn to Peace from the Eirene of Aristophanes*, a high-minded cantata for solo soprano, contralto, and baritone and orchestra (1886), although this was hardly the case with the boisterous fiddles in the Klezmer barn dance and the Greek wedding song in the Thiasos Theatre Company's 2001 production (fig. 1.8), nor the eclectic blend of pop, R&B, and electrified Beethoven that enlivened the powerful *HeartBEAT*, an adaptation of *Peace* by the Mosaic Youth Theatre in Detroit (2002) (see fig. 1.9).

The *brekekekex* chorus from *Frogs* has exerted a continuing fascination, notably in André Bloch's opera on the legend of the Sleeping Beauty, *Brocéliande* (1925), whose score includes choruses of frogs and toads that sing with onomatopoeic noises certainly suggested by Aristophanes.[71] Yet of the plays that form the focus of this volume it is undoubtedly *Birds* that has inspired the most diverse musical responses. These have included Hubert Parry's music for the Cambridge Greek play in 1883, and the fanciful, cerebral opera *Die Vögel* by Walter Braunfels (op. 30, described as a 'lyrisch-phantastisches Spiel'), performed in Munich in 1920. Most recently, the birds have sung to an idiosyncratically electronic and percussive score, with prominent cello, composed by Ed Hughes (the librettist was Glyn Maxwell), that The Opera Group, in association with I Fagiolini, took on British tour in 2005.

The strong historical relationship between *Birds* and musical innovation, indeed, prompted the performance of suites from some significant scores at a special concert which was held during the conference at which most of the papers published here were delivered. The music was performed in Magdalen College auditorium by a woodwind quartet and the tenor voice of Peter Brown, one of the directors of the APGRD.[72] The concert programme included selections from the music that accompanied Planché's adaptation, with the addition of suites of music written for the same play by three significant twentieth-century figures in the USA, Greece, and England. When still a student in 1938, Leonard Bernstein composed the music for *Birds* at Harvard, for a wind quartet plus string quartet, harp, and percussion.[73] It was in this score that Bernstein first experimented with the new harmonies and strange rhythms that he had encountered listening at Harvard to the Hornbostel collection of recordings of Asian, African, and other non-European music.[74] The arresting woodwind music written by Manos Hatzidakis for Karolos Koun's *Birds* at one point parodied the music of the Greek Orthodox Church, as Van Steen's

FIG. 1.8 (above). Thiasos Theatre
Company's 2001 production of *Peace*.
FIG. 1.9 (left). Mosaic Youth Theatre's
production of *HeartBEAT*, 2002

essay describes (p. 160), and was the official reason for the censoring of the play. In the same year, 1959, the soon-to-be-famous comedian Dudley Moore wrote the score for a production of *Birds* in English by Oxford University Dramatic Society. The score was pre-recorded for the live performance of the play in the garden in Christ Church, and a tape recording made at the time is in the possession of the APGRD. Moore himself played the violin (deliberately flat) to a version of 'The Blue Danube', and other tunes included Walton's 'Crown Imperial' and the pop song 'Rockin' Robin'.

For a playwright not one note of whose original musical accompaniments survives (unlike, for example, Euripides, several fragments of melody by whom have been rediscovered on musical papyri),[75] Aristophanes has maintained a formidable presence not only in the comic theatre and imagination of posterity, but in its music too. And a book on performed Aristophanes that went to press in 2006 would be remiss if it failed to mention that Aristophanes reached surely his widest audience ever in May of that year. Aristophanes' choruses of frogs and birds danced vigorously to music arranged by Dimitris Papadimitriou at the 51st Eurovision Song Contest, held in Athens' vast Olympic Indoor Stadium. In spectacular costumes, and supervised by the famous theatre director Fokas Evangelinos, they leapt athletically around a temporarily erected dancing space while the international votes were counted. Tens of millions of television viewers from all over the enlarged Europe of the third millennium, in addition to non-European countries such as Israel that have traditionally (if rather bafflingly) taken part in the competition, will have been introduced to Aristophanes for the first time. Thanks to the Greek organisers of this international television event it is no longer only W. S. Gilbert's very model of a modern major general in *The Pirates of Penzance* (1879) who can boast of his superior erudition in saying that he is acquainted with 'the croaking chorus from the *Frogs* of Aristophanes'.[76]

Notes to Chapter 1

1. See e.g. T. G. A. Nelson (1990), Levin (1987).
2. This point is made with sustained passion and vigour in Silk's aptly entitled study *Aristophanes and the Definition of Comedy* (2000), especially in chs. 2, 7, and 8. See also Slater (2002), 1–21. The sense that Aristophanic plays are in some sense themselves self-conscious explorations of the history and theory of comedy is also often expressed in theatrical practice. A recent example was an adaptation of *Birds* in New York City, which invited spectators to think about comic history by identifying the heroes with Stan Laurel and Oliver Hardy, and to consider theoretical arguments about comedy by resurrecting Aristophanes to complain about modern notions of comedy. The production was David Gordon's *Aristophanes in Birdonia*, performed at the Danspace Project at St Mark's Church, 131 East 10th Street, in January 2006.
3. At the conference which gave rise to this volume, Masaru Sekine from the University of Waseda delivered a fascinating paper entitled 'Aristophanes and Kyogen: Comedies of Ancient Greece and Japan'; see also Sofer (2003). On Japanese fiction see Cohn (1998).
4. Sameh Mahran, playwright, quoted in Kolk and Decreus (2005), 162; El-Ramly (2005); see also Leezenberg (2005), 197, 201.
5. See e.g. Schechter (1994) on impersonation; Thiercy (1986) on carnival. There are some excellent remarks on the breadth of Aristophanes' legacy in Cartledge (1990), 72–76.
6. Shakespeare: Norwood (1968 [1931]), and Miola (1994). W. S. Gilbert: see below, pp. 84–85.

Beckett: see Reckford (2002) on echoes of *Birds* in *Waiting for Godot*. Dürrenmatt: Schmitz (1989) and Riedel (2000), 322.

7. See e.g. Lesky (1963), 425.

8. See e.g. Minturno (1563), translation by Anita Grossvogel as excerpted in Lauter (1964), 74–86, at pp. 81–82; Dover (1968), 147; Csapo (2000). For a short, accessible, and pellucid account of Menander's important relationships with both Aristophanic comedy and Euripidean tragedy, see Brown (2001), pp. xii–xv. There are some excellent cautionary remarks on the limits to our understanding of the evolution of Greek comedy in Henderson (1995).

9. Literary Criticism: Grube (1965), ch. 2. Freedom of speech: see Cartledge (1990), 76 on Salman Rushdie and Tony Harrison; Halliwell (1991); Henderson (1998); Brockmann (2003); Saxonhouse (2006). Platonic irony: Nehamas (1998), part I. Folktale and fiction: Sifakis (1992). German classicism: Hille (1907) and Hilsenbeck (1908); for some of the traditional comparands in the earlier decades of the 20th c. see G. Murray (1933), p. viii.

10. On Science Fiction see Suvin (1979), 55, 87, 94, 99. Dada and Jarry: Trachtman (2006). Comedy and imperialism; beast fables: Cook (1949), as excerpted in Lauter (1964), 475–96 at pp. 479, 493. Joan Littlewood's encounter with Aristophanes when directing Ewan MacColl's adaptation of *Lysistrata* in 1947 (written in the late 1930s), under the name of *Operation Olive Branch*, proved a formative influence on her own theatre works including the satirical protest musical *Oh! What a Lovely War* (1963).

11. 'This arid field' is how Erich Segal (1996), p. xxi, described the entire history of scholarship devoted to the influence of Aristophanes.

12. Solomos (1961), published in English translation in 1974; Russo (1962), published in English translation in 1994.

13. The topic's central status in contemporary scholarship is likely to be confirmed after the delivery and publication of Helene Foley's forthcoming Sather Classical lectures (2007) on the performance of Greek theatre in the USA.

14. See Hall, Macintosh, and Wrigley (2004).

15. Hall, Macintosh, and Taplin (2000); Macintosh, Michelakis, Hall, and Taplin (2005).

16. See Riedel (2000), 220; Holtermann (2004), 127–29.

17. e.g. Srebrny (1984); Flashar (1991); Hartigan (1995).

18. Holtermann (2004). See also Süss (1911), Rechner (1914), L. E. Lord (1925).

19. Gamel (2002).

20. See Harvey and Wilkins (2000); Zimmermann (1998), 188–201; Revermann (2006), 299–319.

21. On which see also, in particular, the very different conclusions drawn by J. R. Green (1985) and Taplin (1987), esp. 97–102.

22. For bibliographical resources, see especially J. R. Green (1989); (1991); (1994); (2002).

23. Further discussion and up-to-date bibliography in Taplin (2007), part I.

24. See further Taplin (2007), part I.

25. A. Hughes (1996).

26. Revermann (2006), 70–71.

27. For a collection and discussion of the relevant ancient evidence in English translation, see Csapo and Slater (1994), 103–85; see also MacDowell (1995), 7–26. There is a clear and succinct account of the chronology of Aristophanes' comic productions, including both lost and surviving plays, in Cartledge (1990), pp. xiii–xviii.

28. Hypothesis to *Frogs* Ic, which claims that the 4th-c. Dicaearchus, a student of Aristotle, was the source of its information.

29. See Revermann (2006), 73; MacDowell (1995), 297–300.

30. See the excellent discussion of Revermann (2006), 75–86. The two different versions of *Peace* may lie behind the confusing identities of the personnel portrayed on the only vase-painting that has sometimes been discussed in relationship to this play, a beautiful Attic red-figured kalyx-krater (Vienna 1024; fig. 25a–b in Stafford 2000, who discusses this and other late 5th-c. Athenian visual images of Eirene on p. 188).

31. *IG* II². 3091. See further Csapo (2004); E. Hall (forthcoming).

32. *Moralia* 853 A–854 D. On this text see Hunter (2000); Revermann (2006), 86.

33. Translation taken from G. Murray (1933), 216.

34. I owe this reference to the late Nan Dunbar, distinguished editor of *Birds* (1994), who wrote to me about it at the time of the conference; see also E. Hall (2002*b*), 30–31 and n. 103.

35. Winter (1933), 224–25; 219 n. 10. For papyrus texts of Aristophanes see also N. Gonis in *The Oxyrhynchus Papyri*, lxvi (1999), nos. 4510–21, with a reference to all previously published papyri on p. 118.

36. On the Aristophanic presence within Lucian see also Branham (1989), esp. 14–20.

37. See below, Giannopoulou, p. 313; Van Kerchove (1974). On the Renaissance, Enlightenment, and Romantic tendency to discuss Aristophanes in conjunction with Lucian see also Riedel (2000), 57, 150–52.

38. *Plutus* was performed in Latin and in Greek at Zwickau in 1521, and in Greek at Zürich in 1531 (Boas (1914), 16).

39. Antonio Sebastiano Minturno, Bishop of Crotone, wrote in his influential *L'Arte Poetica*, published in Venice in 1563: 'I would very much like that our writers imitate Aristophanes for the ancient and the Latins for the New Comedy. Because, thanks to our scholars, those among them who do not know Latin or Greek can read them in our language although not exactly as in the original, but enough to guide them on their way' (trans. Anita Grossvogel excerpted in Lauter (1964), 74–86, at p. 79).

40. Le Loyer (2004).

41. See e.g. Cave (1979), 35–78; Scolnicov (1989); Perret (1992). There was an even earlier French imitation of *Wasps*, entitled *Les Guespes attiques, traduite du grec d'Aristophane par Jean Vernou*, which was published in Paris in 1545, but it has apparently not survived: see Le Loyer (2004), 20 n. 1.

42. T. Le Fèvre (1659).

43. H. Trevelyan (1941), 60. See also Grumach (1949), 306–09.

44. H. Trevelyan (1941), 91 and nn. 1–2 detects traces in his work and diary of *Ecclesiazusae* and *Frogs*. See also Atkins (1995), esp. 244.

45. See Bruford (1950), 299–319; Prudhoe (1973), 65–84.

46. Boyle (1991), 336.

47. Goethe (1987), 685.

48. The translation is quoted from Bruford (1962), 130.

49. These two images are conveniently reproduced in Knudsen (1949), 87, 89.

50. See especially Atkins (1995) and Riedel (2000), 169 on the profound Aristophanic reverberations in Goethe's masterpiece *Faust* (published between 1808 and 1832).

51. Goethe (1987), 686.

52. Werner (1975), 469–70.

53. See Goethe (1987), 336.

54. Two allusions in contemporary authors suggest that *Frogs* was indeed staged for the edification of Friedrich Wilhelm IV, under the direction of either August Kopisch or Ludwig Tieck. For a discussions of the meagre evidence, see Rieks (1993), 124 with n. 23; Holtermann (2004), 313. There had also been a version of *Clouds* performed at the Paris Odéon in 1843 or 1844.

55. Werner (1975), 483. On the other hand, in the early 1870s, the Aristophanes scholar Julius Richter had written 'Aristophanic' comedies with titles such as *Die Ungeziefer* (*The Vermin*, 1872, which is reminiscent of *Frogs*) and *Die Schwalben* (*The Swallows*, 1873); these were virulent right-wing attacks on the views of communists and social democrats, written in ancient Greek in order to speak to a particular and well-defined élite intelligentsia.

56. Solomos (1974 [1961]), 274.

57. See Riedel (2000), 151–52; Holtermann (2004), 74–76.

58. See esp. Hardwick (2004).

59. See e.g. Anon. (1895).

60. See especially Kotzamani (1997); (2005), 241–43. The most important productions were Max Reinhardt's in Berlin (1908) and Nemirovich-Danchenko's at the Moscow Art Theatre's Musical Studio in 1923.

61. On Stein's *Oresteia* see Fischer-Lichte (2004), 344–52; Michelakis (2005), 7, 18.

62. See Riedel (2000), 346–50.

63. Michelakis (2002).

64. See Revel-Mouroz (2002), 102; Durvye (2002), 85.

65. 'Wer Metrik lernen will, soll mit Aristophanes anfangen' (Wilamowitz 1922, 95).

66. L. P. E. Parker (1997), 297.

67. Michael Silk, for example, rather played down Aristophanes' skills as a lyric composer in an influential article (1980).

68. L. P. E. Parker (1997), 15.

69. On which see recently Beta (2002).

70. See further Beta (2001).

71. See R. L. Smith (2006). Indeed, in the case of *Frogs* as well as *Birds* it is often the music that has been remembered long after memories of other aspects of the productions have faded. At Dulwich College's annual Greek play in the earlier years of the 20th c., *Birds* and *Frogs* were two of the favourite plays staged. Mr Doulton's musical compositions, played by a full orchestra with brass and a harp, made a considerable impact, especially the 'solemn march in *The Frogs* for the Eleusinian worshippers' (Leake 1938, 127). But the frogs' cry of *brekekekex koax koax* has a tradition of its own: see e.g. Hans Christian Andersen's tale of 1835, 'Tommelise' (in English known as 'Thumbelina'), in which the toad's son, on seeing the heroine in her walnut shell, can say only 'koax, koax, brekke-ke-kex!' (Andersen n.d. i. 68).

72. On 17 Sept. 2004. The instrumental performers were Helen Clarke, Benjamin Skipp, Edward Littleton, and Benjamin Wardhaugh, who arranged the music for woodwind quartet. A CD recording of the concert is available for consultation at the APGRD.

73. Commissioned by the Harvard Classical Club for the production (1939) when he was a student (score available in the Leonard Bernstein Archive), as was his music for *Peace* in 1941. The *Birds* was very important to his development since Aaron Copland attended the production and as a result encouraged Bernstein to pursue a career as an orchestral conductor. See Peyser (1987), 51.

74. Peyser (1987), 39–40.

75. Transcriptions of the musical papyri relating to Greek tragedy are to be found in West (1992), 283–326 and Pöhlmann and West (2001); see also E. Hall (2002*b*), 5–24, 30–35.

76. See further below, p. 84. I would like to thank all my colleagues at the APGRD — Scott, Fiona, Pantelis and Amanda — for their comments and other help in the writing of this Introduction, but especially Peter Brown for some searching comments and Oliver Taplin, who allowed me to see Part I of the text of his forthcoming *Pots and Plays* (2007), as well as heroically stepping into the breach and giving an impromptu paper on the ancient vase record at the conference itself.

PART I

❖

Precedents

CHAPTER 2

The Ups and Downs of Aristophanic Travel

Ewen Bowie

Introduction

If Aristophanes and his rivals in the fifth century BC were important for the literary imagination of the second and third centuries AD, it was hardly, if at all, as a result of performances of their comedies. Accordingly, although this chapter will address three aspects of Aristophanes' reception in the second and third centuries AD, and one of these, naturally, is performance, by contrast with other parts of this volume performance will be the least prominent aspect in my discussion. The other two aspects I address are (*a*) reading and (*b*) reworking in a text entirely or primarily intended for reading. A full assessment of the impact of Aristophanes on the Greek cultural life of the second and third centuries AD would also have to discuss exploitation of his work by the scholars and lexicographers Moeris, Pollux, and Philetaerus, but this is not the appropriate place to advance that investigation.

The most interesting aspect for the culture of the second and third centuries AD is reworking in a text entirely or primarily intended for reading, and I shall keep this until last. Moreover, to some extent performance and reading need to be taken together and are (in a sense) prior. In my discussion I bear in mind this volume's special focus on *Peace, Birds,* and *Frogs,* but comparison with other plays and with other forms of reference to them will occasionally be appropriate.

Performance and Reading

From the second half of the first century AD, the Greek world enjoyed increasing economic prosperity — thanks largely to peace imposed by Rome — and this prosperity was accompanied by a cultural renaissance. To the cities of mainland Greece (pre-eminently Athens, Sparta, even the Roman colony Corinth), and of what had been and was still perceived as Ionia (Smyrna, Ephesus, Miletus), were now added not just the scores of cities founded in Asia Minor, the Levant, and Egypt by Alexander and his successors, but dozens more which imperial policy encouraged to develop on the basis of villages or scattered populations. The Greek-speaking populations of these cities defined their Greekness not least by an education founded on reading of canonical Greek texts of the eighth to fourth centuries BC:

familiarity with these texts was expected in participants in dinner parties, and by viewers of paintings and sculptures, at lectures of philosophers or sophists, and by readers of any texts with pretensions to high culture.

It is clear that in this period such educated Greeks (for whom the term *pepaideumenoi*, 'educated', was widely used) were aware what Old Comedy was, knew that Aristophanes, along with Cratinus and Eupolis, was one of its major exponents, and had read enough, whether in complete texts or in anthologies, to quote, to refer to, and to recognize the titles of plays and lines from them. The table in the Appendix (pp. 43–49 below) presents some of the evidence, but such investigation could be carried further. Overall it is clear that New Comedy, and above all Menander, was used much more in education and was much more read — as is demonstrated by the distribution of papyri. I also incline to the view that it was only New Comedy that was performed, though the interpretation of the evidence is not easy.[1] But our literary texts of this period — with the exception of the Greek 'ideal' novels — are far less tilted in the direction of New Comedy; moreover, while allusions or quotations in some authors are too few to be the basis of an argument, and while some authors have a particular reason for their choices, it does seem that Aristophanes and other poets of Old Comedy gained ground during the second century. The most plausible explanation for this is that there was an increasing consensus among the creators of prose literature that they should aim to write in a Greek as near to fifth- and fourth-century Attic as possible, and Old Comedy was perceived as an uncontaminated source of Attic vocabulary and syntax.[2]

Learned Citation

To give an impression of the importance of Old Comedy for the period, relative to the importance of Menander, I offer some details of its citation in the speeches of Dio of Prusa (a philosopher and sophist active between c.AD 70 and 112), of Aelius Aristides,[3] and of Maximus of Tyre (a philosopher and sophist active in the reign of Commodus, i.e. AD 180–92).

Dio of Prusa cites or mentions Aristophanes three times,[4] Cratinus twice,[5] Eupolis once,[6] and the poets of New Comedy not at all.

Aelius Aristides refers twice to Eupolis' play *Demes*, on one of these occasions using the phrase 'a certain comic poet'.[7] At another point in the same speech he cites two other fragments of Eupolis,[8] the very well-known fragments 102 and 103; elsewhere he twice alludes to fragment 102;[9] Aristides does not name the poet on any of these occasions. In another speech,[10] Aristides quotes a line from a comic poet which is attributed by a scholion (marginal comment by an ancient scholar) in the manuscripts of Aristides to Eupolis' play *Maricas*: but Aristides, perhaps correctly, must think it was from Cratinus,[11] and it is from Cratinus' *Chirons* that he goes on to quote another single line, naming the title but not the poet.[12] Aristides alludes to or cites Cratinus four more times: at 3.154 in the edition of Friedrich Lenz, continued posthumously by Charles Behr, he cites fragment 229 without naming the poet; at 2.72 Lenz–Behr he cites fragment 324, naming Cratinus, then at 3.51 Lenz–Behr he again cites the same fragment but without naming him. At 34.51 in the edition of

Heinrich Keil (still used for speeches not included in Lenz–Behr) he cites fragment 364 and attributes it to Cratinus, but he does not specify from what play it comes.

Aristides alludes to or cites Menander with similar frequency, i.e. five times or fewer: 3.665 Lenz–Behr names Menander and refers to fragment 432 in the edition of Kassel and Austin (KA); 7.5 Lenz–Behr alludes without name to fragment 146 KA (which may or may not be by Menander); 2.168 Lenz–Behr may allude (using the phrase 'a certain poet') to fragment 2 of the *Girl Possessed*; 3.133 Lenz–Behr cites a line 'of the comic poet', fragment 506 KA, which may be from Menander;[13] 2.237 Lenz–Behr alludes to fragment 642 KA without naming the poet. In his *Sacred Tales* Aristides also narrates an incident in which he dreamt that somebody came with a work of Menander, which he interpreted as a sign he should 'stay' — in Greek, *menein* (47.51 Keil).

Maximus of Tyre refers to Aristophanes five times,[14] seems to allude to one passage of *Clouds* concerning the pallor of Chaerephon,[15] and cites a passage from *Frogs*[16] (see the table in the Appendix); he cites Eupolis once or perhaps twice.[17] He cites Menander once (5.7, fragment 363 KA) and other New Comedy not at all.

Of these three orators, then, only Aelius Aristides cites Old and New Comedy with equal frequency: Dio and Maximus (though of course the figures are tiny) draw far more on Old Comedy than on New.

Lucian

After Aristides I bring onto my metaphorical stage a writer who has been much more influential and admired in post-Renaissance times, when knowledge of some of his more Aristophanic texts affected the way Aristophanes was adapted for performance (see p. 28 n. 37 above), but who probably made rather less of an impression in his own time, and certainly in late antiquity and Byzantium: Lucian of Samosata. I confess to having been profoundly shocked recently when I heard Lucian referred to as 'an obscure Greek author' by an otherwise articulate and well-informed academic in a radio programme about Henry Watson Fowler, author of *Modern English Usage* and, in collaboration with his brother Francis George Fowler, of an important four-volume English translation of Lucian's work.[18] I assume that to most readers Lucian is widely enough known not to need a long introduction. I offer, then, just a brief reminder of some key facts.

Born in around AD 120 in Commagene's capital Samosata on the river Euphrates — now, perhaps symbolically, submerged under a huge Euphrates-valley lake — Lucian received a good tertiary Greek education in rhetoric and philosophy: we do not know where this was, although Antioch, Tarsus, and Ionia are all possibilities. He seems then to have embarked on the career of an epideictic sophist that attracted Aelius Aristides and so many others. Despite some claimed success in this career (perhaps only in western provinces), Lucian developed a form of rhetorical entertainment very different from the standard declamations, *meletai*, in which orators, *rhētores*, adopted the *persona* of a fifth- or fourth-century Greek politician, usually Athenian, and purported to persuade a citizen assembly of a certain course of action in relation to glorious moments in Greek history — Marathon,

Salamis, Leuctra, resistance to Philip of Macedon. Like such *rhētores*, Lucian's main performance was sometimes preceded by a taster, a *prolalia*, thematically linked to the main course; but that main course in Lucian's case was a satirical romp, often mocking the sophists and philosophers who performed in the same theatres and concert-halls as Lucian, and quite often in dialogue form. It is impossible to be sure which of Lucian's surviving works were initially presented orally, and if so on how many different occasions. What we have in our manuscripts was clearly suited to circulation in the form of a written text for reading, and some works may never have been intended for oral delivery. But that some *were* intended for oral delivery seems certain, and it is these that offer part of the legitimation of the inclusion of Lucian in a research project focused on performance.[19]

The other axis of legitimation is the contribution of Attic, and especially of Aristophanic, Comedy to Lucian's new art form. In a much-quoted passage of the dialogue *Twice Prosecuted* Lucian has the character *Dialogos*, Dialogue, claim in his accusation of him in Zeus' court that

> he stripped me of that tragic and self-controlled mask, and put another upon me that was comic and satyric and little short of ridiculous. Next he took to the same place as me and penned in with me Mockery, and Iambus, and Cynicism, and Eupolis and Aristophanes, men who are formidable in their abuse of what is respectable and in their jeering at all that is right. Finally he even introduced ... one of the Cynics of old called Menippus ... (*Twice Prosecuted* 33)

This is a persuasive account of the sort of literary pedigree Lucian might have been ready to acknowledge in his genre-crossing *mimēsis*. To try to sort out which elements in Lucian's deformation of philosophical treatises, biographies, and dialogues are attributable to Old Comedy, which to early Greek iambic poetry, and which to Hellenistic Menippean satire is not a task to be undertaken in this essay. What I want to focus on is the range of Lucian's exploitations of Old Comedy, and ways in which it is exploited by him.[20]

First, an ancient reader might ask why only Eupolis and Aristophanes are mentioned, and not the third member of the gang of three, Cratinus. Part of the answer may be that Lucian was aware that he cited lines of Cratinus rarely or not at all: the only mention of Cratinus by name in the Lucianic corpus is in the spurious *Long-Lifers* 25, where Cratinus is claimed to have lived to ninety-four years old and to have died shortly after staging his comedy *Wine Flask* (*Pytinē*). This was the play of Cratinus known to anybody who knew anything of Cratinus at all, and another part of the answer to the question 'Why is Cratinus not named in *Twice Prosecuted* 33?' is that the whole structure of the dialogue is actually modelled on Cratinus' immensely successful play, as was seen long ago by Kaibel:[21] in that play, the female characters Comedy and Inebriation seem successively to have accused the playwright of abandoning them after cohabitation, probably in the formal structure of the rhetorical contest (*agōn*) that is a regular feature of Old Comedy; the two accusatory speeches of Lucian's 'Rhetoric' (*Rhētorikē*) and 'Dialogue' (*Dialogos*) rework this schema. With his characteristically light touch Lucian prepares for *Dialogos*' claim to have been penned-in with Eupolis and Aristophanes by having *Dialogos* describe himself as previously 'air-walking high up in the clouds' (*Twice*

Prosecuted 32): that takes us straight to Socrates' line in *Clouds* 225 'I am air-walking and am meditating on the sun'; and if we were ever in danger of not seeing this intertext, the phrase 'high up in the clouds', gives us a nudge.[22] This is a line that Lucian alludes to twice elsewhere: at *You are a Prometheus* 6, likewise in a self-referential discussion of Lucian's marriage of serious/pretentious philosophical dialogue with its debunker Comedy; and in *Icaromenippus* 13, where it is wickedly put in the mouth of the philosopher Empedocles. Finally, an audience or reader of *Twice Prosecuted* 32–33 will almost certainly know that *Wine Flask* was the play that won first prize in the Dionysia of 424/3 BC when the first version of Aristophanes' *Clouds* only came third.

The *Twice Prosecuted,* then, may owe more to Cratinus' *Wine Flask* than to any play of Aristophanes. It would certainly be rash to try to explain the role of Hermes, who appears as a character in this and in ten other Lucianic works, as showing the influence of *Peace*; and although the dialogue's setting is on Olympus, no emphasis is laid on the problems or excitements of mortal travel to this elevated court-room (as use of *Peace* would lead us to expect).

Twice Prosecuted is far from being the only dialogue in which Lucian uses the Old Comic *agōn* (contest) as a device to structure his pieces and to evoke classical Comedy. He reworks it in several different ways. Two other good examples are *Fisherman* and *Zeus the Tragic Actor.*

In *Fisherman* a character in some way representative of Lucian, Parrhesiades (Frankness-son) is pursued on-stage, as it were, by a group of irate philosophers who form a sort of chorus. This evocation of a *parodos* (entry of the chorus) is followed by an *agōn* which involves a formal trial, and the piece is concluded by a scene in which imposters are attracted by baits of food and gold and fished (hence the title) by the protagonist Parrhesiades. Several features evoke *Acharnians*: the entry of the philosophers (including their cry 'Pelt, pelt ... ', cf. *Acharnians* 281–82), Parrhesiades' suggestion that he will have to take refuge with Euripides (3, cf. *Acharnians* 394), and his effective defence of his actions as having been just. But that the great philosophers turn out to have been allowed to come up from Hades to take part in the debate (14) reworks a motif from a well-known Comedy of one of Aristophanes' rivals, Eupolis' *Demes*, in which dead politicians were resurrected to advise Athens in a political crisis.[23]

In *Zeus the Tragic Actor* Zeus calls an assembly of the gods to address the emergency of mankind's desisting from divine worship as a result of the preaching of the Epicurean philosopher Damis. Eventually the issues are mock-seriously hammered out in an *agōn* between Damis and the Stoic philosopher Timocles. The notion of a divine audience for a mortal debate might ultimately be traced to *Frogs,* whereas the idea of the gods facing a crisis because sacrifices have been interrupted reworks the unfriendly feathered blockade of Olympus in *Birds*.[24]

Some other works have a comparably Aristophanic patina. A prime exhibit must be *Icaromenippus*, in which Lucian's character Menippus tells an unnamed friend, addressed regularly as 'My dear friend', *ō hetaire,* of his recent journey to Olympus via the moon, a journey whose purpose was to discover which of the contradictory views of philosophers concerning the gods was nearer the truth. To get up to heaven he strapped onto himself the right wing of an eagle and the left wing of a vulture (*Icaromenippus* 10). The idea that with wings he might fly to heaven was encouraged by his desire to get there and by 'the storyteller Aesop showing that the heavens were accessible to eagles and dung-beetles, and sometimes even to camels' (*Icaromenippus* 10). This is manifestly a reworking of lines from the opening sequence (*prologos*) of *Peace*:

> DAUGHTER   And what is your idea, so as to yoke a dung-beetle
>   and drive it up to the gods, daddy dear?
> TRYGAEUS   In the stories of Aesop it was discovered to be the only one
>   among the winged creatures to have reached the gods.
>   (*Peace* 127–30)

This is one of very few references to Aristophanes' *Peace* in literary texts of this period. Plutarch has only one quotation,[25] Aelius Aristides has none; the seven citations in Athenaeus and eight in Pollux is a low score for these scholarly squirrels. It is surely in Lucian's *Icaromenippus* to provoke us to think about the relationship between Menippus' fantastic journey in *Icaromenippus* and that of Trygaeus in *Peace*. And whereas the real author Menippus in the early third century BC may have composed a work involving some sort of journey to the underworld, perhaps following or influenced by a part of the *Silloi* of Timon of Phlius that may have taken this form,[26] there is no evidence that either Menippus or Timon composed a work involving a journey to heaven. This fusion of Aristophanes and Menippus has a good claim to being an innovation of Lucian.

There may also have been a hint at Aristophanic pedigree a little earlier in *Icaromenippus*. The first stage in Lucian's Menippus' quest had been to enrol himself in an expensive philosophy graduate school: 'I thought I should learn to be a lofty-chatterer and get to know the orderly arrangement of the universe' (*Icaromenippus* 5). The word 'lofty-chatterer', *meteōroleschēs*, is attributed by a scholiast on *Peace* 92 to Aristophanes' *Clouds,* and since it does not appear in our revised *Clouds* it is a possible fragment of the first *Clouds*. The edition of Kassel and Austin points out that there could be a confusion with *meteōrophenakas* (*Clouds* 333) or *meteōrosophistōn* (*Clouds* 360), but the appearance of *meteōroleschēs* in *Icaromenippus* 5 does something to support an Aristophanic use of that particular word. Either way, the word's use at *Icaromenippus* 5 asks us to recall Aristophanic send-ups of philosophers in one (or both?) of his two versions of *Clouds*. But it also, as the scholiast may have seen, triggers a recollection of *Peace* 92: 'Where on earth is your lofty prattle taking you?' So *Peace* is on Lucian's literary agenda by the time he wrote *Icaromenippus* 5. A little later, as we have seen, at *Icaromenippus* 13, Empedocles is given an allusion to Socrates' line in *Clouds* 225, 'I am air-walking and am meditating on the sun'.[27] This helps us to continue to relate Lucian's debunking of philosophers and comic treatment of the gods to an Aristophanic model. The same may be the function of the probable allusion to the Aristophanic Socrates' argument against the justice of Zeus at *Clouds* 398–402 that we find in *Zeus Refuted* 16.

So much for upstairs. Now for downstairs. Lucian takes us to the Underworld more than once. Although in Lucian's Underworld readers who knew Timon of Phlius and the historical Menippus may have been able to pick up reworkings of these writers that elude us, it is clear that Lucian keeps the descent to the underworld (*katabasis*) of Aristophanes' *Frogs* in play too. In *Sailing Down or The*

Tyrant, the first speaking characters are Charon, Clotho (one of the Fates), and Hermes; the scene is the outer bank of the Styx. Hermes is late with his new batch of dead — they have been delayed because a tyrant has escaped from the column. A Cynic philosopher, eager to get to Hades, and the tyrant himself, Megapenthes — as reluctant as the Cynic is eager — join the dialogue (*Sailing Down or The Tyrant* 7 ff.). Charon's boat is just about to sail when a poor cobbler Micyllus whimpers that he is being forgotten:

> Tell me, Clotho, and do you take no account of me? Or because I am poor, must I for that reason also embark last? (*Sailing Down or The Tyrant* 14)

This is a clear allusion to *Frogs* 87 (=107 =115), a phrase spoken repeatedly by the slave Xanthias, waiting under his heavy burden while Heracles and Dionysus chatter about tragedians; 'and they take no account of me.' Another couple of allusions to *Frogs* follow soon at section 18, to lines 198 and 273.

The same intertext, 'and they take no account of me', is used to close the dialogue *Charon or Watchers*, in which once more the usual suspects Hermes and Charon are the only interlocutors. Hermes takes Charon high up to observe what silliness is being perpetrated on earth — summed up at the end by Charon in the words 'kings, golden bricks, hecatombs, battles: but they take no account of Charon' (*Charon or Watchers* 24). One function of this intertextuality is subtly to bring the place of the action back to the banks of the Styx.

It is not so clear what is happening in *Runaway Slaves* 28 (set in divine space), where a master complains that his former slave Cantharus is now a philosopher 'but no account is taken of us'.[28] I doubt, however, if this casual use should be taken to invalidate the claim of productive intertextuality made for *Sailing Down or The Tyrant* and *Charon or Watchers*. Rather Lucian's *mimēsis* of canonical texts, like that of some of his contemporaries (e.g. Longus), operates on two levels: sometimes intertextuality invites the reader/audience to recall the classical context and use it in interpreting the text in hand, at other times a phrase simply contributes to the classicising cultural and linguistic wallpaper.

I now turn to another katabatic dialogue, *Menippus or Consultation of the Dead*. That also has fleeting allusions to two Aristophanic plays, *Birds* and *Frogs*. First, near its beginning, when Menippus' unnamed interlocutor — addressed, just as in *Icaromenippus,* as 'My dear friend', *ō hetaire* (e.g. at the end of §1) — comments on Menippus' bizarre outfit 'What is the point of his outlandish get-up — the felt cap, the lyre, the lion-skin?' there is clear allusion to Dionysus in *Frogs* 45–47. Shortly the interlocutor asks Menippus the purpose of his recent expedition to the Underworld, saying he would gladly hear '... what was the intent of your downward journey'. This sounds like a reworking of Peisthetairos' question to the astronomer Meton at *Birds* 994: 'What is the intent, what the loose-fitting boot of your downward journey?' Lucian may be drawing a reader's or audience's attention to the point that his opening with a dialogue between a major and a minor character is one of no doubt several ways in which he is refashioning Aristophanes: such a prompt might be especially timely in a dialogue whose mixture of prose and verse, together with a main character called Menippus, might have given the false impression that Lucian's *mimēsis* was simply of the historical Menippus.

My last Lucianic text is *True Narratives*. At first sight this is a text that can owe little to Old Comedy — a first-person narrative satirizing tall stories in historians, parodying the *Odyssey*, and raising questions about the nature of novelistic fiction. But it is precisely the issue of fiction that may be behind the Aristophanic touch in *True Narratives*. Towards the end of the section that Lucian, adopting a historiographic manner, marked off as 'Book One', his first-person narrator tells of the last stage of his long aerial journey, which will be succeeded by an ocean adventure.

> Setting off on the next day, by this point we were sailing near the clouds: and indeed there we also caught sight of the city Cloudcuckooland and marvelled at it, but we didn't land on it, for the wind prevented us. However their king was said to be Coronus son of Cottyphion [as it were, Crowe son of Blackbirdikin]. And I called to mind the poet Aristophanes, a man clever (*sophos*) and truthful and groundlessly disbelieved in respect of what he wrote. (*True Narratives* I. 29)

This brilliant salvo invites us to reassess what we have been reading. We had been prompted at the start of Book One to see as intertexts Homer's *Odyssey*, the classical historian Ctesias, and the Hellenistic writer of a utopian travellers' tale Iambulus. We had also discovered Herodotus to be in Lucian's sights.[29] We had also been told emphatically that Lucian was writing about what he had neither seen nor experienced nor heard from anybody else, and furthermore things neither existing at all nor capable of existing in the first place — so readers should by no means believe them (*True Narratives* I. 4 end). Now Lucian professes to admire the cleverness (*sophia*) and truthfulness of Aristophanes. In the context of a professedly fictitious narrative we are perhaps entitled to add a negative before the claim to Aristophanic truthfulness: but we need not, and Lucian may be cross-referring to Aristophanic comedy at the expense of philosophers, comedy with which his other intertexts show him to be in sympathy. We certainly need not negate Lucian's attribution of cleverness to Aristophanes — and at the same time we are invited to admire Lucian's own cleverness. Lucian has been taking his narrator on an aerial journey that can be argued to have *Peace* and *Birds* in its complex literary pedigree. We had been given a tiny hint to look out for Aristophanic material, when he said near the beginning that

> each of the things investigated alludes not without touches of comedy (*ouk akōmōidētōs*) to some of the ancient poets, historians and philosophers who wrote up many outlandish and mythical things. (*True Narratives* I. 2)

But I suspect few readers, even connoisseurs of Lucian, will have confidently linked his fantastic sky-trek with *Peace* and *Birds* until they encountered the reference to Cloudcuckooland at I.29.

On a micro-level Lucian also displays his cleverness by giving the city a king with a birdy Homeric name (Coronus, *Iliad* 2.746), and a patronymic that introduces a bird *not* in Aristophanes' *Birds*, whose spelling in good Attic (*kottuphos*) is different from its spelling (*kossuphos*) in the common Greek (*koine*) that was used in everyday life in Lucian's world. It is on several levels, then, that Lucian reworks Aristophanic comedy, and this reworking is much more pervasive than the few specific intertextualities might suggest.

Antonius Diogenes

Another writer of fiction may also, however, be important both for *True Narratives* and for second-century exploitation of Aristophanic comedy. At least so Photius thought in the ninth century AD: towards the end of his summary of the *Incredible Things beyond Thule* of Antonius Diogenes (*Bibliotheca, Codex* 166) he claims that this work is the 'fount and root' of Lucian's *True Narratives*, and indeed was a paradigm for the loves, abductions, and adventures of the novels of Iamblichus, Achilles Tatius, Heliodorus, and Damascius (111[b]35–42). The proposition that Lucian in his *True Narratives* drew heavily on *Incredible Things beyond Thule* was believed by Rohde in 1876 but was vigorously criticized by John Morgan two decades ago.[30] Strong as Morgan's case was, I do not think it proved the matter, and I still think that *Incredible Things beyond Thule* was one of the many texts in Lucian's mind when writing *True Narratives* and one that he would expect some readers to recognize.

Wherever the truth on this may lie, Antonius Diogenes merits attention in himself.[31] It is very hard to work out from Photius' summary either the structure or the tone of Antonius Diogenes' work. The main characters are Deinias, an Arcadian who travelled with his son Demochares *via* the Black and Caspian Seas and the sources of the Tanais (the river Don) to Thule, and Dercyllis, a rich girl from Tyre who had also travelled there with her brother Mantineas, fleeing the persecution of an evil wizard with an Egyptian-sounding name. There Deinias starts an affair with Dercyllis, and there too Mantineas seems to have several liaisons. Numerous sub-plots involving minor characters are recounted to Deinias on Thule, as too are Dercyllis and Mantineas' travels, which involved visits to Crete, Etruria, Spain, Aquitaine, Sicily, and Thrace. In Italy Dercyllis' travels included a *katabasis* which allowed an exchange with her dead servant Myrto, now in the Underworld — apparently at Lake Avernus near Naples. All this — and much more — is narrated by Deinias (when he and Dercyllis have returned to Tyre) to an Arcadian ambassador Cymbas who is trying to persuade Deinias to return to Arcadia. Ultimately — in the penultimate column of Photius' summary — we discover that Deinias' narrative was written down, on his instructions, in duplicate on cypress tablets by one Erasinides, Cymbas' companion: one set of these tablets was taken to Arcadia by Cymbas, the other was buried with Deinias in Tyre, there to be discovered by Balagrus after Alexander's capture of Tyre, and reported by him to his wife Phila, daughter of Antipater. At this point too we discover from Photius that Antonius Diogenes prefaced his 24-book work with a letter to Faustinus, saying that he had gathered together *Incredible Things beyond Thule* and dedicated the *dramata* to his sister Isidora. He then says that he is a poet of Old Comedy, and that even if he is fabricating things incredible and false, yet he has the testimony of older writers concerning the majority of the stories he has told ...

> And he says of himself that he is a poet of Old Comedy (*kōmōidias palaias*),[32] and that even if he is fabricating things that are incredible and fictitious, nevertheless for the greatest number of the stories he has told he has the testimonies of earlier writers, from which he has assembled these with toil. (*Bibliotheca, Codex* 166, 111[a]34–38)

Let us take stock. These two letters seem to have prefaced the whole work, and the narrative as a whole seems to have been encapsulated in, or been further prefaced by, a letter from Balagrus to his wife Phila. It is hard to see Old Comedy here. The various adventures seem further to have been nested in a Chinese box structure. Again, little to suggest Comedy. So what is Antonius Diogenes playing at?[33] I guess — and it must be a guess — that four elements may be relevant. First, the element of fantastic travel, which at one point came close to the moon (111^a7); second, the *katabasis* of Dercyllis; and third, the opening and perhaps further handling of the story: 'There is brought on stage (*eisagetai*) a certain Deinias who has travelled far from his native city in the quest for knowledge together with his son Demochares'. Although this is far from the only place that the Greek term *eisagetai* is used by Photius in summarizing the plots of work of prose fiction, it would particularly suit a quasi-dramatic frame: I am tempted to guess that the work opened with a dialogue — an exchange between the protagonist Deinias and a minor character, his son. An exchange between a father and a son opens *Clouds* and is played out near the start of *Wasps* (and seems likely to have formed part of Aristophanes' first play, *Banqueters*); exchanges between central and minor characters setting out on a quest open both *Birds* and *Frogs*. Perhaps this was a striking way in which Diogenes set himself in an Old Comedy tradition.[34] But a fourth element may also be at issue: a black, almost grotesque humour — as when the evil wizard Paapis eventually catches up with Deinias and Dercyllis on Thule and condemns them to die each day and regain life the following night by spitting publicly in their faces (110^b4).

Even if any of this is correct guesswork, it must be admitted that the Old Comedy component of Diogenes' work is small. If Photius were right, however, that the element of fantastic travel in Diogenes influenced Achilles Tatius, Iamblichus, and Heliodorus, the ultimate impact on European literature would be significant, since it seems clear that it was from Heliodorus (via Cervantes) that picaresque adventure narrative moved into early modern prose fiction.[35] But can Photius be right?

Arguably we can set Antonius Diogenes in a literary context with much greater assurance than when John Morgan wrote sceptically in 1985. Glen Bowersock pointed out in his Sather lectures, published 1994, that only at Aphrodisias does epigraphy attest the combination of the Roman *nomen* Antonius and the Greek name Diogenes.[36] Bowersock also revived the idea of Hallström that the Faustinus addressed by Diogenes was the Faustinus to whom Martial dedicated Books 3 and 4 of his epigrams.[37] Following this up I have argued recently that Antonius Diogenes' choice of title and narrative *mise en scène* might be partly a consequence of Agricola's circumnavigation of Britain and its publicization by Tacitus in his *Agricola*.[38] We may, therefore, be dealing with work of shortly after AD 98, a work written by somebody from a city, Aphrodisias, that had already produced at least two of the earliest three novelists known to us, Chariton and the author of the *Ninus* romance — on my chronology, in the 50s and 60s AD respectively — and a city that had close and regular links with Rome and with the Roman imperial family. That Roman link might even allow Diogenes to know Petronius' *Satyrica*, and would certainly extend the possibility of his familiarity with satirical epigram, both Greek and Latin, enjoying at this period a considerable vogue in Rome and in the province

Asia.[39] It is far from improbable that encounters with these forms of comic literature prompted him to seek material from Attic Old Comedy as well. Perhaps, too, he reacted against the stuffy criticisms of Old Comedy's lack of taste and its addiction to silly linguistic humour in the essay attributed to Plutarch (of which only a précis survives) comparing Aristophanes and Menander.[40]

Conclusions

Two important Greek prose-writers of the first and second centuries AD, then, Lucian and Antonius Diogenes, are to some degree influenced by Aristophanic Comedy, and particularly by the travel plots of *Peace, Birds* and *Frogs* — though, because its chief character is a version of Plato's Socrates, *Clouds* is very prominent too. In each case Aristophanes is only one of a number of earlier writers refashioned to create a new and fresh brand of literature. But without that influence each end-product would have been different. In Lucian's case the knock-on effect in later Greek writing was small, and it was only with the Renaissance — and above all with Erasmus (see below, Steggle, this volume pp. 54–56) — that the Aristophanic component of Lucian's prose was extensively read and less extensively imitated.[41] As to Antonius Diogenes, Photius' claim that he influenced other novelists may have at least some truth. The travels in our first extant Greek novel, and perhaps the first ever to be written at all — Chariton's *Chaereas and Callirhoe* — are less exotic and bizarre than those of his successors, and our current chronology shows that Achilles Tatius, Iamblichus, and Heliodorus are indeed later than Diogenes: the input of fantasy from Aristophanes into Antonius Diogenes may have been one reason for the greater place of paradoxography in the presentation of travel by these later 'sophistic' novelists.

Some details may also suggest that the later Greek novelists kept Old Comedy in mind. The narrator in Achilles Tatius' *Leucippe and Cleitophon* presents a curious description of the priest who hurls invective at Cleitophon's opponent and rival Thersander at book 8.9 as 'an emulator above all of the Comedy of Aristophanes'. The end of Book 6 of Heliodorus' *Aethiopica* has a grotesque scene in which an old witch impales herself on a spear that by chance protrudes from the battlefield where she has been interrogating the corpse of her dead son (6.15.5): there are no linguistic pointers to Old Comedy, but the scene in *Acharnians* where Lamachus is reported as having been wounded by a stake which was part of a ditch-fortification (*Acharnians* 1178–81) comes immediately to my mind. There may be more such allusions yet to be found in the novels.

If a simple explanation were to be appropriate for the success of an originally dramatic genre, Aristophanic comedy, in shaping later non-dramatic texts, it would foreground its combination of verbal dexterity,[42] and hilarious flights of fancy.[43] Although initially conceived for a staged performance, this combination proved to retain its magnetism for writers aiming at a reading public and for these readers themselves.

Appendix

The table on the pages following is intended to give a skeletal account of the distribution of quotations between different Aristophanic comedies in Dio, Plutarch, Aelius Aristides, Lucian, Maximus of Tyre, Pausanias, and Athenaeus. A few fragments cited by Athenaeus but by no author in the Appendix are not included. Abbreviations used:

Fr.	Fragment
KA	Kassel and Austin (1983–), *Poetae Comici Graeci*, 8 vols.

PLUTARCH
Alc.	*Life of Alcibiades*
Cim.	*Life of Cimon*
Mor.	*Moralia*
Nic.	*Parallel Lives: Nicias and Crassus*
Per.	*Parallel Lives: Pericles and Fabius Maximus*
Them.	*Parallel Lives: Themistocles and Camillus*

LUCIAN OF SAMOSATA
Amor.	*Amores*
Bis acc.	*Bis accusatus* = *Twice Prosecuted*; also known as *The Double Indictment or Trials by Jury*
Cat.	*Cataplus* = *Sailing Down or The Tyrant*
Charon	*Contemplantes* = *Charon or Watchers*
Dem. enc.	*Demosthenis encomium* = *Encomium of Demosthenes*
Fugit.	*Fugitivi* = *Runaway Slaves*
I. conf.	*Iuppiter confutatus* = *Zeus Refuted*
Icar.	*Icaromenippus or The Sky-Man*
Imag.	*Imagines* = *Images*
Necyom.	*Necyomantia* = *Menippus or Consultation of the Dead*
Pisc.	*Piscator* = *Fisherman*
Prom.	*Prometheus es in verbis* = *You are a Prometheus in Words*
Ver. hist.	*Verae historiae* = *True Narratives*
Zeus trag.	*Iuppiter tragoedus* = *Zeus the Tragic Actor*

Aristophanes	Dio of Prusa	Plutarch	Aelius Aristides
Acharnians		503: *Mor.* 71 D (1 line) 524–7: *Per.* 30. 3 (4 lines) 1111, 1124: *Mor.* 853 C	42: 2. 380 504: 33. 5 514: 3. 408 530: 3. 124 531: 3. 51 531–3: 3. 79 555: 2. 59 1062: 2. 380 1131: 28. 19
Knights	42–3: 32. 6	50–1: *Mor.* 497 B (2 lines) 79: *Mor.* 517 A (line) 137: *Mor.* 804 C 358: *Nic.* 4. 7 (line) 437: *Mor.* 853 C 454–5: *Mor.* 853 C 815: *Them.* 19. 4 (half-line) 1056: *Mor.* 337 E (line)	General: 3. 631 1321: 20. 19
Clouds 1			
Clouds 2		983: *Mor.* 439 E (line)	General: 51. 18 249: 3. 104 284: 44. 1 555: 4. 47 961–5: 3. 155 964: 2. 380 967–9: 3. 155 971–2: 3. 155 983: 2. 380 984–5: 3. 155 993: 2. 115 993–4: 2. 380 995: 31. 10
Wasps		44–6: *Alc.* 1. 7 (3 lines) 1033 (= *Peace* line 756): *Mor.* 807 A	10: 4. 4 1019ff.: 41. 11 1030: 48. 93 1043: 28. 93 1046–7: 28. 94

Aristophanes	Lucian of Samosata	Maximus of Tyre	Pausanias	Athenaeus
Acharnians	280–300: Pisc. 1 504: Zeus trag. 21 530–1: Imag. 17, [Dem. enc.] 20			85: 130 F–131 A 459: 479 B 524: 570 A 606: 314 F (borrowing) 786: 374 F 872: 112 F 875: 388 B, 395 E 889: 299 A 1092: 646 D
Knights				83: 122 A 92: 782 C 124: 460 C 160: 94 D 198: 460 C 300: 94 C 356: 94 D 361: 311 CD 599: 483 D 631: 367 A 662: 328 E 864: 299 BC 1094: 783 F 1178: 94 D 1289: 446 DE
Clouds 1	?Fr. 401 KA: Icar. 5, [Amor.] 54			395 KA: 479 C
Clouds 2	General: Pisc. 14, 25 144–5: Prom. 6 225: Prom. 6, Bis acc. 33, and Icar. 13 252: Prom. 6 266: Prom. 6 320: Prom. 6 398–402: I. conf. 16 830–1: Prom. 6	General: 18. 6 103ff.: 32. 8		103: 188 C 109: 387 A 122: 367 B 339: 64 F 362: 216 A 455: 94 F 559: 299 B 665: 374 C 961: 380 F 983: 345 F 1196: 171 C
Wasps				330: 385 D 493: 315 C 510: 299 B 511: 396 A 855: 424 C 884: 90 A 1127: 329 B 1208–9: 179 AB 1214: 179 B 1216: 641 D

Aristophanes	Dio of Prusa	Plutarch	Aelius Aristides
Peace		756 (= *Wasps* line 1033): *Mor.* 807 A	
Birds		639–40: *Nic.* 8. 3 1296: *Mor.* 843 E (line)	445: 1. 350 1334: 42. 5
Lysistrata		1140–1: *Cim.* 16. 8 (1.5 lines)	155: 3. 665 1072: 3. 315
Thesmophoria-zousai		455–6: *Mor.* 853 C	
Frogs		(354–7: *Mor.* 348 D?) 1425, 1432–3: *Alc.* 16. 3 (3 lines)	736: 29. 28 785: 32. 34 1515: 32. 34
Ecclesiazousai			
Wealth			650: 44. 17
Fr. 645 B Kock			3. 133
Babylonians (Babylonioi)		Fr. 71 KA: *Per.* 26. 4	
Farmers (Georgoi)		Fr. 102 KA: *Nic.* 8. 4 (4 lines)	
Storks (Pelargoi)			
Broilers (Tagenistae)			

Aristophanes	Lucian of Samosata	Maximus of Tyre	Pausanias	Athenaeus
Peace	127–30: *Icar.* 10			27: 173 A 122: 111 A 143: 486 E 540: 424 B 788: 393 C 804: 343 C 916: 485 A
Birds	'Nephelococcugia': *Ver. hist.* 1. 29 994: *Necyom.* 2		149: 5. 5. 3	67: 386 F 101: 397 D 249: 388 B 269: 397 D 304: 388 E 566: 325 B 695: 57 D 707: 388 B 761: 388 B 884: 397 E 1377: 551 D
Lysistrata				203: 502 B 549: 90 B
Thesmophoria-zousai				457–8: 680 CD
Frogs	87f., 107, 115: *Charon* 24, *Cat.* 14, *Fugit.* 28	92–3: 25. 3		134: 66 B 294: 566 E 1304: 636 E
Ecclesiazousai				707: 77 D 843: 110 A 1117: 691 B
Wealth				179: 592 D 720: 67 C 812: 229 E 1005: 170 D 1128: 368 D
Fr. 645 B Kock				
Babylonians (Babylonioi)				Fr. 67 KA: 86 F
Farmers (Georgoi)				Fr. 105 KA: 111 B 106 KA: 460 D 110 KA: 75 A 120 KA: 650 E
Storks (Pelargoi)				Fr. 448 KA: 387 F 449 KA: 368 D 452 KA: 247 A
Broilers (Tagenistae)				Fr. 505 KA: 677 B 507 KA: 418 D 513 KA: 422 F 516 KA: 410 B 517 KA: 171 AB 520 KA: 96 C, 107 F, 110 F, 374 F 521 KA: 285 E 522 KA: 110 F

Aristophanes	Dio of Prusa	Plutarch	Aelius Aristides
Telemessians (*Telemesses*)			Fr. 544 KA: 47. 16
Thesmophoria-zousai 2			
Three-Phallused (*Triphales*)			
Women in Tents (*Skenas kata-lambanousai*)		Fr. 488. 1 KA: *Mor.* 30 D	
Fr. 598 KA	52. 17		
Fr. 714 KA			
Fr. 720 KA			32. 32
General	33. 9		

Aristophanes	Lucian of Samosata	Maximus of Tyre	Pausanias	Athenaeus
Telemessians (*Telemesses*)				Fr. 545 KA: 49 C 550 KA: 308 F
Thesmophoria-zousai 2				Fr. 333 KA: 104 E 334 KA: 29 A 336 KA: 690 C 347 KA: 117 C 352 KA: 619 A
Three-Phallused (*Triphales*)	Title: *Fugit.* 32			Fr. 556 KA: 525 A
Women in Tents (*Skenas kata-lambanousai*)				Fr. 491 KA: 286 F
Fr. 598 KA				
Fr. 714 KA				
Fr. 720 KA				
General				

Notes to Chapter 2

1. One important text is a speech of P. Aelius Aristides of Hadrianutherae and Smyrna, one of the top declaimers ('sophists') whose rhetorical teaching and epideictic performances were very prominent in Greek cultural life of the second and third centuries AD: his speech 29 Keil (translated by Behr (1981–86), 140–46), entitled *On the Banning of Comedy*, seems to have been delivered in Smyrna between AD 157 and 165 and to be countering a proposal for the introduction of some entertainment akin to Old Comedy into the Dionysia at Smyrna. For a good discussion see C. P. Jones (1993), 40–41.

2. One indication of this is the extensive use of Aristophanes by lexicographers, on which I hope to publish information elsewhere.

3. On whom see footnote 1.

4. *Knights* 42–43 at 32. 6; fragment 598 at 52. 17; unless otherwise stated, fragments of Attic Old Comedy are cited by their number in the magisterial edition of Kassel and Austin (1983– ; abbreviated KA), where Aristophanes' fragments are to be found in vol. III.2 (1984), Cratinus in vol. IV (1983), and Eupolis in vol. V (1986). There is an unspecific reference to criticism of Athenians by Aristophanes, Cratinus, and Plato at 33. 9.

5. Fragment 313 at 56. 2 (Kassel and Austin note that von Arnim thought the name might have entered the text from a marginal note) and the general reference at 33.9 (see preceding footnote).

6. Fragment 234 at 32. 6, not by name, and immediately after citation of *Knights* 42–43.

7. 3. 365 in the edition of Lenz and Behr; the other citation is at 3.487 Lenz–Behr.

8. 3. 51 Lenz–Behr.

9. At 27. 15 Keil and 30. 19 Keil.

10. 28. 92 Keil.

11. Cratinus fragment 306 in the edition of Kock (1880–88), but Kassel and Austin assign it to Eupolis (fragment 205).

12. Fragment 255: Kassel and Austin note that again in 28. 95 Keil Aristides implies these are the beginning and end of the same play.

13. But cf. Aristophanes fragment 645 B in Kock.

14. 3.3 in the edition of Trapp (twice), 12.8 Trapp, 18.6 Trapp, 39.5 Trapp (all referring to *Clouds* and Socrates' response in Plato's *Apology*).

15. *Clouds* 103 ff. at 32.8 Trapp.

16. *Frogs* 92–93 at 25.3 Trapp.

17. At 14.7 Trapp *Flatterers*; at 32.8 Trapp he alludes to *Cities* fragment 253 Kassel and Austin (as well as to Ar. *Clouds* 103 ff.).

18. Fowler and Fowler (1905).

19. On Aristophanes and ancient oratory see also above, p. 8. For the many ways in which Lucian exploits earlier and especially classical literature to construct his own literary creations Bompaire (1958) remains fundamental, especially the sections 'Création rhétorique. Composition: B — éléments comiques' on pp. 320–30, 'Création rhétorique. C. Thèmes comiques et mimiques' on pp. 361–65, 'Thème de l'Hadès' on pp. 365–78, and 'La recréation comique: humour, parodie, pastiche' on pp. 587–655. In addition to these sections, there are many acute and relevant observations throughout Bompaire's work, e.g. on the contribution to the *Timon* of the informers (*sukophantai*) of *Acharnians* 818 and 910 and *Plutus* 850–958 (p. 208 with n. 1); of the *agōn* of *Plutus* 489–954 to *Timon* 36–38 (p. 254); of *Thesmophoriazusae* 561 to *Dialogues of Courtesans* 1 and 4 (p. 364); on the importance of Old and Middle Comedy for Lucian's techniques of parody (on pp. 601–02, 627) and for his use of compound words, often neologisms (on p. 629), of parodic official formulae (on p. 638) and of lists (e.g. *Peace* 1000 ff., cf. *Podagra* 117–24, on p. 642). The development and modification of Bompaire's observations by Anderson (1976a) and (1976b) also remain an important contribution to Lucianic scholarship.

20. For tabulation of 5th-c. comic poets cited in Lucian see Sidwell (2000), 151–52, with some remarks on p. 138 about exploitation of Comedy that goes much further than indicated by these citations. Note also Ledergerber (1905).

21. See also Hirzel (1895), ii. 302–03: Bompaire (1958), 253 is unduly sceptical.

22. Even though Lucian's word for 'clouds', *nephōn* (in the genitive case), is a slightly different form from that in the title of Aristophanes' *Clouds* (*Nephelai,* the genitive of which is *nephelōn*).

23. For further discussion and documentation of verbal echoes see MacLeod (1991), 258–63.

24. For fuller discussion see Branham (1989), 167–77.

25. *Peace* 756, on Cleon surrounded by flatterers, at *Advice on Running a City* 807 A.

26. See Lloyd-Jones and Parsons (1983), nos. 775–840, with the editors' note on no. 775.

27. There may also be a reworking of Trygaeus' recognition of Ion of Chios at *Peace* 835; cf. Anderson (1976*a*), 24.

28. Cantharus is attested as a real name, but the noun *kantharos* means 'dung-beetle', and indeed is the term used to refer to Trygaeus' dung-beetle in *Peace* from the play's very first line.

29. e.g. *True Narratives* 1. 7 reworks Herodotus 4. 82. For a detailed commentary on *True Narratives* see Georgiadou and Larmour (1998).

30. Rohde (1876), Morgan (1985). See also Reyhl (1969), criticized by Anderson (1976*b*), 1–7.

31. For a good introduction, a translation of Photius' summary, and editions and translations of fragments (quoted and preserved on papyri), see Stephens and Winkler (1995), 101–72.

32. For the use of *kōmōidia palaia* as a technical term for Old Comedy (more often *kōmōidia archaia*) cf. Aristotle, *Nicomachean Ethics* 1128[a]22.

33. For a full and stimulating exploration of the issues see Stephens and Winkler (1995), 102–09.

34. Photius 109[a]7 also refers to the work as *dramatikon,* relating it in some degree to drama — but this may be his own term, not that of Antonius Diogenes.

35. Doody (1996).

36. Bowersock (1994), 38–39.

37. Ibid. 37–38, Hallström (1910): I am grateful to Professor Kathleen Coleman for directing me to Hallström's article.

38. E. L. Bowie (2002), 58–60.

39. For Greek satirical epigram in this period see now Nisbet (2003).

40. *Moralia* 853 A–854 D. On this treatise see also above, p. 8.

41. For the influence of Lucian in Renaissance Europe see Steggle and Hall (below, this volume), as well as Robinson (1979), 65–163 and (on Erasmus and Fielding) 165–235.

42. Note the dexterity, *dexiotēs,* claimed by Aristophanes at *Acharnians* 619, *Clouds* 548, *Wasps* 1059, and his insistence that his plays rely on their verbal qualities, at *Clouds* 544.

43. Note his vaunting of 'new ideas/forms (*ideas*)', at *Clouds* 547.

CHAPTER 3

❖

Aristophanes in Early Modern England

Matthew Steggle

As other essays in this volume demonstrate, it is no longer possible to adhere to the traditional model of the reception of Aristophanes, according to which Greek Old Comedy is almost unknown until a nineteenth-century 'rediscovery' of Aristophanes. The reception of Aristophanes is part of a far more complicated cultural picture. This chapter takes as its focus one specific setting for that reception: early modern England, and, in particular, the early modern theatre of Shakespeare, Jonson, and their contemporaries. It aims to pose the question: what are we doing when we read early modern texts, particularly comedy and satire, against Greek Old Comedy? To some extent, perceived resemblances between (for instance) Jonson and Aristophanes can always be read as the product of broad cultural tendencies that speak to the deep structures of drama. And yet, it will be argued here, there is also particular cultural currency in allusion to and imitation of Aristophanes at this date, which could be considered a specific technique used for a specific effect. Renaissance culture was interested, quite particularly, in one aspect of Greek Old Comedy: the fact that it offered a precedent for a drama that satirized living people by name on stage.[1]

By far the most influential texts in this respect are two references by Horace, one in the *Satires*, and one in the *Ars Poetica*, a fundamental work for almost all Renaissance statements about poetics. As translated by Ben Jonson, Horace's discussion of Greek Old Comedy runs as follows:

> To [Greek tragedy] succeeded the old Comoedy,
> And not without much praise; till libertie
> Fell into fault so farre, as now they saw
> Her licence fit to be restrain'd by law:
> Which law receiv'd, the Chorus held his peace,
> His power of foulely hurting made to cease.[2]

But another passage of Horace claims Greek Old Comedy as a validating precedent, again specifically for the personal satire of his own genre. Horace argues that he must be entitled to use satire to attack people, since this what Greek Old Comedians did to improve the morals of their Greek audiences:

> The Poet *Aristophanes Eupolis,* and *Cratine,*
> And aunciens moe, whose interludes are saust with sayings fine,
> If any person were mislyude in theft or leachers lore,
> Or wher a roisting quareller, they woulde display him sore...[3]

While it appears that these two allusions contradict each other entirely, what is interesting is what they have in common: the belief that Greek Old Comedy was not centrally 'about' obscenity, or mythic power, or civic identity, but about the legitimacy (or otherwise) of personal satire. The Renaissance reception of Aristophanes very much takes its cues from these two allusions to his work.

Indeed, the Aristophanes known to the Renaissance is not the same as the Aristophanes known to the twenty-first century. This is not because of changes in the constitution of the corpus of his works, although many of his classical colleagues — notably Menander — have had their reputations transformed during the last century by the rediscovery of previously lost texts. On the contrary, all of Aristophanes' eleven surviving plays were in print by 1515, and although fragments have been added from various sources, especially papyrological finds, no further complete plays have subsequently come to light. Nor has any fresh biographical evidence. The *Life* that accompanied the early editions has remained unchallenged and without the appearance of significant contradictory evidence up to the present day.[4] Rather, the difference lies in the paradigms and expectations that accompany the reading of Aristophanes. These differences are sufficiently large to cause trouble to those few studies that have been done on the relationship between Greek Old Comedy (also known in the Renaissance as *Vetus Comedia*) and the comedies of the Renaissance. In particular, during the twentieth century, academic perceptions of Aristophanes were formed by the work of scholars such as Francis Cornford and Arthur Pickard-Cambridge: investigations into the anthropological significance of the rituals that lie behind Greek drama. A generation of critics attempted to apply these insights to drama and literature. Amongst these, by far the most influential in examining Greek Old Comedy's new-found intellectual respectability was Northrop Frye's *Anatomy of Criticism*.[5]

Frye developed a taxonomy of comic roles, proposing terms to denote four basic types, which he named, respectively, *eirōn* (self-deprecator), *alazōn* (impostor), *bōmolochos* (buffoon), and *agroikos* (churl). Furthermore, he distinguished two tendencies in comedy: Old Comedy, in which one central figure sets about building an entire society in the face of serial opposition, and New Comedy, in which young love triumphs against opposition, usually of a parental nature, by means of intrigue, discoveries and twists of plot. Using these generalisations, Frye provided a useful intellectual framework within which to think about categories of drama. His legacy can still be seen in recent works such as Leo Salingar's study of Shakespeare's comic patterns or Robert Miola's study of Shakespeare and classical comedy, which both set out to analyse deep structures and patterns in Shakespeare in terms of their classical predecessors.[6] The problem is that some subsequent critics have tended to assume that Greek Old Comedy has *always* been regarded as if it were Fryean Old Comedy. And, as the Renaissance fascination with Horace's invocations of Greek Old Comedy shows, while Renaissance writers were well aware of the origins of Greek Old Comedy in ritual, and were interested too in its structure, these concerns were secondary, for them, to its importance as a phenomenon that legitimated personal satire.

As a preliminary to my argument, it is important to survey the presence of Aristophanes in Renaissance English culture and in a wider European context.

The *editio princeps* of Aristophanes, comprising nine of his eleven surviving plays, was issued by the Aldine Press at Venice in 1498, and the other two plays followed in 1515. Within the Aristophanes corpus, *Wealth* continued to be (as it had been through the medieval era) a clear leader in terms of popularity.[7] It was printed in Latin translation at Parma in 1501, and ten different translations of the play were in circulation by 1550.[8] Progress into England and English Universities was also swift. By 1517 Bishop Richard Fox's statutes for Corpus Christi College, newly established at the University of Oxford, included Aristophanes in the list of Greek authors to be studied, and in 1520 demand at Oxford was strong enough for the bookseller John Dorne (whose records happen to survive) to sell a dozen copies of a Latin translation of *Wealth* within two weeks of obtaining them.[9]

In 1536, *Wealth* was staged in Greek at Trinity College, Cambridge, in a production which was deeply controversial, since proponents of a revised Greek pronunciation, including Sir Thomas Smith, were using the play as a vehicle to display their method. Ten years later, but also at Cambridge, the future 'mage' and astrologer John Dee was involved in a visually spectacular production of *Peace*, seemingly again performed in Greek. Dee's account of this production is interesting, partly as a first-hand account of what happened, and partly for the interpretative frame in which it is inserted:

> I was, out of St. John's College, chosen to be Fellow of Trinity College, at the first erection thereof by Henry the Eight: I was also assigned there to be the under-reader of the Greek tongue, Mr Pember being the chief Greek reader then in Trinity College. Hereupon I did set forth (and it was seen of the University) a Greek comedy of Aristophanes, named in Greek *Eirene*, in Latin *Pax*, with the performance of the Scarabeus flying up to Jupiter's palace, with a man and his basket of victuals on her back: whereat was great wondering, and many vain reports spread abroad, of the means how that was effected... They which yet live, and were hearers and beholders, they can testify, more than is meet here to be written, of these my boyish attempts and exploits scholastical.[10]

Ascent, in various senses, is the clear theme of Dee's discussion here of his own achievements. Like a good magician, he does not reveal how he achieved the effect which he claims so dazzled his audience (the scholarly consensus being that it was the use of a man-powered crane of some sort, perhaps inspired by the explicit reference to the crane operator in Aristophanes' play at 174–76). What is interesting, though, is that there is clearly a certain cultural prestige, a useful exoticism, to staging a Greek comedy, rather than a merely Latin one. Although academic productions of Aristophanes in England were rare in comparison to productions of Plautus and Terence, they did from time to time take place: Aristophanes was both read and sometimes performed at English universities.[11]

Even further down the educational system, Aristophanes was not unknown to the syllabus. As early as 1511, in the influential educational treatise *De Ratione Studii*, Erasmus recommends him as an aid for teaching Greek:

> In this category [as aids for teaching Greek prose] I would assign first place to Lucian, second to Demosthenes, and third to Herodotus; again, among the poets, first place to Aristophanes, second to Homer, third to Euripides. For Menander, to whom I would have given even the first place, is not extant.[12]

FIG. 3.1. Detail from title page of Erasmus, *Adagiorum chiliades* (1515)

Both here and in his frequent citations of Aristophanes in the *Adagia*, Erasmus speaks of Aristophanes in the same breath as the other classics. The praise of Aristophanes as a stylistic model was taken up by later writers including Roger Ascham, and Erasmus' advice about putting Aristophanes on the syllabus is followed by later theorists.[13] In 1523 the Spanish humanist Juan Luis Vives recommended that Aristophanes be read at an early stage in a pupil's education in Greek. So did Sir Thomas Eliot in 1531, intending Aristophanes to be read by pupils aged between seven and ten. Records survive of a teacher at Winchester School in the mid-1560s using Aristophanes' *Wealth* as a source of moral exempla to be defended syllogistically.[14]

The prominence of extracts from Aristophanes is also noteworthy throughout Erasmus' *Adagia*, the influential series of compilations of classical proverbs and idioms which served, in James McConica's phrase, as 'an invaluable quarry for the revived classical culture of Europe'.[15] Aristophanes's extraordinary status within classical culture as presented in the *Adagia* can be seen from the following table, compiled from data collected by M. M. Phillips, of the commonest sources cited in the final version of the work.[16]

Author	References	Author	References	Author	References
Cicero	892	Horace	475	Athenaeus	356
Homer	666	Plautus	475	Lucian	335
Plutarch	618	Plato	428	Aristotle	304
Aristophanes	596	'Suidas'	392		

For Erasmus, at least, Aristophanes was one of the most important classical authors in existence, and the frontispiece of the 1515 *Adagia* even features a picture of a smiling Aristophanes, seemingly poking fun at his neighbour in the tree of wisdom, Euripides (fig. 3.1). However, Erasmus' praise of Greek Old Comedy is not always uncritical — at one point he praises Lucian for '[r]eviving the sharpness of Old Comedy, while stopping short of its abusiveness'.[17]

More forthright dispraise of Aristophanes can also be found. Robortello's 1548 treatise on comedy had been dismissive:

> Plutarch also, in that little book in which he compares Menander with Aristophanes, produces evidence enough for one to perceive that Old Comedy is not much esteemed and that much more praiseworthy is the New Comedy whose author is Menander, whom our Terence above all has imitated.[18]

In a similar vein, Scaliger's *Poetices Libri Septem* (1561), although positive about Aristophanes' vigour and invention, did associate him detrimentally with democracy, anarchy and personal satire.[19] Laurence Humfrey, writing in the early 1560s, alluded to the often-repeated story that the patristic writer St John Chrysostom had learned his Greek style from study of Aristophanes, but did not consider that this made Aristophanes any the better: 'A poete nevertheles, bothe nippynge in taunts, and wanton in talke, & no lesse hurtfull to honestye'.[20]

Thanks to references in canonical classical authors such as Horace, Aristophanes is known *about*; thanks to the *Adagia,* excerpts from Aristophanes are well known; on the other hand, by other yardsticks Aristophanes arguably remained marginal to Renaissance culture. English translations were slow to come: the earliest is Thomas Randolph's free adaptation *Hey for Honesty*, printed in 1651 (see further Hall and Wyles, this volume). With the exception of the lone 1593 Greek text of *Knights* produced by the Oxford University Press (*STC* no. 751 in Pollard and Redgrave (1976–1991)), *Hey for Honesty* is also apparently the first printing of Aristophanes in England in any form. Aristophanes is an author commonly known about, but only on rare occasions actually read.

This picture, in which Aristophanes is both a revered classical author and also potentially open to criticism as culpable of libel, provides the rival paradigms that underlie Renaissance thinking about his legacy. These opposed views are both quite distinct from modern perceptions of Aristophanes. And it was upon the second of these two Renaissance views that Stephen Gosson, English humanist and renegade playwright, took his stand in a series of antitheatrical pamphlets published in the years 1579–82, written against the new phenomenon of the professional playhouse.

The antitheatrical controversy marking Elizabethan England provides a useful conceptual bridge between the world of the universities and the world of the professional theatre. It also provoked, directly or indirectly, most of the theorizing about drama written in English in the sixteenth century: and Aristophanes, along with Greek Old Comedy, constituted an important touchstone throughout the debate. Gosson uses this touchstone in his rejection of the idea that drama is morally improving, referring back as he does to Horace's *Ars Poetica* and to *Satires* 2. 1. 82–83:

> ... it appeareth by antiquitie, that the *Poets* which were before, had another meaning: for as any man had displeased them, to reuenge theire owne cause they studied to present him vpon the stage, there did they ruffle, and taunt;

scoffe, and nippe; thunder, and lighten, and spue vp their counning to deface
him. Whereupon grewe one of the lawes of the twelue tables, that no man
should be so hardie as to write any thing, whereby the good name of any bodie
might be hurte.[21]

Poets, he claims, write against vice not out of sorrow or compassion, but out of
'mallice: for so *Eupolis* handled *Alcibiades*: or of corruption, as *Aristophanes* dealt with
Socrates and *Cleon*.'[22] Thus, for Gosson, Aristophanes is a central example, relevant
to contemporary practice, for confounding comedy with satire and representing real
living people in comedies. Even some defenders of the stage did not seek to defend
Aristophanes, and William Webbe, for instance, abandoned him to the Puritans:

> After the time of *Homer* there began the firste Comedy wryters, who
> compyled theyr workes in a better stile, which continued not long before it was
> expelled by penalty, for scoffing too broade at mens manners, and the priuie
> reuengements which the Poets vsed against their ill wyllers. Among these was
> *Eupolis, Cratinus,* and *Aristophanes*; but afterward the order of thys wryting
> Comedies was reformed and made more plausible: then wrytte *Plato (Comicus),*
> *Menander,* and I knowe not who more.[23]

For George Puttenham, another defender of poetry, Satire was the parent of both
comedy and tragedy. Satire was anonymous, vituperative monologue by people
disguised as satyrs to avoid reprisals, and it taxed men by 'expresse names'.[24] This
art form developed into dialogues and then into comedy, although the participants
remained disguised 'with hatts and capps':

> But as time & experience do reforme euery thing that is amisse, so, this bitter
> poeme called the Old *Comedy* being disused and taken away, the new *Comedy*
> came in place, more ciuill and pleasant a great deale, and not touching any
> man by name, but in a certaine generalitie glancing at euery abuse, so as from
> thenceforth fearing none illwill or enmitie at any bodies hands they left aside
> their disguisings and played bare face.[25]

For Puttenham as for other writers, then, the most salient feature of Old Comedy is
that it involved personal satire. A later comment by Puttenham about Old Comedy
runs counter to all that is known about the medium's performance conditions, and
indeed to the internal evidence provided by the plays themselves, but fits with
imagery one finds elsewhere conflating Greek Old Comedy with English medieval
drama: Old Comedy was played

> in the broad streets vpon wagons or carts vncouered, which carts were floored
> with bords & made for remouable stages to passe from one streete of their
> townes to another, where all the people might stand at their ease to gaze
> vpon the sights. Their new comedies or ciuill enterludes were played in open
> pauilions or tents of linnen cloth or lether, halfe displayed that the people
> might see.[26]

In Puttenham's imagination, at least, Greek Old Comedy is an archaic, medieval-
looking form rather than a relevant concern to the theatre of his 'today'.

By contrast, Thomas Lodge, another defender of the stage, did argue for the
utility and relevance of Aristophanic practice. In a brief history of the stage, Lodge
attacked Gosson personally, concurring as he did so with Puttenham's view that

Comedy grew out of satire, and appealing not to the *Ars Poetica* but to Horace's
Satires:

> Whereupon Eupolis with Cratinus and Aristophanes began to write, and with
> ther eloquenter vaine and perfection of stil dyd more seuerely speak agaynst the
> abuses then they; which Horace himself witnesseth. For, sayth he, ther was no
> abuse but these men reprehended it; a thefe was loth to be seene [at] one [of]
> there spectacle[s], a coward was neuer present at theyr assemblies, a backbiter
> abhord that company; and I my selfe could not haue blamed you (Gosson) for
> exempting yourselfe from this theater; of troth I should have lykt your pollicy...
> And if we had some Satericall Poetes nowe a dayes to penn our commedies, that
> might be admitted of zeale to discypher the abuses of the worlde in the person
> of notorious offenders, I knowe we should wisely ryd our assemblyes of many
> of your brotherhod.[27]

Whether being championed by Lodge or shunned by the other writers on poetics,
the idea of Aristophanic comedy was certainly something to be reckoned with in
Renaissance English culture.

Before moving on to the plays themselves, further context can be provided by
examining some non-dramatic Elizabethan authors who asserted that they were
copying Aristophanic practice. In the 1590s, there was no shortage of writers
claiming to be the new Aristophanes. Thomas Nashe wrote, 'Thee I imbrace,
Aristophanes, not so much for thy Comoedie of the clowd, which thou wrotst
against philosophers, as for in al other thy inuentions thou interfusest delight with
reprehension...'[28] The comparison between Nashe's work and Greek Old Comedy
— in that they both offered dangerously personal satire — was drawn by at least
one other contemporary observer. Francis Meres wrote in 1598, 'As Eupolis of
Athens vsed great libertie in taxing the vices of men: so doth Thomas Nash, witness
the broode of the Harueys!'[29]

Joseph Hall, whose *Virgidemiarum Six Bookes* appeared in 1598, also experimented
with donning the mantle of Greek Old Comedy. Again, the point at issue was the
question of whether his satires were based upon real people.

> Ech points his straight fore-finger to his friend,
> Like the blind Diall on the Belfrey end:
> Who turnes it homeward to say, this is I,
> As bolder *Socrates* in the Comedy?
> But single out, and say once plat and plaine
> That coy *Matrona* is a Curtizan,
> Or thou false *Cryspus* chokd'st thy wealthie guest
> Whiles hee lay snoring at his midnight rest,
> And in thy dung-cart did'st the carkasse shrine
> And deepe intombe it in *Port-esquiline*.[30]

As for the source of the anecdote about Socrates standing up during a performance
of *Clouds*, to identify himself with the character Socrates that was portrayed therein,
it could have been derived from one of a number of classical sources: Davenport
suggests Aelian or Plutarch.[31] But two things are of particular interest here.
First, Aristophanes was associated not with religious fertility ceremonies but
with satire of real people in society. Secondly, defenders of Aristophanes and of

the practice of personal satire argued that this satire was legitimized by Socrates' acquiescence in it.

This is the context in which we come to Ben Jonson's references to Aristophanes. This is not a new topic, since numerous imitations and possible imitations of Aristophanes in the works of Jonson have been collected, by a succession of scholars starting with John Upton in 1749.[32] Upton's discussion, in particular, includes amusing commentary on the famous opening line of *The Alchemist*, which begins, 'I fart at thee', which he likens to Aristophanes' use of *katapardein*: 'our learned comedian does not deal in vulgar *English* expressions, but in vulgar *Attic* or *Roman* expressions.'[33]

Nor was Upton actually the first to suggest a link between Jonson and Aristophanes. Commendatory poems in Jonson's lifetime compared him with Aristophanes, and indeed Jonson himself at various times both claims and disavows Aristophanic precedent. Clearly, there is something of a case to answer here concerning the parallels between Jonson and Aristophanes: both authors practise violently surreal and rather highbrow comedy; indeed, at one point a Jonson character quotes Aristophanes in the original Greek. These features have received a certain amount of critical attention. Yet much of the work that has been done in this area has tended to treat Greek Old Comedy as if it were always an equivalent of Fryean Old Comedy. The longest works on the subject of the link between the two authors are full-length studies by Coburn Gum and by Alifki Lafkidou Dick.[34] Gum's work is a series of comparative essays, an exercise in praising Aristophanes at the expense of Jonson. It views Jonson's works as attempts to emulate Old Comedy. Chapter IX, 'Why Jonson Failed', is typical: Jonson, argues Gum, did not possess '[t]he Greek spirit', and '[h]is failure was perhaps inevitable, for Jonson was no Greek.'[35] In particular, Gum does not really consider personal satire — which, as we have seen, is surely central to Renaissance perceptions of what Greek Old Comedy is all about.

One should therefore begin by establishing that Jonson had certainly read Aristophanes. His copy of the 1607 edition survives, sadly without significant marginalia.[36] Among Jonson's numerous references to Aristophanes, this chapter will restrict itself to three comedies: *Every Man Out of his Humour* (1599), *Poetaster* (1601), and *The Staple of News* (1625). Chronologically, these bracket the four 'middle comedies' which are generally reckoned to be Jonson's greatest plays, for which they form an important context.

Every Man Out of his Humour is Jonson's early comic manifesto. It employs a 'GREX, or CHORUS', consisting of the two figures of Mitis and Cordatus, who, despite their names, behave entirely unlike their Greek counterparts, instead serving as a rather grumpy onstage incarnation of the audience.[37] At the start of the play, they discuss what is to come:

MIT.   How is't?
CORD.   Faith, sir, I must refraine to iudge, only this I can say of it, 'tis strange, and of a particular kind by it selfe, somewhat like *Vetus Comoedia*: a worke that hath bounteously pleased me, but how it will answere the generall expectation, I know not.

MIT.	Does he obserue all the lawes of *Comedie* in it?
CORD.	What lawes meane you?
MIT.	Why, the equall diuision of it into *Acts*, and *Sceanes*, according to the *Terentian* manner, his true number of Actors; the furnishing of the *Scene* with GREX, or CHORUS, and that the whole Argument fall within compasse of a dayes businesse.
CORD.	O no, these are too nice obseruations.
MIT.	They are such as must be receiued, by your favour, or it cannot be authentique.
CORD.	Troth, I can discerne no such necessity.[38]

Cordatus then goes on to give an account of the genesis of comedy, following in most important respects Donatus, with additional circumstantial details derived from 'some Renaissance critic':[39]

'tis extant, that that which we call *Comoedia*, was at first nothing but a simple, and continued *Song*, sung by one only person, till SUSARIO inuented a second, after him EPICHARMUS a third; PHORMUS, and CHIONIDES deuised to haue foure Actors, with a *Prologue* and *Chorus*; to which CRATINUS (long after) added a fift, and sixt; EUPOLIS more; ARISTOPHANES more then they: euery man in the dignitie of his spirit and iudgement, supplyed something. And (though that in him this kinde of *Poeme* appeared absolute, and fully perfected) yet how is the face of it chang'd since... [40]

Thus Jonson appeals to Aristophanic precedent, largely in order to authorize his claim to freedom from precedent in general. And the ensuing play has very little to do with any sort of love-comedy conventions in the '*Terentian* manner' which Mitis expects: it is more like a series of satirical sketches than a conventional play, in which a large cast of oddballs parade their oddities until, in a final catastrophe, they are all driven 'out of their humour' by the play's director Asper. There is certainly an Aristophanic flavour to this structure, but more noticeable than the parallels with Aristophanes are the differences from Terence.

In the light of the evidence about what Aristophanes tended to mean in Renaissance discussions, one might then also expect some references in *Every Man Out* to the personal satire for which Aristophanes was notorious. Indeed, Asper himself addresses the audience at the beginning of the play, warning them, in effect, that they may be like Socrates in the audience at *Clouds:*

If any, here, chance to behold himselfe,
Let him not dare to challenge me of wrong,
For if he shame to have his follies knowne,
First he should shame to act 'hem.[41]

Indeed, there are allegations of personal satire marking the discourse surrounding *Every Man Out* as a whole. John Aubrey, writing seventy years later, records a story that one of the buffoons, Carlo Buffone, constituted a personally satirical attack on a man named Charles Chester, who is named and attacked in various 1590s verse satires as well: and it has been argued that the supporting evidence for Aubrey's claim is strong, based on similarities between what Carlo says and does, and what the historical Charles Chester is alleged to have said and done. Chester was a celebrity of late Elizabethan England, and seems to have been fair game for personal attack.

A particularly useful piece of supporting evidence, indeed, is provided by Jasper Mayne, who writes in a commendatory poem to Jonson years later that in *Every Man Out* 'Carlo' was presented truly: and that even if any injustice had been done, it would have been a legitimate use of 'th'old Comicke freedome' as exemplified by Aristophanes' attack on Socrates.[42] So in the case of *Every Man Out*, there is at least some evidence that the invocation of Aristophanes at the start of the play is there to validate not just a freedom from conventional ideas of plotting, subject-matter, and style, but in particular a form of personal satire on the stage.

Two years after *Every Man Out*, Jonson returned to the technique of personal satire, writing *Poetaster*, a play set in ancient Rome in which the hero, no less a person than the poet Horace, functions as a thinly disguised mouthpiece for Jonson himself.[43] The personal satire comes in the form of Crispinus and Demetrius, two incompetent jobbing playwrights who are enemies of Horace, and who bear a striking similarity to Jonson's enemies Thomas Dekker and John Marston, against whom he waged, at the turn of the seventeenth century, the acrimonious public confrontation that became known as 'the War of the Theatres'. In particular, Crispinus (Marston) is depicted as being addicted to pretentious vocabulary. They are put through a series of indignities, culminating in Crispinus being administered an emetic which makes him vomit up all his pretentious vocabulary — as in the climactic scene of *Frogs*, the joke depends upon imagining words as having a material existence and mass.

Jonson's use of personal satire in this way was clearly controversial, and provoked an answer-play by Dekker, *Satiromastix* (1601), which reinvents Crispinus and Demetrius as honest and reasonable writers and Horace/Jonson as an egotistical *prima donna* out of his depth in eleventh-century England. Jonson's own defence of his satirical practice can be found in an 'apologetical dialogue' added to the 1616 printing, in which the author argues against the accusations of his interlocutor Polyposus that there is literary precedent for personal satire against one's enemies.

> POL.   O, but they lay particular imputations —
> AUT.   As what?
> POL.   That all your writing, is meere rayling.
> AUT.   Ha! If all the salt in the old *comœdy*
>   Should be so censur'd, or the sharper wit
>   Of the bold *satyre*, termed scolding rage,
>   What age could then compare with those, for buffons?
>   What should be sayd of ARISTOPHANES?
>   PERSIUS? or IUVENAL? whose names we now
>   So glorifie in schooles, at least pretend it.[44]

So once again, Jonson is using Aristophanes as the provider of a culturally prestigious precedent for personal satire on the stage. In particular, this version of Aristophanes is mediated through the Horace who is the central character of the play.

The third play to be considered is *The Staple of News*, long categorized among Jonson's 'dotages', and slowly regaining ground as a centre of critical interest.[45] Its basic conceit is the idea that information can be treated as a commodity, and at the eponymous staple — a sort of news supermarket — news of all sorts can be bought and sold. This, obviously, partly constitutes a satire on the emergent news industry of the 1620s, and in particular the revolutionary idea that you could have a weekly news bulletin, that there would be some news every week. But the point is that the titular motif of the 'Staple' is not about printing — it is about the commodification of information in the abstract. Into this environment is introduced a motley group of other characters, including Lady Pecunia, an allegorical representation of Wealth, and Penny-Boy senior, a miser with a strange obsession with justice, all loosely tied together by a plot about an inheritance.

The motif of the Staple certainly recalls the Phrontisterion of Aristophanes' *Clouds*. Both present scenes in which a novice enters the lair of a trickster and conjurer, whose particular speciality lies in offering a whole raft of new and strange ideas. The novice is told a series of marvels, some clearly false, others merely far-fetched. Both dwell upon the lexical complexities of the new ideas. In *Clouds* this shows up in the terrible jargon used by the philosophers: in *The Staple of News*, it occurs when Penny-Boy Junior is told about the emissaries: 'Emissaries? stay, there's a fine new word, *Thom*! Pray God it signifie any thing ...'[46] In both cases, money is inextricably linked with the operation: Strepsiades is trying to evade payment of his debts, and at the Staple all concerned are attempting to court Pecunia. And both establishments end up violently destroyed: the Phrontisterion physically demolished by Strepsiades, the Staple mysteriously blown up.

Furthermore, Lady Pecunia clearly recalls on some level the eponymous hero of Aristophanes' *Wealth*, although there is a whole tradition of allegorical personifications of wealth in which Aristophanes is only one element: clearly, Jonson's closer sources include Lady Pecunia in Barnfield's *The Encomium of Lady Pecunia* (1598), Lady Munera in Spenser's *Faery Queen*, Book V, Money in the anonymous *The Contention between Liberality and Prodigality* (pub. 1602), and other examples in Dekker's *Work for Amourers* (1609) and *The Massacre of Money* by Thomas Andrew (1602). There are some verbal parallels with Aristophanes' *Wealth*, but they are not entirely clear and decisive: the best is

> All this *Nether-world*
> Is yours, you command it, and doe sway it:
> The honour of it, and the honesty,
> The reputation, I, and the religion
> (I was about to say, and had not err'd,)
> Is Queene *Pecunia*'s: For that stile is yours,
> If mortals knew your *Grace*, or their owne good.

> WEALTH.   What are you saying? Men make their religious sacrifices on my account?
> CHREMYLUS. Yes. Whatever there is bright or beautiful or that pleases men, comes about because of you. And all the world is subject to Wealth.[47]

Observations about the power of money all tend to possess such a strong family resemblance that it is difficult to distinguish any one source, a situation further muddied by the fact that *Wealth*'s maxims about money were circulating independently in the sixteenth century, used as an educational aid.[48] It would be easy to make a list too of differences between Pecunia and Wealth: Pecunia is neither blind, old, ragged, nor male, which are the distinguishing features of

Wealth in *Wealth* as against these other allegorical personifications of wealth. What she *does* like Wealth, and unlike most of the other personifications of Money discussed here, is to change, and finish the play vowing to be better: but, again, one should hesitate to argue that this indicates influence. Aristophanes is one element which goes towards making up this composite figure.

Rather more definite is the scene at the end of Jonson's play, in which Penny-boy Senior, who is losing his reason as a result of losing Lady Pecunia, holds a trial of two of his dogs; this, as William Gifford noted long ago, is certainly modelled upon Aristophanes' *Wasps* and the dog-trial in that play. One could pursue verbal parallels, and indeed verbal differences, since in general, for instance, the Jonson play is more interested in the psychology of character, and much darker in tone, but this is only part of the story: what is interesting is that this is an imitation of Aristophanes that sticks out like a sore thumb.[49]

If *The Staple of News* is made up of elements from three Aristophanes plays — the Staple itself from *Clouds*, Lady Pecunia from *Wealth*, and the dog-trial from *Wasps* — then, in the light of Jonson's other references to Aristophanes, one might expect personal satire to be associated with the play in some way. And this is, indeed, the case. The play represents on stage under his own name a living contemporary, the printer and newsmonger Nathaniel Butter, and the fact that his own name is used makes this one of the frankest satirical attacks on a living individual in all extant Renaissance drama.[50]

Nathaniel is a clerk in the Staple of News. The Register names him within a few lines, passing a customer over to him: since she is a butter-woman, it is Nathaniel she must consult. The 'butter' pun, strongly implying Nathaniel's surname, is one that will crop up over and over again. In particular, it is a favourite with the four Gossips, who are another onstage audience. At one point a Gossip wishes the Staple to open, and adds: '...would *Butter* would come in, and spread it-selfe a little to vs.'[51] The ensuing twenty lines contain the word 'butter' no fewer than fourteen times, as the Gossips go into a series of excruciating jokes about the sort of butter they might expect. All of this is nonsensical unless Nathaniel is a representation of Nathaniel Butter.

The activities of Nathaniel through the rest of the play must, therefore, be interpreted in the light of his nature as a satirical representation of a living contemporary while he assists in the Staple's propagation of lies of various sorts: and the play has a nasty punishment in store for him when the Staple mysteriously explodes. 'My Fellow', says his colleague, 'melted into butter'.[52] (Jonson does not content himself with imagining the punishment and reformation of his satirical victim, as he did in the texts produced during the War of the Theatres: nothing less than total liquefaction will suffice here.) Introduced as Butter and dissolved as Butter, Nathaniel is therefore a representation of Nathaniel Butter, and the role of the Aristophanic echoes in this play is partly at least to support and defend this transparent satirical attack.

To return to the question with which this essay started: when we see resemblances between Renaissance comedy and Aristophanes, are we seeing evidence of broad cultural tendencies that speak to the deep structures of drama? Or are we seeing authors who know the works of Aristophanes, writing for an audience who also know Aristophanes, and who are making specific intertextual allusions to those plays? In the case of Jonson, in particular (and, I would argue, in the case of other writers as well), the second of these alternatives is often the case. Renaissance constructions of Aristophanes are remarkable for their stress not on the issues that tend to dominate modern perceptions of his work — civic discourse in the wider sense, metatheatre, sexualized humour, plot shapes, or ritual elements — but instead, on his representation of named living individuals on the stage, and this is a perception which is itself shaped and influenced by Horace's allusions to Aristophanes' work. In the case of Jonson, certainly, imitation of Aristophanes' form goes hand in hand with imitation of Aristophanes' satirical practice. Jonson, like other practitioners of Renaissance comedy and satire, had an enduring interest in the author whom Laurence Humfrey had called 'bothe nippynge in taunts, and wanton in talke, & no lesse hurtfull to honestye'.

Notes to Chapter 3

1. See Süss (1911), L. E. Lord (1925), B. R. Smith (1988), and Holtermann (2004); on the context of Renaissance classical education as a whole, see Bolgar (1954); Clarke (1959).
2. Ben Jonson, *Horace His Art of Poetry*, 399–404, cited from Jonson (1925–52), viii. 348.
3. Horace, *Satires* 1. 4, cited from the translation of Thomas Drant in Drant (1567), B6^v.
4. Lefkowitz (1981), 105–15.
5. Cornford (1993; first published 1914); Pickard-Cambridge (1953); Frye (1957), especially 43–45, 158–86.
6. Salingar (1974), 26; Miola (1994).
7. Curtius (1953), *passim*.
8. L. E. Lord (1925), 109.
9. Baldwin (1944), i. 103, 106; for Dorne, see Madan (1885).
10. A. H. Nelson (1989), 155, 964–65.
11. T. L. Smith (1963–83), ii. 176–77; French (1972), 24; Boas (1914), 16–17; L. E. Lord (1925), 155. For Continental plays of this period that used Aristophanes as a model, in one case for a vicious personal attack on Bishop Eck, see L. E. Lord (1925), 108–11.
12. Erasmus, *De Ratione Studii* in Erasmus (1978), 669.
13. Ascham (1570), fos. 57^r, 59^v.
14. Baldwin (1944), i. 191, 197, 335–36.
15. McConica (2004).
16. Phillips (1964), 393–403.
17. Dedication to Lucian's *The Dream, or The Cock,* quoted and translated by Duncan (1979), 29. Throughout this period Lucian and Aristophanes are often paired with each other.
18. Herrick (1950), 229; for Scaliger, see 85–86.
19. Sidnell (1991), 98–110.
20. Baldwin (1944), i. 316.
21. The pamphlets are collected in Gosson (1974), quotation from 165; for Gosson in the context of antitheatrical history, see Barish (1981).
22. Gosson (1974), 167.
23. Webbe, cited from G. G. Smith (1904), ii. 236.
24. Puttenham, ibid. 35; the etymology that linked satire to satyr, not to *satura,* a mixture, held general sway throughout the Renaissance until the pathbreaking work of Casaubon (1605).
25. Puttenham, cited from G. G. Smith (1904), ii. 34.
26. Ibid. 37–38.
27. Lodge, cited from G. G. Smith (1904), vol. 1, 81.

28. Nashe (1958), i. 285.
29. Meres, *Palladis Tamia,* quoted from G. G. Smith (1904), ii. 323.
30. Joseph Hall, *Virgidemiae* IV. i. 49–58, in J. Hall (1969).
31. Davenport's note at J. Hall (1969), 196, referring to Aelian, *Varia Historia* 2. 13, and [Plutarch], *de Lib. Educ.* = *Moralia* 10 C–D.
32. Upton (1749).
33. Ibid. 47.
34. Gum (1969); Dick (1974); Dick shares Gum's assumptions, Fryean vocabulary, and methodology, and does not need separate discussion.
35. Gum (1969), 117, 73.
36. Aristophanes (1607); McPherson (1974).
37. See Jonson (2001), Introduction, esp. 18–24. The edition also has a comprehensive review of recent criticism.
38. *Every Man Out,* 'Induction', 229–45.
39. Ben Jonson (1925–52), ix. 427: a more exact source still proves elusive, although Jonson has been shown to be drawing on Minturno later on — see Snuggs (1950).
40. *Every Man Out,* 'Induction', 250–61.
41. *Every Man Out,* 'Induction', 140–43.
42. For Aubrey, Mayne, and evidence about the historical Chester, see Steggle (1999).
43. On *Poetaster* and personal satire, see Jonson (1995), Introduction; Cain (1998); Bednarz (2001).
44. *Poetaster,* 'Apologetical Dialogue', 184–92.
45. See, for instance, Sanders (1998).
46. *The Staple of News,* I. 2. 48–49.
47. Ibid. 2. 1. 38–43: *Wealth,* 142–46 (my translation).
48. Baldwin (1944), i. 335.
49. *Wasps,* 891–1008; *The Staple of News,* 5. 4.
50. See Frank (1961), 1–18; Raymond (1993), 3–4; for the extreme rarity of representations of living individuals on stage under their own name, see Steggle (1998).
51. *The Staple of News,* 'Intermean' 2, 51–52.
52. *The Staple of News,* 5. 1. 49.

CHAPTER 4

❖

The English-Speaking Aristophanes
1650–1914

Edith Hall

Introduction

In Chs. 5 and 6 it will be seen that as early as the 1650s an Irishman could use
Aristophanes to criticize English imperialism, while by the early nineteenth
century the possibility was being explored in France of staging a topical adaptation
of Aristophanes. In 1817, moreover, Eugène Scribe could base his vaudeville show
Les Comices d'Athènes on *Ecclesiazusae*.[1] Aristophanes became an important figure for
German Romantics, including Hegel, after Friedrich Schlegel had in 1794 published
his fine essay on the aesthetic value of Greek comedy.[2] There Schlegel proposed
that the Romantic ideals of Freedom and Joy (*Freiheit, Freude*) are integral to all art;
since Schlegel regarded comedy as containing them to the highest degree, for him it
was the most democratic of all art forms. Aristophanic comedy made a fundamental
contribution to his theory of a popular genre with emancipatory potential.[3] One
result of the philosophical interest in Aristophanes was that in the early decades
of the nineteenth century, until the 1848 revolution, the German theatre itself felt
the impact of the ancient comic writer: topical *Lustspiele* displayed interest in his
plays, which provided a model for German poets longing for a political comedy, for
example the remarkable satirical trilogy *Napoleon* by Friedrich Rückert (1815–18).[4]

This international context illuminates the experiences undergone by Aristophanic
comedy in England, and what became known as Britain consequent upon the 1707
Act of Union. This chapter traces some steps in the English-language reception of
Aristophanes and his plays between the mid-seventeenth century and 1914. The
material has previously been so little researched that the major part of the exercise
inevitably takes the form of excavation of evidence and narrative. It nevertheless
argues that the excitement associated with Aristophanes during the English
Interregnum, Restoration, and briefly in the theatre of Henry Fielding, disappeared
by the mid-eighteenth century. Aristophanes became dissociated from live theatrical
performances, a result of the paradox whereby he was at that time identified as a
mouthpiece for inveterate political reactionaries, while simultaneously creating
profound unease in moral conservatives. This uncomfortable situation pertained
until the revived appreciation, in the late nineteenth century, of Aristophanes both
as a socio-political vehicle and as a performable playwright.

The Aristophanes of the late eighteenth and nineteenth centuries, in the English-speaking world, was a peculiar beast. His status as pillar of classical history and poetry was confirmed after Thomas Arnold read him at the age of forty and added him to the curriculum read at Rugby School;[5] he also constituted a major cultural signpost, the presence of which everyone dealing with either ancient Greece or comedy felt obliged to acknowledge.[6] On the other hand, as Jenkyns is correct in concluding, 'of all the great Greek writers Aristophanes had the least influence' on the nineteenth century.[7] One reason was certainly that Aristophanic drama was suspected on account of its obscenity. But another reason was its almost uncontested possession by men who espoused traditional, even reactionary political opinions. Such men rarely participated in the professional theatre, and Aristophanes, several of whose plays were unavailable in English translation until well into the nineteenth century, was read by few outside the male, educated élite. He was seen as an establishment-minded 'right-wing' satirist for the whole period from Fielding to Matthew Arnold. This constituted a major difference between the reception of Aristophanes and that of Greek tragedy, which was often used both in performance and translation to articulate progressive causes, and to express criticism of those holding the reigns of power, from as early as the late seventeenth century.[8]

With the exception of Christopher Wase's royalist translation of Sophocles' *Electra* (1649), Greek tragedy did not attract the loyal followers of the Caroline court.[9] It was not until after the Restoration that Thomas Stanley, another ardent royalist, and the first translator of *Clouds* into English (1655),[10] published his edition of Aeschylus (1663).[11] In contrast with the tragedians, Aristophanes had therefore acquired aristocratic associations by the mid-sevententh century. His presence of course lurks behind Jonson's plays (see Steggle, this volume),[12] but, in addition, the three English-speaking literary individuals drawn to Aristophanes in the mid-seventeenth century were all sympathetic to the Stuart monarchy; their sensibilities were indeed anti-republican, but also morally liberal. A translation of *Wealth*, probably by an Irishman, published in 1659 will be discussed by Wyles in the next chapter, but an even earlier translator of *Wealth* was the cavalier dramatist Thomas Randolph. Randolph styled himself one of the 'Sons of Ben' (Jonson), and became the man responsible for the earliest English-language version of any Aristophanic play. His *Ploutophthalmia Ploutogamia*, otherwise known as *A Pleasant Comedie: Entituled Hey for Honesty, Down with Knavery* was written in the early 1630s, and probably performed in a private venue. It is an adventurous transposition of *Wealth* to a setting in Caroline London, and welds the ancient plot to contemporary satire, the victims of which include dour, corrupt Roundheads, the Levellers, avaricious Anglican clerics, and the Pope himself.[13] Several allusions display Randolph's familiarity with other Aristophanic plays, for example Plutus' remarks about utopian dreams of castles in the air.[14]

Randolph's knowledge of *Wealth* informed some of the other comedies that he staged. His *Aristippus*, performed at Cambridge between 1625 and 1626, is inspired by *Clouds* as well as Plato's *Symposium* (a text which has always played an important role in drawing attention to the figure of Aristophanes), and involves a simple-minded youth attending an academy run by a fraudulent and bibulous philosopher.[15] One of the demotic characters in his mildly moral comedy *The Drinking Academy* (which involves an Aristophanic father–son conflict over money), believed to have been performed between 1626 and 1631, imitates *Wealth*; the play also contains a divine epiphany in the final act.[16] Had Randolph survived to the Restoration, rather than dying young in 1635, the picture of Aristophanes in England would have looked fuller and different. It is in Randolph, moreover, that we first find an identification of Aristophanes with the defence of theatre art at the time when it began to come under pressure from the Puritan lobby. *Aristippus* opens with a personification of the Show herself being summoned from the underworld, since 'Shewes having beene long intermitted, and forbidden by authority for their abuses, [she] could not be raised but by conjuring'.[17] In poems where he talks in coded terms about the Puritan assault on theatre, Randolph uses the poetic disguise of ancient bards such as Orpheus: in *The Song of Discord* he laments the silencing of the poets, reflecting that from now on his only 'quire' will be provided by 'a set of frogs' singing in discordant competition with their cantor.[18]

In the years leading up to the closure of the theatres in 1642, Thomas Randolph's *Aristippus* was not the only theatrical performance to offer arguments in defence of its own medium. In 1633 James Shirley's extravagant masque *The Triumph of Peace*, performed against a set designed by Inigo Jones at Whitehall, presented a compliment to Charles I and his Queen, Henrietta Maria, by using personifications of Eirene and Eunomia in order to demonstrate the legal establishment's loyalty to the king. This was in the aftermath of William Prynne's assault on the theatre — and Henrietta Maria's involvement with it — in *Histriomastix* (1633). The masque mingled several features that Shirley (an accomplished Greek scholar) may have acquired from knowledge of Aristophanes, especially the elaborate bird costumes, and the divine epiphany of 'Irene, or Peace, in a flowery vesture like the spring [... and] Buskins of greene Taffata'.[19] The association of Aristophanes with the defence of the theatre itself became explicit during the later years of the Interregnum. This emerged in an entertainment produced by William Davenant, once a leading cavalier dramatist who had also been patronized by Henrietta Maria. As a result he had later found himself in the Tower of London. But after his release and marriage, in 1655, to an enterprising French widow, he began with her gingerly to test the boundaries of the proscription on stage performance by producing crypto-theatrical entertainments that were not labelled as such.[20]

As early as May 1656, Davenant presented a performance neutrally entitled *The First Days Entertainment at Rutland-House*, which consisted of 'Declamations and Musick; after the manner of the Ancients'. The Rutland House venue was his own home in Aldersgate Street, London (near the modern Barbican). A prologue apologized for the 'narrow room', and those present were invited to regard it as a way 'to our Elyzian field, the *Opera*' (the first appearance in the English language of this crucial word to denote a fusion of drama, recitation and song). The figures of Aristophanes and Diogenes the Cynic declaimed respectively for and against the value of public entertainments by 'moral representations'.[21] Persons representing a Parisian and a Londoner then delivered speeches, interspersed with appropriate music, on the merits of their respective capital cities. The entertainment carefully distinguished itself from a stage play, by making the declaimers remain seated, keeping to long speeches rather than dialogue, and abjuring either elaborate costumes or props. At the end there were songs 'relating to the Victor' (i.e. Oliver Cromwell). No official criticism resulted, and in the autumn Davenant staged *The Siege of Rhodes*, part 1, which is regarded as the first true English opera.

In the Rutland House *Opera*, Diogenes spoke first, criticizing all forms of entertainment. Aristophanes followed with this lament:

> This discontented Cynick would turn all time into midnight, and all learning into melancholy Magick. He is so offended at Mirth, as if he would accuse even Nature her self to want gravity, for bringing in the Spring so merrily with the Musick of Birds.[22]

No attempt at impartiality is evident: Aristophanes not only refutes Diogenes point by point, but is given the more attractive and persuasive speech, for example when he describes the power of theatre to translate its audience, in imagination, to any site in the world — a power which outrages Diogenes:

> He is offended at Scenes in the Opera, as at the useless Visions of Imagination. Is it not the safest and shortest way to understanding, when you are brought to see vast Seas and Provinces, Fleets, Armies, and Forts, without the hazards of a Voyage, or pains of a long March? Nor is that deception where we are prepar'd and consent to be deceiv'd. Nor is there much loss in that deceit, where we gain some variety of experience by a short journey of the sight. When he gives you advice not to lay out time in prospect of Woods and Medows, which you can never possess, he may as well shut up his own little Window (which is the Bung-hole of his Tub) and still remain in the dark, because the light can only shew him that which he can neither purchase nor beg.[23]

There is little engagement with the plays of Aristophanes, beyond a passage which defends artistic representation of 'the shining heroes' on the ground that they offer moral examples, which 'encourage your endeavours for perfection';[24] this section reiterates points first made in the history of literary criticism by Aeschylus in Aristophanes' *Frogs* (e.g. 1039–41, 1053–56). But it was Aristophanes whom Davenant chose to defend *all* the performing arts at this crucial moment in their history: Aristophanes became the mouthpiece for the apologia of a royalist man of the theatre frustrated in both the political and the creative spheres.

Davenant went to France to join the soon-to-be-crowned Charles II in March 1660, and was rewarded upon the Restoration by receiving a patent allowing him to manage a new theatrical company at Dorset Gardens. In the Restoration theatre he was the dominant figure, renowned for innovations in scenic effects, for the training of actresses, and for heroic dramas with a royalist bias. Although it is important to remember the political appropriation of Aristophanes by Burnell and Randolph, it is memories of Davenant's Aristophanes that lie behind the handful of Restoration comedies that eighteenth-century critics felt intuitively had been informed by Aristophanes. Two comedies by Edward Howard (who had in 1664 written one of the most anti-Cromwellian plays of the Restoration, *The Usurper*) echo Aristophanes. *The Women's Conquest* (1669) portrays the Amazons' subjugation of the men of Scythia, and in *The Six Days Adventure; or, the New Utopia* (1671),

Howard dramatises a community in which constitutional power alternates between the sexes. When the women assume government, they create an egalitarian republic, endow themselves with the right to initiate courtship, and establish a court to regulate male love crimes. This is reminiscent of *Ecclesiazusae*, while the men's stratagem of refusing the women love inverts the plot of *Lysistrata*.[25] But there may also be an echo of *Birds*, when the character Mr Peacock appears in a costume of feathers, which he claims he has ordered from the Indies, no other part of the world being sufficiently 'airy'.[26]

   The Six Days Adventure was one of several plays attacked in *The Rehearsal* (1671) by George Villiers, Duke of Buckingham. This in turn was felt to have taken from another Aristophanic play, *Frogs*, its idea of examining contemporary tragedy through performed parody.[27] Villiers was a libertarian aristocrat, who (despite a complicated political past) was a favourite of Charles II at the time he wrote *The Rehearsal*, having overseen the execution of no fewer than twenty republican conspirators in Yorkshire in 1663–64. *The Rehearsal* satirized John Dryden and what are presented as the sententious and pretentious tragedies of the Restoration. The play concerns a playwright named Bayes (in reference to Dryden, then Poet Laureate), who attempts to stage a play made up of excerpts of existing heroic dramas. Buckingham set out to puncture what he saw as Drydenesque bombast; most of the excerpts in the play-within-a-play are taken from his dramas, especially *The Conquest of Granada*, in the second preface to which Dryden had upbraided his fellow playwrights for staging immoral heroes and low sentiments: Buckingham's play, in a sense, is the old theatre biting Dryden back. Through *The Rehearsal*, *Frogs* came to inform distantly a whole category of eighteenth-century plays about the theatre, besides Richard Brinsley Sheridan's reworking of *The Rehearsal* for his play, *The Critic* (1779), where the target was the inflated self-importance of theatre criticsm. An important example by Henry Fielding will be discussed in the next section.

Aristophanes and the Theatre under Walpole

Despite the underlying influence of Aristophanes on some Restoration comedy, the impossibility of staging his plays in anything like an authentic state in the British theatre before the late nineteenth century is underlined by the fate which befell the solitary attempt, in 1716–17, to produce Terence's far less alien *Eunuchus* in English translation at Drury Lane; the production was a commercial disaster and did not survive the third night.[28] Aristophanes' association with the Stuart dramatists may partially explain his disappearance from comic culture after the Glorious Revolution until the 1720s. Yet by 1726, Jonathan Swift, in Ireland, was adopting imagery from Aristophanes' *Clouds* in *Gulliver's Travels* (1726).[29] In London, the Whig opposition against the influence of the first Prime Minister, Robert Walpole, was producing theatrical writers, such as John Gay, whose insouciant plays directed satire against the incumbents of the highest offices in the land. It is unsurprising, therefore, to find some scholars suspecting at least an implicit debt to Aristophanes in Gay's *The Beggar's Opera* (1728), especially in the tone taken by the chorus leader Matt of the Mint, and some of the lyrics sung by Jenny Diver, leader of the other

FIG. 4.1. Frontispiece to Lewis Theobald, *Plutus: or, The World's Idol* (1715)

'chorus' of 'Women of the Town', who fuse imagery from the animal world with biting satire.[30]

That the plays of Aristophanes were felt to give low-class characters an irreverent voice is confirmed by Lewis Theobald's unctuous dedication of his 1715 translation of *Plutus* (fig. 4.1) to the then enormously powerful Duke of Argyll (a political maverick who, though loyal to the Hanoverian succession, behaved as if he were monarch of Scotland). Theobald apologised for the rudeness of the fifth-century slaves, which resulted from 'the Liberties allow'd to the Characters of their Slaves'.[31] Theobald, a mild Tory, later plundered Aristophanes when writing a scene for working-class characters in *Orestes*, a musical comedy based on Euripides' *Iphigenia in Tauris*. In Act III scene 3 Orestes' sailors consider their future on this remote shore. They are theatrical descendants of Trinculo and Stephano in *The Tempest*,[32] but the communist colony they design is informed by *Birds* and *Ecclesiazusae*, in addition to *Wealth*, which Theobald had translated.[33]

Theobald's *Orestes*, moreover, followed the première of Henry Fielding's very different stage play of 1730, which had adapted *Frogs* (fig. 4.2). Fielding's version of *Frogs* is supposedly a puppet-show entitled *The Pleasures of the Town*, which constituted a play-within-a-play in *The Author's Farce*, performed in the spring in the Little Theatre in the Haymarket. In fact, the cast list shows that the alleged puppet-show was performed throughout by live actors *pretending* to be puppets — a conceit not untypical of Georgian popular theatre. The frame play *The Author's Farce* was extremely popular, being performed no fewer than forty-two times (an outstanding success in those days) between 1730 and its Drury Lane season in 1733–34;[34] it was also possible to watch it at a booth erected in a fair in London-Spa Fields in the autumn of 1735.[35] Although a light-hearted piece (in the Prologue it is stressed that 'The aim of Farce is but to make you laugh'), it reveals the difficulties facing Fielding.[36] Italian opera, although ridiculed, was popular; Walpole's scrutiny of the stage was growing more oppressive, and as a result neither tragedy nor comedy seemed to be producing significant playwrights able to say anything substantial.

The hero of *The Author's Farce* is Mr Luckless, a failed tragedian, whose maudlin and pretentious verses provide much mirth in Act II scene 1, where they are subjected to quotation and bathetic comic analysis reminiscent of the contest in *Frogs*.[37] Fielding is perhaps lamenting the poor education of many of his audience when the impecunious Luckless complains that to talk of money to a dramatic author is as useless as talking 'Latin or Greek to him';[38] but in the end Luckless's fortunes are saved by the silly farce which opens in Act III — one hears here the echo of Statius' remark that Statius, for all the excellence of his epic poetry, would have starved had he not sold a mime to the players — and continues to the end, where the world of the farce and the real world fuse in a comic denouement. The embedded show, *The Pleasures of the Town*, stages a contest in Hades between different types of entertainment and literature (as represented by Don Tragedio, Sir Farcical Comic, Dr Orator, Signior Opera, Monsieur Pantomime, and Mrs Novel). The judge is the Goddess Nonsense. First there is a journey across the river Styx with Charon, the addition of a Bookseller and a Poet to the literary confusion, and the dance, inspired by Euripides' Muse in *Frogs*, of a black female castanet-

FIG. 4.2. Henry Fielding: line engraving by James Basire after Hogarth

player.[39] Subsequently the competitors strive to outdo each other in increasingly inane parodies of their own style and linguistic register. Perhaps the most distinctly Aristophanic item actually draws on another comedy, *Birds*: Dr Orator sings a three-stanza lyric beginning 'All men are birds by nature, sir', of which the first two refrains sing of the owl's 'hooting, | Hooting, hooting' (repeated three further times), and the raven's 'croaking, | Croaking, croaking'.[40] But a more subtle set of Aristophanic echoes is to be heard in Signior Opera's air for an abandoned heroine, 'Barbarous cruel man, | I'll sing thus while I'm dying; I'm dying like a swan'; this includes extensive repetition and melisma in the phrase 'on the *high* — – — roads*', which must have been suggested to Fielding by the details in the parody of Euripidean monody.[41] According to the original cast list, Signior Opera was played by 'Stopler', a fine singer going by the name of either Charles or Michael

Stoppelaer. He sang in Handel's operas as well as comedy, and specialized in an elevated style of singing for comic purposes: one of his other roles was that of Cantato in the humorous *Bayes' Opera*.[42]

Fielding returned to Aristophanes when looking for a platform from which to deliver anti-Walpole Whig polemic. Despite being traumatized at Eton, Fielding had picked up considerable respect for ancient Greek literature, and in 1742 he published the translation of *Wealth* on which he had collaborated with William Young. In the preface Fielding developed his ideas about the possibility of a political comedy. Walpole had passed the Licensing Act in 1737 in order to curb political attacks on his premiership in the theatre, especially Fielding's satires that were playing to packed houses at the Little Theatre in the Haymarket: these had included *Historical Register for the Year 1736* in March 1737, and in April *Eurydice Hiss'd* (whose katabatic theme probably drew on Aristophanes' *Frogs*). Since Walpole could now refuse a licence to any but the most anodyne of comedies, the legislation put Fielding out of business and drove him into attacking Walpole by other means.

The preface to *Wealth* also gave Fielding a place in which to attack the genteel drama known as Sentimental Comedy and associated with Colley Cibber. This drama was compliant, middle-class, and consciously avoided controversial subject-matter: Fielding prescribes the reading of Jonson and Aristophanes as the antidote to its cloying mires. In the notes Fielding draws a parallel between Walpole and ancient demagogues who 'make use of popular interest, and the character of patriotism, in order to betray one's country'.[43] The translation may have informed Fielding's own unfinished comedy *Jupiter's Descent on Earth*.[44] But its real impact was more subterranean, since it was much studied by later comic writers and theorists, keeping just alive the possibility of an Aristophanic mode of social and political criticism even when such a concept was inimical to both the government and the stage.[45]

Counter-Revolutionary Aristophanes

In the 1740s and 1750s, the actor and dramatist Samuel Foote encouraged the use of his soubriquet 'the English Aristophanes', but his claim to this title rested not on any identifiable debt to Aristophanes' plays, either in specific allusion, institutional target, or subterranean adoption of plot, episode, or character. Instead, what seemed to make people regard Foote as 'Aristophanic' was his apolitical brand of satirical revue, involving *ad hominem* jokes and mimicry at the expense of what we would call 'celebrities'. There is no notion of citizenship or public responsibility to be discovered underlying his comedies. Despite the lip-service Foote paid to Aristophanes' contribution to 'Greek virtue', he saw no further than those passages in the ancient plays which adumbrated his own brand of personal (not political) satire.[46] But Walpole had effectively put a stop to political comedy on the London stage, and the dangerous *moral* reputation of Aristophanes was confirmed in the publication (1759) of the book that brought him to the widest audience so far. This was the English translation, by several individuals including Charlotte Lennox, of the Jesuit scholar Father Pierre Brumoy's *Le Théâtre des Grecs* (first edition 1730). Volume III contains a long 'Dissertation on Ancient Comedy'. Other materials are appended, including a competent version of *Frogs* (the first to appear in English) by the accomplished Hellenist Gregory Sharpe, and plot summaries of all Aristophanes' plays. The troubled reputation attaching to Aristophanes is conveyed by the opening section, 'reasons why Aristophanes may be reviewed without translating him entirely'; here Brumoy admits that he was doubtful about meddling with comedy at all, on account of Aristophanes' 'licentiousness', which struck him as 'exorbitant'.[47] In his discussion of *Lysistrata* the reader discovers that Aristophanes had disgraced the noble freedom of his comic muse by a shocking depravity, and by the abominable pictures he had created, which would for ever render him the horror and execration of every reader who had the least taste for modesty and sentiment.[48]

Following the French Revolution, however, the moral repugnance of Aristophanes was forgotten as the politically conservative Aristophanes emerged in Francis Wrangham's *Reform: A Farce, Modernised from Aristophanes* (1792). Wrangham later became a moderate Whig, and there has been some confusion about his political intentions at the time when, as an undergraduate, he penned this satirical text. The actual dialogue is short, and placed in the mouths of the revolutionary Tom Paine and John Bull, an archetypally commonsensical Englishman, who are identified in the Introduction as Chremylus and Plutus.[49] Paine tries to persuade Bull to support his proposals for abolishing the monarchy and economic equality; Bull (a believer in ordinary decency, and a victim of both the decadent, overpaid monarchy and grasping radicals) wins the argument. He counters with reminders that revolution causes suffering, that Paine has proved himself unpatriotic during his involvement with American revolutionaries,[50] and that the French Revolution was problematic. The satire presents an unmistakable case against what it presents as the specious appeal of Paine's reformist rhetoric.[51]

By 1836 the counter-revolutionary Aristophanes had been promoted to protest against all the reforms instigated by the Whigs, especially the Great Reform Act of 1832, which had massively extended the franchise. The reforms were celebrated in the same year in a play that was dependent, rather, upon Greek *tragedy*, Thomas Talfourd's *Ion*;[52] it is fascinating to compare the less flattering parallels with democratic Athens being perceived through the application of an Old Comic lens. The Aristophanic complaints against the reforms were expressed in the skilful, reactionary *The Possums of Aristophanes, Recently Recovered*, published in 1836 in the popular new Tory literary organ, *Fraser's Magazine for Town and Country*. The unnamed author is likely to be the effective founder of the magazine William Maginn, a brilliant classicist and parodist of Greek and Latin authors.

The Possums is presented as the newly rediscovered first version of Aristophanes' *Clouds*, which, it is claimed, featured a chorus of possums. This allows the author to introduce a supercilious note about the North American 'negro' minstrel song, *Possum up a Gum-Tree*.[53] The reader is informed that while Aristophanes had satirised a new school of philosophy in the revised *Clouds*, in *Possums* his target had been 'the new school of politics and legislation. He was, as every school-boy knows, an aristocrat; and the *Possums* breathe the very spirit of genuine Conservatism'.[54] That in *The Possums* Aristophanes had prefiguratively targeted the classes newly franchised in 1832 is proposed when the audience is sneeringly told that the Pheidippides figure, 'Sophoswipos', spends his time at the Mechanics Institute.[55] The equivalent of Socrates is Micromegalus, apparently a thinly disguised Earl Grey, Prime Minister between 1830 and 1834, who had presided over some of the most far-reaching reforms in British history: not only the Reform Act, but the Poor Law Amendment Act and the Abolition of Slavery in the Colonies.[56] Grey/ Micromegalus practises twirling in order the better to legislate:

> My thoughts forsake the past, and learn to waltz
> With notions yet unheard of. Then, new schemes
> For public good arise. For public good
> Is not like sluggish ponds, that stand all still,
> And rot for want of motion: public good
> Changes its aspect daily. So the laws
> That guard it must change daily too.[57]

Micromegalus requests that his chorus of Possums expound their 'thoughts on policy' and 'legislative principles', to which the Possums respond, unintelligibly, in blatant imitation of an Aristophanic animal chorus, 'Ullaboo, ullaboo | Lillibu, lillibu, lillibulero'. (*Lillibullero*, of course, was a popular song that since the Glorious Revolution had often been used to satirize the sentiments of Irish or other rebels against the British monarchy and government).

In the realm of scholarship and translation, too, Aristophanes remained the preserve of dyed-in-the-wool reactionaries. John Wood Warter, for example, the author of a translation of *Acharnians, Knights, Wasps,* and *Birds* published in 1830, was a churchman whose austerely conservative leanings — both moral *and* political — struck even his contemporaries.[58] Moreover, the debate about how to translate Aristophanes was conducted not from opposite sides of the political fence, but by two gentlemen who represented different brands of conservatism, and it was published in the conservative press. One of them, Thomas Mitchell, was an academic whose editions of Aristophanes develop the indictment of Athenian democracy which he had found in William Mitford's *History of Greece* (1784–1810). It was Mitford's position on the Athenian constitution, especially his identification of the democracy with the dangerous reforms suggested by contemporary radicals, that Mitchell's editions 'strongly perpetuated', as Turner has shown.[59]

Mitchell's edition of *Frogs* (1839), with its notes in English, became a chief conduit through which Victorian men had access to that play at school and university. Its introduction stresses the problem presented to Athens by the demagogues, 'the real deformity daily developing itself'; in democratic Athens, 'the last knave was welcome as the first'; Cleophon was 'clearly not of true Attic origin [...] and perhaps not even speaking the language correctly', and it was the 'innate vices of the Athenian constitution' that enabled such a man to put himself in power (iv).[60] In a note ostensibly dealing with the political views of Aeschylus, Mitchell takes the opportunity openly to inveigh against democracy as a political ideal and opinion;[61] the volume, of course, was published just a few years after the great Reform Act of 1832, at a time when the Chartists' appeal for universal male suffrage had attracted the support of a prominent sector of the middle class. Thucydides, Xenophon,

Aristophanes, and Plato, says Mitchell, offer 'so complete a view of the effects of this form of government [...] in the two great questions of civil freedom and moral excellence, that it must be to sin with the eyes open, if any portion of the world allow men of small attainments, and not always the most upright principles, to precipitate it into such a form of government again'.[62] Here Aristophanic commentary becomes a weapon in the war against advocates of universal suffrage.

The detailed comments Mitchell made offer more in this patrician vein. When Xanthias speaks up during the dialogue between Heracles and Dionysus (*Frogs* 82–83), 'the vanity of an indulged lacquey [*sic*] exhibits itself'.[63] The same superior censure of the serving class emerges in Mitchell's remarks on the dialogue between Xanthias and the underworld slave.[64] In particular, Mitchell takes exception to Xanthias' remark that masters can afford to be magnanimous, if all they do is *pinein* and *binein* (drink and fornicate, *Frogs* 701–03); he proposes that the whole dialogue must itself be accompanied by the drinking of the slaves, on the dubious ground that the sort of remarks they make are rarely made except under the influence of alcohol:

> And do our two lacqueys hold a *dry* colloquy? Forbid it every feast of Bacchus, of which we ever heard! forbid it all the bonds which have tied lacqueyism together, since the world of *man* and *master* began?[65]

The text of *Frogs* is also used by Mitchell to inveigh against the socially corrupting aspects of Euripidean tragedy, which were often mere 'vehicles of sophistry, philosophy, misogynism, democracy, and blasphemy'.[66]

Yet throughout the nineteenth century, the man whose name was most likely to have been cited in association with Aristophanes was John Hookham Frere (fig. 4.3). His lively and readable verse translations towards the end of the nineteenth century helped the drive to stage Aristophanes; they were still being published in the Everyman series as late as 1945. The popularity of Frere's translations resulted partly from what is still is his impressive attempt to present them as performable playscripts, with elaborate stage directions extending even to descriptions of masks: that offering a performable text was his intention is clear from the title page of his *Birds*, which says that the translation is 'Intended to convey some notion of its effect as an acted play'. But even more important were his keen wit and poet's ear, above all his sense of rhythm, which make the translations satisfying to speak; indeed, as the first English author to write mock-heroic *ottava rima* in his 1817 poem 'Whistlecraft', he had already exerted a formative influence *as a poet* on a crucial text, Byron's *Don Juan* (1819–1824), as well as Shelley's translations of the *Homeric Hymns*.

The son of a high Tory magistrate and MP, Frere came from old-fashioned gentry stock. At Eton in the 1780s, he befriended the future Prime Minister, George Canning, and was elected MP in 1796. In 1797 Frere joined the contributors to the influential *Anti-Jacobin*.[67] It owed much of its fame to verses written by Canning and Frere, some of them parodies of poets who supported the opposition, such as 'The Friend of Humanity and the Knife-Grinder', which mocked Robert Southey's idealization of the poor and those who supported the French Revolution.[68] The time spent on this journal was crucial to the development of Frere's buoyant, sceptical, conservative comic sensibility. After succeeding his friend Canning as

FIG. 4.3. Engraving of John Hookham Frere (1769–1846)

Under-Secretary of State in the Foreign Office, he took up appointments in Lisbon and Madrid, but in 1808 a disastrous set of events curtailed his public career. In 1818 he moved to Malta permanently, and sought solace in translating Aristophanes and another poet inherently appealing to disgruntled conservatives — Theognis.

His work on Aristophanes was already in progress when he wrote the canonical nineteenth-century critical discussion of the principles involved in translating Greek comedy, in a long review of Mitchell's translation.[69] The essay argued persuasively against Mitchell's archaizing imitations of Jacobean comic language in favour of up-to-date vernacular idioms which offered living correlatives to the styles adopted by individual characters in Aristophanes, and as such laid the foundations for all successful subsequent translations of ancient comedy. It was published in the self-consciously Tory periodical *Quarterly Review* for July 1820.[70] Frere's own lively translations, which he had privately printed, were essentially complete by 1830.[71] During the decade when he wrote them, he became depressed by news of radical agitation in Britain, and penned diatribes on the subject of Canadian insurgency, bemoaning 'that tendency to Democracy, which is said to be so lamentably prevalent in new settlements'.[72]

These views affected his translations of Aristophanes, in which he even objected to the canonization of the assassination of the Peisistratids 'by the democratic fanaticism of the Athenians'.[73] He also resents the right of poorer Athenians to serve on juries where they could become 'the arbiters of the lives and fortunes of their subjects and fellow-citizens'.[74] His unusual interpretation of *Frogs* sees the intelligent slave Xanthias as representing not the slaves freed at Arginusae (a politically liberal-minded interpretation he had found Brumoy's *Le Théâtre des Grecs*), but the exiled aristocrat Alcibiades, whose 'genius and abilities might have relieved' the Athenians; Frere thinks this would have been at only the relatively minor cost of submitting to a more dictatorial government![75]

Aristophanes as Conservative Victorian

Frere's translations helped to keep Aristophanes on the curriculum at both schools and universities throughout the Victorian period: Charles Bristed read all eleven comedies for the Cambridge tripos in the 1840s.[76] The importance of Aristophanes to British male education is underlined by the enthusiasm of Alexander Forbes, a colonial administrator in India, for collaborating with Dalpatram Dahyabhai on a translation of this particular author into Gujarati (see Vasunia, in the following chapter). Yet, despite the routine inclusion amongst the sculptures of the Grand Front of the new 1808 Covent Garden Theatre of the figure of Aristophanes alongside Menander, the Muse of Comedy, and Aeschylus,[77] on only one occasion until the 1870s was Aristophanes in any danger of actually returning to the stage. The exception was an adaptation of *Birds* in 1846, penned by the most intuitively conservative writer of Victorian burlesque, James Robinson Planché.

Planché's pro-establishment mentality is underlined by his appointment in 1854 to no less a ceremonial office than Rouge Croix pursuivant at the College of Arms, which entailed accompanying Garter missions and appearing, in full regalia, on state occasions. But back in the 1840s Planché was a prominent playwright, who attempted to repeat the success of his classically derived burlesque *The Golden Fleece* (1845) with an Easter entertainment at the Haymarket, based on an ancient Greek comedy.[78] *The Birds of Aristophanes: A Dramatic Experiment in One Act, being an humble attempt to adapt the said 'Birds' to this climate, by giving them new names, new feathers, new songs, and new tales* (fig. 4.4). Planché was inspired by the idiomatic verse forms he found in Frere's translation, first issued publicly in 1840. *Birds* may also have been chosen because of its famous bird-noises and low level of obscenity, and Planché may have been aware that Goethe had staged this play in late eighteenth-century Weimar (see above, 'Introduction', pp. 11–14). Euelpides and Peisthetaerus appear in the updated personae of Jackanoxides and Tomostyleseron, 'Hellenized' forms of the proverbial Jack Noakes and Tom Styles. Planché subsequently complained that

SCENE FROM THE NEW CLASSIC BURLESQUE OF " THE BIRDS OF ARISTOPHANES," AT THE HAYMARKET THEATRE.

FIG. 4.4. Scene from Planché's *The Birds of Aristophanes* (1846)

his intention had been to ascertain 'how far the theatrical public would be willing to receive a higher class of entertainment than the modern Extravaganza of the English stage'.[79] In his memoirs he claimed that he had been trying to 'open a new stage-door by which the poet and the satirist could enter the theatre without the shackles imposed upon them by the laws of the regular drama'; he had contemplated no less an ambitious scheme than 'to lay the foundation for an Aristophanic drama, which the greatest minds would not consider it derogatory to contribute to'.[80]

Yet *The Birds of Aristophanes* failed, despite the lofty motivations, the lavishness of the production, and the excellence of the cast. The primary problem was that making comedy out of comedy was not the way of the early Victorians: the point of the laughter in burlesque, burletta, and light opera was always that it parodically reworked an *elevated* prototype.[81] But it is more significant that, although a romp, Planché's *Birds*, politically speaking, is a reactionary one. After the establishment of the new bird city, problems are created both by human immigrants and by some of the lower-class birds, who become restive and demanding.[82] The rooks want a rookery because they 'can't afford to live in Peacock-square'; the sparrows are mutinous, and the geese demand a common on health grounds. Jackanoxides is unsympathetic, scornfully asking 'What can it signify what sparrows think', and pointing out that geese are 'always cackling for a commonwealth'.[83] The King of the Birds tells Jackanoxides that he was misguided in trying to build a paradise for inferior creatures: why did he think it was rational to 'stir inferior beings up to treason? | ... | And make each goose believe itself a god?'[84] The play concludes with a regal epiphany of Jupiter, who rebukes all birds and men 'Who discontented ever with their lot, | Sigh only to be something they are not', and advises them to 'fear the gods and trust the wise'. In the context of the far-reaching reforms of the previous decade, and the continuing agitation of the 1840s, the conclusion of this light-hearted adaptation of Aristophanes must have come over as an admonition against constitutional aspirations of any radical nature at all. Planché's *Birds*, despite its aesthetic ambitions, perpetuated the reactionary tradition in which Aristophanes had found his exclusive home since the 1790s.

There were several similar conservative manifestations of interest in Aristophanes. When in 1850 Henry Longueville Mansel, a philosophy don at St John's College, Oxford, wrote a curmudgeonly satire protesting against Whig proposals to reform universities, he adopted Aristophanes' *Clouds* as the vehicle for his diatribe against innovation.[85] George Trevelyan may later have developed into a reform-minded Liberal politician, but little other than cliquey elitism is to be found in his comedy *The Cambridge Dionysia*, written at Cambridge in 1858 when he was an undergraduate. It involves Trevelyan falling asleep while reading the article 'Dionysia' in Smith's *Antiquities*;[86] this device introduces a play which takes place in the Old Court at Trinity College. An updated version of *Wasps*, full of in-group jokes and references to alcohol, it closes with the suggestion that a particular policeman be punished: a sense of the intellectual level can be gained from the last line: 'Break his head, and shave his whiskers, and suspend him from the lamp'.

Aristophanes was still beloved of elitist Oxbridge youths articulating vendettas as late as 1894, when Oscar Wilde was attacked in the satirical drama *Aristophanes at Oxford*. It was officially penned by 'Y.T.O.', a troika of undergraduates led by Leopold Amery (who was to become a staunchly conservative politician and journalist), then preparing for Classical Mods. Their motivation is described in the 'Preface' as 'an honest dislike' for *Dorian Gray*, *Salome*, and 'the whole of the erotic, lack-a-daisical, opium-cigarette literature of the day'; there is what would now be called a homophobic innuendo in their claim that they have never seen Wilde himself except surrounded 'by a throng of admiring Adonises'.[87] (By the middle of the next year, Wilde had been sentenced to two years' hard labour.) An even more disreputable instance of Aristophanic imitation must be the novel *Simiocracy* (1884) by the Conservative MP Arthur Brookfield, the most politically incorrect fable of all time. It tells how the Liberal Party enfranchises orang-utans, and imports millions from Africa in order to retain power. *Simiocracy* fuses Aristophanic material (especially *Birds* and *Ecclesiazusae*) with the conventional contents of a genre invented in the 1860s, known as 'prehistoric fiction'.

The Old and the New

This chapter has shown how uniform became the long line of typical targets of 'Aristophanic' satire between Wrangham and the attacks on Oscar Wilde — Tom Paine, republican ideals, democratic reforms, widening of the suffrage, constitutional change, social egalitarianism, university modernization, avant-garde literary authors, enfranchisement of the imperial masses. Yet at the time Brookfield was penning *Simiocracy*, there appeared the first glimmerings since Fielding of a more popular, and also performable Aristophanes. Aristophanes was always perceived as funny enough: indeed, Lemprière's *Dictionary*, widely consulted in the nineteenth century, described Aristophanes as 'the greatest comic dramatist in world literature' on the criterion of his wit: 'by his side Molière seems dull and Shakespeare clownish'.[88] But that humour was still suspected of succeeding at the expense of moral probity. The sensibility of those creating the editions from which nineteenth-century English-speaking boys learnt their Aristophanes can be gleaned from Mitchell's comment on *Frogs* 8, where he remarks that obscenities 'which an Englishman shrinks from uttering' came as easily to ancient Athenians as to 'a modern Frenchman'.[89]

The crucial antidote was the emergence of the notion that Aristophanic humour, however bawdy, also possessed intellectual weight and moral or social utility. Few had agreed with Edward Lytton Bulwer when he had argued, during the reformist zeal of the 1830s, for the establishment of a political theatre modelled on that of classical Athens, in which Aristophanes' plays had fearlessly dramatized the specific issues of his day.[90] It is true that John Ruskin, who took his own aesthetic angle on Aristophanes, was a rare defender of his picturesque qualities, which in the 1850s he had even placed on a par with those of Aeschylus.[91] This defence, however, arose only 'at the cost of taking away the fun'.[92] Most people failed to see that Aristophanes had anything serious to offer, except a satirical mouthpiece to political conservatives lamenting the encroachments of lower orders on their privileges.

A new chord was struck in 1869, with Matthew Arnold's essay 'On the Modern Element in Literature'. Arnold introduced the notion of Aristophanic comedy's claim to *veracity*, and he paid him the compliment of pairing him with Sophocles, his (and most mid-Victorians') favourite Greek tragedian. Aristophanes' distinction was to have regarded humanity 'from the true point of view on the comic side':

> He too, like Sophocles, regards the human nature of his time in its fullest development; the boldest creations of a riotous imagination are in Aristophanes [...] based always upon the foundation of a serious thought: politics, education, social life, literature [...].[93]

Arnold's contemporaries described his own public self-presentation as involving self-conscious playfulness, vivid comedy, personal abuse, and even 'low buffoonery',[94] and when Browning allowed Aristophanes to defend the social utility of his theatrical medium in *Aristophanes' Apology* (1875), he may have intended the ancient poet to represent Arnold.[95]

Fundamentally based on Plato's *Symposium*, Browning's long poem describes Aristophanes turning up with his drunken *kōmos* after the first performance of *Thesmophoriazusae*; he and Browning's ancient Greek heroine (loosely modelled on his deceased wife Elizabeth Barrett Browning, but expressing many of his own views) deliver speeches in defence of Aristophanic comedy and Euripidean tragedy respectively. And it cannot be denied that the poem contains a vision, Arnoldian or not, of a perfect democratic comedy aimed at uncovering truth and nurturing virtue: an ancient Megarian comic actor is envisaged as travelling around on his actors' wagon, complaining that 'Skin-flint starves his labourers! | Clench-fist stows figs away, cheats government!' Moreover, Aristophanes claims that he can prove that comedy is 'coeval with the birth of freedom'. But throughout the poem, the portrayal of Aristophanic comedy is compromised by Aristophanes' (and Browning's) fear of the mob.[96] The very popularity of Aristophanes, the broad social base from which his supporters derived, ultimately seem to repel Browning, who prefers the idea of a maligned, isolated Euripides, losing competitions as he produced tragedies dramatizing timeless verities. For the core of his argument is that comedy must engage with the contingent and parochial and is therefore always at the mercy of political circumstance, whereas the universality and generality of tragedy can allow it to transcend the cultural impoverishment and petty tyrannies of its own day.[97]

George Meredith disagreed. Meredith is the first English-speaking individual to produce a theory of comedy that is adequate to account for Aristophanes. His Aristophanes is underpinned by a sense of citizenship which is finally free of the sexual conservatism that had hampered critics since the Puritans. Meredith's deservedly famous essay *An Essay on Comedy and the Uses of the Comic Spirit* was first delivered as a lecture on 1 February 1877 at the London Institution.[98] After lamenting the state of the contemporary comic stage, he asks:

> But if the Comic idea prevailed with us, and we had an Aristophanes to barb and wing it [...] there would be a bright and positive, clear Hellenic perception of facts. The vapours of Unreason and Sentimentalism would be blown away before they were productive.[99]

Like Arnold, Meredith regarded Aristophanic comedy as possessing the potential to reveal to any age the *truth* about itself. One way in which it could do this was by offering an education, even to the least educated or perceptive members of the public. Aristophanic comedy could rupture 'the link between dull people, consisting in the fraternal agreement that something is too clever for them'; this link is 'equivalent to a cement forming a concrete of dense cohesion, very desirable in the estimation of the statesman.'[100] Meredith here comes close to saying that comedy, if it imitates Aristophanes, has a democratic potential because it protects the masses from the lies fed them by those in power. For Meredith, the Comic Spirit 'makes the future possible by [...] the revelation of division, conflict, forward-movement, potentiality'.[101] It is the spirit born of humankind's united social intelligences.

Admirers of Meredith's sophisticated theoretical rehabilitation of The Comic tend these days to neglect his then-famous novels, dealing with class snobbery and sexual repression, behind which lies a momentum generated by his exploration of the history of comedy. *An Essay on Comedy*, indeed, was written in preparation for *The Egoist: a Comedy in Narrative* (1879).[102] Now acknowledged as his masterpiece, the 'Prelude' to this novel articulates Meredith's idea of comedy as 'the ultimate civilizer'. Like the German Romantics before him, Meredith regarded Comedy as a liberating force in society, but now society was to be defined in a much wider way that accommodated his dream of universal male and female suffrage. The first sentence of *The Egoist* reads, 'Comedy is a game played to throw reflections on social life', and with verbal brilliance the narrative draws on the traditions of stage comedy, especially Molière and Congreve, but simultaneously engages with intellectual issues such as evolution, imperialism, and women's liberation. Meredith's recent biographer has argued that this idiosyncratic fusion also explains the curious title of his subsequent novel *The Tragic Comedians* (1880); the central figures are caught up in a drama that turns into a tragedy, but the irrationality of their conduct makes them comical.[103] It is the serious undertow of Aristophanic humour that consistently appealed to Meredith, who was also an advocate of sexual frankness and regarded as extremely harmful to women society's refusal to discuss the sexual needs and behaviours of both sexes.

By the early 1870s, signs of Aristophanes can also be felt in another venue of comic expression — the opera librettos penned by W. S. Gilbert. It was on account of the consistent (if subterranean) dialogue with the Aristophanic tradition of theatre that Gilbert was claimed at the beginning of the twentieth century to have been 'The English Aristophanes';[104] certain aspects of his irony, parody, and excoriation of pretension do indeed suggest that their author had given Aristophanes' legacy a considerable amount of thought. In a classic study, Edith Hamilton juxtaposed several passages from Gilbert and Aristophanes in order to reveal their similarities, above all in the delineation of verbal nonsense and elevated style.[105] Gilbert was an admirer of Planché,[106] and echoes of *Birds* are to be heard already in *Thespis* (1871), the first work on which Gilbert collaborated with Arthur Sullivan: Thespis and his troupe of travelling actors take over Olympus from the immortals.[107]

The famous song 'I am the very model of a modern Major-General', sung by the Gentleman-Officer Stanley in *The Pirates of Penzance* (1879), provides the following as evidence for his wide-ranging erudition:

> I can tell undoubted Raphaels from Gerard Dows and Zoffanies,
> I know the croaking chorus from the *Frogs* of Aristophanes.[108]

But the Aristophanic chords sound loudest in *Princess Ida*, Gilbert's travesty of Tennyson's 'The Princess'. In an earlier, less frolicsome 1870 version of the Tennyson poem, he had used music by Offenbach, but he rewrote the libretto as a comedy, *Princess Ida*, for Arthur Sullivan (Savoy Theatre, 1884). The intervening years had seen the publication of Benjamin Bickley Rogers's spritely translation *Lysistrata*, in diverse rhythms, under the contentious title of *The Revolt of the Women* (1878); this may have encouraged Gilbert to revisit *The Princess*. The influence of *Lysistrata* behind Gilbert's second portrayal of Tennyson's University for Women at Castle Adamant is palpable, especially in the humour when the women try to exert self-control in order to keep themselves away from men: the emancipated students

are going to do without them, 'If they can — *if they can!*'[109] The very obscenity of
the comic drama which underlies Gilbert's take on Tennyson's story is alluded to
when Melissa asks 'what authors should she read | Who in Classics would proceed,'
and Lady Psyche, Professor of Humanities, responds:

> If you'd climb the Helicon
> You should read Anacreon,
> Ovid's *Metamorphoses*,
> Likewise Aristophanes,
> And the works of Juvenal:
> These are worth attention, all;
> But, if you will be advised,
> You will get them Bowdlerized![110]

At exactly the same time as Browning, Meredith and Gilbert were turning their
back on the hoary question of Aristophanes' licentiousness in order to focus attention
on his social utility, Aristophanic comedy was enjoying its earliest known British
performance in the English language. It was in the early 1870s that Professor Henry
Charles Fleeming Jenkin directed a performance of *Frogs*, in Hookham Frere's
translation. This engineer and Renaissance man ran a private theatre in his Edinburgh
home, which also performed works by the realist nineteenth-century dramatist
Guillaume Augier, Racine, Shakespeare, and Greek tragedies; for these he used the
translations of Lewis Campbell, Professor of Greek at St Andrews and a key member
of the company (along with the young Robert Louis Stevenson).[111] *Frogs* seems
to have been the first Greek play that they performed, and Fleeming Jenkin later
recalled that it 'had been costumed by the professional costumier, with unforgettable
results of comicality and indecorum'.[112] The Edinburgh productions exerted an
influence that extended to Oxford through Lewis Campbell's relationship with
Benjamin Jowett, and they precipitated the new craze of the 1880s for the production
of ancient Greek plays in ancient Greek.[113] The passion for Aristophanes was
confirmed by the spectacular production of *Birds* at Cambridge in 1883 (see further
Wrigley, this volume). There is another vivid connection between the Edinburgh
productions and the new craze for Greek plays: the programme to the 1883 *Birds*
informs us that the parricide was played by Mr Austin Fleeming Jenkin of Trinity
College, Cambridge, the eldest son of the very man responsible for the pioneering
experiments with performing Greek drama in Edinburgh in the previous decade.

   The revived interest in ancient comedy as drama owed much to the cultural
presence of Frere's performable Georgian translations, the texts actually acted in
Edinburgh, which also provided the 'cribs' used in connection with some of the
Oxford and Cambridge productions.[114] The particular choice of comedies is also
significant. While in Germany the 'woman' plays *Lysistrata* and *Ecclesiazusae* were
adapted for political purposes by the last decade of the nineteenth century,[115] in
Britain the male environment of the universities, the longstanding aversion in that
environment to transvestite acting, and the perceived need to avoid obscene or political
material, all contributed to an inevitable attraction towards Aristophanes' more
intellectual comedies *Birds* and *Frogs*. An additional consideration was a fascination
with spectacular animal choruses offering potential to costume designers.[116]

As Fiona Macintosh has demonstrated, the Aristophanic undertow to George Bernard Shaw's *Major Barbara* (1905), which engages with social controversies, reflects the impact made on its author by Gilbert Murray's translation of *Frogs* (1902): the moral hero Cusins becomes identified, through the Aristophanic undertext, with Euripides himself.[117] Yet the revival of interest in Aristophanes traceable to the 1870s continued to run on its two separate tracks — either as a presence lurking behind social critique expressed in other media and genres, such as Browning's dramatic monologues, Meredith's novels, and Shaw's new school of comic theatre, or in performance in the rather anodyne new tradition of academic performance. It was not to be until February 1914, when *Acharnians* was staged at Oxford with the encouragement of Professor Murray, that an academic Greek play was consciously felt to be political. *Acharnians* was promoted as an 'unmistakeable vindication of peace',[118] and the music reflected the current international situation; the chorus of Marathonomachs sang the jingoistic songs 'The British Grenadiers' and 'Rule Britannia'; the Athenian allies were melodically represented by 'La Marseillaise', and the Spartans by 'Wacht am Rhein'.[119] This was not just topicalization; it was topicalization with at least a half-hearted agenda. Fifty-nine young men took part; it would be telling to discover how many were dead four years later.

Yet this chapter must conclude at the first moment when a British performance of a play by Aristophanes was involved in trying to effect social change, and that had been in 1910, four years prior to the Oxford *Acharnians*. The pivotal production was not a peace play, nor an academic favourite such as *Birds* or *Frogs*, but a London staging of the long invisible *Lysistrata*. There is not a great deal to be said about the history of this comedy in Britain, at least between the Restoration and its submerged presence in *Princess Ida*; its sexual content had kept it firmly away from the public eye to exert a closet fascination over generations of young male Greek scholars. Its prurient associations led directly to Aubrey Beardsley's privately printed version (1896), with its luxuriantly obscene drawings designed to appeal to a male homosexual audience.[120] The comedy's notoriety meant that it would have been almost impossible to stage it before the arrival on the British scene of the suffragette movement. When Edwardian women at Oxbridge colleges braved Aristophanic waters, one respectable possibility was to imitate their menfolk by staging the intellectual comedy *Frogs* (so Somerville College, Oxford, in 1911).[121] Another had been to adapt *Birds* as *The Bees*, the Girton College, Cambridge second-year entertainment in 1904 (see fig. 19.3); this featured two heroines named Peitheteira and Euelpide leaving Cambridge University because it refused to let them graduate officially, and founding the feminist Beebuzzborough College instead.[122] But by 1910 the London theatregoing public had become accustomed to women of the theatre, who had long been prominent voices in support of female suffrage, performing in ancient Greek dramas that gave women shocking things to do and say: the scandalous production of *Medea* at the Savoy Theatre in 1907 was a particular case in point.[123]

When Gertrude Kingston became the lessee of the Little Theatre in the Adelphi, London, she was no stranger to assertive ancient Greek heroines, having in the 1880s performed as Penelope in the English-language version of G. C. Warr's *The Tale of Troy*, as Clytemnestra in Aeschylus' *Agamemnon* (also in Warr's translation),[124]

LYSISTRATA

A MODERN PARAPHRASE
FROM
THE GREEK OF ARISTOPHANES

BY

LAURENCE HOUSMAN

Photograph by Messrs. Alexander Corbett, Orchard Street, W.

Miss Gertrude Kingston in the Title Rôle of Lysistrata.

LONDON:
THE WOMAN'S PRESS
156, CHARING CROSS ROAD, W.C.
1911

FIG. 4.5. Laurence Housman, *Lysistrata*, 1911: Gertrude Kingston in title role

and as Helen in the 1905 *Trojan Women* that Harley Granville Barker directed in Gilbert Murray's translation. In this performance she had notoriously peeled off her flame-and-gold *himation* in an attempt to seduce Menelaus, leaving the gleaming fabric 'coiled like a serpent across the stage'.[125] Her 1910 season at the Little was inspired by the Royal Court's introduction of highbrow drama to a commercial audience, and thus opened with Aristophanes' *Lysistrata*, in which she played the title role (fig. 4.5). Kingston herself was as interested in the sartorial dimension of Aristophanes as the polemical: she later recalled that she had 'opened the Little Theatre with *Lysistrata* amid forty or fifty good-looking young women on the steps of the Acropolis in bright hues and gaudy gold and silver designs'; she had herself dressed in a much more sober grey *chitōn*. Here she was following the advice Edward Burne-Jones had given her when he designed the clothes for her performance as Penelope, suggesting that she accentuate her presence by the striking sobriety of her costume.[126] As Lysistrata, however, the more mature Kingston did relieve her grey tunic with a sky-blue *himation* ornamented with golden stars.[127]

The translator, however, saw the production as offering a purely political opportunity. Laurence Housman produced the script at great speed in the aftermath of a censorship scandal: his feminist play *Pains and Penalties*, about the divorce inflicted on Queen Caroline in 1820–21, was refused a licence and banned from public performance.[128] Laurence, the militant brother of the poet A. E. Housman, had helped found the Men's League for Women's Suffrage in England in 1907.[129] Like the Women's Social and Political Union (WSPU), the Men's League engaged in protest strategies that included civil disobedience and hunger strikes. He saw *Lysistrata* as a 'play of feminist propaganda which offered lurid possibilities', and a vehicle for jokes about women's exclusion from the suffrage.[130] These were appreciated by reviewers from sympathetic quarters of the press.[131] Six months later Kingston directed a scene from the play as part of a matinée organized at the Aldwych by the Actresses' Franchise League and the Women Writers Suffrage League; the performance was enhanced by 'carefully planned typical interruptions from the audience',[132] similar to the audience participation which had enlivened the performances of Elizabeth Robins's suffragette drama *Votes for Women!*[133] The Woman's Press published Housman's translation in 1911, and North American suffrage groups also performed it.[134] The English-speaking Aristophanes, only lightly adapted, had finally rediscovered a voice of immediate relevance in what is surely his most appropriate context — performance in live public theatre.[135]

Notes to Chapter 4

1. Scribe (1817).
2. Holtermann (2004), 91–101.
3. Schlegel (1958 [1794]).
4. Friedrich Rückert was a trained classicist who had worked on *Birds* at the University of Jena in 1811: see further Holtermann (2004), 127–29, with the review by E. Hall (2004c).
5. Jenkyns (1980), 61, 79.
6. For the ubiquitous presence of Aristophanes in all attempts to define comedy, see above all Silk (2000).
7. Jenkyns (1980), 79.
8. Hall and Macintosh (2005).
9. See Wase (1649), with Hall and Macintosh (2005), 162–65.
10. Stanley's version was intended to illuminate the figure of Socrates; it was originally published in his *The History of Philosophy* (1655), and omits the parabasis and the debate between the two *Logoi*. It also compresses some other passages, edits out 'words of [...] anatomical or physiological forthrightness' (Hines 1966, 35), while reflecting the terse concision of Ben Jonson's lyrics.
11. Hall and Macintosh (2005), 101.
12. Perrotta (1954), 876 suggests that Jonson's *Poetaster* uses *Frogs*, *Cynthia's Revels* imitates both *Plutus* and *Wasps*, and that *Epicœne, or the Silent Woman* also owes something to *Plutus*.
13. See Randolph (1651), 2 (disparaging reference to 'Round-headed citizens'), 17 (joke against the Levellers), the whole of Act II scene 5 (caricature of Dicaeus the avaricious parson), and 45–46 (the irreverent portrayal of the decadent Pope).
14. Randolph (1651), 7.
15. Randolph (1630).
16. Randolph's *The Drinking Academy* was first published in 1924, and a superior edition followed in 1930.
17. Randolph (1630), 1.
18. In 'The Song of Discord', included in Randolph (1652), the author imagines himself as the ancient poet, in exile from a hostile world, teaching the birds to sing.
19. Shirley (1634), 12. There is an even clearer Aristophanic undertext to Shirley's satirical poem *The Common-Wealth of Birds* in Shirley (1646), 34–35. It is interesting that Shirley must have worked alongside Henry Burnell when in 1640 they overlapped for at least some months at the Werburgh Street theatre in Dublin.

20. See Dane Farnsworth Smith (1936); id. and Lawhon (1979); Hall and Macintosh (2005), 36–37.
21. For Aristophanes' declamation see Davenant (1657), 21–40.
22. Ibid. 25–26, ll. 492–500.
23. Ibid. 37–38, ll. 767–92.
24. Ibid. 31–32.
25. D. Hughes (1996), 165.
26. Howard (1671), 18.
27. See in Rymer (1693), 24: 'Amongst the Moderns, our *Rehearsal* is some semblance of his *Frogs*'. Rymer also thought that Thomas Wright's *The Female Vertuosos* (1693) bore some relation to *Clouds* (ibid.).
28. Doran (1888), i. 342.
29. See further Nordell (2000), who also identifies Aristophanic material in Swift's *A Tale of a Tub* (1704).
30. See e.g. Griffin (1959), 91–93, who also points out that in his *Zara*, produced in 1736, Aaron Hill required moralizing 'COMIC CHORUSSES' between the acts, a practice justified in the prologue in a sung dialogue between a man and a woman; she assures the audience that the chorus was 'the custom, ye know, once of Greece'.
31. On Theobald as translator of Aristophanes, see further R. F. Jones (1919), 10–11; Hall and Macintosh (2005), 55–57.
32. Ingram (1966), 117.
33. Theobald (1731), 41–43.
34. See Scouten (1961), pp. cxl, 45.
35. The booth was that owned by Yeates, Warner, and Hinds; see the record for 23 Sept. 1735 in Scouten (1961), 505.
36. See Hall and Macintosh (2005), 60.
37. See Fielding (1903), 213–14.
38. Ibid. 223.
39. Ibid. 233–35.
40. Ibid. 244.
41. Ibid. 249.
42. See Highfill, Burnim, and Langhans (1991), 289.
43. Fielding and Young (1742), 86, 57.
44. See Cross (1918), i. 386; Hines (1966), 165.
45. It was still the translation of choice seven decades later, reproduced by e.g. Valpy (1812), alongside other translations of *Clouds*, *Frogs*, and *Birds*; it was still quoted copiously in a mass-market translation published in 1874 by Bohn's Classical Library: Hickie (1853–74).
46. See Dircks (2004).
47. Brumoy (1759), iii. 131–36. Brumoy is also caustic about Anne Le Fèvre's (Madame Dacier's) praise of Aristophanes, expressed in her preface to her 1684 translation of *Wealth*, while he praises Jean Boivon's popular recent translation of *Birds* (1729).
48. Brumoy (1759), iii. 358.
49. Wrangham (1792), p. vii. Kaloustian (2004) seems to me to be entirely mistaken in assuming that *Reform* is in any respect sympathetic to Tom Paine.
50. Wrangham (1792), 29.
51. Ibid. 9–13. Wrangham positioned his own politics carefully within *Reform*, since the criticism of the corruption in the British court, and the implied support of the anti-slavery campaign in the notes, sit alongside a judicious assertion of patriotism and self-distancing from the radical end of British republicanism.
52. Hall and Macintosh (2005), 282–315.
53. Anon. (1836a), 286 n.
54. Ibid. 285.
55. Ibid. 288.
56. Hall and Macintosh (2005), ch. 11.
57. Anon. (1836a), 294.

58. See Courtney (2004).
59. Turner (1981), 209.
60. T. Mitchell (1839), pp. iii, iv.
61. Ibid. 396–404.
62. Ibid. 397.
63. Ibid. 20.
64. Ibid. 147, 149, 162.
65. Ibid. 147.
66. Ibid. 182.
67. For Frere's contributions to *The Anti-Jacobin*, see Canning and Frere (1991). After a brilliant career of eight months *The Anti-Jacobin* was brought to a close on 9 July 1798.
68. For the text of this poem see Canning (1825), 8–9.
69. For the longstanding respect the essay commanded, see e.g. the remarks of the critic in the *Pall Mall Gazette* for 29 Nov. 1867, cited in Frere (1874), i. 179.
70. Vol. 23. The review is more accessible in Frere (1874), ii. 179–214. I hope to discuss Frere's essay and its impact in greater detail in a later publication.
71. Frere (1874), iii. 188, 206, 208.
72. Ibid. 216, quoted from a letter of 26 Apr. 1830.
73. Ibid. 118.
74. Ibid. 244.
75. Ibid. 270–72. Moreover, just like Mitchell, Frere transparently recycles Mitford's views on the Athenian democracy, even regularly recommending the reader of his translations turn to a particular page in the historian for a fuller account of what was 'really' happening in Aristophanes' Athens (see e.g. his introduction to *Knights*, his notes on Cleon's treatment of the Spartans taken at Pylos, and on *Frogs* in Frere (1874), iii. 66, 89, 91, 277, 299, 309).
76. Bristed (1852), 255.
77. See Hall and Macintosh (2005), 268–69 with nn. 11–15.
78. Ibid. 342–47.
79. Planché (1846), 'Preface'.
80. Planché (1872), vol. ii, 80.
81. Hall and Macintosh (2005), 355–66.
82. Planché (1846), 24–25.
83. Ibid. 25.
84. Ibid.
85. Mansel (1873).
86. William Smith (1842). *The Cambridge Dionysia* was published in Trevelyan (1869).
87. 'Y.T.O.' (1894), p. vi. The satire synthesizes scenes from several Aristophanic comedies, but *Frogs* and *Clouds* are the most dominant. Its most memorable moment is the conflation of Agathon's monody from *Thesmophoriazusae*, the parody of Euripidean monody in *Frogs*, and also Dionysus' rowing scene, when 'O.W.' himself arrives. He is to be imagined 'in a canoe [...] reclining on cushions, smoking a gold-tipped cigarette and occasionally idly paddling; and sings' (p. 18). At the end of the satire Wilde is put on a mock-trial by a combination of fellow-students and ancient philosophers on unspecified charges.
88. The first edition of this much republished work of reference was published in 1788.
89. T. Mitchell (1839), 3. On bowdlerization and expurgation of such texts, see further Dover (1988), 276, 278–94, and Brown (2006).
90. Bulwer (1833), ii. 141.
91. Ruskin (1856), iii. 193.
92. Jenkyns (1980), 79. Ruskin (1856), iii. 105, for example, contrasts mere fatuous jesting with 'the bright, playful, fond, farsighted jest of Plato, or the bitter, purposeful, sorrowing jest of Aristophanes'.
93. Arnold (1960–77), i. 29.
94. See the material collected in Dawson and Pfordresher (1979), 210, 95–96, 92.
95. McCusker (1984), 786–87.
96. Lines 977–78, 1784.

97. From this perspective, at least, Ryals (1976), especially 282–83 is probably correct in perceiving, behind the arguments that Browning's Euripides uses to criticize his Aristophanes, the influence of Thomas Carlyle's Transcendentalism.
98. It was published in the *New Quarterly Magazine* in April 1877, and in book form in 1897.
99. Meredith (1919), 69.
100. Ibid. 70.
101. Lindsay (1956), 233.
102. It was serialized in the *Glasgow Weekly Herald*, June 1879–Jan. 1880, and also published in 3 volumes in 1879.
103. M. Jones (1999), 149–50.
104. See above all Sichel (1970 [1911]).
105. Hamilton (1970 [1927]); see especially her comparison (pp. 120–21) of Aristophanes' Euripides in *Acharnians* with Lady Blanche's ontological speculations in *Princess Ida*.
106. See above all Granville-Barker (1932).
107. Thanks to Fiona Macintosh for pointing this out to me. On *Thespis*, see further E. Hall (2002*b*) and Hall and Macintosh (2005), 386–87.
108. Gilbert (1994), 121.
109. On the degree to which Gilbert was concerned in *Princess Ida* to make serious feminist points, see Baily (1973), 80.
110. Gilbert (1994), 271–72.
111. See further Hall and Macintosh (2005), 449–52.
112. Fleeming Jenkin (1887), i, p. cxxvii.
113. See especially Easterling (1999); Hall and Macintosh (2005), 430–87.
114. See e.g. Frere (1892) and (1897).
115. See Holtermann (2004), 263–64 on Adolf Wilbrandt's 1892 play *Frauenherrschaft* ('Women in Power'), a fusion of *Lysistrata* and *Ecclesiazusae* first performed in Cologne in 1895. In the same year both *Birds* and a version of *Ecclesiazusae* were also performed in Berlin.
116. See Cecil Smith (1881). In 1892 the play chosen by OUDS for performance in the New Theatre, Oxford was *The Frogs*, reviewed in e.g. *The Athenaeum* no. 3358 (March 5th 1892). This production had a great impact on many involved; Lady Evans actually dedicated her book *Chapters on Greek Dress* (1893) to OUDS 'in memory of their performance of 'The Frogs of Aristophanes' the previous year'.
117. Macintosh (1998); see also Hall and Macintosh (2005), 492–508.
118. 'Argument' to the programme held in the Bodleian OUDS collection of cuttings (G. A. OXON. b. 8). Any political resonances heard in the much earlier (1886) stage revival of *Acharnians* in Philadelphia, where the play had been performed in Greek by students from the University of Pennsylvania, seem to have looked backwards twenty years to the American Civil War, according to Pearcy (2003), 308–09.
119. In his subsequent study of Aristophanes, Murray (1933) himself described the political directness of Dicaeopolis' message in *Acharnians* ('an extremely daring play', 29) as without parallel in any later theatrical tradition (31): 'It would have been quite impossible in any country of Europe during the late war, for a writer, however brilliant, to make a speech on behalf of the enemy in a theatre before an average popular audience...an attack on the national policy in the midst of a performance in a national theatre. And if impossible in our time, it would scarcely have been possible in any other period of history.'
120. The edition, moreover, provides notes exactly specifying the nature of the sexual positions mentioned in the Greek text. For sympathetic treatments of the obscenity in Aristophanes in two homosexual authors in the late 19th c., Swinburne and J. A. Symonds, see Jenkyns (1980), 280–81. Beardsley's translation was also, however, important as the first faithful and unexpurgated translation of *Lysistrata* into the English language.
121. This production was rehearsed under the aegis of Gilbert Murray, a frequent visitor to Somerville College at the time.
122. Anon. (1904), 16–17, 5–6, 8–9, 16–17.
123. See Hall and Macintosh (2005), 511–19.
124. Kingston (1937), 62–67.

125. Ibid. 184. It was George Bernard Shaw who had suggested her for the role of Helen, as he emphasizes in a letter he wrote to her on 14 Apr. 1905, reproduced ibid., 184–85. Perhaps she became attracted to Greek comedy as a result of her close friendship with Shaw, who wrote to her in the same letter that Murray suspected him 'of craving to use his poetry as the jumping-off-place for shrieks of laugher' (ibid.).
126. Ibid. 63.
127. Ibid.
128. Besides Housman's autobiography (1937), the only book-length study of this fascinating Englishman remains Engen (1983), which is focused on Housman's important contributions as a book illustrator, and is rather limited in its discussion of his literary and political achievements.
129. He was swayed by the arguments presented to him by his sister Clemence: see Mix (1975).
130. See Housman (1937), 247; Tylee (1998), 149.
131. *The Englishwoman*, 8 (1910); 'The Greek Suffragettes' in *Votes for Women*, 3 (17 Mar. 1911), 386.
132. *Votes for Women*, 3 (25 Nov. 1910), 130.
133. See Tylee (1998), 149. On the relationship between Robins' play and Euripides' *Medea*, see Hall and Macintosh (2005), 512–13.
134. Tylee (1998), 149.
135. I should like to thank Ashley Clements, Chris Weaver, Amanda Wrigley, and especially Fiona Macintosh for help in the preparation of this chapter.

❖

PART II

Excursus:
Publication as Performance

CHAPTER 5

❖

Publication as Intervention:
Aristophanes in 1659

Rosie Wyles

Introduction

In 1659, in a London of closed theatres and on the brink of the Restoration, a translation of Aristophanes' *Plutus* was published. *The World's Idol; or, Plutus the God of Wealth, A Translation from Aristophanes by H. H. B.*, printed together with the author's 'Short Discourse' upon it, has not gained the attention it deserves. One explanation for this neglect is that the controversial issue of the identity of its author has distracted attention from the work's true importance. For this version of *Plutus* is an invaluable document for three reasons. First, it represents a landmark in the reception history of Aristophanes because it offered a fresh approach to the way in which dramatic material might be used to make a political statement, even in an era when theatrical activity was curtailed. Secondly, it offers a direct account of a Christian's attitude towards the ancient Greek pagan Classics in the seventeenth century. Finally, it has a place in the debates surrounding the colonization of Ireland, and presents an individual's critical view of the English colonial ventures of the time.

The issue of authorship arises from the uncertain identification of H.H.B. He has traditionally been identified with the Catholic playwright Henry Burnell, although there is no *positive* evidence that I know of for the certain ascription of the work to him. Burnell, an Irishman descended from an Old English family, became a key figure in the Kilkenny Catholic Confederacy, formed after the 1641 Irish rebellion. Burnell's opposition to English military interventions in Ireland was expressed above all in his 'tragicomedy' *Landgartha*, the first known performed play by an Irish writer. It was acted to great applause on St Patrick's Day, 1640, in the New Theatre in Werburgh Street, Dublin. The plot of the play, taken from the Danish historian Saxo Grammaticus, treated the conquest of Sweden by Regner, King of Denmark, whose queen, Landgartha, gave the title to the piece. But at the time of the production Charles I's position was speedily weakening, and *Landgartha* was a thinly disguised allegory about Anglo-Irish relations; it represented 'a last-ditch attempt to define a possible relationship between two cultures spiralling towards war', as a recent historian of the Irish theatre has put it.[1] Shortly afterwards the theatre was closed and the man who had built it and employed Catholic playwrights,

Thomas Wentworth, Lord Lieutenant of Ireland, was beheaded for treasonable acts including the fostering of Catholicism. Burnell himself became part of the Kilkenny government in internal exile that tried to keep alive the possibility of a Catholic state and theatre, but this dream was killed off along with Charles I in 1649.

    There are two other playwrights of this period with the initials H. and B. One of these is Henry Burkhead, whose vivid Senecan drama *A Tragedy of Cola's Furie; or, Lirenda's Miserie* (1646) reveals him to have been another Irish Catholic, passionate critic of English atrocities in Ireland (the play even includes passages spoken by victims in the Irish language), and supporter of the Kilkenny Confederacy. The other candidate is the Englishman and Latin poet (who certainly also knew Greek) Henry Birkhead. Between these three candidacies there is little to choose. The implied criticism of English activities in Ireland certainly seems more appropriate to Burnell and Burkhead, although the Englishman Birkhead had strong Catholic leanings, having been converted temporarily by a Jesuit at an impressionable age.[2] H.H.B.'s briefly stated stance on Spanish imperialism, however, might seem more plausible in Birkhead, although by 1659 it will have been shared by most people outside Spain (see further below). Yet it is questionable whether the identity of the author really matters, since it is possible to analyse the significance of the publication even without this information. When asking why this play was published, we need look no further than the author's own explanation in his Discourse. In the discussion which follows I therefore simply refer to 'H.H.B.' or 'the author'.

Using Aristophanes Politically

Even before considering the content of the Discourse, there can be little doubt on the part of the potential reader that the author of this publication intended to make a political statement about contemporary affairs. Three significant elements announce this intention. First, the very nature of the material suggested a political agenda. Entertainment, and specifically theatre, was a deeply politicized issue. The closure of theatres and restrictions on public entertainment under the Puritans had created a climate in which the publication of any stage play, albeit one which was presented as a translation for reading, could not be perceived as anything other than a politically charged act. Moreover, the figure of the playwright Aristophanes had long been associated with the court theatricals enjoyed by Charles I and loyal followers of the Stuart monarchy (see further Hall, this volume).

    The second indication that this publication was to be of contemporary significance is the choice of alternative title: 'The World's Idol'.[3] The use of an alternative title at this date is of course not remarkable in itself, but the particular choice of the term *Idol* will have implied that the text underneath the cover was likely to contain a political — even controversial — subtext. From the very first days of the religious tensions that led to the Reformation, 'idolatry' had been central to the rhetoric of religious attack and counter-attack. The impact made on the ideological and semantic significance of the word 'idol' by the activities of Protestant iconoclasts on the European mainland, from the mid-sixteenth century onwards, can hardly be overestimated. The term had received a fresh new charge after the Long

Parliament's Ordinance of 28 August 1643, ordering the removal of 'all monuments of idolatry and superstition' from places of worship. In 1659 the worship of idols was still a live issue, as the volley of mid-seventeenth-century publications devoted to the topic demonstrates. Yet crucial amongst these publications is the Quaker activist Edward Burrough's 1658 polemic *A Testimony against a great Idolatry committed: and a true mourning of the Lord's servant upon the many considerations of his heart, upon that occasion of the great stir about an image made and carryed from one place to another*, namely at the funeral of Oliver Cromwell. Who were the worshippers of idols now? By 1659, the year of the publication of *The World's Idol*, the term had therefore acquired potent political resonances of a new kind. The word indicated the presence of a controversial perspective, and so to use it in the title of publication was a form of battle-cry, a signal that the author was ready to engage.[4] A politically neutral translator of Aristophanes (although such a thing is almost unimaginable at this date), who merely wanted to offer an uncontroversial English translation of this play, would certainly avoid using the word 'Idol' in the title and would not, as our author has done, have made a concerted effort to include it.

The use of the title 'The World's Idol' should therefore be recognized as a deliberate marketing strategy. It at once categorizes this work as a certain sort of publication — in other words, one that has something to say politically. This title aims to interest and attract a particular readership: those, like Edward Burrough, who were embroiled in the religious and political debates of the time. The targeting of such a readership reveals H.H.B.'s intention to use his translation as a means to influence political thinking. This didactic intention behind the publication of the comedy is made explicit in the title-page of this work, which contains the couplet:

> Some dare affirm that Comedies may teach
> More in one hour than some in ten can preach.

This couplet constitutes the third signal that H.H.B.'s translation is intended to make a political point. Collectively the choice of material for publication, the choice of alternative title for the work, and the couplet given in the title-page prepare the reader for a play invested with political meaning. It is rather surprising, therefore, to find that the play which follows is strikingly faithful to the Aristophanic original. This really is, as it promises to be, 'a translation from Aristophanes'. It is only on reaching the short Discourse which explains the significance of the comedy that the political message intended by the publication of the play becomes fully apparent.

The uniqueness of H.H.B.'s approach to the Aristophanic material can be illustrated by contrasting it with the approach which Thomas Randolph takes in his very different response to Aristophanes' *Plutus*. His adaptation *Ploutophthalmia Ploutogamia; or, Hey for Honesty, Down with Knavery*, based on the same Aristophanic material, had been published just eight years before in 1651.[5] While Randolph is free in his translation of the Aristophanes and includes many explicit contemporary references in his play, the author of *The World's Idol* gives as accurate a translation as possible and produces a scholarly edition which even includes marginal notes on certain words in the original Greek.[6]

While fidelity to the original does not preclude the making of a political statement, it does necessitate the development of a new approach to the use of drama to be able to do so. The superficial difference between *The World's Idol* and Randolph's *Hey for Honesty*, which is a difference in the extent of alteration and adaptation, is actually symptomatic of a fundamental difference in approach to the use of drama to make a point. Randolph indicates to his audience the political significance of his play by introducing explicit contemporary references, for example to Roundheads, into it. In contrast, in H.H.B.'s *Plutus*, the significance of the play only becomes clear in the Discourse, which is intended to help the reader understand why this play has been translated in the first place. What we have in these two published responses to *Plutus* is therefore alternative models for the political exploitation of Aristophanic material in the mid-seventeenth century.

Another way to term this difference in approach would to be to consider it in relation to the tradition of Ben Jonson. Jonson, who had exploited Aristophanic material (see Steggle, this volume), served everywhere as a model for subsequent playwrights. Significantly, Randolph claimed himself to be one of the 'sons of Ben', and John Bermingham, in his poem praising *Landgartha*, makes a similar claim for Henry Burnell:

> And, though thou *England* never saw'st: Yet, this
> (Let others boast of their owne faculties,
> Or being Sonne to *Iohnson*) I dare say,
> That thou art farre more like to *Ben*: then they
> That lay clayme as heires to him, wrongfully:
> For he survives now only, but in thee
> And his owne lines; the rest degenerate.[7]

Playwrights were evidently vying over the claim to be the true heir of Jonson, and yet our author makes no attempt in his Discourse upon his own play to insert himself into this competition, nor to present himself as working in a Jonsonian tradition. Nor is there any reference to Randolph's recently published reworking of *Plutus*. The sense of rivalry that comes across so strongly in Bermingham's poem is not found in the Discourse upon *The World's Idol*. This suggests an author who is not primarily concerned with whether or not his work will be judged a major contribution to the world of comic drama, theatre, or entertainment. He is not interested in being the next Jonson, since the way in which he aims to teach with drama is entirely different. It is a less direct approach, which depends on reading. If *The World's Idol* were indeed actually performed, then, if the audience were to understand its political point they would have to read, or be read, the discourse upon it. The emergence of this alternative approach to the political use of drama may therefore be seen as a response to the particular historical circumstances.[8]

'A Short Discourse upon the Preceeding Comedy'

The Discourse, then, provides the essential means by which H.H.B. transforms the Aristophanic material into a political critique of contemporary relevance. The 'Short Discourse' (which is actually more than six thousand words long) is printed at the back of the edition, filling pages 33–46. The author writes in a scholarly and serious style with the purpose of explaining to the reader the significance of the play. The following extract illustrates the style of the discourse and introduces the essential idea explored within it:

> *Plutus*, the Tipe of *Wealth* and *Plenty*, is said by *Jupiter* to be deprived of his Eyes, for aspiring to enthrone himself in his power and wisdome, that which at the first we read threw down the Angels, and next to them him, and in him that posterity that was created almost as happy as those Angels; so that *Plutus* with his *eyes open* may allude to us *Adam* in his *Innocency*, his *blindness* our *fall*; and his being brought to *Esculapius* his Temple to receive his sight again, may not unfitly emblem to us our seeking of a *Saviour* to bring us into that State again we fell from: But yet further then in this consideration, which I hope will offend no body, we will not use comparisons, but proceed to our intentions, which are to consider the *World* as it stood with *Plutus* his eyes *open,* and as it now stands with his eyes *out.* (pp. 33–34)

The author is explicit in stating that the essential motivation for translating Aristophanes' *Plutus* is that it is capable of being interpreted as a representation of the Fall of Mankind and the Restoration of the world to its first estate. This passage is one of the few in the Discourse to address the pervasive assumption that *Plutus* correlates to the Fall/Restoration model. Once the outline of such an allegorical reading has been set up by the author, the details are left to take care of themselves, and H.H.B. is true to his promise: 'But yet further then in this consideration, which I hope will offend no body, we will not use comparisons'. In the rest of the Discourse, therefore, more specific details of how aspects of the play fit the model are given only when they add strength to the general argument. Hence it is almost in passing that on pages 40–41 and 43 specific references to the play are made. These references augment the outline of the allegory given in the introductory passage, and offer a more detailed view of how the author sees Aristophanes' expressing 'the suddain reconciliation of the world'. He argues that Aristophanes shows this in the following details: the just man gaining the rich attire of the Sycophant, the Old Woman being put out of countenance for expecting a lover at her age, and Mercury being refused his customary office as patron of the Arts.

While the intelligibility of *Plutus* as a play about the Fall/Restoration seems to be considered by the author to be almost self-apparent; the nature of the Fall/Restoration and its relevance to his own society in his view merits further discussion. The author tells us that his intentions 'are to consider the *World* as it stood with *Plutus* his eyes *open,* and as it now stands with his eyes *out*'. A consideration of the 'Fall' invites a general consideration not only of the state of the world but even more fundamentally the state of man. The author forecasts this as a topic of particular interest when he gives as a reason for choosing *Plutus* that 'amongst the ancient Fables, I find none that better unfolds the nature and state of Mankind then this'. The Discourse, which follows, examines the question *what is man?* What was his first estate — that is, what are the limits set by nature? What caused the decline from this state? The answers to this question are tillage, subjugation, wealth, and poverty. It is in the introduction into the argument of the term *tillage* that the peculiar relevance of *Plutus* to the Irish situation becomes apparent. The motif of tillage is of course found in both the biblical tradition of the fall (Genesis 3: 23) and in the Classical tradition of the decline from the golden age (see, for example,

Hesiod, *Works and Days* 109–26). Yet by the time of the Irish rebellion of 1641, there was already a longstanding convention of justifying English expansion into 'Celtic' territory on the ground that only English 'civility', which was promoted by tillage, towns, and commerce, could save the pre-agricultural savages, eking out an inactive and miserable existence in untilled woods and bogs. The very term *tillage* will also have insinuated the idea of the hated plantations, areas of land confiscated from Irish landowners and given over to English and Scottish Parliamentarian soldiers.

The Discourse also offers reasons for the changed nature of thoughts (natural causes, diet or education), the nature of belief (knowledge and the soul), the possibility of the return to the first estate, reconciliation of the world as illustrated in *Plutus*, and finally describes the wrong of presuming to civilize 'barbarians' with art and invention and of imposing Christianity on those from whom God is content to receive 'universal worship'. The primary function of the Discourse, therefore, is to explain the significance of the play through the use of allegory. It is this allegory which mediates the division between the play world and the real world — the play can only comment on the real world through the filter of the Fall/Restoration idea. An analysis of how the author relates the Fall/Restoration idea to his own world in 1659 is therefore crucial to understanding what is being 'said' by this translation. But before offering such an analysis, I should first like to consider how H.H.B. justifies the use of this ancient Greek text, and what this tells us about attitudes towards the Classics in the seventeenth century.

The Christian Aristophanes

An important part of the Discourse, which the author develops before the allegorical reading is even proposed, is concerned with justifying the choice of material through which the author wishes to teach a lesson. The justification of the use of a 'fable' written by Aristophanes reveals the general attitude of the author towards the place of pagan Classics in his society. There is a distinct note of apologia in the explanation behind using an ancient fable from a pre-Christian society. But the potential 'problem' of using an ancient Greek play to illustrate a Judaeo-Christian idea is circumvented by a skilful reconciliation of the two traditions, which sets up a dialectic between them. The author accomplishes this reconciliation by constructing a view of Christian knowledge of a type that would soon afterwards, as a product of British Enlightenment thinking, be associated with the so-called Whig school of history: according to this view, earlier societies may have known the 'Tipes and Figures' of God's truth which subsequently acted to 'usher in' Christianity. Thus the fables of ancient societies are seen to pre-figure the perfect Christian knowledge, as set down in the Holy Scriptures, which the author's present age has the privilege of enjoying.

This reconciliation, along with its implied teleological continuum, forms the justification not only for the choice of material for translation but also, implicitly, for the use of examples from a wide range of ancient works, invoked throughout the Discourse to support its argument. So, for example, the author appeals to the observations of Herodotus and Diodorus Siculus to make the point that Man does not need bread in order to survive (p. 37). These references contribute to the scholarly style of the work: just as the marginal notes beside the play itself demonstrate a knowledge of Greek, so too the author can comfortably quote directly from the ancient Greek (and provide a translation for the less learned reader). His knowledge of ancient Greek authors is extensive; the authors to whom he refers, besides Herodotus and Diodorus, include Hesiod, Pythagoras, Antiphanes, Xenophon, Cassius Dio, and Menander. At the point of inclusion of some of these authors the 'continuum perspective' is reasserted, for example. through the hope that ancient philosophers 'were Divines, and are now Saints' (p. 44). This perspective allows references to ancient authors to sit comfortably alongside references to the Old and New Testament in the Discourse. Thus the works of ancient Greek authorities, and in particular Aristophanes, can be appropriated by our author as models for Christian thought and ultimately as vehicles through which he can comment on his contemporary society.

Anti-Colonial Aristophanes

The author's tone in commenting on his contemporary society is wary: there is nothing so overt as contemporary reference within the play itself, and even the allegorical reading, proposed in the Discourse, is cautiously accompanied by the hope that it 'will offend no body'.[9] Yet for all his caution the author has a definite message to convey, as an analysis of the discussion of the Fall/Restoration idea makes clear. Though much of the discussion is of a generalized nature and seems to be included either due to the author's own digressive nature or by virtue of tradition, the contemporary relevance increases as it hones in on the theme of subjugation and dominion.[10] As the Discourse progresses it is this theme which emerges as the most prominent concern of the author and the focus of all discussion. What emerges is that it is colonization, in its various guises, to which the author wishes to draw attention and indeed criticize in this published translation of *Plutus*.

In the author's schematization, the evils of colonization are the ultimate result of the Fall. This is made explicit in the assertion that for Man to be able to return to his first natural state, it will be necessary to 'put down all rule, and power, and authority; that is, what ever we now call Propriety and Right' (p. 35).[11] This initial claim is developed in the rest of the Discourse, which discusses what this 'Propriety' (i.e. property) is, how it arose and why it must be put down. According to the arguments presented, pride and self-opinion taught Man to 'practice Tiranny and blood-shedding over other creatures' and 'the next thing that followed was persecution and slavery of one another' (p. 36). Then 'when man, or a few men, by Strength or eloquence had subdued many, the next thing that followed, was that unhappy thing we call Propriety'. This 'Propriety', far from keeping away Poverty, in fact thrives on the notions of Wealth and Poverty and the impossibility of men ever feeling satisfied that they have an equal part in any social division of economic resources.

In the author's own time people had been subdued by 'Strength and eloquence'. The form that the eloquence took emerges from the arguments he presents in the

Discourse. The author explicitly attacks those 'whose natures are under bondage of education' for despising 'the rest who stand free, with the title Barbarous' and for 'praying for them as a lost people, wishing to have them brought home to their own condition'. This justificatory argument — that the savage stands in need of civilizing — is a *topos* which has been used by colonial powers across the ages. But it had also been exploited, both explicitly and implicitly, by the English in justification of their actions in Ireland.[12] With the claim of barbarism went the patronizing desire, identified by H.H.B., to bring the Irish 'into their own condition'; this is epitomized in the expressed desire of Sir John Davies, who had been involved in an official capacity in Ireland since 1603 (first as solicitor-general and then from 1606 as the attorney-general), that the Irish would 'in tongue, and heart and everyway become English so there would be no difference or distinctions but the Irish sea betwixt us'.[13]

The applicability of H.H.B.'s comments to the English attitude towards the Irish cannot have been lost on the contemporary readers. This would have been felt all the more keenly in H.H.B.'s observation that those wishing to civilize 'lost people' assume superiority either through their knowledge of 'Art and Invention' or through 'religion' and thereby exert their authority over others. Religion, of course, was a dangerous issue in the wake of the Cromwellian conquest, whereby nearly all Catholic-owned land had been confiscated under the terms of the 1652 Act for the Settlement of Ireland, and given to English settlers. The practice of Roman Catholicism was banned. But in the case of 'H.H.B.', his criticism of the use of 'Art and invention' can more clearly be seen as alluding to England's own policies towards her dominions. The dangerous potential of art and invention to be used as tools of domination result in there being no place for them in H.H.B.'s imagined reconciliation of the world. He argues that Aristophanes had represented this in his play as the rejection of Mercury from his customary office. H.H.B's translation of the line where Mercury makes his request allows us to be even more specific about what is meant in the discourse by 'Art': Mercury asks (line 1161), 'let me then be the inventer of your Playes and Musiks, how say you, to that?' This invites the question of how plays and music had played a role in 'civilizing' Ireland in the first half of the seventeenth century.

The building of the Werburgh Street theatre in Dublin provides a striking example of exactly this policy of exerting cultural superiority as part of a programme of colonization. Sir Thomas Wentworth, Lord Deputy of Ireland 1633–40, oversaw the building of this playhouse as 'one in a series of key projects' in his general programme 'for Dublin's social upgrading'.[14] The cultural and ideological significance of the original erection of the Werburgh Street theatre in Dublin cannot be overestimated. The implications of this programme of social upgrading made the theatre building a symbol of the colonist's power. The attitude behind the enterprise is epitomised in the importing of an Englishman, James Shirley (on whom see further Hall, this volume, p. 68), to be the resident playwright. What is surprising is how during the short time of its existence the theatre undoubtedly became more 'inclusive', especially when the Anglo-Irish Catholic Henry Burnell was hired and put on his cryptic *Landgartha* there; but in its original intention this theatre provided a conspicuous example of Art being used as a means to claim cultural superiority and thereby assert authority over others.[15]

In addition to this concrete example of the principle of domination by Art being put into practice, the connection between theatre and empire had long been established metaphorically. John Speed's *Theatre of the Empire of Great Britain*, first published in 1612, had circulated throughout the known world. In this publication Speed presented maps of the kingdoms of Great Britain, together with descriptions of the people who lived in them. The cartography and ideological bias of the descriptions made this publication into a powerful 'tool of colonization'.[16] For the purposes of this discussion, what is of particular interest is the way in which Speed chooses to describe his work. The metaphor of his work as a theatre extends beyond the title. The title-page gives the details of the work encased in a surrounding illustration of a classical style theatre-building façade with a statue in each alcove to represent each ancestral race of the English: there appears a Dane, a Roman, a Briton, a Saxon, and a Norman. The work itself is referred to as a Theatre in the contents page which is headed with the statement, 'The British Empire containeth and hath now in actual possession, those many and renowned kingdoms and principalities described in this our Theatre'. Finally, in the prologue the author plays on the same metaphor by saying: 'O great was the attempt to assay the erection of this large and laborious Theatre' and claims himself 'not worthy to hew (much less to lay) the least stone in so beautiful a building'. It seems only too appropriate that cartography, one tool of domination, should describe itself metaphorically through theatre which seems in practice, for example at Werburgh Street, to have constituted another.

The extended use of this metaphor, in a highly influential work embodying the colonial enterprise and attitudes, presents an appropriation of theatre which stands in direct opposition to the use which our author — whether Henry Burnell, Henry Burkhead, or even Henry Birkhead — is trying to make of it. There is however a critical distinction to be made between the respective appropriations. The Englishmen's use of theatre, whether literal or metaphorical, was grounded in the emblematic force of the physical building, while our author, as must be clear from the nature of the work and constraint of the times it was written in, could not hope to use a theatre building to this effect and instead offers this book to be read: play together with discourse. He sees no place for the plays and music of Mercury in his ideal world, but in the meantime he would fight against those who would abuse Art for imperial ends in the best way he could, and that is with Art. If he could not actually stage plays in order to argue the case of the Irish, then he would do the next best thing: publish a canonical ancient comic dramatist associated with politics and polemics — Aristophanes — instead.

But the English and their actions in Ireland are not the only target of criticism; it emerges that H.H.B. also wishes to voice concern over Spanish activity in the Indies. This concern becomes apparent when discussion turns to the criticism of the second means of domination: religion. H.H.B. explicitly argues against Christianity being used as a pretext for colonization and forcibly imposed by one nation on another. The specific example he gives of Christianity being imposed as part of a colonial enterprise is 'in the conquest over the *Moors* and *Indians*' (pp. 43–44). The treatment of the Moors by the Habsburg rulers of Spain had certainly had its own rhetorical value in the debate over how to proceed in Ireland: Sir John Davies, appointed Solicitor-General of Ireland in 1603 (see above, p. 101), had used the example of the Habsburg transplantation of the Moors to justify some of the worse crimes committed against Catholics during the Ulster plantation.[17] But the reference here had an additional specific relevance by 1659, when *The World's Idol* was published, for the allusion to Spanish *conquistadores* in the West Indies concerns a different imperial venture altogether.

The fear that Spain was aiming at a universal monarchy had been a dominant influence on English foreign policy in the early 1650s, culminating in the launching of an attack on the Spanish West Indies in December 1654 in a policy known as 'the Western Design'. On an ideological level, what was actually a struggle between the English and the Spanish for imperial dominance predictably produced art and literature in English that portrayed the Spaniards as cruel despots throwing their weight around the globe and imposing their particularly restrictive brand of popery on innocent indigenous peoples. The most famous example of such anti-Spanish propaganda was probably the opera by Sir William Davenant (on whom see further Hall, this volume, pp. 68–69), *The Cruelty of the Spaniards in Peru* (1658). When H.H.B. — whoever he was — mentions the cruelty shown towards the Indians, he is implicitly — and controversially — aligning the colonial cruelties inflicted in the past on Ireland with those currently being inflicted on native peoples by the barbarous Spaniards across the Atlantic.[18]

Conclusion

The World's Idol holds an extremely important place in the reception history of Aristophanes. At a time when the production of stage plays was banned altogether, the very act of publishing a translation of a comedy by this particular dramatist represents an intervention in the controversies about the moral status of theatre. But the edition is a testimony to the potential for even the most faithful translation of Aristophanes to be used as a means of commenting from an oppositional viewpoint on contemporary political affairs. The model, which H.H.B. employs, therefore marks a new direction in the way dramatists might use Aristophanes. The Discourse, along with the allegorical reading it proposes, reveals the contemporary relevance of the play as the author saw it and intended his readership to see it. It works, indeed, in a way equivalent to the non-textual signs at a stage performance of a faithful translation: contemporary relevance can be implied by aspects of acting and design even when the script is carefully not 'topicalised'. That is, in a manner of speaking the Discourse turns the play into an effective performance of a political stance. Through the Discourse we discover an author who, with strikingly modern ideas, felt passionately about both religious intolerance and the brutalities involved in colonization, and chose to publish Aristophanes in order to express these controversial views. His decision to use Aristophanes' *Plutus* in an era when this poet had never even previously been published in a freestanding English translation required some justification on his part, but nevertheless he seems to stand by the conviction that 'Comedies may teach more in one hour than some in ten can preach' and judges Aristophanes' the best comedy for the task.

Notes to Chapter 5

1. Morash (2002), 9. The British Library catalogue ascribes *The World's Idol* to Henry Burnell. Rankin (2004), in her *Oxford Dictionary of National Biography* article on Burnell, notes the lack of evidence for this ascription, and also points out that Burnell is last heard of signing a petition in 1654 to request dispensation, on the plea of sickness, from the order to transplant to Connacht after the confiscation of his lands. An argument against Burnell has been made on the basis that he was once said never to have gone to England (see John Bermingham's dedicatory poem in the front matter of *Landgartha*, quoted below), and H.H.B.'s Discourse suggests that he had (p. 42). Yet eighteen years lay between *Landgartha* and *The World's Idol*, surely plenty of time for Burnell to have visited London.

2. To 'H. B.' (probably Henry Birkhead, 1617–96) there is also attributed *The Female Rebellion*, a 17th-c. dramatic satire (not published until 1872) in support of hereditary monarchy set amongst the ancient Amazons and Scythians. It has no obvious Aristophanic input despite the suggestive title. Tantalizingly, on the Restoration of Charles II, an H.H.B. wrote *A Poem to his Majestie on His landing*, which is imbued with classical allusions, but nothing further is known about the author of this work.

3. This is the first use of this English title for Aristophanes' play. Over half a century later, Lewis Theobald followed H.H.B.'s example by sub-titling his translation of the same play (on which see further Hall, this volume, pp. 72–74) *The World's Idol*.

4. Apart from the primary associative overtone of 'idol' as a word of religious significance and controversy, there is the possibility that for some the 'idol' was suggestive of the idea of disruption to monarchical regime; in this period 'idol' could be used to describe pretenders to the throne (*Oxford English Dictionary*, s.v. 'Idol' 7). This ambiguity of language extends also to the use of 'restoration'. 'Restoration' is used by the author in his Discourse (on which see below) to describe the return of Man to a state of innocence, but this word also carried the meaning of restoring a person to his or her former political position (*Oxford English Dictionary*, s.v. 'Restoration' 1b). There appears, then, to be a pervasive terminological ambiguity, which allows for two levels of meaning for those who wanted to look for them; the obvious and primary engagement is with religious concepts, but this engagement is enriched by the political undertones to the language.

5. Randolph's play, published in 1651, had actually been written in the early 1630s. See further Hall, this volume, p. 67.

6. Indeed 'W. G.', the printer of H.H.B.'s play, seems to have specialized in the publication of this sort of erudite edition. The following year (1660) he published Samuel Pordage's famous translation of Seneca's *Troades*.

7. Bermingham's poem is included amongst the front matter of the edition of Henry Burnell's *Landgartha* (Dublin, 1641).

8. On the implication of the figure and plays of Aristophanes in the mid-17th-century debates about the legitimacy of the theatre, see further Hall, this volume.

9. It is only at the very end of the Discourse that the division between the play and the contemporary world of the author is allowed to collapse, when H.H.B. draws a parallel between the clergy of his own day and the priests in *Plutus*.

10. So, for example, the long discussion of the evils of tillage (on which see further above, pp. 98–99).

11. The question of 'Propriety and Right' and the limits to them in Man's natural state had, spurred on by the extraordinary political circumstances of the Interregnum, become a preoccupation amongst political philosophers of this period. Of particular note is Sir Robert Filmer's *Patriarcha*, written before his death in 1653 but not published until 1680. In this work he set out the theory that paternal politics and political power both descend from Adam. Both Hobbes and Locke

contested Filmer's theory; see further Milton (2004). The language used in the Discourse on *The World's Idol* suggests that the author, albeit with a different axe to grind, wishes to engage in the same debate and to defend the altogether different position that Man in his natural state did not have power over others at all.

12. On the representation of the Irish as barbarians see Ohlmeyer (1998), esp. 130–31; Hadfield and McVeagh (1994).

13. Davies (1612), 272. Davies's policy in Ireland rested on his belief in the civilizing power of law and institutions, which he sought to use as a means of maintaining control there. On the attempted Anglicization of Ireland see Canny (1996). The rhetoric for conquest, as Canny shows (see esp. 165), had also been based on the argument of the necessity to civilize barbarous people, not for their own good, but to prevent their ways from causing degeneracy amongst civilized people.

14. Fletcher (2000), 261.

15. For the changes in the management's attitude and repertoire in the Werburgh Street theatre, see further ibid. 267–77.

16. For maps as a 'tool of empire' see Ohlmeyer (1998), 140, and (2000), 8–9.

17. See Ohlmeyer (1998), 135–37 with n. 46. Ireland of course remains an important subtext in the Discourse at this point, since, as Ohlmeyer shows, in Ireland the imposition of Protestantism had become a key index of civilization.

18. For England's foreign policy in the 1650s, see Pincus (1992). Another aspect of propaganda discussed by Pincus which seems worth considering is the caricaturing of the Dutch as materialistic after the failure of the proposed Anglo-Dutch alliance in the early 1650s. 'Wealth' had become an established player in the political game of blame propaganda. This could only add to the appeal of Aristophanes' *Plutus* as a potential vehicle for political criticism.

CHAPTER 6

❖

Revolutionary Aristophanes?

Charalampos Orfanos

Introduction

Hardly any ancient Greek plays were staged in Paris during the years of the Revolution. Although eighteenth-century dramatists often wrote plays on Greek subjects, set in Greek contexts, their sources and models were predominantly Roman.[1] In the case of Greek comedy, if one sees the Consulate as the last stage of the French Revolution, the unique exception to what we may call the 'silencing' of ancient theatre is François-Benoît Hoffman's *Lisistrata ou les Athéniennes*. This play was an adaptation of Aristophanes' *Lysistrata*, performed in the Théâtre Feydeau in Nivôse of the 10th year of the Revolution (22 December 1801–20 January 1802). This was during the final negotiations for the peace treaty of Amiens, conducted from 5 December 1801 to 27 March 1802, between France, Spain and the French-controlled Batavian Republic (Netherlands) on the one hand and Great Britain on the other. According to its subtitle, *Lisistrata* is a *Comedy in one act and in prose, mixed with satirical songs and imitating Aristophanes' play; its performances have been suspended by Order...*[2]

The author, François-Benoît Hoffman, who was born in Nancy in 1760 and died in Paris in 1828, was a minor dramatist. He only wrote about thirty short plays, and was more widely known as a literary and theatre critic whose articles appeared in the *Journal des Débats*. Nonetheless, his complete works include a few celebrated opera librettos, such as Luigi Cherubini's *Médée* (1797), directly inspired by Seneca's play,[3] and Étienne-Nicolas Méhul's *Adrien empereur de Rome*, a particularly popular (if dramatically nonsensical) opera.[4] His collaboration with Méhul, one of the most prominent French composers during the Revolution and the Empire, proved to be the determining factor in his career.

Although Hoffman had clearly attempted to clean up and ameliorate the effect of his Aristophanic model both politically and morally, the Consulate's censors could not tolerate his *Lisistrata*: its fourth performance was its last.[5] Unfortunately, there is no trace of any official report, since the archives including the censorship decisions for that period probably disappeared in 1871 when rebels burned down the police headquarters during the Paris Commune.[6] Thus the only source for Hoffman's misadventure is the play's first edition, where he defends himself against censors and critics in his preface and footnotes. Through a study of *Lisistrata* and of its relationship with its ancient model, I shall try to find out why this unique attempt to put Aristophanes on stage was aborted, arguing that this is in keeping with Napoleon's stated desire 'to finish the revolution', asserted two years earlier, immediately after he overthrew the Directory and replaced it with the Consulate by means of the coup known as 'the 18th Brumaire' on 9 November 1799.[7]

Démobilisettes, ancient and modern[8]

Although the core of the plot is preserved (the subject in both plays is the imaginary first 'strike' in Western history), and the adaptation does not modernise the context of the action, Hoffman in fact limits himself to the Prologue and the Cinesias scene of Aristophanes' *Lysistrata*. His comedy is divided into fifteen scenes and punctuated with nineteen songs, most of them adapted from celebrated opera arias and tunes.[9] The only Aristophanic character remaining in the adaptation is Lisistrata herself, who is married to an Athenian general, Mérion. Lisistrata's niece, Carite, takes the place of Calonice as the second character. Her husband's name is not Cinesias but Darès.[10] Lisistrata's servant, Machaon — a Scythian, named after an Iliadic hero — is himself married to Thaïs. The antagonism between the chorus of old men and the chorus of women, fundamental to Aristophanes' plot, is replaced with a perfect symmetry between groups of younger and older women, who complement one another: eight distinct characters form each age group. Lisistrata explicitly takes responsibility for and justifies this symmetry in the beginning of scene iii. When her niece asks why she is so concerned with equal rights of representation, the protagonist declares (p. 6):

> In order to avoid any reproach of partiality. All women [i.e. those present on stage] must equally desire their husbands' return. The older ones, because they have no time to lose; the younger, because they want to save time.

The Spartan Lampito has no counterpart in Hoffman's play, and nothing equivalent to the audacious occupation of the Acropolis is being planned; apparently, the author did his best to avoid the real political issue, relating to the Peloponnesian War, by reducing his *Lisistrata* to a purely domestic plot, free of embarrassing 'external' enemies. On the other hand, there is also a distinct absence of internal antagonists, since, with the exception of Mérion, the men are not menacing to women. They are instead merely flabbergasted at the strike and rather guileless. The removal of the play's adversarial tenor helps to maintain the perfect politeness of the language used in the dialogue and exchanges.

The first scene exposes the play's main issue and the motive behind Lisistrata's action. It is by far the richest scene in terms of arias, since there are four within three pages. It is precisely these songs that introduce the audience to the issue: the collective despair of Athens after ten years of war (aria no. 1) is exemplified by the individual despair of Carite, who has not seen her husband for two years (arias nos. 2 and 3). Lisistrata infers that the war is an obstacle to the survival of mankind 'both positively and negatively', since many men are dying in the battlefields and others are kept away from their wives (aria no. 4). In scene ii, Machaon announces the arrival of the group of women invited by Lisistrata. Although the slave seems to be nothing more than a traditional character of stage burlesque, his final aria (no. 5), at the same time, ironically confirms that war is contrary to common sense, by reducing this view to its simplest mode of expression — the sung opinion of a barbarian slave who is wiser than the free Greeks. In scene iii, Lisistrata is invited by Carite to name the female conspirators.

The chorus march on stage in scene iv, singing their *Hymn to Silence* (aria no. 6). This song is the first instance in this play of gendered self-criticism with a comic effect, a central feature of Aristophanes' *Lysistrata*: discretion is needed in order to ensure that the conspiracy meets with success. But discretion, according to the conventions of this comic world, is not compatible with femininity, since women are presented as characteristically talkative. When they invoke the divinity of silence, their very self-consciousness is as funny as the reason for the invocation. This long scene (pp. 7–17) develops the core of the plot. The comic theme of both Aristophanes' *Lysistrata* and the new *Lisistrata* is the contradiction between the peace project, which is a creditable goal in itself, and the means implemented to reach that goal — that is, the sex strike. Far from being remotely feminist in its thrust, scene iv is actually full of subtle jokes about nymphomania, the most ludicrous among all of women's inherent flaws. The comic equation thus consists in the correction of women's stereotypical faults (loquacity and nymphomania) in order to obtain peace, which is advantageous for all humans, both male and female. But, unlike Aristophanes' play, where both husbands and lovers are treated identically as objects of the women's desire and therefore targets of their strike, Hoffman progressively introduces the idea of female infidelity, not as a joke but a threat. The threat gradually increases during the course of this scene: if the husbands persist in making war, their wives will inevitably make love with someone else! When Lisistrata asks six of her accomplices whether they are ready to make any sacrifice whatsoever in order to ensure the return of their husbands, their answers sound like an accumulation of evidence for their moral feebleness. This comic progression begins with the allusive mythological dream of the young Cyane and reaches a crescendo with the explicit threat of Mélite (p. 13) and the warning given by Astioche, who belongs to the group of older women. Thus the comic effect of the anaphoric injunction 'my husband *must* come again'[11] is considerably enhanced. The oath song closes the scene.

In scene v, Machaon announces to the women what Lisistrata had already predicted in scene iv, just before the oath (p. 14): the army is coming back home under the terms of a three-day truce. The women confirm their commitment to their project once more. After being invited by her husband Machaon to help him with housework (scene vi), Thaïs reveals the conspiracy to him (scene vii). The conspiracy section closes with a comical comment about the impotence of the modern male as opposed to the vigour of his ancient counterpart (pp. 20–22).

Scene viii, a confrontation between Darès and Carite (pp. 23–31), is a toned-down and expurgated version of the famous Aristophanic episode in which Cinesias tries to convince Myrrhine to satisfy his burning — and perfectly visible — desire (*Lysistrata* 864–958). By the time Darès leaves the scene, he has decided to ask General Mérion to put an end to the conspiracy initiated by his own wife (pp. 28, 30). Scenes ix to xiii introduce the final *agōn* of Hoffman's play, between Lisistrata and Mérion. In scene xiv, the general refuses to kiss his wife, pretending that he had sworn to keep away from her until the Spartans are defeated. Lisistrata falters in her plan; she is upset because of Mérion's indifference, which seriously undermines her self-confidence and her belief in her own sex appeal. When she finally manages to give her husband a kiss, her accomplices protest, accusing her of committing perjury. In the last scene, Mérion reveals that what permitted the return of the army was in fact a peace treaty, not a truce.

Generally speaking, the transition from one scene to another seems credible and dramatically justified. Nevertheless, the play leaves an unpleasant aftertaste of implausibility, mainly because of a major dramaturgical weakness: does Mérion feign indifference in order to punish his wife for the conspiracy, as suggested by the author in his Preface (p. 11), and by the fact that Mérion is only informed late about the conspiracy?[12] Or had he really sworn chastity until the enemies could be defeated? The latter assumption is in contradiction with Mérion's final statement that a definite peace treaty had been signed *before* the army's return to Athens (p. 40). But the former assumption is dramatically inconsistent, because in this case Lisistrata's statement about the truce in scene iv (p. 14, confirmed by Machaon in scene v, p. 17) is left without justification. In other words, if the peace treaty had been signed before the return of the army, why the desperate sex strike initiated by Lisistrata? In the last scene, Mérion himself does not feel very comfortable about the plot (p. 41):

> Yes, what I'm telling you is precisely that peace is made. I wanted to defer the announcement, but now I understand how important it is for you to know.[13]

Obscenity

> Last but not least, it is to you that I'm offering [this little book], you honest and enlightened men of letters who examined my play and gave me your opinion, not orders; you, who were grateful to me for having concealed [the crudeness of] Aristophanes' *tableaux*, and, since I hadn't gone beyond the bounds [of decency] as dictated by the greatest masters, allowed my *Lisistrata* to be put on stage. But I am not offering it to you, women of loose morals, young ladies of easy virtue; in public, you would find in it too much; in private, too little. I am not offering it to you either, severe critics, sorrow moralists, scrupulous readers, people of taste that Molière revolts, nor to you, too penetrating spirits, who never see in a book what the author actually presents, but only what you have on the brain.[14]

These are the final words of the dedication introducing the 1802 edition of the play. As announced in this excerpt, Hoffman consciously amends Aristophanes' immorality, while pretending that, if the women had lovers, they would not be so eager to see their husbands back from the battlefield (Preface, p. xi). It is informative to compare this moralizing inflexion of the original dramatic situation with a famous passage in the Greek *Lysistrata*, which, of course, is omitted in the adaptation (107–10):

> And not the slightest glitter of a lover!
> And since the Milesians betrayed us, I've seen

> Not even one of those eight-inch dildos,
> Which used to be our leather relief.[15]

Hoffman insists emphatically on moral decency. In scene iv (pp. 8–9), for instance, the repetitions imitated from the original oath scene (*Lysistrata* 212–36) are free of any hint of an erotic subtext. But, as we have seen earlier, the audience progressively discovers in tandem with the younger women's reactions to Lisistrata's position, and mostly through the songs, that pledges of chastity are not eternal. The return of the husbands becomes more and more urgent:[16] with adequate diction and gesturing it is easy to imagine the refrain 'il faut que mon mari revienne' as a sexual suggestion, and indeed, it seems that the imposers of censorship understood it as such. Women may be neither lascivious nor immoral, but there is a limit to their patience. Cyane's mythical kidnapping dream and her misgivings about marital fidelity in Osiris' oracle (aria no. 8, p. 12) sound as if she is assuming a philosophical position in relation to the problem of sexual frustration. Mélite — and Lisistrata — eventually sing the refrain in the opposite sense (p. 13, aria no. 10):

> MÉLITE   *S'il tarde encor quelque tems...*
> LISISTRATA   — Eh bien?... Achevez donc... Ah! J'entends.
> *Vous aurez peur qu'il ne revienne.*

Yet when the sequence of events based upon this aria is in fact achieved, the general impression is that hundreds of lovers constantly harass the women. Whereas in *Lysistrata* women lack lovers for the same reason that they miss their husbands, in *Lisistrata* every male still available in Athens relentlessly besieges them.[17]

   As I pointed out earlier, Hoffman raises the question of the decline of the city: in war many people get killed and many others are prevented from having children (p. 3 with footnote; p. 10). There is certainly an echo here of what were in Hoffman's time very recent debates on the demographic issue;[18] by emphasizing this point, however, the author was laying himself open to moral rather than philosophical criticism. If we are to believe him, these are the two major points that seemed lewd to critics. But there was another point that shocked them, and that was the abundant use, mainly in the Darès–Carite scene, of the substantive 'baiser', interpreted as euphemistically alluding to the infinitive of the main verb in the French language that designates sexual intercourse. Hoffman defends himself in a footnote (p. 26):

> What is Darès asking for? A kiss ... What is Carite refusing to give him? A kiss. What's all this about, after all? A kiss. A kiss, that's all I said. It's not my fault if your imagination is lewder than my pen! ... The public laughed and applauded, they called for an encore. But the scrupulous made a great fuss, turning the noun into a verb. I have never fallen into this error.

Apart from these rather mild indecencies, there is nothing that could justify the prudish reaction of Napoleon's police agents. If one of them were zealously religious, the oath by Juno might have shocked him too. Even if it has nothing to do with the explicit description of sexual practices mentioned in the oath of Aristophanes' *Lysistrata*, this funny little poem, self-curse rather than promise of chastity, was intended to be a parody of a prayer form or *Gebetsparodie*,[19] since the tune was probably a pastiche of the most celebrated hymn to Saint John the Baptist (p. 17, aria no. 14):

> *Non, sainte Junon,*
> *Non,*
> *Qui jure par ton*
> *Nom*
> *Ne trompe jamais;*
> *Mais,*
> *Si pourtant mon serment*
> *Ment,*
> *Punis mon forfait,*
> *Et*
> *Pour percer mes deux*
> *Yeux,*
> *Tiens tous tes*
> *Traits*
> *Prêts.*[20]

To sum up: if we take Hoffman's assertions literally, we must deduce that the play was suspended for moral rather than political reasons. Nevertheless, a hint inserted in a curious 'Avertissement' at the beginning of the volume makes a threat against the censors to the effect that the play will not be restaged until they renounce their arbitrary 'corrections'. It also points to a second intervention by censors, *after* the performances had been stopped, intended to amend the text *in a new way*. One way of interpreting this is that the critics and censors attacked the play exclusively on moral grounds, resulting in a unique police order interrupting the performances. If this is the correct interpretation, it requires no further analysis. Indeed, this interpretation would mean that the enigmatic formulas of the 'Avertissement' (*'new* censorship [...] corrections of a *new kind*') should be understood as nothing more than boasting. The author would have been attempting to weave an autobiographical narrative bond with *Adrien*, Étienne Méhul's controversial opera which had been proscribed in 1792. On that occasion, too, Hoffman had refused to follow the censor's recommendations and to amend his politically suggestive libretto. If this were true, the 'Avertissement' should be taken as a kind of parabasis, a comic poet's act of self-praise, similar to Aristophanes' self-praise in *Acharnians*, *Clouds*, or *Peace*. Yet the most paradoxical element in Hoffman's defence against the charge of obscenity is precisely that he never shelters behind his ancient model. His strategy consists solely in emphasizing that his play is quite recent and yet much more decent than Molière's comedies and other classics of the French repertoire. He seems to forget that Aristophanes, his direct and explicitly asserted model, is much older than Molière (p. xiv):

> Are you ready to excuse immorality and indecency in comedies just because they are old? Such reasoning would indeed be quite futile. The effect that a play has doesn't depend on production? The impression that it makes isn't renewed each time that it is put on stage? If it is dangerous, if it is indecent, should one check its date, to know whether one must blush or not?

Politics

On the other hand, if one assumes that there were two kinds of censor, as stated in the 'Avertissement', the following sequence of events should be considered a serious possibility: the first intervention was an official one and it compelled the troupe to interrupt the performances for (undoubtedly political) reasons on which the author was not allowed to comment. This was because they were covered by some kind of 'official secrets' policy linked to the diplomatic negotiations and military action still in progress in January 1802. The only trace of this repressive measure is its mention in the 'Avertissement'. The second intervention would have aimed at amending the text morally, probably after the incriminated passages had been modified. This must be the censorship that Hoffman was alluding to when deploring its 'innovative character' in the 'Avertissement' or when castigating the 'scrupulous people' in his footnotes.[21] Indeed, he had the perfect right to talk about this unofficial pressure, since the play's performances had already been interrupted 'by [official] order'.

Actually, there are several anachronistic allusions to the contemporary political situation in this French play. For instance, the war against Sparta that Lisistrata tries to stop has, at the beginning of the play, already lasted for ten years (p. 1: 'dix ans de succès balancés', 'dix ans de tapage, de combats de carnage'; p. 2: 'dix mortelles années'). The detail is not consistent with ancient history, since Aristophanes' *Lysistrata* was staged in 411 BC, twenty years after the beginning of the Peloponnesian War. But it is perfectly in keeping with contemporary chronology, since the French Revolutionary Wars had been waged since precisely 1792.[22] As I pointed out earlier, the war is condemned as undermining the reproductive balance of the human race (p. 10); it is also, in a very careful formulation, presented as running counter to common sense by Lisistrata's Scythian slave, a convinced pacifist (p. 6, aria no. 5):

> Although I know that our brave soldiers
> Go to meet the Creator as they go to lunch,
> I never had the slightest intention of following them,
> For the Gods ordered me to live
> So that to serve my country.
> I'm pious, I obey.[23]

Eventually, Mérion, the providential man (named after Meriones, another Iliadic hero, half-brother of Idomeneus), announces the end of the war at the end of the play (p. 40):

> You swore to be cruel as long as war continues. Well, I'm telling you that it is not a truce that I'm announcing to you, but a peace treaty, signed, concluded, perfect and solid.[24]

The praise of Napoleon is clear, and yet it is not unambiguous. Just before his final announcement, Mérion had broken his own oath: in spite of the promise supposedly made to his soldiers to abstain from any pleasure until Sparta had been entirely destroyed (p. 36), he had finally kissed his wife (p. 39). More than the licentiousness of the play, which is not really scandalous, what must have seemed challenging to Napoleonic decorum is the combination of mild sexual allusions with overt pacifism and, above all, with the weakness of character attributed to General Mérion.

Moreover, comedy as a genre was currently at the centre of much wider questioning of the relevance of theatrical representation in general. Fumaroli explains that the origins of this questioning can be traced back to the Christian mistrust of theatre as theorized by Bossuet and Nicole at the end of the seventeenth century; Goldzink has also brilliantly demonstrated that the Enlightenment tended towards a sense of shame in relation to the joyful comic expressivity of the new era and that therefore, paradoxically, the 'Enlightened' atheist position on theatre was quite similar to its Christian antecedent. Together they form a kind of continuum that we may call the *Querelle* of the comic, a phenomenon which lasted into the 1800s and was best formulated in the liberal, counter-revolutionary criticism of Greek comedy formulated by Madame de Staël.[25] According to Goldzink's analysis,

> As the upshot of a century so rich in tragedies, thanks to Voltaire, La Harpe's comedy looks rather miserable. Most cheerful in our eyes, the eighteenth century wanders about, sorrowful at heart, always dissatisfied, hesitating between different versions of the Comic — moral, sentimental, or buffoon. Too much cheerfulness shocks it, too much wit freezes it, too many tears in the laughter irritates it. Even before looking at itself, dismayed, in the mirror of the Revolution, the Enlightenment, so proud of its ideas, began by failing to recognise itself in its comedies. It is possible that this weakness is only a symptom.[26]

In the particular case of Aristophanes, the most eloquent writer to slate him during the eighteenth century was an enthusiastic advocate of comedy, Nicolas de Chamfort, who demonstrated in an academic essay that he apparently had learnt his Plutarch quite well, for it is ultimately from this ancient literary critic that his class-conscious critique of Aristophanes was inherited:

> For Molière, the comedy was to be found in works of another kind [...]. The irony of Socrates, so perfectly preserved in Plato's dialogues [...] belongs to a really theatrical figure; and in this sense, the comic poet of the decent people was the sage of Greece, Aristophanes being nothing more than the buffoon of the common people.[27]

Conclusion

In Aristophanes, the women eventually obtain a ceasefire. In Hoffman's play, because of the feebleness of their leader, they just surrender by giving up their strike and by delegating their peace-making power to men, since the author's aim is to restrict women to their traditional role, as defined by the domestic plot-type enacted in boulevard comedy.

The ancient Greek archetype may have been licentious, but its rehash was not. Hoffman's play probably shocked Napoleon's agents because of its offhand, irreverent treatment of war, too serious a subject to laugh about, even on the eve of a truce. 'Comedy for me is as if someone was trying to force me to be interested in gossip. I can understand your admiration for Molière, but I do not share it,' Napoleon said.[28] Nevertheless, it was certainly not Napoleon's personal *goût* that dictated the censor's attitude towards the play.

There is an eighteenth-century contradiction between, on the one hand, theoretical positions that rejected theatre in general and comedy in particular, and on the other hand the proliferation of troupes, theatres, and plays during the revolutionary period. But this contradiction is only a superficial one. By the end of the eighteenth century, theatre, broadly defined, had become a phenomenon in daily life, and people (Parisians at least) saw themselves as real, rather than metaphorical 'actors' on the political stage. People exhibited exactly the same excited and exalted responses at assemblies and on the barricades as they did in theatres, and they were unusually receptive and reactive at this time to all forms of performance.[29] Thus, from a political point of view, theatre in Paris during the Revolution was comparable to theatre in fifth-century Athens: these were both contexts in which popular sovereignty could assert itself. This is the reason why theatrical performances were often subject to similar treatment as the press.[30] In this sense, the treatment meted out to this rather mediocre attempt to put Aristophanes on stage, namely the police order that brutally interrupted the performances of Hoffman's *Lisistrata* (whatever the exact reasons for and circumstances behind the order), was an instance of collateral damage that occurred as a result of the First Consul's will to 'finish the Revolution'.

Notes to Chapter 6

1. There is evidence for some attempts to stage Greek tragedies during this period, but none ever met any success: Euripides' *Hecuba*, for instance, in a translation published before the Revolution by Belin de Ballu (1783), was performed ten years later, on 13 Mar. 1793 at the Théâtre de la Nation. But it was never restaged. The three most celebrated Ancien Régime operas with Greek titles that were still being performed during the Revolution have so little to do with the original Greek plays that the librettists do not even mention their sources: *Œdipe à Colone*, composed by Antonio Sacchini (Marie-Antoinette's favourite composer) to a libretto by Nicolas-François Guillard, was performed continuously from 1 Feb. 1787 (at the Opéra) until 1830 (a total of 583 performances); see Hyslop (1945), 352. Another adaptation by Guillard, the libretto of Gluck's celebrated *Iphigénie en Tauride*, first performed in 1779, was even more successful — it was as popular as the first Euripidean opera by Gluck, *Iphigénie en Aulide* (libretto by M. F. L. Grand Bailli du Roullet, first performed in 1774). For Cherubini's *Medea*, see below. The most successful attempt to put an ancient theatrical text on stage seems to have been an adaptation of Plautus' *Menaechmi* by Cailhava (1791). Staged in January 1791, it was performed all year round, then regularly restaged from September 1795 onwards (source: César database, http://cesar.org.uk). The author of the adaptation recognizes in his Preface the difficulty of his task: 'No doubt, it's quite dangerous nowadays to risk a Comedy of the ancient kind. In this genre, imagination, rejecting any ornament that has nothing to do with Thalia, makes it a rule to be constantly fertile, vivid, full of ups and downs, and yet quite simple' (Cailhava (1791), p. vi). Some years later, in 1797, the same author apparently failed to put Aristophanes on stage. There is actually no trace in the sources of any performance of his *Athènes pacifiée*: Cailhava (1796/7). According to his Preface, the author pretends to put politics on stage, but the result is moralizing scholarly nonsense. See Jacob (1843–45), no. 2076; Cailhava's potpourri is now available on the Gallica website: http://visualiseur.bnf.fr/Visualiseur?Destination=Gallica&O=NUMM-108740 (accessed 22 Aug. 2006). Plutarch served more than once as a source for aesthetically, morally and politically acceptable subjects: see Viala (1997), 114. On the Roman heritage in

French revolutionary culture, see Raskolnikoff (1990) and (1992), 262–313; Momigliano (1950). For a complete list of French translations and adaptations of Greek drama until the mid-20th c., see Horn-Monval (1958). For a detailed quantitative analysis of theatre during the Revolution, see Kennedy, Netter, McGregor, and Olsen (1996).

2. First print: Hoffman (1802). Henceforth all references to the play inserted in the main text will be to this edition. The last words of the volume's subtitle is 'by Order', printed on a separate line in small capitals and followed by suspension dots. Edition available on the Gallica website: http://visualiseur.bnf.fr/Visualiseur?Destination=Gallica&O=NUMM-84958 (accessed 22 Aug. 2006). Complete works: Hoffman (1829). All translations are the author's own unless otherwise stated.

3. See Trentin (2001).

4. First staged in March 1792, this three-act opera was censored: see Jacob (1843–45), nos. 273–301. The performances were suspended after Hoffman's refusal to amend the script according to the revolutionary censorship's instructions. He probably changed his mind later. The cover of its later edition does not mention the 1792 performance; the new version was first performed on 4 June 1799 (i.e. 16 Prairial of the 7th year), in the Théâtre de la République. I can see hardly anything in this text that could be taken as hinting at a pro-monarchical stance: the Roman emperor Hadrian is presented as a lustful, completely amoral tyrant. He arrogantly tries to seduce and then incessantly harasses a princess, whom he has taken prisoner during a military campaign in Parthia, while deceiving his own fiancée, before suddenly changing his mind at the last minute. In 1802, the play had been restaged for an extensive run. The author always regarded this as his masterwork.

5. Until his address to the Conseil d'État (9 April 1809), which announced that censorship should be systematized by 1810, Napoleon's position on censorship is quite ambiguous; see Locré (1819). Unofficially, the police exercised control upon every publication and performance, and yet the Emperor seemed to condemn censorship in favour of 'organization' of culture in a letter addressed to Joseph Fouché, his Police Minister (12 prairial year XIII = 1 June 1805). As far as theatre is concerned, he explained more clearly what he meant by 'organization without censorship' when suggesting to Fouché that he commission Raynouard to write on ancient subjects. In another letter to Fouché, four years after *Lisistrata* had been censored, he feigned ignorance of his administration's habits (15 January 1806): Napoléon (1858–70), x. 325, 337; xi. 124.

6. There is no trace of *Lisistrata* in the inventory of Krakovitch (1982), which bears on the manuscripts of the plays (F18 581–668) and the official reports of the censors (F21 966–95), nor in Thalie, the electronic catalogue of the manuscripts of plays and related official reports of censorship preserved in the Centre Historique des Archives Nationales in Paris. For the entire period, only 171 manuscripts have been preserved. But we know that 80 boxes containing manuscripts of plays submitted for police approval, together with other printed material seized on the public thoroughfare, disappeared in May 1871.

7. Proclamation made by Napoleon to the Consuls on the 24 Frimaire year VIII (19 Dec. 1799), inserted in the Constitution of the 22 Frimaire (13 Dec. 1799): 'Citoyens, la Révolution est fixée aux principes qui l'ont commencée, elle est finie'.

8. 'Démobilisette', modelled on 'suffragette', is the brilliant translation of Lysistrata's name by Debidour (1965).

9. The provenance of each tune is clearly stated in the 1802 edition.

10. A man named Dares, the Trojan priest of Hephaestus, is mentioned in the *Iliad* 5. 9, but Hoffman's hero is more likely to have been named after Dares the Phrygian, the enigmatic author of the late Latin *History of the Destruction of Troy*, written or translated from a Greek original in the 6th c. AD and published in France by Mlle Le Fèvre in 1680. See Fry (1998), 231–87; Fumaroli (2001), 208.

11. See the next section.

12. 'Mérion [...] warned about that scheme, thwarts it by a comic ruse: he pretends to be as indifferent to his wife as she had sworn to be to him.'

13. 'Oui, la paix est faite, vous-dis-je: je voulais différer de vous l'apprendre; mais je vois combien il est important pour vous de le savoir.'

14. Hoffman (1802), p. vi.
15. Later in the Prologue, according to the original oath, Aristophanes' women swear to keep away *first* from lovers and *then* from husbands (Ar. *Lys.* 212–13).
16. The music of this aria is borrowed from *Les Fraises*, a translation into French of a German play for children: Schmid (1833); see Jacob (1843–45), nos. 3719, 5059.
17. It is interesting to observe the reversal of this tendency in modern productions, since nowadays the obscenity of the play is often the very reason why it is staged. This has been the case recently, in a Parisian production eloquently entitled *Lysistrata (la grève du sexe)* (the sex strike). Text: Garma-Berman and Bianciotto (2005). Obscenity is also the main feature of modern Greek productions of the play.
18. For the optimist point of view echoed here, see Condorcet (2004); for the pessimist one, see Malthus (1798).
19. For a discussion of this issue in Aristophanes, see Kleinknecht (1967).
20. 'No, Saint Juno, no; who swears by Juno never deceives. Nevertheless, if my oath lies, punish my sin and get your arrows ready to pierce my eyes', to the tune of 'Ut queant laxis', syllables from which were used to name the notes of the medieval hexachord and in modern Romance languages designate the notes of the scale.
21. See footnotes on pp. 3, 11, 26, 31, 33, 35.
22. Hoffman is perfectly aware of this inconsistency; see p. 9.
23. 'Je sais que nos braves soldats | vont à la mort comme au repas; | mais je n'ai garde de les suivre, | car pour bien servir mon pays, | les Dieux m'ont ordonné de vivre: | je suis pieux, et j'obéis.'
24. The praise is completed in the 'exodos' song (p. 42): 'D'un vainqueur l'on chante la gloire; | mais que l'on aime le guerrier | qui dans le champ de la victoire, | fait croître et fleurir l'olivier! | Si son bras étonnait la terre, | ses mains la couvrent de bienfaits [...] | Honneur à qui fait bien la guerre. | Amour à qui fait bien la paix.'
25. Fumaroli (2001); Goldzink (1992); for an analysis of Staël (1991 [1800]), 115–29 (on Greek comedy), see Goldzink (1992), 93–111. Cf. D. Marshall (1986); Avlami (2000), 299–305. On laughter as a central issue in the 18th-c. philosophical debate, see also Andries (2000).
26. Goldzink (1992), 24. Cf. Frantz (2000). For a description of the atmosphere in the theatres, perceived by the Committee of Public Safety as 'schools of the Revolution' and a 'supplement to public education', see Hyslop (1945). Cf. Tarin (1998); Quéro (2000), 67–83.
27. Chamfort (1824), 9–10. See Goldzink (1992), 86–88.
28. Quoted in Albert (1902), 188.
29. See Hyslop (1945) and Friedland (2003), 258–94.
30. See Graczyk (1989).

CHAPTER 7

❖

Aristophanes' *Wealth* and Dalpatram's *Lakshmi*

Phiroze Vasunia

Aristophanes in Nineteenth-Century India

'For an over-modern reader', notes one handbook of Gujarati literature, 'much in his poetry comprising of 650 pages in two volumes will seem to be verbal jugglery, Salvation Army jingle and claptrap'.[1] In his own time, the work of Dalpatram Dahyabhai, who lived from 1820 to 1898, was widely appreciated both within the circles of the Gujarat Vernacular Society (GVS), to which he belonged, and among the wider public. According to the Society's official report, Dalpatram's elegiac poem 'Forbes Viraha', which was about the loss of his friend Alexander Kinloch Forbes, sold 1,500 copies within a few months of publication. The Society's journal, *Buddhiprakash*, which Dalpatram edited from 1855 to 1879, sold 76,680 copies by the year 1865. His work on Gujarati prosody went into twenty-two editions and sold 91,000 copies, which is a surprising figure for a work of this type.[2] The play *Lakshmi*, which was Dalpatram's (largely prose) translation into Gujarati of Aristophanes' *Wealth*, and which he wrote with the assistance of Forbes, had sold almost a thousand copies by the late 1860s, and it went into four editions. It is this play *Lakshmi*, and the collaboration between Dalpatram and Forbes, that form the subject of my essay.[3]

Whether *Lakshmi* was performed in the live theatre of Ahmedabad in 1850, when the play was published, is not clear. But if it was indeed not performed, the history of *Lakshmi* would be consistent with the early reception of the Athenian playwright in Britain since it seems that, from the middle of the seventeenth century to the early twentieth century, Aristophanes' plays were edited, annotated, and translated, but seldom acted out on the live theatrical stage. In her essay in this volume, Edith Hall explains the situation of the English Aristophanes by saying that 'this was a result of the paradox whereby he was identified simultaneously as a mouthpiece for inveterate political reactionaries, while creating profound unease in moral conservatives'.[4] Dalpatram's conservatism was certainly very different from that of the early English translators: he was one of a number of reformers who were trying to modernize the social behaviour of Indians in the second half of the nineteenth century, and his text fits well into this overall schema of moral reform. Whether or not he can be called a 'moral conservative', his poetry often assumed a didactic voice and sought to 'improve', as he put it, the morals and behaviour of the Gujarati people.[5]

The relative infrequency with which Aristophanes' *Wealth* was staged for over a hundred years should not be taken to imply that the play was unpopular at all times: Dalpatram's translation is part of a dazzlingly rich Aristophanic tradition in which this particular Greek drama holds a privileged status. *Wealth* was perhaps the most read drama of Aristophanes in late antiquity, and it survives in over 150 medieval manuscripts, while fragments are preserved in several papyri. It is placed first in the important Ravenna manuscript (gr. 429), which contains all eleven plays, as well as in the Venetian manuscripts. According to K. J. Dover, 'In nearly all manuscripts which contain more than one play *Wealth* comes first and most Paleologan manuscripts contain only the trio *Wealth, Clouds, Frogs*'.[6] *Wealth* occupies the first place in the *editio princeps* of Aristophanes, namely, the Aldine edition of 1498 by Markos Mousouros. Moreover, it was among the first works from Greek antiquity to be translated into Latin during the Italian Renaissance as well as the first Greek play to be performed in England (in Cambridge in 1536), the first play to be adapted into English (as the *Ploutophthalmia Ploutogamia* by Thomas Randolph), and the basis for four of the nine translations that were written in England before 1800.[7] If Dalpatram's collaborator, Forbes, was sufficiently moved to recommend the play to the Gujarati poet, he could have himself studied *Wealth* in any number of versions, not least the school edition of 1834 by Henry Parker Cookesley that was based on Wilhelm Dindorf's text and that 'carefully omitted every verse or expression which would shock the delicacy of the most fastidious reader'.[8]

'The Plutus is, perhaps, next to the Clouds, the best of Aristophanes' productions.'[9] So wrote Charles P. Gerard in the preface to his verse translation of the play, published in 1847, three years before the appearance of Dalpatram's version. Various other explanations have been offered for the historical success of the play. One translator, Edmund F. J. Carrington, in his own verse translation of 1825, explained the play's popularity by observing that the 'subject [... was] general, and therefore, one which would be received with an equal share of interest in all ages, and under all circumstances of event'.[10] In fact, several readers agreed on this point, that the play had a universal appeal and that its humour was less rooted in contemporary contexts than other Aristophanic comedies. In his account of the influence of Aristophanes, Louis E. Lord wrote, 'To understand it the audience needed no erudite knowledge of fourth century Athens but only an acquaintance with those ills to which all flesh is heir.'[11] More recently, Stephen Halliwell has said that 'the comedy appears to float relatively free of Athens of the 380s, and requires much less historical exegesis than any other surviving Aristophanic play in order to be made intelligible to cultures remote in time and place from the classical Athenian polis.'[12]

Complementary to the view about the play's generality and timeliness is the suggestion that Aristophanes meant to deliver a 'moral lesson' to contemporary Athenians. 'In its extant form', Richard C. Jebb wrote, in 1910, for the eleventh edition of the *Encyclopaedia Britannica*, 'the *Plutus* is simply a moral allegory.'[13] This reading, too, is a leitmotif that recurs through the play's reception, with one commentator after another referring to the morality and virtue of the dramatic 'message'. Since Dalpatram's work has also been analysed for its moral vision, it is worth underscoring this feature of Aristophanic reception. As with *Lakshmi*, however, the moral reading of *Wealth* should not obscure the play's meaning in political and social contexts. Of the range of texts that could be discussed in this light, one might mention two works already discussed by Hall above: Henry Fielding's collaboration, with William Young, on a translation of *Plutus*, and *Reform: A Farce, Modernised from Aristophanes*, attributed to Francis Wrangham; the latter offers a version of selected lines from *Wealth* (112–246) in which the entire dialogue is assigned, along with a plethora of annotation, to Thomas Paine and John Bull.[14] One might also mention the *Pluto* produced at Nuremberg in 1551 by the 'mastersinger' Hans Sachs (the inspiration for Richard Wagner's *Die Meistersinger von Nürnberg*): among other things, the drama portrays 'a Jew reduced to the utmost depths of despair by the wholesome financial order which is introduced by the God of Wealth after the restoration of his eyesight'.[15]

If Aristophanes' *Wealth* and Dalpatram's *Lakshmi* were composed in very different contexts, *Lakshmi*, as an episode in reception, enhances the significance of reading Aristophanes' last play in terms of its political and ideological valences. Of course, *Wealth* has not been lacking in interpreters who have considered its political implications. As James McGlew suggests, for instance, 'Chremylus invites his audience "to laugh at poverty" and dream of escaping it in a way that reaffirms Athenian democratic identity and celebrates the decision-making powers of the collective demos.'[16] From a different perspective, David Konstan and Matthew Dillon have described *Wealth* 'as an active intervention in the ideological instabilities of the Athenian city-state'.[17] The Gujarati *natak*, or 'play', also reminds audiences of the entanglement of Aristophanes' drama in contemporary Athenian debates, even as it draws attention to its own situatedness in nineteenth-century British India.[18]

On a literalist reading of the two plays, it would perhaps be easy to enumerate the similarities and the differences. In Aristophanes' *Wealth*, Chremylus is a farmer who has fallen on hard times and Cario is his slave. On the advice of the Delphic oracle, he takes home with him the first person he encounters as he departs from the sanctuary. As Chremylus and Cario discover, this person is Wealth, old, blind, and decrepit. Chremylus supposes that if the god had his eyesight restored he would distribute money to the good and not to the wicked. Chremylus and Cario eventually restore Wealth's eyesight in the temple of Asclepius and, by the end of the play, they are attempting to install the god on the Acropolis as the custodian of Athena's treasury. In the course of the play, the two men meet Blepsidemus (a friend of Chremylus), Poverty (a horrible hag), an informer (or 'sycophant'), an old woman, her young lover, the god Hermes, and a priest of Zeus. All of the action takes place on an Athenian street in front of Chremylus' house.

In Dalpatram's *Lakshmi*, Dhirsinh is a landlord who has fallen on hard times and Bhima is his servant. On the advice of the divine Lord Mahadev, he takes home with him the first person he encounters as he leaves the temple. This turns out to be the goddess Lakshmi, old, blind, and decrepit. Dhirsinh supposes that if the goddess had her eyesight restored she would distribute money to the good and not to the wicked. Dhirsinh and Bhima eventually restore Lakshmi's eyesight in the temple of Dhanvantri (the physician of the gods) and, by the end of the play, they are attempting to install the goddess in a temple. The play closes with a song and a brief coda of four lines of verse. In the course of the play, the two men meet Daji (the village headman), Bhaichand (a lawyer), a scavenger or wretch (a figure of poverty), Lavinga (a female servant?), Dhanpal, Dolatkhan (a slave), Shastri (a priest), Desai (an informer), the old woman Fatma, her young lover Juvankhan, the god Hanuman, and Gosai (a member of the priestly community). All the action takes place on a street in front of Dhirsinh's house in a Gujarati village.

It is not hard to see the many superficial similarities and correspondences between the two plays, but let us attempt to understand rather the nature of the 'adaptation'.[19] The different circumstances of the composition are signalled to the reader in Dalpatram's prologue. The prologue, which is narrated in the first person by an authorial voice, immediately proclaims the status of Athens in England and Christian Europe as well as among the Greeks. It begins:

> About three hundred and fifty years before the birth of Vikramajit, there was a city named Athens in the country of the Greeks. On the whole, the Greeks were well-read. But there were no people as wise as the Athenian people anywhere else [in Greece]. In that city, there were many poets and other good writers of books. Even after the passage of so many years, the children in all the schools of England and of other Christian countries learn the books of those great, well-known poets. Therefore, people say that the woman named Athens is dead, but that even today she gives life to the world in the form of knowledge. In those days, the people of that country worshipped many gods and also made statues of them and had them installed in attractive temples. Those statues were well decorated and the temples were also worth looking at. Some of the temples are still there, but the worship of their gods has completely stopped. People have taken away the statues of the gods to England and other countries.[20]

In a shift that only makes sense within the reality of British rule in India, this Gujarati passage traces a movement from an Indian marker (the legendary king Vikramajit, who often serves as a point of reference in Hindu chronology) at the beginning to an English one at the end. Significantly, the pedagogic importance of Athens for Indians is indicated by the pedagogic importance of Athenian culture for the English and other Europeans. Also significantly, the issue of religion is introduced early in the prologue, with the pointed suggestion that the desolation of the temples of Greece has been caused by the removal of statues by the English and the Europeans. One does not quite know what to make of this deprivation of Greek temples, given the lapidary nature of the last sentence, but perhaps the narrator is alluding to the authority, whether religious, capitalist, or imperial, that has transferred from Greece to England. If the shifting lines of this passage converge on one point, that point seems to be England, in terms of pedagogy (school children) and the accumulation of cultural capital (statues).

It is, therefore, all the more striking that in the drama that follows no direct mention is made of England. Aristophanes' *Wealth* makes very specific references to individuals and events in the fourth century BC. But the village in which the action of *Lakshmi* unfolds is largely set in a timeless past and is the home of several stock characters of Indian, and specifically Gujarati, folk theatre: the landlord, the servant, the priest, the village headman, and so on. The playwright justifies his decision in the prologue by saying that he has set aside Greek traditions, and 'used the traditions of the Hindus, so that the Gujarati people can properly understand' the play.[21] There are very few intimations here of the world of the factory and the machine that we shall encounter in Dalpatram's poem 'Invasion of Hunnarkhan'. Yet the traditionalist cast of *Lakshmi* is countered by the language of modern social reform that is used in the main body of the text and in the prologue. Readers of the play may conclude, the narrator says, that people must 'not earn wealth through injustice, immorality, and slander'.[22] The idea that wealth is to be earned through honest means seems banal, but it should be set against the larger canvas of social reform that was being attempted by the educated middle class and the intelligentsia in the nineteenth century.[23] The reformist background is what gives the charge to jokes made in the play about differences in caste; or to the outsized greed of Brahman priests; or to the satirical complaint about the Jadeja Rajputs who poison their infant daughters because they wish to have male rather than female offspring.[24] Thus, the play attempts to work contrapuntally: it simultaneously campaigns for reform along modern lines and relies on a nostalgic and impossible vision of the simple village.

When the outside world intrudes on the village community, nevertheless, Dalpatram's play casts this intrusion in terms that are startlingly reminiscent of the colonial world of mercantile Ahmedabad. Consider his reading of a moment in Aristophanes' *Wealth* when the Informer tells the Just Man about the nature of his occupation.

> INFORMER   Gods above, must I put up with this, with their outrageous
>   conduct toward me? I'm terribly hurt that an upstanding patriot
>   like me should be mistreated.
> JUST MAN   You, an upstanding patriot?
> INFORMER   Second to none!
> JUST MAN   Very well then, I have a question for you.
> INFORMER   Ask away.
> JUST MAN   Are you a farmer?
> INFORMER   Do you think I'm crazy?
> JUST MAN   A businessman, then?
> INFORMER   Sure; at least, I claim to be when the occasion arises.
>   (*Wealth* 898–903)[25]

After describing himself as upstanding (*chrēstos*) and patriotic (*philopolis*), the Informer continues this exchange by saying that he works for the benefit of the city. In *Lakshmi*, the informer Desai also claims to work for the benefit of the government and the people.

> DESAI   Since my birth, whatever work I have done has been for the
>   benefit of the government and the welfare of the people. There is
>   a saying that virtue and vice are brothers. These people here are
>   mocking me today.
> BHIMA   You've worked for benefit and welfare?
> DESAI   Yes, yes. No one has done the work that I have done.
> BHIMA   Then answer my question.

> DESAI   What's your question?
> BHIMA   Are you a farmer and has the world benefited from your growing
>   enough grain?
> DESAI   Do you think I'm like a farmer?
> BHIMA   Have you ruled over foreign countries for the benefit of people?
> DESAI   No, nothing like that, but sometimes I have composed documents
>   for the repayment of debts.   (*Lakshmi*, scene 5)[26]

Where Aristophanes places the Informer in relation to a businessman (*emporos*), Dalpatram raises the issue of rule over foreign countries. Indeed, the context in which the exchange takes place between Desai and Bhima points to an expectation that rule by foreign countries can be beneficent to the governed. The implicit parallel between the useful businessman, in Aristophanes, and foreign rule, in Dalpatram, is further telling in so far as it combines two themes that are important to Dalpatram's work. It is, of course, consistent with the Gujarati poet's attitude to British rule and his acceptance of the capitalist ideology of Ahmedabad's business élite, and it is part of a political economy in which industry, commerce, and colonialism are supposed to sustain each other and lead to an improvement in the lives of people.

    The texture of the village is enhanced by Dalpatram's use of popular language and humour. 'Dalpatram's characters are not always as clearly individualized as Chaucer's,' Krishanlal Mohanlal Jhaveri wrote, 'but he has a finer sense of the thinking and feeling and moralizing of the common people and of the rich texture of the social scene of his time, and the total impression which his body of poetic work produces is one of abounding energy of life and of the poet's inexhaustible interest in observing it.'[27] But if Dalpatram appropriated the popular, he also naturalized it and gave it the feel of the eternal. As Mikhail Bakhtin suggested, the popular can be dangerous, offensive, rude, or vulgar, and it needs mediation, and has to be domesticated and presented in such a way that it is rendered acceptable. That, in a sense, is the effect of much in Forbes' treatise *Ras Mala*, which is presented by the author as a sympathetic account, but is also a mediated rendition of manners and customs of Gujaratis. Dalpatram himself became widely known for his use of popular or folk forms and metres in his poetry and prose writings, and he offers an example of folk lyrics in the song that concludes the play.

> The wasp is flying in the celebration hall,
> The drum-beats are rolling
> In the procession of Lakshmi.
> How will it go without Grandfather?
> Grandfather Dhirsinh is there
> In the procession of Lakshmi.[28]

While he was familiar with the traditions of Sanskrit, Vraj, and medieval Gujarati poetry, and while many of his compositions reveal these influences, several of his poems are also written in a fluid vernacular, and they became renowned, to quote one reader, for their 'catchy rhymes, verbal tricks, wit, cleverness, homely illustrations and simple representation'.[29] Nevertheless, Dalpatram also offered up a version of the popular that was stylized, carefully demarcated, and often moralizing in its intent. So even though *Lakshmi* drew on the indigenous Gujarati tradition of the *bhavai* drama, the play for the most part avoided the 'gross vulgarity, open indecency, public obscenity' that characterized the genre.[30] Accordingly, in his version, Dalpatram takes out much of the flatulence, the sexual banter, and the scatological references of Aristophanes' play.[31]

Here is a passage from the opening scenes of the Greek comedy:

CHREMYLUS	That's right. And what's more, it's through you that people have anything radiant, fine, or charming. Everything's in the service of wealth.
CARIO	In my case, it was for small change that I lost my freedom and became a slave.
CHREMYLUS	And I've heard that Corinthian courtesans, when a poor man makes a pass at them, pay him no mind, but if he's rich, they right away offer him their arse.
CARIO	And I've heard that boys do the same thing, not for their lover's sake but for the money.
CHREMYLUS	But not the decent ones, only the whores; the decent ones don't ask for money.
CARIO	For what then?
CHREMYLUS	A good horse, or hunting dogs.
CARIO	No doubt they're ashamed to ask for money, and cover up their sluttiness with fancy words. (*Wealth* 143–59)

And here is Dalpatram's interpretation of this passage:

DHIRSINH	Of course. And what's more, in this world, anything good or socially respectable is attained only through wealth, is it not? It is said, 'All virtues are harboured in wealth.' [The quotation is in Sanskrit.] Therefore, all virtues are harboured in Lakshmi.
BHIMA	Yes, lord, you may remember that you paid for me with just a little money. At that time, I was poorer than you.
DHIRSINH	What's more, I have heard that if a poor person goes to a prostitute, he is driven away, but if a wealthy man goes, he is welcome.
BHIMA	What's more, without wealth, many men of the Vadnagara caste die unmarried. I will recite a song about that:

> *Oh god, why was I born into the Nagar caste? I can't see a sari with red patterns hanging on the wall opposite.* (*Lakshmi*, scene 1)[32]

The joke in Aristophanes about Corinthian courtesans and boy-lovers, which is mirrored in *Lakshmi* by a remark about a prostitute, is clearly rooted in a particular ancient Greek context. Dalpatram does not develop the humour in any literalist manner in the context of his Gujarati village, but rather he sets aside the male–male lovers and redirects the sexual valence of the original into a point about marriage within the terms of the caste system. The frustrated man of the Nagar caste is so low down on the social scale that he needs money to attract a wife, and without wealth, he has no chance of seeing a wife's red sari in his own home. Moreover, the Sanskrit line uttered by Dhirsinh is not a repudiation of the popular tone of the play but a confirmation of it. Classical Sanskrit confers its ancient and sacrosanct authority on Dhirsinh's claim, but the claim itself is the opposite of what the audience would expect to find in an ancient religious text. The mode of classicism used here is, therefore, counter-traditional and part of the humour.

The question of sexual behaviour resurfaces toward the end of the action in both Aristophanes and Dalpatram. In the Greek play, a young man (he is called *neanias*) stops visiting an old woman because, with the onset of wealth, he does not need to turn to her for money. In Dalpatram's play, the audience also encounters an old woman and her young lover, but with a twist: the old woman Fatma and her erstwhile lover Juvankhan are both Muslims and they speak in Hindi rather than Gujarati. Whereas in Aristophanes the unfortunate woman once went out at the time of the Great Mysteries, for instance, in Dalpatram she is said to have gone riding on her wagon during the festival of Id.[33] Dalpatram seems to have been unwilling to present the old woman and her adulterous young lover as Hindus, like many of the other characters in his play. (Even in his play, Juvankhan is an adulterous man with a wife rather than the professional gigolo of Aristophanes.) The only other explicitly Muslim character is Dolatkhan, who also speaks in Hindi and is described as a slave (*gulam*).[34] He wants to know when the goddess of wealth will be visiting his house.

Islam was a problem for Dalpatram as it was for several others of the Hindu intelligentsia in Gujarat. Several members of the Gujarat Vernacular Society considered the Gujarati language spoken by Muslims in Gujarat, as also by Parsis, to be impure or deviant in some way.[35] In his poem on industry ('Hunnarkhanni Chadhai'), Dalpatram suggested that the learning and wisdom of people in Hindustan lessened with the arrival of Muslims. To be sure, in another poem, called 'Forbesvilasa', which recalled a literary event convened by Forbes in 1852, Dalpatram did not blame the death of Sanskrit on Muslim invasions, as some others had done, but rather saw the fading of 'the language of the gods' as a long process that occurred over centuries.[36] He may well have disagreed with Forbes, who thought that the 'tall minaret of the Moslem' in Ahmedabad was a symbol of Islamic intolerance.[37] Moreover, Muslims are not the only immoral characters in *Lakshmi*, and Hindus of various backgrounds are said to be thievish, gluttonous, or criminal. Nevertheless, it is striking that sexual immorality in *Lakshmi* is ascribed so clearly to a Muslim couple. Islam is also an irruption in the temporal frame given to the village of *Lakshmi*. It disturbs the archaic nature of the community in so far as the village can be located not in the pre–Islamic period but only after the advent of Islam in western India. The presence of Islam in *Lakshmi* clarifies the boundaries around the imagined village community and places limits on the context in which the group can be situated.

The conception of the village in *Lakshmi* as a Hindu community radiates out from practically every page in the script. Beginning with the eponymous goddess and ending with the procession to the temple, the play's action is pervaded by references to Hinduism and Hindu culture. As Forbes noted, this was a Hinduism that could laugh at itself. The god Hanuman, who appears with the news of Rama's fury, is described by Dalpatram in terms that make him out to be an even more gluttonous, selfish, and scheming deity than Hermes in Aristophanes' play. The play might even have offended certain segments of society. Yet the sharpness of the satire should not obscure the essentially Hindu construction of the community, in its priests, temples, deities, rituals, and practices.

Dalpatram himself followed a particular kind of Hinduism, namely, that associated with the Swaminarayan group, which had distanced itself from certain Vedic dogmas. Dalpatram was attracted to the group at the age of fourteen when he met Swami Bhumanand, who was a disciple of the founder, and the aspiring poet gave his Vedic father such a shock that the latter became an ascetic and withdrew from society. According to the followers of Swaminarayan, 'Over the centuries, the cult of devotion [in the Vaishnava tradition] was taken to extremes of erotic emotionalism which weakened people's moral sense. The Swaminarayana teaching was a reform movement against this moral loosening, stressing good conduct and social morality as [the] necessary foundation of the practice of true devotion'.[38] Considered from this perspective, *Lakshmi* is not an encouragement to social or religious licence, despite the behaviour of its characters, but rather a working through of a moral vision of Hindu culture. In that sense, it is perhaps true to say that the socio-moralistic perspective precedes and shapes the literary exploration rather than the other way around. The self-presentation of his drama is very different from the self-presentation of those artistic creations — the films of Federico Fellini, for example — that suggest organic development, from one scene to the next, without a cohesive or stable teleology. With Dalpatram, the ethical or moral point is made emphatically, from the beginning, and the play trails in its wake.

The Context of Colonial Gujarat

Dalpatram was one of a group of intellectuals who helped contribute to the shaping of a regional Gujarati identity in the period.[39] For intellectuals such as Dalpatram, this regional or communal identity was linked, in turn, to the idea of the Indian nation, and the articulation of the Gujarati community occurred in the context of an emergent nationalism and worked through the language of nationalism. The precise forms assumed by this language were important, and will need to be considered again. But it should be noted that, for Dalpatram and others, these regional impulses were also connected to discourses of modernity, and the claim to group identity was also voiced as an aspiration for modernity (in relation to widow remarriage, for example, or female infanticide). As Partha Chatterjee puts it, the provincial intelligentsia 'constructed through a modern vernacular the new forms of public discourse, laid down new criteria of social respectability, set new aesthetic and moral standards of judgment, and, suffused with its spirit of nationalism, fashioned the new forms of political mobilization that were to have such a decisive impact on the political history of the province in the twentieth century'.[40]

Scholars such as Chatterjee have noted that these discourses of modernism arose in the colony and they have further noted, without denying agency to the colonized, that these discourses gained definition and consequence through an engagement with Western or European political thought and social philosophy. There is an apparent paradox about this movement in so far as modernism borrowed some of its content from the colonizers and, at roughly the same time, also contributed to anti-colonial movements. This paradox can be explained, at least in part, by the nature of colonial rule in India. The colonial rulers themselves instituted a liberal regime and a civil society within the contact zone but then placed limitations on the extent to which natives were able to participate in that society and enjoy its benefits. The frustrations of the natives were marked precisely by their unwillingness to accept the conditions and parameters of colonial society and by their corresponding attempt to forge an identity along lines different from those projected by the imperial power. However, it is important to state that not all reform movements were anti-colonial and that some were supportive of the colonial establishment. In the city of Ahmedabad, for example, many prominent Gujarati intellectuals who claimed to have an agenda for social reform also colluded with the British and supported colonial rule.

Contact with western European literature and ideas was more restricted in Ahmedabad than it was in such other cities as Bombay and Calcutta, and hence the forms of nationalism that developed elsewhere out of an engagement with European thought were more muted in Ahmedabad and more closely linked to a sense of a regional Gujarati identity. When the British took control of Ahmedabad in 1817, the city had lost some of its local prominence thanks to the promotion of other centres by the Mughals and Marathas, but it was still of economic importance. The British strategy for Ahmedabad was to encourage commerce and industry and not to foster the development of English-language universities and presses in the city, which remained without these institutions in the nineteenth century. The British gave financial incentives to the business classes, cut back on certain taxes, and attempted to regularize some practices.[41] The business and commercial élites of Ahmedabad were prepared to work with the new European power so long as it secured their own interests, and by the end of the nineteenth century they successfully turned the city into a major centre of the textile industry. 'Thus', as Svati Joshi says, 'in spite of its entry into the age of industrial technology, Ahmedabad in the nineteenth century remained socially, intellectually and politically, largely conservative as it responded to issues and events in a practical and pragmatic manner'. She adds, 'It was Dalpatram, more than anyone else, who was to provide the most powerful and influential literary articulation of this conservative pragmatic ideology'.[42]

Dalpatram often spoke approvingly of British rule; his literary compositions appealed for modernist reform and contributed to the fashioning of the community (Gujarat) and the nation (Hindustan). If regional literary themes, nationalist sentiment, and a modernizing zeal are evident in much of Dalpatram's poetry, it is nonetheless important to understand that he seldom targeted the British openly in his writings. There are passages in his poetry where he complains about conditions under British rule, but they are not very frequent. In July 1855, he linked his favourite themes of industry and reform with British rule in India, when he wrote the following in the journal *Buddhiprakash* ('Advent of the Intellect'), which he edited: 'The improvement of one's country means that, as in England, people are efficient in knowledge and industry and work together [...] With the advent of rule, so much reform has taken place. The daily improvement in knowledge and roads that we see is because of British rule.'[43] After the uprising of 1857 and the transfer of power to the crown from the East India Company, he remarked on the improved law and order situation: 'No one now dare hold even a she-goat by the ear against her will.'[44] That attitude is close to another in his poetry where he wrote that 'the British regime is so good that the evil-doers are punished and the rest are happy'.[45] In 1885, he was decorated by the government with an impressive-sounding title, Companion of the Order of the Indian Empire.[46]

In 1851, the year after he wrote *Lakshmi*, Dalpatram recited in Surat an allegorical and not quite coherent poem of 160 verses on the 'Invasion of Hindustan by the King of Industry' (*Hindustan upar Hunnarkhanni Chadhai*) in which India, or Hindustan, was conquered because of its deficiencies in machinery and technology.[47] While the poem can be read as a call for unity and for the modernizing of the nation, it both refers to the goddess of wealth and also notably leaves out of its critique a consideration of the economic and political conditions brought about by conquest and foreign rule. Instead, the poet appears to reproach Indians themselves for their numerous failings and asks them to convey Lakshmi to their land again. According to the poem, Hunnarkhan (*hunnar* = 'industry'), who rules an empire that is called Vilayat (which can mean variously 'foreign realm', 'England', or 'Europe') and that is as large as England and China, invades Hindustan. Hindustan was under the sway of Lakshmi, and had an abundance of *vanraaj* (raw cotton) as well as opium and *majith* (a fruit used to make dyes and medicines). But the country seems unable to repulse the foreign king Hunnarkhan. The reasons for the country's weakness, the poet says, are the lack of industry and the lack of unity; indeed, Unity, or Mandalik, is in deep slumber, and fails the nation. The country is impoverished by the invasion, and Lakshmi herself is taken away from the land by Hunnarkhan. When Hunnarkhan's minister, Yantrakhan (*yantra* = 'machine'), warns the king about the enemy's resources, Hunnarkhan replies that his forces are strong even against Lakshmi because he has at his disposal the tools of mechanized industry, including the printing press and other machines. He says, 'A thousand scribes of Lakshmi write together, our single press does the job.' Whereas the goddess only has four arms, Hunnarkhan's machines have that number several times over: 'If Lakshmi has four arms, we have twenty.'[48] The narrator calls on his readers to defeat the invading Yantrakhan, set aside their ignorance, superstition, and idleness, and use machinery and modern inventions for their own upliftment. The poem offers an intriguing vision of imperial aggression and internal indolence, but does not open the door to the suggestion that the imperial adversary may be responsible for the poor condition of the homeland. In fact, Yantrakhan tells Hunnarkhan that his main threat is the British, who have introduced machines, schools, and libraries to India, and who may arrest the king and hand him over to Indians.[49]

An important factor in analysing Dalpatram's poetry is the British involvement in the study of regional Indian literature, and especially Gujarati literature. In the middle of the nineteenth century, a few colonial administrators in western India encouraged the study of the Gujarati language and literature. Dalpatram was associated with the Gujarat Vernacular Society from an early date, and served as the assistant secretary from 1855 to 1879.[50] But the Society, which was established in Ahmedabad, in December 1848, was instituted largely by British officials, among whom were civil servants such as Forbes. In the early years of the Gujarat Vernacular Society, most of the members of the executive committee were British, and few natives served in an official capacity. It was only gradually that the number of Indians on the committee increased in the second half of the nineteenth century. The British role in facilitating the study and dissemination of Gujarati literature was acknowledged by Gujaratis themselves in later years when control of the Society ceded to natives. One member, Mahipatram Rupram Nilkanth, said in the 1880s, 'The Society [...] owes its birth to European friends (the late Hon'ble A. K. Forbes and others) of this country. It was nurtured and brought up by them and was afterwards handed over as it were to us (natives) for keeping it alive and making it grow [...] We must now show that we are fit to conduct its affairs. Let this be an instance of Self-Government.'[51] As the speaker's remarks indicate, the promotion of a regional Gujarati culture and Gujarati identity by the British could be accepted without qualification, but it could also be made to serve native demands for self-rule.

The association between Forbes, who lived a relatively short life from 1821 to 1864, and Dalpatram needs to be considered a little more closely. The title page of *Lakshmi* says that it was written by Dalpatram 'with the assistance of Mr A. K. Forbes' and 'printed by the Gujarat Vernacular Society'. Forbes met Dalpatram in 1848 when he was collecting Gujarati manuscripts and attempting to study the folk songs and chronicles of the region, and they were both also connected with the GVS from its founding. They read Gujarati poetry together for two hours a day, and it was thanks to his contact with Dalpatram that Forbes became exceptionally fluent in the language and deeply versed in the literature and history of the region.[52] Dalpatram himself won awards for his essays from the GVS, and one of the earliest prize-winners, which was about ghosts and spirits (*Bhoot Nibandh*), was translated into English by Forbes and published by the Society in 1850. This essay was then incorporated into the last chapters of Forbes's magnum opus on Gujarat, *Ras Mala* ('A Garland of Chronicles'), which appeared in two volumes in 1856. *Ras Mala*, which quickly gained renown as a study of Gujarati culture and history, was itself translated into Gujarati in 1869 by another scholar, Ranchodbhai Udayaram. H. G. Rawlinson, who introduced a new edition in 1924, invoked Thucydides and called the book 'a work for all time, a *ktēma eis aei*, which will always find an audience, "fit but few", among those who love the chivalry of mediaeval India'. It was Dalpatram who, by Forbes's own admission, helped the Scottish judge to cut across colonial and racial barriers and gain access to local traditions and folklore.[53]

While Dalpatram was giving Forbes assistance in his studies of Gujarat and Gujarati, Forbes was instrumental in advancing Dalpatram's career. In October 1850, Forbes wrote to the GVS and asked the managing committee to publish a collection of Gujarati proverbs edited by Dalpatram as well as *Lakshmi*. He said, 'I have the pleasure of forwarding to you the MSS of "Lakshmi" — a Guzerati comedy of Dalpatram Daya, being an adaptation of the Plutus of Aristophanes already accepted by you. [...] Both the Lakshmi and the Proverbs appear to me to be valuable works, & such as are likely to retain a position in the literature of the Province even should that literature be very far improved.'[54] Whether or not Forbes's judgement has been borne out by posterity, the GVS published both manuscripts, and Forbes continued to support his associate's work for the rest of his life. Forbes's own papers contain a translation into English of a scene from *Lakshmi* as well as a detailed summary of the comedy.[55]

Dalpatram's perspective on the relationship can be understood in light of the poetry he wrote about Forbes. When the association between Forbes and Dalpatram was cut short by Forbes' early death in 1864, Dalpatram published an elegy called 'Forbes Viraha', which U. M. Maniar described as 'probably the first "elegy" of the English type' in Gujarati poetry.[56] The highly stylized poem is imbued with the language of loss and separation (the word *viraha* means 'separation'), as if the narrator were parted from his beloved. He asks, 'Now who shall address me as "my dear"?' He is pained to visit the places that he had once frequented with Forbes and heartbroken by his letters. The narrator laments the passing of his companion and, in a suggestive moment of self-referentiality, writes of 'the mast of poetry broken down'.[57] In another telling passage that connects with a major concern of the poet, he observes that the poor are sad at the passing of Forbes because 'wealth' (*lakshmi*) has passed with him into heaven.[58] If the literary merits of the poem are widely accepted, the verses can nonetheless also be interpreted in the terms of the social reform movements in which Dalpatram was involved. Social reformers among the British and the Indians were attempting to regulate the traditions of ritual lament, especially as practised by women. In *Ras Mala*, Forbes himself had compared the lament of Gujarati women to the laments of Greek tragedy and had thereby demarcated them as alien and archaic.[59] By carrying out the work of mourning in an 'English' elegiac form, Dalpatram was both paying tribute to the memory of his lost friend and enacting an appropriately modern gesture of lament.

Forbes also intervened in the reception of *Lakshmi* in a manner that was helpful to its author. It is difficult today to find much information on the staging of the drama or the reaction to it, though historians of Gujarati theatre have referred to the play in passing. But *Lakshmi* caused some hubbub in the 1850s, and Forbes wrote the following in a letter to a British member of the GVS:

> We come now to Lakshmi which you tell me is considered to be too keen
> in its satire and too severe upon all sects of Hinduism except that of Swami
> Narayan to which the author belongs. I am not surprised at this nor do I
> see any great cause for regret in it. Many of the people in Ahmedabad were
> excessively alarmed at the appearance of Bhut Nibandh and if it had not been
> for Dalpatram's adroitness in telling them with so much apparent simplicity
> but real irony that all these things which their Bhaktas teach were no doubt
> very true formerly it is exceedingly possible that not an individual would have
> read his work.[60] Lakshmi is in fact what it professes to be an adaptation of
> Aristophanes' Plutus and as such it is hardly necessary that the adapter should
> excuse the keenness of its satire — In their own farces which are common at
> the present day no great respect is shown by the Guzeratis to any one & Shri
> Krishn himself is ridiculed in no measured terms — There is a specimen of this
> in Section LI. [?] of Bhut Nibandh —[61]

The reaction of Hindus to Dalpatram's play appears to have prompted a communication to Forbes, who expresses neither surprise nor regret at the purported anxiety among Hindus. Forbes implies that, just as Dalpatram was attempting to rid people of their old superstitions and fears in his earlier work, so the poet was satirizing conventional pieties in a manner no different from contemporary Gujarati drama. Forbes's contradictory point is that the Gujaratis of his own time were old-fashioned enough to be alarmed by Dalpatram's attempts to change their attitudes to ghosts and spirits and modern enough to handle satire about religion. But Forbes's letter can also be understood as a reading of the play since it is this very balance between two contrasting positions on modernity that Dalpatram explores in his 'adaptation' of Aristophanes' *Wealth*.

Forbes's letter should be interpreted in the light of the claim on the title-page of *Lakshmi* that he helped Dalpatram in the writing of the comedy. Dalpatram received no formal education beyond two years in a primary school, and he is reported not to have been able to speak in English, though his poetry is peppered with English words and phrases throughout.[62] His knowledge of the Aristophanic play came from Forbes, who studied from 1840 to 1843 at Haileybury, the training college for civil servants of the East India Company. I have considered elsewhere the study of Greek and Latin at Haileybury,[63] and for the moment let me note that the most influential versions of Aristophanes (though not of *Wealth* per se) in the England of Forbes's youth were written by Thomas Mitchell and John Hookham Frere, both of whom came from Tory backgrounds. In discussing the conservative biographies of Mitchell and Frere, Hall has remarked above on the anti-democratic tendencies of both writers. She quotes a telling remark made by Frere in a letter to his brother Temple in 1830 where he complains in relation to the Canadian colonies about 'that tendency to Democracy, which is said to be so lamentably prevalent in new settlements'.[64] (Sir Bartle Frere, who was the Governor of Bombay in the 1860s and the official 'Patron' of the Gujarat Vernacular Society at a time when Dalpatram and Forbes were both active members, was the nephew of John Frere, with whom he often corresponded on various subjects, including Aristophanes. He saw to the publication of his uncle's poems during this decade and also narrated the life of his relative in a lengthy 'Memoir', in which the letter quoted above appears.[65]) Given that these writers were, in Hall's words, 'dyed-in-the-wool reactionaries', it is scarcely surprising that Forbes, whose official job was to help administer the British Empire in India, took to Aristophanes and returned to the Greek playwright in nineteenth-century Gujarat. What is notable, however, is the transformation of the conservative Aristophanes in a colonial context.

Dalpatram's writings indicate that in his politics he was comfortable with the bourgeoisie of Ahmedabad as he was with the British officials of the GVS. Joshi observes that 'Dalpatram's literary politics [...] forms an integral part of the business ethic of the élite of Ahmedabad'.[66] She quotes a passage from *Buddhiprakash* of April 1868 in which the poet considers the power of writing:

> The power of writing a book is the best and most precious. Only a fortunate scholar receives this gift. And those who have got this gift have become immortal [...] Valmiki, Vyas and Shankar, Homer, Shakespeare and Milton [...] Kings have also written books and seem to be eager to include their names in the class [of writers ...] Bhartruhari, the kings of Udaipur, Julius Caesar, our Queen Victoria [...] Similarly, people of the upper classes at whose temple the goddess Lakshmi keeps her residence, have also considered the class of writers the best and shown eagerness to include their names in that class [...]

Dalpatram continues:

> Lakshmi is the material part of the body of this 'rising' country and Saraswati
> [goddess of the arts] the spiritual part. Without the spirit, Lakshmi is like a
> corpse [...] We also pray to god that the people of the upper classes and kings
> are capable of, if not being writers themselves, at least of judging writers; and
> let there be a confluence of Lakshmi and Saraswati and let its constant flow run
> through the country.[67]

Dalpatram is already writing here as if he were forging a literary programme
for Ahmedabad, and for Gujarat, in the second half of the nineteenth century.[68]
What is extraordinary about this programme is how it recasts the cultural location
of moneyed Ahmedabad as a potential breeding ground of the hybrid. Here are
Europeans as well as Indians, writers as well as kings, the old as well as the new.
The mixed nature of Dalpatram's prayer is, in turn, part of an attempt to stake
out a claim for the greatness of literature: even monarchs want to write books,
he says, even the kings of Udaipur as well as 'our' Queen Victoria. Nevertheless,
Dalpatram's mosaic of knowledge, class, and money also shows that for him literature
is inseparable from power and wealth. As with kings and queens, 'the people of the
upper classes at whose temple the goddess Lakshmi keeps her residence' deeply
value literature. Literature and the art of writing are worthwhile, according to
Dalpatram, precisely because they appeal so deeply to the rich and the powerful.
Literature thus functions within a worldly fabric out of which it cannot be torn.
Yet the country needs not just literature alone in order to function healthily, nor
even just wealth alone, but a confluence of both literature and wealth. Less an
affirmation of patronage, Dalpatram's statement is more an acknowledgment that
for him literature and knowledge circulate within certain social contexts, which,
in his case at least, are shaped by mercantile and political élites.

The passage from *Buddhiprakash* returns us to the status of European literature
for Dalpatram. Aristophanes occupies no special place for Dalpatram and does not
feature prominently in his writings, and in fact no other Greek or Latin work
appears in any substantial form in the Gujarati poet's oeuvre.[69] Since Dalpatram
had small English and less Greek, his knowledge of the Aristophanic comedy must
have depended on the collaboration with Forbes. To Dalpatram, Aristophanes and
the Greek poets were part of the European tradition, as his prologue also made
clear, and hence they belonged in the same line of writers as Homer, Shakespeare,
and Milton. The title-page proclaims that the play is based on an 'English' book.
It was in this Anglo-European tradition that he placed the comic playwright and,
despite the seeming barrier of language, it was with this tradition that he had a
lifelong relationship in his own poetic compositions. If, as a reformist intellectual in
bourgeois Ahmedabad, he was attracted to a story in which wealth and its societal
impact were central themes, and if, as an exponent of indigenous and popular verse
forms, he was moved to work out Aristophanes' logic in the environment of a
small, traditional Gujarati village, it was as an admirer of the culture of Europe, to
which, in his eyes, England clearly belonged, that Dalpatram was drawn to a story
composed in the far-off European past. Whether from Forbes or his own studies,
Dalpatram understood the singular authority given to the ancient Athenians by

modern Europeans. When he wrote in his prologue that the woman named Athens may have passed away, but that 'even today she gives life to the world in the form of knowledge', he was acknowledging the remarkable position occupied by ancient Greece in the European tradition.

Through the use of that figure, lastly, Dalpatram offered a model for the reception of the classical Greek past when he said that the Athens of antiquity breathed life-giving knowledge into the present. Dalpatram clearly thought of literary culture and the old verse forms as dynamic, fecund, and malleable, and indeed much of his work gains its colour and quality from the lively manner in which he combines the traditional and the modern. There is a vital homology between the Athens of the prologue and the Saraswati (as goddess of literature and the arts) of the passage in *Buddhiprakash* since they are both said to infuse a moment with spirit and vivacity. The two examples also explore life and death in the context of the artistic tradition: in the former case, Athens is a dead woman who has transmitted knowledge to the living present; in the latter, Saraswati represents a spirited, spiritual force, without whom Lakshmi would remain but a corpse. Literature was not an inert and bloodless thing, for Dalpatram, but a vigorous enterprise that was capable of lighting and nourishing the spark of life. The poet who, in an age of empire, courted the favour of *mahajans*, maharajas, and sahibs knew that Lakshmi served little purpose if she did not also help the cause of a literature that both enlivened and enriched the individual.[70]

Notes to Chapter 7

1. The quotation comes from Shastri and Lal (1974), 68, and closely follows Maniar (1969), 37.
2. Shastri and Lal (1974), 69.
3. The complete works of Dalpatram (*Dalpat Granthavali*) were published in five volumes by the Gujarat Sahitya Academi, in Gandhinagar, from 1999 to 2001. References to Dalpatram's work in verse (*Dalpat-kavya*) and in prose (*Dalpat-gadya*) are to this edition, unless otherwise stated. For the text of *Lakshmi*, see *Dalpat-gadya* part 1, 1–40 (Dalpatram (1999b)). I am grateful to Harshad Shah for his help with the English translation of Dalpatram's play. In accordance with the publishers' guidelines for this volume, I have quoted from Aristophanes and Dalpatram in translation and not provided texts in Greek or Gujarati. The resulting metaliterary and metalinguistic displacements are worth considering further, but can only be alluded to here.
4. Hall, above, p. 66. See *Dalpat-gadya* part 1, p. 40: Dalpatram (1999b).
5. The key word is *sudharo*; see also Mukta (1999), 33.
6. Dover (1972), 4. The Paleologan dynasty ruled in Byzantium from 1261 to 1453.
7. See L. E. Lord (1925), 104, 107–13; Sommerstein (2001), 34–35; Halliwell (1998), pp. lx, 201. For the early English productions of Aristophanes' *Wealth*, see Lever (1946) and B. R. Smith (1988), 168–77. *Wealth* may also have been the first play of Aristophanes to be translated into French; see Delcourt (1934). For the manuscript tradition of Aristophanes' *Wealth*, see Di Blasi (1997a) and (1997b); for the manuscript tradition in general, see e.g. White (1906a) and (1906b). The bibliography in Austin and Olson (2004), pp. xcix–civ, relates to the texts and editions of Aristophanes' *Thesmophoriazusae*, but also contains many items that are relevant to the texts and editions of Aristophanes' plays in general, from 1516 to the early twenty-first century.
8. Cookesley (1834), p. iii. For the German reception of Aristophanes in the 19th century, see Holtermann (2004).
9. Gerard (1847), p. iii.
10. Carrington (1825), p. iii.

11. L. E. Lord (1925), 155.

12. Halliwell (1998), 210.

13. *The Encyclopaedia Britannica*, 11th edn. (Cambridge), ii. 500.

14. For both these works, see Hall, above, pp. 74–76.

15. L. E. Lord (1925), 110.

16. McGlew (1997), 36–37.

17. Konstan and Dillon (1981), 371.

18. For Indian plays that resisted imperial authority in British India, see Solomon (1994) and Bhatia (2004).

19. One obvious difference, namely, the gender of the eponymous wealth-giver, turns on the divergence of religious traditions. It is nonetheless significant that in Dalpatram's play, Lakshmi is female and the Poverty figure is male, whereas in Aristophanes, Plutus is male and Poverty is female.

20. Dalpatram (1999*b*), 2.

21. Ibid.

22. Ibid. 3

23. See Raval (1987), esp. 123–27.

24. For the jokes about caste and female infanticide, see Dalpatram (1999*b*), 8, and for priests ibid. 24.

25. Translations of Aristophanes' *Wealth* are based on the Loeb edition of Jeffrey Henderson (2002).

26. Dalpatram (1999*b*), 30.

27. Jhaveri (2003), 197.

28. See Dalpatram (1999*b*), 39–40. These are the opening verses of the song that concludes *Lakshmi*. The song continues: 'How will it go without Uncle? | Uncle Dajibhai is there | In the procession of Lakshmi. || How will it go without Aunt? | Aunt Fatmabai is there | In the procession of Lakshmi. || How will it go without the priest? | The priest Shashtribawa is there | In the procession of Lakshmi. ||| How will it go without the lawyer? | The lawyer Bhaichandbhai is there | In the procession of Lakshmi. || How will it go without the informer? | The informer Desaibhai is there | In the procession of Lakshmi. || How will it go without the family-deity? | The family-deity Hanuman is there | In the procession of Lakshmi. || How will it go without the scavenger? | The scavenger Wretch is there | In the procession of Lakshmi.'

29. Maniar (1969), 38.

30. Jhaveri (1924), 181; see also Sheth (1979), 57–58.

31. Dalpatram (1999*b*), 38: Gosai refers to Dhirsinh as the 'high-fornicator'.

32. Ibid. 9.

33. *Wealth* 1013–16; *Lakshmi*, scene 6. The use of Hindi rather than Gujarati by Fatma, Juvankhan, Dolatkhan, and Gosai can be compared to the use of non-Attic dialects by characters in Aristophanes' plays, although, of course, Hindi and Gujarati are distinct languages and not just dialects of one language.

34. *Lakshmi*, scene 4.

35. Isaka (2002).

36. For the poem, first published in *Buddhiprakash* (1857), see Dalpatram (2000), 149–231. The following extract is also quoted in Pollock (2001), 394: 'All the feasts and great donations | King Bhoja gave the Brahmans | were obsequies he made on finding | the language of the gods had died. | Seated in state Bajirao performed | its after-death rite with great pomp. | And today, the best of kings across the land | observe its yearly memorial.'

37. Forbes (1856), i. 387–88.

38. Jhaveri (2003), 190.

39. See Isaka (1999); cf. Yashaschandra (1995).

40. Chatterjee (1993), 35–36.

41. Gillion (1968); for Surat, cf. Haynes (1991).

42. Joshi (2004), 331.

43. *Buddhiprakash*, July 1855.

44. From Dalpatram (2000), and quoted in Maniar (1969), 5.

45. 'Rajyaprashansa', Dalpatram (2000), 3.

46. N. K. Singh (2000), 277.

47. For a text of the poem, see Dalpatram (2000), 48–60.

48. Dalpatram (2000), 53, vv. 43, 46.

49. Dalpatram (2000), 55, v. 84.

50. For a history of the Society, see Parekh (1935) and Raval (1987), ch. 4.

51. *Annual Report of the Gujarat Vernacular Society* (1883), 9; also quoted in Isaka (1999), 102; and cf. *Annual Report of the Gujarat Vernacular Society* (1884), 11.

52. See A. K. Nairne's memoir in Forbes (1878), vol. 1, xvii.

53. H. G. Rawlinson, in Forbes (1924), vol. 1, xvi. See Sherry Chand and Kothari (2003) for an exploration of the mode of history implicit in Forbes' *Ras Mala*.

54. India Office Records, British Library: European Manuscripts, Mss. Eur. D 481(b), 230–31.

55. Ibid. 218–26.

56. Maniar (1969), 43. For the poem, see Dalpatram (2000), 231–55.

57. Ibid. 232, v. 1.

58. Ibid. 233, v. 4.

59. Forbes (1878), 635–36. See Mukta (1999).

60. A sentence has been struck out here, and is only partly legible: 'In the case of Lakshmi [...] of the author that the satire is too pungent for present digestion'. In the margin, there appears the following comment (which contains an unattributed quotation from Isaiah 46: 1): 'The sensitiveness thus exhibited is perhaps only a proof that "Bel boweth down, Nebo stoopeth"'.

61. India Office Records, British Library: European Manuscripts, Mss. Eur. D 481(b), 219–20.

62. Jhaveri (2003), 191.

63. See Vasunia (2005).

64. Frere (1874), i. 216; quoted in Hall, above, p. 79.

65. See the letters in Festing (1899); the poems are in Frere (1867); the 'Memoir' takes up all vol. i of Frere (1874); and see the *Report of the Vernacular Society of Gujarat, For the Year 1860 to 1864* (Bombay, 1865). Bartle Frere attended Haileybury in 1832 and 1833, a few years before Forbes; he appears to have had the latter ('though a good man in his way') replaced as Resident in Kathiawar in the 1860s; see Martineau (1895), i. 447–48. On Bartle Frere, see in general Martineau (1895) and Ranade (1990).

66. Joshi (2004), 342.

67. Quoted ibid. 342–43; translation modified.

68. This attitude is consistent with the self-reflexive passages in *Lakshmi*, such as the enigmatic concluding stanza that is written in the traditional *savaiya* metre: 'The human mind is a play-actor. It dances in the body day and night; sometimes, it dresses as a king and acts as a guardian of the country; sometimes, it acts as a poor man holding a beggar-bowl, and sometimes as an old person, a young person, or a child. The pandits see the human body as a delightful play-house', Dalpatram (1999*b*), 40.

69. The engagement of Gujarati poets with the classical European tradition is briefly discussed in Tripathi (1958) and with the English tradition in Maniar (1969).

70. I should like to thank Edith Hall for suggesting this topic and for her help with the essay. A preliminary version of the paper was presented to the Department of Classics at the University of Pennsylvania. I am grateful to Sheila (Bridget) Murnaghan for the invitation and for her hospitality, and to the audience in general for criticism and comments given on the occasion. My deep thanks as well to Barbara Goff and Miriam Leonard for their advice and suggestions.

PART III

❖

Revival to Repertoire

CHAPTER 8

❖

Aristophanes Revitalized!
Music and Spectacle on the
Academic Stage

Amanda Wrigley

The Performance Context

In the modern history of staging Greek plays, Oxford is less famous for its strong tradition of staging Aristophanic comedy than for the 1880 *Agamemnon* which had been staged as a local attempt to prove that undergraduates, who had long been suffering under a ban against acting by the authorities, could be 'perfectly serious and artistic in getting up theatricals'.[1] In order to appreciate the significance to cultural history of the subsequent revivals of Aristophanes at the University, which began with *Frogs* in 1892, it is essential to put them into their immediate performance context. Although the ban against undergraduate acting in 1869 was in spirit only a renewed enforcement of the 1737 Licensing Act, which forbade dramatic performance at the University and within five miles of the city,[2] the immediate reason for it was the link made very publicly between the lively and irreverent transvestite classical burlesques which had been all the rage in Oxford in the second half of the 1860s,[3] and the trial of key figures in London's cross-dressing and homosexual *demi monde* for various 'felonies' at the close of that decade.[4] Towards the end of 1870s student groups such as the Philothespians began testing the water with small, private productions of comic and burlesque drama,[5] but it was when the undergraduate (and later famous actor-manager) Frank Benson approached Benjamin Jowett, classical scholar and Master of Balliol, with a view to performing *Agamemnon* in the hall of the College, that the recent experimental undergraduate theatricals were taken to a new and public level.

The impact of the 1880 *Agamemnon* was not merely local: the wave of productions of Greek tragedy and myth (whether in the original language or in English translation) stimulated by it enabled the late-Victorian theatre-going public to witness life being breathed into ancient Greek texts — almost as if the performances were Frederick Leighton paintings come to life, or dramatized versions of *tableaux vivants*. As Macintosh discusses, factors both within and beyond academia contributed to the craze for staging Greek tragedies at this time, but significant indeed was the way in which archaeological discoveries in the ancient lands of the Mediterranean — on display in the British Museum and reproduced pictorially in the national press — stimulated the Victorian 'viewing culture' into embodying antiquity and ancient dramatic characters on their stages.[6]

Whereas the fashion for beautiful and solemn stagings of tragedies seems to have brought the *idea* of Greece alive in the late-Victorian imagination, via the embodiment of ancient dramatic characters on stage in a way which was akin to the static visual art forms, the tremendously successful production of *Frogs* in Oxford in 1892 marked a significant step in the realization that Greek *comedy* could be 'revitalized' in its own way too, via the long-established British tradition of comic and musical drama (especially burlesque) which had been so popular locally in the commercial Victoria Theatre at Oxford and in private undergraduate performances. One local reviewer of this production even concluded that Aristophanic comedy was better suited to modern audiences than Greek tragedy:

> To those who could lay aside all thoughts of archaeology it was even valuable towards the understanding of Aristophanic humour, which burst through again and again, even where overlaid with local and temporal conceptions. As compared with the two latest revivals at Oxford and Cambridge — the *Alcestis* and the *Ion...* — it suggested that Greek tragedy, unless the very greatest, is not so well adapted to the appreciation of the modern audience as the comedy of Aristophanes.[7]

This opinion, echoing sentiments aired a decade earlier in response to a production of *Birds* in Cambridge,[8] perhaps contributes to the sense that 'Social Philhellensim' of the sort that had been fashionably playing out on (especially) London stages for some years now was for some at least experienced as not a particularly vibrant phenomenon. It even came to be ridiculed as being somewhat pretentious: as Hall and Macintosh conclude with regard to the decline in interest in staging classical burlesque on the popular stage, 'Watching popular entertainers dressed up as ancient Greeks perhaps seemed less hilarious than watching progressive members of the educated classes doing so in all seriousness.'[9] 'Aesthetic Hellenism' too came under fire at this time: as represented by male poets of this generation it received perhaps its most aggressive attack in the play *Aristophanes in Oxford: O.W.* Produced anonymously for Oxford's Eights Week in 1894, it included a scene which — drawing on *Frogs* — took Oscar Wilde, perhaps the most flamboyant Aesthetic Hellenist of them all, down to Hades in his 'fairy skiff' and left him there to his fate (see further Hall, above, p. 81).

Frogs Translated and Interpreted

It is striking that the widely influential 1880 *Agamemnon* was not followed by a sustained interest in staging Greek tragedy within Oxford itself: only in 1887 did OUDS resolve to tackle a Greek play, and the appeal of Euripides' *Alcestis* at that point may have been the scope for humour offered by its 'pro-satyric' elements. By 1892, one senses that if the students felt that the time was right for a Greek play, then it might as well be funny.[10] Thus did they hit upon the idea of staging

Greek comedy in Oxford for the first time, and such a successful departure was the production of Aristophanes' *Frogs* in 1892 that OUDS would not turn to tragedy for their Greek play for some decades.[11] For a startlingly imaginative interpretation of the comic potential of the text through, on the one hand, the musical score and, on the other, the 'stage business' offered the audience a dramatic experience that was not only more complex than tragedy but also vividly different, drawing on a long tradition of comic drama on the British stage, and in many particulars echoing the five decades of cultural familiarity with the conventions of classical burlesque, including burlesque of Greek tragedy. The music written by the composer and music historian C. Hubert H. Parry (1848–1918), an allusive feast which drew on classical and modern Italian opera, Beethoven's symphonies, English airs, popular waltzes and music hall, offered the audience a clear and recognizable non-verbal 'language' for an understanding of the play. Similarly, 'stage business' — which might be described as acting 'between the lines' of the Greek text, with facial expression, gesture, movement, and the physical interaction between actors, stage properties and set — provided a vigorous visual 'drama' which provided yet another level of interpretation of the Greek text. More so than with tragedy was 'stage business' an active tool of communication owing to the greater freedom (and necessity) within comedy for its exploitation: see fig. 8.1 for contemporary sketches which give us some indication of the nature of the activity on stage for several key scenes. The lively music and 'stage business' added up to quite an unusual experience for the Greek play-going audience. Although one or two critics were hesitant about the introduction of a degree of topicality into both the comic content (e.g. recognizable musical motifs) and the style of delivery of the play (with its obvious debt to classical burlesque and comic opera), the majority agreed that it was a brilliant step in the full interpretation of the Aristophanic text for a modern audience.

The lively and well-received score which Parry had written for the 1883 production of *Birds* in Cambridge was doubtless the prime recommendation of the composer for the first Greek comedy in Oxford.[12] A great measure of the success of the 1883 production was attributed to the score, with one critic noting that 'the composer is an interpreter of the first importance for a considerable part of a not-too-Greek audience.'[13] The Cambridge *Birds* had been envisaged and produced on a grand scale, and the production demonstrated the central importance not only of music but also of the visual aspects for the successful staging of Greek comedy. The most arresting aspect of the production was the birds' beautifully executed costumes (illustrated in fig. 1.6, above, p. 19): canvas wings, painted with the actual markings and attached to the *chitōn*, could be extended at will; and elaborate head-dresses with beaks protruding from foreheads were fashioned from bird-plumage.[14] Although 'stage business' was clearly recognized as an important conduit for the communication of the humour, with 'amusing by-play' and 'laughable stage business' mentioned in reviews,[15] at this early stage in the 'revitalization' of Aristophanes in Britain such accounts indicate that the 'business' was less robust than it would be in *Frogs* a decade later.

The 1892 *Frogs* and the later OUDS productions of Aristophanes (*Knights*, 1897; *Clouds*, 1905; *Frogs*, 1909; *Acharnians*, 1914), together with the earlier experiments

FIG. 8.1. Scenes from the 1892 *Frogs* at Oxford

on which they built — at Cambridge (*Birds*, 1883), Blackheath (*Acharnians*, 1883, discussed by Hall, above, pp. 18–19), and Pennsylvania (*Acharnians*, 1886) — were of more consequence than amateur theatricals in élite academic environments might normally be expected to be because they made an important contribution to the widespread cultural realization that Aristophanes performed in ancient Greek could be hugely funny and enjoyable.[16] At this time Greek plays on 'Oxbridge' stages were social and cultural events of some cachet, and the national (and sometimes international) press was attentive in reviewing them. The particular success of *Frogs* in 1892 was reported widely and in great detail, and remained in mind as a benchmark for the successful staging of Greek comedy for some years.[17] That the 1892 *Frogs* seems to have been put on when the time was ripe — within Oxford and perhaps even beyond — for new direction and fresh vigour in the staging of Greek plays as they were being staged in tragic revivals seems to be supported by the plethora of Aristophanic productions which are observed to follow closely on its heels.[18]

This was also the moment when English-language productions of Aristophanic plays in the academic sphere pick up the early, if sporadic, experiments in staging Aristophanes in other European modern languages, notably French, German, Italian, Polish and modern Greek.[19] Women are noticeably absent from the casts of Aristophanic productions in ancient Greek in Oxford and Cambridge, but they are particularly visible in the trend to stage the comedies in English translation, especially on academic stages, from the beginning of the twentieth century: for example, see Hall (above, p. 86) on the productions of *The Bees* (a loose adaptation of *Birds*) by the women of Girton College, Cambridge in February 1904; and *Frogs* in Gilbert Murray's translation performed by the women of Somerville College, Oxford, in 1911. Furthermore, it is important to note that — just as the 1904 adaptation of *Birds* by the women of Girton is very likely to have been inspired by the second production of that play as the Cambridge Greek Play, in ancient Greek, less than three months earlier — the Somerville women no doubt took their inspiration from the most recent OUDS Greek Play, which was *Frogs* staged (for the second time) in 1909. But the greatest spur to women in academia may well have been the appearance of Gertrude Kingston as an English-speaking Lysistrata on the London stage (see Hall, above, pp. 86–88). The very fact that women were beginning to appropriate Aristophanes for themselves by building a new tradition for staging his plays in adaptation and translation — in the very Universities where their more fortunate male contemporaries were staging him in the original language — in itself suggests a degree of socio-political engagement which simply does not arise in the early examples of the all-male, academic productions in ancient Greek. At Oxford, women students were by this time an important and visible presence, but they were far from being able to enjoy full equality with their male peers, allowed to study, but not to take degrees and graduate.[20] Nor could they as students act for OUDS (despite the injunction against male undergraduates taking the female roles), a fact which clearly stimulated these productions in their own all-female colleges where they had the freedom to chose to act the plays in translation, in spite of the fact that some of them at least would have been familiar with ancient Greek.

FIG. 8.2. Caricature of John Ruskin and John William Burgon (1867)

Knowledge of Greek language and literature had been central to the Oxford curriculum for several centuries: close familiarity with the literary remains of ancient Greek culture was an obligatory requirement for, and marker of, membership of this élite academic environment, but it was also used playfully and irreverently as a reference point for contemporary discourse of matters local and national. Most of the locally printed and much circulated caricatures which offered a satirical commentary on University life in the second half of the ninettenth century, for example, make some verbal or pictorial reference to classical literature or history: see fig. 8.2, which uses the poets' contest in *Frogs* as visual comment on the debate surrounding the next incumbent of the Professorship of Poetry. Fig. 8.3 is the illustration used on the front of the Oxford weekly magazine (1883–1973) which, in portraying students in 'classical dress' and describing their extra-curricular activities in terms of two of the three branches of Greek education, strongly implies that an equivalence is intended between the lives of Oxford undergraduates and the young men of ancient Greece. Examples abound of academic Oxford positing itself, and being understood as, the 'English Athens' — in other words, the cultural capital of the nation, and even, by extension, the British empire.[21] Such total immersion in the cultural, literary and linguistic remains of ancient Greece which gave rise to use of classical language and literary reference in humorous and satirical contexts, combined with the local undergraduate taste for musical, comic, and burlesque drama, presented a particularly fertile cultural context for the appreciation of the musical, visual, and topical comic feast that was Aristophanes' *Frogs* in 1892.

> *Undergraduates in the Dress Circle.* Increases one's respect for one's Tutor, doesn't it, to see him wedged in the Pit and reading the English side of the crib?
>   There's a Reader and a Professor doing the same, not to mention an ex-President of the OUBC! I suppose they have to construe the English!
>   'At *The Frogs*', *The Oxford Magazine*, 2 March 1892, p. 217.

The 'crib' referred to in this quotation is the acting edition of the Greek text which had been substantially cut for performance and published alongside an English version in the style of a facing-page translation. Line numbers were not printed, probably to draw attention away from the fact that much of the Aristophanic play was missing.[22] Direct sexual references had been entirely excised: for example, lines 56–59 where Heracles quizzes Dionysus on the object of his desire ('For a woman? ... Or a boy? ... Was it for a man? ... Did you get it on with Cleisthenes?').[23] The cruder scenes also disappeared (for example, 479–90 where Dionysus defecates through fear and then cleans himself up; also the stock examples of broad humour in 6–11, in addition to the scenes involving the female characters of Maid and Innkeeper (503–604), 'in order to relieve the OUDS from the necessity of filling those parts'.[24] The most severe cut, however, was of more than two hundred and fifty lines from the poets' contest in order, it seems, to maintain the comic pace of the drama for the audience.

The English version, which was printed facing the Greek text, is substantially that of John Hookham Frere, whose popular translation had been widely accessible in print since 1839,[25] with the choruses freshly translated to fit Parry's music by David George Hogarth and Alfred Denis Godley who were both fellows and tutors at Magdalen College, the former in archaeology and the latter (who was also well known for his light verse) in classics. This facing-page translation was written in verse, like burlesque, and at points Hogarth and Godley amended or even retranslated Frere's lines in order, it seems, to make it read more like burlesque: they italicize Frere's words '*abroad*' and '*aboard*' to bring out the humour of the rhyme, for example; and retranslate lines 221–22 to make Dionysus, who is at his oar, punningly declare that 'Every part of me is rawing' (which might more literally be rendered as 'My bottom's getting sore!').[26] The book was on sale in Oxford in advance of the performance for two shillings, and a review of it in *The Oxford Magazine* expects that it 'ought to keep any audience *au courant* of all the scenes'. The reviewer goes on to declare that if the production is a success it 'will be due, in no small degree, and in more ways than one, to the editors of this *libretto*'.[27] The reviewer in *Black & White* estimates that the Aristophanic text, 'to at least half [of

Fig. 8.3. Header for *The Oxford Magazine*, 1892

the audience], must have been well-nigh unintelligible'; and *The Academy* confirms that 'many who were unacquainted with Greek' were indeed present.[28] Indeed, with regard to the ability of the audience to understand ancient Greek spoken aloud, it is notable that when OUDS produced *Frogs* again, in 1909, the following 'Paean' was printed in *Varsity*:

> This year 'tis not to be! William [Shakespeare], go to!
> Not ours the fragrant parlance of this land!
> This year all must applaud the jokes they do
> Not understand! [...]
> All those who e'er the Classic Drama woo'd
> Will surely speed to Oxford from afar
> And leave delighted, having understood
> καὶ, ὀυ [*sic*] and γὰρ.[29]

The excerpt from *The Oxford Magazine*'s skit on the audience response to the 1892 production (excerpted above), which portrays even scholarly reliance on the right-hand, English side of the crib, suggests that libretti in hand were likely to have been far from an uncommon sight amongst the audience. It may not, therefore, be too outlandish to say that this was — in a sense — an English-language performance of the play, translated into English on the page before the audience member's eyes (much as audiences might today rely on surtitles at the opera or at recent Oxford Greek Plays). The colloquial and lively English version was, then, as crucially important to the success of *Frogs* as the 'translation' of Aristophanic humour via music and stage business, which will be the subject of the next section.

Music and Stage Business

> *A Voice on the Stair.* Well, I never thought there was anything so good in Greek.
> Why, it might almost have been Gilbert and Sullivan!
>
> 'At *The Frogs*', *The Oxford Magazine*, 2 March 1892, p. 217.

The cover of the theatre programme for the 1892 *Frogs* is notable for its beautiful, stylized illustration of Charon in his boat surrounded by lapping waves and jumping frogs which artistically leap out of the frame to serve as decoration in the border (see fig. 8.4; and fig. 8.5, below, for the illustration on the reverse of the programme). The artist was Charles Wellington Furse (1868–1904), one of the leading portraitists of the day and brother of the stage manager Michael Bolton Furse, who also played Heracles. The illustration refers to the early scene of the play which was absolutely key in setting the mood for the reception of the production by the Oxford audience. Rowing was the sport with more undergraduate participation than any other in Oxford, and in the nineteenth century most undergraduates would have rowed at some point in their student career.[30] Moreover, the production coincided with Torpids, the intra-University rowing races. The scene between Charon and Dionysus was therefore naturally played in the manner of a rowing coach and a new undergraduate out 'tubbing' (practising rowing) on the river. Such was the local and topical interpretation of the scene that *The Athenaeum* doubted that it 'would have been understood at Athens, since it depended for its immense success with the audience upon their personal knowledge of the ways of rowing men on the Isis and the Cam',[31] and its resonance amongst the Oxford audience supported a comical article in *The Oxford Magazine* which portrays Charon as a friend of an undergraduate who, on watching Torpids, remarks 'if they want to win they'll have to row like H — '.[32]

The playing of this scene was found to be incredibly effective and funny, and it was clearly one of the most memorable parts of the entire production: 'the enthusiasm [...] was uproariously sympathetic'.[33] All reviews single out this scene for particular mention, but none goes into detail about how it was actually staged; just as frustratingly, the extant photograph of the set for this scene lacks actors (fig. 8.6). We must presume that there was some fine comic acting for the audience to respond with the 'enthusiastic uproar' that was reported,[34] and — at the risk of stating the obvious — it is worth noting that the tone and volume of vocal delivery, facial expression, gesture, and vigorous movement (of actors, and — we might imagine — the boat) in this scene would have been very far removed from what the audience had experienced in the rather solemn and serious renderings of Greek tragedy on the contemporary stage, and exactly what they had become familiar with in the fifty-year tradition of classical burlesque. The music at this point was considered by some to be one of the best parts of the score, when the frogs with their 'irritating refrain' comment contemptuously on the lesson on rowing taking place in from of them.[35] A special article reviewing Parry's music in *The Times* tells us that the frogs' utterances at this point are 'absurdly associated with the theme of "Le parlate d'amor" from [Gounod's] *Faust*'.[36] Even the published translation

FIG. 8.4. Programme cover for the 1892 *Frogs*

FIG. 8.5. Design on reverse of programme for the 1892 *Frogs*

received praise in this scene for improving on Frere by rendering *antibas* (202) by the 'proper technical equivalent' of 'off your stretcher!', and for the burlesque pun on the word 'rawing'.[37]

Although *The Times* found 'continual amusement' in the vacillation between the effeminate portrayal of Dionysus on the one hand and the 'Herculean' Dionysus on the other,[38] a local reviewer in *The Oxford Magazine* was unhappy with the 'slim and girlish' portrayal of the god, with his 'mincing airs and gait', 'trotting across the stage on tiptoe'. He also considered it quite wrong for him to be wearing the *chitōn*, 'that severely beautiful garment', and 'a little unecessary' for Herakles to grab hold of said garment as he uttered the word *gynaikōn* ('of women', 157) in his description of the Eleusinian Mysteries.[39] The 'grossly effeminate' Dionysus also offended the reviewer of *Black & White*, who considered that the actor had taken 'Mr Dan Leno — of the Drury Lane Pantomime — as his model, and needless to say he fell far short of his original'; with similar dissatisfaction the *Temple Bar* review likened Dionysus to an 'elderly shrew with the finical airs which one associates with the Widow Twankay of provincial pantomimes'.[40] It is clear, therefore, that the portrayal of Dionysus strongly suggested the transvestite acting tradition of the comic, and perhaps especially the burlesque, stage. The import of such a stock comic performance into a Greek play did not cause anxiety for everyone, and indeed the negative criticism in *The Oxford Magazine* drew two protesting Letters to the Editor in the next issue. One wrote to say that the actor's 'mincing airs and gait' had actually been 'highly amusing'; and Hogarth (the archaeology scholar who had worked on the script and translation) himself wrote to defend at length the portrayal of Dionysus as 'something between Postlethwaite and a fussy old maid' on the basis of Herakles' use of the word *krokōtos* to describe the god's attire (a saffron-coloured robe worn by female mortals and Dionysus and his followers, 46).[41]

Reviewers also use the word 'effeminate' of the portrayal of Euripides, who was clearly 'acted' as a poet in the recognizable 'Aesthetic' mould.[42] The poets' contest is said to have pitted the 'refined, effeminate latter-day Euripides' (clothed in pinks and greens) against the 'antique, massive, virile Æschylus' (in greys and browns).[43] *The Academy* too notes the contrast between the 'rugged vigour of Aeschylus and the mincing refinement of Euripides'; Euripides is described as a 'lily-loving æsthete' in *Temple Bar*; and *The Athenaeum* comments that 'the whole bearing of Euripides [...] revived the fading memory of Bunthorne', the Aesthetic poet character satirized in Gilbert and Sullivan's comic opera *Patience, or Bunthorne's Bride*.[44] The critics generally agreed that no fault was to be found in the actor's performance here; but the poets' contest left many unhappy. The prevailing idea in the reviews is that it had been a mistake to act Aeschylus as a 'gentleman', since this placed the burden entirely on the actor playing Euripides to bring out the contrast between them.[45] Such discussion in the press indicates that a coherent way of representing the poetic contest was as problematic in 1892 as it has been found to be since (see Gamel, below, pp. 213–14, on the replacement of the two ancient poets with Shakespeare and Shaw). Parry's music, however, is roundly considered to have saved the day here, glossing over any sense of deficiency in character acting with its clever use of recognizable motifs to carry the comic sense and humour: for example, Euripides borrows from Gluck's *Orfeo* to poke fun at the choral songs of Aeschylus; and Aeschylus takes off Euripides to the accompaniment of flute and castanets, and mixes a popular music-hall melody with Verdi's 'La Donna è mobile' and pieces from the See-Saw Waltz.

As Hall discusses above (p. 84), the dramatist W. S. Gilbert — whose most famous works are the comic operas to Sullivan's scores — has sometimes been seen as the English Aristophanes. Somewhat conversely, this 1892 staging of Aristophanes was said by several reviewers to borrow from Gilbert and Sullivan's comic operas — a view which further reinforces the link in the Victorian frame of cultural reference between these two types of comic theatre. For example, 'The dances of the Chorus at Oxford', one review declared, 'would hardly have been what they were [...] but for various operas by Gilbert and Sullivan'.[46] Parry even pays Sullivan a direct compliment by incorporating a musical phrase from *Ivanhoe* at the point when the chorus speak of the man (Aeschylus) who has written more very beautiful tunes for singing than anyone else to date (1254–56 in Sommerstein's 1996 revision).[47] The chorus in the later OUDS production of *Knights* in 1897 was considered to be even more in the comic opera style: 'So far from circling round a Dionysiac altar, they made their first entrance from all sides of the stage, and on hobby-horses, and their evolutions throughout were conducted with a view to ludicrous effect. The acting was treated in the same spirit.'[48]

The same critic concludes, without satisfaction, that *Frogs* had been 'merely a veiled way of producing a modern burlesque under the cloak of the Greek author'.[49]

The reviewer in *Temple Bar* goes further: 'If the members of the OUDS want to show their powers in burlesque, why experiment on the unfortunate Aristophanes? They could find greater opportunities, and a more obvious theme, in some selection from the Gaiety *répertoire*.'[50] The importance of music and of 'stage business' in creating the humour in *Frogs* (and later productions of Aristophanes at Oxford) stimulated many more reviewers to apply the phrase 'modern burlesque' to this presentation. Unlike traditional classical burlesque with which the theatre-going public had become familiar over several decades, these Aristophanic productions sought not to deflate or poke fun at some other genre or type of person, but, rather, they resembled burlesque in the comic use of the musical score and visual spectacle (including dancing, gesture, facial expression, and other use of the body, scenery and costume, and imaginative 'stunts') as essential parts of the creation of the humour.[51] Aristophanes was, in this way, a vehicle for a similar sort of comic experience that the audience had for some time enjoyed in the contemporary theatre. Indeed, *Black & White* declared Aristophanes 'the first great master of burlesque',[52] and *The Athenaeum* considered that it was 'not impossible that this success may cause intending writers of burlesque to revert to Aristophanic devices'.[53]

Leaving aside the portrayal of Dionysus, one aspect of burlesque staging which was notably absent from the 1892 *Frogs* was transvestite acting: the maid and the innkeeper scenes were (as noted above) excised from the text to remove the necessity of filling those parts. Indeed the largely male casts of many Aristophanic comedies was probably a contributory factor in the choice of Aristophanes for OUDS's Greek plays henceforth.[54] The necessity of giving the plays in ancient Greek meant that opportunities for linguistic jokes, especially puns — so readily seized upon by English-language burlesque writers — were largely absent on stage (although not, as has been shown above, from the English-language 'libretto'). One outside-the-drama example of this — to which the audience reacted with hilarity — occurred after the final performance of *Frogs*: a bunch of carrots was thrown to Dionysus for the 'donkey' standing by his side, and he thanked them with the (similar-sounding) Greek word *charites*.[55] This, the very last time that the 1892 *Frogs* brought the house down, rather sums up the spirit of classical burlesque which infused the whole production and made it so readily and completely enjoyable for the audience.

> A performance more closely resembling the ancient *Frogs* of Aristophanes would have been very different, but such a performance would not have reproduced the chief characteristic of the original — it would not have pleased the public.[56]

Frogs certainly did please the public. *The Times* declared it 'a genuine success such as could hardly have been anticipated in the production of a Greek play before a modern audience'.[57] That it was a considerable departure from Greek plays as they had hitherto been staged is noticeable in a few critics' rather hesitant observations in the vein that, whilst it may have been amusing, it 'certainly was not classical', and that the methods employed had even 'abandoned the whole *raison d'être* of putting these works upon the stage':[58] indeed as one commentator some years later wrote, 'The *Frogs* of 1892 was perhaps the funniest of all these [Aristophanic] revivals. But not the least funny part was the way in which some of the critics shook their heads over the "tomfoolery". "*This* Dionysus! *This* Attic Comedy! Shocking! Positively indecorous!" [59] The high jinks and lightness of spirit, the energetic shifts in tempo and period in the score, and the noisy laughter from the audience certainly contrasted markedly with the serious, beautiful, and 'archaeological' stagings of tragedy and their largely reverential reception. The realization that Aristophanes could be thus, and so successfully and enjoyably, staged seemed to offer a continuation of the early and mid-Victorian tradition of staging Greece according to the aesthetic framework of burlesque, alongside and in addition to the more reverential late-Victorian attitude to the *idea* of Greece as it had been mediated through painting and staged tragedy. Indeed, the juxtaposition of these two visions of classic drama had been very precisely and it seems presciently expressed in the *Frogs*-inspired debate on the rival merits of Euripides and Aristophanes in Browning's *Aristophanes' Apology* (see above, Hall, pp. 83–84).

Towards the political

Although the revived Aristophanes had his high-minded detractors, as Browning's Aristophanes had been criticized by Balaustion, the genie had been let out of the bottle. The topical interpretation of the Greek text — so necessary to 'get at' the comedy — through the music, acting, and stage business, spoke to the audience about things which they recognized from their own culture: rowing coaches and contests, the sexual and artistic issues surrounding the Aesthetic movement, phrases from a variety of musical genre, the playing of the corpse as if he was come alive from one of Edgar Allan Poe's stories — and the importance of this layer of interpretation in the staging of *Frogs* in 1892 is that it made Aristophanes' humour work in *performance*. These leaps of imagination which some feared took the Aristophanes out of the 1892 *Frogs* were simultaneously recognized by most others as the necessary leap away from Aristophanes which brought the audience closer to the spirit, and perhaps the experience, of late fifth-century Athenian comedy. It was indeed 'not classical' — whatever the Victorians meant by that since, of course, it could never be — but it was Aristophanes fully revitalized via the stage traditions of British classical burlesque and musical comedy.

Indeed it is in the music that can be discerned one of the few clues to the connection between this rather anodyne academic production and the increasing sense that Aristophanes might be performed with a political agenda. For Parry's *Frogs* score contained one or two contemporary political resonances of a serious kind: for example, the chorus' song shifts from the tune of a polka to Henry Duprato's 'Boulanger' March when they move from honouring the Eleusinian gods to politics — with one reviewer declaring the March 'a most excellent *motif*' for this passage. [60]

This adumbrated the more serious political agenda underlying the music he was later to compose for *Acharnians* at Oxford in 1914 which resonated most strongly with the worsening international situation at that tense time: 'while *The Acharnians* is not in itself the most exciting of the comedies of Aristophanes, its talk of wars and rumours of wars, of "jingoists" and peace parties, of alliances and scares of invasion, give all sorts of obvious opportunities to a composer who is out for fun. ...

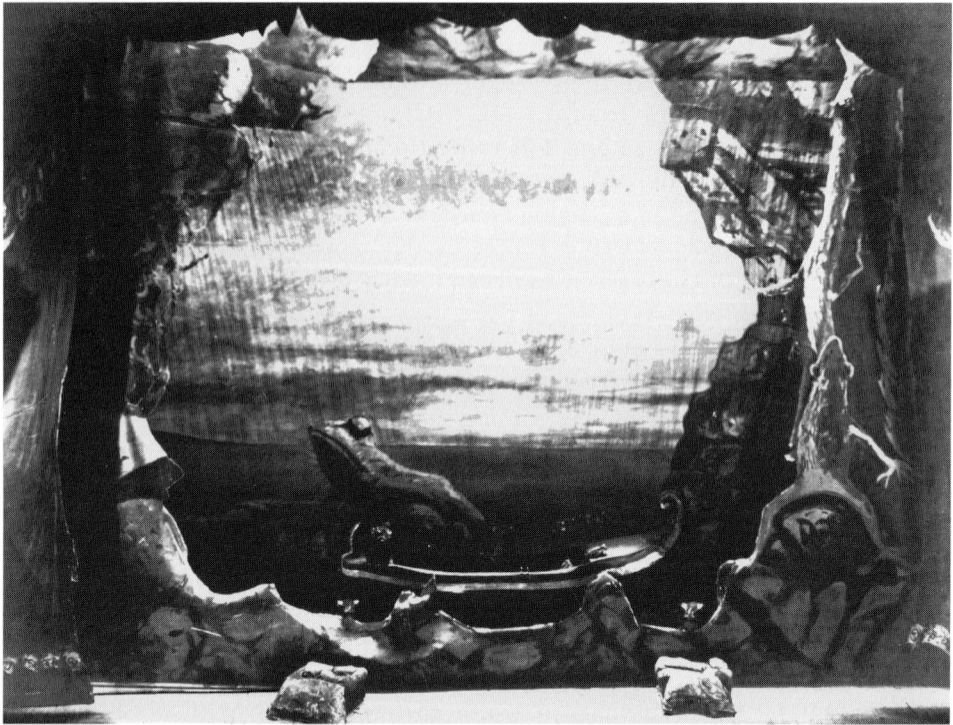

FIG. 8.6. Set for boat scene in the 1892 *Frogs*

[Parry] marked down the chief points which give some sort of parallel to the politics of to-day, and he picked up a dozen or more tunes from the street, the music-hall and the opera, to become the motives [*sic*] of individual characters, of parties and various points of view, weaving them together into a deliciously complicated musical argument'.[61] The music was, therefore, both 'a perfect riot of good fun' and a startling current commentary on international politics.[62] Another important figure, Gilbert Murray, had both the ancient play and the contemporary situation very much on his mind: as Professor of Greek he gave a lecture on *Acharnians* at Somerville College in connection with the production, and this took place just days after he had chaired the inaugural meeting of the Oxford University War and Peace Society, the stated aim of which was 'to find the best way out of the race [for armaments], and to discuss whether this way is by war or peace'.[63] Some months after war had broken out the biblical scholar Alexander Nairne of King's College London felt the political application of Aristophanes so keenly that he wrote a letter to *The Times* suggesting that his own Christian rewriting of *Peace* 991 ff., beginning 'O Thou that makest wars to cease in all the world', might be worthy of including in Church prayers for peace.[64]

The necessity of staging Greek plays in ancient Greek on the academic stages of Oxford and Cambridge went hand in hand with the rapid assumption of music and 'stage business' as modes of interpretation and communication of the comic force of the plays. Furthermore, the audiences for these late Victorian and early Edwardian academic productions discovered with relish that the comic drama of Aristophanes could be very successfully staged according to long-established comic and musical theatrical traditions, and that this resulted in an experience very different from that offered by solemn and beautiful stagings of tragedy. The 1892 *Frogs* was the prime example of such 'revitalization' of Aristophanes as comic drama in Britain during this period. It was inevitable that, once English-language productions on the commercial stage had shown that Aristophanes could be performed with reference to the socio-political issues of the day, even academic productions of Aristophanes delivered in ancient Greek would begin to find a language with which to refer to contemporary world affairs, thus bringing Aristophanes' political messages to bear on the problems of the modern world. It is not surprizing that the political resonances of these plays in ancient Greek for a largely anglophone audience found their 'voice' through Parry's allusive and eloquent music. The stage was now set for a brand new chapter in the full comic, musical, and political revitalization of Aristophanic comedy in the rest of the twentieth century.[65]

Notes to Chapter 8

1. Adderley (1888), 20.
2. See Carpenter (1985), 10.
3. At least two of the undergraduate dramatic groups active in the 1860s turned to Greek tragedy and mythology for their burlesques: the Shooting Stars, for example, staged *Fair Helen: A Comic Opera, Ariadne; or, The Bull! The Bully!! And the Bullion!!!*, and *Pentheus*; and the St John's College Amateurs put on *Iphigenia; or Sail!! The Seer!!! And the Sacrifice!!* and *Agamemnon at Home; or The Latest Particulars of that Little Affair at Mycenæ*. See Hall and Macintosh (2005), 303–04.
4. At least one of the Oxford undergraduate actors — Martin Luther Cumming, who starred in several of the Shooting Stars' burlesques owing to his skill in transvestite acting — was named in court and in the press. See further Wrigley (2008).
5. For the detail, see Adderley (1888) and Mackinnon (1910), ch. 3.
6. Macintosh (2005), 141. See also Challis (2005).
7. Anon. (1892*j*).
8. 'It is a fact, though it may seem a paradox, that Greek comedies are, in many respects, better adapted than tragedies for the modern stage' (P. Gardner (1883), 381). 'Attic comedy, however, cannot fail to have the advantage over tragedy for purposes of representation before a modern audience', Anon. (1883*b*).
9. Hall and Macintosh (2005), 387.
10. Scenes from Greek comedy, perhaps especially the poets' contest in *Frogs*, had for many decades been recited and staged on special occasions (e.g. prize-giving days) at British public schools. In 1836 Benjamin Jowett had himself, as a schoolboy at St Paul's, played the part of Dionysus arriving at Hades with 'comic distress' (Anon. 1836*b*). The 1892 *Frogs* seems to have stimulated schools to stage the entire play, often with Parry's music (e.g. St John's School, Leatherhead, 1895; Dulwich College, 1895 and 1898).
11. The plays given in ancient Greek were *Agamemnon* (1880), *Alcestis* (1887), *Frogs* (1892), *Knights* (1897), *Clouds* (1905), *Frogs* (1909), *Acharnians* (1914), *Rhesus* (1923), *Clouds* (1928), and *Oedipus Tyrannus* (1932). On the history of Greek drama on Oxford stages see further Hall and Macintosh (2005), index s.v. 'Oxford University', and Wrigley (2008). The early performance of a Greek comedy in Cambridge did not in the same way tip the balance away from tragedy on a long-term basis: for discussion see Easterling (1999), and for data the APGRD Database (www.apgrd.ox.ac.uk/database). (It is worth mentioning that productions of Latin comedy were popular in Oxford in the second half of the 16th c.; and there was a production of Terence's *Eunuchus* in 1762/3: see especially Boas (1914)).

12. Parry's first choral commission had been *Scenes from Shelley's Prometheus Unbound* for Gloucester's Three Choirs festival in 1880; Charles Villiers Stanford, who had performed this work in Cambridge in 1881, commissioned him to write the music for the 1883 *Birds*. That was his first commission to write music for a Greek play; and following the 1892 Oxford *Frogs*, he went on to compose the score for the 1900 Cambridge *Agamemnon*, and the 1905 and 1914 productions of *Clouds* and *Acharnians* in Oxford. See further Radcliffe (1983), Dibble (2004).

13. Edwards (1909), 546. Parry's scores were published (see e.g. Parry 1892 and 1914), and often enjoyed an independent life in the concert repertoire. The Bridal March for *Birds* even became a popular piece for weddings through the 20th c.: see Kerr (1965).

14. Easterling (1999), 31 describes how samples of birds' skins from stuffed specimens in the Museum of Zoology were sent to the costumiers.

15. Anon. 1883*a*.

16. On the 1883 *Birds* see Easterling (1999); on *Acharnians* in 1886 see Pearcy (2003). Cambridge had seen Aristophanes performed at least twice before: *Plutus* was staged at St John's College in 1536; and in 1546 the mathematician Dr John Dee put on *Peace* at Trinity College. See above, pp. 54 and 118. Evidence for other pre-20th-c. stagings of *Peace* has yet to come to light, beyond a tantalizing illustration of a scene in costumed performance (on a modern stage, identified as such by its banisters) in a review of the 1881 Harvard *Oedipus* (Anon. (1881), 229).

17. For example, in 1914: 'Greek plays ... may not always achieve the *succès fou* which attended the first production [in Oxford] more than a score of years ago of *The Frogs*, when crowds who did not understand a word of Greek thronged to see the *spectacle* and enjoy Sir Hubert Parry's delightful musical *pot-pourris* and parodies' (Anon. (1914*c*)).

18. APGRD Database, s.v. Aristophanes.

19. Weimar in 1861 saw a play of Aristophanes staged in German translation. Later that decade, *Wealth* (1867/8) and *Clouds* (1868) were given in modern Greek in Athens. *Wealth* (1873 and 1880), *Ecclesiazusae* (1877), and *Lysistrata* (1892) were staged in the vernacular in France. Fleeming Jenkin's English production of *Frogs* was given in Edinburgh in the late 1870s (see Hall, above, pp. 14, 17, 85), and in 1882 there was an Italian production of *Wealth* in Milan. The early Polish tradition of staging Aristophanes in translation, especially in the old university town of Kraków, deserves further investigation: the Jagiellonian University productions of *Knights* (Rycerze, 1905), *Frogs* (Żaby, 1906), *Birds* (Ptaki, 1907), and *Wasps* (Osy, 1910), for example, were prefigured by the 1873 *Knights* (Rycerze) by Teatr Krakowski, and the 1895 *Lysistrata, czyli Wojna i Pokój* (*Lysistrata, or War and Peace*, a Polish translation of Maurice Donnay's version) by Teatr Miejski (Municipal Theatre), a company that would henceforth stage both Aristophanes and Greek tragedy on a regular basis. For more information and sources see the APGRD Database, and on the Polish productions Srebrny (1984). Thanks to Allen Kuharski for help on sources for Polish productions.

20. Full membership of the University was not opened to women until 1920, and of OUDS not until 1964. See Hurst (2006).

21. This self-congratulatory phrase comes from William Camden's 16th-c. *Britannia*: 'the most famous University of Oxford, in Saxon Oxenford, our most noble Athens, the seat of the English Muses, the prop and pillar, nay the sun, the eye, the very soul of the nation; the most celebrated fountain of wisdom and learning, from whence Religion, Letters and Good Manners, are happily diffused thro' the whole Kingdom' (quoted in Dougill (1998), 36 from Thomas (1903), 258).

22. Including ll. 905–1118, 1151–97, 1215–36, 1279–1303, 1323–64, 1395–1406, 1437–45. Hogarth and Godley (1892), Preface, p. v: 'Act III has been shortened by the excision of the first part of the Poets' contest, dealing with purely literary criticism, and occupying over 200 lines. The other parts of the contest have been curtailed considerably, on the ground that almost all their point lies in sustained parody of plays either lost or not sufficiently known to a modern audience; or in personal allusions not intelligible now-a-days'.

23. My translation. Ibid. 8.

24. Ibid., p. v.

25. On Frere see Hall, above, pp. 77–79.

26. Hogarth and Godley (1892), 9 (*apedēmeis/epebateuon*, *Frogs* 48), and 23.

27. Anon. (1892*h*).

28. Anon. (1892*c*); H. F. Wilson (1892).
29. H.F. (1909).
30. Brock and Curthoys (2000), 521.
31. Anon. (1892*g*). The Isis is the local name for the River Thames as it runs through Oxford; the Cam, of course, is Cambridge's river.
32. Anon. (1892*a*).
33. Carr (1898), 62.
34. Anon. (1892*g*).
35. Anon. (1892*j*).
36. Anon. (1892*i*). At that time in England opera was sung in Italian even if the original libretto was in French or German; but this Italian version of 'Faites-lui mes auveux' has retained currency as an independent aria.
37. Anon. (1892*h*); Hogarth and Godley (1892), 21 and 23 respectively. The stretcher is the board against which the rower pushes his feet when pulling the oar(s).
38. Anon. (1892*f*).
39. Anon. (1892*j*).
40. Anon. (1892*c*); Anon. (1892*e*).
41. Letters to the Editor, *The Oxford Magazine*, 9 Mar. 1892, 231. The poet Postlethwaite was one of the recurrent characters in George du Maurier's 'anti-aesthetic' cartoons for the magazine *Punch*, the target of which was what he regarded as 'the effeminacy and absurdity' of aesthetes (Ormond (2004)).
42. For example, as typified by Swinburne, Rossetti, and — retrospectively — Wilde.
43. Quotations: Anon. (1892*f*). Costume detail: Anon. (1892*d*). *The Times* attributes the dresses to Alan Mackinnon and A. E. Haigh, but *The Queen* acknowledges the help of the classical archaeologist Maria Millington Lathbury (Lady Evans) of Lady Margaret Hall, Oxford, in (at least) ensuring 'that the draping should be correct and graceful'. A close association is suggested by the dedication of her book, *Chapters on Greek Dress*, published the following year, to OUDS 'in remembrance of their performance of the *Frogs* of Aristophanes' (Evans (1893)).
44. *Patience* premièred at London's Opera Comique in 1881. Quotations from H. F. Wilson (1892); Anon. (1892*e*); Anon. (1892*g*).
45. Anon. (1892*g*).
46. Ibid.
47. Anon. (1892*b*).
48. Carr (1898), 63.
49. Ibid. 64.
50. Anon. (1892*e*).
51. See Hall and Macintosh (2005), ch. 13, 'The Ideology of Classical Burlesque'.
52. Anon. (1892*c*).
53. Anon. (1892*g*). Cf. 'Of the whole play, but especially the latter part, it may be said that if it were not so good, so skilfully moderated, it would run the risk of breaking into broad burlesque', Anon. (1892*f*).
54. Although it should be noted that in OUDS's Shakespearean productions lady amateurs (e.g. wives of academics) took the female roles.
55. Carr (1898), 62–63, reproduced in Mackinnon (1910), 184–85.
56. Anon. (1892*g*).
57. Anon. (1892*f*).
58. Carr (1898), 64. For another example see Anon. (1892*e*): 'the audience [forgot] at once the antiquity and the nature of the play. In fact, they modernised the performance. The applause evoked when the actors leaned more than usually towards latter-day farce amply testified that this effect was produced. Surely the object should have been to present the comedy, as far as possible, in its pure form . . . to reproduce the *Frogs* in a classical spirit, and, when circumstances allowed, in a classical shape. Otherwise the artistic value of these productions disappears, and there seems, indeed, no reason why they should be given at all.'
59. Anon. (1905).
60. Anon. (1892*g*). For discussion of Boulanger see Bridges, Hall, and Rhodes (2007), 365–68.

61. Anon. (1914*a*). The reviewer goes on to describe one of Parry's typical musical puns: 'The Overture is brought to a brilliant climax by the first three notes of the National Anthem, which are the same as the opening of the Marseillaise, starting from the accent, and so we get a peace alliance or an *entente cordiale*.'

62. Anon. (1914*b*).

63. *The Oxford Magazine*, 12 Feb. 1914, 194.

64. Nairne (1915).

65. First thanks go to Edith Hall, who a full five years ago encouraged me to delve into the history of Greek plays on Oxford stages and who has provided valuable advice and suggestions on this chapter. I am also particularly indebted to Oliver Taplin for his constant encouragement of my book on that subject (Wrigley (2008)), especially when the Balliol Players' lorry seemed to be taking a long time to appear at the brow of the hill. For advice on earlier versions of this chapter I am grateful to Peter Brown, Fiona Macintosh, and Pantelis Michelakis; and to Debbie Challis and Don Chapman for help on particular points. I thank Colin Harris of the Bodleian Library's Modern Papers Reading Room for his indefatigable help over several years, and for introducing me to the Oxford caricatures and letting me see his in-progress Shrimpton catalogue (which is worthy of publication in its own right as a document for the social, political and cultural history of Oxford).

CHAPTER 9

❖

From Scandal to Success Story: Aristophanes' *Birds* as Staged by Karolos Koun

Gonda Van Steen

'Made in Greece'

One morning in May of 1946, Giorgos Vlachos wrote up his plan: to lift Greece out of its Civil War conflict and disastrous economic situation, the Greeks should aggressively promote ancient drama to the Western Europeans and to the Americans.[1] This tactical use of revival productions of classical tragedy as propaganda tools would prevent the British from terminating their financial and military aid programs for Greece. And, if the Greeks toured the United States with productions of ancient drama, perhaps the Americans could be coaxed into complementing or taking over entirely Britain's role as the financial sponsor of Greece. The Americans could become the new patrons of a war-torn country that was badly impoverished but that had, until then, been able to stop the communists from ascending to power. Vlachos published his 'great idea' in the leading conservative Greek daily newspaper of the time, *Kathimerini*.[2] His political colours were well known, and he was not without an audience for his views. Vlachos was, after all, the owner of *Kathimerini*. He wrote and published at a time when the political climate was set by successive western-assisted, right-wing national governments, which were preoccupied with containing or repressing communism.

   Ancient drama was part of Greece's 'cultural capital' (to use a notion established by Pierre Bourdieu).[3] Apparently, Vlachos' recommendations for a national cultural policy (i.e. a foreign policy) had him thinking more about capital than about culture. He certainly cared about theatre but understood this exchange more in business terms than as an artistic challenge: the better the export product, the greater the return in monetary benefits. Vlachos had the details all worked out: the director of the National Theatre of Greece (Ethniko Theatro) would prepare a few plays that 'sold' and take those on tour to Western Europe and the United States to woo goodwill for a nation in distress. Or, in Vlachos' glorifying words, the purpose of the company's international tour would be to 'reinspire the great public of the nations that now direct the world's fate with the spirit of ancient Greece'.[4] Vlachos was ready to entrust this goal to Dimitris Rontiris, the then newly appointed but controversial director of the National Theatre (a director at the National from 1946 until 1955). The 'grand tour' would promote ancient drama as the unique export product of Greece based on the classic argument for continuity from ancient through modern Greece: because of the impeccable pedigree of the modern Greeks, which was taken for granted, their revival productions of classical theatre were nothing less than *survival* productions. Following careful preparation and study, the modern Greek productions of ancient drama would stand out as unique, exclusive, and unquestionably 'authentic' (a high-voltage word since its use by the critical theorists Horkheimer and Adorno, but liberally applied in Greece of the 1940s and 1950s). If all later performances had really lapsed from the — idealized — original performance, then modern Greek performers and directors could best undo the nefarious effects of such lapses. Modern Greek artists could lead the way and show the world how classical theatre was to be presented. Vlachos' advice revealed a positivistic approach to reading and meaning. At the end of the long quest for the one and only 'right' meaning stood, for him, the modern Greek interpretation. It was therefore only proper, he argued, for the end product to bear the label 'Made in Greece' (he actually used the English words), in the same way in which the honey of Hymettus was labelled for export overseas. 'Made in Greece' functioned as the logo or business card for a bold commercial as well as artistic enterprise: its highly priced final product would be a stage production of a classical tragedy that was the best on the market and that shed the best possible light on modern Greece.[5]

Vlachos' public reasoning opened the door for western-style capitalism and neocolonialism to engulf revival drama. But New World versus Old World relations of dependency and debt also played a part in his rationale, and in the broader symbolic economy. The international tour, Vlachos argued, would generate tremendous goodwill among nations that owed a spiritual debt to Greece (and were still aware of it), and would translate into the guaranteed result of financial and military aid for Greece. The modern Greeks had to play the trump card of the better-known classical tragedies that many westerners had read and studied in school. Because of the long tradition of humanistic studies and philology and, in particular, the intensive instruction in the classics in Britain and the States, Vlachos could reasonably expect to tap rich reserves of benevolence toward modern Greece as the 'legitimate' heir to ancient Greece. The physical presence of Greek actors and artists in the targeted host countries would help to remind westerners of their historical debt, and would place some pressure on their governments to assist in rebuilding an exhausted Greece. Recent history teaches us, however, that the British government discontinued its aid programs to Greece around this time. But in March 1947, US President Harry Truman prevailed upon the American Congress to grant massive military and economic relief aid to Greece's right-wing national government. The Americans presented their role of Greece's new patrons as part of a larger program of support that they extended to 'free peoples' threatened by internal (i.e. communist) subversion.

It was not the art of the Greek National Theatre, however, that swayed the Americans to make Greece the first focus of the Truman Doctrine and Marshall Plan funding.[6] The theatre's propaganda tour did not take place until 1952. From mid- to late-November 1952, the Greek National Theatre made its first appearances in New York, where it presented two tragedies of Sophocles, *Oedipus* and *Electra*. The lead actors were Katina Paxinou and her husband Alexis Minotis, who had both worked in the United States before: Paxinou played the title role of Sophocles' *Electra*, which was directed by Dimitris Rontiris. Minotis directed the *Oedipus* production, in which he also played the lead role, while his wife played Iocaste. A. C. Sedgwick, author of the introductory article 'Authentic Classics from Athens' in *The New York Times*, stated that the National Theatre was scheduled for two weeks of performances in modern Greek at the Mark Hellinger Theatre in New York City.[7] Just as Vlachos had hoped, Sedgwick projected an exceptionalist idealism onto Greece that pivoted on ancient drama: '[People] will be seeing the best thing of its kind ever submitted to the public'. Sedgwick picked up, however, on the tour's nationalist aim, promulgated by its star actors:

> A theory which the Minotis are pleased to expound is that there is a conscious and unconscious similarity between the Greeks of today and those of classic times who lived in the same climate, were warmed by the same sun, marveled at the same nature, gazed upon the same sea around them, had the same emotions, and a language which in spirit, if not in actual word formations, is the same.[8]

Two post-production review articles in the *New York Times*, both by critic Brooks Atkinson, praise the execution of the chorus and, in general, lend support to Vlachos' perspective on ancient drama. A first review of the *Electra* ends with the telling words: 'Now we know that Sophocles' *Electra* is more than a schoolbook myth. The National Theatre of Greece knows how to transmute it into a tragedy that still retains heroic stature after nearly 2,400 years of squalid history.'[9] The second article, a review of the *Oedipus* production, concludes: 'In mastering the function of the chorus, the Greek National Theatre has mastered the art of playing Greek classical drama as a whole.'[10]

These events capture, in a nutshell, some of the contemporary theatrical priorities. First and foremost, theatre, and especially the National Theatre of Greece, had a nationalist and patriotic mission to fulfil — 'patriotic', that is, in the definition of the successive pro-western, anticommunist, right-wing national governments. Vlachos summed up the 'long-standing' mission of the National Theatre, with the political conservative Rontiris recently placed at the helm, in three characteristic words: *Ethnos, technē, euprepeia*, or 'Nation, art, and decorum'.[11] He explained that the first part of this mission was the National Theatre's obligation to be a 'weapon (*hoplon*) in the hands of the State'. To be more successful, then, at appealing to foreigners through art and 'propriety', the National Theatre had to go back to its 'roots' and exploit the 'best' of ancient Greece. Taking modern Greek plays on tour would have been unthinkable in Vlachos' mind. Taking Aristophanes on tour would have been just as inconceivable. He and many of his contemporaries in key positions of power and influence considered it 'patriotic' to make classical tragedy the centrepiece of a nationalist propaganda tour and to ban Aristophanes, because of his 'lack of decorum', or his notorious 'immorality'. Dirty laundry was best kept indoors. So the selection of plays proposed by Vlachos as early as May 1946 was a predictable, 'patriotic' selection and part of it was realized on the actual tour six years later: Vlachos had proposed Sophocles' *Oedipus*, *Electra*, and *Antigone*, and Aeschylus' *Persians*.[12]

It must give us some pause to see the makers of opinion and policy barter ancient plays in this way, and steer postwar Greek revival tragedy towards aggressive fundraising for the conservative and indeed reactionary reconstruction of their country, which excluded a substantial part of the Greek populace. Vlachos worked in conjunction with Rontiris: the two held leading positions (whether administrative or artistic) in the National Theatre for many years, and would have called themselves good 'patriots'.[13] However, just as many performances of classical plays have been applauded for being *classical* rather than for being good performances, so did many Greeks of the postwar era applaud 'patriotic' theatre primarily for its stated 'nationalist' or 'national-minded' qualities. The combination of ancient drama and conservative patriotism proved, for many years, impregnable, even though it was far more convincing politically than artistically.

Cultural Capital in Aristophanes?

In the late 1940s, there was no room for Aristophanes to play the role of goodwill ambassador for Greece. There was hardly room for him domestically, let alone on a showcase tour abroad. Attic comedy did not enter the stately halls of the National Theatre building until 1951, when two antiquarian-style productions of Aristophanes appeared during the same year. Critics and policy-makers, however, did not see enough potential in the arch-conservative *Lysistrata* staged by Linos Karzis and his Thymelikos Thiasos to incorporate it into the nationalist cultural policy. The 1951 production of *Clouds*, directed by Sokrates Karantinos and the National Theatre, raised many objections, too: the playwright and this play, in particular, were still seen as somehow complicit in the trial, condemnation, and death of Socrates — not exactly a cause for Greek pride.[14] But the first voices went up, too, of prominent critics and intellectuals who could reconcile themselves publicly, even if still reluctantly, with the prospect of occasional, conventional stagings of Attic comedy.[15] This would be an Aristophanes presented before a (preferably) well-educated public, but not before the broad masses. In many ways, this Aristophanes would continue to be a guilty pleasure for classicists and connoisseurs, who would appreciate that a director, trained in revival tragedy though not in comedy, pursued textual, historical, and archaeological accuracy and set the priorities of form and convention above those of content, style, or relevance.

But, while the critics and the intelligentsia argued, Aristophanes had been given a new lease on theatrical life by Karolos Koun (1908–87), who had started to experiment with Attic comedy at Athens College as early as 1932. At this American-sponsored boys' high school, where Koun taught English, he had successfully directed a group of creative students performing *Birds* (1932, 1939), *Frogs* (1933), and *Wealth* (1936).[16] Here, Koun first developed his signature style, which would render him famous as the 'master' during the next decades. Koun's rudimentary but earnest early attempts evolved into a coherent performative response to the challenges posed by Aristophanes and the irregular modes of his reception in Greece until then. At the helm of his Art Theatre (Theatro Technis, founded in 1942 as an independent theatre company), the avant-gardist Koun himself embodied perhaps the most successful transition from stage amateurism to professionalism in Attic comedy. Both for the director and for Aristophanes, the first positive results of this transition began to show by the mid-1950s, when professional and subsidized productions of the Greek classics also became a permanent reality. Meanwhile, Koun gained slow but steady repute for his pioneering productions of Shakespeare, Brecht, the Theatre of the Absurd, and neo-realist native Greek theatre. He opened up these genres to the dedicated ensemble of young actors with which he surrounded himself at the drama school of his Art Theatre, while he educated the postwar Greek theatre-going audience in the new modes and expressions of international drama.

In 1956, Alexis Solomos, one of Koun's former students at Athens College and then a young director at the National Theatre, started to bring regular productions of Aristophanes to the newly inaugurated Athens and Epidaurus summer Festivals.[17] This breakthrough was possible because Solomos had reached the higher ranks of the Greek theatrical establishment, had received an education in classical comedy from Koun, and had managed to calibrate precisely the tenor of Aristophanic humour.[18] Solomos allowed himself no vulgarities and relatively few verbal anachronisms, but he did adopt some visual and aural anachronisms in his use of comic props and music. He succeeded in rendering even Aristophanes' women's plays acceptable: they were among his first productions (*Ecclesiazusae*, 1956; *Lysistrata*, 1957; *Thesmophoriazusae*, 1958; and *Frogs*, 1959). Well before 1960, Solomos had managed to institutionalize the 'suspect' poet with shows that remained at all times elegant, mundane-cosmopolitan, 'clean', 'civilized', and, above all, 'proper'.[19] Especially for Aristophanes' women's plays, this was an incredible development: within half a century, these plays had moved from salacious or marginal, semi-pornographic spectacles for male patrons and actors only to huge public performances by mixed casts of the official National Theatre, for mixed audiences at the government-sponsored summer festivals.[20] Solomos's productions of Aristophanes met the standards set by the state's investment in classical drama as cultural capital, by the 'sacred' nature of the monumental ancient theatre sites, and by the pressure of the expectations of increasing numbers of foreign visitors to Greece. They met the stakes of 'patriotism' and of the growing tourist industry vested in the big outdoor productions in Epidaurus or at the Herodes Atticus Theatre in Athens.[21]

Scandal

Imagine the shock, then, when in the summer of 1959 Koun and his Art Theatre brought a première of Aristophanes' *Birds* to the Herodeion that flouted all the written and unwritten norms that had by then emerged from modern Greek revival productions of classical comedy. Let us first have a look at the incident that shook the opening performance of a production that went on to achieve near-mythical status in the world of Greek theatre. The incident took place before the eyes of more than three thousand theatregoers and, as part of the official Athens Festival,

set off all the alarm bells. In one scene, the protagonist, Peisetaerus (played by
Dimitris Chatzemarkos), called on a priest to sacrifice a goat to the gods. Quite
unexpectedly, the actor who played the role of the priest, dressed in the robe of a
modern clergyman, began chanting in the familiar notes of Byzantine ecclesiastical
music, but without altering the content of Aristophanes' original mock prayer to
the Olympian gods of Nephelococcygia. Koun's parody-of-the-parody shocked
some spectators, who showed their disapproval of this 'sacrilege' with cries
of *Aischos!* ('disgraceful', 'shame', 'enough!'). Most of the audience, however,
applauded enthusiastically. Chatzemarkos saved the scene by breaking off the
mock prayer, but the atmosphere in the Herodeion remained tense during the rest
of the performance.

The consequences of this incident, however, could not be avoided. The next day,
Konstantinos Tsatsos, a prominent intellectual and leading politician who acted on
behalf of Prime Minister Konstantinos Karamanlis, banned the three remaining
scheduled performances of Koun's 'anticlerical' *Birds*.[22] Tsatsos notoriously stated,
'The play performed yesterday, insufficiently rehearsed, constituted a distortion
of the spirit of the classical text, while some of its scenes were presented in such
a way as to offend the religious sensibilities of the people'.[23] Tsatsos, who charged
Koun with abusive and indefensible distortions, had been among the spectators in
the Herodeion, and he had taken offence at the production's implicit criticisms of
the Greek Orthodox Church and its alliance with the conservative, pro-American
Karamanlis. Even though the Greek penal code could punish blasphemy against
sacred symbols, this formal act of censorship, inconsistent with democratic
principles, baffled most Greeks and was widely seen as an infringement of the civic
right of freedom of speech and an affront to artistic expression.[24]

The press named or shamed Tsatsos. What it did not state, however, was what
the Karamanlis administration found more subversive than the religious offence:
the production's militant leftist and anti-western language. Key to the scandal
was Koun's use of the boldly anti-government and anti-American translation of
Birds by the poet, playwright, and journalist Vasilis Rotas (1889–1977). A known
communist activist, Rotas had sharpened the play's language, ideological attacks,
and socio-political relevance through connotations that had been noticed before but
that had hardly, if ever, been given expression on the official stage. Rotas' acting
version employed bold anachronisms denouncing US missiles, hand grenades,
and military bases and airports, as well as icons of current American culture from
cowboys to Einstein. The opposition had attacked Karamanlis before for allegedly
betraying the cause of Hellenism to the United States and to the North Atlantic
Treaty Organization (NATO, which Greece entered in 1952), but had seldom done
so in such a dramatic manner. Moreover, Rotas exploited the première's date of 29
August 1959, which was, to the day, the ten-year anniversary of the defeat of the
Left in the mountains of Grammos and Vitsi that had brought an end to the Civil
War. Official state rhetoric cast this final stand-off as the decisive victory over evil
communism. Rotas countered and spoke through an Aristophanes involved in
Greek and international cold-war politics. His biting topical language and pointed
anti-Americanism reminded the audience that the Greek Left did not consider itself

defeated. The defiant Rotas knew the power — and perils — of resistance drama all
too well: in the 1940s he had himself managed one of the partisan theatre troupes
constituting the 'Theatre of the Mountains'.[25] The première's interdiction was thus
another act of rightist suppression of left-wingers who had publicly shown that
leftist militancy and sympathies were still alive. The authorities rightly perceived
the 1959 première (and possible repeat performances) of this *Birds* as dissident
acts aimed against them. That the Art Theatre had opened the production in the
spotlight of the official, state-sponsored Athens Festival, geared also toward foreign
visitors, exacerbated the incident's public impact. The danger was real that such a
scandal might jeopardize the relatively new institution of the festivals altogether.
As an unforeseen result of the official ban, Koun and the contributors to his *Birds*
would find a new political aim in the vital cause of defending political freedom and
self-expression.

Tsatsos' decision was labelled hypocritical by the leftist paper *He Auge* (*The
Dawn*) on 1 September 1959. On its front page, the paper printed the observation
by Athanasios Tsouparopoulos, 'What Cleon could not do to Aristophanes [i.e.,
prevent him from speaking out publicly], Konstantinos Tsatsos managed to do, all
under the cover of democracy!' The journalist claimed that the politician saw in
Aristophanes' satire, and in his presumed revolutionary ideas, a powerful threat to
the establishment. Therefore, Tsouparopoulos continued, the 1959 production was
banned not because the people disliked the opening performance but because the
government disliked it. By punishing Koun, the minister wanted to set a precedent,
to make everyone understand that interpretation of Aristophanes had to follow
certain rules. For the incensed journalist, however, this act of censorship would
stand as a monument to the climate of obscurantism fostered by the authoritarian
Karamanlis administration. In a highly ironic passage, Tsouparopoulos wrote:

> Aristophanes 'has been threatening the established order' for the past two
> or three years, with his comedies, with his crude language, and with his
> revolutionary ideas. He managed to sneak inside the 'precinct of Helleno-
> Christian civilization', but all he does is speak sarcastically about the sacred and
> the holy. First of all, he glorifies peace, which makes him intolerable. He calls
> on us Greeks, 'liberated from civil fighting and from wars to bring peace into
> our midst!' And when did he do that? On the very same day when the cannons
> of Lycabettus shook the Acropolis inviting the people to celebrate the 'joy' of
> the Civil War! Ah, that is too much, Mr Aristophanes! Add those theories about
> wealth and poverty, about cruel injustice, and about social changes that must
> take place ... And finally, ... there is his ridicule of the Olympian gods, along
> with his allegations at the very opening of the *Birds*: 'We took the dark road back
> to a place without petty politicians and law courts, without sycophants, critics,
> or police forces ... '! [his ellipses] What is that all about?! How can a regime
> that is based on sycophancies, police forces, and petty politicians ... tolerate all
> of that? So, get out of here, Mr Aristophanes! We ain't dumb birds!

The official ban on Koun's production caused a terrible uproar: newspapers wrote
about the incident for weeks, interviewed all parties involved, took sides publicly,
and began running cartoons.[26] Leftist newspapers continued to attack and ridicule
Tsatsos, who was nicknamed 'the Chicken' (*i Kota*) in an amusing reminder of

Koun's *Birds*. The ancient Greek word *ornithes* still exists in modern Greek, but now means 'hens'.[27] Because the term *ornithes* occurs in both languages, users from 1959 could comically lower the *ornithes* of the classical title to the level of ordinary (female) chickens. This meant, too, that newspaper commentators and illustrators could outdo themselves in chicken-related allusions, and they did not hold back. Phokion Demetriadis became the most renowned cartoonist to immortalize Tsatsos in newspaper caricatures and to keep the memory alive of one of his sadder interventions in a long and otherwise distinguished political career. For years, Tsatsos was portrayed either accompanied by a chicken (on a leash) or as a short man with a chicken head or body. Thus Aristophanes' comic and political influence extended far beyond the physical boundaries of the stage to the forums of the Greek press, popular representation, and, in particular, the thriving culture of political cartoons. The latter enjoyed greater licence than many other media and public channels.

The 1959 production of the *Birds*, the first big scandal of the official Athens Festival, not only shook the foundations of the Karamanlis administration but had a long-term impact on politics and theatre as well. Its dissident contents and the unforeseen protests it spurred became critical public issues in stage politics from the late 1950s through to the mid-1970s. The treatment of the 1959 *Birds* revealed how easily representatives of the ruling elite took offence, and how little sense of humour they often displayed. It also indicated how political the fare of the Art Theatre really was, even though the Aristophanes of Koun and Rotas showed no apparent desire to overthrow the government or to substitute anarchy for law and order. The playwright's comic licence was abruptly curtailed. The producer and the translator had not been granted dramatic liberty, but both had assumed it, aware of the risk, when there had seemed to be a political opening for an unfettered comic revival stage. The direct ban on Aristophanes' comedy corroborated leftists' belief in the poet's mission: his ability to take on the artistic and public functions that in a free Greece would have been performed by a variety of genres and civic organs.

Koun and Stage Populism

Koun had commissioned the acting version of the *Birds* from Rotas, whose politics of translation were more outspoken than his own. Many forward-looking artists and intellectuals, including Koun, belonged to neither the hard-line leftist or rightist camp, yet during an international communist scare, and the internal exigencies that brooked no negotiation, they were readily suspected of subversion or conspiracy against national security. Throughout his career Koun insisted that for him and for his drama school, the Art Theatre was a unique artistic vocation, a task of and medium created by the intellect, not influenced by one-sided party politics. His work was, above all, thought-provoking more than politically committed or politically provocative. Historical circumstances, however, compelled Koun's Aristophanic theatre to become profoundly socio-political, ask hard-nosed questions, and give disturbing answers concerning Greek culture and ideology.

Identifying with the ancient playwright, Koun assumed a more engaged, topical-political, or even sceptical stance, often confronting the taboos and prejudices of the time. Because the real reasons for banning the 1959 production of the *Birds* were political, the climate of anticommunist fear and distrust affected not only Koun, Rotas, the actors, and other artistic contributors, but even Aristophanes. The latter became *Aristero*-phanes, 'the one who reveals himself as leftist', in a caustic remark of Voula Damianakou, journalist and wife of Rotas. Aristophanes, whose name gives away his sympathies, she sarcastically continued, was to suffer exile or death for his lifelong communist tendencies and for his leftist associations with the common Greek people and with their language and culture.[28]

Damianakou alluded to Aristophanes' allegiance to the people's language as sufficient ground for the charges against him and his translator. The association of the *written* use of the Demotic tongue with the political Left and with communism had been deeply ingrained in the mind-set of the Greek public since the first decades of the twentieth century. In the opinion of the progressive camp, the pursuit of Demoticism was part of a broader programme for the social and intellectual liberation of the illiterate bulk of the populace, currently debarred from an educational system that stressed religion, classical studies, and the use of the formalist Katharevousa language. Whereas contemporary authors often intended their writings in the popular language to signal their left-wing, democratic sympathies, adherence to the 'purist' tongue maintained its older connotations of political conservatism. From 1911 on, when the Katharevousa of Greece's new constitution was decreed the official language, this classicizing idiom had increasingly been equated with the Right and its western-Hellenic nationalism, as well as with the preservation of the élitist status quo. Language-based ideological codes of 'proper' morality and of Hellenic-style patriotism set the terms by which subsequent sociolinguistic issues would be argued and political affiliations would regularly be judged. Within the twentieth-century Left–Right polarity, the official language policy of 1911 fuelled the conservatives' rejection of Demoticism as a tool of Marxism and communism, as well as their promotion of Katharevousa as proof of 'national-mindedness.' This self-styled *ethnikophrosyne*, or patriotism in the rightist definition, was thus proclaimed by Greek defenders of the old social, political, and linguistic order, who joined in the *ethnike parataxis*, or 'national camp'. The Right further de-Hellenized the likes of Rotas and Aristophanes and branded them as 'unpatriotic,' 'antinational' (*antethnikos*), or 'anti-Greek,' equating the writers, their language, and the entirety of their writings.

During the cold war, Attic comedy — irreverent towards established religion, local authority, and foreign allegiance — reemerged as an art form more committed to overlooked traditions than to canonical histories or master narratives, and ultimately capable of reasserting Greek popular self-esteem. Through the 1959 incident, Aristophanes himself became a powerful, stirring symbol of the resilient vitality and stubborn struggle for freedom of the suppressed Left. In the interstices of the public imagination of the late 1950s until the mid-1970s, he represented the dissident Greek character, combining the qualities both of a modern Romaic standard-bearer and of a classical genius of universal 'wit' (*pneuma*). The term

'Romaic' denoted the popular Greekness of recent centuries; as an ensemble of cultural values, *Romaiosyne* was heavily promoted from the 1920s onward. Not only did the shared Romaic 'spirit' thrive on liberty, but the very thought of restraint, whether in the theatre or in the realm of government, was antithetical to its nature and therefore had to be resisted. Aristophanes' *pneuma* mobilized the Greek people with its call for a proud national culture and politics that refused subservience. Romaic nationalism, the Left, and Aristophanes, now committed to a larger social mandate, joined forces to broach such progressive topics as broad Demotic and artistic outreach, the improvement of intellectual and wider civic life, and even minority (re)empowerment. Against this ideological backdrop, the official silencing of the liberals Koun and Rotas was equated with an attack on the enduring underground support for the Left, which resorted to the comic revival stage as one of the few remaining public outlets for discontent. Even though it was only a one-off performance in the 1959 season, Koun's *Birds* thus managed to provoke intense debates and conflicts that touched on fundamental questions of Greek identity and destiny.

Koun's production came at a time when intellectual collisions were taken so seriously that they became creative, established novel theatrical concepts and forms, and engendered a new collective socio-political imagination. Koun approached Aristophanic comedy through the method of what he called Greek Folk Expressionism, with the purpose of turning *Birds* into a feast for the eyes, ears, and popular mind.[29] This modernist paradigm engaged Koun in a lifelong search for remnants of native popular culture: it stressed the continuity and unity of the vernacular, rather than the learned Greek heritage, and legitimized the Romaic and folkloric element of indigenous Greekness. This professed continuity of affinities between the ancient and modern popular spirit inspired (and occasionally declined into) a back-to-the-roots folksiness in which Koun genuinely believed but sometimes became mere lip-service when imitated by others. Koun's aesthetic movement disclosed an alternative transhistorical continuum linking the modern Greek *people* to the legacy of the Golden Age — a modernist position increasingly common among artists and intellectuals after the Asia Minor debacle of 1922. As a problematic geared towards tradition and performance, Koun's Folk Expressionism reinvented Aristophanes, thereby turning his oeuvre into a grassroots form of modern Greek theatre and culture. From this movement, the *laïkos* (popular) poet emerged as the champion of the Greek people and of the political Left. This 'folk Aristophanes' handed contemporaries a key to overlooked layers of the more recent Greek past, and encouraged artists like Koun to set out on a quest for Greek authenticity through Attic comedy. The playwright and his antiheroes functioned as channels of direct access to the *laïkotita* (populism) and *Romaiosyne* of the autochthonous people of a pristine and unchanged rural Greek landscape. As these protagonists also conditioned the traditionalist narrative and image of the struggling *laos* (people), Koun extended the history of stage populism by centuries in just a few strokes. Meanwhile, Greek audiences, especially the lower and middle classes, grew increasingly well acquainted with Attic comedy, and by extension with ancient drama, in new, interactive ways. Koun's innovations altered not only how Aristophanes' plays were treated on stage, but also how new productions were interpreted by critics and by reading and theatregoing audiences.

The early twentieth-century Romaic popular tradition had begun to appropriate Aristophanes and had made him transgress official morality and ideology.[30] In Koun's hands then, the poet came to symbolize the new appreciation for an indigenous Greek civilization that included native spectacle, Karaghiozis shadow theater, and folk music (*rembetika* music and song). This appreciation, however, stemmed more from recovery and rediscovery than from any first-hand experience of indigenous and topical Greekness: it tended to come, not from those who lived native culture in rural Greece, but from those who, like Koun, remembered it with nostalgia while residing in rapidly urbanizing city centres. By 1959, the enduring and at times artificial search for popular and Romaic national character contravened the rightist government's pro-western political and cultural orientation. For the idealists who promulgated the myth of the people then, Koun's 1959 production of *Birds* promoted the folk spirit and popular language and art, all aspects that had long been branded as unpatriotic interests or activities. For the detractors of 'fake-lore', or critics of the myth of the myth, the instant applause and recognition that the première received from the younger generations of spectators, in particular, was politically motivated and had hardly anything to do with their (questionable) appreciation of 'indigenous' Greekness. The conservative stage director and critic Aimilios Chourmouzios, for instance, who had years of experience in the world of Greek theatre and revival drama (at the National Theatre), averred that Koun's première was a success mainly with younger people, but contended that their approval was no more than a political act, 'the mobilization of taste'.[31]

Critics and scholars are unsure as to whether Koun, when he was a student at the Sorbonne in Paris, had the opportunity to see the famous 1928 satirical revue *Birds,* by Charles Dullin.[32] Dullin, the modernist French actor, director, teacher, and proponent of folk theatre, envisaged a *théâtre du peuple*: at his Théâtre de l'Atelier (founded in 1922), he strove to create (leftist) politicized 'theatre of the people', and experimented with popular and physical forms of performance. Koun shared with Dullin, whom he admired but to whom he seldom referred, the conviction that the theatre had to broaden the social basis of its audience. One may track the influence of Dullin's Atelier also in many aspects of the composition and innovative practice of Koun's Art Theatre and in the high demands that 'the master' made on its members.

The bombshell dropped by Koun's 1959 production contained within it all the germs of previous and subsequent Aristophanic controversies centering on morality, politics, language, aesthetics, and the viability of performance. In one quick stroke, Aristophanes fell back on his role as taboo-breaker, which he had been playing for most of his reception history in modern Greece. Yet the outcry now had nothing to do with sexual immorality or with the poet's stereotypically unruly, overheated women — the longstanding anxiety. The scandal had everything to do with political offence, under the cover of religious transgression. However, this *Birds* was also a political firebrand because it destroyed ideological self-confidence and uprooted right-wing stability at the worst possible time: just when the authorities had grown convinced, after seeing the comic revival productions of Solomos and the National Theatre, that Aristophanes, too, could be exploited as a winning ticket, as part of the country's cultural capital.[33]

A Makeover for Success

The tensions that provoked the official ban against Koun's *Birds* of 1959 did not exist in isolation from religious concerns or the production's aesthetics and theatrical viability. Even though Koun's long involvement with Attic comedy should have made for a better-prepared critical reception, the critics showed themselves not well versed in the realities of Aristophanic performance. They reacted mainly with political comments or took issue with very specific aspects of Koun's artistic conception. Koun and his contributors did not respond much to the aesthetic criticisms at first, but did adopt changes afterwards, and set the production on the road to unquestioned success. Koun made careful changes to the musical style and spectacle of rhythms, movements, and sounds. As in his score for Koun's 1957 production of Aristophanes' *Wealth*, Manos Chatzidakis preferred modern Greek folk tunes and Anatolian dances in a lively and playful composition to any ancient-style choral music and comic dance, artificially reconstructed on the basis of very scant evidence. Despite the growing popularity of the *rembetiko* music, however, Hatzidakis' score of *Birds* failed to engage the audience at the opening performance. The main reason for its lack of success was that it had been poorly rehearsed. The composer then made some revisions to the original musical score, which was also better executed on later occasions.[34] The balletic choreography of the Helleniko Chorodrama of Rallou Manou did not please the public of 1959, largely because score and dancers' movements were not coordinated. Newspaper reviewers noted that the actors' parts were often obscured by an overload of music, song, and dance. Koun then asked Zouzou Nikoloudi to step in as choreographer, which led to radical changes in movement by 1962. Nikoloudi's new choreography featured popular dance motifs that suited the production's folk atmosphere as well as its music. Assisted by Nikoloudi, Koun created the comic chorus anew, and found convincing solutions to the dramaturgical problems it poses: he made his bird-actors semiprotagonists and dared to give them centre stage (fig. 9.1). Their dynamic ensemble oscillated between lyricism and animal revelry, free from artsy self-consciousness. Koun's production of *Birds* has rightly been commended (and often imitated) for endowing the complex classical chorus with new verbal, visual, and musical lustre. The 'master' broke the monotony of the traditional chorus and let it play a truly modernist role (fig. 9.2).

The audience did not know what to make of the stage and costume designs of artist Yiannis Tsarouchis. Tsarouchis' plain and flimsy-looking sets flouted convention, which demanded a solidly constructed backdrop with three entrances opening onto a raised stage. They fitted, however, squarely within the tradition of folk spectacle and improvised popular entertainment. Tsarouchis' earthen-coloured bird costumes looked poor, shabby, and hastily fabricated.[35] They completed the overall impression of an unfinished and disorganized production. Many spectators,

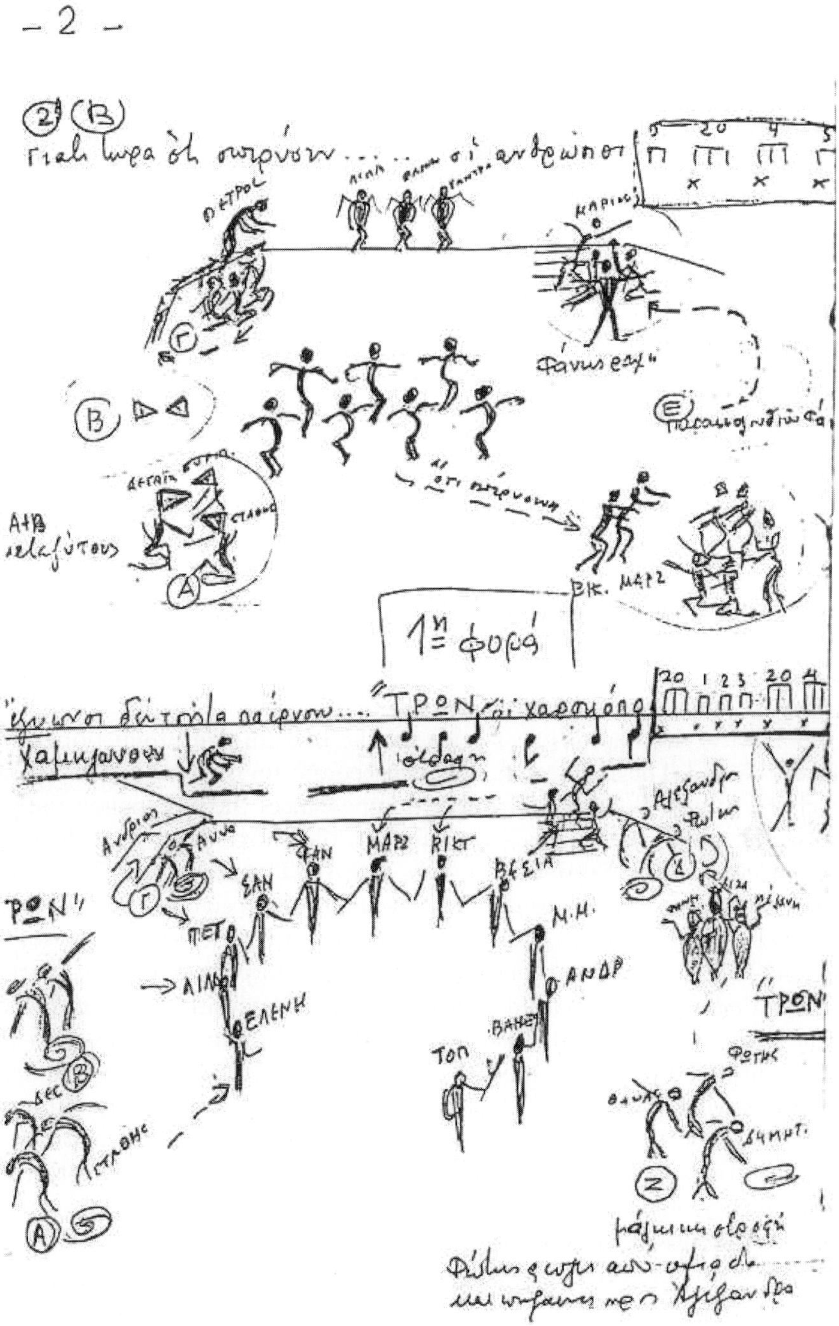

FIG. 9.1. Sketch for the bird chorus's movement centre stage, 1997

however, had expected to see some of the opulence of bourgeois theatre and its overload on props and accessories — expectations that Solomos' style had managed to fulfil. Tsarouchis' work was perceived as an act of iconoclasm that went beyond a clash of new aesthetic values with old theatrical conventions. Again, the production exposed a raw nerve that measured this act of heresy more in the terms of political subversion than of aesthetics. The public and the critics altogether missed the connections with the attire and movement of African ritual dancers, from which Tsarouchis had drawn inspiration. Today, the costumes of Tsarouchis strike us as almost surrealistic. In the later reception of Koun's *Birds*, they have been widely praised for turning the production and, in particular, the choral parts, into an intoxicating feast of colours and images.

The condemned *Birds* moved from being Koun's largest failure to becoming his greatest triumph. Against all initial expectations and despite a consistent lack of state support, the controversial production became *the* most important comic revival of the Art Theatre and arguably the biggest landmark in the modern Greek reception history of Aristophanes. From 1960 onwards, with popular curiosity sharpened by the earlier ban, the improved version of Koun's *Birds* earned broad public approval. Since most of the 1959 detractors (who had written in the heat of the moment) changed their minds, they helped transform the première from a 'disgraceful act of vandalism' into a proud source of Greek cultural capital. With Aristophanes' *Birds*, the Art Theatre rapidly moved from the wings of Greek dramaturgy to centre stage and began an impressive international run. Invited to Paris in 1962, Koun's *Birds* won the Théâtre des Nations first prize for the best foreign production. Later, as part of the World Theatre Season, the same comic revival was performed at the Aldwych Theatre in London. Through its appearances there, it caused the British theatre world to reconceptualize, in particular, the choral parts of ancient drama. In London, as in other European capitals, the Art Theatre's production achieved overwhelming success, even though the move indoors affected the way in which the choruses were executed. Koun was the first to take the modern Greek Aristophanes abroad on multiple occasions *and* to competitions and playhouses of worldwide repute. His *Birds* placed Koun and comedy on the international tour circuit, which, from the early 1950s onwards, had been reserved for tragedies presented by the National Theatre. From 1965 onwards, *Birds* was often featured on a double bill with the Art Theatre's new production of Aeschylus' *Persians*. Thus the comedy appeared alongside the tragedy that yielded more cultural capital than any other classic.[36] Aristophanes had entered a more visible, mainstream, and international reception history of ancient drama.

Despite the accolades gathered, the new, freed *Birds* appeared at neither the Athens nor the Epidaurus Festivals, which were forbidden territory for Koun's play until after the collapse of the military dictatorship (1967–74). The production's exclusion became the most prolonged and most complex instance of stage censorship in Greece in recent decades. Following the coup until the downfall of the colonels, the Art Theatre continued to suffer the repercussions of its earlier clash with the establishment. Shortly after the putsch, representatives of the newly installed junta demanded that the company return home from a tour to London and cancel a

FIG. 9.2. Koun's chorus of birds taking centre stage (1962)

scheduled performance of *Birds* at the Lycabettus Theatre in Athens. After sixteen years' suspension from the summer festivals, Koun's legendary production finally saw its first state-sponsored repeat performance at Epidaurus in 1975. By then, the foreign laurels that *Birds* had gained made it draw huge numbers of Greeks and tourists to the ancient theatre.

By 1975, the long-forbidden *Birds* had become the *cause célèbre* of the Art Theatre and of all advocates of artistic licence. No play other than the *Birds* could then have expressed the same cry for *complete* freedom of speech, because its symbolic dimension of ideological dissent had been attached by recent modern Greek history rather than inherited from classical antiquity. The rightist animosity against Koun's première, which was both qualitatively different from and similar to the junta's political pressures and distortions, had become a constitutive impulse of the play's reception history, submerging its modern prototype in the service of later demands: this semi-autonomous *Nachleben* heavily advertised Aristophanes' indomitable popular-national spirit that resisted antidemocratic oppression of any kind, including that of the military dictators. The Greeks credited Aristophanes' comedy with helping to shape the world's oldest democracy, and they invoked him again as they installed a new democracy on the same Greek territory. The comeback of the free *Birds* production, which symbolized regained freedom of speech and fully restored democratic rights, dramatically relegated the junta era to the past. Also, it was permitted on the official stage under a new Karamanlis regime (1974–81) and at the outset of the presidency of Konstantinos Tsatsos himself. For Tsatsos and Karamanlis to allow Koun's performance of the *Birds* at Epidaurus was an important public step: they displayed the goodwill of their right-wing New Democracy Party (founded in 1974), while distancing themselves from the censorship rules enforced by the recent military dictators. The 1975 repetition functioned as an instant measure of the proclaimed liberalism of the new, post-junta rule of Karamanlis. The *Birds* production now bespoke not only cultural capital, but also the value of 'democratic capital'.

The production of Koun's *Birds* in 1975 expressed an overwhelming sense of optimism at the prospect of exploring the paths of progress and liberalization in the arts after a long period of *stasis*. Anny Koltsidopoulou, writing in the leftist periodical *Anti*, described its political and aesthetic statement:

> [I]t was a symbol of and a wish for rebirth, an uplifting move, and a starting-signal to shake off the museum-style traditional form that, with very few bright exceptions, has weighed down the interpretation of ancient drama until today.[37]

Self-Referentiality, Idealization, and Restoration

A cartoonist by the name of Niarchos ominously predicted that Tsatsos' name and interference would remain associated with the reception history of Koun's *Birds*. Niarchos' cartoon (fig. 9.3), reprinted on the front page of a 1999 special issue of the satirical journal *To Pontiki* (*The Mouse*), incorporated a billboard or poster that announced the *Birds* as a work by the 'duo Aristophanes and Tsatsos'. Tsatsos walks up to Aristophanes to affirm that he, too, now owns rights to the play.

As the *Birds* and other comic plays were subsequently revived in Greece, they proved crucial in establishing an intricate web of communicative connections and dialectic relations, just as Aristophanes himself had related to Euripidean tragedies over a long period of time. The notion of stage dialectics describes this web connecting living dramatic productions; comic stagings have not been isolated theatrical events but have instead responded to one another in the public forum of the summer festivals and through a rich tradition of reperformance. The modern Greek custom of putting on multiple repeat performances of older productions has enhanced such dialectics, whether of a verbal, paraverbal, or visual nature.[38] Also, repeat performances have been able to offer audiences information about the main characteristics of a première, of its first impact, and of a company's typical approach to the ancient poet. Thus stage dialectics can easily come about between entire phases, or fashions, in the dramatic reading of Attic comedy. With every repetition, as with every novel production, collective and individual knowledge of the comic revival tradition is confirmed as well as (re)fractured, so that the image of the play and its author can be assembled anew.

In a first phase, Koun's *Birds* soon stood at the centre of this process of continuous re-membering.[39] The numerous repetitions of the comedy that the Art Theatre mounted after the dictators' demise became highly self-reflexive. Here, the public's knowledge of the première was key to new anachronistic jokes far removed from

ΤΣΑΤΣΟΣ : Πρέπει νὰ ἐμφανιστοῦμε μαζὶ στὴν πρε-
μιέρα, κύριε ᾿Αριστοφάνη. ῎Εχω ἀποκτήσει κι᾿ ἐγώ δικαιώματα
στὶς..... ὄρνιθες !...

FIG. 9.3. Cartoon by Niarchos of 'co–authors' Aristophanes and Tsatsos

Aristophanes' ancient original, though not from the 1959 incident and its aftermath. In the opening scene of the Art Theatre's 1975 revival, Peisetaerus and his sidekick Euelpides announced that they went looking for a 'land without juntas'. The scene with the priest and his parody of Orthodox liturgy was by far the most successful, and it became obligatory for this and other Greek productions of *Birds*. The 1986 and 1987 repeat performances of Koun's play still featured the same priest. In the later version, intertextual references to the scandal of a generation earlier formed the basis of comic stage dialectics. Lazanis, alias Peisetaerus, declared to the priest (but in fact to the youth among the spectators): 'You are young and you do not remember what we suffered twenty-eight years ago!' — a line that elicited tremendous applause. Thus individual words and lines assumed meanings that were new and significant yet shared, with the latest stage adaptations of *Birds* aiming at as much of the original effect of Koun's production as audience taste and understanding would allow. Levels of self-referentiality and idealization were further intensified by

Koun's insistence on working with as many of the first protagonist-actors as possible in his repeat performances of *Birds*. He did, however, introduce younger actors to the production by casting them in minor roles until he judged them ready for promotion to the leading parts. For nearly three decades, Koun's *Birds* functioned as a training school for most actors attached to the Art Theatre. Indirectly, Aristophanes' comedy became central to the career development of a generation of Greek stage professionals, including not only actors but also producers, musicians and composers, set and costume designers, choreographers, technicians, and so on. Thus, a wide range of Greek theatre professionals and amateurs have rewritten and fed off Koun's work on Aristophanes.

Yet the reception of Aristophanes' *Birds* entered, in a second phase, a process of idealization and careful restoration. From 1962 onwards, Koun's *Birds* was thought to have reached a state of perfection that no other comic revival would be able to surpass. The Art Theatre's play had shaped a historical moment and had become *the* example of a compelling interpretation of Aristophanes. As Koun's version gained control over the ancient text, Aristophanes merely receded to the background of philological and historical reception. Paradoxically, Koun's *Birds* achieved, over the years, something of the permanence and even the sacred status typically attributed to ancient texts rather than to modern adaptations. His 1959 première (in the 1962 'edition') became a 'text' in its own right: not in the literal sense defined by eighteenth- and nineteenth-century philologists, but in the eyes of those contemporary theatre practitioners for whom the verbal and visual language of Koun, rather than of Aristophanes, stood as fixed.

So compelling was the Art Theatre's version of *Birds* that for nearly thirty-five years few other paths lay open for exploring this classic. Only since the early 1990s have a small number of diverse readings of the same comedy finally found suitable forms of their own; they dispelled the taboo against altering the play's 'objective' and 'lasting' interpretation, which had been cast, paradoxically, in Koun's single and determinate mould. From the early 1960s until the late 1980s, the mere handful of new adaptations of Aristophanes' *Birds* could only be partially successful. Stage directors avoided presenting *Birds*, because they feared that their own production would inevitably be compared unfavourably with the standards set by Koun. Many critics have admitted that contemporary Greek producers need a certain 'audacity' to revive *Birds* anew. The 'anxiety of influence', which Harold Bloom defined in the realm of poetry, weighed heavily on the contemporaries and successors of Koun. Even Solomos, a director more than capable of formulating an innovative, coherent reading of a dramatic text, failed to shake off the burden of *Birds*' recent past in his 1979 production with the Greek National Theatre. In this realm of the revival of the revival production, time and socio-political change was needed to have new aesthetic approaches prevail over the older political meanings of the prototype.

The model quality of Koun's *Birds* restricted not only outsiders but also insiders. The heirs of his Art Theatre still occasionally repeat the by now over-forty-five-year old production. They stay as close as possible to their 'master's' creation, in a show of homage that paradoxically subverts any natural evolution in the reception of *Birds*, whether of Koun or Aristophanes. Under the pressure of scandal, success, and nostalgia, the in-house repetitions of the *Birds* have *not* become entangled in new and diverse webs of signification: they are not allowed to change anything in the original version. The Art Theatre has even deliberately preserved the translation, decor, costumes, and music used in what was, in fact, the 1962 revision. The Greek audience –unrealistically — wants to share in the old experience and become part of the eventful history and dramatic career of the *Ur*-production.

In 1997 Giorgos Lazanis and Mimis Kougioumtzis joined together to present by far the most repeat performance of *Birds* as a memorial event. On the occasion of the tenth anniversary of Koun's death, they restaged the original production twice at the Epidaurus theatre. A total of nearly sixteen thousand spectators gathered to partake in a veritable flashback of Greek cultural history. The 1959 *Birds* had gained the 'agelessness' of a classic; it had also become uncomfortably authoritative in its own right. Lazanis and Kougioumtzes, who cast themselves as indebted disciples and loyal heirs of Koun, saw it as their duty to move the public of 1997 closer to the 'master', rather than bringing Koun — let alone the classical playwright — closer to his latest audience. Like the *auteur* filmmaker, Koun had become the 'author' of a production that was decidedly his. He had presented the less-familiar ancient text in unsettlingly familiar guise, and his underlying vision had stamped *Birds* with the seal of his ownership. Even as the formal ban initially curbed Koun's directorial freedom, the general licence of Greek 'authorial theatre' could not be revoked. Through the play's subsequent success, Koun essentially legitimated even the marginal producer's right to press his or her own ideas in reviving the classics. In the spirit of commemoration, cast members, theatre critics, and journalists discussed the 1997 repeat performances in terms reminiscent of the rhetoric of 'respect', which had typically been accorded to ancient *tragedy* by conservatives in the past. New constraints were imposed, not externally as a result of any excess of familiarity, but via inherited modes of exaggerated 'faithfulness' that demanded verbal and visual literalism. This respect made of the most value-laden achievement of Aristophanic revival theatre the touchstone against which repeat performances would be measured, but simultaneously deprived Koun's essentially revisionist *Birds* of its chances to build a new logical cohesion and to discover its psychological depth, motivation, and relevance to the changed world of the late twentieth century. In Foucauldian terms, Aristophanes thereby redefined but also expanded the established canon.[40] His comedy reinscribed its own history, affirmed the received Greek legacy, and even produced its own language and power dynamics in terms of 'paying respect'.

Postscript

By the late 1970s, most Greeks — and even conservative critics — recognized that the creative use of ancient comic materials opened up challenging artistic and socio-political avenues that were more promising than the reduction of comedy to a state of artificial preservation for its value as cultural capital. Thus Aristophanes could more and more freely be used as a vehicle of criticism and introspection. By way of insights gleaned from the classical playwright, issues of current public concern were

FIG. 9.4. Caricaturist Dimitris Chantzopoulos refers to *Birds* in 1994

tabled for debate and scrutiny. Aristophanes' utopias could more openly, and more productively, be contrasted with the faulty realities of contemporary Greece. The poet could function as a key to the country's recent past and present state and help to define the position of various classes of Greeks within the nation. Influenced by the example of the Art Theatre, and anxious to assert themselves with common Greek audiences, directors, actors, and artists were quick to exploit what they believed to be the modern, new-leftist dynamics of *all* the plays of Aristophanes. They recognized the political weight of seemingly innocent translations, adaptations, and individual allusions and realized the poet's potential for dissident transgression under different historical conditions. These heirs and successors to the 1959 scandal, drawn both from within and from outside the Art Theatre, enhanced the revisionist and indeed disruptive force of the comic revival stage and, in the process, called forth anew the occasional outburst of enmity from staunch defenders of the current socio-political order. Aristophanes' *Birds* provided the caricaturist Dimitris Chantzopoulos, for

FIG. 9.5. Greek postage stamp, 1987

instance, with a means to denounce Andreas Papandreou and the aloofness that tainted the years of his mid-1990s administration (fig. 9.4).

In addition, the directors, translators, performers, composers, and artists of the new democratic era were keenly interested in those aspects of Aristophanes' language and stagecraft that their predecessors had toned down, in particular his ribald wordplay and parodic diction. Over time, the demand for literal or 'faithful' translations diminished, and new renditions that deployed the slang of the city or of a vibrant youth and pop culture appeared. Like Koun, contemporary Greek interpreters of the comic playwright have based their methods on modern audience responses and sensibilities and much less on the principles that have guided more conventional approaches to classical tragedy. Spyros Evangelatos, for instance, has been emphasizing, not the rural or folkloric, but the urban and tragicomic dimensions of Attic comedy.[41] Trends during the last quarter of the twentieth century included also the development of innovative regional Greek theatre and moves toward explicitly western-oriented, postmodern, techno-savvy, or sensational productions of Aristophanes. To make the ancient comedies more relevant for modern audiences, some directors have modified their socio-political humour, while others have made the plays completely contemporary by supplying full modern equivalents for the political, literary, and artistic victims of Aristophanes. The women plays have often become feminist, militant, or political, and displayed heightened social and global awareness. Aristophanes thus consistently reached broader audiences than did any classical tragedian, especially among the popular strata of Greek society. Koun's

Birds of 1959 marked the beginning of a new Greek debate about the comic stage and theatre aesthetics that has lasted through the 1990s and through the start of the twenty-first century and that, whenever it could, integrated politics or spilled over into that domain.

Since the 1970s, however, Aristophanes' plays have not been divorced, either, from the pragmatic, organizational, and marketing aspects of translations, stage adaptations, summer festivals, commercial promotions, and the like. Occasional repressive influences returned in the form of government control, the pressure exerted by media reports, the devouring system of star performances (by the popular stars of theatre and especially television), and the at times stifling training methods practised by established drama schools. Yet it is important to note that a diachronic exchange has continued to operate on the modern Greek stage between the works of individual directors and the older and even the younger generations of critics. Many audience members participate in this discourse: they read and discuss theatre reviews; they follow up on revival productions and repeat performances, they take active memories from one show to the next, and they buy into the book market of a huge output of drama-related popular works, from professional and political (auto)biographies to actors' memoirs and confessional gossip. But time and again, Aristophanes' role as a cultural icon in modern Greek society, politics, literature, and the arts has been confirmed: the poet has functioned both as a source of legitimacy for less-established cultural, artistic, and political values and as a forum to negotiate and renegotiate the desirability and consistency of such values. Nothing could better capture this modern Greek investment in Aristophanes' 'democratic capital' than a postage stamp issued in 1987 by the Republic of Greece. Modern Greek does not use the common Latin-derived word for 'republic', but uses the word *demokratia* instead. The postage stamp reproduced above (fig. 9.5) sports an image of a popular Aristophanic actor (Christophoros Nezer) accompanied by the words 'Hellenike Demokratia'. These refer as much to the Republic of Greece, in the official designation of the Greek state system since 1974, as to the values of democracy derived from classical Hellas.[42]

Notes to Chapter 9

1. The Civil War of 1946–49 saw the internecine strife between embattled Greek nationalists and communists over the social and political hegemony of liberated Greece.
2. Vlachos (1946).
3. Bourdieu's theory can be conveniently accessed in English in Bourdieu (1993). For a recent interpretation of revivals of ancient tragedy produced by the Greek National Theatre in the light of Bourdieu's theory, see Roilou (1999).
4. Vlachos (1946). In an illuminating article, Mavrogeni (2002), 347 and *passim*, stressed that the international tour of select ancient plays was also supposed to jumpstart the development of mass foreign tourism to Greece.
5. Vlachos made the latter arguments in a detailed follow-up article, published two years later and entitled 'A Parenthesis. The National Theatre' (Vlachos 1948). See also the response of Ploritis (1948).
6. For images of what Greece looked like after the first substantial amounts of American aid had come in, see the photo reportage published in the *The National Geographic Magazine*: Williams (1949).

7. The tour group, fifty persons strong, kept an open agenda: 'If they [the first fifteen performances of 'these famed ... classics'] meet with favor they will be shown in other American cities', Sedgwick (1952) announced. The tour was indeed extended. See Martin (1952). The sketch on the front page of the Sunday edition of *The New York Times* of 16 Nov. 1952, which accompanied Sedgwick's article, depicts a scene from the *Oedipus* play in which Minotis as Oedipus confronts Paxinou alias Iocaste. A dozen of the male chorus members stand by. All are dressed in ancient-style costumes. Here, Al Hirschfeld, the illustrator for *The New York Times* who was widely acclaimed for his theatrical drawings, revealed his love of the line and his fascination with Greek drapery, in particular.

8. Of course, anyone who read or heard Karolos Koun explicate his reassessment of ancient drama in the light of his vision of Greek Folk Expressionism could not but be struck by the similarities. Koun's aesthetic manifesto was reprinted in full or in abridged form in nearly all playbills issued for comic revivals staged by his Art Theatre. This long 'theoretical' statement can be found also in Van Steen (2000), 159–61. For more information on Greek Folk Expressionism, the case for modern Greek exceptionalism made by Koun and many of his disciples, and the artistic and ideological consequences, see below and Van Steen (2000), 161–78. Minotis and Paxinou applied their version of the argument for continuity through the more popular tradition to perhaps the least palpable areas of classical theatre. They did so with a touch of chauvinism that spoke louder than any presentiment of inconsistency. They maintained that the translations that they employed, Ioannis Gryparis' Demotic rendition of Sophocles' *Electra* and Photos Politis' translation of *Oedipus Rex*, 'caught the spirit of the ancient tongue to a degree that no other language could approximate'. They even hazarded a similar continuity theory in the area of least certainty, ancient Greek music. The Minotis couple called the musical scores (by Dimitris Mitropoulos for *Electra* and by Paxinou herself for *Oedipus*) 'supremely suitable, being in the perennial Greek tradition and deriving from the great dirges, the like of which can be heard even today in the wild, mountainous areas of Crete and the Mani'. These quotations are taken from Sedgwick (1952).

9. Atkinson (1952*a*).

10. Atkinson (1952*b*).

11. Vlachos (1946).

12. All three suggested tragedies of Sophocles still figured in Vlachos (1948). There, however, he dropped Aeschylus' *Persians* but added Euripides' *Alcestis*.

13. Vlachos laid out his credentials somewhat before identifying his more specific guidelines in Vlachos (1948).

14. On the long-standing modern Greek and foreign qualms about Aristophanes' role in the conviction and death of the 'father of rationalism', see Van Steen (2000), ch. 1 and *passim*.

15. The debate is reflected in a string of contemporary newspaper articles and in a special issue of the periodical *Hellenike Demiourgia* (edited by Melas 1952). On Karzis and Karantinos' approach to classical comedy, see further Mavrogeni (2002), 348–50; Van Steen (2000), 197, 198–99, 200, 226, 255 n. 10.

16. See further Van Steen (2000), 127, 155–57.

17. Since the mid-1950s, ancient drama has been the artistic commodity of the annual state-funded summer Festivals of Ancient Greek Drama at Athens and Epidaurus, at which impressive open-air performances have proved their commercial potential, partly through their appeal to international tourists. On the institutional structures and origins of the Athens and Epidaurus Festivals, see further Van Steen (2000), 194–96.

18. Mavrogeni (2002), 350 argued that, after 1951, revivals of ancient tragedy paved the road for revivals of comedy by abandoning first the antiquarian, museum-style approach. The path, however, had been cleared by Koun since the 1930s. Because of the Occupation and the Civil War, the 1940s were a lost decade for Greece. Work on Aristophanes could only resume in earnest in the early 1950s.

19. On Solomos's treatment of Aristophanes, see further Van Steen (2000), 197–98, 199–204, 226–27, and *passim*. See also Mavrogeni (2002), 351–52.

20. From about 1900 until the 1930s, women were excluded from the transvestite productions of the 'women plays'. Mainstream theatre companies would have nothing to do with this kind

of Aristophanes. On the hazardous road taken by the 'women plays' to respectability in the modern Greek performance tradition, see Van Steen (2000), ch. 3, and, more recently, Van Steen (2002).

21. See also Mavrogeni (2002), 350–51.
22. Within the administration of Karamanlis' conservative National Radical Union (ERE), Konstantinos Tsatsos held the formal position of minister of the presidency of the government, and accordingly had oversight of interior cultural affairs. A former professor in the philosophy of law at the University of Athens, Tsatsos was a critic, friend, and brother-in-law of the poet Giorgos Seferis, with whom he had engaged in a modernist-aesthetic dialogue on poetry and on the nature of Hellenicity (*hellinikotita*) in 1938 to 1939. Under a second and more liberal post-dictatorship administration of Karamanlis (1974–81), Tsatsos became president of the Hellenic Republic.
23. All translations from modern Greek are my own, unless otherwise noted.
24. On church-influenced acts of censorship against theatre plays, which intensified after 1957 and resorted to laws issued under the Nazi occupation of Greece, see Mavrogeni (2002), 353 n. 43, and Van Steen (2001).
25. See further the study by Myrsiades and Myrsiades (1999).
26. For a detailed analysis of the scandal, its political context, and the immediate outcry, and also for more cartoons, see Van Steen (2000), ch. 4.
27. The modern Greek word for 'birds' is *poulia*, but it is seldom used to refer to Aristophanes' comedy, except perhaps in children's versions of the play. The generic, non-gendered modern Greek word for 'chickens' is *kotes*.
28. Damianakou (1960), 78. For a more extensive quotation of Damianakou's cynical parody of the rhetoric of contemporary anticommunist paranoia, see Van Steen (2000), 131.
29. On Koun's folk conception of the *Birds* and other Aristophanic comedies, see also Glytzouris (2001), 589–90.
30. See further Van Steen (2000), ch. 3.
31. Chourmouzios (1978), 292.
32. See Kangelari (2005), 31; Van Steen (2000), 251 n. 41.
33. The outcry was therefore more politically motivated than Mavrogeni (2002), 353–54 leads one to believe. Mavrogeni's general conclusion (p. 355), however, is more to the point: she sees the patriotic conception of revival drama opposing the folk interpretation of Aristophanes, with the two clashing in the 1959 *Birds*.
34. Hatzidakis' score was recently re-released in a remastered version, together with a booklet (Minos-EMI 7243 522324 2 0). See also http://www.hadjidakis.gr.
35. For more information on Tsarouchis' sets and costumes, see Kontogiorgi (2000), 109–14.
36. On the cultural-historical and philhellenic values attached to *Persians*, see Van Steen (2007).
37. Koltsidopoulou (1975), 51.
38. This is not to say that the practice of public reperformance was rare or non-existent in antiquity. In the 4th c. BC, the Hellenistic period, and the Roman Empire (where they were usually performed in different ways, in sung recital or as danced pantomime), some classical Greek tragedies were revived in urban centres (which increasingly built their own theatres), at festival competitions, in provincial villages, and in private for audiences of elite spectators. On these topics, see Easterling (1997), Revermann (1999/2000), the collection of essays in Easterling and Hall (2002), and Hall and Wyles (forthcoming). However, the nearly uninterrupted flow of modern Greek repeat performances, which began with the summer festivals of the mid-1950s, gained much in intensity from the plays' return to the same official locations (Athens and Epidaurus), which were frequented regularly in antiquity by many of the first spectators.
39. While it would be rewarding to study the various forms of intertextual stage dynamics to which Koun's *Birds* has been subjected, I refer here for a more detailed analysis to Van Steen (2000), 141–45.
40. See the warnings made by Jonathan Miller (1986), 109 against this danger of canonization by repeat performances and revivals of the same production.
41. For more on Evangelatos' treatment of Aristophanes, see Van Steen (2000), 215–18.
42. For more extensive references, see the bibliography section attached to Van Steen (2000), 259–73.

CHAPTER 10

❖

The Use of Masks in Koun's Stage Interpretations of *Birds*, *Frogs*, and *Peace*

Angeliki Varakis

'Greekness', Masks and Folk Aesthetics

> The Greek cultural heritage is so vast that no one really knows who is going to
> be called to carry out its designs in practice. [...] Anyone who takes the trouble
> to look into this endless adventure will learn a lesson of great value. Our folk
> song can, in the sensitivity of one and the same person, throw fresh light on
> Homer and fill in the meaning of Aeschylus.[1]

The poet Giorgos Seferis, who would win the Nobel Prize, delivered these lines
as part of a speech made in 1947 at the opening of the folk painter Theophilos'
first exhibition at the British Institute in Athens. A decade later, Karolos Koun
presented his first professional Aristophanic production, *Wealth*, in which Greek
popular songs were indeed sung to communicate the meaning of an ancient poet,
thus transforming the comedy into a modern Greek event inspired by live popular
traditions.

   Just like Seferis, Koun trusted in the value of a live popular language that would
revive the spirit of the ancient plays in a simple but truthful manner, thus producing
an experience that could engage his present-day audience. In his view, the primitive
artistic forms and oral practices of the changeless rural environment would allow for
the effective communication of the ritual and lyrical dimension of the text through
the creative appropriation of traditional folk customs, sounds, rhythms, colours and
songs. As he declared in the early stages of his career:

> Our aim is to create a stage with a Greek tradition. [...] We shall be guided
> by the customs and images that one can still find in Greece as symbols of the
> spirit and life of modern times. Through these symbols, plenty of which have
> survived from antiquity up to recent times, we shall approach ancient Greek
> drama.[2]

Koun's interest in the ideal of the primitive stemmed from a wider tendency which
started to develop in Greece during the inter-war period. Intellectuals who had
received education elsewhere in Europe, who belonged to the Modernist movement

and would later be recognized as the 'Generation of the Thirties', became increasingly interested in rural village customs that could inspire their personal creativity and simultaneously create a new cultural identity for a troubled nation. Greece had just come through a devastating war with Turkey in 1922, and it became a matter of urgency for the progressive intelligentsia and avant-garde artistic circles to provide the nation with a new cultural selfhood that instead of depending solely on ancient Greek civilization would link all periods of Greek history.[3] Seferis, a leading figure of the Generation of the Thirties, displayed this tendency in a long debate about Hellenism which he conducted with Professor Konstantinos Tsatsos. Tsatsos charged Koun with 'using abusive and indefensible distortions' when presenting his stage version of *Birds* in 1959 (for further discussion of which see Van Steen, this volume). In Seferis' view, there was a distinction between people like Tsatsos, who wished to interpret ancient tradition through foreign sources, and those who looked within their own land and souls to discover the Hellenic spirit. The first tendency manifested a superficial attempt to tackle the ancients, while the second reflected a far deeper and more meaningful effort to understand the ancient Greek psyche. As Seferis stated, the creation of European Hellenism had happened long before, and this type of Hellenism was perhaps already in a process of dying, but 'our own "Greek Hellenism", if I may be permitted so to call it, has not yet been created and has not yet recovered its tradition'.[4]

In the realm of theatre, the 'Delphic Idea' developed by Eva Palmer-Sikelianou and Angelos Sikelianos combined elements from the culture of classical Greece (costumes, masks) and Byzantium (music) to create productions of ancient drama that attempted to recover the ancient Greek spirit; in the late 1920s and early 1930s the director Photos Politis meanwhile developed an interest in popular Greek forms of performance.[5] The desire to capture the essence of 'Greekness' also characterized the field of visual art, becoming apparent in the work of painters and stage designers. The artists Giannis Tsarouchis, Nikos Hadjikyriakos-Ghikas, Nikos Nikolaou, Giannis Moralis, D. Diamantopoulos, and Giorgos Mavroidis were among those who expressed this tendency by combining Modernist precepts in painting with themes and style inspired by archaic sculptures and mosaics, Byzantine religious paintings and more recent paintings by folk artists such as Theophilos and Kontoglou. The masks in Koun's early work at the Laiki Skini (for example, the *Alcestis* of 1934),[6] and later Aristophanic productions for the Art Theatre (Theatro Technis),[7] resonate with this peculiar mixture of archaic art and modern Greek tradition, especially thanks to the work of his stage designers Yannis Tsarouchis and Dionysis Fotopoulos. The folk painter Kontoglou was also pivotal in Koun's development as a theatre practitioner and a key inspiration for the creation of the Art Theatre's aesthetic principle of 'Greek folk expressionism'.[8] In numerous interviews, Koun admitted to the influence exerted upon him by Kontoglou, and to how he 'fell in love with Greece' through the primitive simplicity of the artist's folk paintings.[9]

Koun's position regarding the issue of 'Greekness' became visible to the broader public in 1957, when he announced the advantages that could be enjoyed by Greeks when reviving ancient plays in a way that reflected Seferis' vision of a new tradition based on the notion of Greek Hellenism. As he stated:

Even though centuries have passed and our race has changed through the ages, we cannot ignore the fact that we live under the same sky, under the same bright sunlight, and on the same land. The same geological and climatic conditions affect and form our everyday life and thought. [...] The images and feelings created in our minds today draw shape and colour from the same natural landscape that surrounded our ancestors. The living elements that surround us today will help us understand and feel the thought and poetry within the ancient plays much more than any historical study regarding the exterior form of ancient drama.[10]

The director was making an ideological and political statement implying that Greek people should recover their past in a genuine Greek folk form. The land and nature of Greece were crucial in giving rise to particular emotions and thoughts, and therefore people of different ages who lived on the same land could present strong similarities with each other. The revival of Greek drama was no longer a matter of historical knowledge but a matter of confidence in the fact that, since the interpreters were Greek, the works created out of their souls could not be anything but Hellenic.

For example, in Koun's view, the correct way to stage the carnal mode of Aristophanic comedy was by means of Greek performers. The Greek people were more sensual and expressive than Western Europeans so the vulgarity of the plays and excessive behaviour of the comic characters would seem more natural and less offensive when presented by actors who shared the same high-spirited temperament that had characterized the ancient performers.[11] His appreciation of 'Greekness' also justified making analogies between ancient and modern performance traditions, notably between Aristophanic comedy and the popular shadow theatre known as Karaghiozis, a feature evident in his 1976 production of *Acharnians* where the leading character adopted the distinctive physicality of the shadow-puppet hero. The 'Greekness' of both types of performance was directly relevant to, and inspired by their natural environment; they thus shared the same spirit. As Antonis Glytzouris has observed with regard to this tendency, 'By reducing the notion of 'Greekness' to a mythical symbol, every Greek historical period could from now on interpret another.'[12] But Koun also acknowledged other, non-Greek, sources on which he was prepared to draw in his continual search for the magic that is theatre. This is partly relevant to his understanding of Greek culture as an amalgam of western and eastern elements, which is often ascribed to the country's unique geographic position, located between Western Europe and the Middle East.

Koun's desire to capture the essence of 'Greekness' as conveyed in the pure environment of the rural countryside gave rise to productions grounded in modern ritual activities and popular raw emotions rather than archaeological formality or spectacular effects. The latter were a key characteristic of the lavish National Theatre (Ethniko Theatro) performances of Alexis Solomos, which were deeply influenced by the western popular entertainment practices characteristic of bourgeois theatre.[13] Within nine years of his first production in 1956, Solomos had presented eight out of the eleven Aristophanic plays, using grandiose spectacle and impressive choreography, in an attempt to attract the urban audiences that would gather every summer in Epidauros.[14] Although Solomos's productions were rich in spectacle they lacked the totality and organic quality of Koun's performances, which were primarily rooted in the body of the performer. One could argue that the stylistic dissimilarity between the National Theatre and Art Theatre productions stemmed from the different way in which the directors read the popular element in Aristophanic theatre. For Solomos, the popularity of classical comedy was connected to its entertainment value, as expressed by means of a spectacular choreography and a famous leading actor, whilst for Koun it was associated with the earthy and sensual quality of the ancient roles, reflecting his deeper contemplation of the origins and nature of comedy.[15]

The mask was crucial to Koun's wider project. It was the surreal and primitive mask used in popular festivities, in its double capacity as both an aesthetic object and ritual device, that became the perfect means for fulfilling his vision of a sensual and ritual Aristophanes. As Koun admitted, although the masks in rural festivities bore no resemblance to the comic masks used in antiquity, they still contained an earthy quality and presented a scruffy, shabby appearance that was appropriate to the process of uncovering of comedy's carnal mode and carnivalesque mood.[16] Koun's masks, especially in his comic performances, are deeply imbued with this sense of being well worn. Each mask was unique and even the masks worn by the chorus were distinguished from each other by subtle variations in their design.[17] This variety, in combination with the energetic physicality of the performers, added a playful and anarchic ambience to the performance, which was in line with Koun's general disapproval of 'military' formality in the staging of ancient drama. In his view, strict formality was an alien concept for the Greeks because even within a traditional pattern of collective movement there was room for spontaneity.[18] This sense of imperfection and individual creativity was further stressed in the festive world of Aristophanes.

Masks also allowed for the effective communication of the poetry that constituted the text. Their use by the chorus would help the actors deliver the lyrical parts in a more focused way, whilst encouraging them to behave as an organic entity. This was not irrelevant to the director's belief that one of the most important elements of the performance was the text, and more specifically the poetic lines uttered by the chorus.[19] The face of the performer, if presented unmasked and naked, might through its expressions and varied grimaces have distracted the audience's attention away from the poetry of the play. The concealment of the face, on the other hand, automatically made the spectator focus on what was said rather than who was saying it.[20] The idea of the mask as a concealment device that helps the actors maintain an impersonal aspect was a justification for Koun and the Art Theatre's persistence in using the half-mask, especially in tragic performances. Instead of employing full masks, which were devices to reveal characters, for the presentation of a chorus Koun preferred using half-masks. In most of Koun's productions the lower face of the performer remains visible, whereas in ancient theatrical performances the mask functioned virtually as a helmet that covered the whole face and head. In this respect, Koun's use of masks appears closer to Brechtian theatre than to ancient Greek theatre. The actor does not vanish behind the mask, in order to allow a fresh identity to emerge, but instead becomes a 'vocal medium of expression' similar to a

FIG. 10.1. Clockwise from top right: scenes from *Peace* (1977), *Birds* (1962), *Frogs* (1966)

storyteller. On various occasions, Koun admitted the pivotal role of modern theatre and Brecht in his interpretation of Greek drama and use of the mask. [21]

The mask's appearance in Koun's professional productions of *Birds, Frogs,* and *Peace* corresponded to live images found in the Greek countryside and other live festivities (fig. 10.1). Simultaneously, its attachment to the dynamic presence of the chorus and other symbolic figures transformed it into an object of a true ritual celebration that energized the bodies of the performers and overall atmosphere of the comedy. In each production, the use of masks was connected with the director's ritual reading of the choral sections, which incorporated a distinctive aesthetic quality inspired by the nature of the chorus and characteristic setting of the play. For example, the masks in the 'upstairs' comedies *Peace* and *Birds* were more festive than the half masks used to represent the underworld initiates in *Frogs*, which conveyed a more tragic impression.

Birds: The Mask as Surreal Element in an 'Oneiric' Performance

Koun considered *Birds* to be a dream-like drama with a surreal dimension created by the presence of a non-human chorus. He also regarded the movement, appearance and sound of the zoomorphic figures to be one the main attractions of the comedy when presented on stage. This was the key reason for the director's later reservations about certain performance aspects of the controversial production (discussed in detail by Van Steen, this volume) that stressed the socio-political side of the play at the expense of its fantastic dimension. As he remembered many years later:

> We made direct references to real political personalities in the 1959 production of *Birds*. This prompted the immediate reaction of the government that forced us to cut them out. Maybe this was for the best, because today I consider such references spiteful. One finds them appealing at first but then regrets having used them. It makes you feel sad. Things and situations change and this is the reason why I do not agree with direct political references to the present.[22]

Influenced by the production's negative reception, Koun searched for an appropriate form that would expose the utopian side of the play, and decided to make a number of modifications to the initial performance. The director's emphasis on the political aspect of the comedy was set aside, while the lyrical and fantastic dimension became a priority, and was transmitted via the vigorous presence of the chorus. The prioritization of the play's visual side and performers' corporality was also partly a reaction to the production's touring appearances at international festivals, where the non-Greek audiences would have difficulty understanding the details of the text. The responsibility for relaying the Greek and surreal spirit of the play therefore came to rest upon the use of colours, sounds, rhythms, and movement. [23]

In the 1962 version of the comedy, the physicality of the chorus was transformed from an orderly and traditional style of movement into 'a spectacle of animal revelry', whilst the costumes of the birds were refashioned from a naturalistic style to a more surreal design that suggested people wearing an animal disguise as they engaged in ritual practices (see fig. 10.1 above, and fig. 9.2 in Van Steen's chapter, p. 169). The pivotal role of the chorus in the creation of an appropriate mood was emphasized by making it move within a plain set and on a bare raised platform. The reviewer Ploritis described the choreography and costumes of the improved *Birds*:

> This year the production of *Birds* is more complete and rhythmic, with a number of improvements. The most important difference between the earlier and present production is that the weakness of the choreography has been corrected. This year the choreography of Zouzou Nikoloudi is perfectly adjusted to the rhythm of the music and spirit of the directorial approach [...] the costumes by Yannis Tsarouchis have been refashioned so as to retain their fine simple lines, but they are enriched with colours and shapes suitable for the fairy-tale quality of the play.[24]

In the costumes worn by the chorus, the faces of the birds did not come across as the most important element for identifying each one's individual nature; the faces now seemed to be parts of the bodies. The members of the chorus masked their eyes as if they were wearing spectacles. They also wore a hat that varied in shape and size from performer to performer, with colourful artificial feathers that connected the head aesthetically to the body. Even though a mask did not cover the eyes of the performer, the costume still appeared effective in concealing identity and establishing a visual bond between the faces of the birds, especially when seen from a distance. Like the carnival eye-mask, the head pieces obscured the individual expression of the performer as generated by the eyes in combination with the eyebrows. In an open-air theatre, the mask would have been the most visible element of the performer's face, thus concentrating the audience's gaze towards the eyes of the bird.

It is interesting to reflect on why Tsarouchis did not choose to mask the nose of the performer, which is usually the most dominant feature of a bird-like image. In Tsarouchis' designs, the impression of a bird was produced mainly through the costume and the physical movement of the actors, and this is connected with the African rituals that inspired him. As he noted:

> In our first attempt at staging *Birds* [...] I asked a Greek professor in London [...] to translate from an English ornithology book the names of the birds into modern Greek. All the costumes of the birds were inspired by real pictures and were very naturalistic. As I continued working I realized that I was mistaken, and that naturalism is not always the best solution for theatre, especially ancient Greek theatre. [...] In the second version of the production the naturalistic costumes became more fantastic, but the final and most perfect version was when the set and costumes found, in my personal opinion, the correct style, after exploring African costumes that appear in rituals.[25]

Even though the shapes and forms of the costumes were inspired by exotic ritualistic celebrations, their earthy colours highlighted the aesthetic ideal of Greek Folk Expressionism. It was the colours rather than the shapes that connected these animal images to the more classical figures of the gods, who emerged in the performance with large head masks. Koun intentionally masked these mythical figures with tall masks in order to distinguish their heroic status from that of the human characters and chorus. For example, Iris was represented by a sizeable pale mask inspired by classical art and sculpture; it had a straight nose and well-balanced features, but no detailed expression (this personal style of the designer Tsarouchis is also evident in other portraits and masks by him). The pale face, and angel-like costume, with ribbon in the hair, lent the goddess a subtle, delicate appearance, whilst the size added an imaginary feel to the entire image (fig. 10.2).

The other three large masks, belonging to Poseidon, Heracles, and the Triballian deity Trivalos, were grotesque, had more detailed expressions and were bronzed. The mask that represented the barbarian god Trivalos was the darkest, and it was this, in combination with his wide mouth, that indicated his exotic origin. These masks functioned as headpieces in the same manner as they did in antiquity, and their overall design seemed to have been inspired by images of large masks found at festivals. As an English reviewer observed when describing the figures of the Gods: 'The comic masks of the indignant gods revealed to me the link between the masks of old Greek drama and pâpier-maché fairground giant-heads.'[26] Their large size and festive quality assisted in the suggestion of the small mythical community of Gods and invited the spectator to enter a dreamlike world reminiscent of children's fairytales. Unlike the birds that gained their dynamic through their continuous motion as a scattered group, the grand figures of the gods, with simple and contained movements, were equally effective in creating a surreal feel, especially when seen alongside the unmasked and more realistic figures of the comic protagonists.

FIG. 10.2. The figure of Iris in Koun's 1962 *Birds*

Frogs: Masks as Mystical Objects within an Exotic Ritual

By the time *Frogs* was performed at the theatre of Herodes Atticus in 1966, Koun had achieved overwhelming success and international recognition for his seminal productions of *Birds* (in the 1962 version) and also Aeschylus' tragedy *Persians* (1965). It is therefore essential to see the function of the mask in his *Frogs* in the context of his earlier landmark works, and as a continuation of his systematic efforts towards creating a total theatre grounded in folk ritual activities. In the 1965 staging of

FIG. 10.3. The chorus of frogs in Koun's 1966 *Frogs*

Persians, the masked chorus had been used as a prime means for the communication of the emotional poetry of the ancient play. The passionate images expressed in Aeschylus' poetic language were transformed into physical representations through the various formations of the chorus' bodies, which exploited in the most effective way the corporeal possibilities of the text. The chorus's central position stressed the ritual side of Greek drama, summoning up a theatre of religious meaning where the masked actor was not a reciter of choral speeches but a true initiate who suffers and expresses himself physically on stage, evoking the chthonic and pagan elements of Greek theatre. The melodies of Yannis Christou, eastern in feel, orchestrated in a highly emotional way the physicality of the chorus, emphasizing the passion within the words of the text and bodies of the performers.

Koun was accused by Stathis Dromazos, a famous Greek reviewer, of misreading the light-hearted role of the initiates in the comedy *Frogs* and treating them in a similar manner to that used for the dramatic representation of the tragic chorus in *Persians*. Dromazos believed that by staging the members of the comic chorus of *Frogs* in a ritualistic fashion, the director stressed their identity as followers of Dionysus, but failed to highlight their dramatic purpose within the play. Dromazos noted that for this comic performance Koun had used the same famous composer, Yannis Christou, as in his *Persians*, and expressed the view that the oriental tunes led the comic chorus to a Dionysiac frenzy with mystical undertones, wholly inappropriate to the satirical spirit of the lyrics. This resulted in a stylistic inconsistency between the tragic representation of the choral sections and the buffoon-like acting of the main characters.[27]

Koun stressed the Dionysiac nature of the choral parts not only by way of movement and exotic music but also by using masks and costumes (designed by Chloe Georgaki-Obolensky) inspired by images found in primitive rituals (see fig.

Whilst the 1976 production of *Acharnians* was based on an elaborate analogy with modern Greek shadow theatre, in *Peace* the visual references to Karaghiozes were less obvious. This was partly due to the use of different clothing. The traditional Anatolian *vraka* (type of baggy trouser) that was worn by shadow theatre characters and was used to represent the characters in *Acharnians* was replaced by a more universal rural costume code (fig. 10.4). As a result, the image of Trygaeus and that of the chorus evoked the western image of a rustic clown, with his distinctive red nose and shabby attire. Similarly, the raised stage platform no longer referred to the linen screen of shadow theatre, as it had in *Acharnians,* but represented a domestic village household. The full-headed masks used to represent the abstractions of the comedy (Peace, Festival, and Harvest — *Eirene, Theoria,* and *Opora*) added a topical feel, connecting the performance to local festivities and living forms of Greek celebration (fig. 10.5).

This time the production did not merely use modern folk forms to present the Aristophanic play, as was the intention in *Acharnians,* but aimed at the actual recreation of a folk festival on stage. The distinction between theatre and life consequently became less clear. The world of the play, especially towards the end of the performance, became a real celebration in which the audience took an active part. As Koun noted:

> Our objective is to achieve the active involvement of the audience within the celebration that the poet brought to the stage, because that is how the people of classical Greece perceived and staged their plays. This is why we try to make use of all the appropriate situations of the text in order to create a direct contact between the performers and the audience. When the scene encourages something like this to happen, we 'spray' the spectators with wheat or water. And at the end of the play we throw sweets and cake to the audience. Just like Dario Fo and modern popular theatre I create an intimate relation with my audience. We also throw to the spectators small pieces of paper with the word Peace spelled on it in all languages. This is our objective. We wish to involve the audience. This direct contact is essential in order for the spectators to receive the message of Peace.[30]

The presence of masks and large puppets, more than in any other of his productions, invited the audience to enter the illusion of a real celebration. They functioned primarily as uplifting elements of a true folk carnival reflecting in the most effective way Koun's appreciation of the popular mask as a live element of traditional festivals. The structure and nature of the play *Peace* encouraged a festive approach. Just as in a carnival parade, each group of masked characters that visited Trygaeus was connected in a satirical way to a deeper political or social meaning. Moreover, the play ended with a great celebration similar to the climax of a carnival. Owing to the variety of images the sources of inspiration for each group were not strictly Greek. The symbolic meaning of each individual or group of characters guided the creative imagination of the mask-maker and pointed in different directions. For instance, the masks and images of the arms–sellers were inspired by American cartoons, thus satirizing in an indirect manner the United States and its role in the world.[31]

Some reviewers disagreed with the production's extreme use of folk festive traditions, and criticized Koun for presenting a one-sided interpretation of

Aristophanes. In their view, his persistence in embracing forms from folk tradition hindered the display of the text's multiple messages and threw light only on the celebratory and visual dimension of the comedy.[32] As Kostas Georgosopoulos, a famous Greek reviewer, characteristically remarked, 'The performance had a clear set of objectives but failed to display the full meaning of the Aristophanic text. [...] Aristophanes is theatre and not an illusion of life as demonstrated through Koun's recreation of a folk festival on stage'.[33] Although many may disagree with Georgosopoulos' critical remarks, he had a valid case when he implied that Aristophanes remained in the background, with the director's scenic language becoming the key text.

Within thirty years, Koun had managed to project a complete and recognizable system of interpreting Aristophanes with a clear aesthetic view based on primitive culture, raw emotions, and oral popular practices. He thus created a new play-text which on many occasions proved to be more important than Aristophanes' ancient original. The monumental stage interpretation of *Birds*, as Van Steen persuasively argues in this volume, 'became a text in its own right' through its numerous restagings.

Koun's Aristophanic productions have remained alive even after his death, and most performances mentioned in this chapter have been restaged a number of times in an attempt to keep Koun's vision for a folk Aristophanes in existence.[34] In an innovative project, which constitutes the most extreme example of this tendency, a performance entitled *Theatro Technis Karolos Koun — Half a Century of Aristophanes*, was performed at the Ancient Theatre of Epidaurus in 2004 in the framework of the Greek Cultural Olympiad.[35] In this particular production, the textual coherence was no longer important; what mattered was the revival of powerful scenes and unforgettable moments from the comedies of Aristophanes as mounted by the Art Theatre in performances formerly directed by Karolos Koun and his students Giorgos Lazanis and Mimis Kougioumtzis. The individual gems that made up this mosaic were selected from landmark productions that still serve as benchmarks for the genre. It is debatable whether the restaging of these vigorous scenes, with all the inevitable changes that have been effected through the passage of time, retained the vitality of the initial performances. One thing that is certain, however, is that the success of the performance was now dependent on the skills of montage, thus marking the beginning of a new, postmodern phase based on the nostalgic reconstruction of the Art Theatre's artistic achievements in the revival of Aristophanes.

Notes to Chapter 10

1. Seferis (1967), 8.
2. Quotation from the theatre programme for the Laiki Skini's production of *Alcestis* in Athens, December 1934. All translations from the Greek are my own, unless otherwise stated.
3. For more on the 'Generation of the Thirties' see Vitti (1989), and Van Steen (2000), 153–54.
4. Seferis (1967), 94.
5. For a more detailed account of the modern Greek theatre's attempt to recover the Greek popular element see Glytzouris (2001), 553–601.
6. The theatrical company and drama school Laiki Skini ('Popular Stage') attempted to promote

both Greek popular culture and popular theatre. The idea originally came from an intellectual, Dionysios Devaris, who was impressed by Koun's innovative stagings at the American College in Athens and saw in him the ideal person to bring his vision into life. The creation of the company took place in the winter of 1933–34, and the first play to be performed was *Erophili* (1934). The stage designer Yannis Tsarouchis was also invited to join the company and help in the creation of the sets and costumes. The idea of the school was to enrol young amateur actors who came from the working class and had in many instances abandoned school. According to Koun, within these young deprived people you could find genuine strong emotions that were expressed with honesty and with none of the restrictions imposed by the rules of good manners. The Laiki Skini's search for genuine forms applied to all aspects of a production, including costumes, sets, music, dance and acting.

7. The Art Theatre was founded in 1942 and was a continuation of the efforts made by the Laiki Skini. The first performance to be staged by the newly established company was Ibsen's *Wild Duck*, which opened on 7 Oct. 1942.

8. This was an aesthetic theory encouraging the display of Greek popular culture in its 'purest' form as it appears in unchanged rural life, folk traditions, and older Byzantine religious paintings and ancient pottery.

9. At a later stage Koun admitted that his early obsession with the aesthetics of popular iconography, as communicated through Kontoglou's paintings, prevented him from seeing or being inspired by anything else. This is apparent in Koun's very stylized productions at the Laiki Skini, which were based on colour and shapes. Koun's early stylized theatre would turn into the exact opposite in his 1977 production of *Peace*, where the intention was the creation of an illusion of a festival on stage (see pp. 188–91).

10. This is an extract from Koun's famous speech regarding ancient theatre, delivered on 4 July 1957 at an international conference on theatre held at the Theatre of Herodes Atticus. The speech has been reprinted in full in nearly all programmes issued for comic and tragic revivals of the Art Theatre, and can also be found in Koun (1997), 33–36 and (1981). Also in Van Steen (2000), 159–61.

11. Koun (1997), 81. Koun followed a similar line of thinking when explaining why Shakespeare should be interpreted by English people: see ibid. 61.

12. Glytsouris (2001), 543.

13. The first two attempts to reintroduce Aristophanes to the modern Greek public after a long pause in the revival of classical comedy were the National Theatre (Ethniko Theatro) production of *Thesmophoriazusae* (1951), directed by Sokratis Karantinos, and the Thymelikos Thiasos production of *Lysistrata* (1951), directed by Linos Karzis. In both productions full masks were used to cover the performers' faces, whilst the costume and choreography were inspired by images depicted on ancient pottery.

14. All the Aristophanic productions that were presented by the National Theatre during the period 1956–70 (*Ecclesiazusae* in 1957, *Lysistrata* in 1957 and 1960, *Thesmophoriazusae* in 1958, *Frogs* in 1959, *Acharnians* in 1961, *Wasps* in 1963, *Peace* in 1964, *Knights* in 1968, and *Clouds* in 1970) used Alexis Solomos as director, G. Vakalo as stage and costume designer, and Tatiana Varouti as choreographer.

15. Both Solomos and Aimilios Chourmouzios (artistic director of the National Theatre, 1955–64) agreed that the most comparable type of theatre was the popular, episodic *Epitheorisi* ('Review'), because of its loose plots, satirical nature, and musical interludes, which contain both singing and dancing. It also provided space for improvisation and direct contact between the comedian and the spectator. However, they both acknowledged that the Aristophanic text contained a level of poetry that the sketches of the *Epitheorisi* could never reach. Koun, on the other hand, approached Aristophanes as an earthy comedy with a sensuality that could be experienced in Greece's folk festivities: see Koun (1997), 96.

16. Ibid.

17. The best source of images of these masks is Fotopoulos (1980).

18. Koun (1997), 66–67.

19. Ibid. 59.

20. For a detailed account of the use of masks by the Art Theatre's Greek choruses see Kougioumtzis (1989), 139–42.

21. Koun (1997), 112, 116.
22. Koun (1985).
23. Koun (1997), 40.
24. Ploritis (1962).
25. Quotation from Fotopoulos (1986), 264.
26. Buckle (1964).
27. Dromazos (1993), 155–59. The critical review initially appeared in the leftist newspaper *He Auge*, 26 July 1966.
28. These masks and costumes were destroyed the following year in a fire at Patras during a tour of the production. This could partly explain why it was never restaged during the following decades.
29. Fotopoulos (1989).
30. Koun (1997), 98.
31. The best source of these images is Fotopoulos (1980).
32. See Varopoulou (1977) and Georgosopoulos (1982), 157.
33. Georgosopoulos (1982), 157.
34. *Birds* (1959, 1960, 1962, 1964, 1975, 1985, 1987, 1988, 1997), with designs by Yannis Tsarouchis, music by Manos Hatzidakis, and choreography by Ralou Manou (1959), and in the later versions by Zouzou Nikoloudi. *Acharnians* (1976, 1981, 1982, 1985, 1986, 1987, 1988). *Peace* (1977, 1978, 1989) with the designs of Dionysis Fotopoulos and music by Christos Leontis.
35. The production was created and directed by Giorgos Lazanis, Kostis Kapelonis, and Theodoros Grampsas. The sets and costumes were made by Dionysis Fotopoulos, and the choreography was designed by Maria Kynigou. The choreographies for the historic productions were by Zouzou Nikoloudi, Maria Kynigou, Natasha Zouka, Eleni Vakalopoulou, Konstantinos Rigos, and Roula Koutroumbeli.

CHAPTER 11

❖

'Aristophanes is back!'[1]
Peter Hacks's Adaptation of *Peace*

Bernd Seidensticker

On 14 October 1962 the Deutsches Theater in Berlin presented the première of Peter Hacks's adaptation of Aristophanes' *Peace*;[2] the director of the play, Benno Besson, celebrated one of the greatest, if not in fact the greatest success of his career, which was rich in successes.[3] The audience applauded for forty-five minutes and critics reacted enthusiastically. The play was shown over the course of no fewer than twelve theatre seasons in more than 250 performances, and road tours spread the fame of the production throughout Germany and Europe.[4] Until Peter Stein's *Oresteia* no other German production of an ancient play was ever received with such enthusiasm by critics and audiences. Hacks's adaptation was put on stage by a large number of theatres not only in East and West Germany, but also in other European countries and even in the United States;[5] it also inspired other dramatists to adapt Greek and Roman comedy for the contemporary stage.[6]

From a later perspective, Peter Hacks's play appears to have been the starting-signal and catalyst for the rich reception of classical material in the German Democratic Republic. Until 1962, productions of Greek tragedy or comedy in translation or free adaptation had been rare;[7] the 'Greek' plays of Sartre, Giraudoux, and Anouilh, of Wilder and O'Neill, which in the first two decades after World War II were very successful in the West, were mostly criticized in the East;[8] and with the exception of Bertolt Brecht, no major East German dramatist had ever tried to write a play with subject-matter from classical antiquity.[9] In subsequent years, Heiner Müller, who soon was to become the most important German dramatist of the second half of the twentieth century, began his lifelong work with Greek and Roman material,[10] and a number of younger authors followed suit.[11] The creative reception of classical antiquity quickly 'invaded' all areas of artistic production and became a favourite means of expression for authors, painters and composers.[12]

For Hacks, the adaptation of Aristophanes' *Peace* was 'the beginning of a wonderful friendship' with antiquity, attested by a long series of Greek and Roman plays. This comprised both adaptations and his own dramas, among which we find pieces on such well-known subjects as *Amphitryon* and *The Death of Seneca* as well as plays on more obscure topics such as *Omphale* and *Prexaspes* and even a play on the medieval nun and poetess Hrotsvit of Gandersheim, with the title *Rosie träumt.*[13]

Yet Hacks' acquaintance with antiquity had come about rather by accident. In 1961 he was commissioned by the Deutsches Theater 'to dust off an Aristophanic comedy',[14] and he selected *Peace*. It is not known whether the decision was reached in discussions with Besson or made by Hacks on his own.[15] In his critical review of Fritz Kortner's film version *Lysistrata*, which was made for television and broadcast on 17 January 1961, a year before the production of *Peace*, Hacks gave two reasons for the renaissance of Aristophanes. These were inferred from the recent productions of *Peace* in Warsaw, Paris and Berlin, and of *Lysistrata* in London:[16] 'The first reason lies in the timeliness of the subject-matter [...] and the second in its treatment.'[17]

Timeliness and form of treatment: one feels reminded of Brecht, who justified his decision to produce an adaptation of Sophocles' *Antigone* on the grounds that 'the subject-matter could obtain a certain topicality and posed interesting artistic tasks'.[18] Indeed, it was Brecht who had persuaded Hacks (and Besson) to come to Berlin and work with him at his newly founded theatre, which soon became the most famous theatre in East Germany, the so-called Berliner-Ensemble (BE); moreover, Hacks's early plays, which he had written while still in Munich, had earned him the title 'Brecht's most intelligent pupil'.[19] But by the end of the 1950s he began to disengage himself from the master and went his own way.[20] In an essay entitled 'About the play of tomorrow',[21] he abandoned the epic-sociological theatre of the 1950s; this was a type of theatre from which his friend, the dramatist Heiner Kipphardt (who at this time also worked as dramatic adviser at the Deutsches Theater), once said, 'the audience could learn how an ironworks or a canning factory works'.[22] Hacks's formulation was no less ironic: 'Authors who claim that the real problems lie in our everyday life, declare only that their real problems lie in everyday life'.[23] He called, instead, for a new form of drama, which he felt was already emerging and which he characterized by the catchphrase 'Streben nach Größe' (pursuit of greatness): 'Together, intensely and insistently, the new generation of German dramatists work on the recovery of great stories and on the artistic forms of great representation. These two tasks belong together, but they are not identical.'[24]

In a short text about Heiner Müller's first experiments with blank verse, Hacks described the immense task that East German dramatists faced:

> The socialist dramatist begins his work after more than a century of bourgeois destruction of poetic resources, after a century of destruction of the fable, destruction of character, destruction of beauty. His job is dialectical and revolutionary reconstruction.[25]

The means by which the reconstruction could take place were defined by Hacks as 'artistry, brilliance, fantasy'.[26] And he went on, wittily, to express the tensions between himself and the famously bespectacled Brecht that underlay this characterization of the means of poetic reconstruction: 'When I had arrived at this point, a critic came into the room, looked at me through his quadrangular glasses and said: "It smacks of classicism." '[27] Here the breaking away from Brecht was still implicit, but nevertheless obvious; it was one year later, in a short essay on Brecht's aesthetic theory, that Hacks committed (to use the influential terminology of Harold Bloom) every rising literary star's inevitable act of aesthetic 'parricide':[28]

> Brecht's reality was the reality of the first half of the twentieth century. Our
> reality is different; our methods and techniques therefore have to be different
> from Brecht's, if they want to be Brechtian methods and techniques.[29]

Hacks here showed respect for Brecht's achievements, but insisted that the master
had to be left behind: 'Like every human achievement, Brecht's accomplishment
is historical. It is transient and everlasting. Its continuation can only be secured by
means of negation and not by means of prolongation.'[30] Closely connected with this
turn to a socialist classicism (*sozialistische Klassik*) there was also a re-evaluation of the
literary tradition. In 1956 Hacks had attacked some early indications of a tendency
towards socialist classicism with the argument that 'the rule of the working class is
not reached at the moment when the working class has adopted the forms of the
bourgeois class and of feudalism, but at the moment when it creates its own forms'.[31]
Yet by four years later he no longer understood socialist art as the negation of earlier
forms of art, but called instead for their creative preservation and development.

For this radically new definition of the dramatist's task Hacks could appeal to
a concept which was called 'cultural inheritance' (*kulturelles Erbe*) or 'acquired
tradition' (*erworbene Tradition*).[32] This theory, which was developed and propagated
by the cultural bureaucracy of the GDR during this period, was based on Lenin's
fourth thesis on proletarian culture, according to which 'Marxism had won its
historic significance as the ideology of the revolutionary proletariat because, far
from rejecting the most valuable achievements of the bourgeois epoch, it has, on
the contrary, assimilated and refashioned everything of value in the more than two
thousand years of the development of human thought and culture.'[33] At the fifth
congress of the central committee of the East German Socialist Party (SED) in
March 1951, moreover, the regime had heralded the realization of a fully developed
socialism ('Sieg der sozialistischen Produktionsverhältnisse') and had granted poets,
painters, and composers greater artistic freedom.

Hacks could easily and safely inscribe his call for a revival of the great classical
dramatists into this political context.

> The respect for greatness shown by the new German dramatists changes their
> perspective on the history of literature. They now look further back than to
> the few years of bourgeois decadence. From a high ideological vantage point
> they clearly see the peaks Aeschylus, Aristophanes, Shakespeare, Goethe,
> and Büchner, and don't take the hills Ibsen and Hauptmann for the real
> mountains.[34]

During the years that followed, Hacks therefore dealt with the 'elephants' of literary
history, as he called them, in both theory and practice: he tackled Shakespeare,[35]
Goethe,[36] and Aristophanes. *Peace* was the first classical play Hacks adapted, and
Hacks described Aristophanes, in his review of Fritz Kortner's *Lysistrata* (see above),
as 'the greatest comic poet of all time', 'inventor of every basic comic situation,
creator of a type of comedy that was not equalled before Shakespeare'.[37] In the same
essay Hacks also talks about the adaptation of Aristophanes for the modern stage:

> He is ineffective, if we try to put him on stage in correct translation. The
> more pedantically we hold on to him, the more thoroughly we abandon him.
> Faithfulness is betrayal. The reason for this paradoxical truth lies in the fact that

FIG. 11.1. Chorus and musicians in Hacks's *Der Frieden*, 1962

most of his qualities cannot be reproduced. We are not able to imitate them, so
we must try to comprehend and reproduce them by our own means.[38]

In this particular version, Hacks, who knew no Greek, used a number of
nineteenth- and twentieth-century translations;[39] since he used them very freely,
his text of course strays far from the original wording. However, Hacks perfectly
comprehended the essence of Aristophanic style, the colourful mixture of different
elements and registers, and reproduced it effectively. His text — like the Aristophanic original — fuses pointed and witty brevity with exuberant fullness,
lofty poetic imagery with crude scatology and obscenity, low colloquialism and
paratragic pathos, idiomatic terms and artificial neologisms.

Apart from the verbal puns, which are difficult to transfer from one language to
another, Hacks preserved most of Aristophanes' jokes and comic situations. Rather
than toning down the scatological and sexual jokes and allusions, he actually
intensified them, and in some places he was inspired by his Greek prototype to
vary or expand the original in a truly Aristophanic manner and tone, as for example
in the Hierokles scene (1052–1126). In Aristophanes, Hierokles does not get the
coveted part of the sacrificial meat, but is instead walloped and chased away by
Trygaios and his slave (1119–26); in Hacks's version, he is offered his very own flesh
at the end of the scene. The slave who assists Trygaios at the sacrifice puts a plate
under his feet, and the stupid priest greedily thrusts his big knife into one foot. The
scene could have been invented by Aristophanes himself.

Just as successful as the transformation of language and jokes is the attempt to reproduce the metrical variety of the original.[40] In many of his plays Hacks revealed himself to be a master of verse. In *Peace* he worked with a constant alternation of verse and prose. Within the verse sections, blank verse dominates, but there are several other metres used alongside it. Hacks's text has the daughters of Trygaios speak in pure trimeters;[41] for the first appearance of Trygaios he uses anapaests,[42] in the parodos a trochaic metre,[43] and in the parabasis a mixture of dactyls and anapaests.[44] Whereas in all these cases the choice of metre appears to be inspired by the original, in the songs Hacks worked with both classical and modern forms of stanza. Thus the chorus (fig. 11.1) recite their prayer to Hermes in an Asclepiadean stanza,[45] known from Horace, and later, when they receive Opora, they sing a song in the Sapphic strophe.[46] But for the work-song, with which Trygaios and the chorus accompany their dragging of Eirene out of her prison (she retains her Greek name because *Frieden* is masculine), and for the little love-song, which Trygaios in the German version sings at the beginning of the second part, Hacks has chosen simple folksong forms.[47]

The action of the play is preserved to a large extent. Besides a short prologue, which Hacks added in order to introduce the initial situation,[48] the first part — up to the parabasis — is virtually identical with the Greek prototype. In the second part we find a fairly large number of interventions, all of which serve to tighten the loose, episodic structure of the Aristophanic original,[49] which was criticized by both Hacks and Besson.[50] Thus Hacks not only cuts the second parabasis (1127–90), which interrupts the series of Punch and Judy scenes rather inorganically, but also the sketchy scene with the sickle-smith and potter (1197–1209). Moreover, he reduces the number of arms-dealers (1210 ff.) to two, and he only brings on one of the two boys near the end (1270 ff.). Of greater importance than these cuts and modifications is a rearrangement in the sequence of scenes: in Hacks's version, the arms-dealers are the first who come to complain about the peace; only then does the greedy oracle-seller Hierokles appear. By this arrangement it is — in Marxist terms — the economic basis of war which is criticized first, and only then the ideological superstructure. Furthermore, in Hacks's *Peace* Trygaios does not chase away the boy who only knows war poetry, but instead teaches him a little song in praise of peace.[51] The poet thus creates an effective contrast with the two rather negative preceding scenes and a gliding transition to the cheerful end of the play. Peace can only be secured by a successful re-education of youth — and Trygaios can finally enjoy his young bride.

The programme note introducing the play on its first performance in the Deutsches Theater in Berlin presented a pointed summary and indicated the tight two-part structure which Hacks had tried to elicit from the much looser original:

> The comedy *Peace* shows:
> One cannot celebrate peace, before one has produced peace [sc. part I]
> To produce peace costs organized effort
> One can not enjoy peace, before it is functioning [sc. part II]
> In short:
> In the struggle for peace there is no sweet without sweat.

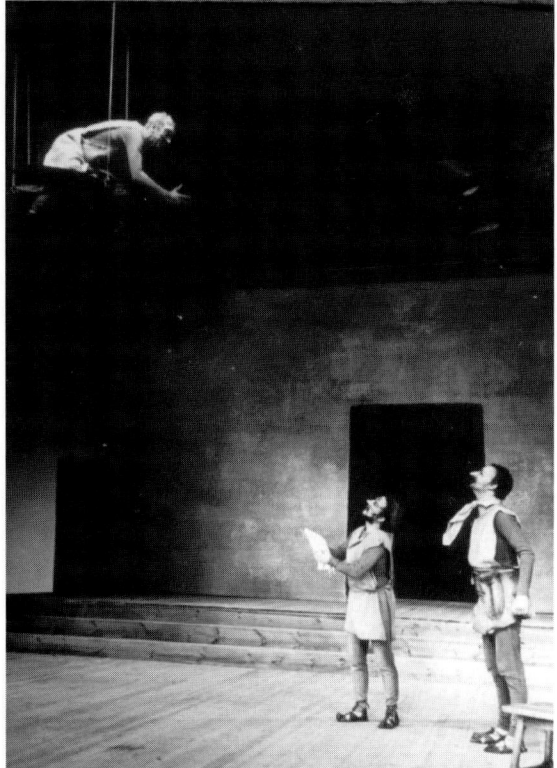

FIG. 11.2 (above).
Trygaios on the beetle
in *Der Frieden*
FIG. 11.3 (below).
Trygaios speaks from
the beetle's back in
Der Frieden

Whereas transposition, cuts, and modifications in the slapstick scenes primarily serve to tighten the dramatic structure of the second half of the play, the appearance of Zeus, which Hacks added at the end of the Hierokles-scene, apparently functions to create a closer connection between the two parts of the play. In Aristophanes' *Peace,* the conflict between Trygaios and Zeus is confined to the beginning of the play. When Zeus does not answer his prayers, Trygaios decides to fly up to Mount Olympus and force him to put an end to the war (see figs. 11.2 and 11.3), if need be by prosecuting him for treason (57–59, 62–63, 103–08), only to learn that Zeus threatens with death everyone who wants to free Eirene from her prison (371–72). After Trygaios has returned to earth this strand in the play is forgotten. But in Hacks's version, when Hierokles enters he immediately informs Trygaios about Zeus' anger at the agreement between Hermes and Trygaios; at the end of the scene, when Trygaios serves him his own feet, the oracle-seller calls on Zeus to come and take revenge for the outrage. And Zeus indeed appears in a black cloud and threatens to crush Trygaios with a thunderbolt. When Trygaios, however, calls on Eirene to save him, it suffices that the goddess opens her eyes to make the ruler of Olympus drop his thunderbolt and retreat.

Whereas all these and other minor modifications in the second half of the play function to tighten its structure and strengthen its thematic unity, most of the other changes that Hacks made were in response to the difficulties modern audiences have in understanding details of Aristophanic drama.[52] Sometimes Hacks adds an explanation to a name or fact, but normally he cuts or replaces everything which presupposes familiarity with material of which the normal contemporary spectator would not have knowledge. Cuts remove almost all references to fifth-century politicians, generals, living and dead poets, and other notorious Athenian personalities, as well as to mythological and literary figures; the same holds true of the parody of oracular style in the Hierokles scene, the literary quotations in the scene with the two boys (or rather, in Hacks's play, the single boy), and Hermes' long analysis of the origin and development of the Peloponnesian war (1070 ff., 1270–1304, 632–48).

Yet, in contrast, in his review of Kortner's *Lysistrata* Hacks insists that the adaptor of an Aristophanic play should 'leave the church in the village' (as the German proverb goes) 'and Athens in Greece.' 'One ought not simply to update Aristophanes.' The simple substitution of contemporary events for ancient ones would only drag comedy down to the level of cabaret.[53] Hacks, therefore, confines himself to a few topical allusions, and, in a number of places, he takes the liberty of making ironic sideswipes.[54] These may be directed against the stinginess of the theatre for which he works as author and dramaturge; some are at the critics, who 'cannot hold down a fresh and hearty dish, unless it has passed through the teeth and bowels of several creatures'; some are at the members of the board of censorship: 'there are people who say disgusting things and there are people who hear disgusting things'. Other swipes are at politicians; when the coryphaeus critically remarks that Hermes and Trygaios are not helping to drag Eirene out of her prison, the quarrel gets reduced to the level of a stichomythic exchange:

FIG. 11.4. War in *Der Frieden*

TRYG.	What? You dare to call leadership laziness?
COR.	To set a good example is the best advice.
HERM.	For a good overview one needs a high position.
COR.	It is not the man of high station whose head is upright.

Only in a few places does Hacks bring the Peloponnesian war closer to his audience. Thus the coryphaeus praises the longed-for peace with the words, 'no more bombs in the daytime / no more fires at night.' When Hermes explains to Trygaios why Eirene does not want to talk to him, he states,

> Now, Greek, listen to why she is so disgruntled.

Three times, she says, trust has been broken with her. Not once, not twice, but thrice it happened that she was forgotten in her bed.

With these words Hacks alludes to the three wars which Germany waged between 1870 and 1871, 1914 to 1918, and 1939 to 1945.[55] When Hermes points out how inferior had been the leaders that Trygaios had 'wobbled along' with, Trygaios defends himself on the ground that those leaders 'were gasolined [*benziniert*] a long time ago', a reference to the stories that after their suicides the corpses of Hitler and Goebbels had been doused in petrol and burned.[56]

But such topical allusions are rare. On the whole Hacks could rely on the fact that at the beginning of the 1960s, at the height of the Cold War and shortly after the building of the Berlin Wall, with the confrontation of Russian and American tanks at Checkpoint Charlie, peace was a hot topic; the audience could and would draw the parallels between the ancient Greek play and the present without much help. The critical analysis of the economic and ideological causes of war, which Hacks added to the scenes with the arms dealers and with Hierokles, will also have sounded rather familiar to an audience trained in Marxist theory. In his review of Kortner's *Lysistrata*, the topicality of the subject-matter was the first of the two reasons Hacks gave for the renaissance of Aristophanes:

> In the middle of the century we, who are in doubt whether we live in the time after or before the final world war, do understand the poet of one of the earliest world wars. Once again the word peace has grown beyond the sphere of political decisions and has become the most important ethical concept.[57]

And in a short text, which he wrote for the production of his *Peace* in Göttingen, Hacks declared that 'the Greeks already ask questions which we still ask, and like everyone who asks a question for the first time, they ask them with particular freshness and intensity'.[58]

The second reason which Hacks gave for the relevance of Aristophanes is the treatment of the subject-matter. For Hacks, Aristophanes was a master of poetic resources, and he characterized these in his essay about the drama of tomorrow as the poetic means of tomorrow — artistry, brilliance, fantasy: 'The audience, tired of dull tendentious realism, gets from Aristophanes what it wistfully longs for: the unity of fighting spirit and poetry.'[59] With these words Hacks attributed to the audience a desire which undoubtedly prompted many poets and artists in the GDR to work with stories, figures, themes, and motifs derived from classical antiquity. An essential impulse lying behind the astounding breadth, variety and quality of the reception of antiquity in East Germany was the attractive potential it offered for evading the aesthetic constraints of socialist realism, the official artistic doctrine of the regime. A related reason was that ancient material could be used creatively as a vehicle for more or less open criticism aimed against political, social, or cultural developments that could not be voiced explicitly. Lyric poets such as Günter Kunert,[60] and dramatists including Heiner Müller,[61] in addition to many other authors, made extensive use of this form of expression, a coded response to repressive cultural conditions which the literary critic Hans Maier, using a term coined by Lenin, has called the 'language of slaves' (*Sklavensprache*) or 'the language of Aesop' — the clever slave of ancient fable.[62]

In Hacks's version of *Peace* there are traces of this technique. At the beginning of the 1960s he had suffered considerable problems with the mandarins of the Department of Culture. He had to rewrite his play *Die Sorgen und die Macht* (*Worries and Power*) twice.[63] Other plays could not be staged or were quickly taken off the programme. The satirical comments about critics and censorship in his *Peace* were certainly understood by the audience as his answer to criticism of his work,[64] and the same holds true for the parabasis, the first part of which Hacks took over almost unchanged. The lines in which the chorus praise Aristophanes for having created a new and grandiose form of comedy sound like a pleading for the socialist classicism that Hacks was promoting at that time;[65] when the Aristophanic chorus praises their poet's fight against the monster Cleon (751 ff.), Hacks, to evoke his own controversies with the cultural bureaucracy, only had to excise Cleon and generalize the sentiment expressed by the lines, transforming them into 'the eternal battle of art against the mighty, which the artist always loses, but which art always wins'.[66]

At the end of the first part of the parabasis (Hacks cut the second part completely) there was an inconspicuous but significant change. Whereas the Aristophanic chorus asked the jury to honour the poet's poetic and political achievements — that is, to award him the first prize in the competition (765–74) — Hacks adds an idea which can be found in many ancient texts from Ibycus to Horace, but not in Aristophanes:

> 'Honour him, you authoritative bald heads, and honour your selves in honour-ing him. Attach a small label to his winged name and he will carry it to the stars. By supporting him make your changes eternal.'

The bald heads, which Aristophanes also addresses together with men and boys as part of the audience, come by means of the qualification 'authoritative' to refer to the leading politicians of the regime, whose 'changes' (that is, the socialist revolution) Hacks promises to make eternal, if his art is supported and promoted instead of being restricted.

The sideswipes at politicians, critics, and censorship up to this point have already been rather general and lacking real bite (see above p. 200); and here it appears that Hacks does not use the ancient text to criticize the mighty and their politics. To be sure, the chorus praise the poet who 'dares to attack the powerful', and speak of 'the perpetual battle between art and power', but then all they do is ask for acknowledgement and support. And since these lines are the only addition to the Aristophanic parabasis and conclude the appeal of the coryphaeus to the bald heads, we may safely assume that Hacks attached some importance to the request. His final goal apparently is not 'the perpetual fight against the mighty', but the patronage of the regime.

Hacks's wish came true; not immediately perhaps, but in the long run.[67] The sensational success of *Peace* certainly contributed to the fact that, after all his problems with the cultural bureaucracy, Hacks was finally accepted and honoured. In 1965 he received the Weiskopf prize, bestowed by the Academy of Arts of the GDR, and from the 1970s onwards he was the most performed dramatist in the state.

In the programme to the production of his *Peace* in Göttingen, Hacks explained the enormous success of Aristophanes in these words: 'We, who try to bring about a happy ending, feed on the energy and cheerfulness of a poet for whom a happy ending was imaginable.' And the sentences that follow confirm the result of my interpretation of the end of the parabasis, namely Hacks's political and ideological loyalty to the regime in the GDR. In complete conformity with official propaganda, he stresses the imminent realization of a socialist utopia. 'Scientific socialism theoretically (for a hundred years) and practically (over the time taken by a few party conventions) has opened the era in which virtue flourishes. By following its calculations we are pulling the rope, and out of the well comes Peace and — finally reconciled — the sisters Productivity and Pleasure. Out of the well rise peace and happiness' (fig. 11.5).[68]

It is hard to believe, however, that the enormous success of the production in 1962 can be attributed to the audience sharing such a conviction: socialist reality was too grey for that. But apparently the play, with its celebration of peace and all the physical pleasures of life, with its exuberant *joie de vivre* and bawdy sexuality, touched a nerve that was very much alive at the time.[69] As many critics emphasized, it was this dimension of the play that Besson's production highlighted. In the archive of the Academy of Arts in Berlin there is a short manuscript by Besson with the title 'The battle for peace as sensual desire' ('Der Friedenskampf als sinnliches Bedürfnis'), in which the director defines the goal of his production as follows: 'The audience should learn to love peace the same way Trygaios loves her, as [one loves] a woman, whom one desires ardently, as [one loves] the air, which one must breathe as [one loves the] sun, which creates our life.' In the same text, Besson — like Hacks — stresses the importance of preserving and presenting the audience with its distance from the ancient play, notwithstanding its topicality. It is in the Brechtian tradition that he insists 'that the many means and instruments of the theatre — as for example machinery, masks, stylisation and exaggerations — must indicate that the people who on the stage get peace out of the deep hole into which it has been thrown, are not identical with us.' A year before his own production, Besson had seen Jean Vilar's Paris staging of *Peace*,[70] which had presented Trygaios as an identifiably French winegrower. Besson, in contrast, decided against this type of strategy and instead chose 'to preserve the spirit and style of the old work of art.'

As I said at the beginning, the production was a sensational success for the director Benno Besson, who moved into the first rank of European directors overnight, and for Peter Hacks, who became the most frequently performed dramatist in the GDR. It was also a stunning success for Aristophanes, who prior to Besson's production had rarely been produced in Germany.[71] And this was despite the relative success, in 1908, of the first professional production of an Aristophanic play — Max Reinhardt's *Lysistrata*, in the same Deutsches Theater which was later to present Hacks's adaptation of *Peace*.[72] There had been fifty-seven performances of *Lysistrata* in its first season alone. Apparently Reinhardt also added a prologue, written by Hugo von Hofmannsthal, no less. Subsequently there were some minor productions of *Lysistrata* in the interim between the Reinhardt production and, fifty years later, Rudolf Sellner's anniversary production. Using Wolfgang Schadewaldt's translation, Sellner's production was mounted at the festival in Schwetzingen and subsequently taken to Darmstadt and Berlin and to the World Fair in Brussels.[73] Yet Aristophanes did not achieve his real breakthrough until Besson produced Hacks's adaptation of *Peace* four years later. Over the course of the following twenty-five years, Hacks's version was staged by almost every theatre in the GDR. There

FIG. 11.5. Eirene with Herbstfleiß and Lenzwonne in *Der Frieden*

are records of forty productions, totalling 716 performances between 1962 and 1987,[74] and the Hacks boom inspired a number of other productions which used translations of Aristophanes.

After the reunification of Germany, Hacks's *Peace* disappeared from the repertoire of German theatres almost completely. Just one production (in Recklinghausen in 1994–95) preceded the most recent revival in 2001. It was then that Besson's daughter Katharina Thalbach, a well-known actress and director, presented her own version in honour of her father's eightieth birthday. It was based partly on Hacks and partly on Aristophanes. But the feat achieved by the original version could not be repeated: Benno Besson's production remains the only real successful production of an Aristophanic comedy to have been performed in modern Germany.

Notes to Chapter 11

1. 'Aristophanes ist zurück' was the phrase used by Hacks to entitle his discussion of Fritz Kortner's TV movie *Die Sendung der Lysistrata* (1961), quoted here from Hacks (1977), 92. Here and in the following all translations are mine.

2. Unpublished material relating to Besson's production of Hacks's *Peace* can be found in the archives of the Deutsches Theater in Berlin and of the Akademie der Künste (Academy of Arts) in Berlin; there is no video recording of the production, nor of any part of it, but a soundtrack survives (soon to be published, together with photographs). The photographs in this chapter (on which see the List of Illustrations, pp. x–xv above) follow the sequence of scenes. In the

Deutsches Rundfunkarchiv Babelsberg there is also a radio play which closely follows the theatre production (archive no. 3000778X00).

3. For further information about Besson, see e.g. A. Müller (1967), Regie International (1988), Macasdar (1995), Besson (1998a) and (1998b), and Cornaz (1998).

4. Kuschnia (1986), 288.

5. See below pp. 204–05 and n. 74.

6. For example, Joachim Knauth's production *Die Weibervolksversammlung* (Aristophanes' *Ecclesiazusae*) in 1965; *Der Maulheld* (Plautus' *Miles Gloriosus*) in 1968; *Lysistrata* in 1975; Egon Günther's production of *Das gekaufte Mädchen* (Plautus' *Mercator*) in 1965; Armin Stolper's *Amphitryon* in 1965–66.

7. See Kuckhoff (1969). Of some importance were the free translations and adaptations of Euripides' *Medea* (1957–58), *Trojan Women* (1957) and especially of Aeschylus' *Persians* (1961–67) by Mattias Braun; see Trilse (1979), 130–43; E. Hall (2004a), 174–75.

8. Mittenzwei (1978), 526–27.

9. Brecht also transformed his radio play *Verhör des Lukullus* (1939) into a libretto for an opera (1951), and wrote an adaptation of Shakespeare's *Coriolanus* (1952–53); see also Ilse Langner's *Iphigenie kehrt heim* (1948) and *Klytämnestra* (1949), as well as Joachim Knauth's *Die sterblichen Götter* (1960).

10. See Riedel (2000), 352–62, and, for bibliography, 477–78.

11. See e.g. Karl Mickel's *Nausikaa* (1967); Hartmut Lange's *Der Hundsprozeß* — *Zwischenspiel* — *Herakles* (1965–67); *Die Ermordung des Aias oder Ein Exkurs über das Holzhacken* (1971) and *Staschek oder Das Leben des Ovid* (1972); Stefan Schütz's *Odysseus' Heimkehr* (1972), *Die Amazonen* (concerning Antiope and Theseus, 1974); *Laokoon* (1979), *Spectacle Cressida* (1984). See the treatments of Riedel (2000), 363–65 (on Lange and Schütz) and 370–71 (on Mickel); Lange's *Herakles* is also dicussed by Riley (2004), 114 and n. 2.

12. Riedel (1984) and (2000), with comprehensive bibliography; Seidensticker (1999).

13. *Rosie Dreams*. For a complete list of Hacks's 'classical' plays, see Riedel (2000), 346–52.

14. See 'K.L.' (1965) and Kipphardt (1989), 197.

15. In 1962, at a climax of the Cold War, *Peace* appears to have been an obvious choice; for the political and cultural context of the production see Gysi (1984).

16. Hacks could have added Karolos Koun's famous production of *Birds* in 1959, on which see the chapters by Van Steen and Varakis, this volume.

17. Hacks (1977), 92.

18. Brecht (1965), 68.

19. Demetz (1973), 162.

20. For Hacks's gradual cutting of the umbilical cord that attached him to Brecht, see Scheid (1977), 79–119; Mittenzwei (1978), 528–31; Stucke (2002), 20–27.

21. 'Über das Stück von morgen', in Hacks (1977), 58–75.

22. Kipphardt (1989), 83: 'Dabei lernt der Zuschauer in der Regel den Arbeitsvorgang eines Eisenhüttenwerks oder einer Konservenfabrik recht gut kennen.' Hacks refers to the plays written in the official style of socialist realism as 'Industriestücke', or 'industrial pieces'.

23. Hacks (1977), 62.

24. Ibid. 59; see also his essay on *Peace*, 'Götter, Welch ein Held! Zu *Der Frieden*', ibid. 341–45, with his plea for the 'great character'.

25. 'Über den Vers in Müllers Umsiedlerin-Fragment', ibid. 83.

26. Ibid. 66.

27. Ibid.

28. 'Die Ästhetik Brechts', ibid. 76–77.

29. Ibid. 76.

30. Ibid.

31. Hacks (1956), 120.

32. See e.g. Weimann *et al.* (1970).

33. Lenin (1970), 308.

34. Hacks (1977), 60.

35. See 'Hamlet ohne Geheimnis', ibid. 153–58; in 1965 Hacks produced an adaptation of *Henry IV*; see Trilse (1981), 174–80; M. Mitchell (1990), 109–22.

36. Goethe plays: *Das Jahrmarktfest in Plundersheim* (1973); *Das Gespräch in Hause von Stein über den abwesenden Herrn von Goethe* (1974); *Pandora* (1979); see Trilse (1981), 233–46.

37. Hacks (1977), 95.

38. Ibid.; see also his essay 'Über das Revidieren von Klassikern' (On the Revision of Classic Authors) in the same volume, 197–212.

39. Pietzsch (1966), 11, reports that Hacks in an interview said, that he used 'at least five translations', but it is not known which ones he consulted.

40. Schütze (1976), 116–17; Scheid (1977), 148 ff.; Goldsmith (1985), 107; Stucke (2002), 85 ff.

41. Hacks (1963), 13: 'O schlimmer Vater, ganz unmöglich dünkt uns dies. / Was wir gehört, das Seltsame, nun sehn wir's zwar, / Doch was wir leider sehn, wir glauben's nimmermehr.'

42. Hacks (1963), 11: 'Willst Du sachte wohl fliegen. Sachte, du Aas, / Eile langsam, ich will's. Wer am Anfang schon,/ Eh die Flügel noch warm und geübt das Gelenk, / Solche Sprünge macht, landet schwerlich am Ziel.'

43. Hacks (1963), 22: 'Sind schon da. Und kamen schleunig / Und in ungeheuren Haufen.'

44. Hacks (1963), 40: 'Nämlich ein Wort für den Dichter scheint einzulegen mir nötig / Und zu fordern den Preis ihm, ihr Herren vom Stab, / Den ihr andern Komödienschreibern, talentlosen, / mit berechtigtem Abscheu verweigert. Ihm aber sicher gebührt er.'

45. Hacks (1963), 28: 'Hermes, herrlicher du, schon den Trygaios uns, / Denk nicht seines Vergehns, denke der Ferkelchen, / Quiekend so appetitlich, / Die wir willig dir spendeten.'

46. Hacks (1963), 46: 'Wie, wo Orpheus singt, aus dem Wald die Hirsche / Treten wir auch heraus zu dir, Trygaios. / Sicher nach den Göttern der Erste bist du, / Friedenserretter.'

47. Hacks (1963), 45: 'Die Sonne hat dich süß gemacht, / Die Sonne und der Wind./ Ich will dich pflücken heute nacht, / Rote Traube von Korinth.' For Hacks's handling of music and dance see Stucke (2002), 86–89.

48. The coryphaeus deplores that the war will not end, but can only lament: 'Und ich steh hier und kann nicht mehr tun als / Hier stehn und jammern und den Bart mir raufen / Und an die Brust mich schlagen und mit gram- / erstickter Stimme schrein: es ist Krieg. Es ist Krieg. / O Götter.' The prologue thus not only introduces the theme, but the helplessness and desperation of the coryphaeus serve to contrast with Trygaios' optimism and determination.

49. Stucke (2002), 90–97.

50. The archive of the Academy of Arts in Berlin holds a number of notes in which Besson and Hacks criticize the dramatic structure of the play.

51.

TRYGAIOS:	Die Oliven gedeihn.	[The olives thrive.]
KNABE:	Der Krieg ist vorbei.	[The war is over.]
TRYGAIOS:	Es tönt die Schalmei.	[The shawm sounds.]
	Der Frieden zog ein.	[Peace has marched in.]
	Wir würzen den Wein	[We are spicing the wine]
	Mit Zimt und Salbei.	[with cinnamon and sage.]
TOGETHER:	Die Oliven gedeihn	[The olives thrive.]
	Der Krieg ist vorbei.	[The war is over.]

52. Goldsmith (1985), 112–17 presents an instructive example of Hacks's technique of transformation (Aristophanes' *Peace* 361–84 and 400–27, compared with Hacks (1963), 26–29).

53. Hacks (1977), 93.

54. Cf. Stucke (2002), 44–65.

55. Goldsmith (1985), 109.

56. Stucke (2002), 51.

57. Hacks (1977), 92.

58. Ibid. 343.

59. Ibid. 92.

60. See Kunert (2002) and Maaz (2002).

61. Heiner Müller openly talked about this technique in an interview as early as 1982, when discussing his *Philoktet* (H. Müller 1982, 77): 'In the early sixties one could not write a play about Stalinism; one had to use a kind of model [...] if one wanted to ask the real questions. The people here understand that quite quickly.' A paradigm of poetic *Sklavensprache* is Müller's poem 'Geschichten von Homer' ('Tales of Homer'), reproduced in English translation in H. Müller

(1989): the controversies and disputes that rage about the true meaning of the Homeric poems, and the lies that are told about them, can never obscure the unbending power of truth, a sure arrow.

62. See Lenin (1966), 466, 468.

63. See e.g. Scheid (1977), 51–58; Jäger (1986), 2–15.

64. See above p. 201–02.

65. Hacks (1977), 58–75; Scheid (1977), 100–19; Stucke (2002), 20–27.

66. Hacks (1963), 41: 'Sah er sie sitzen, griff er sie an, in dem ewigen Streit der Kunst gegen die Großen, / Den immer der Künstler verlor, den stets die Kunst noch gewann.'

67. Scheid (1977), 85–91.

68. Hacks (1977), 344.

69. Schütze (1976), 122–23; Stucke (2002), 97–100.

70. On which see further Bastin-Hammou, this volume, p. 249.

71. On the reception of Aristophanes in Germany see Süss (1911), Friedländer (1969), Holtermann (2004), and above, 'Introduction' to this volume.

72. On Max Reinhardt's production of *Peace* see Flashar (1991), 126.

73. For the Schadewaldt/Sellner production, see ibid. 202–03.

74. These statistics are based on the 'Werkstatistik des deutschen Bühnenvereins (1956–2002)': see also Fix (1970).

CHAPTER 12

❖

Sondheim Floats *Frogs*

Mary-Kay Gamel

Contemporary Performance

Aristophanes is a hard act to follow. Menander, Plautus, and Terence have a rich and ongoing influence on European and American drama, from the tenth-century plays of Hrotsvit of Gandersheim to contemporary television situation comedies.[1] Few playwrights working in English, however, have adapted Aristophanes' plays or tried to write Aristophanic scripts.[2] The main reason is obvious: these plays are full of topical allusions to Athenian political, social, and theatrical life which are difficult for later audiences to understand. *Frogs* is especially rare, and commercial productions are practically unknown.[3] Yet there is one American adaptation of *Frogs* which has a sixty-year history extending to 2004. *The Frogs*, 'freely adapted from Aristophanes by Burt Shevelove, even more freely adapted by Nathan Lane', with music and lyrics by Stephen Sondheim, was presented by Lincoln Center Theater at the Vivian Beaumont from 22 July to 10 October 2004 (fig. 12.1).[4] This version, which played at a major New York theatre, was arguably the most significant American production of Aristophanes in many years. In what follows I shall trace the interwoven strands of the text, music, and performance of this adaptation as it developed.[5]

Studying this production can offer a classicist much more than the chance to compare a contemporary with the ancient version (a comparison which almost always regards the later as inferior). Productions and adaptations of classical drama should not be measured only by 'fidelity' or 'authenticity', especially when these are defined in terms of 'archaeological correctness' (that is, by criteria such as the use of literal, uncut translations; sets, costumes, music, and movement inspired by Greek sources; the use of all-male casts, and so forth). David Wiles says that most of those 'who engage with Greek drama feel (a) that they have touched on something authentically Greek which is worth bringing to the present, and (b) that there is something in the present which they would like to bring to the ancient text'. Yet 'what seems authentic to one generation seems stilted, ill-researched and irrelevant to the next'.[6] Authenticity needs to be defined by a production's relation to its audience, not by its formal similarities to the script, or to the original production, which will always remain in the realm of the imaginary. Studying a contemporary production offers us the chance to experience an ancient play

FIG. 12.1. The cover of *Playbill* for *The Frogs*, 2004

not *sub specie aeternitatis*, but in a particular material representation at a particular time and place, and with a wealth of information about producers and performers which is unavailable for ancient productions. Experiencing an ancient play in modern performance allows us to examine its reception by an audience of diverse backgrounds and capabilities.[7] Whereas scholars are trained to decipher the *single* correct meaning of a text, studying a modern production vividly demonstrates the *variety* of audience responses it arouses. Finally, experiencing a modern production of an ancient play allows us to explore the connections between the production and

FIG. 12.2. World première of Shevelove and Sondheim's *The Frogs*, 1974

its historical and social context. Such connections are easier to discern than they are when examining productions from the past; 'there is always a tinge of mourning and nostalgia in the study of lost performance'.[8] Such exploration can also help us understand the ancient play better.[9] Seeing *The Frogs* in 2004 made me feel Aristophanes' play more powerfully and think more deeply about both similarities and differences between the 405 and 2004 productions.

The Frogs of Shevelove (1941, 1974)

In 1941, Burt Shevelove, then head of the Yale Dramatic Association, wrote and directed a version of *Frogs*. His central production concept involved Charon and Dionysos rowing across the Exhibition Pool in the Payne Whitney Gymnasium,

while the Frogs, played by members of the Yale swimming team, swam around the boat. In 1974 Shevelove, now teaching at the Yale School of Drama, asked Stephen Sondheim, with whom he had collaborated on *A Funny Thing Happened on the Way to the Forum*, to write songs for his version. The musical version was produced by the Yale Repertory Theatre, again at the pool, again with the swim team (see fig. 12.2).

The 1941 script is not available; the 1974 script, published in 1975, follows the plot of Aristophanes fairly closely in a one-act structure.[10] Shevelove's version, however, notably softens many of the hard edges of Aristophanes' script. Obscenities and references to bodily parts, functions, and sex (e.g. 8–11, 479–90, 543–46, 739–40), already less frequent in *Frogs* than in other plays of Aristophanes,[11] are thoroughly cleaned up; at one point, for example, Dionysos primly declares he's going to 'partake of some nookie' (p. 63).[12] Instead of mocking the wimpy god, Herakles welcomes him and helps him act more masculine: 'Walk like this. Could you be a little less graceful?' (p. 27). Shevelove's Hades is not at all grim, but a place of perpetual self-indulgence. Pluto is a jovial host, and Xanthias says, 'You dead certainly know how to live' (p. 80). Shevelove increases the metatheatrical references in the original: the Initiates (here called the Dionysians) 'loved the theatre and never came late' (p. 24);[13] Dionysos tells Herakles, 'You can't go about like that. People will think you're in a play' (p. 25); when Charon says the trip across the Styx takes all night, Dionysos gestures at the audience: 'They haven't got all night' (p. 35); Hades is 'not unlike earth [...] The lighting is different' (44); 'Everything is falling into place. Like a well-made play' (p. 56), and so forth.

Shevelove's most radical revision is to eliminate the political references in Aristophanes' script. Aristophanes' Dionysus is initially uninterested in politics; he goes to Hades for artistic reasons, seeking the playwright Euripides, who had recently died, because he considers the poet 'skilful' or 'clever' (*dexios*, 71), one who 'takes risks' (*phthenxetai* [...] *parakekinduneumenon*, 98–99), and uses bold metaphors (100–02, 105).[14] But in the parabasis (a feature of Aristophanic comedy in which the chorus members step out of character and address the audience directly) the chorus says that drama should 'give good advice and instruction to the city' (686–87) and they proceed to do so. Scholars differ about exactly what advice the chorus is giving; their range of responses no doubt reflects that of the original Athenian audience.[15] But clearly it is *political* advice, with references to the restoration of citizens exiled after the oligarchic revolution of 411 and the restoration of democracy in 410. It is important to remember that fifth-century Athenian theater was state-sponsored, and that various events in the Festival of Dionysus reminded audiences of the connections between drama and politics.[16] Given the historical moment of the play's production in 405, as the Peloponnesian War moved towards its terrible conclusion, political implications seem inescapable, and the Underworld setting throws a dark shadow over the events. Finally, the fact that the Athenians decreed Aristophanes a crown and a re-performance of the play for this particular advice demonstrates that they considered it truly political.[17]

When Dionysus reaches Hades, after various adventures, his desire to bring Euripides back to the upper world is challenged by Aeschylus, and a major contest takes place between the two playwrights, with Dionysus as judge (830–1478). In

the contest, much attention is given to artistic questions — dramaturgy, poetics, and metrics, but Aeschylus is characterized throughout as a poet who inspires audiences to martial virtues and traditional values (923–38, 1013–44). At 1008 he asks his opponent, 'why should anyone respect a poet?' Euripides answers, 'for skill and good advice, because we make people in the cities better' (1009–10), but he has already shown that he thinks 'good advice' is individual and intellectual rather than public and political: 'I taught [the audience] domestic matters' (*oikeia pragmata*, 959). At the end of the contest, however, Dionysus changes course radically, declaring that he came to Hades to get a playwright 'so that Athens could be saved and continue to stage the dramatic festivals' (1418–19). He then asks the two playwrights for political advice; Aeschylus gives more straightforward answers than Euripides, and Dionysus chooses him (1471). As Aeschylus departs, Pluto urges him to 'save our city with your fine counsels, and educate thoughtless people' (1501–03). Slater argues that it is

> profoundly wrong to treat [*Frogs*] as a meditation on aesthetics alone, an extended lament on decline for a literary golden age. The political issues that become evident at the end of the play are implicit in its concerns from the beginning. [...] Dionysus begins with a purely instrumental view of role-playing [... then learns] he can no longer be a layabout on shipboard [...] but has to learn the fundamental Athenian skill of rowing. [...] In the second half of the play [...] spectatorship [...] is not a purely passive pursuit, but one that requires the right kind of active contribution.[18]

In Shevelove's version, when Herakles suggests that there is more at stake than the future of the theater ('Everything's in terrible shape. We have need of a lot more than a dramatist'), Dionysos retorts 'But I am the god of drama' (p. 21). Although Shevelove increases the metatheatrical moments, he eliminates all the parallels in Aristophanes' script between Athens and Hades, as well as all criticism of the audience (274–76, 772–83, 804–10, 909–10, 954–55, 989–91, 1083–98). The most striking change involves the playwrights' contest. This contest, with its many allusions to Athenian dramaturgy, poetics, and metrics, is the central problem faced by contemporary stagings of this play, and productions have tried quite different solutions to it.[19] Shevelove substitutes George Bernard Shaw for Euripides and Shakespeare for Aeschylus.[20] The great advantage of using Shakespeare is English-speaking audiences' acquaintance with his plays and easy recognition of famous passages. In the case of Shaw, the playwright was still alive in 1941, and in 1974 his plays were still very much a part of the English/American intellectual and theatrical scene. Even today, Shaw's plays are frequently produced, and even if quotations from his plays are less familiar, his prose style, and the distinctive polemic tone of the quotations chosen from his plays clearly distinguish him from Shakespeare. Nevertheless, the use of 'classic' British rather than contemporary American playwrights does not have the immediacy the Athenian playwrights had for Aristophanes' audience.

Almost immediately after he meets Shaw, the playwright's indignation and acerbic tongue begin to upset Dionysos, who is especially worried about offending the audience. He asks Shaw to be 'civil' (p. 85) and instruct the audience 'painlessly'

(p. 87) but Shaw will have none of it: 'It is no more possible for me to do my work honestly as a playwright without giving pain, sir, than it is for a dentist. Morals are like teeth, sir, the more decayed, the more it hurts to touch them' (p. 87). Whereas in Aristophanes' *Frogs* Aeschylus is much fiercer than his Euripides, Shevelove's Shakespeare is 'gentle' and 'pleasant' (p. 88) until Shaw's sharp insults offend him. Dionysos keeps a fight from breaking out by setting 'an agon' (p. 101) of quotations on various topics such as Woman, Man, and Love.[21] The stage directions specify that 'Shakespeare never refers to the book in his hand. Shaw is constantly being handed books by his seconds' (p. 103). Shaw continues to denounce the theatre audience and Dionysos gets more and more upset with him: 'must you be so brutal?' (p. 111). While Aristophanes mixes in hilarious parodies of Aeschylus and Euripides, Shevelove makes the contest less funny by using actual quotations from the playwrights. Some of the Shakespeare quotations have a distinctly melancholy strain, such as 'Love's not Time's fool, though rosy lips and cheeks | Within his bending sickle's compass come' (Sonnet 116). Most important, Shevelove's choice of playwrights *reverses* the stances of the Greek opponents, with Shakespeare standing for humanism, emotional power, and poetry, while Shaw represents engagement with social and political questions.

For the final round the topic is Life and Death. Shakespeare offers two speeches from *Measure for Measure* capped off by the song 'Fear no more the heat o' the sun' from *Cymbeline*. Dionysos now tells Shaw that he has lost: 'no one listens to wise and witty people [...] not many listened to you' (p. 117). When Shaw complains that Dionysos is 'honoring voluptuous reverie over intellectual interest, and romantic rhapsody over human concern' (p. 115), the god answers, 'the theatre needs a *poet*. A great big poet. [...] Someone to lift audiences out of their seats' (p. 120). Dionysos and Shakespeare now recross the Styx as the Dionysians urge them to 'bring a feast of words to a hungry earth' (p. 124) and they stand in front of the audience 'with great smiles on their faces' as the lights fade (p. 126). There is no feast of words, and no suggestion of what the audience might be when lifted out of their seats, except some vague remarks about improving the environment: 'the followers of Demeter will do something about the land and the followers of Poseidon will do something about the sea. Yes! And what wonders Apollo will work with the sun. All this can happen' (p. 121). Shevelove's turn away from the political dimension of Aristophanes' *Frogs* is especially striking in the 1974 context, the year in which President Nixon was forced to resign because of the Watergate scandal, when the United States had been embroiled for years in the Vietnam War, and many theatre artists were responding to the war and to the social and political conflicts it had created.[22]

The Frogs of Sondheim (1974)

Stephen Sondheim is the most important, most interesting, most complex musical-theatre composer in the United States, 'the single most important creative force in the American musical theater from the 1960s through the 1990s'.[23] He is not, however, the most popular or the most often produced. His works, sometimes called 'new' musicals or 'concept' musicals, take on very different subjects, including a Victorian barber seeking revenge (*Sweeney Todd*, 1979), the creation of a *pointilliste* painting (*Sunday in the Park with George*, 1984), and revised fairy tales (*Into the Woods*, 1987).[24] His lyrics are dazzling, with complex rhythms and rhyme schemes, especially internal rhymes.[25] In a new song he wrote for the 2004 production of *The Frogs,* for example, the manly Herakles tries to teach wimpy Dionysos to 'Dress Big':

> You gotta look messy,
> Not saucy,
> Less dressy,
> More bossy,
> Be mussy,
> Not glossy.
> (*Dionysos strikes a pose*)
> Too fussy!
> (*He strikes another*)
> Too Fosse.
> You don't talk, you growl.
> You don't mutter things, you roar 'em.
> As for matters of decorum, ignore 'em.

Sondheim's musical styles too are sophisticated and remarkably varied: the domestic comedy *A Little Night Music* is written primarily in 3/4 time, while *Assassins* uses different kinds of American music to reflect the various historical moments it depicts. Sondheim is generally more appreciated by critics than by audiences, but not universally; his work is often criticized for its dark themes, hyperintellectuality, inaccessibility, lack of feeling, lack of melody.[26]

By 1974 Sondheim had written the lyrics to *West Side Story* (1957), *Gypsy* (1958), and *Do I Hear a Waltz?* (1965), and both lyrics and music for *A Funny Thing Happened on the Way to the Forum* (1962), *Anyone Can Whistle* (1964), *Company* (1970), *Follies* (1971), and *A Little Night Music* (1973). He was working on *Pacific Overtures* (1976) when Shevelove asked him to write songs for a revival of *The Frogs*; Sondheim now says he was not interested, but obliged because he owed Shevelove a favour.[27] The score of *The Frogs* has never been published, but audio recordings of both the 1974 version and the 2004 version are available.[28]

Broadway musicals rarely address political issues in any but the broadest, most general terms.[29] In Sondheim's work, as in that of more conventional composers, direct political comment is practically unknown, yet many of his works raise social and political questions.[30] *Night Music* and *Sweeney Todd* deal with class, privilege, and gender relations. *Pacific Overtures* focuses on Perry's 1853 expedition to Japan, which used gunboat diplomacy to force the opening of the island to foreign influences. *Assassins* (1991) features eight historical figures who tried to assassinate US Presidents.[31] In these works, the political implications are woven into the fabric of the music drama, and left to the audience to explore. Sondheim's songs for *The Frogs*, I argue, move Shevelove's script in tougher, more thought-provoking, more political directions — but in the same subtle and ironic way as in the composer's other works.

At the beginning of Aristophanes' *Frogs*, Dionysus and Xanthias share a meta-theatrical moment as they discuss whether to use the 'usual jokes' (1–18). Sondheim provides a metatheatrical song called 'Prologos: Invocation and Instructions to the Audience'.[32] They ask the gods' blessing: 'You who look down on actors [...] And who doesn't? Bless this yearly festival and smile on us' (p. 6) and ask the audience not to talk, cough, open candy, or be offended:

> If we are crude, please,
> Don't sit and brood, please.
> Let's not be too strait-laced
> — The author's reputation isn't based
> On taste. (p. 10)

Sondheim even pokes fun at his own well-known disinterest in writing 'hummable' songs: 'if, by a sudden miracle, | a tune should appear that's lyrical | don't hum along' (p. 9). But political allusions are mixed with the metatheatre: they also forecast 'Bacchanales and social comment' and promise to 'signal you when we're serious (it's in the second half)' (p. 9).

Sondheim's works frequently focus on an ensemble of characters, a practice which foregrounds social context and social issues and has led one critic to compare his use of the chorus to Greek drama.[33] In 1974 Sondheim was becoming interested in contrapuntal writing,[34] and most of the songs in the 1974 version correspond to choral numbers in the Greek, including the Frogs' chorus (208–68), the hymn to Iacchos (316–459), and the parabasis (674–737). The composer makes significant changes, however, in each of the original songs, and creates important connections between them. His Frogs declare themselves happy Philistines:

> Not your hoity-toity intellectuals,
> not your hippy-dippy homosexuals,
> Just your easy-going, simple,
> warm-hearted, cold-blooded
> frogs
> of the pond
> and the fronds we never go beyond. (p. 38)

and spell out a philosophy of complacency and conservatism in which the answer to all problems is 'Whaddaya care the world's a wreck? | Leave 'em alone, send 'em a check, | sit in the sun and what-the-heck, | Whaddaya wanna break your neck for?' (p. 39). If the result is entropy —

> While the world may not know what it needs
> It proceeds,
> And in time
> Will be
> Sublime,
> All bogs
> And weeds
> And frogs
> And beautiful slime. (p. 43)

— so be it.[35]

The lyrics of the next song, the Dionysians' hymn to their god, suggest kinship between the passive Frogs and the woozy Initiates:

> Dionysos, we are come to join you
> in a shout of joy at the only shrine
> where you come benighted and leave benign
> [...] Wine helps the edges blur,
> wine lets the mind escape,
> [...] wine eases tension — what an invention is wine! (pp. 50–51).

They praise Dionysos:

> for the hazy vision that sees through all
> [...] for the happy fog that dissolves recall
> [...] in the sacred rite
> which begins at five and goes on all night' (pp. 52–53).

The opposition between Dionysos trying to make things better and the chorus seeking self-indulgence and maintaining the status quo continues as the Dionysians celebrate life in the Underworld with 'Evoe for the Dead':

> They do an awful lot of drinking, the dead.
> They have a truly endless evening ahead.
> What with the dancing and the eating
> and the laughing and the drinking,
> there's no problem in retreating
> from the awkwardness of thinking,
> Plus that ever present smidgen of dread
> Down here among the dead.

And here Sondheim inserts a very Aristophanic comparison between the dead and the audience: 'Like up there among the dead!'[36] As with the Frogs' song, this celebration of bourgeois complacency and hedonism is tinged with irony.

The opposition between activism and passivity in these songs reaches its peak in 'Parabasis: It's Only a Play'. Sondheim casts this number as a double address to the audience. A character called the Hierophantes praises Dionysos and Herakles for taking action and reproves the Dionysians: 'He's off to clean the Augean stables. You wouldn't do it, but he's doing it now' (p. 78). Pluto, on the other hand, is a ruler who 'lets us do as we please. Funny, isn't it, how we always get the leaders we deserve' (pp. 78–79).[37] The Dionysians answer that Herakles is 'only a myth' and advise 'Let the leaders raise your voices for you. | Let the critics make your choices for you' (p. 79), concluding each interchange with the refrain 'Don't worry, relax. | It's only a play'. When the Hierophantes warns 'The great god Chaos, father of darkness, once ruled the earth. He was overthrown. He could return' (p. 79), they respond:

> Well, words are merely chatter,
> And easy to say.
> It doesn't really matter,
> It's only a play.
> It's only so much natter
> Which somebody wrote. [...]

>Don't worry.
>Relax.
>On with the play. (pp. 79–80)

The melody of the title line creates a musical shrug. This interchange can be interpreted in quite opposite and equally compelling ways. On the one hand, from the perspective of death, lived reality is evanescent and not worth getting excited about; on the other, passivity and failure to act are deadly. This deeply ironic moment, which raises metatheatricality to what I would call a philosophical level, is entirely appropriate for the deep questions raised by Aristophanes.

The competition between Shaw and Shakespeare pits intellectual against emotional appeal, prose against verse, and finally speech against song. (All Aristophanes' references to Euripides as a proponent of 'New Music' have been dropped.) Shakespeare wins the competition by singing the first two stanzas of 'Fear no more' from *Cymbeline* (the *only* time in Sondheim's career that he has set someone else's lyrics):

>Fear no more the heat o' th' sun,
>Nor the furious winter's rages,
>Thou thy wordly task hast done,
>Home art gone, and ta'en thy wages.
>Golden lads and girls all must,
>As chimney-sweepers, come to dust.
>Fear no more the lightning-flash
>Nor th' all-dreaded thunder-stone.
>Fear not slander, censure rash.
>Thou hast finish'd joy and moan.
>All lovers young, all lovers must
>Consign to this and come to dust.
>(IV. ii. 258–69)

Instead of a call to action, this song with its lute-like accompaniment continues the melancholy strain in the quotations Shakespeare uses during the *agōn*. Death is depicted as liberation from life's pain as well as its pleasures, while the melodic line follows a melancholy, irregular rising and falling arc, pausing for a poignant melisma on 'must' and achieving harmonic closure only on the second 'come to dust'.[38] Here again, as in 'It's Only a Play', words and music offer a complex perspective which transcends both simple passivity and simple activism. Why did Sondheim choose to set this song? Perhaps because it is had not often been set by other composers? Those who know the *Cymbeline* context — the song is sung as two people are buried, one of whom will turn out to be alive — may find a parallel with Shakespeare and Shaw, or even to the theater, that 'fabulous invalid' who never really dies.

Overall, Sondheim's songs for *The Frogs* add several crucial dimensions to the play. As a lyricist Sondheim is one of very few able to equal Aristophanes' linguistic and poetic brilliance.[39] Because he is also a brilliant composer he allows audiences to experience this play as it was designed to be experienced — as a music drama.[40] We can never come in contact with Aristophanes' plays as the original audiences did, but we know that music radically changes the nature of a theatrical production, taking the discourse to a different plane (see further Silk's chapter, this volume).[41] In conventional American musicals, songs express the feelings of, and delineate, particular characters, and their connection with the audience is powerful but straightforward. Sondheim characters, however, 'feel many things at once — "sorry-grateful", as one song [in *Company*] phrases it'.[42] In *The Frogs*, Sondheim's choral songs function as those in Aristophanes do — punctuating the spoken scenes, offering complex emotions and contrasting points of view, provoking audiences to think. Banfield notes that musically *The Frogs* is unusual even within the Sondheim oeuvre: 'Sondheim takes risks with his imagination by keeping as few creative props as possible from his regular milieu, and [...] builds up what can only be described as an authentic world, verbally comic yet ritually strange and impressive through its music, which steers well away from Broadway'.[43] The American musical, as Mordden says, 'was not supposed to challenge its public's self-perception' or tell them they 'must let go of unfeasible dreams' or challenge 'the unfulfilled promises of the past'.[44] But such a challenge, such a mixture of tones and moods, is especially appropriate for a modern rendering of Aristophanes' *Frogs*, with its dark setting. That play ends with hope for a renewed Athens, but, with the hindsight of history, we know this was not to be.

Sondheim's work can be seen as provocative, even idealistic, rather than cynical, misanthropic, or pessimistic.[45] In 1974 Sondheim made a statement very much like what Aristophanes has Euripides say in *Frogs*: 'People ask me why I continue writing for the stage. The answer is simple: the theater is the only dramatic medium that acknowledges the presence of an audience. [...] I believe it's the writer's job to educate the audience [...] to bring them things they would never have expected to see'.[46]

The Frogs of Lane and Sondheim (2004)

The 1974 production of *Frogs* had some serious problems, mostly caused by the swimming-pool setting.[47] Since then *The Frogs* of Shevelove/Sondheim has been staged infrequently, usually at swimming-pools (although the script includes alternate dialogue for dry productions); the British première took place in a pool in Acton in 1990. Nathan Lane, a very well-known Broadway and film actor, played Pseudolus in an important Broadway revival of *A Funny Thing* in 1996. He first became interested in *The Frogs* in 1979, and performed Dionysos in the 2001 recording of the songs. He then started revising and expanding the Shevelove script, and convinced Susan Stroman to direct, who convinced Sondheim to revise some of the songs ('Parodos: The Frogs', for example, was greatly expanded) and add new ones. The poster proclaimed 'a new musical' (as on the programme: see fig. 12.1 above).[48]

Lane moulded the script into a two-act structure typical of American musicals.[49] The first act lengthens the trip to Hades, climaxing with the Frogs' song (which ends at l. 268 in the 1533-line Greek script, and on p. 43 of Shevelove's 126-page script). Lane naturalized the Frogs' effect on Dionysos by having the god explain that he's terrified of the creatures, and added a spectacular first-act ending when Dionysos is swallowed by a giant frog. He condensed the second act, eliminating sections Shevelove had kept from the original, such as the monsters (pp. 47–48), the beating of Dionysos and Xanthias to find out which is the god (pp. 69–71), and quite a lot of the playwrights' *agōn*, including most of the references to other playwrights (pp. 82–84).[50] Lane added many jokes, mostly one-liners like 'My name is Xanthias. That's Greek for "second banana"'; Herakles says the quickest way to Hades is 'a hemlock and tonic'; Charon emits a drumroll of maxims involving the word 'Hell'; Pluto says 'Down here R.I.P. means let 'er rip!' and so forth. He also provided new allusions to contemporary pop culture, such as cellphones, Viagra ('the god of perseverance'), and *The Lion King* (on Dionysos, Herakles' lionskin 'looks like the Circle of Life that stopped': see fig. 12.3).

Where the 1974 production featured songs for the chorus, most of the new songs are performed by individual characters or duos — 'I Love to Travel' by Dionysos and Xanthias, 'Dress Big' by Herakles, 'All Aboard' by Charon. A song and dance for Pluto and the Hellraisers called 'Hades' has replaced 'Evoe for the Dead'. The most striking addition is Dionysos' announcement that he has another reason for his trip to Hades — to see his dead wife Ariadne; he sings her a romantic ballad, and she appears in the second act. These new songs move away from the earlier choral songs towards the traditions of more conventional American musical comedy.

Lane's primary motivation for working on Shevelove's script and advocating for a production was political: 'after September 11th [...] I started to think, There's something in this piece right now. [...] There's something idealistic about the notion of someone believing that the arts can make a difference. [...] I found it moving, in light of what was going on in the world'.[51] The stage directions in the 2004 script specify that Dionysos and Xanthias (not yet identified as such) come through the curtain to give the 'Invocation and Instructions'. The curtain then opens to reveal the chorus, in Greek costume, standing in front of a large Greek vase. They give a rather pedantic lecture about the Athenian production of the play ('there were only three actors with a variety of masks and a large chorus who broke up the loosely plotted story with songs, dances, slapstick, spectacle, and the author's opinions on contemporary topics') while 'a distant but ominous rumbling' begins and grows louder till the chorus says, 'having been at war for too long, the people feared that one more attack might bring life as they knew it to an end', whereupon the vase cracks in half and smoke pours out.

From this point on Lane's script is closely connected to the time and place of its 2004 production — New York City, three years after the terrorist attacks of 2001. He moves Dionysos' announcement of his mission to earlier in the show, and now the god tells Xanthias that he will 'bring back to earth a brilliant writer who can speak to the problems of our society and give us comfort, wit and wisdom. And also challenge our complacencies. We have been starved of food for thought.' There is only one direct allusion to the current US president, when Charon warns of 'the Big Bully Bush Frog that makes pre-emptive strikes and then forgets why it attacked in the first place'. Most of the political references are indirect, yet clear — to the Iraq occupation ('The Peloponnesian War still rages on, Xanthias. A war we may not be able to win. A war we shouldn't even be in'); Bush's inarticulateness ('Words seem to fail them. Even the simplest words'); and his regime's manipulation and intimidation of the public ('Our leaders have filled us with fear. And that's

FIG. 12.3. Dionysos and Xanthias in *The Frogs*, 2004

the way they like us. Frightened and vulnerable. So they can do as they please').[52] Lane's attempt to combine political issues with comedy goes against the American tendency to consider serious drama as the only appropriate vehicle for political content.

The end of the play echoes the beginning, as two actors come through the curtain and face the audience. There is a pause, then Dionysos says to Shakespeare, 'Say something!' Lane has Shakespeare respond with Edgar's words at the conclusion of *King Lear* (V. iii. 323–24): 'The weight of this sad time we must obey: | Speak what we feel, not what we ought to say.' This continues the portrait of the melancholy Shakespeare established earlier, and he says nothing further, perhaps because he feels there is no hope. But Dionysos now addresses the audience, reprising the 'Invocation' in calling on them to take action:

> Don't just shrug,
> Content to be a conscientious slug.
> It's fine to feel contented, safe and snug.
> But soon enough contented turns to smug.
> Don't shovel what's uncomfortable
> Underneath the rug.

> Speak up! Get sore!
> Do something more than just deplore.
> Don't sit and brood, please,
> Learn to be rude, please.
> There's just too much at stake.
> And now is simply not the time to take
> A break.
> So shake
> Your ass!
> I know, I know, that sounds a little crass.
> But, citizens of Athens,
> If you're smart,
> Don't sit around while Athens
> Falls apart.[53]

Politically and artistically, the revival of Shakespeare is less important than that of Dionysos, a god of theater who tries to save his city and country with fine counsels and to educate thoughtless people. As Sondheim's songs did for Shevelove's script in 1974, Lane's additions — looser plot, increased jokes, direct political comments, metatheatricality used for political effects — move Shevelove's drama in a more pointed, more political, more Aristophanic direction. Lane's revisions also bring the Shevelove script closer to conventional musical comedy, but this does not have to be seen as a concession to audiences' ignorance. Aristophanes too drew on his audience's familiarity with the conventions of comedy, such as the 'usual jokes' at the beginning, the alternation of speech and song, the *agōn*, and so forth. The combination of musical numbers in the 2004 version more closely resembles the Aristophanic mix of low comedy and high seriousness, and the new, more conventional songs draw attention to the strangeness of the choral songs. Even the addition of Ariadne as Dionysos' love interest — a completely un-Aristophanic note — enriches the mixture of familiar and unfamiliar elements.

The combination of such elements creates interesting tensions. Virilla the Amazon makes a smooth transition from telling Dionysos (as Herakles) that he's let himself go — 'Step away from that dinner table, honey, just step away' — to asking where Hippolyte's girdle is and suggesting he stole it 'to go with those sandals'. Like the scene in which Herakles tries to get Dionysos to act masculine, this fits perfectly with Dionysos' effeminacy. But in a play that explicitly criticizes war Dionysos' choice of Shakespeare is jarring. The modern audience may not know that Shaw was a pacifist whose plays depict war more negatively than Shakespeare's,[54] but in Shevelove's version Dionysos first asks Shakespeare for 'All the world's a stage', while Lane has him begin by requesting Henry the Fifth's words before the Battle of Agincourt! Mendelsohn complains that Lane has ignored the fact that in Athens it was the conservatives who were peaceniks and the extreme democrats who were imperialist warmongers. The greater problem, however, is that the choice of Shakespeare, who will 'touch people's hearts as well as their minds' and 'remind people what's right with them as well as what's wrong with them', comes across as a sentimental move which contradicts Lane's call to the audience to 'Get sore!'.[55]

The Frogs of Stroman (2004)

Many of the staging aspects of the production of *The Frogs* at Lincoln Center realized the potential inherent in the Shevelove/Sondheim/Lane script. Susan Stroman is a prominent Broadway choreographer whose breakthrough show was *Contact* (2000), followed by the megahit *The Producers* (2001). Lane was an excellent choice for Dionysos: he came to the role trailing clouds of glory as the reigning Broadway clown. Lane's performance was criticized for being too tentative, but weakness and uncertainty are appropriate to a god whose domain is in decline, and they prepare for his recovery of assurance and self-awareness at the end of the play.[56] As Xanthias, Roger Bart brought memories of his performance with Lane in *The Producers*. Charon was the wonderfully dry John Byner while Peter Bartlett as Pluto was a charming old queen without a hint of menace.

Some of the production choices worked well. The design echoed Dionysos' first lines, 'The time is the present. The place is ancient Greece' by mixing Greek and modern elements. The set included a cornice, initially crowned by a small temple, which projected over the stage below. The downstage of the Vivian Beaumont was round (probably less to suggest a Greek *orchēstra* than to accommodate a turntable for the travel scenes) while the upstage changed to different locations. As the cracking urn at the beginning suggested 9/11, at the end the skyline of Manhattan — indeed, the skyline at Ground Zero — and the Statue of Liberty appeared on the cornice. Dionysos and Shakespeare were coming back to save New York and, by extension, the United States.

Other choices were less effective. The costume designer spoke about his research,[57] but some of the wigs were more Flavian than Greek, and Virilla the Amazon looked like a female gladiator; overall, the look might best be described as 'Hollywood Graeco-Roman'. Hades had a similar mix of elements: although Pluto complains that 'it was really the Christians who decided that Hades was a place of punishment', a lot of fire effects were used. Perhaps the idea was to take the symbolism out of the flames and make them only a theatrical effect; in his song celebrating Hades Pluto sings 'It's got flash! It's got flair! It's got spectacle to spare!'[58] Stroman's answer to a question much debated by scholars — do the Frogs actually appear during their song? — was an emphatic yes, with Frogs both on the floor and on the cornice, singing and dancing, some leaping thirty feet via bungee cords, in the biggest production number of the show (see fig. 12.4).[59] There were two problems with Stroman's choice, however. First, the song's witty, significant lyrics got lost in the chaos. These include a wicked parody of Jerome Kern's 'Old Man River' — 'You and he, you sweat an' strain, bodies all achin' an' racked wid' pain' — which demonstrates that the Frogs' taste in musicals is also conservative! Second, the complacent, passive stance in the Frogs' song was completely at odds with their energetic staging. In his review Beye notes, 'the paradox of an aggressive insistence upon their do-nothing conservative agenda. [...] One is tempted to read the energy of the chorus set against the hesitating, timid manner of Dionysos as a kind of clichéd portrait of present-day conservative assurance versus the wishy-washy unfocused liberal agenda'.[60]

FIG. 12.4. Dionysos and the leaping frogs in *The Frogs*, 2004

In the 1974 script only two terms, 'Frogs' and 'Dionysians', are used to identify the chorus, and these groups are connected not only by their personnel but also by their philosophy. The 2004 production had many more subgroups — Greek chorus, Hellraisers, Shavians, etc — each with different costumes and wigs. Similarly, the production never made explicit the connection between rulers on earth and the indulgent Pluto who gives his citizens just what they want so they will 'never have to fret about fate'. In the Parabasis, instead of the Hierophantes haranguing the chorus, Dionysos and Pluto argued unheatedly center stage: D. 'Our leaders won't tell us the truth. [...] P. 'I think the truth is terribly overrated', and Pluto even got the last word.

Stroman's production was entirely too civil with the audience, with no Aristophanic mockery and few of Sondheim and Lane's challenges to their self-perceptions. The Beaumont audience was never provoked to think of themselves as the smug Frogs or the drunk Dionysians or the happy dead who have the leaders they deserve. Part of the problem was the 'archaeological correctness' of the setting and costumes. During the Parabasis, the chorus were dressed in Greek costumes and held masks on sticks before their faces; as they exited at the end of the song they reversed the masks to reveal frog faces. This made a connection to the Frogs, but before the reversal the masks all had images of *Dionysos*. Since those singing 'It's only a play' do not share Dionysos' sense of purpose and desire for change, this choice made little sense. It would have been far stronger to have the chorus resemble the audience. Similarly, the scenic backdrop to the playwrights' contest was a shot of the Beaumont seating areas filled with audience members wearing *Greek* dress.

If instead they had worn contemporary New York street clothes, their advice might have had some of the power of, for example, 'The Ladies Who Lunch' from Sondheim's *Company*, with its mockery of rich New York women filling their lives with empty activities and booze — 'another long, exhausting day, another thousand dollars [...] a matinee, a Pinter play, another vodka stinger' — which ends by calling on the audience to 'Rise! Rise! Rise! Rise!' in recognition of the song's accuracy and/or to make a change. *The Frogs* in 2004 was much too civil with its audience (except perhaps for Bush backers). Winer (2004) says rightly, 'Shaw is quoted here: "All great truths begin as blasphemy". We could have used more of that.'

Beyond the Reviews

The Frogs of Shevelove/Sondheim/Lane/Stroman received a mostly negative response from the critics. Most judged the production by the standards of the well-made play, criticizing the loose structure and the mix of themes and styles.[61] About Aristophanes and Greek drama most knew little and cared less.[62] Only Beye, Brustein, Dale, and Finkle found the mixture of elements purposeful and exhilarating.[63] None of the reviewers took into account the limitations imposed on a non-subsidized commercial theatre.

At the beginning of this essay, I said that studying the 2004 production brought out both similarities and differences between it and the 405 production. I shall end with one difference and one similarity. The idea that a *playwright* could actually make a difference in the real world made sense in 405 Athens, and it still made some sense in 1941 and 1974 USA.[64] In 2004, when *The Frogs* played only to audiences who could afford $95 tickets, it made almost no sense.[65] Moreover, for Dionysos to choose Shakespeare — the most frequently produced playwright in the United States — is predictable and politically quietist. Sondheim's songs deserve to be set free from Shevelove's script. I suggest it is time for a new version of *Frogs*, perhaps one in which stages the debate between playwrights who do political theater in different ways, such as Tony Kushner vs. Tim Robbins, or Alan Bennett vs. David Hare. Another possibility would be to change media. Beye suggests pitting Playhouse 90 against 'reality TV'; other possibilities would be a duel between a right-wing country-western singer and Bruce Springsteen, or between filmmakers who produce different kinds of political films, such as Michael Moore, Oliver Stone, Steven Spielberg.[66]

On the other hand, the mixture of tones and meanings in the 2004 production seemed to me utterly right, with warnings of disaster and calls to political action balanced by low comedy and by strains of doubt and questioning. Can anything really be done? Is anything worth doing? Is it so bad to 'thrive just by staying friendly and alive'? Maybe life really is 'only a play'. Maybe death really does offer a 'home', a peaceful end to both 'joy and moan'. Reckford acknowledges the dark notes in Aristophanes' script: 'the "bubblesplashifications" of which they are so proud may suggest the ephemeral nature of all human creations'. 'And yet, that song swelling up from the depths [...] suggests that other power of imaginative creations, to live on and to move the spirit from beyond the waters of death'.[67]

Live performance does more than 'suggest', it *embodies* the power of imaginative creations to live on. Hall argues: 'Theatre is uniquely poised to make the future seem potentially *controllable*, or at the very least susceptible to intervention. [...] All art can narrate or represent revolution, but only drama has the potential to *enact* through both form and content radical, optimistic, changes in power relations which would be impossible in the society producing the drama'.[68] In the case of the 2004 production of *The Frogs*, a change in the power relations dictated by the corporate managers and the media which serve them was enacted (however briefly) by contemporary artists who felt a 'longing' for an Aristophanes play and brought it back (however changed) from the dead, and by audiences who were moved to laughter and thought, agreement and disagreement.

The 2004 Lincoln Center production closed on 10 October 2004. Once the new script and the new score are published, *The Frogs*, like all of Sondheim's other works, is sure to be produced widely, and without the political, economic and artistic constraints that Broadway imposes.[69] *The Frogs* 2004 is dead; future *Frogs* are waiting to be born.[70]

Notes to Chapter 12

1. For discussions of the connections between New Comedy and modern film and television, see Cavell (1981); Konstan (1988); Karnick and Jenkins (1995), 63–86. Horton (2000) discusses both Old and New Comedy in his guide. The first collaboration of Burt Shevelove and Stephen Sondheim was *A Funny Thing Happened on the Way to the Forum* (1962), based on three plays by Plautus; its original title was *Roman Comedy*.

2. This scarcity is even more striking when compared to the wealth of Greek productions documented by Van Steen (2000). The production history of Athenian tragedy has been extensively examined: see Burian (1997); Colakis (1993); Dunn (1996); Flashar (1991), who includes comedy very much in passing; Foley (1999); Garland (2004); Hall, Macintosh and Taplin (2000); Hall, Macintosh and Wrigley (2004); Hartigan (1995); McDonald (1992) and (2003); Macintosh (1997) — significantly, there is still no *Cambridge Companion to Greek Comedy*; Steiner (1984). Walton (1987) and Wiles (2000) include both tragedy and comedy. The reception of Athenian comedy has to date received little attention — an oversight this publication will help correct. Recent English-language adaptations of Aristophanes (many unpublished) include Arrowsmith (n.d.), Bolt (2005), Calandra and Coates (1990), Drake (2001), Gamel (2000) and (2006), Gelbart (2002), Glore with Culture Clash (1998), A. Green (n.d.), Harrison (1992), Margraff (2002), Muldoon (1999), O'Brien (2002a), D. Parker (n.d.), Robic (1994), and Taylor (n.d.). A. R. Gurney describes his play *The Fourth Wall*, written in 1992 and later revised in response to current political events, as Old Comedy. On 3 March 2003, readings of *Lysistrata* took place worldwide as a protest against the upcoming American invasion of Iraq. *Acharnians* was performed in New York in October 2004. Composer Mark Adamo's *Lysistrata, or The Nude Goddess* premièred at Houston Grand Opera in March 2005 and was performed at New York City Opera in March 2006. *Saturday Night Live* resembled Aristophanes in its topicality, satire, and loose structure, and Euben (2003) argues that the American TV comedy series *The Simpsons* has Aristophanic elements.

3. See the statistics compiled by Wrigley in the APGRD Database (www.apgrd.ox.ac.uk/database).

4. Throughout I refer to Aristophanes' play as *Frogs* and the Shevelove/Sondheim version as *The Frogs*.

5. Mr Sondheim has told me that the 1974 script was entirely Shevelove's and the lyrics and music entirely his (personal communication, 1 July 2006). I attribute all the script changes in the 2004 version to Lane, and all the production choices to director Susan Stroman. Such an articulation is

different from many of the reviews of *The Frogs* in 2004, even thoughtful ones like Mendelsohn's (2004), which made little distinction between the textual, musical, and production aspects of the show. On the other hand, theatre is a collaborative art, and choices made in one area of production always affect other areas.

6. Wiles (2000), 179.

7. Including not only the professional critics but other audiences, such as the Sondheim fans who frequent the fansite 'Finishing the Chat' (http://www.sondheim.com/community) or the ladies at the next table having dinner after the matinee. As Edith Hall says, 'To do Performance History is to excavate a different kind of Influence of the Classics, a more popular, demotic, and incomparably more widespread influence' [than that represented by elite authors and readers] (E. Hall (2004*b*), 81–82).

8. Armstrong (2002), 293. This is not to deny the importance of historical studies, only to argue that the study of contemporary productions is also crucial. Sarlós (1989) insists that past performance should not only be studied but reconstructed; Pearson and Shanks (2001) offer a dialogue between theater and archaeology; Fenton counters, 'The stage cannon, fired in salute, that caused Shakespeare's Globe to burn down, taking with it all his production books, leaving us guessing about so much — that fire did us all a great service. It released the plays into the free republic of our imagination' (Fenton (1996), 17).

9. Revermann (2006), 47. See Foley (1999) and (1999/2000). Given (2002) draws on Sondheim to discuss Aristophanes. I would add that working on new translations and adaptations is even more revelatory than seeing such productions.

10. Shevelove (1975). All page references refer to this text unless otherwise stated.

11. See Henderson (1991) for discussion of obscenities in Aristophanes.

12. Shevelove's few obscenities are quite witty, as when Herakles says he's off to clean the Augean Stables. Dionysos: 'No shit.' Herakles: 'Unfortunately, that is not the case' (p. 28).

13. This is a reference to the song 'The Lady is a Tramp' by Rodgers and Hart. I owe this insight to Judy Hallett.

14. References to Aristophanes' *Frogs* are to Dover's edition (1993); English translations are mine. For a detailed discussion of the issues involved in the contest between Aeschylus and Euripides see Dover's introduction, 10–37.

15. See Hubbard (1991), 205–10, Goldhill (1991), 201–21, Dover (1993), 69–73, and McGlew (2002), 163–70 for various views, as well as Van Steen's discussion of modern Greek productions (Van Steen (2000), 178–80).

16. See Goldhill (1991).

17. See Sommerstein (2003) for a discussion of the decree and the restaging.

18. Slater (2002), 205–06.

19. A production at the University of California, Berkeley in the 1960s projected 'footnotes' onto the set explaining the references. A 1989 production at the University of California, Santa Cruz, directed by Audrey Stanley, changed Aeschylus and Euripides to American playwrights Eugene O'Neill and Tennessee Williams. Unfortunately, the audience found the quotations from their plays just as obscure as they would have the original quotations.

20. In 1949 Shaw published a very brief play (his last) called *Shakes versus Shav*, in which the two playwrights, played by puppets, fight with quotations and fists. At the end Shav says 'Peace, jealous Bard: | We both are mortal. For a moment suffer | My glimmering light to shine' but Shakes responds 'Out, out, brief candle!' and darkness falls (see Shaw (1949) or (1950)).

21. I thank John Given for sharing with me his very useful list of quotations from Shakespeare and Shaw used in the Shevelove/Sondheim *Frogs*.

22. American plays influenced by the Vietnam War include Barbara Garson's *Macbird!* (1966); Terrence McNally's *Botticelli* (1968); John Guare's *Muzeeka* (1968); Maria Irene Fornes's *The Red Burning Light* (1968); Arthur Kopit's *Indians* (1969); Michael Weller's *Moonchildren* (1970); David Rabe's *The Basic Training of Pavlo Hummel* (1969), *Sticks and Bones* (1969), and *Streamers* (1970); Luis Valdez's *Soldado Razo* (1971); Romulus Linney's *The Love Suicide at Schoffield Barracks* (1973); Adrienne Kennedy's *An Evening with Dead Essex* (1974); see Reston (1985).

23. Adler (2000), 37.

24. The bibliography on Sondheim is immense. On his life and oeuvre see Banfield (1993), Citron

(2001), Goodhart (2000), Gordon (1990) and (1997), Gottfried (2000), Guernsey (1974) and (1985), Hischak (1991), Horowitz (2003), and Secrest (1998) — although these studies contain almost no mention of *The Frogs*. Discussions of Sondheim's contributions to American musical theater at various stages of his career include Block (1997), J. B. Jones (2003), Kislan (1980), D. A. Miller (1998), Mordden (1984), Singer (2004), and Steyn (1999).

25. Sondheim first achieved fame as a lyricist when at age twenty-five he was hired to write the lyrics for *West Side Story*, but says 'I find lyric writing one of the most unpleasant professions in the world, whereas music is fun — not that it isn't hard, too. [...] I was trained and started out as a composer, and I fell into lyric writing, so to speak. I wanted to do both, but music was my joy' (Sondheim (1991), 14). For very detailed analyses of Sondheim lyrics and music through *Into the Woods*, see Banfield (1993). Davis (2006) categorizes Sondheim lyrics in the light of classical rhetorical figures.

26. For a trenchant critique, see Steyn (1999), 128–45; for more favourable views, see Goodhart (2000), 3–33 and Cronin (1997).

27. Guare (2004), 10.

28. A concert recording of the 1974 score was released in 2001 by Nonesuch Records under the title *The Frogs/Evening Primrose (2001 Studio Cast)* (= Sondheim (2001)). The audio recording of the 2004 production was released as *The Frogs (2004 Broadway Cast)* by P.S. Classics (= Sondheim (2005)).

29. There are American musicals which raise social issues, such as racism (*South Pacific*, 1949; *Ragtime*, 1998), domestic violence (*Carousel*, 1945), drug use and AIDS (*Rent*, 1996), gang violence (*West Side Story*, 1957), lynching (*Parade*, 1998), and even political ones (*Of Thee I Sing*, 1931), but they usually do so in a very abstract, non-confrontational way. The 1967 counter-cultural musical *Hair* includes the burning of draft cards, while *Miss Saigon* (1991) uses the Vietnam War as the backdrop for a romantic melodrama. *Avenue Q*, which opened in 2003 and is still playing on Broadway, takes on current issues in a directly satirical way.

30. See Swayne (2005), 157–58.

31. Mordden (1984), 187 discusses the social commentary in Sondheim's musicals through *Sweeney Todd*. Fisher (1997) locates *Follies* and other Sondheim works in the social and political context of 1970s America. Arblaster (1992), 295 calls *Overtures* Sondheim's 'most political to date' but does not explore its connections to the Vietnam War. Scott Miller (1997) discusses connections between the artistic and political implications of *Assassins*. Sondheim maintains, however, that at least in the case of *Pacific Overtures*, 'I couldn't have been less interested in politics' (Secrest (1998), 280).

32. A version of this song was composed in 1965 as the opening for *A Funny Thing Happened on the Way to the Forum*, but rejected by director George Abbott and replaced by 'Comedy Tonight' (Zadan (1986), 71).

33. Fraser (1997). About his songs for *The Frogs* Sondheim says 'One of the things that made it hard to write the score is that the numbers are arbitrary. I was brought up to make songs carry character and plot forward. In Aristophanes, it's quite the reverse — you take a moment and savor it' (Guare (2004), 10).

34. Swayne (2005), 31.

35. In a note included in the 2005 recording Wendy Wasserstein recalls that the 1974 Frogs, 'with their synchronized swimming [...] bore a frightening resemblance to all the clean-cut, mechanized President's men'. The lyrics of this song were augmented for the 2004 production, in which this was a huge production number right before the intermission; those lyrics are available in the booklet which accompanies the 2005 audio recording (Sondheim (2005)).

36. 'Evoe for the Dead' does not appear in the 1975 script, but is included on the 2001 recording (Sondheim (2001)).

37. The 2001 audio recording does not include the Hierophantes' words, and in the 2004 performance and the 2005 recording this character does not appear. 'Evoe for the Dead' does not appear in the 1975 script, but is included on the 2001 recording (Sondheim (2001)).

38. Duffin (2004), 142 provides the score of an Elizabethan setting. A few modern British composers including Gerald Finzi, Kenneth Leighton, and Ralph Vaughan Williams have set the poem, but none of these songs is well known. Banfield (1993), 53 comments, '[Sondheim's] song is

intimately familiar in style and address and yet still in keeping with the harmonic world of the rest of the score with its euphony of fourths and fifths'. Niall Slater points out to me that this song is often performed (as a reading) at actors' funerals.

39. See Silk (2000), chs. 3 and 4, on Aristophanes as a wordsmith, with special attention to his variety of modes. For very detailed analyses of Sondheim lyrics and music through *Into the Woods*, see Banfield (1993).

40. As I write this sentence, I wish that readers could listen to the music I am trying — inevitably inadequately — to describe. Like the productions they discuss, performance studies need to be multi-mediated.

41. Too few productions of ancient Mediterranean comedy include music. The London Small Theatre Company's production of *Frogs*, available on video, uses a combination of doo-wop and patter songs *à la* Gilbert and Sullivan; these are funny and effective, but they never achieve the range of Aristophanes' lyrics or Sondheim's songs. On the potential Aristophanes offers to musically sensitive directors, see further Silk, this volume.

42. Mordden (1984), 188. Adler (2000), 37 argues that in 'Exodos: The Sound of Poets' in *The Frogs* Sondheim expresses his 'own artistic credo' in the lines 'Bring a sense of purpose, | Bring a taste of words, | Bring a sound of wit, | Bring the feel of passion, | Bring the glow of thought | To the darkening earth'.

43. Banfield (1993), 53.

44. Mordden (1984), 188, 190, 195.

45. See Cronin (1997).

46. Zadan (1986), 368.

47. The swimmers dripped water on the playing space, causing actors to slip and fall. Also, says Sondheim, 'You couldn't hear anything. Jonathan Tunick, who orchestrated it, said afterward that he hadn't taken into account how reverberant the swimming pool would be, and it sounded like a urinal' (Guare (2004), 10). In 'Prologos: Invocation and Instructions to the Audience' Dionysos warns 'As for applause, please, | when there's a pause, please. | Although we welcome praise, | The echo sometimes lasts for days' and the chorus responds 'Days, days, days, days, days, days, days, days' (Shevelove (1975), 8).

48. Another term is 'revisal', used for a work which makes it to Broadway after major revisions.

49. The 2004 script has not been published, but Philip Rinaldi provided me with a copy of the working script used at the Beaumont, for which I am extremely grateful.

50. Shevelove (1975).

51. Guare (2004), 5.

52. The Bush administration, and especially the Iraq war and occupation, have provoked widespread theatrical responses (e.g. Justin Butcher, *The Madness of George Dubya*; David Hare, *Stuff Happens*; Tony Kushner, *Only We Who Guard The Mystery Shall Be Unhappy*; Tim Robbins, *Embedded*, Sam Shepard, *The God of Hell*, Gillian Slovo, *Guantanamo*; see Wren (2004)). On British theatre's political use of Greek drama in 2004, see Billington (2004).

53. Lane (2004*a*).

54. See Holroyd (2004), Brustein (2004).

55. Lane (2004*a*).

56. M. Murray (2004) asserts that Lane's Dionysos had 'none of the conviction, authority, or even stage presence that helped establish him as a major comic actor'. Brustein (2004) commented, 'his performances have never impressed me as equal to [Zero Mostel, Phil Silvers, Bert Lahr] in largeness or madness [...] his love affair with the folks out front (and theirs with him) has been a little too promiscuous to sustain that hard-boiled, brazen independence of style necessary for great clowning. There was always a hint of sentiment bubbling on the edges of his quavering tenor that threatened to weaken the tensile strength required for farce'. Blistein agreed: 'Lane (both the writer and the performer) pulls what I consider to be Aristophanes' most significant punch, the fact that Dionysos is as much a buffoon as he is an acute literary critic. The subtext to *Frogs* is: Can you really trust *this* guy to restore Athenian theater to its prior glory?' (personal communication from Adam D. Blistein, 9 Aug. 2004). The argument that Dionysos 'finds himself' in the course of the play is made by Segal in a now-classic article (1961). Herakles teaching Dionysos how to walk in a 'heroic' way (pp. 26–27) is reminiscent of the scene in the

film *The Birdcage* (1996) where Armand Goldman (Robin Williams) teaches his partner Albert Goldman (Lane) to walk like John Wayne. But by then Lane was already studying Shevelove's version, so perhaps the influence went the other way.

57. Long (2004), 24.

58. The 1997 Disney film *Hercules* uses similarly fiery iconography for Hades, but to convey the menace of its king (Hercules' nemesis in this version). That film also starts with a Greek vase which metamorphoses.

59. On the question whether the Frogs appear during their song see C. W. Marshall (1996), with bibliography. Russo (1994), 205 argues that Aristophanes, knowing the challenges of the second half, indeed the 'impossibility of staging and dramatizing the debate and the artistic sentence, [...] wished to compensate the spectators in advance by offering them a major spectacle, animated and varied in style'. But then he insists that the Frogs do not appear!

60. Beye (2004*b*).

61. Scheck (2004): 'a hodgepodge'; Ryan (2004*b*): 'schizoid quality'; Teachout (2004): 'ill-crafted book'; E. Gardner (2004): 'an awkward marriage of goofy humor and earnest social commentary'; Brantley (2004): serious elements chafe 'against the surrounding glitz and vulgarity'; Als (2004): 'any verbal depth and insight in the argument are lost in the predictable pyrotechnics of babes and boobs'. See also the very funny parody by Varod (2004).

62. Als (2004): 'Euripides and Aeschylus — the "philosophical" and "political" voices of their era, respectively'; Feingold (2004): Lane's Dionysos 'needs a poet not only to save the theater, but to save the world — a notion that Aristophanes, for all his faith in the political potency of theater, would have hooted down'; Barnes (2004): Aristophanes' play is 'neither particularly funny nor especially meaningful'.

63. Finkle (2004): Lane signals 'that he's aware of what he's doing and is going to keep doing it'; Lane and Stroman 'have honored the spirit, if not every letter' of Aristophanes; Dale (2004): 'such a clash of styles usually spells death for a musical, but Stroman seems to have embraced this crazy quilt of a concept'.

64. The 1941 production received a very strong response, including an editorial in the *New York Times*; the 1974 show became legendary, at least in theatre circles. Nowadays, the idea that a *theatrical* production could have such an effect is of course absurd — on anything other than a local audience (which was of course the audience for whom Aristophanes was writing).

65. Jeff Henderson points out to me that the two-obol price of admission in Athens was not cheap: it was a labourer's daily pay.

66. Beye (2004*b*). For further suggestions, see English (2005).

67. Reckford (1987), 412–13.

68. E. Hall (2004*b*), 78–79.

69. Sondheim's works do not need elaborate productions; in fact simpler ones may serve them better. John Doyle's brilliant 2005 production of *Sweeney Todd* with all the actors/singers playing instruments demonstrates this; so did Brad Shreve's production of *Assassins* at a University of California, Santa Cruz dining hall in 1999.

70. Special thanks to the organizers of the 2004 conference 'Aristophanes: Upstairs and Downstairs' for their invitation and for the stimulating events which gave rise to this volume. For their help in preparing the 2004 presentation and this essay, I owe great thanks to Charlie Beye, John Given, Christopher Grabowski, Judy Hallett, Jeffrey Henderson, Tom Lehrer, Steven Padla, Rick Pender, Philip Rinaldi, Niall Slater, Paul Sosbee, the staff of Visual Resources at McHenry Library, University of California, Santa Cruz, and Amanda Wrigley. Very special thanks — as always — to Tom Vogler.

PART IV

❖

Close Encounters

CHAPTER 13

❖

Freeing Aristophanes in South Africa: From High Culture to Contemporary Satire

Betine van Zyl Smit

It is 1996 in South Africa. The scene is set in Hades. A choice has to be made as to which poet has the most inspirational message for the citizens of the time. The arbiter is not the god Dionysus, but the audience. Democracy has been in action everywhere in the country since the successful transition from the apartheid regime two years before: now it has come even to the theatre! The audience at the Thom Theatre at the University of Stellenbosch are invited to exercise their democratic rights. They have to choose the best, not from a choice between Euripides and Aeschylus, but between four local writers, to bring inspiration to the living. In this play, *Paradox*, an adaptation of Aristophanes' *Frogs*, Aristophanes has been freed from the shackles imposed on him as one of the representatives of the western classical tradition. His comedy has been appropriated and transformed into a product that reflects South Africa in the last decade of the twentieth century. A glance back at the history of the reception of Aristophanes in South Africa shows that he has not always enjoyed this freedom. Greek drama was introduced into South Africa as part of the lasting legacy of colonialism, both Dutch and British. Written drama did not exist in the country before the advent of the settlers from Europe. It is thus unsurprising that the whole canon of western classical literature was incorporated into the schools and universities.[1] The study and production of plays also reflected this. During the course of the twentieth century, Greek drama came to form part of the syllabus of schools of drama at the different universities. Aspiring actors, playwrights and directors were thus familiarized not only with tragedy, but also with comedy, and specifically with the plays of Aristophanes.[2]

In his valuable study of the reception of Greek drama in Africa, *The Athenian Sun in an African Sky*, Wetmore devotes only two pages to 'Aristophanes in Africa'. He remarks that the tendency around the world to privilege tragedy over comedy, 'especially for adaptation', is even more pronounced in Africa.[3] In fact, Wetmore maintains that 'apart from a handful of professional and university productions in the admittedly Eurocentric culture of South Africa (there are, after all, no Zulu, Xhosa, or Sotho adaptations, for example, only English and Afrikaans), there is very little, if any, adaptation of Aristophanes' works into African contexts. Even performances of translations of the Greek originals seem fairly nonexistent.'[4]

Wetmore's statement, especially the vagueness of his language in the phrase 'fairly nonexistent', reflects the lack of reliable information on performances in Africa. For South Africa the situation is better, although the information lies scattered in various small archives, newspapers and libraries. This chapter traces the performance in South Africa of the three Aristophanic comedies that involve anabatic or katabatic adventures, *Peace*, *Birds* and *Frogs*. In spite of Wetmore's mention of only a 'handful' of productions of Aristophanic comedies in the country, there are enough examples of these three plays to provide material for a study of the development of the reception of Aristophanes in South Africa. Barring *Lysistrata*, which seems to have been the Aristophanic comedy most frequently produced,[5] *Birds* and *Frogs* appear to have been the most popular with directors.

The production of Aristophanic comedies in South Africa has been predominantly at universities, where, as we have noted, they form part of the training of students. The professional Afrikaans travelling companies that toured the smaller towns in the early part of the twentieth century, and the amateur theatre societies, probably could not afford to present classical theatre as their general fare. Commercial theatre in the country has apparently not viewed these plays as sufficiently popular to warrant production, while the 'community theatre' and 'workers' theatre' that started emerging in the black communities in the 1960s, as part of the cultural and political struggle, had their own agenda based on their social and political situation. However, the four performing arts councils that were established in 1963, one in each of the four provinces into which the country was then divided, staged several productions of the plays under discussion. These productions were probably the most influential in introducing the comic playwright to a wider audience in South Africa. But the brief of these councils was 'to present the whole spectrum of dramatic art [...] both in English and Afrikaans', and thus effectively excluded performance in indigenous African languages.[6] Until 1977 all the staff involved in performance, as well as the audiences, were white.

Birds, a celebrated flight of fancy, is rated by many as representing the pinnacle of Aristophanes' art. Erich Segal calls it 'the fullest expression of the comic dream' and 'Aristophanes' masterpiece'.[7] The audacity of the poet's imagination and the scope that it provides for adaptation probably account for its popularity. Two productions especially deserve attention as representing the two approaches to staging Aristophanes that are notable in South Africa. The first is that of the Drama Society of the University of Cape Town in 1965, and the second the adaptation by André P. Brink for the Performing Arts Council of the Transvaal (PACT) in 1971. Both these productions stimulated considerable interest and are consequently well documented. The Cape Town production was directed by Peter Kleinschmidt, a young West German, who had been invited to the Cape for the first time two years before to stage Ionesco's *Rhinoceros*. Kleinschmidt was to be one of the most important interpreters of Aristophanes for Cape Town audiences, as he would later also direct *Frogs* (1977) and *Peace* (1983). Kleinschmidt's first invitation had been arranged by Donald Inskip, who was involved in the management of the

FIG. 13.1 (above). Pisthetairos, Hoopoe, and Euelpides in Kleinschmidt's *The Birds* (1965).
FIG. 13.2 (below). Pisthetairos and Iris in Kleinschmidt's *The Birds* (1965).

University's theatre.[8] Inskip and his colleagues aimed at 'presenting as wide a spectrum of work from the international repertoire as possible', and had several times invited directors from abroad who could bring 'novelty, freshness and [...] theatrical worth and effectiveness' to their productions.[9] Kleinschmidt's work was obviously highly regarded in Cape Town as his frequent subsequent engagements indicate.

It is therefore of interest to consider Kleinschmidt's views on the performance of Aristophanic comedy, as they are revealed in his pronouncements and style of direction. The programme notes to the 1965 *Birds* production in Cape Town quote Kleinschmidt's belief that the comedy should be interpreted 'as though it had been written yesterday'.[10] Further views of the director were revealed during two lectures given under the aegis of the Classics Department to provide information to the general public on the background to the work of Aristophanes.[11] The director believed that *Birds* could only be produced in a democracy, for only then could the audience react in the way that the Athenians had. The reporter (D. Pelteret) commented that Kleinschmidt apparently understood a democracy to be a state where a certain amount of self-criticism was allowed. South Africa at the time could not by any stretch of the imagination be classed as a true democracy.

Kleinschmidt further believed that Aristophanes was a showman and that the play should be a spectacle. Yet it should be presented in as contemporary an idiom as possible. This underlay the choice of the translation by the American William Arrowsmith, which had appeared in 1961. Its jokes and idiom had immediate contemporary resonance, although they might be dated in ten years' time.[12] The insistence on contemporaneity was carried on to the composition (partly by Kleinschmidt) of jazz music for the play, but stopped short of modern dress as that might 'get too close to definite individuals, and Aristophanes' characters were still types'. There seemed to be no attempt by the director to incorporate any local elements into his production. The actual style of presentation also indicates Kleinschmidt's interpretation. For *Birds* he chose an eclectic approach, preserving some elements of ancient performance, such as the masks, but introducing contemporary ingredients such as jazz (fig. 13.1).

This production of *Birds* had a highly successful run. The student newspaper *Varsity* reported that for the two and a half weeks of the season 'Packed houses were a feature.'[13] Three aspects of the reception of this production in the press are noteworthy. The first was the exceptionally wide range of publications that covered it, amongst others *House and Home*,[14] the *South African Jewish Times*,[15] *Die Burger*, *The Cape Times*,[16] *The Cape Argus*,[17] *Sunday Chronicle*,[18] *Sunday Express*,[19] and *News Check*.[20] The second striking feature is that the reviews were uniformly enthusiastic. The third was that the reviews were remarkably similar in aspects of the production that they selected for comment.

The cultural importance of the play was highlighted by reviewers noting that this was a Greek comedy dating from more than two thousand years ago. All agreed that the German director had brought a special expertise, thus enhancing the cultural value of the show. Its excellent acting, music, costumes (see fig. 13.2) and effects were generally praised. It was noted that no local touches had been introduced, but that it had rather been presented as part of Western culture; the lively Americanisms in the translation made it contemporary in language, but completely timeless in feeling. One reviewer paid special attention to the 'liberal sprinkling' of four-letter words.[21] This was an unusual feature on any South African stage at that time, but the critic considered that the words were not offensive and fitted in well with the general liveliness and boldness of the play. It is interesting to note that when the students of the University of Cape Town's Drama Department presented the same play in the same translation fifteen years later, but with a South African slant, it evoked sharp criticism. One reviewer stated that the attempt to present the play as commentary on local conditions spoilt its subtlety and conciseness.[22] Another spelt out his objection more plainly: 'By using Afrikaans accents and mannerisms for the gods' delegation who come to negotiate with the birds, the play is clearly being used as an allegory for a similar usurpation of power which could arise in this country. But it is a powerless allegory, trite in its statement, and scarcely justifying the banalities used for its implementation.'[23] One cannot isolate the added local ingredients as the sole cause of this play not succeeding, but it certainly did not grip the imagination of reviewers and audiences as its predecessor had done.

The 1965 production of *Birds* was undoubtedly experienced as a cultural highlight in Cape Town. In addition to the extensive press coverage and the lectures organized at the University, an article by the distinguished classicist Professor T. J. Haarhoff compared the satire and humour of Gilbert in his operas with that of Aristophanes.[24] Another very long review article in the student newspaper, while generally praising the production, presented detailed criticism of the choice of translation.[25] The author found the American slang already somewhat dated and objected to the introduction of obscenities not even hinted at by Aristophanes. His gravest disapproval was however for the deliberate mistranslation of scientific terms in Meton's speech (999 ff.). This is treated at length and compared with a literal translation of the Greek text. Although this discussion would perhaps not have appealed to the general public, it does show how serious a preoccupation this production was to a section of the public.

Birds has also proved a popular choice at the Drama School of the University of Natal in Durban, where it was staged in 1966, 1973, and 1982. However, none of these productions drew public attention comparable to that of the new version presented by the Performing Arts Council of the Transvaal's Youth Theatre, an Afrikaans adaptation by André P. Brink with the title *Die hand vol vere* (literally *The hand full of feathers*). The Afrikaans title is an idiom for something light or worthless and thus signals the playful approach of this version. Brink followed the structure of Aristophanes' comedy closely, but transformed the characters into contemporary South Africans, while the scene was set somewhere in Africa. This approach in itself satirized the policy of B. J. Vorster, then Prime Minister, of trying to forge contact with other African countries, a policy known as 'beweging uitwaarts', literally 'movement outward'.[26] Euelpides was renamed Pistorius, a 'verligte' ('enlightened'), and Pisthetairos' new name was Van der Merwe, a 'verkrampte' ('cramped'): 'verlig' and 'verkramp' were the terms coined at that time to indicate somewhat progressive politicians on the one hand and ultra-conservatives on the other. Pistorius and Van der Merwe had left South Africa because of drought, new taxes, hire purchase contracts, land bank loans, petrol prices, inflation, the price of bread, the price of butter, the South African Broadcasting Corporation, immigrants, and sundry other complaints. They hoped to find a new country, but shortly after arriving they tried to persuade King Hoepoe that their new country must have a name, that a high wall had to be built to separate the North from the South so that a toll would have to be paid to pass through, that national festivals with appropriate longwinded speeches would have to be organized and that the country must have a flag. The colours chosen for this flag, by means of plucking feathers from three different birds, were yellow, green, and black, the colours of the African National Congress, which at that time was of course a banned organization. Strangely, none of the reviewers of the play even noticed this. To those who recognized the colours and what they stood for, the chorus' cry of 'Viva Viva Viva Kammabokmakierieland!' must have had an added dimension,[27] especially if they knew that the bokmakierie was a green and yellow bird with a black band under the throat. They would then also have been conscious of a second meaning to Pistorius' remark: 'There it is. Our flag of freedom.'[28]

As in the Greek comedy, a series of visitors who try to gain something from the new state arrived. Brink adapted the originals to satirize contemporary South Africans and their preoccupations. Thus the priest became a parody of a Dutch Reformed Church minister, a bombastic hypocrite whose sermon was interrupted by commercials. The poet was Wurm Wurmse, a poet of the 1970s; he represented a gentle satire on the poet Breyten Breytenbach, a personal friend of Brink, and a writer regarded as one of the most innovative Afrikaans poets of the time, but *persona non grata* to the South African government. Prometheus was now called Promethes, which suggested the widely used nickname for a longstanding member of the Nationalist cabinet, Piet 'Promises'. Iris became Iris Nixonhower, thus changing her status from that of divinity to a North American national. Poseidon, Triballos, and Heracles were replaced by three delegates from the United Nations. This last change made fun of the preoccupation of the South African government with what it regarded as the interference of this organization in the country's internal affairs. The chorus of birds sang songs adapted from Afrikaans popular and folk music.

This play was put on in two phases. The first version, staged in Pretoria, was directed by Carel Trichardt and was not as well received as the second, directed by François Swart, and performed in Johannesburg three months later before being taken on tour.[29] Reviews in the press were generally favourable. It was praised as 'folk satire',[30] and even claimed to represent an Afrikaans version of the rock musical *Hair*; the whole cast was commended for the tasteful and witty way in which they kept the audience in stitches.[31] However, there was one reviewer who complained that the play was all Brink and no Aristophanes, and asked whether Brink needed a great writer behind whom he could hide.[32] This indicates the latent hostility to Brink on the part of conservative Afrikaners. They had already been scandalized by some of his daring novels in the previous decade, when he had become conspicuous as a prominent member of a new wave of Afrikaans writers, the Sestigers.[33] Public comment on *Die hand vol vere* was unexpectedly passionate, as is evident from a number of letters published in the Afrikaans daily *Die Transvaler*. Part of the performing arts councils' mission was to take performances to smaller towns in the provinces. After its run in Pretoria and Johannesburg, the play was presented in the Western Transvaal and it was from here that some outraged letters came.

N. R. van Zyl, a Dominee (Dutch Reformed Church minister) of Christiana, wrote to express his disquiet that a play of such a kind could be presented.[34] He called on parents and the youth to oppose the trend and questioned the comedy's educational and moral value. His letter demonstrates that he considered the portrayal of beauty and the expression of elevating sentiments to be prerequisites for the arts and that in his view it was the task of PACT to bring such art to the people. His condemnation of the play was due to superficial Puritanism. He objected particularly to women wearing jeans and men with long hair. His letter expressed moral indignation at the smutty language, suggestive jokes and puns, and patriotic suspicion at the lampooning of serious matters like the laws of the country, national customs, and even the Publications Control Board. Dominee van Zyl warned that PACT risked losing the support of schools and churches if it continued with this kind of play. That was no idle threat, for at that time, when most men in prominent positions in the Afrikaans churches and in the provincial education departments were members of the Afrikaner Broederbond, such censure could be put into practice.

Dominee van Zyl's letter was supported and followed by another from A. M. de Lange of Potchefstroom.[35] His indignation was even more strongly expressed, and his letter opened: 'It was brutal, unclean, sacrilegious.' He declared that he was prepared to tolerate satire of the state, the government, the laws of the country, and public bodies like the Publications Control Board if those responsible were to regret their offence sincerely and apologize. However, the lampooning of God, idolatry, making fun of Christian congregations, and other excesses were a sin against the Holy Ghost. De Lange saw the play as a tool of the Communists to subvert innocent minds. He complained about vulgar, suggestive, sex-laden dances, and psychedelic music, and demanded that PACT should be called to account for the abomination. This tirade was supported by another letter from one who simply signed as 'a parent'.[36] This writer supplemented the attack of the previous letters by casting suspicion on the character of the playwright. He stated that filthy language and sacrilege were what one should expect from one who had publicly declared that he was an atheist. This storm in a teacup, which encapsulated so much of what passed as public morality in white apartheid South Africa, had, in the meantime, drawn the attention of a national Sunday newspaper.[37] It gleefully ran the story of a scathing attack launched on PACT by the Dutch Reformed Church and school boards 'for dishing up vulgar, foreign, sex-loaded hippie cult material to the youth'. Reports indicated that not only in Christiana, but also in Bloemhof, the local ministers, congregations and school boards were united in condemning the play and had written to PACT to protest. PACT answered that it had not been their intention to shock anyone and that the play was pure satire.

A subsequent letter from R. Engelbrecht of Pretoria at last contributed a note of sanity.[38] After refuting De Lange's attack in detail by citing examples from the

Fig. 13.3. Aeacus and Dionysus in *Die Paddas*, 1977

play, he reminded readers that *Die hand vol vere* was an adaptation of Aristophanes' *Birds*, written in 414 BC, and speculated that Aristophanes would have been most amused if he had known that he would still inflame tempers in such a distant future. Yet this did not prevent the sad conclusion of the fracas, when, as the same newspaper reported a few weeks later, the Transvaal Education Department had refused to approve the performance of *Die hand vol vere* for schools.[39] Perhaps the hand of Dominee van Zyl had reached from Christiana to Pretoria. The irony is that none of the professional reviewers, nor the self-appointed moralists, noticed the one factor that would have made Brink, the director, and even PACT, criminally culpable — namely the display, as the symbol of freedom, of the colours of a banned organization. Those in the know must have had the last laugh! By transforming Aristophanes' satire of Athenian life into a send-up of contemporary South Africa, Brink started the process of freeing Aristophanes from the fetters of being regarded with awe as a 'classic'. In his use of earthy, everyday Afrikaans Brink also domesticated the Greek writer and brought him to the notice of many whose views were rigidly conditioned by the tenets of Afrikaner and Christian nationalism.

While Brink's play contains many indigenous elements (the Afrikaans language and scores of contemporary South African references and resonances), there were probably equally many, of another part of South African life, in the only version of Aristophanes I could trace in a black African language. Thus far I have been able to discover that there was a production in Zulu based on Aristophanes' *Birds*. The playwright, Themi Gwala, used the Aristophanic concept of creating a better society (in this case, an enslaved people liberating themselves from enslavement by finding a new world) for his play called *Izinyoni*, which is the Zulu word for 'birds'. The Durban newspaper *The Daily News* reported on 2 May 1974 that the play would be staged at the Casa Cinema in Port Shepstone, a small town south of Durban, the following Sunday at 5 pm in aid of the newspaper's LEARN Fund. It is also indicated that the performance would be open 'to the African, Indian and Coloured race groups'. This is a sharp reminder that during the apartheid years theatres were segregated, and that it was only in 1977 that theatres were opened to all race groups.

In these circumstances, one would have imagined that the new world that the people in *Izinyoni* would be shown to be seeking would be connected with political freedom, but according to the short piece in the paper it was 'the Western way of life'. Further particulars reveal no more than that the play was based on the history of the Zulu people and that Gwala had composed songs for the play which combined Western and Zulu styles. Although I have not been able to gather more information about this adaptation, it is, however, proof that Wetmore is not correct in his assumption that Aristophanes has not appealed to Africans. The difficulties involved in obtaining information about this African version bear out Orkin's observation of the obstacles that black playwrights face in getting their work published,[40] and especially underline the lack of reviews of 'performances from the oppressed classes' appearing in the white daily newspapers.[41]

A final example of the reworking of *Birds* into a South African context is *Boklied*, a play by Breyten Breytenbach.[42] This play also caused a furore when it was first staged at an Afrikaans Arts festival in 1998. Objections were made to nudity and simulated copulation on stage, but critics found it a compelling exploration of the position of the artist in contemporary society. There is a complex interplay between the second act of Breytenbach's new work and the text of Aristophanes' *Birds*, which has been explored in detail by P. J. Conradie.[43] He concludes that the true theme of the second act is an exploration of the poet's craft ('digterskap'), and particularly the cheerful and imaginative sides of it. In this respect it complements the fantasy of Aristophanes' comedy.

When one considers that only two of Aristophanes' comedies have been published in Afrikaans translation,[44] while the number for Greek tragedies is at least fourteen,[45] it seems that Wetmore was correct in concluding that the comedies of Aristophanes have had less appeal than Greek tragedy. Nevertheless, the publication and production of *Die Paddas*, an Afrikaans translation of *Frogs*, again brought the Greek playwright to the fore in Cape Town in 1977 (fig. 13.3). This production was the second play of Aristophanes to be directed in Cape Town by Peter Kleinschmidt, this time for the Cape Province Performing Arts Board (CAPAB). In his preface to the published version of *Frogs*, the translator, Merwe Scholtz, set out the principles according to which he worked. He did not use the Greek text, but a number of German and English translations. The final product was vetted by a classicist.

FIG. 13.4. Donkey, Xanthias, and Dionysus in *Die Paddas* (1977)

Scholtz stressed that his work was a translation and not an adaptation. In this he respected the approach of the director, and he refers to Kleinschmidt's reasons for not attempting to modernize the play in any way: 'The future is a past that projects itself over the present. The theatre deals with the past — and the more carefully and sensitively this is done, the better the theatre accomplishes its meaningful task — to be the guardian of the future.'[46] Kleinschmidt believed that respecting the conditions under which the play was originally produced, rather than pretending that it was a contemporary work, would best enhance the audience's appreciation of the play's meaning and structure. It is clear that he was still viewing Aristophanes as enshrined in his Greek past. The translator nevertheless made some concessions to facilitate the audience's understanding of the play, including the addition of some background information. He also incorporated parts of the parabasis of *Acharnians* into that of *Frogs*, since he thought that the earlier play carried the same theme, but in a form more accessible to a modern audience.[47]

In an interview published in a Cape Town newspaper, Kleinschmidt reiterated his view that theatre should help organize the future by looking carefully at the past,[48] and that theatre should better the life of people. It is clear that in spite of his refusal to modernize the play, Kleinschmidt believed his audience capable of interpreting its message and applying it to contemporary circumstances. In the same interview he deplored the number of what he termed 'West End-type' productions in Cape Town, on the grounds that they had little relevance to reality and would make audiences incapable of appreciating worthwhile plays. He thought that this type of show should not enjoy state subsidy. Asked about his views on censorship, he said that he opposed it, but that it could be circumvented and could sometimes even be beneficial as it forced writers to become more sophisticated. Indeed, since this was a production of CAPAB, *Die Paddas* enjoyed the benefit of the generous subsidy and an impressive and lavish show could be staged. One newspaper reported that in order to accommodate the enormous set, three rows of seats had been removed from the front of the theatre.[49] Nearly a ton of soil and real plants had been brought in to create the swamp. Although four actors were used for all the speaking parts, fourteen more actors were employed to make up the two choruses (the frogs and the initiates), while the donkey was played by the huge athlete John van Reenen (fig. 13.4).

The Nico Malan theatre where it was staged had recently been opened to all race groups, and one reviewer urged all Afrikaans-speakers not to miss the production.[50] Indeed, the play ran for three weeks and received much acclaim from reviewers in both Afrikaans and English newspapers. However, a letter from Dr A. Blumer in the Afrikaans newspaper *Die Burger* cast a new light on the reviews. He noted that all three Cape newspapers, although praising the translation and production lavishly, were curiously similar in content. Each contained a paraphrase of the play, and comments on the staging, the actors, the décor, and costumes. Yet none even mentioned the exciting end of the play or discussed the director's aims. The very lameness of the reviews, so shrewdly observed by Blumer, suggests that Kleinschmidt was over-optimistic in his belief that a modern audience would be able to interpret the message of the play and apply it to contemporary circumstances. What would this have meant? If one considers that in *Frogs* the state is in danger and that wise counsel is needed to put it on the right course, it would not have been difficult to infer a simple application to South Africa. The preceding years had seen what were regarded as 'terrorist organizations' coming to power in the former Portuguese colonies in the area, covert South African military involvement on the Namibian–Angolan border, the continuation of the Rhodesian war of independence, and, internally, the Soweto uprising of 1976. It would be hard to deny that the South African state needed wise counsel to guide it.

A similar failure to reach the local population with the message of the play marked Kleinschmidt's third and last production of Aristophanes in Cape Town, *Peace* in 1983. This comedy has not often been performed in South Africa, but Kleinschmidt directed, under the aegis of CAPAB, an Afrikaans translation by Nerina Ferreira.[51] Kleinschmidt followed his declared policy of privileging the original text, but a number of anachronistic elements were introduced, notably a VW Beetle as the vehicle to transport Trygaeus to heaven, and the god Hermes dressed in a winged business suit. This production also enjoyed good publicity,[52] but the reviews were less enthusiastic and *Die Burger* printed a short article expressing disappointment and stating that this was not the kind of show to attract audiences to the theatre.[53] Again, given that the theme of the comedy is the quest for peace, it should have been easy to construe the play as an allegory of what South Africa needed, but none of the newspaper critics even hinted at such a suggestion.[54]

The performing arts councils continued relentlessly in their set pattern, making occasional concessions such as the opening of its theatres to all population groups in 1977 and even staging a few 'progressive' South African plays, such as Athol Fugard's *Boesman and Lena*. Yet the real growth point and interest had shifted elsewhere, to the theatre of protest and to indigenous South African productions that were often multiracial and multicultural. These were put on at venues like The Space in Cape Town (founded in 1972) and The Market Theatre in Johannesburg (established in 1976).[55] As Temple Hauptfleisch, a specialist in South African theatre, has succinctly put it, by the mid-1980s this new wave of creative energy had 'usurped the central position in the theatrical system, ousting performances of European and American classics and even box-office successes to the periphery. Serious theatre in South Africa, in the 1980s and early 1990s, primarily consisted of indigenous productions of indigenous works, cast in a non-formal format.'[56]

This explains why, after the rather moderate success of *Vrede* (*Peace*) in 1983, there seem to have been no further major productions of Aristophanes' comedies. The students of drama at the University of Natal in Durban were staging his work at regular intervals, with some references to contemporary South Africa included in their versions of *Frogs* in 1986 and 1988. However, the inauguration of the new regime in the country seemed to energize students and inspire them to take a fresh look at the Greek classics. Within the space of two years there were two productions that brought new life to Aristophanes in South Africa, freed him from being treated with too much respect and gave him a voice in the idiom of the new South Africa. The first was a performance by University of Cape Town drama students of an adaptation of the *Frogs*.[57] It had been reworked from David Barrett's Penguin translation (1964) by two members of the lecturing staff, and included plenty of innovative local touches, documented by one classical scholar who reviewed it thus:

> Whereas the references to Aristophanes' contemporaries were retained in the dialogue scenes, some clever updating for South African spectators had been introduced into the separate choral sections, particularly in the *parabasis*. The names of Cleisthenes, Archedemus, Phrynichus and Cleigenes were replaced (not always by wholly appropriate analogues, but ten out of ten for effort and ingenuity) by those of Terre'blanche (leader of the Afrikaner Weerstandsbeweging, a group of White rightwing extremists), Rajbansi (slippery Indian politician), Verwoerd (promulgator of *apartheid*, assassinated in 1966), and Mangope (Black puppet leader of the former *homeland* of Bophuthatswana, who refused to participate in the recent elections). The resonance of these references helped to transmit something of the political flavour of Aristophanic comedy. Certainly, the chorus leader's impassioned appeal for constructive engagement by all Athenians recalled President Nelson Mandela's stirring inauguration speech, delivered only three days before the production opened, urging reconciliation and nation-building.[58]

This version of *Frogs* thus openly and explicitly made Aristophanes a participant in the change in South Africa.

Yet a more radical reinterpretation of *Frogs* was *Paradox*,[59] produced by the drama students at the University of Stellenbosch in 1996. The adaptation of this Afrikaans version was by Chris Vorster, who also directed. Vorster preserved the outline of the Greek comedy in that a slave and a godlike figure (here simply 'W'),[60] both women, undertake a journey to the Underworld to bring back a poet. But much of the original text was changed, supplemented, or deleted. A Master of Ceremonies (a female student in a tuxedo) served as a narrator and link between the audience and the actors. The large cast was overwhelmingly female, a woman taking the role even of Heracles, here called Herak. The ancient Greek practice of male actors playing all roles, even those of women, was thus neatly reversed. Pluto became a 'Bitch Goddess' who presided over a rave club. Many aspects of the new dispensation were satirized, including the new South African Broadcasting Corporation, affirmative action, and even the abolition of the death penalty. Afrikaans had become 'the forbidden language', but was used in a lively and irreverent way in the show.[61] Music and dance of all kinds served a variety of purposes, mostly satirical. There was a merciless critique of the musical *Les Misérables*, which had been playing to capacity houses in Cape Town for a much longer season than local plays could command.

The climax was, however, the democratic selection of the most inspirational poetic utterance. Instead of a contest between two poets, there were many in the rave club who offered their contributions, mostly rather banal. Some parodied the Bible and the old national anthem, others told feeble jokes, but everything was solemnly uttered to the strains of Verdi's *La Traviata* playing softly in the background. Vorster's radical innovation was to introduce the audience as judge. To facilitate selection, five 'poetic' declarations had been printed on the programmes, which thus became mock ballot papers, although the vote was by a show of hands. This was a cheeky updating of Aristophanes,[62] which made him part of the new South Africa and freed him from the cultural grandeur with which he had traditionally been associated. The further implication of this romp was that it was no longer Dionysus who presided in the theatre. In the modern world, the theatre, it argued, is ruled by its public. The underlying theme of the play was the importance of keeping theatre culture alive.

The reception of Aristophanes in South African theatre has undergone an astonishing evolution which in some way parallels the political changes in the country. The comic playwright whose work was fifty years ago considered in some way sacrosanct, as part of the great western heritage, has now become, like the rest of that heritage (Greek tragedy and Shakespeare are good examples), a storehouse from which ideas and plots may be taken and transformed into a local product with deep resonances of the past. Yet, at the same time, the dominant aspects of the canonical ancient comedies — satire of contemporary life and a celebration of the powers of the theatre — have been retained.

Notes to Chapter 13

1. Hauptfleisch (1997), 35: 'The Anglo-European canon of dramatic works was simply appropriated as the South African canon for study and the models for emulation — even by the literate African population of this country.'
2. I would like to thank Paul Regenass of the Artscape Archive, Chris Weare of the Drama Department of the University of Cape Town, Petrus du Preez and Gaerin Hauptfleisch of the Centre for Theatre and Performance Studies at the University of Stellenbosch, and Mervyn McMurtry of the Department of Drama and Performance Studies at the University of KwaZulu-Natal for access to their archival material.
3. Wetmore (2002), 52.
4. Ibid. 51.
5. *Lysistrata* and *Frogs* are the two Aristophanic comedies which have been published in Afrikaans translation: J. P. J. van Rensburg (1970) and Scholtz (1978).
6. Orkin (1991), 245. He quotes from a publication of PACT, the Performing Arts Council of the Transvaal.
7. E. Segal (2001), 85. See also Arrowsmith (1961), 7.
8. He held the chair of French at the University of Cape Town from 1932, and later became Vice-Principal. He was very actively involved in drama and the management of the University's own theatre, the Little Theatre.
9. Inskip (1972), 103.
10. This opinion is also expressed in an interview Yvonne Bryceland held with Kleinschmidt, published in *Cape Times* on 31 July 1965: 'The problems expressed in the play are so commonplace that people will think [...] that this comedy was written some months ago'.
11. *Varsity*, 18 August 1965.
12. William Arrowsmith's insensitivity even for his time to racial issues became conspicuous later, when in the 1980s his 'updated' and 'topical' translation of *Thesmophoriazusae* attracted criticism in North America on account of his decision to make the Scythian slave archer speak in a way suggestive of an African-American: see further E. Hall (2006), ch. 8.
13. *Varsity*, 28 August 1965.
14. July–August 1965.
15. 3 Aug. 1965.
16. 30 July and 6 Aug. 1965.
17. 23, 28, and 29 July; 2 and 6 Aug. 1965.
18. 8 Aug 1965.
19. 8 Aug. 1965.
20. 13 Aug. 1965.
21. Terry Herbst in *The Sunday Express*, 8 Aug. 1965.
22. E. Wessels in *Die Burger*, 25 Aug. 1980.
23. P. Mitchell in *The Argus*, 22 Aug. 1980.
24. In *The Cape Argus*, 16 Aug. 1965.
25. See 'Wings are Wonderful Things', *Varsity*, 11 Aug. 1965.
26. Brink (1971), 1: 'Pistorius: Ons beweeg uitwaarts' (literally: 'Pistorius: we are moving outward').
27. This is Brink's equivalent for Nephelokokkugia. The literal meaning of Kammabokmakierieland is 'pretend country of the bokmakierie', a yellow and green bird with a black band under the throat (the *Telophorus zeylonus*).
28. Brink (1971), 25: 'Daar's hy. Ons vlag van vryheid'.
29. Aart de Villers in *Die Vaderland*, 16 July 1971, 8: 'Hand vol vere het tot sy reg gekom' [*Die hand vol vere* has come into its own']; see also 'P.R.B.' in *Die Transvaler*, 21 July 1971, 8: 'Flink sêgoed laat kraai van plesier' ['Sturdy repartee makes one cry out for pleasure'].
30. Eben Meiring in *Die Burger*, 28 July 1971.
31. Aart de Villiers in *Die Vaderland*, 16 July 1971, 8.
32. 'H.J.' in *Die Transvaler*, 9 Apr. 1971, 4.

33. The Sestigers, the 'generation of the sixties', used modern literary styles and techniques to explore themes such as sexual freedom, racial tolerance, and secularization.
34. 27 Aug. 1971.
35. 7 Sept. 1971.
36. 13 Sept. 1971.
37. *The Sunday Times*, 12 Sept. 1971.
38. *Die Transvaler*, 16 Sept. 1971.
39. Ibid. 20 Oct. 1971.
40. Orkin (1991), 120.
41. Ibid. 212.
42. Literally 'goatsong'.
43. Conradie (1998).
44. *Lysistrata* translated by J. P. J. van Rensburg (1970; above, n. 5), and *Die Paddas* translated by Merwe Scholtz (1978).
45. See van Zyl Smit (2003), 4–9.
46. Scholtz (1978), 11 (my translation).
47. Ibid. (1978), 12.
48. Interview with Garth Vardal in *The Argus Tonight*, 12.
49. *Die Burger*, 14 July 1977.
50. 'C.S.' in *Rapport*, 31 July 1977.
51. *Vrede* (it has not been published).
52. For instance, a long article by G. van W. Kruger in *Die Burger*, 22 Aug. 1983, on the background of the comedy.
53. 27 Aug. 1983.
54. The published responses included 'Magical Greek Satire' by Mark Swift, *The Argus*, 26 August 1983; 'Nie heeltemal vrede nie' ['Not entirely peace'] by Kerneels Breytenbach, *Die Burger*, 26 August 1983; 'Kaapse Vrede vir oog en oor' ['Cape Peace for eye and ear'] by Coenie Slabber, *Rapport*, 28 August 1983; and 'Aristophanes' Anti-War Play' by Robert Greig, *The Cape Times*, 25 August 1983.
55. It is interesting that both the Market Theatre in 1974 and The Space in 1977 put on adaptations of *Lysistrata* that incorporated distinctly South African elements.
56. Hauptfleisch (1997), 60.
57. For a detailed discussion of this performance see the review by Mezzabotta (1994).
58. Mezzabotta (1994).
59. The title puns on the pronunciation of the Afrikaans word for 'frogs', 'paddas', which is often colloquially pronounced 'parras'; see e.g. Vorster (1996), 12.
60. Sometimes it is suggested that she represented Winnie Madikizela-Mandela, divorced wife of President Mandela, who is satirized for benefiting from the fame of her husband (ibid. 9).
61. See ibid. 1.
62. In a metatheatrical moment, the Master of Ceremonies said that they had 'raped' the original text enough: see ibid. 25.

CHAPTER 14

❖

Aristophanes' *Peace* on the Twentieth-Century French Stage: From Political Statement to Artistic Failure

Malika Bastin-Hammou

Introduction

If we consider professional productions of Aristophanes in France, it is clear that throughout the entire twentieth century his comedies were performed immeasurably less often than works by the Greek tragic poets. Every year there are at least five professional stagings of Greek tragedy in France, whereas Aristophanes was only produced on about sixty occasions during the whole period between 1900 and 2000. In my opinion, the reason for this is not a particular French generic taste for tragedy. I suggest, rather, that this phenomenon is to be related to the distinctive French political and economic organization of culture, which leads directors to feel that they have a political and educational duty to fulfil through their theatrical productions. This, I think, is the pattern that can be inferred from the the history of the twentieth-century productions of Aristophanes' *Peace* in France.

As a matter of fact, *Peace* was staged more frequently than any other Aristophanic comedy between 1900 and 2000 in France.[1] Plays like *Lysistrata* and *Ecclesiazusae* may have had a brief period of glory in the 1960s and 1970s, but they are no longer staged. Other comedies were hardly ever performed (*Thesmophoriazusae* was performed only once, and, as far as I know, *Frogs* was never produced at all). *Peace*, on the other hand, has long enjoyed the favour of French directors, especially in the subsidized theatres, even though it is certainly not considered to be Aristophanes' best play. Directors and journalists stress the length of the second part and criticize the scatological jokes, and especially the dung-beetle. So why have there been so many productions? The most important reason, I think, is political. *Peace* is felt to be the most political (in the modern, polemical sense), of Aristophanes' comedies: it is perceived to be a play with a message. Directors tend to turn to it in situations of political crisis.

Indeed, the chronology of the stagings of *Peace* in France reflects in a straightforward manner the French experience of military conflict. The first twentieth-century production, by Charles Dullin, was staged in December 1932,[2] just a month before Hitler became the chancellor of the Weimar Republic.

Subsequently there were, however, no significant productions of *Peace* until 1961. But within two years from that date, *Peace* was staged no fewer than three times. The first production was by Jean Vilar in 1961; this was followed in 1962 by two productions. One of these was initiated by Michel Fontayne in collaboration with Antoine Vitez, and the other by Tibor Egervari and Hubert Gignoux. These dates occurred, of course, at the height of the war in Algeria. The next production, by Marcel Maréchal, took place in 1969 in Lyon, and was related to the war in Vietnam. And the same Maréchal staged *Peace* again in 1991, this time in Marseille, during the Gulf War.

   Directors generally acknowledge that they produce this comedy for political reasons. For Jean Vilar, *Peace* was not only politically but theatrically interesting: 'The framework is excellent and the poetry beautiful.'[3] For Gignoux, since arriving at a state of peace was the most urgent problem facing France in the 1960s, it was interesting to see how the Greeks had faced that same problem.[4] But why Aristophanes, and why *Peace*, rather than *Lysistrata* or *Acharnians*? Because, says Vitez, this comedy is 'politically effective'.[5] As for Maréchal, he argues that Aristophanes is less 'dangerous' than modern writers: in 1991 he actually cancelled his staging of Jean Genet's controversial *Les Paravents* (*The Screens*, originally written in 1961 in direct response to the Algerian situation) because of the war in the Gulf, and decided to stage *Peace* instead. It is, however, true that it is not possible to relate the two stagings of *Peace* between 1991 and 2000 directly and immediately to any specific war, and neither of them made a claim to contain an explicit political message: one of these was directed by Michèle Heydorff in 1995, and the other by Anne Torrès in 1998.[6] An attempt will be made to explain this particular phenomenon later. But at this point in the argument it is appropriate to examine how the specific readings of *Peace* by its several twentieth-century French directors affected the choices they made regarding the text, the performance, and the ideological meanings that they attempted to convey.

Text: From Adaptation to Translation

Anybody who ever decides to stage Aristophanes, in any venue, has to face the question of the text. It offers at least three fundamental challenges. What should one do with the political allusions? What should one do with the obscenities, which cumulatively create the effect of what has been euphemistically known, since Jeffrey Henderson's pathbreaking book by that title first appeared in 1975, as the Maculate Muse? What should one do with the choral odes? And, as it happens, the very nature of the humour and structure of *Peace* makes these questions more than usually pressing. French directors have offered different answers to the problems at different points in the century. But it is possible to discern a general evolution, which I believe can also be noticed in the case of Greek tragedies, from adaptations to translations.

   Charles Dullin, Jean Vilar, Tibor Egervari, and Michel Fontayne each either wrote his own translation or commissioned one.[7] It is not until 1969 that a director, Marcel Maréchal, used a translation made by a classical scholar, and that was the version by Victor-Henry Debidour, a professor in Lyon.[8] Nor was this translation made to order, since Debidour had independently translated and published all Aristophanes' plays in 1965–66. But Maréchal read them, appreciated them and as a result contacted Debidour, who began to work with the actors. This was, I think, a major development. Maréchal not only used an actual translation, rather than a loose adaptation, but was actually proud of doing so: 'nous voulions monter la pièce d'Aristophane, et non une quelconque adaptation' ('we wanted to stage Aristophanes' comedy, and not any adaptation').[9] Similarly, in 1998 Anne Torrès agreed to work hand in hand with a classicist named Claire Nancy. This type of collaboration marks an evolution not only in terms of the directors' practice, but also of the entire conception, I think, of a translation for and in performance. Using a translation has become a sign or 'proof' of a particular kind of authenticity (even if, most of the time, directors still adapt that translation).

This is particularly clear if one considers how political allusions are treated. Dullin used an adaptation written by François Porché. One critic wrote, 'Everything is in Aristophanes. M. Porché only puts in a living and warm language the translations of specialists. And from time to time he adds something about the trenches or the cost of life',[10] while the return of *Peace* causes 'a crash of steel'.[11] Porché also wrote his own parabasis. According to our current standards, this constitutes not a translation but an adaptation, yet Dullin and the critics agreed that such an adaptation is in a sense 'faithful' to Aristophanes, because 'it makes it universal'.[12] In comparison, the three stagings of the 1960s were less naive than Dullin's: they did not aim at anything 'universal', but all three had different ways of adapting the text to current events.

In 1961, Jean Vilar did not not pretend to be faithful. He called his text an 'adaptation libre', a 'free adaptation'. Indeed, he quoted famous emblematic phrases used by Général de Gaulle, such as 'je vous ai compris' and 'hélas, hélas, hélas'.[13] The text used by Vilar mentioned generals, Algerians, socialists, and torture. It was seriously to underestimate the topical rewriting which had gone into the text to allege, as Bertrand Poirot-Delpech did in *Le Monde*, that Vilar had only changed proper names![14] Vilar was perfectly aware of the problem: he says that he never wanted to 'modernize', but simply to make the play relevant to contemporary events, a principle which would mean that Aristophanes' comedies should be retranslated every ten years, or, even better, each time a director decides to stage them.[15] The year after, Antoine Vitez also wrote an adaptation, but of another type. One could, I think, call it a Brechtian adaptation, yet it is interesting to note that Vitez did not want to call it an adaptation but an *imitation*. Rather than change the text, he added explanations. The coryphaeus explained the Peloponnesian War background, so that the spectators could understand, without transposing the war to another time and place. 'In fact, it is not Vitez but the spectator himself who adapts the play', said director Michel Fontayne.[16] In consequence, his entire production did not 'adapt' but 'explain': the costumes were Greek, but they did not aim at historical recreation. They just evoked Greece, and thus put some distance between the real world of the spectators and the entire production.

When it comes to the question of the treatment of the political allusions by the director Marcel Maréchal, it becomes very interesting because Maréchal staged

Peace twice in his career, once in 1969 in Lyon (at the Théâtre du Cothurne) and another time in 1991 in Marseille (at the Théâtre de la Criée). In 1969, as we have seen, he used the translation of Debidour, claiming that he could not see the point of adapting it. He collaborated with Debidour, and indeed defended his choice of text against the alternative of the respected Budé translation, which had been made for scholars (a somewhat absurd comparison since nobody had ever wanted to staged the Budé translation)![17] In 1991, however, the text he used, which he claimed to have taken from Vilar, topicalized the political allusions: one could hear the voice of President François Mitterrand, and the words 'SCUD' and 'Patriot missiles'. Maréchal chose to 'feed the play with the words, whether terrible or funny, of current events', as a critic wrote in *Le Monde* at the time.[18]

One might relate this new approach to the relative failure of his first production of *Peace*. But the first production, in fact, also adapted parts of the text. Maréchal admits that he had indeed made a few necessary cuts, consisting of political and literary allusions 'which do not mean anything to us any more.'[19] He also made a few changes, 'with the blessing of the translator'.[20] To put the situation concisely, while the first directors claimed their adaptations to be faithful to the *spirit* of the ancient comedy, recent ones claim to be faithful to its *text* — even if they change it from time to time. This marked a new turn in the conception of translation, and in the relations between directors and classicists. Moreover, I think that the more recent stagings of tragedies and comedies corroborate and consolidate this turn: it seems that directors do not commission adaptations any more, nor do they use existing translations; what they now prefer is to commission entirely new *translations*, and are willing to work alongside classical scholars, not only in respect of the actual performance text, but in respect also of their general understanding of the plays and the staging of them.[21]

Performance: Beetle, Gods, Chorus

When it comes to performance, *Peace* raises several problems which are of course also the very reasons that make it so interesting to directors. *Peace* is theatrically stimulating for two major reasons: its distinctive use of machinery, and the role it gives to the chorus. Considerable challenges are presented by the dung-beetle that flies in the air thanks to the *mēchanē*, by the gods who stand on a different horizontal level from the humans, and by the goddess *Peace,* a mute statue that needs to be excavated. Some directors, such as Heydorff or Vilar, have shown themselves to be particularly fond of machines, while others have been rather less sophisticated. Dullin's dung-beetle was an actor climbing stairs; but the lights nevertheless gave the feeling that this actor-beetle was flying. Vilar used a giant dung-beetle with a sophisticated contraption hanging in the air, from the theatrical roof-flies, thanks to four steel ropes.

As for the gods, both Maréchal in 1969 and Tesson in 2002 chose to use puppets to represent them. The goddess Peace herself raises two problems: both her own physical presence and her cave. Dullin, accustomed to dramatic illusion, had a hard time trying to come to terms with what he saw as Aristophanic 'incoherence': as he commented, 'It is hard to understand how Peace can be in a cave in the sky, and how Trygaeus can gather the Greeks there to free her.'[22] From Dullin's particular realist perspective, the goddess Peace must be represented as an almost naked young woman. Maréchal used a striptease artist, and Vilar a model freed by workers from her bunker. But Fontayne, on the other hand, has interesting thoughts about the goddess. Everybody, even Aristophanes' contemporaries, noted that she does not utter a single word, while one would expect her to make a speech.[23] Fontayne said that at first he wanted a lovely young woman, chosen because of her beauty. But then he realized that he had to give the role to a real actress, who plays the role of a type of peace that would love to speak, but just can't do it. And this actress should not look like a model, but more like a peasant girl. When it comes to the chorus, what makes the chorus of *Peace* so different from other Aristophanic choruses is the famous scene in which Peace herself is liberated through the 'hauling' scene. This has definitely stimulated the imaginaton of directors, probably because it allows the participation of the spectators and thus realizes on stage the political message that directors want to convey, and provokes the kind of reflection that they want to encourage in their audiences. Dullin actually asked the spectators to help, while Vilar directly addressed the spectators, brought them on stage, subjected them to accusations and even blamed them for the loss of peace.

Ideology

Yet even if *Peace* is visually interesting, it is primarily on account of the ideological statement that they want to make that directors have usually chosen to stage this comedy. It is not surprising that the message that they wish to convey is almost always a political one relating to war. The most famous stagings of *Peace* all allude directly to a specific war. Dullin staged his *Peace* in 1932, and it is striking how much his production became an occasion and a pretext for the critics to take political stands. The reviews they wrote were long, and all took similar positions which were critical of the League of Nations and diplomatic activity. Indeed, the criticisms directed at Dullin were exclusively political, and never aesthetic. One journalist disliked the fact that the chorus of Greeks attempting to free Peace were only the French spectators, and did not include the Germans, Italians, and Russians.[24] And the same slippage between theatrical and political judgements can be noted in the case of every production of *Peace*. The critics of performances of this play all regard the choice of Aristophanes as concealing a clever directorial strategy for escaping censorship. Dullin may not actually have made this decision explicit, but the other directors all explained their choice in an attempt to pre-empt critical reactions. This applies to Maréchal especially, who first produced *Peace* during the Vietnam War and again during the Gulf War. In 1991, however, it was not censorship that scared him, but the fear of provoking riots. This fear is ultimately what prevented him from reviving Genet's *Les Paravents*: 'I did not want to see the National Front gather at the gates of the theatre of La Criée', he said, explaining his decision to cancel Genet in favour of *Peace*.[25]

These directors all chose to stage *Peace* because of an international situation. But two productions do not so easily fit this interpretative framework. When Anne Torrès directed *Peace* in 1998, the international situation was not perceived as particularly sensitive or painful to the French people. Even though she alluded from time to time to the war in Bosnia, the war Torrès was concerned with was, instead, the social, indeed the 'civil' war within the French state. Her production gathered together both professional actors and amateurs. But she mostly aimed at bringing together people who came from entirely different social backgrounds. Indeed, this production used Aristophanes as a pretext for another agenda — this time a class-based one — even more clearly than the other, more topical performances discussed earlier in this chapter. Torrès says that this experience was interesting because of what happened before the rehearsals, and during the pauses, when people drank coffee and smoked cigarettes. Then, she has said, it became possible for the unemployed worker to converse with a doctor.[26] Her words constitute a powerful expression of a what is actually a rather fantastic and idealistic view of the potential and power of drama.

Torrès's production was financed by the Ministry of Culture, which made the claim at the time that 'culture belongs to everybody'. What 'culture' denoted, for the two-year duration of this project, was, of course, the Greeks. Indeed, the project in its entirety was given the title *The Greeks*: it took place in Neuhof, a poor neighbourhood of Strasbourg. In the first year of the project Torrès staged Euripides' *Trojan Women*, and the second year Aristophanes' *Peace*: through these productions she aimed in some way to 'share' culture with local audiences. Both Euripides and Aristophanes have of course developed reputations for being somehow 'universal' in their messages. But the point was mainly to educate: Brigitte Sabourin, from an agency working for social integration, observed that the rehearsals taught those participating 'to be on time'. Theatre practice is clearly a pretext here. And Aristophanes and Euripides are also pretexts. They embody 'culture' and are supposed to be hard to understand, and it is for these reasons that they are selected. In this type of project, nobody takes the spectators into consideration. The point is not the quality of the final performance, but what happens during the process. It is highly significant that this was the only production amongst those discussed in this chapter that did not integrate the spectators into the play. The fantasy of social reconciliation did not extend beyond the stage. The spectators were forgotten, and the directors became social workers.

To conclude, I should like to compare the only 'private' production of *Peace* of which I have heard. It represents, in almost every respect, the opposite of Torrès's production. It was directed by Michèle Heydorff in 1995, and engaged with no identifiable or specific political or social concerns. It made no allusion to any war, and contained no obvious political message, but simply offered a depiction of a pastoral, village utopia. It was part of the festival *Wine and Utopia* held in the Minervois, a wine-producing region of Languedoc in the south of France. Each performance was preceded by country meals with substantial amounts of wine. Then the performance took place in a wine-producing château, a different one on every occasion. This festive phenomenon represented, of course, the other fantasy embodied by Aristophanes, the one that French journalists always like to relate to

Rabelais: the image of Aristophanes as 'bon vivant'. It is a fantasy version of rustic authenticity, the indulgence of a kind of agrarian pleasure at which the ancient Greeks are supposed to have been especially adept. These performances shared with Torrès's project a dream of gathering different people together, this time around a collective feast. The spectators, here, were not forgotten: on the contrary, they were expected to play their part by joining in the meal and by drinking and celebrating together. But — also as in Torrès' production — the text of Aristophanes became a mere pretext for something else altogether.

These two productions of *Peace* did not enjoy any great success, either at the box-office or in critical reception, because this was not their aim: their purposes were different. It is far more important and striking that none of the other stagings of *Peace* (apart from Dullin's, the first one) achieved any great success either. This failure to make an impact in the theatre is also not a general Aristophanic phenomenon: it is specific to *Peace*. Neither Aristophanes' *Birds* nor his plays about women shared in this misfortune. My guess is that the relative failure of *Peace* in comparison with the other plays by Aristophanes is related closely to the very reasons why directors have decided to stage it. Most of them had previously directed Greek tragedies, and all of them wanted to 'make the audience think'.[27] Perhaps their very lack of success indicates that trying to make audiences think is not always such a good idea, after all.

Notes to Chapter 14

1. These data come from BN-Opale+, the databank of the 'arts du spectacle' in the Bibliothèque Nationale de France (http://catalogue.bnf.fr). I thank Professor Evelyne Ertel and Romain Piana for having helped me with the productions not included in BN-Opale+. The archives come from the BNF, département des Arts du spectacle, Paris, and from the Bibliothèque de la Maison Jean Vilar, Avignon.
2. There seems to have been an earlier production at the Théâtre de l'Odéon in 1921, but I have been unable to track down any information about it.
3. Quoted from Olivier (1961).
4. Ibid.: 'Parce que c'est notre plus urgent problème et qu'il me semblait intéressant de montrer à la fois comment il se posait aux Grecs et jusqu'à quel point il se pose à nous de la même façon, de montrer à la fois ce qui n'a pas changé et ce qui a changé'.
5. Ibid. 'A mon sens, c'est cela le ressort fondamental de la pièce: faire pression. Évidemment, nous avons des moyens moins grands qu'Aristophane, nous allons toucher moins de spectateurs.'
6. I shall not consider here Stéphanie Tesson's production in 2002, which used my translation. For details see Hammou (2002).
7. Charles Dullin staged François Porché's adaptation at the Théâtre de l'Atelier, Paris, in December 1932: see Porché (1933). Jean Vilar wrote his own translation (a 'transposition moderne', published as Vilar 1961), and staged it at the Théâtre National Populaire de Chaillot, Paris, in December 1961. Tibor Egervari staged Hubert Gignoux's (unpublished) adaptation and staged it at the Comédie de l'Est, Strasbourg, in 1962. Michel Fontayne staged Antoine Vitez's 'imitation' at the Théâtre Quotidien, Marseille. Vitez's text has not been published in France, but it was translated into German in 1964. The 'manuscrit dactylographié' [1962] can be consulted at the Institut Mémoire de l'édition contemporaine (IMEC, Fonds Vitez, VTZ2. H2). See Vitez (1995).
8. See Debidour (1965).
9. Maréchal (1969).
10. Brisson (1932).

11. Ibid.

12. Ibid.

13. These phrases came from his famous speech of 23 April, the day four generals made a putsch in Algeria. It was in the course of this speech that de Gaulle arrogated extensive new power.

14. 'Contrairement à ce qui semble d'abord, toutes les allusions font mouche, le texte d'origine n'a guère été sollicité'. But, one reads further: 'Jean Vilar ne fait que déplacer de peu le trait de la caricature, qu'adapter les rosseries, que circonstancier les apostrophes au peuple' (Poirot-Delpech 1961).

15. 'Moi, je ne souhaite qu'une chose: c'est que tous les théâtres, dans l'année qui vient, montent *la Paix*, avec une adaptation chaque fois différente!'. Quoted from Olivier (1961).

16. Quoted from Olivier (1961).

17. 'Nous voulions monter la pièce d'Aristophane et non une quelconque adaptation. [...] Aussi avons-nous choisi la traduction de V. H. Debidour (livre de Poche) qui a su retrouver [...] les équivalences modernes qui font de cette œuvre non pas une planche d'anatomie figée à l'usage des seuls érudits, mais un texte véritablement populaire, brûlant de jeunesse et d'actualité' (Maréchal 1969). The Budé translation was the work of Hilaire Van Daele (Coulon and Van Daele 1924).

18. Schmitt (1991).

19. See Maréchal (1969): 'Nous nous sommes bornés à faire quelques coupures nécessaires (attaques personnelles, souvent obscures même pour le spécialiste, anecdotisme politico-littéraire qui n'a plus aucun sens pour nous) et quelques légers changements, ceci en accord total avec le traducteur. Mais nous avons préféré dans tous les cas la coupe franche à l'adaptation.'

20. Ibid.

21. This trend started in 1994, with the new translations of the novels of Dostoyevsky by André Markowicz. People realized a translation could totally change their perception of a text. His translations for the stage, sometimes in collaboration with Françoise Morvan, also convinced directors of the usefulness of new translations. In 2004, Les Solitaires Intempestifs, the publisher of contemporary drama in France, started a new collection dedicated to translations, called *Traductions du XXIe siècle*. This series published both Markowicz and Morvan's translation of Chekhov and Platonov, and my translation of Sophocles' *Antigone* for the director Jacques Nichet.

22. See *Feuilleton du Journal des Débats*, 26 December 1932.

23. See e.g. Eupolis fr. 62 and Plato Comicus fr. 86, both in the edition of Kassel and Austin (1983–).

24. 'L'adaptation aurait pu remplacer ces peuples de la Grèce par les peuples de l'Europe [...] Les Allemands, comme les Argiens, ne tirent-ils pas en sens contraire? Les Russes s'unissent-ils à nos efforts? Et les Italiens? Et les Anglais? Et les Américains? [...] Ma critique ne porte que sur l'impression que nous retirons de la Paix française, d'être seuls en jeu' (*Feuilleton du Journal des Débats*, 26 December 1932).

25. Schmitt (1991).

26. Quoted from 'Des amateurs jouent Euripide', *L'Alsace*, 10 September 1997.

27. In a recent and very stimulating book on the modern performances of Greek tragedies, Patricia Vasseur-Legangneux (2004: 17), points out how directors have long interpreted Greek tragedy as a political and ritual performance, a reading which led them to the dream of spectator participation: 'Ils ont rêvé d'un théâtre dont l'espace créerait une vraie participation du public, d'un théâtre dont le contenu politique le ferait réfléchir, d'un théâtre de conventions affichées, sans illusions.' I think this approach to Greek tragedy has also influenced productions of comedies.

CHAPTER 15

❖

Poetry and Politics, Advice and Abuse: The Aristophanic Chorus on the Italian Stage

Martina Treu

'I am We'
African proverb

A Troubled Marriage

An Author for the Stage: such is the significant subtitle, as it appears in English, of a well-known Italian book on Aristophanes first published in 1962 by Carlo Ferdinando Russo.[1] We all owe much to him, and to a very few other authors of the 1960s and 1970s, especially Solomos and Taplin, since their work resulted in a far greater value being placed ever since — by scholars and theatre practitioners everywhere — on the *performance* of classical drama.[2] Yet Russo's approach to Greek comedies was at the time of the publication of his book a striking exception, perhaps especially in Italy, where the worlds of classical scholarship and live performance very rarely met. For to Russo, Aristophanes' art lay in far more than the production of masterpieces of literature. Aristophanes' works are *theatre*, in all senses. As Russo later confided in a friend, the reason why he could conceive such a book and write it in that innovative way, from the perspective of a theatre practitioner, was above all his experience of the company where his wife worked; she was a set designer, and introduced him to the distinctive world of the professional theatre.[3]

In the third millennium, many years after its original publication, Russo's book is now itself something of a 'classical' text for Italian students. And yet this distinctive approach to the study of the ancient theatre remained, for a long time, less utilized in Italy than elsewhere. Russo's legacy remained a treasure available to a privileged few until very recently. *His* Aristophanes actually encountered many obstacles within Italian culture. It took quite a long time before he began seriously to be considered 'an author for the stage' by either theatrical audiences or by scholars. It is was only in the late 1990s that a very few books taking a similar angle began to be published in Italy, especially those by Umberto Albini, Diego Lanza and by one or two other scholars who shared Russo's respect for and skilful treatment of theatrical matters, and were able to address comedy as well as tragedy.[4]

So much for scholarship: what about the live theatre? During the twentieth century, the real potential of Aristophanes' art was almost inaccessible to Italian audiences. It is of course true that Greek and Roman dramas have been staged in the ancient theatres of Southern Italy since 1914.[5] But until recently, especially in large-scale productions, tragedy played by far the major role. It was only seldom that a comedy was performed. Latin authors — which seem more 'polite', at least superficially — have, especially in minor theatres, often been preferred. The more obscene plays by Aristophanes are sometimes selected for revival, only to have their performances cancelled later. His works have been scarcely tolerated, and sometimes virtually banned according to the intuitive criteria and sensibility of the bourgeois audience, itself under the strong influence of the Catholic Church.[6] A few fortunate audiences have almost clandestinely had the occasional chance to see a comedy of his. But most of Italy remained totally unaware of any Aristophanic productions.

Up to a point this situation has slowly begun to change, and Aristophanes can now count on receiving a little more attention. His comedies (at least some of them) can be seen more often today than previously. But it is a rare piece of luck to encounter him for the first time in performance, and thus to watch a play of his before ever reading one. Many years ago, exactly this happened to me, and it was therefore entirely natural for me to see Aristophanes as 'an author for the stage'. Subsequently I read Russo's book, and I met the scholars whose books I have already mentioned, Albini and Lanza. For the past ten years I have been studying Aristophanic comedies both as a theatre practitioner and a scholar, and my work has progressively come to focus on the chorus.[7] Here I draw on my previous research in order to analyse the Aristophanic chorus and its role in some Italian productions.

Chorus *versus* Actors

I consider the chorus and the actors in Aristophanes as two forces acting in a dynamic ensemble: both contribute to the success of the show, especially in the earlier comedies. Every play is a unique combination of the two, the result of a different balance between them.

Each plot begins and ends with a real situation, generally of *crisis*. The leading actor's aim is to escape from the crisis — to find a solution, however bizarre the solution may be. Indeed, the more bizarre and absurd the solution, the better the comedy will be. But Old Comedy is often based on an allegory, and Aristophanes wants his audience to see below the surface (which consists of a distinctive, personal story about an individual character) to what lies deep beneath it: the contemporary history of Athens and its entire citizen body. The chorus itself is allocated that responsibility: it plays a major role in some choral sections such as the parabasis (the exclusively choral passage, with no actors on stage, traditionally dedicated to personal abuse and to the poet's own self-advertisement). But the chorus also uses other parts of the comedy in order to remind the audience what is really at stake in the real world. Generally (and rather simplistically) speaking, the actor leans toward fantasy, the chorus towards reality.

The allegory is particularly evident in *Knights* (424 BC) and *Wasps* (422 BC). Both comedies are strongly characterized by two parallel dimensions: one dimension presents the fictitious plot acted out by the individual characters (Demos and his servants in *Knights*, the struggle between a father and a son in *Wasps*); the other dimension is presented in the form of the profound message delivered by the chorus. In the earlier comedy the chorus of knights is in charge of making the allegory clear: they speak of the 'City' instead of 'Home', they treat Demos not as an individual man but as the collective citizen body of Athens. Moreover, they constantly attack the real target of the comedy, Cleon the politician, who is disguised as a fictitious character named Paphlagon or 'the Paphlagonian'. During the course of the entire comedy the real name 'Cleon' is mentioned just once, by the chorus itself, thus tearing the illusionist veil maintained by the pervasive allegory (976). Two years later, in *Wasps*, Aristophanes assigned the same function to the chorus, who reveal the political struggle that lies behind the 'domestic' story. Throughout the comedy the chorus reminds the audience of the politicians who really take advantage of trials — Cleon above all — so that a strong significance is lent to the personal names of the two main characters (Philocleon, Bdelycleon) and to their political and social role in reality.[8]

In brief, the chorus is always ready to recall reality — and dispense advice and abuse — whenever a political, symbolic or social matter is involved. The chorus, thanks to its superior authority, can also be used as a weapon. It regularly points out to the city who is to blame for the present situation and who should be driven out as a scapegoat: Cleon, the warmongers, illegitimate or otherwise irregular citizens, pretend patriots, and so on.[9]

Yet scholarly study of the reception of Aristophanes has paid much more attention to the principal actor and to those aspects of the comedy which he oversees. The neglect of the chorus is partly a result of the historical development of comedy: for most scholars, the comedy contemporary with them uses techniques based on great performers, while the chorus has in fact disappeared. Aristophanes' individual characters, besides, are so strong and powerful — especially those impersonated by the principal actor or *prōtagonistēs* — that it becomes all to easy to underestimate the real weight of the other components of the show.

I have found this actor-centred attitude to pervade both critical works and staged performances, at least in Italy: during my research I discovered less analysis of the chorus than I expected, especially in comparison with the large amount and wide variety of Aristophanic studies; many Italian scholars, besides, are interested in the lyrics or appearance of the chorus rather than in its dramatic role, and most of them focus on particular aspects of its language, such as metaphor, imagery or obscene vocabulary. Moreover, on those occasions in which the chorus does become the specific matter under discussion, more attention is generally paid to poetry rather than politics, to advice rather than abuse, to fantasy, once again, rather than reality. That is the reason why, as an act of poetic justice, I devoted my first book to the dramatic functions of the chorus, especially to vituperation and instances of aggression.[10]

The Definition of *Elsewhere*

When it comes to performances, there is a perfect correspondence between scholarly attitudes and stage productions in Italy: the major role is always played by actors rather than by the chorus, both in tragedy and comedy. The chorus's contribution to the action tends to be more formal than substantial, especially if compared with what is suggested by the text. This happens, moreover, even in productions of the earlier comedies such as *Acharnians* and *Knights*, where the chorus is a major and well-developed character in its own right: it displays aggression, threatening behaviour, and violence interactively with the individual roles. In the later comedies, where the chorus participates in a more minor portion of the text, productions neglect it even more, often reducing it to a single character or a simple theatrical voice. Most of the time, generally speaking, the role of the chorus on the Italian stage is merely ornamental, or restricted to offering entertainment largely unrelated to the central action.

The same general discrimination against the chorus operates in the case of production of the three plays which provide the focus of the current book — *Peace*, *Birds* and *Frogs*. But the chorus in these plays is also condemned to a strange and special destiny. This seems to be somehow connected to the distinctive feature of these comedies, which is the requirement for the set to indicate a remote Elsewhere in a non-terrestrial dimension, whether it is the upper air or the Underworld. This other-worldly quality of course offers an opportunity for a director or designer to imagine and create a whole new world on stage — far too attractive an opportunity to pass by. But the result all too often is that the set completely dominates the general conception of the show, and indeed overwhelms the other elements. Indeed, the set(ting) is sometimes the main reason why a director chooses a particular comedy to revive, almost regardless of its specific content.

But who is it who defines and shapes the physical setting? Seemingly, it is the individual actors: they travel from one place to another, and they are the very impulse which generates the journey and the plot itself. In ancient theatre the definition of time and place seems mostly to have been provided by words, rather than by scenography or set design. Such verbal description is mainly a privilege of the leading characters: through their eyes the audience can experience unknown worlds, and through their words the Elsewhere literally creates itself, as the plot develops. Moreover, since their purpose is always egocentric, they keep pretending to do everything by themselves. But they cannot, since they have to encounter the Others. Aristophanes' new worlds — far above or below the visible surface of the Earth — are anything but deserted lands. Indeed, they are quite busy and crowded with people: some are familiar and friendly, some are strange and even dangerous. They are the alternative vision, the 'other side' of Athens, whether dark or bright. No matter how hard the central characters try to leave their city, whether they loathe or love it, they still keep finding it in other places. And the chorus is always a part of it, indeed quite an important one. But exactly what sort of entity is it?

A Switching Identity

Each of Aristophanes' choruses consists, first and foremost, of citizens, and they always remember that. So did the ancient Athenian audience, and so should we. The fictitious role assumed by actors in Aristophanes is like a second dress; it can come in many varieties, but it is always transparent. The actor and the chorus can change it between one comedy and another, or within the same comedy, according to Aristophanes' desires and dramatic needs. I define this type of identity as a 'switching' one. Such a phenomenon is alien to our theatre conventions, so it is often extremely puzzling to scholars, directors, and audiences, who can easily misunderstand it. Let us look at where the character of the chorus is first asserted: the parodos, its entrance song in Greek comedy.

As marking the 'big entrance' of the chorus, the parodos is in itself a very important section of any ancient comedy.[11] It is in the parodos that the chorus is able to define itself, gather information about the plot, and begin to help or fight the leading character. The parodos can often be divided into sections, each one devoted to one or more functions. It thus deserves serious attention, and should be thought about in as much depth by theatre practitioners as by scholars. Very few Italian directors, however, think it is worth paying a *chorodidaskalos*, a choreographer and a music director, to teach the chorus how to act, move, and sing appropriately in each phase of the parodos.[12]

A good example is the parodos of *Peace*: it is quite complex, and it is even more charged with symbolic force than the rest of this symbol-rich drama. Its function is clearly to deliver one single message: the help of every single citizen, not only of Athens but of all Greece, is required if the war is to end. Just like Dikaiopolis in *Acharnians*, Trygaeus wants peace, but this time he cannot get it alone and keep it all for himself. So he calls to his aid a chorus of men of all sorts, from numerous Greek city-states. They are all strangers in the strange 'Elsewhere' world where Peace is incarcerated, as Trygaeus is. But they are not all alike. The parodos is thus vital in order to see on whom Trygaeus can count for support, who is struggling for peace, and who works against it. It is only the peasant-farmers, in the event, who actually cooperate to free the goddess.

How can a modern director show a message of this kind being delivered by a group with such a multiple identity? Perhaps he may choose to simplify it, by isolating single individuals or groups who stand apart or leave — one by one, as their names are called out — until only the peasants finally remain on stage; some scholars have indeed suggested this solution.[13] But most of the time the way that this particular chorus takes shape gets completely lost, along with its message. In many performances, such as the one in 1992 at Vicenza's Teatro Olimpico, the members of the chorus were all identical: a group of clones or replicants of Trygaeus.[14]

The Chorus as Chameleon

The choruses of *Birds* and *Frogs* are also both blends of symbolic and realistic features. But another set of problems arises from their very nature, which is zoomorphic and therefore not human. Ideally, they should conduct a sort of dialectical, mutual exchange with their supernatural surroundings: from their environment they gain characterization, charm, and emotional potential, but at the same time they themselves lend power and attractiveness — in a word, life — to a world that would otherwise be virtually a pure vacuum, or dead land. For the same reason, in performance, such choruses entail the director's taking a great risk: that the chorus will be too much conditioned by the scenographic decisions governing each show, or even that they will be so assimilated to the scenography as to become *a part* of it. Sometimes they even seem like a chameleon: well integrated, but almost camouflaged and virtually invisible,

The metaphor is indeed appropriate to the zoomorphic choruses of *Birds* and *Frogs*. Their original symbolic role is often forgotten or misunderstood. The concern of most directors seems to have a single focus: how the chorus should be costumed. It may be true that the costume created an important impact even in Aristophanes' time, but so did the dance, music and songs that are unfortunately often missing from the Italian stage. The greatest effort is demanded from costume designers and scenographers, sometimes at vast creative and economic expense. Then the work is over: most directors seem no longer interested in the chorus members, and little concerned about how they should move or talk or sing.

As for *Birds*, there is a praiseworthy exception in the case of Gabriele Vacis, whose major concern is always the chorus whether he is working on tragedy or comedy. The chorus of his *Uccelli* was part of a real ensemble: actors, professional singers and instrumentalists performing live, altogether, on stage. So the parodos was not a parade of gorgeous costumes, but a profoundly powerful scene. While the chorus members entered, the audience gradually began to hear and feel the instinctive suspicion of birds towards men and their growing menace. Soon the parodos degenerates into a fight of great effect between the chorus and the actors, thanks to their skill at mimicry and physical energy of the players.[15]

In the most recent Italian production of *Birds*, however, the parodos was again more of a parade than a fight, and the one time the chorus made a significant appearance in the whole comedy.[16] And a similar pattern emerged even in the version of *Birds* recently produced by the colourful and dynamic ensemble which is the distinctive trademark of the Teatro della Tosse, a company who produce Aristophanic comedies in spaces around their town, Genoa, other than recognized theatres. The performance in question was their *Gli Uccelli e altre Utopie* (a play written and directed by Tonino Conte, and 'freely inspired by Aristophanes' comedies', but above all by *Birds*).[17] The show took place on the Diga Foranea, a dam in the very centre of Genoa's large harbour. Here the chorus seemed to melt — almost absorbed, again like a chameleon — into the context itself, which was enriched by the gorgeous scenes, costumes. and sculptures of the late, great artist Emanuele Luzzati.

The Underworld as a Looking-Glass

An even harder task, for a director, is addressing the problem of how to bring the first chorus of *Frogs* on stage. The comedy is named after these creatures, which have a mysterious but highly symbolic relationship with the Underworld.

They are of course in one sense an element of the set, as inhabitants of the ponds surrounding the watery route to Hades. The whole set in itself is a real challenge for a scenographer, who must work under a double influence, needing to respond to such hints as are offered by Aristophanes' text, but also to the literary and cultural reception of the play and traditional representations that came after it, which are extraordinarily rich in images. As a chorus the frogs live a very short life, like Malherbe's rose: *l'espace d'un matin*, the time taken by the parodos. And it is not even a flight or fight or lively scene as in *Birds* or *Acharnians*. In some productions the frogs have even been invisible, just a voice; they have also been reduced to a single representative, and have not moved at all, as in Ronconi's production.[18]

And yet in most productions the frogs are unforgettable, and the reason is not just the sheer noise and energy that they expend in this single ode. There is some kind of perturbing quality to their mocking and adversarial form of expression. Maybe that is the reason why Dionysus seems so aggressive and nervous: it is not just a joke. The frogs stand at the entrance of the Underworld; and a threshold is always a symbolic and frightening place, from the Greek myths to Kafka's *The Trial*. The frogs also sing a hymn to Dionysus and remind him that they are somehow his double, his other 'self' in the Underworld.

A similar function can be recognized in the second chorus, the Initiates: they too are linked to Dionysus (perhaps to the god, rather than to the stage character that bears his name, whom they do not recognize). The typical elements of his cult, such as the ritual jokes, are constantly referred to in their parodos. The association with the god also lends their words a supernatural and divine authority. Not only in the parodos but throughout their contributions they deliver political advice and abuse, especially directed against bad or false citizens. In the poetic competition (*agōn*) between Aeschylus and Euripides the verdict is up to Dionysus, not to them; but they clearly support Aeschylus' case. Ronconi understood this partisan stance clearly, and had the good idea of giving Euripides a second chorus, a group of people dressed in black, in order to counterbalance the white chorus of Initiates. He can be seen as having split the chorus in order to create a concrete, visible ideological opposition (as Aristophanes himself does in other comedies, from *Acharnians* to the parodos of *Peace* discussed above). So Ronconi lent an even greater emphasis to the winner: Dionysus brings Aeschylus back to his city, which needs him more than ever.

The same message is expressed in the parabasis once again: Athens must be saved at any cost. *Frogs*, like all the other plays, is bound to its precise historical moment. The journey of Dionysus, the contest of poets and the entire plot bring us back to where we started. So the tight connection between the city and its double in the Underworld is made clear once more. We see Athens through a looking-glass. And no reflection, upstairs or downstairs, can be rendered in the absence of the city which is itself reflected.

FIG. 15.1. Farì prays to Zeus in Martinelli's *All'inferno!*

An Italian Aristophanes

The best illustration of this point is also our last. The illustration is drawn from none of our three comedies and it is not even a text written by Aristophanes. It is a mixture of some Aristophanic plays with a personal 'director's cut' — Marco Martinelli's *All'inferno!* Martinelli is a well-known Italian playwright and director, considered by many people in Italy, including myself, to be the true heir of Aristophanes.[19] His motto in staging Aristophanes is an African proverb, 'I am We'. The actors of his company — Teatro delle Albe/Ravenna Teatro — together form a real chorus, both in everyday life and in performance: they are a bunch of people who share the same dreams and living conditions. The text by Martinelli is not just a mixture of Aristophanic comedies, but a brand new play in its entirety. The title is significant: *All'inferno!*, which means *To Hell!* The plot, essentially based on *Plutus*, tells the story of two poor people of today. The actors are actually real immigrants from Senegal, who came to Italy looking for wealth, or at least for enough money to survive (fig. 15.1).

In the play they go to the Underworld to look for the God of Wealth and they find a job in a weird motorway restaurant called 'Infernord' ('North-Hell'). This absurd and nasty place turns out to be Hell indeed, but it is amazingly and miserably similar to our current Northern Italy. The two men work as slaves twenty-four hours a day, and they meet strange people (some are characters from *Clouds*, *Knights*, and other comedies). They constantly remind us of the thousands of immigrants who try to reach Italy every year, following a dream or an illusion that does not come true in reality. Today the conditions of immigration are getting worse and worse. Boatfuls of would-be immigrants leave places in the South and the East and sometimes sink as they try to go North, to the Promised Land of Work and Slavery. But War is crossing the sea again, and Terrorism is increasingly striking back. No wonder Martinelli feels the urgent need to put Aristophanes' comedies on stage (figs. 15.2 and 15.3).

Moreover, he has been working with youngsters for years, in his 'Non-School' at Ravenna Teatro, and also with non-professional actors. They are mostly boys, local inhabitants of ghettos or suburbs or dangerous areas, such as African cities, the South Side of Chicago, and Scampia (a notoriously poor district on the outskirts of Naples, where high unemployment favours any kind of criminal activity, the Government is absent or seen as an enemy, and the rule of law is entirely unknown). One exception is the project called 'Arrevuoto [in Neapolitan dialect, Upside-Down] Scampia-Napoli'. This project is consciously directed at helping a community with a large multicultural population of disaffected youths, and is indeed sponsored by the municipality of Naples and by Mercadante-Teatro Stabile di Napoli. The challenge is to give a second chance to these youths, to the suburbs, and to the whole country.[20]

Scampia, 'A Suburb of Athens'

In Scampia, Martinelli works with seventy youngsters. They come from different schools in Scampia and Naples, while some are gypsies of Romany culture. Together they rewrite Aristophanes' text. The title is *Peace!* It is meant as a prayer for a sacred goddess, a plea for a bliss long desired. Peace has become essential, especially here and now, when it is not only Iraq that is in crisis, but increasingly, as it seems, the whole culture of the Mediterranean.

A sign of hope and rebirth through theatre appeared on 21 April 2006 in Scampia, in a recently restored auditorium, and three days later at the Teatro Mercadante in Naples. In the show the youngsters sing, dance, and move as one entity: a real comic chorus. Their words and acting express a mixture of the traditional abuse of Old Comedy with the typical humour of Naples, aggressive and desperate (associated above all with the famous Neapolitan actors Totò and Eduardo De Filippo). The effect is a sort of angry and painful laughter — it is like gulping down a deep intake of breath before sinking back into cruel reality. In the end the kids take the director in their arms and make him fly above their heads. As usual in Martinelli's productions, the final feast leaves you with a bitter taste in the mouth. Someone in the audience is crying. But the last words of the show say, 'If you feel like crying sometimes, don't'. The kids have this written on a wall in their school, named after Elsa Morante. Martinelli borrowed it to pay a personal homage to this beloved Italian writer and to her beautiful poems.

One of these poems was recently staged by Martinelli himself: its title, in English, would be 'The world saved by children'.[21] The director strongly hopes that this will be the case. To make this wish come true, he works with youngsters in many similar projects. Other Italian cities quickly invited Martinelli to bring the

FIG. 15.2 (above). The *agōn* scene from *Knights* in Martinelli's *All'inferno!*
FIG. 15.3 (below). The *agōn* scene from *Wealth* in Martinelli's *All'inferno!*

show on tour, which can only mean that it is indeed time for Aristophanes to come back to Italy. Nowhere can we receive him with open arms better than here. This is Martinelli's hope, and ours too. And we wish Aristophanes himself could see what Italian children are finally beginning to do in his name.[22]

Notes to Chapter 15

1. Russo (1994); 1st Italian edn. 1962; rev. edn. 1984.
2. Solomos (1961); Taplin (1977). See above, Introd. p. 2.
3. Through this connection he met, for example, the Austrian writer Ingeborg Bachmann and the German composer Hans Werner Henze, resident in Italy from the 1950s; their letters from these years are reproduced in Bachmann and Henze (2004); see also Henze (1996).
4. See e.g. Albini (1998) and Lanza (1997).
5. For the history of the production of Greek drama in Sicily see http://www.indafondazione.org.
6. A brief history with some examples of actual censorship may be found in Treu (2002).
7. See Treu (1999) on aggressive parts (*psogos*) and the main functions of the chorus in the eleven comedies), and Treu (2005b), a study of those recent productions of Greek drama in Italy that have been distinguished by a cosmopolitan attitude and have made a deep impact.
8. This function was particularly evident in a 2003 Italian production of *Wasps* (directed by Renato Giordano at the Greek theatre of Syracuse). The director perhaps failed in his target, if he intended (as was rumoured) to attack some Italian judges and bring discredit on the trials which at that time menaced the Prime Minister. But Giordano did not miss the point when he chose to name 'Poet' the single character who attacks Cleon, in the name of the whole chorus, in the parabasis: see Treu (2003b).
9. These matters, for instance, are directly mentioned by the leading actor and chorus again in *Peace* (421 BC), the comedy where the *audience* is most frequently addressed. In *Birds* and *Frogs* a stronger 'transfer' is involved, but the main target of personal abuse is still the same kinds of people: illegitimate, presumptive, and fake citizens (see MacDowell (1993)).
10. Treu (1999).
11. No wonder that in the history of comedy the parodos seems to have been the last choral part to survive in a written form in the whole script, while the other choral sections are just signified by the term *chorou* from *Plutus* to Menander. And in the latter's *Dyskolos* the chorus' entrance is still announced by the character on stage, even if the parodos is not actually scripted.
12. A good model is the *Acharnians* directed by Egisto Marcucci featuring Marcello Bartoli (Greek Theatre of Syracuse, 1994): the chorus moved, danced, and sang in a different way in each section of the parodos and the parabasis, and each choral ode was treated as it deserved.
13. See Treu (1999), 38–40 and Russo (1994), 133–46, 260–61; see also Zimmermann (1996), 182–93.
14. *La Pace*, directed by Arnoldo Foà, Teatro Olimpico, Vicenza, 1992.
15. *Uccelli*, directed by Gabriele Vacis, featuring Eugenio Allegri, Roman Theatre, Spoleto, 1996.
16. *Gli Uccelli*, adapted by Sandro Lombardi, directed by Federico Tiezzi, 2005.
17. Some other Italian directors have created plays by mixing Aristophanes' comedies: for instance Aldo Trionfo (*Viva la Pace*) and Ronconi (*Utopia*).
18. *Le Rane*, directed by Luca Ronconi, Greek Theatre of Syracuse, 2002; and Piccolo Teatro, Milan, 2004. See further Schironi, this volume.
19. *All'inferno!* has not been published yet, but other texts of Ravenna Teatro have been translated into English: see Picarazzi and Feinstein (1997), and Picarazzi (1999). For more information on texts and shows see http://www.teatrodellealbe.com ('Bibliography' and 'Past Productions' sections).
20. For information and images see the online archive of Teatro Mercadante at http://www.teatrostabilenapoli.it (Archivio, Stagione 2005–2006, Progetto Arrevuoto-Scampia Napoli).
21. See Treu (2005a) and Morante (1968). Her most famous novels (*History* and *Arturo's Island*) are available in English.

22. Many thanks to Amanda Wrigley and all the staff of the APGRD for their kind invitation and splendid job they made of the conference; Marco Martinelli and Francesca Venturi of Ravenna Teatro for their constant help and support; Marzia D'Alesio of Teatro Mercadante-Stabile di Napoli and the photographers for their kind permission; Carlo Ferdinando Russo and Sotera Fornaro; and Annalisa Di Liddo, last but not least, for her careful reading and wonderful patience.

CHAPTER 16

❖

A Poet without 'Gravity': Aristophanes on the Italian Stage

Francesca Schironi

Since the beginning of the twentieth century, Aristophanes has enjoyed a certain public profile: I have counted at least seventy-four official productions that have taken place in Italy since 1911. The most popular play by far seems to be *Birds*, which has taken the stage in sixteen different productions. *Clouds* is also reasonably popular, having been staged in twelve different productions. There have also been some interesting rewritings and pastiches of more than one play. But particularly striking is the relative infrequency with which *Frogs* — in my view one of Aristophanes' most engaging comedies — has been produced: it has only seen public performance twice, in 1976 and in 2002.[1]

Indeed, it is one of those two productions of *Frogs* that attracted my attention: the most recent one, directed by Luca Ronconi at Syracuse in May 2002. As most people know by now, this performance excited many discussions, in Italy,[2] as well as abroad,[3] because of widespread suspicion that it had incurred censorship at the hands of Berlusconi's government. I would like to reconsider this episode, not only because it is both striking and ambiguous, but above all because on closer inspection it seems to me a particularly good illustration of how theatre, and in particular ancient Greek and Roman theatre, 'works' in Italy.

The Festival of Classical Drama, which is held each year at the end of May in the Greek Theatre of Syracuse under the aegis of the INDA Foundation (Istituto Nazionale del Dramma Antico), is very famous. It was established in 1914 under the initiative of Mario Tommaso Gargallo. Furthermore, it was the distinguished Hellenist Ettore Romagnoli who provided the translation of Aeschylus' *Agamemnon*, the play which inaugurated the Festival. In 1927, comedy was included in the programme in the form of *Clouds*, translated once again by Romagnoli, and performed in a very orthodox classicizing production, where all the actors except Strepsiades wore masks. Since then the Festival of Syracuse has enjoyed increasing popularity, although more for tragic productions than for comedy;[4] since 2001 it has been held every year instead of every two as before. In 2002 the programme comprised *Bacchae*, *Prometheus*, and *Frogs*; the director was Luca Ronconi, one of the most outstanding directors in Italy, and the artistic director of the Teatro Piccolo in Milan.

FIG. 16.1. First image of set for the Syracuse *Frogs*, 2002

On Saturday 18 May 2002, the evening before the première of this *Frogs*, a reception was held at the house of the prefect of Syracuse, Francesco Alecci. Among the invitees there were Luca Ronconi himself, Sergio Escobar, who was director of the Teatro Piccolo of Milan, the minister of equal opportunity for women Stefania Prestigiacomo, and Gianfranco Miccichè, a Forza Italia official and Berlusconi's right-hand man in Sicily. During the dinner Miccichè approached Ronconi, because he had been informed that in the staging of the *Frogs*, as a backdrop set, there would be four panels with the caricatured faces of Berlusconi, the Deputy Prime Minister Gianfranco Fini, the Northern League leader Umberto Bossi and another member of Fini's party Ignazio La Russa (fig. 16.1). Miccichè argued that it did not seem fair to have those panels, because 'public theatre shouldn't criticize the people who give it money'. The minister Stefania Prestigiacomo intervened in the discussion on Miccichè's side; the quarrel escalated and eventually Miccichè and Prestigiacomo left the dinner.[5]

The next day, Sunday, the play opened, but without the panels. It was Ronconi himself who decided to remove them. At the end of the performance the coryphaea Annamaria Guarnieri pointed her finger towards empty frames. Ronconi, furthermore, made no appearance. Aside from these oddities, however, nothing indicated to the audience that there was any political tension underlying the performance they had attended.

On Monday, 20 May, a press-release by Ronconi was published in which he claimed to have been censored by Berlusconi's government, and added that he wanted to leave Italy.[6] An official communiqué of the government followed in which Prime Minister Berlusconi maintained that he was disappointed that, at Syracuse, 'ancient drama turned into a comedy of errors', and insisted on his government's unawareness of any censorship. He hoped that Ronconi would put the panels back again. 'Of course', Berlusconi continued, 'that portrait of a tyrant with an Aristophanic flavour does not resemble me, but art has the right to choose — and miss — its targets.'[7] The directors of the Piccolo Teatro in Milan made haste to reply and defined the declaration of Berlusconi as an 'act of intelligence and civility'.[8] Notwithstanding Berlusconi's invitation, however, the panels were never put back up again and the show went on.

In an interview given by Ronconi and published in the *Corriere della Sera* on 21 May, the director commented on Berlusconi's declaration in these terms: 'Yes, of course, Berlusconi gave a civilized reply [...]. I am not going to put the panels up again; let's put an end to it. Otherwise it would seem that first there was censorship, then an act of liberality from above. Let's not exaggerate. [...] Berlusconi chose the right tone. Perhaps he understood that the presence of the panels on the stage did not reflect any political provocation or lack of respect.'[9]

To the obvious question, 'and why then did you take them away?', Ronconi answered: 'it was a choice shared by every one of us in order to save the performance. Before any controversy, *Frogs* comes first, as does the right of the audience to follow Aristophanes. As a director and a man of the theatre, I participated in an obligatory choice. Better to avoid surprises, protests, accusations, or who knows what.'[10] And then: 'The panels were a striking element, clearly, but an incidental one. If they had been fundamental to the performances we would have left them where they were.'[11]

This statement, at first quite puzzling (how could part of the set not be 'fundamental'? And how could the director himself say that?), becomes clear in the light of certain choices that had been made concerning the staging at Syracuse. The text of *Frogs* chosen for the performance is basically faithful to the original. The only changes consisted in eliminating those details that were deeply embedded in the Athenian reality of the fifth century BC and thus difficult for a contemporary audience to grasp. The rest however was purely Aristophanes; indeed one could watch the comedy and follow it from the original text. The 'updating' related, instead, to the stage setting and the interpretation of the characters.

Ronconi's interpretation of the set was 'decadent': there was a sense of death and shabbiness everywhere in this Underworld. The set was occupied only by the wrecks of cars (fig. 16.2). This is Ronconi's Hades: a car-cemetery. As Ronconi later explained in a TV interview, this set was designed to be a sort of a mirror of the real city outside the theatre — Syracuse. Therefore the wrecked cars, which were actually taken from Syracuse's dumps, tips and 'car-cemeteries', were intended to offer 'the visual representation' of the 'real' traffic noise of the city (the theatre at Syracuse is indeed in a very busy part of the town and the traffic can be heard when sitting in the cavea).

This decadent and postmodern scenario was in some ways the right set for Ronconi's Dionysus: Ronconi had disempowered this god and lent him a strong,

FIG. 16.2. Second image of the set for the Syracuse *Frogs*, 2002

low-class Roman accent. Dionysus became thus a Pasolini character that, personally, I found rather too extreme. However, especially for an Italian audience, he represented a familiar and ubiquitous type of comic character, associated especially with actors such as Alberto Sordi, Nino Manfredi, and Carlo Verdone. This stock character is always from Rome and, it is usually implied, from a particular district of Rome, Monte Testaccio; in his strong accent he gives voice to a sort of popular wisdom, blended with a rather vulgar slapstick humour. Actually, this proletarian god fitted very well into the postmodern landscape of abandonment embodied by the discarded cars. The same applied to Heracles, defined by one of the actors as 'gone hippy', with golden necklaces and long, coloured hair, with grey roots growing in at the hairline.

What about the panels then? What had the panels of Berlusconi and Co. to do with this scenario? Actually, when watching the performance, one received the impression that Ronconi was right: the panels were not essential. The play, as Ronconi interpreted it, was perfect and complete without them. One had no feeling that there was anything missing, a gap, a void due to censorship. And when the play was performed again in March 2004 in Milan, the apparatus was the same: no panels. Again, the performance was very well received — everyone praised Ronconi's interpretation and Aristophanes' plea that art should be rescued in order to save his decadent society.[12]

The performance we saw at Syracuse and then in Milan was to large extent a convincing one. However, it was convincing not because of those missing panels, nor because of its proletarian and farcical Dionysus, but because of Aristophanes himself, whose text was presented almost intact. In particular, the words of the chorus of initiates sounded extremely relevant to the current Italian political situation:

> Let him be silent and stand aside from our sacred dances
> whoever does not reconcile the opposed parties for the sake of his fellow
>   citizens,
> but fans and stirs them up, craving for his private advantage:
> and whoever accepts bribes when guiding the state tossed by the storm,
> and hands over towers and palaces to the profiteers or smugglers,
> as that wretched one Thorycion does, who, without paying any tax,
> has his sails and the pitch for his boats pass beyond the border under
>   the counter.
> and whoever persuades the rich to pay for his own party,
> and whoever sullies the honest people and then sings his prayers among
>   the priests.[13]

Or, even more striking, the parabasis:

> The last-born, who, up to now, the city
> would not have easily taken at random, not even as scapegoats.
> These indeed we use for everything.
> But at least now, fools, change your habits
> and go back to make use of honest people.[14]

These words were particularly meaningful in the context of contemporary Italian politics, at a time when the Prime Minister was the *parvenu*, self-made Berlusconi. And indeed when these words were expressed (almost unchanged) in the theatre, the reference was, I think, unmistakable. The applause that rose up among the audience afterwards testifies to that. It is interesting, however, to see how Ronconi had these scenes performed.

For Ronconi's choice is revealing here. The chorus of initiates, and in particular the coryphaeus, who pronounced the words above, gave an extraordinarily feeble impression; his voice was tentative, and hopeless. In the TV documentary already mentioned, the actor himself (Luciano Roman) declared that this was done on purpose; as if he, the coryphaeus, were conscious that what he was about to say was condemned to remain unfulfilled, ineffective, without results. Personally I find this choice a missed opportunity. The opportunity to speak out loud was gone in Ronconi's interpretation. And the panels with it. Yes, in hindsight Ronconi was right: those panels were not fundamental at all, at least in his reading of the comedy. We were left with a decadent and clownish Dionysus, a tacky Heracles and a hopeless coryphaeus.

It is not my intention here to judge what happened from a political point of view. Nor do I endorse completely the condemnation of Ronconi's sudden change of mind that appeared in some articles, such as that by Sebastiano Messina, in the 20 May 2002 edition of *La Repubblica*, the most widely read left-wing newspaper:

> Aristophanes should have been there to make us laugh. Unfortunately he was
> not. [...] And so we could only witness a second-rate comedy of false errors,
> in which a director was so brave and daring as to find the figure of tyrant in

> four politicians, but 'in order to stage the play at any cost' becomes a pragmatic
> man of the theatre and destroys his own creation, apart from crying censorship
> after the show.[15]

No, Aristophanes was there. Notwithstanding all the efforts to have his words
spoken feebly by a chorus of resigned initiates, he was indeed still speaking to us.
Aristophanic comedy was still there in all its force — notwithstanding every effort
to turn it into a farce, played by a clownish Dionysus.

Besides all its ambiguities, Ronconi's 2002 *Frogs* provided, above all, an
instructive example of the way in which an Italian audience appropriates ancient
drama. Theatre in Italy, especially in productions of the classical repertoire, is far
less political than other European or American theatre.[16] In particular, Aristophanes
becomes synonymous with humour, and his comedies are appreciated more as
exceptionally forceful dramatic celebrations of fantastic carnival than as seriously
engaged works of art. This is why, I think, that it is *Birds*, among all the Aristophanic
plays, that has enjoyed the most success in Italy.

A recent and very famous version of *Birds* is revealing in this sense: *Gli Uccelli di
Aristofane e altre utopie* (*The Birds of Aristophanes and Other Utopias*), directed by Tonino
Conte and staged in Genoa in 2000 (on which see also the discussion by Treu in
this volume, p. 260).[17] The play is a pot-pourri of Aristophanes: it is a bravura piece
in which a political meaning is scarcely discernible. Rather, Aristophanes becomes
the champion of Utopia. Another such revealing adaptation, this time directed by
Ronconi himself, was *Utopia*, a collage from *Knights*, *Plutus*, *Birds*, *Lysistrata*, and
Ecclesiazusae, staged in Venice in 1975 and characterized by a funfair and carnival
atmosphere. Again, in 1976 the *Frogs* staged at Syracuse was notorious for its non-
committal tone and for its 'carnivalesque' Dionysus, who highlighted the comic
aspects of the play. Revealing in this sense is an article published in *Unità*, the
journal of the Communist Party, by Aggeo Savioli and entitled, 'Aristofane come
Scacciapensieri' ('Aristophanes as Pastime').[18]

And this idea of a utopian Aristophanes, an author whose primary concern is
with a world of fantasy, seems to have come back in the interpretation of *Frogs* in
2002. In the TV interview, the actors and Ronconi himself speak often in terms of
utopia; they seem to think that what Aristophanes does in this play is essentially to
offer a utopian, hence unrealistic, solution to the problem of the decadence of the
present by recalling a dead poet. This might be true, and I am the first to admit that
assessing the true intentions of Aristophanes and the real meaning of his comedies
is an extremely hard task, doomed ultimately to a turn into a dead end. However
it is somewhat puzzling, if not indeed disturbing, that Aristophanic drama is in
Italy mainly reduced to the level of farce or — in the best cases — interpreted as
representing the triumph of carnival. Like the others, Ronconi, a great director
with long experience and a true understanding of classical drama, chose here
consistently to downplay the serious side of Aristophanes. His updating of the *Frogs*
took the form of turning it into a decadent farce. The only open reference to the
political world outside — those panels — was withdrawn before the première and
indeed, as Ronconi himself said, it was not essential to the production. The panels
were 'not essential' because nothing in the rest of Ronconi's staging (from the text

to the set) tried to translate Aristophanes' satire into a modern equivalent. The satiric part remained firmly in the past. We were reminded of contemporary Italy only by the farcical characters, drawn from the Italian movie industry, and by the car wrecks, mirroring Syracuse outside.

Ronconi's choice is understandable, and indeed the decision whether or not to update Aristophanes is a crucial one for any director. Updating surely entails a greater challenge and indeed risk, because any attempt to compete with Aristophanes has a high chance of failure. However, this peculiar compromise, in which the farcical dimension of the production is up-to-date, while the more serious one remains, instead, firmly anchored in the fifth century BC, is not only characteristic of the Italian approach to classical drama, but reveals a great deal about it. The lack of political concern in Italian classical theatre is a complex problem that cannot be exhausted in a short discussion. It involves Italian political and cultural history and is the result of the interplay of several factors.

First, Italy was not a unified country until 1860; our political sensitivity can be defined as 'primitive' compared to that of other European countries with a tradition of unity and political commitment, such as, for example, the UK or France. Our lack of political concern is evident in our recent political history, which has been far more concerned with political gossip than matters of substance; and it is reinforced by our individualism, which often acts as a burden and an obstacle to any serious political engagement.

The second factor is our cultural past. Italy has always considered herself to be the natural heir of the Roman world and, via the Romans, the legitimate heir of Greek culture. And although this sense played a great role in the rediscovery of classical authors during the Renaissance, it later had the contrary effect of preventing any attempt to reappropriate the classics in a more modern way. 'Updating' the classics in Italy is often a synonym for their betrayal. Classics *is* tradition.[19]

The third factor is our school curriculum. Latin and Greek are a permanent part of the Italian school curriculum in high school, a curriculum that was designed during the Fascist era by the philosopher Giovanni Gentile in 1923, and which is still almost the same. Thus, classical culture has always been supported and sustained by the government, and embodied in the state school system. This has led to a link between Classics and the conserving of tradition, if not actually between Classics and political conservatism. While the Italian academics to whom the classical world appeals are generally left-leaning, the spectators who enjoy classical drama in theatres are often more conservative. The Italian audience normally goes to a performance of a classical play with certain expectations, because they often happen to know the play (in the last year of high school, for example, the state curriculum prescribes the reading of an entire play in the original). Thus they do not like it when the text is changed or updated. And this, I would suggest, plays an important role in the choices of directors like Ronconi.

The fourth factor it is important to remember is that the Istituto Nazionale del Dramma Antico is a state institution which has been backed and funded by the Italian government since 1925. The most important festival of classical drama is therefore closely linked with the official establishment. This factor is well illustrated, in conclusion, by another emblematic example: *Wasps* at Syracuse in May 2003. During that period one of the hottest news items consisted of the judicial problems faced by Berlusconi. So the choice of play could have offered a golden opportunity for a 'modernizing' interpretation of Aristophanes. Yet no such opportunity was taken. Everything during that trilogy of plays (Aristophanes' *Wasps* was staged alongside Aeschylus' *Persians* and *Eumenides*) was set firmly in the past.[20]

In comparison with this anodyne production, we should at least give Ronconi credit for having modernized his *Frogs* at all. But modernizing in Italy does not always mean politicizing. And the Italian term 'commedia politica' cannot be translated as English 'political comedy'. A much more accurate translation would perhaps be 'comic politics'.

Notes to Chapter 16

1. For a survey of the most important productions of Aristophanes in 20th-c. Italy see Amoroso (1997).
2. This is a list of articles that appeared in the most important Italian newspapers. In *Corriere della Sera*: Corde (2002), Postiglione (2002*a*), and Postiglione (2002*b*) on 20 May 2002; Galluzzo (2002), Merlo (2002), Postiglione (2002*c*), Postiglione (2002*d*), and Vecchi (2002) on 21 May 2002. In *La Repubblica*: Bolzoni (2002*a*), Bolzoni and Quadri (2002), Jerkov (2002), Messina (2002), and Quadri (2002*a*) on 20 May 2002; and Quadri (2002*b*), Maltese (2002), Luzi (2002), De Marchis (2002), and Bolzoni (2002*b*) on 21 May 2002. In *La Stampa*: Anon. (2002*a*) on 20 May 2002; La Mattina (2002) on 21 May 2002; and M. D'Amico (2002) on 22 May 2002. In *Il Giornale*: Iadicicco (2002) on 20 May 2002; Guarini (2002), Pennacchi (2002), and Veneziani (2002) on 21 May 2002; and Sgarbi (2002) on 22 May 2002. In *Il Manifesto*: Bongi (2002) and Manzella (2002) on 21 May 2002. It is interesting to note that all the newspapers reported the news along the same lines regardless of their political orientation: *Il Giornale* is owned by Berlusconi, and *Il Manifesto* is the mouthpiece of Rifondazione Comunista.
3. Cf. for example Anon. (2002*b*); Anon. (2002*c*); Grimond (2002).
4. Aristophanes has been staged only seven times at Syracuse: *Clouds* in 1927, *Frogs* in 1976, *Acharnians* in 1994, *Thesmophoriazusae* in 2001, *Frogs* in 2002, *Wasps* in 2003, and *Ecclesiazousae* in 2004.
5. As Miccichè explained in the interview to Venanzio Postiglione in Postiglione (2002*b*): 'quando ho detto che l'autore greco non insultava i politici democratici ma soltanto i tiranni, lui mi ha risposto "Tiranni e affaristi". E io: "Vuol dire che Berlusconi è un affarista?". Mi ha risposto di sì. Senza problemi. Allora ho lasciato la cena, me ne sono andato'. (Translation: 'when I said that the Greek author did not insult democratic politicians but tyrants, he replied: "Tyrants and profiteers". So I asked: "Do you mean that Berlusconi is a profiteer?" and he said yes. Without problems. Then I left the dinner and went away'.) Similar explanations were given by Miccichè to Attilio Bolzoni, in Bolzoni (2002*a*). All translations from the Italian are mine unless otherwise stated.
6. Cf. Anon. (2002*a*); Iadicicco (2002); Postiglione (2002*a*); Quadri (2002*a*).
7. 'Ho letto con rincrescimento che a Siracusa il dramma antico si è trasformato in una commedia degli equivoci. Il governo, tutto il governo non sa neanche cosa sia la censura. Personalmente, mi preoccupa anche l'autocensura a dispetto. Spero che Ronconi, un artista da tutti apprezzato per il suo lavoro teatrale, rimetta subito al suo posto quel ritratto di tiranno in salsa aristofanea. Certo che non mi assomiglia, ma l'arte ha il diritto di scegliere, e di sbagliare, i suoi bersagli.' These words were reported by all the major newspapers, regardless of their political orientations: cf. Bongi (2002); Galluzzo (2002); La Mattina (2002); Luzi (2002); Pennacchi (2002).
8. 'Sergio Escobar e Luca Ronconi ritengono la dichiarazione del Presidente del consiglio un atto di grande intelligenza e civiltà, che solo un atteggiamento fazioso, che non appartiene loro, potrebbe non apprezzare nel suo significato'. Cf. Vecchi (2002).

9. Postiglione (2002*c*): 'Sì, certo, Berlusconi ha dato una risposta civile [...]. I pannelli non li rimetto in scena, basta. Altrimenti pare che, prima, ci sia stata la censura e, poi, dall'alto, l'atto di liberalità. Non esageriamo. [...] Ha scelto i toni giusti. Forse ha capito che l'idea dei manifesti sulla scena non nascondeva nessuna provocazione politica e nessuna mancanza di rispetto'. On Ronconi's sudden change of attitude, see Maltese (2002), 17.

10. Postiglione (2002*c*): 'È stata una scelta comune, concordata, per garantire lo spettacolo. Prima di ogni "querelle" vengono *le Rane,* viene il diritto degli spettatori a seguire Aristofane. Come regista, come uomo di teatro, ho condiviso una decisione obbligata. Meglio evitare sorprese, proteste, accuse o chissà cosa.'

11. Postiglione (2002*c*): 'Ma si poteva rinunciare così, senza problemi?' 'I pannelli erano un elemento vistoso, è chiaro, ma un accessorio. Se fossero stati determinanti, fondamentali per lo spettacolo, li avremmo lasciati dov'erano'. Similarly, see the interview with Ronconi in Bolzoni (2002*b*).

12. Cf. Principe (2004); Provvedini (2004).

13. My translation of Raffaele Cantarella's Italian translation of *Frogs* 353–68, as used in performance. My own translation of Aristophanes' *Frogs* 353–68: Let him be silent and stand aside from our sacred dances, | Whoever is ignorant of these sacred words or is not pure in his mind, | Whoever has never seen or danced the rites of the noble Muses, | And was never initiated in the mysteries of the bull-eating tongue of Cratinus, | Whoever likes the coarse jokes not at the right time, | Whoever does not settle hateful civil strife, and is not at peace with his fellow citizens, | But fans and stirs them up, craving for his private advantage: | Whoever accepts bribes when guiding the state tossed by the storm | Whoever betrays a fort or the ships or smuggles forbidden items, | From Aegina, a Thorycion, that wretched tax-collector, | Sending leather oar-pads, sails, and pitch to Epidauros, | Whoever convinces someone to give money to the enemies' ships | Whoever befouls the statues of Hecate while accompanying with the voice cyclic choruses | Whoever is a politician and bites off the pay of the poets | Because he has been ridiculed in the ancestral rites of Dionysus.'

14. Again, my translation of Cantarella's Italian translation of *Frogs* 731. My own translation of Aristophanes' *Frogs* 731–35: 'These citizen we use for everything, | These parvenus, whom before the city | Would not have used easily at random not even as scapegoats. | But at least now, fools, change your ways | And make use of honest people again.'

15. Messina (2002), 14: 'Ci sarebbe voluto Aristofane, per farci ridere. Purtroppo non c'era. [...] Così abbiamo potuto assistere solo a una mediocre commedia dei finti equivoci. In cui un regista così coraggioso, così temerario da individuare il Tiranno in quattro governanti, diventa un pragmatico uomo di teatro e cancella la sua invenzione, "per mandare comunque in scena lo spettacolo", salvo denuncia nel dopo teatro.'

16. Cf. Treu (2002) and (2003*a*).

17. A production by the Teatro della Tosse, which in 1988 produced *Viva la pace,* another pastiche from *Knights, Plutus, Birds, Lysistrata, Ecclesiazusae,* and *Clouds,* which, notwithstanding the pacifist meaning underlying it, still transformed the original into a burlesque. The style of opera buffa was adopted also in *Le donne di Aristophane,* another collage from *Lysistrata, Ecclesiazusae,* and *Thesmophoriazusae* by Giorgio Prosperi in 1969 at Segesta.

18. Cf. Savioli (1976).

19. Famous cases of Aristophanic stagings accused by the critics of having betrayed the original are *Birds* staged at Ostia and produced by INDA with the translation of Ettore Romagnoli in 1947; *Clouds* produced by the INDA and directed by Giulio Pacuvio in 1955; and *Peace* directed by Arnoldo Foà at Segesta in 1967. See Amoroso (1997), 558–60. For some reflections on Italian classicisms, see Rossi (1997).

20. Cf. Treu (2003*b*).

CHAPTER 17

❖

A Version of *The Birds* in Two Productions

Sean O'Brien

I

First of all, I should clarify my relationship to the text. I'm not a classicist by training. I did 'A' level Latin a very long time ago, but I have never studied Greek. My version of *The Birds* was made with the assistance of a literal translation produced by David Gribble and Claudia Wagner of London University — a document for whose help I am extremely grateful, not least because some of the other versions I read seemed designed to ensure that readers would steer well clear of the whole business. I have no particular expertise in Greek comedy, or comedy of any sort. My English teacher in the sixth form was very firm in his view that to complain that Henry Fielding's novel *Joseph Andrews* was not funny — and it still isn't — betrayed a sorry want of understanding of what was meant by comedy. He may have been right.

Given these background facts, I was surprised to find myself being asked to write a new verse version of *The Birds* for the National Theatre's Transformation season, staged in the Lyttleton Theatre in summer 2002. The reason for the invitation seemed to lie in the fact that I was a poet who in recent years had started writing for the theatre. My first play, *Laughter When We're Dead* (2000) was a kind of Jacobean political tragedy set in the near future at a Labour Party conference in the North East. The play was ferociously violent and foul-mouthed and — probably more importantly — it was written in rhyming couplets. When I was originally asked to write a verse play, by Max Roberts of Live Theatre in Newcastle, I took 'verse' to mean what it said. The audience should be able to hear the motor running. There was also the political dimension of my work. Almost all my plays are about politics. My next full-length stage play after *The Birds* was *Keepers of the Flame*, jointly staged by the Royal Shakespeare Company and Live Theatre in 2003, which is about poetry and Fascism. The main interests of my poetry are history, politics and the workings of the imagination. So it made a kind of sense to pair me up with *The Birds*, which is in part about the acquisition and exercise of power.

The idea for a production of *The Birds* at the National in fact came from Mamaloucos Theatre, a circus theatre company run by Matt Churchill. Churchill's idea was that the theatrical potential of the play could be released if performers with circus and in particular aerial skills were used, so that the birds could be seen to fly (see figs. 17.1–2). The production, after its initial staging at the National, would tour in Mamaloucos's big top. This was a logical development from the huge growth in interest in physical theatre in the previous ten years or so, and from the parallel interest in the theatre of spectacle exemplified by Arkaos, Le Cirque du Soleil and British-based companies such as Walk the Plank. It seemed to me that such a production of *The Birds* might also help to bridge the fissure which seemed to be developing between the realm of the theatre and that of language — between the play as written and the play as 'devised', for example, as well as between poetry and the rather atrophied language of many stage plays. It might be possible to attain the best of both worlds, so that the circus would help the play to escape the gravity which in another sense the play would confer on the circus. The production was to be directed by Kathryn Hunter, famous in several areas of theatre — as Lear's fool, for example, as Lee Hall's Spoonface Steinberg, as an exponent of highly imaginative physical theatre, and as a former member of the massively influential theatre company Complicite. The collaboration was ready to begin in October 2001.

II

I remain extremely grateful to the providers of the literal translation, but I soon found that the only way I could understand the play was by beginning to write — by opening the door and going inside. What I brought back was a version, an adaptation, rather than a faithful rendering. From the outset I decided to use rhyming couplets (with some different forms for songs and choruses) because they lent a necessary degree of artifice to the language as performed and — I hoped — would help to audience feel at home with a special case of what was already (by being drama) a special case. The couplet is, as we know, an extremely flexible form, capable of accommodating anything from complex argument, to imaginative evocation, to groan-making doggerel — distinctions which in the event the *Sunday Telegraph*'s reviewer proved unable, sadly, to make for himself.[1] It can also sustain a brisk pace. In this first extract Pez (Peisthetairos) and Eck (Euelpides) present and explain themselves to the audience. They are lost, far from home, and disheartened — the opposite of what we might expect of Greek heroes. The task at this point for anyone making a contemporary version of the play is to incorporate what would not have needed saying to the original audience, who would have recognized these characters a mile off and shared the background of their concerns.

> Pez   ... We love the city but we had to go
> In search of somewhere else, somewhere with no
> Damned bureaucrats and lawyers up your arse,
> Where you can simply sit and watch time pass.
> Of course, while life drags on from day to day
> There is the word we're almost scared to say.
> Good citizens —
>
> Eck   (*sotto voce*) don't talk about the war,

FIG. 17.1 (above). The birds 'in flight' (RNT/Mamaloucos, 2002)
FIG. 17.2 (below). *The Birds* as circus theatre (RNT/Mamaloucos, 2002)

	Because they can't remember what it's for —
	And all they hear is grim, then grimmer news
PEZ	About the fleet we sent to Syracuse...
	We've mortgaged the entire economy
	In order that it might be lost at sea... (p. 7)[2]

There is of course an anachronism here. When *The Birds* was written, the Syracuse expedition was yet to come, but this seemed to matter less than to convey a background hum of anxiety — especially given our own situation following the events of 9/11 — a point to which I'll return.

First, though, Pez and Eck. We recognize these two comedians — lustful, idle, good-humoured, in some sense innocent. They have something in common with Morecambe and Wise, Cannon and Ball, and perhaps Ant and Dec. But despite their roles — the brighter one, the dafter one; the grandiose one, the gormless one — their particular chemistry is unique and will also be affected by Eck's disappearance from the play around the halfway point. I imagine all playwrights have a cast in mind when writing. When I started *The Birds* I wanted to try out the idea of the two comedians as Geordies, because while their discontents are those of Athenian citizens burdened with taxes and obliged to participate in civic life, the colour of their resentments reminds me very strongly of working class bar-room talk. In the pub, revolt and rancour have their say, while everyone knows that nothing much is going to change and that the only certain things are death and taxes. So the actors I thought of were Trevor Fox and Joe Caffrey, stalwarts of Live Theatre in Newcastle, either of whom could take either part. In the event, nothing could have been further from the case. For reasons I'll explain, there's only the odd trace of Geordie speech in the text still, but the hedonism of the North-East remains a strong presence in their voices and attitudes. Newcastle-Gateshead, remember, was then pitching its bid for City of Culture status partly on the back of being a party town. When the comedians meet the Hoopoe, the bird-man asks what they are really seeking:

PEZ	. . . We're looking for a mega party town,
	Entirely occupied with getting down —
	Where party policemen throw away the keys
	Unless you end up guttered on your knees.
	My life's ambition is to puke my ring —
ECK	I'd rather die a pisshead than a king.
	Let's not forget we'll need some canny birds,
	Susceptible to charm and honeyed words,
	In party gear with neither fronts nor backs,
	Some nice lap-dancing nymphomaniacs. (pp. 13–14)

As the epigraph to the play I used a remark made by Corinthian emissaries about the Athenian character. It is referred to by Thucydides in *The History of the Peloponnesian War*: the Athenians, it was said (1. 71), 'are incapable of leading a quiet life themselves or of allowing anyone else to do so'. Here lies the kind of absolute contradiction on which societies seem to depend. The hard-drinking, fornicating wasters turn out — in my reading — to be entrepreneurs, for whom everything is a commercial opportunity, an idea which was to be important in the political context of this version. Pez instantly absorbs the economic implications of the paradisal state; indeed, he understands the economic basis of everything:

> PEZ   . . . The sky, whose other names are heaven and space,
>   Is where the race of birds must build its place —
>   Developmentally unlimited,
>   And bigger than the mind of God, it's said.
>   What better place to let your city rise
>   To rule the world from the all-seeing skies.
> HOOPOE   But how?
> PEZ   By economic means, of course.
>   You call this *air*? I call it market force. (p. 17)

Perhaps the business of dramatic illusion — a subject too large to consider here — does not particularly concern Aristophanes. But it concerns us, or at any rate it concerns me, and when the Hoopoe summons the birds to the meeting with the visitors from Athens I want the beauty of the world he invokes to be more than a formality. We should realize with a pang that this is a place that Pez has not — yet — got his grubby hands on. Thus the Hoopoe, with a nod to W. H. Auden's 'The Composer' (1938):

> HOOPOE   Nightingale, nightingale, mistress mine,
>   Awake and set your holy singing free —
>   For only your gift is an absolute gift,
>   Your voice alone can sing of what will be.
>
>   The gods themselves are listening
>   To your unceasing melancholy note.
>   The gods themselves are listening:
>   Your tender voice is caught in heaven's throat. (p. 18)

Similarly, when the Hoopoe/Chorus Leader recounts the Creation myth — 'We are the oldest creatures: we. | We were, before the gods could be' — there must be a dimension of awe, and here the speaker veers somewhat in the direction of Ecclesiastes in his rendition of the limits of human life compared with the divinity of birds.

> CHORUS LEADER   Are you listening, men,
>   Where you crawl in the half-light?
>   Are you listening, you shadows
>   On loan from the night?
>   You who amount to less than a dream,
>   You flightless, earthbound, clay-footed
>   Momentary things, who only seem
>   To live:
>   You must endure your little lives of pain
>   And then wither like leaves
>   Come to dust, come to death, once again.
>   Are you listening, men? (p. 40)

It would have been a terrible waste of the performers not to emphasize their beauty as well as their skill. The descent of Matilda Leyser's Nightingale by silk rope during the invocation of the nightingale was one example where the sense of the supernatural served to still the surrounding comedy (fig. 17.3).

This account of Creation is, as it were, economically or culturally harmonized with Pez's nakedly acquisitive approach when the birds' tone shifts from the hieratic to the self-admiring:

> CHORUS LEADER   But we would always recommend
> The ultimate in getting high.
> Throw off the bonds of earth, my friend —
> And learn to fly.
> Say one evening at the theatre
> It's some boring tragedy.
> You can easily imagine
> A much nicer place to be:
> You simply slip out for a sandwich
> So swiftly that nobody sees,
> And be safely back in your seat again
> For Aristophanes.
> Perhaps you've got your kippers
> Under someone else's grill:
> With wings you get to have your shag
> And still have time to kill... (p. 42)

III

The plot, then, is wound up. A city of the birds is being rapidly constructed, despite the fact that the birds have never felt the lack of one before, despite the fact that Pez and Eck, the Athenian visitors, have come here to escape their own city. Pez and Eck have adapted physically to the setting with the aid of a miraculous disco biscuit supplied by the Hoopoe — 'a secret psychedelic root | Which blows your mind, then grows you wings to boot.' With mysterious alacrity, bureaucrats, priests, fortune-tellers, poets, and other chancers appear. The role of the poet is one I found especially interesting. In this version he figures as a temporarily tolerated nuisance, surviving somehow on the margins despite the cognitive dissonance which exists between him and the host society, which views his claims to authority and utility as evidence of beggary and fraud. The poet is certainly a figure without authority. All he has is persistence. I was to reflect on this later. When the acting text was cut for length, removing some of the best speeches, I remembered a remark made during an interview with Tony Harrison about his film *Prometheus*, made in 1998. Faced with the suggestion that it was perhaps a little too long, he replied that on the contrary, if he had been able to make it as long as he really wanted it to be, as long as it needed to be, then *Prometheus* would have seemed shorter. For the first time, I felt I really understood his point — though on the opening night *The Birds* — which is quite a short play — ran at a little over three hours. Well, it wasn't the words that did it. Must have been the acrobats.

By the time the play moves towards its climax, Eck has gone from Aristophanes' text, perhaps to take up other parts in the large cast. In the version as played at the

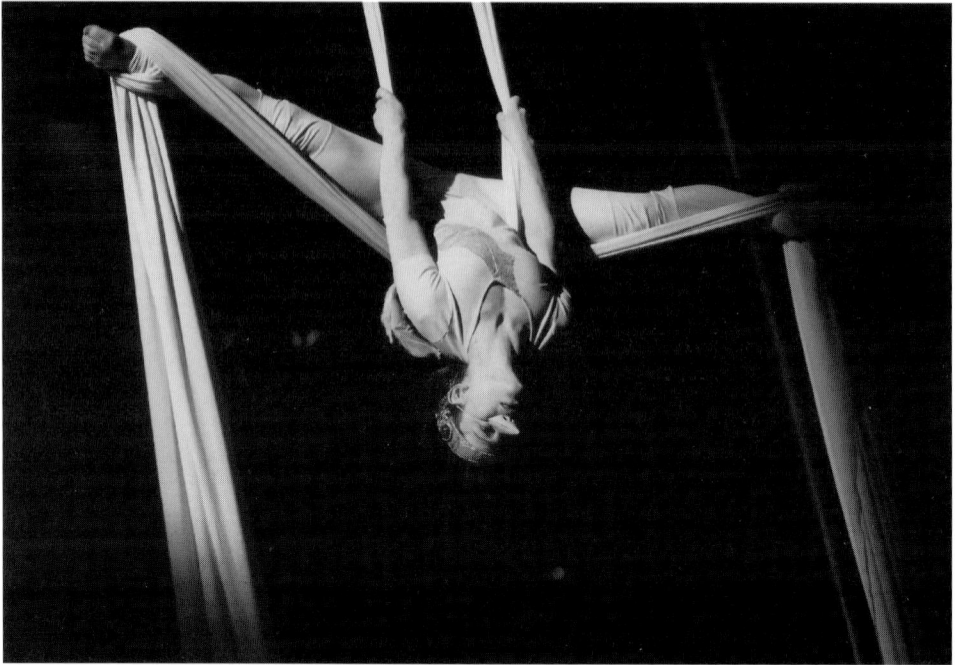

Fig. 17.3. The descent of the Nightingale (RNT/Mamaloucos, 2002)

National he returned as a reminder of Pez's former loyalties, and was rejected, only to return a second time. On the stage he was in fact stabbed by Pez during a final orgiastic party — but by this point there was a marked degree of divergence, to put it no more strongly than that, between the text as written (by me) and the one performed on stage. At one point it seemed a good idea to divide the Chorus into pro- and anti-Pez factions, old and new birds, as it were, in order to make more of the moment when Pez is discovered having a barbecue. The birds turning on the spit are

> Conservatives — a few birds that we've found
> Had formed a clique, a deviant underground
> Opposing this, our new democracy.
> *Holds bird aloft on fork.*
> The traitor feeds the democrat for free! (p. 82)

But by this stage the indisputably breathtaking skills of the cast on trapezes, ropes, silks, and the strop were to some extent permitted to lead the action. The noblest of the birds — 'the sailor's friend, the far-flung albatross' — had made his first appearance flying with his arms/wings wound in cords as he circled the stage seeking a landing place, accompanied by music of melancholy and eerie beauty. Now when traitors and examples were called for, the Albatross was hunted down, crucified, and barbecued by his fellow birds, acting under Pez's command. This raising of the visual and emotional stakes signalled the kind of grim carnival with which the stage version was to close; but it also departed entirely from the realm of the comic and introduced a form of symbolism — the crucifixion — which is, whatever its actual origins, inextricably linked with the birth of Christianity. This seemed to me to deny the necessary otherness of the birds and to impose a moral code which didn't seem to have very much to do with the play. Newcomers to the theatre are always told to bear in mind that it is a co-operative medium. From the writer's point of view this may mean an enlightening interaction with artists from other areas of expertise; or it may mean that people monkey about with the text; or it may mean both — and the last of these was my experience. 'Collaboration' extends to all areas of the theatre. If you write a play about poetry and Fascism, you may discover that those are the two words to which the marketing department is most fearfully and implacably opposed. Collaboration — that's the name of the game.

Certainly, though, it is true that in *The Birds* the theme of *exploitation* was one I wanted to explore. The analogies between economic liberation and development and the fresh subjugation of the alleged beneficiaries were hard to resist — we can recall now that American global dominance had until 9/11 seemed perhaps more likely to be achieved by various economic means rather than enforced by military intervention. I would have been happy to see these suggestions *left* as suggestions for the audience to see, but at some point in rehearsals Pez turned up wearing a cowboy hat, and by that stage the goose, as well as the albatross, was cooked and analogy had been abandoned in favour of agit-prop. The wedding of Pez and Sovereignty was an extended dumbshow in which money rained from the ceiling. Sovereignty herself was the Statue of Liberty. It was probably just as well, at the first performance, that the two rows of American visitors had walked out at the interval.

The Birds is a play famous for its adaptability, which seems to exist in proportion to its enigmatic character. Edith Hall was kind enough to send me an article she had written in 1995 for the *Times Literary Supplement* describing parts of the play's performance history.[3] One famous production — Karolos Koun's in Greece — had been censored in 1959 (see Van Steen, above, this volume). Still nearer to our own time, Silvio Berlusconi was attempting to censor an Italian production of Aristophanes' *Frogs* (see Schironi, above, this volume). This last example, I thought, gave a far more impressive sense of theatre's powers of threat and provocation than the remarks of our own David Blunkett when Mark Ravenhill's *Shopping and Fucking* toured overseas with official backing. Mr Blunkett, you may remember, remarked that Shakespeare didn't need to use all this sex and bad language. One point at which I think our production fell down — although these elements were certainly much enjoyed by the younger members of the audience and by the drama reviewer of *The Morning Star*[4] — was in imposing a layer of 'relevance' on the play, rather than allowing the concluding plot mechanisms to make their own suggestions. I'm referring to the discussion with the deputation of gods led by Poseidon, and to the marriage of Pez to Sovereignty. 'This is a comedy, and comedies end happily', Peter Porter once wrote, managing to suggest something quite different.

When the city is built, Pez and the birds — now his servants — have control of space and establish frontiers with transit fees and immigration checks. The gods are outraged but the tide of public sentiment is running against them. A messenger pictures the situation for Pez:

> ...now the coming thing's birdolatry
> And everybody simply wants to *be*
> A bird. They walk and talk and think like birds —
> So much that they've abandoned words
> In favour of the various species' songs
> And name their children Lark and Currawong. (p. 70)

In this 'model state', the Chorus declares there will be 'some designed for comfort, some for speed — | Grant wings to each according to his need!' This is, I think, the last utterance on behalf of the birds' utopian project. What happens after that is a restoration of the status quo by dynastic contrivance and marriage. It is a question of the old gods finding their range in relation to the parvenu Pez. Poseidon gets off on the wrong — paternalistic — foot entirely, but the solution to the problem, by which the interests of both parties are served and in fact unified, depends on recognizing that Sovereignty need not be regarded as a sacred abstraction, beyond the reach of negotiation. At the bottom of it all lies self-interest. When the marriage is celebrated, the formalities are all in place, but it seems to me that the Chorus's final speech unpicks the 'settlement' by showing that Pez's elevation to divine status forbids us to take any comfort in 'normality'.

I'm aware that I'm likely to be visiting my own preoccupations on the play, but its pragmatism seems to invite that somehow. As well as thematic, my preoccupations are in the first place verbal, and the problem with this particular collaborative production was that the play of language became at times an encumbrance for a cast whose nature was to be in movement, and for whom language was not the primary dramatic material or even within their sphere of competence. In addition the cast was multilingual. It included performers from Brazil, Bulgaria, France, Francophone Canada, Italy, Malawi, Wales, and Essex — and my two Geordie leads were played by an Italian and a south Londoner who happened to be female. I did also feel at times that there was a fear of the audience — a fear that it might be bored by too much language. But this would be a counsel of despair, especially for a poet-dramatist. In the time available to us — and in effect we were rehearsing the equivalent of two plays — we made a start, and the performance gained strength throughout its run. An unfortunate dispute between the National and Mamaloucos scuppered the planned tour, for which advance sales were very strong. If we could match the song of the birds to their powers of flight, I think we might have a formidable version of Aristophanes' *Birds*.

IV

I will end with a short tail-piece about a recent development. In 2005 threeovereden, a small theatre company based in the North-East, decided to stage *The Birds*, and in 2006 mounted a tour of small venues in the region, including The Store, a former Co-op in Dipton, County Durham, now a superb small venue for theatre and music, and the Literary and Philosophical Library in Newcastle upon Tyne. The

FIG. 17.4 (above). Opening scene from *The Birds* (threeovereden, 2006)
FIG. 17.5 (below). Iris scene from *The Birds* (threeovereden, 2006)

rather original choice of the latter was dictated by the closure for rebuilding of both Live Theatre and Newcastle Playhouse at the time. threeoverden are five actors and a musician. The company has a growing reputation for ambitious and imaginative work: their previous production had been *Peer Gynt*, a strong indication that a large cast of characters would not present any obstacles.

The brand of theatre practised by threeovereden, which involves physical comedy, dance, and movement, is certainly physical, but it differs from the National's approach not only in the simplicity of its means but also in the decision to put these theatrical resources at the service of the text, which was — gratifyingly — presented almost uncut, clearly spoken, with a good understanding of the relationship between metre and the natural stresses of speech. This production ran at under two hours (compare the National's epic approach). The inventiveness of threeovereden always served the text, so that the political resonance was there for the audience to consider in the light of their own sense of things, rather than being imposed. The very simplicity of means — flags, occasional comedy wings, a deckchair, with a small raked circular block for most of the action (see figs. 17.4 and 17.5) — had the curious effect of helping to substantiate the fantasy and at the same time of making the performance seems like a civic, rather than an economic occasion. In the light of this experience, I think the version of *The Birds* which I have been describing remains a work in (tantalizingly slow) progress.

Notes to Chapter 17

1. J. Gross (2002).
2. The page references are to the published text: O'Brien (2002*a*).
3. E. Hall (1995).
4. Campbell (2002).

CHAPTER 18

❖

Translating/Transposing Aristophanes

Michael Silk

There are three broad categories of literary translation, classically labelled by John Dryden. In his *Preface to Ovid's Epistles* (1680), the poet-translator Dryden distinguishes: *metaphrase*, a word-by-word and line-by-line version; *paraphrase*, a version of the sense rather than the words; and *imitation*, which — like a jazz improvisation on a given melodic base — looks to create an overall equivalence to the original.[1] In practice, many versions, no doubt, tend towards one of the three categories, whereas others are best located on the borders of two of the three, or else oscillate between two or indeed between all three.

Metaphrase, often called 'literal' translation or (in everyday terms) a crib, is what Housman parodies in his 'Fragment of a Greek Tragedy':

> Oh suitably attired in leather boots
> Head of a traveller . . .

Metaphrase is the way Dryden's own version of Virgil's *Aeneid* begins, with, famously, 'Arms and the man I sing' for Virgil's 'arma virumque cano'. It then carries on with paraphrase. Virgil wrote,

> arma virumque cano, Troiae qui primus ab oris
> Italiam fato profugus Lavinaque venit
> litora — multum ille et terris iactatus et alto
> vi superum, saevae memorem Iunonis ob iram,
> multa quoque . . .

And Dryden,

> Arms and the man I sing, who, forced by Fate,
> And haughty Juno's unrelenting hate,
> Expelled and exiled, left the Trojan shore.
> Long labours, both by sea and land, he bore
> And . . .

where, for instance, Virgil's 'primus' ('first') is left to be understood and, conversely, Dryden's 'unrelenting' is inferred from 'memorem' ('mindful'); where, again, Dryden's 'Fate' is conjoined with 'Juno' (if only by rhyme), but Virgil's is only loosely attached to 'violence of the gods above' (which is elided in Dryden) and that 'violence', rather, glossed with reference to Juno; and where the order of events is adjusted — Fate and Juno first in Dryden, Troy and Italy in Virgil (with 'Italy' itself in Dryden's version elided) — by which point (and there are more points) paraphrase, one might well think, has shaded into imitation.

Dryden's *Aeneid* as a whole, certainly, is as much an imitation as a paraphrase of Virgil; and its imitational response is, on reflection, summed up by its form. When Dryden translates Virgil's quantitative dactylic hexameters into his iambic rhyming couplets ('Arms . . . Fate, | And . . . hate, |'), the new form, however familiar in and from Dryden's own age, constitutes a powerful element of equivalence in its own right, and that very familiarity is itself part of the point. The rhyming couplet is a staple in Dryden's age, as the hexameter is in Virgil's; Dryden is to Virgil, as the couplet is to the hexameter, as the neoclassical is to the classical; and these are the equivalences, not of paraphrase, but of imitation.

When Dryden's successor Alexander Pope produced his *Iliad*, along similar lines to Dryden's *Aeneid*, the great scholar Richard Bentley acknowledged it as 'a pretty poem, Mr Pope, but you must not call it Homer'.[2] Most academic versions of ancient texts operate in the range between metaphrase and paraphrase. Works like Pope's *Iliad* and Dryden's *Aeneid*, for all their intermittent metaphrase, operate largely, and creatively, in the range between paraphrase and imitation, and Bentley is in effect denying academic value to this creative range. In that denial, Bentley seems to me misguided. I would wish to argue for the value, including the academic value, of creative paraphrase-imitation, and, equally, of its equivalent in the sphere of performance.

The underlying logic and goal of metaphrase-paraphrase is the legitimate one of indicating, perhaps shadowing, the isolatable *contents* of the original. The underlying logic of paraphrase-imitation is different, but has its own legitimacy: the goal here is to create an equivalent *dynamic* and *impact*. In a few enviable instances, across the vast experience of translated literature, the two goals are approached, even realized, simultaneously: the great English Bible translations, from Tyndale's to the King James, constitute an uncontroversial case in point. In most instances, the two represent distinct and exclusive goals — and especially so, where the culture gap between source and target is great, where the source and target languages differ significantly in kind, and above all where the original uses the distinctive resources of its own language to add significantly to the *density* of the text.

These complicating factors are present in extreme form with English translations of Aristophanes, as also with English performative versions of Aristophanes. In practice, the most sensitive issue here is the density of the original text. Translators and others tend to suppose that the sensitive issue is the degree of otherness — with the crucial decision, how to reclaim the alienness of the original. This is important, but actually secondary: the crucial decision is how to represent density. On a spectrum, texts are either dense (more or less) or thin (more or less) or in between (which often means stylized). With thin texts — however powerful, like the Greek of the New Testament Gospels — a plausible aim of translation is to locate the semantic centre and reproduce it. The outcome may or may not be satisfying (compare and contrast the great English Bible versions with their recent counterparts), but the aim stands. With stylized texts, like Homer, the best bet may be to recentre on an equivalent stylization — as Logue recentres Homer on a version of Poundian imagism, or as Pope recentres Homer on a neo-Virgilian English Augustanism. With dense texts, involving layers or clusters of effects, the solution may well be to establish a mode that facilitates the creation of new clusters entirely.

Aristophanic text is dense text, full of clusters. A simple example might be Aeschylus' parody of Euripidean lyric (i.e. song) style (*Frogs* 1309–22), where the Greek begins,

> *alkuones, hai par' āenaois thalassēs*
> *kūmasi stōmullete . . .*

and ends,

> *. . . botruos helika pausiponon –*
> *periball', ō teknon, ōlenās.*[3]

Here is Sommerstein's translation of the complete sequence (with the cited parts italicized), firmly in the metaphrase-paraphrase range:

> *Ye halcyons, who jabber amid the ever-flowing waves of the sea,* moistening and bedewing the skin of your wings with its watery drops — and ye spiders in the nooks under the roof who wi-i-i-i-ind with your fingers the loom-stretched bobbin-thread whereon the tuneful shuttle plies its art — where the pipe-loving dolphin leaped at the prows with their deep-blue rams to the oracle and the race-track, bright joy of the vine's blossom, *tendril of the grape that banishes toil and trouble — fling your arms around me, baby!*[4]

The translation — admirable in its way — tells its readers most of what they might reasonably expect to be *told*. All that really *impinges* from the English, though, is that this is florid and flamboyant text, which is hard to follow, not to say cluttered, and eventually not just cluttered, but (in its movement from halcyons to spiders, to dolphins, to oracles, to race-tracks, to grapes, to a child's embrace) confused. No doubt, one gathers a few other points incidentally — notably that the parody subsumes Euripides' inclination to stretch a syllable over several musical notes ('wi-i-i-i-ind') — but the rest is lost. The rest, in fact, is a cluster of points which metaphrase-paraphrase cannot reasonably convey. It is widely assumed that metaphrase-paraphrase is in principle more *accurate* than any other mode of translation: hence its claim to academic propriety. But all metaphrase-paraphrase does (and the more damagingly, with texturally dense originals) is privilege superficial accuracy over fundamental quality — the elucidation of which is an essential academic activity on any reckoning.

In the first place, the Aristophanic Aeschylus' Greek, though rhythmically abstruse, is still rhythmically coherent[5] — but the syllable-stretching points to a certain rhythmical looseness, while the relative coherence that remains presents a blandly absurd contrast with the accelerating incoherence of the contents. Then too, while the English rightly gives us an impression of Euripides' characteristic relish for topographical detail (sea, house, race-track, vineyard),[6] it loses the *force* of the climax — the way that topography is trumped by the high-value human-emotion card, with the (again, in itself) very Euripidean appeal to a 'welcome home' embrace ('fling your arms around me').[7] Then again, there is another implicit tension in the Greek: between (*a*) the huge archaizing of Euripidean style (richly elaborated in traditional high-verse idiom, and flagged negatively by, for instance, the suppression of definite articles and positively by high-style compounds like *pausiponon* and vocabulary like *āenaois*) and (*b*) one or two sly little touches like *stōmullete* ('jabber'), in register a totally untraditional modernism, which points (however unfairly) to Euripides' supposed plebeanizing of tragic idiom.[8] And, not least, all the above is delightfully complicated by the overtone that this is one (older and more traditional) poet imitating another (younger and less traditional) poet, in historical reverse.

I cannot see how this cluster of activity — or indeed even the sense that there is, here, any cluster of activity — could possibly be *conveyed* in metaphrase-paraphrase. And if one wants a comparable effect, the best thing would be to go for full-bloodied transposition and, thereby, an equivalent cluster. Indeed, at the end of the sequence, Sommerstein seems to acknowledge the point, by suddenly (but in his terms arbitrarily) switching from metaphrase-paraphrase to paraphrase-imitation. 'Baby', he writes, for *teknon*, which, metaphrastically, is 'child' — where 'baby', both in itself and particularly as a hanging vocative, irresistibly evokes the distinctive, but conceivably equivalent, world of American popular song ('I can't give you anything but love, *baby*'):[9] on which, more below ...

Translation, even the most literal metaphrastic translation, involves a kind of transposing, from one language to another. This is not the only, or the only relevant, kind of transposing. There is transposing from language to language; there is also transposing from text to performance, from script to stage; and implicit in both is a transposition from one culture — often a past culture — to another culture, such that, at the point of transposition, the past (if past) is necessarily made *present*. Any and all of these transpositions involve translation from absence to presence, from notional to immediate, from the unattainable Other to the experiential-continuous One.

Transposing from past to present raises the venerable issue of historicism. In his *Aesthetic as Science of Expression* (1909), Benedetto Croce, philosopher-spokesman of historicism, states the issue in the form of a question:

> The Madonna of Cimabue is still in the church of Santa Maria Novella; but does she speak to the visitor of today as to the Florentines of the thirteenth century?

Answer, obviously, *no*, but *no* is not good enough for a historicist, and Croce carries on with a plea that the 'visitor' be assisted by 'historical interpretation':

> Historical interpretation labours [. . .] to reintegrate in us the psychological conditions which have changed in the course of history. It revives the dead, completes the fragmentary, and enables us to see a work [. . .] as its author saw it in the moment of production.[10]

The whole issue has been endlessly discussed, in an extensive secondary literature,[11] but the salient, and most relevant, point is simply stated: Croce has neatly outlined the opposite of live theatre and live performance. Yes, of course, there is a time and a place for his kind of 'enabling' (albeit talk of 'reviving' and 'completing' seems,

neatly again, to beg the crucial question), but the outcome of his historicist position
is archaeological fidelity, irrespective of, or without, present effect.

Does the Cimabue speak to the visitor of today as to the old Florentines? *No.*
Consider for a moment Aristophanes' first extant play, *Acharnians*, and Dicaeopolis'
quest for peace within it. Does Dicaeopolis' quest for peace speak to the audience
(or reader) of today as to the Athenian audience of 425 BC? *No*: how *could* it? *We*
know the peace that passeth all understanding, and Tolstoy, and World War I (the
war to *end* war), and subsequent and contemporary wars and peaces, including the
so-called war on terror, whose peace seems beyond attainment; the Athenians knew
none of these. We also know, where they did not know, some of Aristophanes' later
plays, like *Peace* and *Lysistrata*, which present obviously illuminating comparisons
— just as we know Menander and Shakespeare, and Woody Allen and Gabriel
García Márquez (ditto, ditto). We can't unknow these; and why should we want
to try? *Acharnians* looks different in their light — and properly so.[12] Meanwhile,
we know a lot less Greek than the old audience did, and a lot less earlier Greek
literature, and we know a lot less about dramatic festivals in Athens, and about a
multitude of local and topical circumstances — albeit, what we *do* know 'about' in
the area of dramatic festivals and local and topical circumstances, we hardly know
experientially: no, we don't *know* it, we do know *about* it.

To restate: does the past speak to the audience (or reader) of today as to the
audience (or reader) of the past? Obviously not: how could it? but why should we
want it to? Of course we should all like to find out more *about* the past (and not
only if or because our professional status requires us to); of course we should like
access to more texts, more monuments, more records of the past; and of course we
should like 'better' interpretations of the past, as also 'better' understandings of
what 'better' interpretations might involve; but why should we want anything past
to *speak to* us as it might be judged to have spoken to earlier generations, when that
'speaking' can only be remote?

Historicism comes in two main varieties, old (represented here by Croce) and
new (prefigured by Foucault and institutionalized by Stephen Greenblatt, among
others), with the old historicists committed, ultimately, to a belief in the hermeneutic
authority of past consciousness, and the new, to a privileging of the cultural logic, or
rhetoric, of texts in their past contexts.[13] For a historicist, old or new, 'Aristophanes'
is something inherently and necessarily past. But this, fortunately, is not a necessary
position: *fortunately*, because the past, as past, can have only a notional impact,
immediacy, presence. Aristophanes, indeed, may be something irredeemably past;
if so, what a pity; but perhaps we can do something to remedy the situation, by
finding ways to revisit Aristophanes, and give Aristophanes presence, in the light of
the later experience which makes us a 'we' in the first, or last, place.

Modern performance of Aristophanic drama seeks, should seek, to transpose
a notional past to an immediate presence, and to conquer the cultural distance
by whatever equivalence and transposition is judged necessary and appropriate
— bearing in mind that impact is a prerequisite, but that some impacts are more
appropriate than others. In this transposing, one does not try and evade modern
realms of reference: one explores them. What you don't know is assimilated to

what you do know: *this* is like *that* ('discuss') — like, but also, necessarily, unlike (because, if there's no unlikeness, you must have, not likeness, but identity).

If one is to have an equivalent, *any* equivalent, to Aristophanes, it does of course help to decide what Aristophanes is like in the first place — subject, of course, to the pragmatic relativities which are implicated in that 'is' and that 'like'. Most users of Aristophanes, since the Renaissance certainly, have identified him with his satire or his jokes. If one has to identify him with any one thing, better, I would suggest, to identify him with the rich brilliance of his language, which presupposes, correlatively, the sheer joy at the possibilities of living that his best plays and best moments (which are many) convey. In the *Symposium* Plato — who didn't get *everything* wrong — seems to associate Aristophanes, not with satire, but with brilliant, life-enhancing creativity. In terms of recent imaginative experience, Aristophanes may profitably be compared with a wide variety of writers, from Woody Allen to Gabriel García Márquez to (among others) *song*writers in the American tradition of twentieth-century popular songwriting — not, that is, in the post-'50s era of youth culture and protest, but the more adult pre-'50s era of verbal sophistication and demotic immediacy.[14]

What is Aristophanic comedy like? What (if one prefers to say so) can it be made, or shown, to be like, that (in its new immediacy) conveys something of its dynamic, therefore of its impact? — albeit (*yes*: important qualification) a dynamic and an impact you didn't necessarily *see* before the new showing, the new transposing.

Dynamic and impact, I would argue, reside above all in texture, in constituent detail. Yes, it's fine to have a Big Idea that establishes 'relevance' — by, for instance, transposing an Aristophanes anti-war play into a contemporary anti-war scenario — but dynamic and impact depend on detail. And if this is true on the level of translation (as the Euripides parody in *Frogs* serves to suggest), it is no less true on the level(s) of theatrical transposition. Here, as with translation in the ordinary sense, what one needs is a mode of equivalence that provides systematic opportunities for the necessary kind of effect.

One such mode is music; and here the American popular song tradition comes into view again. Where Aristophanic writing is concerned, this tradition of music and song can claim a special relevance: something between a partial kinship and a distinctive potential for its articulation in our times. There would seem to be several considerations here:

(*a*) As already indicated, Aristophanic verbal idiom can be related to the peculiar combination of sophistication and demotic immediacy of that American song tradition at its best (from the early '20s to the early '40s, say).

(*b*) With its alternations of spoken action and (often) high-profile song, an Aristophanic comedy bears a structural resemblance to (many of) the musicals — stage or screen — of this era.[15]

(*c*) Aristophanic comedy is itself not only full of songs (choral or solo), but rich in passages of stylized delivery ('recitative') which in modern terms impinge as musicalized or readily musicalizable as well.

(*d*) It is characteristic of songs in the given American tradition that individual instances are readily evoked, because easily remembered and recognized: they belong, both collectively and individually, to a range of immediate experience. Something similar, no doubt, holds good for various other kinds of music — but no other kind, arguably, is so readily evoked in its particular detail: melodies, titles, phrases, words.

(*e*) Music in general offers large and varied possibilities of effect and allusion. The given range of music offers particular possibilities, arising from its recognizability (see (*d*) above) and the distinctively close association between the melody and the words (including, for instance, the song title) in any given case.

For all its own intermittent musicality (see (*c*) above), Aristophanic comedy is and remains word-dominant. It is not music-dominant, like opera, nor could one possibly hope to find any overall equivalent to Aristophanic comedy in musical terms. There is, instead, a much more plausible possibility: using music — notably, music of the given kind — to help recreate its verbal dynamic, and in particular its verbal density. However, in any performance of Aristophanes in English (or any other modern language), the use of music with any life to it at once raises serious and often pervasive awkwardnesses — if only because of a new, recalcitrant and distracting, triangularity: English (or whatever) words, fifth/fourth-century reference, unrelated music. On the other hand, music attached to the *untranslated* words retains the advantages of musical attachment, without any such awkwardness. In this attachment, 'modern' music becomes a suitably incongruous, recreative, Aristophanic factor (and nothing could be more Aristophanic),[16] in support of the words: the words now take on a kind of protean status, with the music directing their orientation and effect, on the basis of a new equation — between original density and new density of Greek words in newly suggestive musicalization.

★ ★ ★

Between the late 1970s and the mid-1990s, I was closely associated with the annual Greek plays at King's College London. These productions have always assumed performance in Greek; and during my own period of involvement, for Aristophanes in particular a set of coherent procedures was developed, associated with the 'musical' equation, along with other equations associated with the word 'popular', with myself generally in charge of the music.[17] 'Coherent' was itself a big word in this connection; and to me at least it always seemed important to strive for a coherent musical score — coherent, both in itself and vis-à-vis the given conception of the given play.

A representative example was the 1988 *Frogs*, whose London production (in March) was followed by a revised version which (after another London run) went on tour to the USA that autumn (fig. 18.1).[18] There were differences between the two versions, but the music remained virtually unchanged. The idiom of the production included a large element of Art Deco: the set and the publicity materials were straightforwardly Deco, and the music was aligned, both in terms of period and ethos. Art Deco was chosen as a suitably exuberant, yet also stylized, idiom: one that is eclectic, yet also coherent[19] (and Aristophanic comedy is all of these things). In some of the King's productions the music was a newly composed score.

FIG. 18.1. *Frogs* on tour, 1988: the programme cover

Here it was newly arranged but pre-existing music: American standard songs of the appropriate period (mid 1920s to late 1930s). More specifically, the musical idiom covered the range from Tin Pan Alley standard songs to big-band jazz arrangements, but in each case the musical sequences involved songs with impact, with distinctive identities, and with convenient sets of appropriate associations.

It is entirely plausible, but not conventional, to describe such music as, itself, Deco: the term is usually restricted to the visual sphere.[20] The Deco quality of the music of this range is partly a matter of association (just picture a 1930s big-band publicity photograph, with each elegantly tailored musician sitting behind the Deco-shaped and Deco-lettered band logo, raising their instruments in stylized, perhaps sun-ray, formation) — but partly, I would argue, intrinsic. The point is that, during this phase of popular music (including, not least, its popular jazz embodiments), instrumentalists, band arrangers, and even sometimes composers (Gershwin, among others) cultivate the kinds of shapes and especially the often jagged parallel figures and bold symmetries which are all of a piece with the configurations on (say) an ordinary early-thirties light fitting or (say) the magnificent elevator doors inside the Chrysler Building in New York.[21]

The *Frogs* music, though easily identifiable with this continuum, was orchestrated, in the main, for four unaccompanied saxophones — with no other melody instruments and no rhythm section.[22] This would have been an unheard-of line-up in any form of popular music between the wars: our idea was to allude, not reproduce. There was, though, a specific rationale to the instrumentation (see below, pp. 300–01), while in accordance with the principles discussed, the music itself was used largely to accompany — to reanimate and inform — the Greek words, especially the words of the lyrics and, in some cases, the recitative.

From the various sections of *Frogs* music, I shall cite four contrasting examples. The first is the music for the frog-chorus' entrance song (209–68). This was based on a 1928 composition by James Cavanaugh (words) and Harry Barris (music), 'Mississippi Mud'. The song was popularized by the recording made in that year by Paul Whiteman's orchestra, featuring Bix Beiderbecke on cornet, with vocal by the Whiteman Rhythm Boys, a three-man singing group which specialized in jazz-influenced three-part harmony;[23] and our arrangement of the music followed the spirit and sometimes the letter of this and other early versions.[24] Under the influence of the so-called minstrel tradition, Cavanaugh's original words assume a now outmoded conception (celebratory, but patronizing) of the American negro, which might seem potentially distracting, as well as distasteful.[25] But then, we were not actually using the original words, any more than the original song-title, but seeking to evoke the more immediately relevant connotations of both,[26] as a presence. Here are those words, with (as a rough guide to the rhythm) stressed syllables in bold, and each line, as printed here, representing a musical bar:[27]

> When the **sun** goes **down,**
> (The) **tide** goes **out,**
> (The) **dark**ies gather **roun'**
> And they **all** begin to **shout:**
> 'Hey hey,
> Uncle **Dud,**

> It's a **treat** to beat your **feet**
> On the **Miss**issippi **mud**;
> It's a **treat** to beat your **feet**
> On the **Miss**issippi **mud**.'
> **What** a **dance**
> **Do** they **do**! –
> **Law**dy, **how** I'm
> **Tell**in' you.
> **They** don't **need** no
> **Band**;
> They keep **time** by **clap**pin' their
> **Hand**.
> Just as **hap**py as a **cow**
> **Chew**in' on a **cud**,
> When the **dar**kies beat their **feet**
> On the **Miss**issippi **mud**.

The tune that goes with the words is rich in Deco-like jagged parallel figures, which are to some extent implicit in the verbal rhythm, and which are in any case accentuated in the Whiteman arrangement; and these Deco qualities were foregrounded in our version.[28] Both the underlying melody and its treatment, therefore, evoke the requisite idiom. Beyond this, though, the *fun* aspect of the piece is arguably as sympathetic to Aristophanic comedy in general as the specific orchestration (four saxes) is programmatically appropriate to Aristophanic frogs in particular. But most relevant of all, prospectively, is the sense of the suppressed song-title and the words that go with it, as (ideally) evoked by the music. A world of water and mud, of spontaneous *a cappella* music-making in a strange, dim setting ('when the sun goes down'): all this is suitably relatable to the 'song-loving', 'marshy' frogs of the underworld, enjoying the 'harmonious sound' of their own song, not least with endlessly enthusiastic repetitions of their rhythmical croak (*koák koák*), as their victim Dionysus is the first to complain.[29] Meanwhile, in correlative opposition to this enactment, there is an obvious, take-it-or-leave-it, clash of 'classical' Greek words and modern popular music: a pervasive incongruity which becomes a cumulative running joke with each musical item and, *as* an incongruity, a richly Aristophanic presence in its own right.

There is, of course, another set of issues: the precise rhythmic shapes of the new song and the original Greek words. The rhythmic mode of Aristophanes' frog-song is broadly iambo-trochaic ($\times - \smile -$ or $- \smile - \times$ etc.), but with a few contrastive trills.[30] It begins (in transliterated Greek and line-by-line metaphrase):[31]

209 *brekekekek koak koak,*	*Brekekekek koak koak,*
210 *brekekekek koak koak,*	*Brekekekek koak koak,*
211 *limnaia krēnōn tekna,*	(We) marshy stream-children,
212 *xunaulon humnōn boān*	(A) harmonious lyric cry
213 *phthengsōmeth', eugērun emān*	Let us utter, our sweet-voiced
214 *aoidān, koak koak.*	Song, koak koak.

Specifically: after two lines of trochaic croaking ($\smile \; \smile \; \smile - \times - \smile -$: the notional opening $-$ is resolved into two $\smile \; \smile$), we get two more of a syncopated iambic equivalent (× − ◡ − − ◡ −), then a line of (so to speak) equivalent weight, but shifting into a slightly different shape (× − ◡ − − ◡ ◡ − : a choriambic dimeter), before returning to more iambic syncopation and another croak (◡ − − × − ◡ −).

In broad terms, 'Mississippi Mud' is rhythmically related overall, with some specific equivalent ingredients.[32] Thus the opening, '(When the) sun goes down, | The tide goes out' is, in effect, two leading notes (◡ ◡) followed by a sequence (− ◡ − × − ◡ −) equivalent to 209–10 in the Greek. Likewise, the lines 'What a dance | Do they do' impinge as − ◡ − − ◡ −, a syncopated sequence akin to (*lim*)*naia krēnōn tekna* (211). Again, a phrase like 'clappin' their hand' is a rhythmic match for the choriambic − ◡ ◡ − of *-gērun emān* (213).

For all these welcome affinities, though, Aristophanes has not quite — not yet — succeeded in setting out his Greek in precise Cavanaugh–Barris rhythmic patterns. His original words, therefore, need a bit of tweaking — some adjustment and some minimal supplementation — to fit the new music, while the precise phrasings of the music can themselves be marginally adjusted in turn: the Greek is assimilated to the music, but also the music to the Greek. The requisite treatment of the Greek, however, entails two particularly significant, audible, adjustments. If ancient Greek words are to be sung to 'our' music, the rhythmical shapes of the individual syllables must be subject to some reinterpretation in the process of conversion from quantitative metre to musical stress. On top of this, it is surely *de rigueur* that the words should exhibit that indispensable feature of popular songs, namely rhyme.[33] One way or another, then, we end up with this:

> *brekekekek koak koak,*
> *brekekekek koak koak,*
> *age, limnaia*
> *krēnōn tekna,*
> *humnōn boān phthengsōmetha*
> *eugērun, emān*
> *autou xunaulon aoidān,*
> *hēn . . .*

The words are recognizably Aristophanes', only slightly rearranged, and with a couple of minor idiomatic additions — an initial 'come' (*age*) and an emphatic 'our own [song]' (*autou [aoidān]*). The precise correspondence of these revised words to the revised music may be indicated by a syllabified version, with stressed syllables again in bold, alongside the corresponding Cavanaugh word-shapes. After what is now recognizable as a modestly syncopated four-bar lead-in (which, with or without syncopation, is a norm in arrangements of standard songs of the period),

*bre**kekekek** | **koak koak,** |*
*bre**kekekek** | **koak koak,** |*[34]

we get this:

age, limnaia	When the **sun** goes **down**
krēnōn tekna,	The **tide** goes **out**
humnōn boān phthengsōmetha	<.> **lawdy how** I'm **tellin'** you
eugērun, emān	They **don't need** no **band**

*autou **xunaulon** aoidān,*	They keep **time** by **clappin'** their **hand**
hēn . . .	Just . . .

which can be, and was, sung satisfyingly to an adjusted version of the Barris melody, with only a minimally adjusted version of the Cavanaugh rhyme scheme.

Most of our audiences, both in England and America, had little or no Greek. For the Greek-sensitive listener, one potential obstacle to satisfaction, perhaps, is the scale of the rhythmical reorientation of the revised Greek words, as compared with the originals. Although, as indicated, the rhythmical character of the Aristophanic words in Aristophanic sequence is sufficiently akin to the Cavanaugh-Barris words in *their* sequence to make the transposition plausible in the first place, anyone familiar with authorized Aristophanes (or indeed, simply, with authorized Greek) will note that there is, now, no consistent stress-accentuation of what were, in the Aristophanes, heavy syllables, nor any consistent *non*-stress equivalence for original light syllables. More precisely, the sequence cited involves a fair amount of what is likely to strike (certainly) a British ear — an ear used either to a quasi-Latinate stressing of ancient Greek or to a scanning pronunciation or to some pragmatic compromise between the two[35] — as counter-intuitive: *limnaia, eugērun, autou xunaulon.* Many of the revised wordings in the *Frogs* production, as in others, involved a good deal less of this. Given a somewhat syncopated tune and a more than somewhat uncouth (froggy) set of singers, a relatively high degree of rhythmic in- (or per-?)version seemed appropriate to the particular case — and not least, because the 'licence' recalls a recognized practice in popular song-writing itself (not least in the '20s), a faintly defamiliarizing practice known, in the trade, as 'ragging'. 'Fascinating rhythm, I'm all a-**quiver**': the Gershwin line exemplifies, as it describes, the phenomenon.[36]

That last (special?) point aside, the prerequisites for a compositional match would, therefore, seem to be several:

(*a*) the new musical material should have some latent rhythmic affinity with the Greek, if only to allow preservation and foregrounding of key phrases.

In addition, the new music should aspire to the following:

(*b*) the capacity to participate in a new and coherent musical score;

(*c*) the capacity to suggest an appropriate period or idiom (here, the Deco '20s/'30s);

(*d*) the capacity to convey an appropriate mood (here, 'fun');

(*e*) the capacity to convey appropriate theme or content, through the latent associations of the suppressed words, including the suppressed title, of the 'English' original (here, 'mud', 'spontaneous music' etc.).

In addition to which, it is in any event both likely and desirable that:

(*f*) the music in its new setting will be appropriately incongruous — meaning that it can cooperate with the Greek context to enact that open mobility of style which is integral to Aristophanic comic idiom and vision[37] —

just as it is, again, likely and desirable that:

(g) the overall transposition will convey an effect of ingenuity, equivalent to, or at least suggestive of, Aristophanes' own.[38]

These requirements are duly satisfied in the given instance, as in those that follow.

'Mississippi Mud' involves allusions: it helps to be able to identify it under that title. Will the audience *get* the allusions? Maybe; maybe in part; maybe not at all. The more (and the more completely), the better. But even if the audience fail to recognize an allusion altogether, they are still likely to sense and appreciate the presence of an allusion,[39] and in any case feel *some* of the effect of the musical material, not least its appropriate incongruity. In fact, of the prerequisites just listed, any remotely competent auditor should be able to make headway with (b), (c), (d), (f) and perhaps (g). All that is at risk — and it is not frivolous to make the point this way — is (a) and (e), along with, perhaps, the true impact of (g): in effect, the full force of the recreated cluster.

The King's frog chorus made its first appearance (at 209) as a song–and–dance troupe in grotesque, if stylized, frog masks,[40] and it duly re-entered (at 323), still in its masks, as initiates (*mustai*) in the Underworld — with the masks now connoting ritual observance and adding, perhaps, a hint of the sinister to what is, by any standard, a different sort of message. Aristophanes has his chorus sing:

448 *khōrōmen eis polurrhodous*	Let us go to [the] rose-rich
449 *leimōnas anthemōdeis,*	Meadows flowery,
450 *ton hēmeteron tropon*	In our own way,
451 *ton kallikhorōtaton*	[The way] of lovely dances,
452 *paizdontes* [. . .]	Playing [. . .]
454 *monois gar hēmīn hēlios*	Yes, on us alone [the] sun
455 *kai phengos hieron estin,*	And light holy falls,
456 *hosoi memuēmeth(a)* . . .	Us initiates . . .

By the now established logic, a lightly recast version of these words was sung to the 1930 classic (words by Dorothy Fields, music by Jimmy McHugh), 'On the Sunny Side of the Street', whose English words begin,

> Grab your coat and get your hat;
> Leave your worries on the door-step;
> Just direct your feet
> To the sunny side of the street

and end,

> If I never had a cent,
> I'd be rich as Rockefeller,
> Gold dust at my feet,
> On the sunny side of the street.

Thus the newly adjusted Greek equivalent to that final stanza (those last eight bars) now runs,

khōrōmen es leimōnas:	Let us go to [the] meadows:
hieron gar phengos hē-mīn	Yes, [there is] a holy light on us
memuēmenois	Initiates
hēlios t' epesti monois.	And [a/the] sun, upon us, just us.

En route, there are several fairly precise correspondences of sense and shape, typified by the retention of *Frogs* 346, *aposeiontai de lū-pās* (= 'they [the initiates] shake off their griefs'), for line two of the song ('leave your **wor**ries on the **door**-step') — or again by the first word of the final stanza in the new Greek (*hēlios*: 'sun'), to match the corresponding 'on the **sun**-' in the original English.

At the end of the initiates' song, that last superimposition was given a special prominence. The musical orchestration of the number looked back to a classic big-band arrangement by Sy Oliver for the Tommy Dorsey band.[41] Artfully Deco in much of its detail, and (in particular) repeatedly finding opportunities for secondary parallel phrasings where Fields and McHugh had failed to envisage them, Sy Oliver's arrangement reaches its triumphant climax on an exuberantly Deco-ized vocal end:

> On the **sunny**
> On the **sunny**
> On the **sunny** su-**hide** of the **street**.

In our *Frogs*, a minimal adjustment to the already adjusted Greek, by way of accommodating the extra syllable, yielded a suitable equivalent:

> *hēlios te*
> *hēlios te*
> *hēlios te paresti monois.*[42]

There was a similar logic to the choice of song for the choral finale which closes the play.[43] Aeschylus, triumphant over Euripides, prepares to ascend to the world of light with the prayers and good wishes of the chorus (now, in good Aristophanic fashion, a chorus of citizens)[44] ringing in his ears. The original Aristophanic song is in dactylic hexameters, therefore has grand-manner connotations. It begins (1528–29):

> *prōta men euhodiān agathēn apionti poētēi*
> *es phaos ornumenōi dote daimones hoi kata gaiās . . .*
>
> First, a safe journey for [the] poet, as he leaves
> [And] ascends to [the] light, grant, you underworld spirits . . .

Our Aeschylus was dispatched upwards to the strains of a 1922 George Gershwin number (lyrics by Ira Gershwin and Buddy De Sylva), 'I'll Build a Stairway to Paradise' — a number best known, these days, from its revival in the fondly-remembered 1951 Gene Kelly film, *American in Paris*, where Georges Guetary sings it in suitably high-style top hat and tails, ascending a suitably grand-manner spiral staircase, whose black treads turn white, like piano keys, as he steps upwards and onwards. That cinematic ascent was a *coup de théâtre* not quite available to us, but the potential of the evocation was there. Themselves broadly dactylic in rhythmic cast (as in the opening line), the Gershwin lyrics begin,[45]

> **I'll** build a **stair**way to **Par**adise
> With a **new** step **ev'ry day!**
> **I'm** gonna **get** there at **any price;**
> Stand a**side**, I'm **on** my **way!**

while our revised Aristophanes, accordingly, began

> *prōta men euhodiān pote*
> *agathēn ornumenōi*
> *hoi kata gaiās theoi dote*
> *tōi poētēi Aiskhulōi*

with the poet now named as 'Aeschylus', the underworld deities (*daimones*) now called 'gods' (*theoi*), but otherwise eveything much as before.[46] 'Stairway to Paradise' has been plausibly described as 'the first of many major Gershwin songs to posit dance as an antidote to life's travails'.[47] As such, it could claim an additional aptness in the context of the victorious poet's brief, to 'save the city and its drama' (1419), where the metonym for 'drama' (*tous khorous*) points specifically to choral song and dance.

Rather different in kind were the musical items featured in the contest between the two poets, Aeschylus and Euripides, earlier in the play, from which I take my fourth and last example: Aeschylus' critique of Euripidean song-writing (1309–22), with its incongruous collage — the jabbering halcyons, the wi-i-i-i-inding spiders, the dolphin, the race-track, the vineyard — and its yet more incongruous end: the 'fling your arms around me, baby' of Sommerstein's rendering.[48] The song, of course, is literally paratragic, and like so much of Aristophanic paratragedy, it foregrounds collisions between the tragic high and the less–than–tragic low — and, in this instance, the supposedly Euripidean propensity for such lows and, therefore, for such collisions.

One possible kind of equivalence to this kind of collision is to be found in the domain of the classical-musical high. Consider for a moment *Acharnians* again, and Dicaeopolis' phallic song, a triumphant affirmation of male sexuality that is also a celebration of his private peace (263–79). The lyric begins, more or less, on a tragic-lyric high,

263 *Phalēs, hetaire Bakkhiou*	Lord Prick, thou friend of Bacchus,
264 *xunkōme nuktoperiplanēte*	Thou, revel-mate, night-wandering,

then abruptly dips, down to a level that I have elsewhere characterized as low-lyric-*plus*:

265 *moikhe, paiderasta* . . .	Fornicating, boy-loving . . . [49]

In a King's *Acharnians* of 1992, our phallic song sought to enact the sequence. It started high, before falling back into a more demotic idiom; and the opening was made high by virtue of a quotation from the opening bars of the Pilgrims' Chorus from Wagner's *Tannhäuser* —

> **Beglückt** darf **nun** di-ich o **Heimat**, ich **schauen** . . .
> *Phalēs, Phalēs, he-e-etaire Bakkhiou* . . .

The logic here was composite. The point was partly to insist on the elevated features of the sequence, and the abrasive alienness of this elevation in context, partly to evoke the erotic associations of this particular piece of music (the *Venus*berg, *et al.*).[50]

In our *Frogs*, however, any such use of genuinely elevated music would have supplanted the requisite Deco and destroyed the requisite coherence of the chosen musical idiom, while the paratragic preoccupations of *Frogs* as a whole made it less urgent for the tonal highs of our particular bit of jabbering-halcyonic paratragedy to be foregrounded as such. In any case, various distinctive features of this particular lyric called for a more specific solution: the combination of florid detail and emotional end, the sheer eccentricity of the stylistic mix (summed up by the 'jabbering' halcyons themselves),[51] and — not least — the residual sense of chronological dislocation associated with the fact of an older writer purporting to imitate a younger, by way of allusion to a range of old, but not *old*-old, compositions: a range, in fact, of modern classics.

The solution (a complicated one, no doubt) was an unusually allusive, indeed literally backward-looking, American song: a song of slightly earlier vintage than the others, but a song still current into the 1940s, thanks to its association with the larger-than-life singer it was written for. The composers were Sam Lewis and Joe Young (words) and Jean Schwartz (music); the year of composition was 1918; the singer was Al Jolson, first great singer of the American popular song, and a byword for expansive emotion, often (as here) associated with blackface minstrel performance;[52] and the song was 'Rock-A-Bye Your Baby With a Dixie Melody', a distinctive, even extraordinary, concoction, both charming and emotionally shameless. Interpolated into the stage musical *Sinbad*, which ran from 1918 to 1920,[53] the song was to become one of Jolson's best-known numbers, so that, inevitably, he sings it in his two, much later, film biopics, *The Jolson Story* (1946) and *Jolson Sings Again* (1949). But not only is this song utterly over-the-top and associated with an utterly over-the-top performer and mode of performance. It specifically alludes to three earlier minstrel songs by an earlier song-writer, in fact the earliest American popular composer of note, Stephen Foster.

Foster died in 1864, and apart from romantic ballads like 'Jeannie with the Light Brown Hair', was remembered above all for his 'plantation melodies', a series of heavily nostalgic pieces of minstrelsy that included 'My Old Kentucky Home' (1853), 'Old Black Joe' (1860), and 'Old Folks at Home' (1851) — this last, widely known as 'The Swanee River', after the opening line of its celebrated verse ('Way down upon de Swanee Ribber . . .'). Of these Stephen Foster classics, the 1918 'Rock-A-Bye Your Baby' alludes to 'Old Black Joe' by title, to 'Old Folks at Home' under the name 'The Swanee River', and to 'My Old Kentucky Home' by the first line of its chorus: 'Weep no more, my lady, oh weep no more today'. The premise of this new song is that the singer is a black Southern grown-up son singing to his now aged mother (his 'Mammy') in recollection of the songs she sang to him in his black Southern childhood, from which he is now, seemingly, distanced (which is not wholly irrelevant to Euripides' supposed relation to the maternal womb of poetic tradition . . .). Unexpectedly, then, the 'baby' of the title is not — as is usual in American popular songs — a young woman addressee ('I can't give you anything but love, baby'), but instead a male addresser, referring to himself.

The chorus of the song runs:

> Rock-a-bye your baby with a Dixie melody.
> When you croon,
> Croon a tune

From the heart of Dixie.
Just hang that cradle, Mammy mine,
Right on the Mason–Dixon line,
And swing it from Virginia
To Tennessee with all the love that's in ya.
'Weep no more, my lady': sing that song again for me,
And 'Old Black Joe',
Just as though
You had me on your knee.
A million baby kisses I'll deliver,
If you will only sing 'The Swanee River'.
Rock-a-bye your rock-a-bye baby with a Dixie melody.

For *Frogs* purposes, this time, significance resides not in the song's title, but only in the rich diversity of its contents — and the sense of playful allusiveness that they share with the diversities of Aristophanes' 'Euripidean' lyric. The song begins with a traditional nursery-rhyme opening ('Rockabye baby, thy cradle is green . . .')[54] — where, however, 'rock' also points to the world of popular music and specifically dance,[55] a connotation which is duly realized with the imperatives, 'croon' and, especially, '*swing* it [the cradle] from Virginia'. Meanwhile, the little conceit of 'hanging' the cradle on the Mason–Dixon 'line' (the North–South boundary) is as pleasingly outrageous as the rhyming of 'Virginia' with 'that's in ya' — a take-it-or-leave-it bit of phonic violence that contrasts, for instance, with the decorously subliminal pararhyme, in parallel structure, of 'Rock . . . your baby' and 'Weep . . . my lady' that frames the two stanzas.

One way and another, the song was suitably, and richly, incongruous for its new parodic context. Its loose and often unemphatic iambo-trochaic shapes also called for relatively little recasting of the Aristophanic words,[56] and, among much else, the halcyons at the start and the baby embrace at the end were preserved almost intact:

1309   *alkuones, hai par' āenaois thalassēs* . . .
              (**Rock**-a-**bye** your **baby** **with** a **Dixie** **melody**)
              (You) halcyons, who at (the) sea's ever-flowing . . .

1321–22   . . . *pausiponon helika — periball', ō teknon, ōlenās.*
              (**Rock**-a-bye your **rock**-a-bye **baby** with a **Dixie** **melody**.)
              . . . pain-ending tendril: throw round (me), child, (your) arms.

Our Aeschylus performed the piece unaccompanied, with exaggerated Jolsonesque gestures, but with additional miming movements in simulation of each passing item — halcyons, waves of the sea, tendrils — in the Greek. The final mimetic move coincided with a suitably triumphant moment of semantic superimposition between suppressed English 'baby' and the *teknon* of the (eventual and original) Greek. Performance of the 'Rock-a-bye' melody *à la* Jolson demands that, during its emotive last line, the singer sink onto one knee in (as it might as well be) urgent cradling pose, which gives way, finally, to an expansive opening of the arms — in line with the climactic gesture called for by the Aristophanic imperative at the very end (fig. 18.2).

FIG. 18.2. *Frogs* on tour, 1988: Aeschylus, *à la* Jolson, and chorus

★ ★ ★

While occupied, over the years, with these and other transpositions, designed to help an audience *experience* Aristophanes, I became vividly aware of the complexity and the range of the issues associated with transposition, in theory as in practice — and aware, not least, of the peculiar and paradoxical advantages of seeking to convey the density of an Aristophanic text through the 'original' Greek, even — or, often, especially — to Greekless ears and minds. Needless to say, the issue of how to convey unmusicalizable portions of a Greek text remains — but the distinctiveness of the advantages remains too. 'Translating' a text in the ordinary sense of that word, and translating a text into performance for an audience, both necessarily pose the problematic of transposition. And in performance itself, the decision to choose the transpositional mode that we call translation, like the decision to choose a particular mode of translation, is not a given.

Notes to Chapter 18

1. Dryden (1962), 268. 'Improvisation on a given base': Dryden's own music-related phrase is 'to run divisions on the ground-work'.
2. Cited in this form in Hawkins (1787), 126.
3. For *Frogs* citations, text and line-numbering here and hereafter follow Sommerstein (1996), unless otherwise specified.
4. Sommerstein's facing translation (1996: 139).
5. The metre is aeolo-choriambic, with variations; see Parker (1997), 504–07, for full metrical analysis. Parker (ibid. 507) speaks of 'a jumble of cola' — but on the grounds of absent architectonics (for which this lyric indeed scores low), rather than of insufficient affinity of rhythmical elements.
6. The justice of the satire is not my main concern, but such pictorial detail is certainly, in itself, Euripidean: see e.g. Barlow (1971), under the rubric of 'imagery'.
7. Though not purely Euripidean: see e.g. Rau (1967), 146–47, Silk (1988), 98–99.
8. See Silk (1993), 487. In classical Greek, the *stōmul-* word-group is attested almost exclusively in comedy, i.e. is prospectively low usage.
9. The opening line (of the chorus) of 'I Can't Give You Anything But Love', by Dorothy Fields (words) and Jimmy McHugh (music) (1928).
10. Quoted here from the English version of the fourth edition of the Italian original: Croce (1922), 124–26.
11. See e.g. Silk and Stern (1981), 90–107, on the Wilamowitz–Nietzsche spat of 1872/3 and cf. n. 13 below.
12. The classic contention of T. S. Eliot in 'Tradition and the Individual Talent' (1920): Eliot (1951), 15.
13. See, especially (but not only) for new historicism, the lucid account given by Colebrook (1997).
14. For the analogy, see Silk (2002), 183–85, and for a comprehensive account of the verbal sophistication, Furia (1990).
15. In contrast, then, both to the unstructured song-and-dance reviews of the period and to the more fully musicalized and 'integrated' art-musicals associated, in a later age, with, above all, Sondheim. In these terms, classic musicals are far closer to Aristophanic comedy than classic opera is to Attic tragedy — notwithstanding the fact that opera was called into being as a supposed reinvention of Attic tragedy itself. On Aristophanes and the musical, see further Silk (1998), 18–19 and (2002), 268–69, 277.
16. See Silk (2002), 451 (index s.v. 'recreativity').
17. The King's Greek Play began in 1953/4 with a production of *Hippolytus*; it claims (as far as I know, correctly) to be the world's only established annual production in classical Greek. The Aristophanic sequence I was myself associated with consisted of *Clouds* (1977), *Wasps* (1981), *Birds* (1982), *Thesmophoriazusae* (1985), *Frogs* (1988), *Clouds* (1990), *Acharnians* (1992) and *Lysistrata* (1995), together with two more recent productions, *Birds* (2000) and *Ecclesiazusae* (*Women Take Power*) (2006). For most of these productions, my official status was as 'Executive Producer' and 'Musical Designer'. Of the earlier sequence, *Wasps*, *Thesmophoriazusae*, and *Frogs* were staged in London (in March) and restaged (in September/October) on tours of North America.
18. With performances at, or under the aegis of, various universities on the East and West coasts: Brown University; Connecticut College; Haverford College; University of California, Santa Cruz; University of Southern California; Stanford University; University of California, Berkeley.
19. Irrespective of the coherence of individual Deco designs, the overall Deco design movement can claim an unsurpassable coherence, embracing everything from lettering to skyscrapers, jewellery to interior decor, ocean liners to dance formations.
20. In accordance with its symbolic origin in the Paris *Exposition des arts décoratifs* of 1925, from which the name derives.
21. For a pertinent Gershwin example, see the original piano arrangement of the 1922 composition, 'Stairway to Paradise' (on which see above, pp. 300–01).

22. The orchestrating and performing, throughout *Frogs*, was the work of Barak Schmool, then a student at the Royal Academy of Music.

23. The trio consisted of Al Rinker (brother of the better-known singer, Mildred Bailey), Barris himself, and the young Bing Crosby.

24. These include another 1928 Beiderbecke rendition with the Frank Trumbauer Orchestra.

25. Many would put it more strongly, denying 'outmoded', and insisting on the political implications of this problematic tradition: 'minstrelsy was not a form limited to the nineteenth and early twentieth centuries; it is an *ongoing* form of bourgeois appropriation of black culture' (Baraka and Baraka (1987), 328). At the same time, politically conscious critics of the phenomenon are well aware of its ambivalence: 'the ridicule and dehumanization of the minstrel project is a put-down, but also a kind of distorted admiration' (ibid.). The title of Lott (1995), *Love and Theft*, says it all. (See further n. 52 below.) In recent decades, the offensive phraseology common to the songs in, or affected by, the minstrel tradition tends to be adjusted — but mechanically, even meaninglessly. Thus, in post-war recorded versions of 'Mississippi Mud', such as a Bobby Darin–Johnny Mercer version from 1961, the 'darkies' of l. 3 (etc.) are replaced, less offensively but limply, by 'people'. This is a well-attested pattern. A prime instance of such rewording involved the opening words of the Kern–Hammerstein hit, 'Ol' Man River', from *Show Boat*, which premièred in 1927: see Block (1997), 25–27, and Silk (1998), 18.

26. As with (say) metaphor in poetry, where the reader is invited to sense out relevant aspects or associations of the (presumptively equivalent) vehicle and to discard the rest.

27. Albeit in some cases the first words of the *following* lines belong strictly to the *previous* measure. 'Musical bar': the circumstances of the present publication preclude the use of any formal musical notation. 'Original words': my transcription of these and other song lyrics represents a compromise between what is printed in the original sheet music, what is heard on early recordings, and what makes sense on the music-less page. Song lyrics as printed in sheet music do not consistently offer plausible punctuation, plausible lines of verse, or even (sometimes) plausible spellings. Then again, precise wordings (as also precise phrasings and precise pitchings) may differ. On early recordings, for instance, the bracketed 'The' of lines 2 and 3 is sometimes sung, sometimes not; sometimes one is sung, the other not. In addition to these variables, the words printed above are often extended by one or more semi-verbalized eight-bar sequences: see n. 28 below.

28. As anyone familiar with Tin Pan Alley conventions will gather, the Cavanaugh–Barris song has an unusual shape. The norm is shapes of thirty-two bars, in four eight-bar parts, whereas this song has twenty-two, made up of eight plus two-bar tag (corresponding to ll. 9–10), then eight, then four (after which, in some versions, there follows an additional eight-bar section, or two such sections, of, mostly, scat singing). Suffice it to say that an abundance of parallel configurations is provided by the extra two- and four-bar sections.

29. First at *Frogs* 226–27, then repeatedly until his triumph at 263–68. The croak is spelled *koáx*, but the spelling no doubt implies the sound *koák*: Dover (1993), 219, Silk (2002), 191. The principle (though not the particular application) is a familiar one: e.g. Greek /-ng-/ is customarily spelled -*gg*-, but sounds -ng-, and is always, and rightly, so transliterated.

30. See Parker's analysis (1997), 456–67. In these metrical symbolizations, – denotes a heavy syllable, ⌣ a light syllable, × an indeterminate syllable ('anceps': heavy or light).

31. In these and subsequent transliterations of Greek, pitch markers ('accents') are ignored; my macron denotes a long vowel.

32. On the basis of the familiar equation between Greek quantitative shapes and English (etc.) stress patterns.

33. Only a handful of the many thousands of popular songs from the twenties to the fifties involve any eschewing of rhyme. The most notable single instance is surely 'Moonlight in Vermont' (words by John Blackburn, music by Karl Suessdorf, 1944): 'Pennies in a stream, | Falling leaves, a sycamore: | Moonlight in Vermont. || Gentle finger waves, | Ski trails down a mountain side: | Snowlight in Vermont. ||' Even here, there is a sense of parallel repetition ('–light in Vermont') at the stanza's end.

34. The two-bar musical phrase which provided the two halves of this requisite four-bar sequence then became the basis for the agonistic call-and-response routine between Dionysus and chorus that occupies much of 220–68.

35. See Allen (1987), 140–61. Classical Greek itself involved no determinative stress accent, but instead a determinative pitch (on the 'accented' syllables), and an essentially unrelated system of syllabicity for metrical purposes — neither of which are any modern English-speakers' mouths equipped to produce or ears equipped to hear.

36. The second line of (the chorus of) the song 'Fascinating Rhythm' (George and Ira Gershwin, 1924). 'Such "ragging" of words by music — reversing verbal accents, breaking up phrases, splitting words by musical pauses and rhythmic shifts — [. . .] would become prominent features in the lyrics of [. . . the] songwriters of the golden age': Furia (1990), 28.

37. Silk (2002), 102–20.

38. See e.g. my analysis of *Peace* 774–95: Silk (2002), 111–16.

39. This important point is formulated apropos Aristophanic comedy itself by Dover (1972), 189. In any case, the currency, and therefore the recognizability, of many standard songs is perpetuated through use in television commercials and signature tunes, quite apart from specific musical revivals.

40. The chorus was properly visible from the first: cf. Silk (2002), 234–35. In the heyday of Deco, masked choruses are not common, though one is used for the title number of the 1937 Astaire/ Rogers film *Shall We Dance* (music and words, George and Ira Gershwin; director, Mark Sandrich; choreographer, Hermes Pan).

41. With vocals by the Sentimentalists (1944). The year 1944 is late for Deco, in music as in visual design, but the arranger, Sy Oliver, had formed his arranging style with the Jimmie Lunceford band a decade earlier (witness such Lunceford records as 'My Blue Heaven', 1935, and 'Annie Laurie', 1937) and, from 1939, maintained it in a new incarnation with Dorsey. A comparable Oliver arrangement for Dorsey is 'Oh, Look at Me Now' (1941), which sets an almost extravagantly Deco chorus against the more contemporary musical phrasings of the young solo-singer Frank Sinatra.

42. The 'licentious' Sy Oliver phrasing in such a case perhaps recalls, *mutatis mutandis*, the syllable-stretching Euripides of *Frogs* 1314 ('wi-i-i-i-ind'), but an overt allusion to Euripides in this non-Euripidean choral context would have served no useful purpose. Our version and use of the Oliver arrangement was already high on allusiveness, of a quite different kind. That arrangement begins with a usual four-bar introduction, but one that, very unusually, lays out a chromatic pattern of ascending harmonies which is both deeply sensuous and oddly otherworldly. This memorable opening, in simplified form, yielded us a plausible ritual riff to shape the chorus' mystic incantations (first at 316–17). With, as before, a four-saxophone orchestration, we used the riff to create an enigmatic moment of sound and sight, which could then, in properly 'comic' fashion, explode into easier meaning when the song proper began. The chorus (re)entered to the sound of the ascending harmonies, took up stylized prayer postures (with a faintly sinister green light on their masks and outstretched arms), chanted Aristophanic words to the four bars, then, on musical cue, stood, sang, and 'danced' to the suddenly recognizable tune.

43. Itself no doubt *sung* in the Aristophanic original, and reasonably so described by (e.g.) Dover (1993), 383–84 and Sommerstein (1996), 298 (likewise, by implication, Zimmermann (1987), 95), but seemingly treated as recitative (to judge *ex silentio*) by Parker (1997).

44. Compare Silk (2002), 234–35.

45. That is, the lyrics of the chorus of the song: the less well-known verse begins, in broadly trochaic rhythm, 'All you preachers . . .'

46. Minor adjustments include an idiomatic use of *pote* + imperative, 'at long last' (high-style: Sophocles, *Philoctetes* 816 etc.), and epic correption in the last line, as often in Aristophanic dactyls (Parker 1997, 91–92).

47. Rosenberg (1997), 50.

48. Above, pp. 289–90.

49. Translation based on Silk (2002), 182. For 'low lyric *plus*', see ibid. 189–90.

50. It did not go unnoticed that, in this conversion, Lord Prick himself (*Phalēs Phalēs*) moves, in musical pitch, up and down.

51. Above, p. 290 with n. 8.

52. It is plausibly argued that, for Jolson, 'blackface was probably more of a theatricalization than a caricature' (Goldman 1988, 36). Anecdotal evidence certainly suggests that, for his time, Jolson

was no racist (ibid. 171). The ambivalence nevertheless implicit in his own, as in any, 'minstrelsy' (cf. n. 25 above) might be said to invest the Aristophanic-Aeschylean caricature of Euripides with a certain political edge — but one hesitated to make anything of the point. More broadly, the potentially disturbing resonances of both 'Rock-A-Bye Your Baby' and 'Mississippi Mud' might claim a long-range relevance to the political issue of master/slave (in)equality, which is so apparent in this play (explicit at 21–24, 693–96, 738–53; implicit in the prominent role of the slave Xanthias and his successive role-reversals with his master Dionysus). In our production, again, the point was not pursued.

53. Ostensibly a Sigmund Romberg musical, the show also benefited from the insertion of 'Swanee' (1919: George Gershwin's first hit, with words by Irving Caesar) and 'My Mammy' (1918: words by Lewis and Young; music by Walter Donaldson).

54. A rhyme recorded from 1805: Opie and Opie (1951), 62.

55. The word was so used in black American English long before its appropriation by Rock and Roll in the 1950s: cf. Duke Ellington's early signature tune, 'Rockin' in Rhythm' (1931) or the dance, 'The Eagle Rock', alluded to, for instance, in the 1913 song, 'Ballin' the Jack' (words by Jim Burris; music by Chris Smith).

56. Themselves rhythmically, if not loose, then at least elusive: above, p. 289 with n. 5.

CHAPTER 19

❖

Aristophanes in Translation before 1920

Vasiliki Giannopoulou

The following list is a bibliographical survey consisting mainly of published translations of Aristophanes' comedies, as well some particularly important printed editions and adaptations. The normal practice has been to indicate only the first edition, issue, or printing of a particular translation, unless there are particular reasons otherwise. The survey is far from being exhaustive. There are, without any doubt, more translations of the Aristophanic comedies to be discovered (some of which were never published). The list here is drawn from the results of a larger research project, which lists very many more printed editions, commentaries, performances of and scholarly works on Aristophanes that came into being during the same period. This research was commissioned by the APGRD and the ensuing, much longer list is now housed in its collection, while its findings relating to actual performances have also been incorporated into the APGRD Database of Modern Performances of Ancient Drama, published online at www.apgrd.ox.ac. uk/database.

Most of my sources have been electronic databases: OLIS (Oxford Libraries' Catalogue), COPAC (University research libraries in the UK and Ireland), HOLLIS (Harvard Library Catalogue), Karlsruher Virtuelle Katalog (worldwide meta-library catalogue, especially good for European research libraries), and WorldCat (books and other materials in libraries worldwide). The following list includes all the translations that exist in the above electronic databases, except WorldCat, the enormous holdings of which have been investigated in less detail. The information about early translations of Aristophanes into Russian has been kindly sent to me by Dr Dmitry Trubochkin, who has used V. N. Yarkho.[1] These sources have been supplemented by the following books: the massive Italian *Enciclopedia dello spettacolo*,[2] Gonda Van Steen's book on Aristophanes in modern Greece,[3] J. Werner's study of the scholarly reception of Aristophanes in Germany,[4] Solomos' *The Living Aristophanes*,[5] Flashar's *Inszenierung der Antike*,[6] Foster's *English Translations from the Greek*,[7] France's guide to literature in English translation,[8] and Bolgar's *The Classical Heritage and its Beneficiaries*.[9]

The patterns of activity by translators that this exercise has uncovered tell us a great deal about the nature of Aristophanes' presence in the cultural imagination of each period from the Renaissance onwards. There are many early translations of *Plutus* into Latin. Correspondingly, there are several early performances of *Plutus* (usually in ancient Greek). Aristophanes was at this time seen as a moralist; this inoffensive comedy (lacking in personal attack and obscenity), with the allegorical figures of Plutos and Penia, seems to have fitted the Medieval and Renaissance mental framework. Indeed, this continued a trend already established in Byzantine times: as Solomos points out, in the Byzantine era the most famous comedies seem to have been *Frogs* (of which 78 MSS survived), *Clouds* (127 MSS), and *Plutus*, which is recorded in as many as 148 MSS. Of each of the other comedies we possess 28 MSS, but of the *Thesmophoriazusae* only two.[10]

What is really striking is that all eleven Aristophanic comedies were translated into Italian as early as 1545 by two members of the Rositini family, Bartolomeo and Pietro, who also translated Diogenes Laertius and some Hippocratic and philosophical texts. As Professor Michael Silk has suggested to me, this can be explained in the light of the influence on the Italian Renaissance humanists of the Aristotelian canon (i.e. Aristophanes was seen as *the* canonical example of ancient Greek comedy). The humanists were apparently bent on discovering the Aristophanic 'genius' for themselves and on making it accessible to the reading public. Surely, the intellectual, cultural and socio-economical climate in Renaissance Italy (and especially Venice) was ripe enough for the emergence of such a stellar achievement in translation. After the fall of Constantinople (1453) all the archives and manuscripts of ancient Greek literature held there had passed to Italy. It is significant that Markos Mousouros, the editor of the seminal 1498 edition of nine comedies, had immigrated from Constantinople to Venice.

The 1498 Aldine *editio princeps* of nine comedies does not include *Thesmophoriazusae* and *Lysistrata* (fig. 19.1). Aristophanes' scurrility seems to have been an issue. These two comedies were, however, added to the 1515–16 Florence edition of the nine comedies; it is revealing that the editor apologizes towards the end: 'If the reader finds something offensive in the two comedies this is because everything has been printed as it stood in the Greek original without changes'.

Although *Lysistrata* and *Ecclesiazusae* became very popular from the late ninteenth century onwards, at the time of movements for women's suffrage and emancipation, it emerges from this list that it was *Plutus* and *Clouds* that in the earlier centuries of the Renaissance and Early Modern periods inspired overwhelmingly the greatest interest all over Europe. In sixteenth-century Italy, Germany, France, England, Spain, and Switzerland there are translations and/or imitations, as there were performances, of either or both plays. The 1613 performance of *Clouds* in Strasburg also generated the first translation of Aristophanes into German. *Clouds* also provided the first Russian translation of Aristophanes in 1821. *Plutus* was the first comedy translated into French (1560), Spanish (1577), and English (1651); the 1546 Cambridge performance of *Peace* seems to have been something of an exception. It is in seventeenth-century England, France and Italy that there begin to be signs of interest in *Frogs* and *Birds*: the 'peace', 'Cleon' and 'demagogue' plays *Acharnians*, *Knights*, *Wasps* and *Peace* began to make their first significant impact in the late eighteenth century in response to the French Revolution.

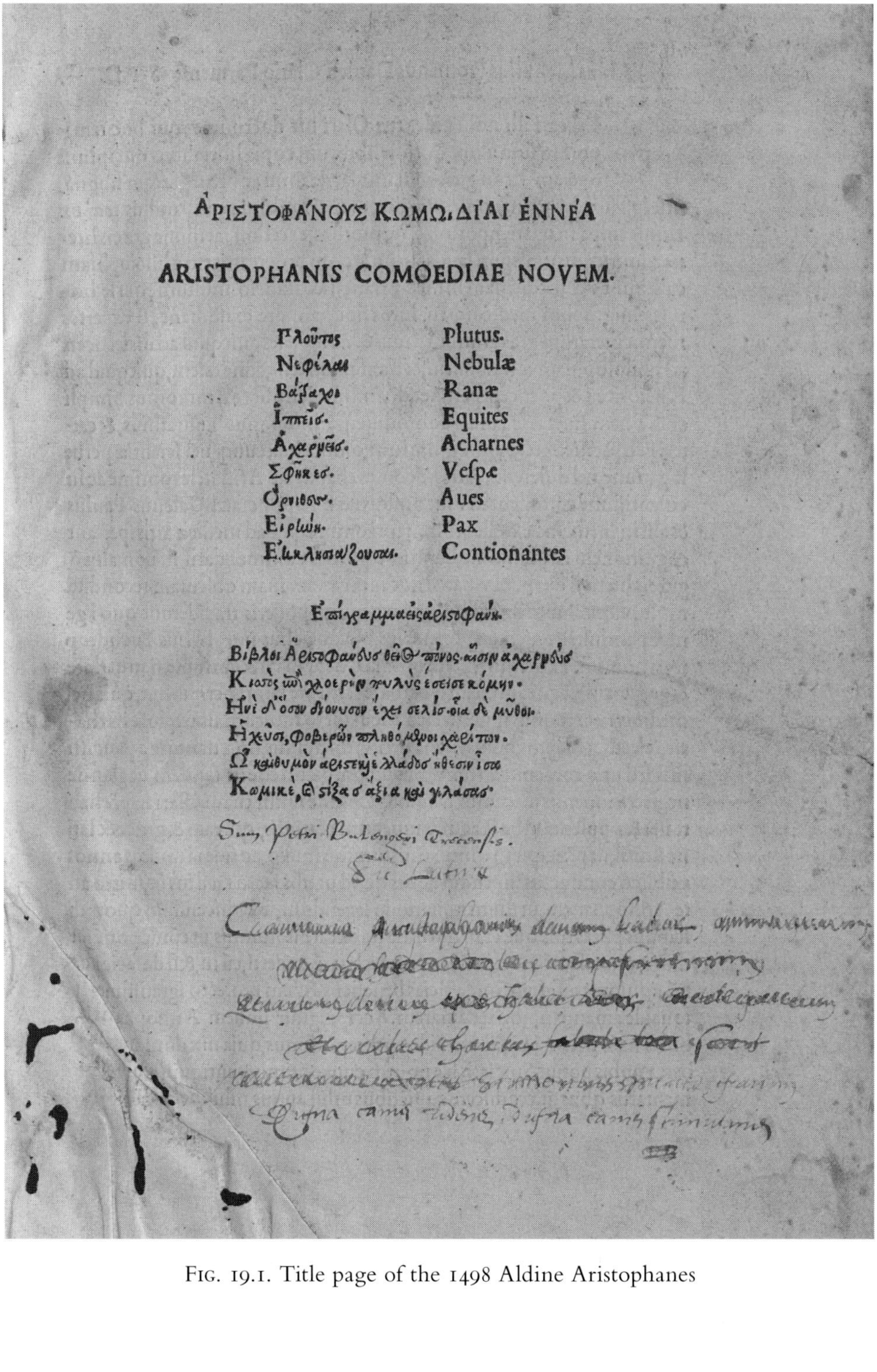

ΑΡΙΣΤΟΦΑΝΟΥΣ ΚΩΜΩΔΙΑΙ ΕΝΝΕΑ

ARISTOPHANIS COMOEDIAE NOVEM.

Πλούτος	Plutus.
Νεφίλαι	Nebulæ
Βάτραχοι	Ranæ
Ἱππεῖσ.	Equites
Ἀχαρνεῖσ.	Acharnes
Σφῆκεσ.	Vespæ
Ὄρνιθεσ.	Aues
Εἰρώνη.	Pax
Ἐκκλησιάζουσαι.	Contionantes

Ἐπίγραμμα εἰς ἀριστοφάνη.

Βίβλοι Ἀριστοφάνους θεῖ᾽ πνεος ἆσιν ἀχαρνεῦσ
Κισσὸς ὣ χλοερὸν πυλὺς ἐσείσε κόμην·
Ἠνὶ δ᾽ ὅσον διονυσον ἔχει σελίσ οἶα δὲ μῦθοι
Ἡ χύσι, φοβερῶν πληθόμενοι χαρίτων·
Ὦ κ᾽θυμὸν ἀριστῆ᾽ ἐλλάδος κ᾽θεσιν ἶσα
Κωμικέ, ὦ σῖζα σ᾽ ἄξια κỳ γλάσσα·

FIG. 19.1. Title page of the 1498 Aldine Aristophanes

Chronological Survey

*c.*1440   Florence
Plutus
The first Latin prose translation of ll. 1–269 of *Plutus* by the Florentine humanist
Leonardo Bruni (1369–1444).[11]

1498   Venice
Aristophanous komodiai ennea = Aristophanis comoediae novem
Edited by Markos Mousouros and Aldus Manutius; preface in Greek and Latin;
the *editio princeps* of nine of the comedies (*Plutus, Clouds, Frogs, Knights, Acharnians,
Wasps, Birds, Peace, Ecclesiazusae*), known as the 'Aldine Aristophanes'; *Lysistrata* and
Thesmophoriazusae were not printed until 1515 (fig. 19.1).

1501   Parma
Plutus; antiqua comoedia ex Aristophane quae nuper in linguam latinam translata est
Translation of *Plutus* into Latin verse by Franciscus Passius.

1504   Italy
Machiavelli writes *Le Maschere* [*The Masks*], a satirical attack on contemporary figures,
said to have been based on *Clouds* and other plays of Aristophanes.[12] The text is lost.

1512   Florence
Performance of *Comedia di Giustizia* by Eufrosino Bonini at the Medici palace; an
adaptation of the first three parts of *Plutus* (ll. 1–801) in five acts.

1515–16 Florence
Aristophanous komodiai ennea
Edited by Bernardo Giunta (Bernardus Iunta), printed by Filippo Giunta; preface
in Latin, text in Greek; contains the same nine comedies as the 1498 *editio princeps*
(see above). This is sometimes found issued with the Giunta edition of the newly
discovered *Thesmophoriazusae* and *Lysistrata* (January 1516): *En tede mikra vivlo
tadenestin; Aristophanous Thesmophoriazousae; tou autou Lysistrate = In hoc pavro* [sic] *libro
haec insunt. Aristophanis Cereris sacra celebrantes. Eiusdem Lysistrate*. Preface in Latin; text
in Greek follows.

1517   Hagenau
Aristophanous eutrapelotatou komikou Ploutos = Aristophanis comici facetissimi Plutus
Edited by Petrus Mosellanus; preface in Latin and in Greek (the argument of the
comedy); text in Greek.

1521   Zwickau
Performances of *Plutus* both in Latin and Greek, directed by George Agricola and
acted by his students.[13]

1524   Basel
Aristophanous komodopoion aristou, Batrachoi = Aristophanis inter comicos summi Ranae
Frogs edited by Ioannes Frobenius; preface in Latin; the argument of the play in Greek,
and text in Greek.

1528   Hagenau
Aristophanis . . . Nubes ac Plutus, comoediæ
Philipp Melanchthon publishes his scholarly edition of *Clouds* and *Plutus*.

1531   Nuremberg
Aristophanis facetisimi comici Plutus
Latin translation of *Plutus* by Thomas Venatorius.
Nuremberg
Pluto dem Gott der reichtumb
Hans Sachs adapts *Plutus* in five acts.

Zurich

Plutus performed in ancient Greek by adherents of Ulrich Zwingli, the Swiss Reformer. Zwingli himself composed the music for the choruses. The 1515–16 Florentine edition of the Greek text was used.[14]

1532   **Basel**

Aristophanous eutrapelotatou komodiai hendeka = Aristophanis facetissimi comoediae undecim

The first printed edition to contain all eleven comedies; text in Greek, preface in Latin; edited by Simon Grynaeus, Professor of Greek at Basel.

1533   **Antwerp**

Aristophanis ... Plutus. A. Chilio interprete. [With] *Podagra Luciani posterior, eodem Chilio interprete*

Metrical translations into Latin of *Plutus* and of the *Podagra* ascribed to Lucian by Adrianus Chilius.[15]

1536   **Cambridge**

Plutus performed according to new rules of pronunciation of ancient Greek established by John Cheke; student actors, at St John's College.[16]

1538   **Venice**

Aristophanis comodiae undecim, è Graeco in Latinum, ad verbum, translatae

Latin translation of all eleven comedies by Andreas Divus, notable for its anticipation of subsequent textual corrections. Reissued in Basel in 1539 (see fig. 19.2), where it was reprinted in 1552; also reprinted in Venice in 1542 and 1548.

1545   **Venice**

Le comedie del facetissimo Aristophane: tradutte di Greco in lingua commune d'Italia

Translation into Italian of all Aristophanic comedies by Bartolomeo Rositini and Pietro Rositini.

1546   **Cambridge**

Peace performed in ancient Greek by student actors at Trinity College; directed by John Dee.[17]

1547   **Paris**

Plutus Aristophanis, comoedia in latinum conversa sermonem, authore M. Cabedio

Plutus translated into Latin by Miguel Cabedo de Vasconcellos (1525–77) who was also the printer/publisher.

1549   **Joachimsthal**

Clouds performed in ancient Greek, directed by [Schulmeister] Eberhart.[18]

Paris

Aristophanous komodopoion aristou Ploutos = Aristophanis poetae comici Plutus

Translated into Latin by Charles Girard.

Paris

Pierre de Ronsard translates at least ll. 462–79 of *Plutus* into French,[19] and also directed a performance of the play at the Collège de Coqueret in either 1549 or 1550.[20]

1556   **Naples**

Coriolani Martirani Cosentini episcopi Sancti Marci: Tragoediae ... Comoediae ...

Latin translation of *Plutus* and *Clouds* by Coriolanus Martiranus, bishop of San Marco Argentano. The edition includes also the Latin translation of eight Greek tragedies, *Odyssey* book 12, the *Batrachomyomachia*, and Apollonius' *Argonautica*.

Utrecht

Aristophanis ... Plutus

Latin translation of *Plutus* by Lambertus Hortensius.

ARISTO

PHANIS, COMICO
rum principis, Comœdiæ undecim,
è Græco in Latinũ, ad uerbum tranſ-
latæ, ANDREA DIVO Iuſtino
politano interprete. Quarum
nomina ſequens indi-
cabit pagina.

BASILEAE,
M. D. XXXIX.

B c VII 689

61.1760 Aul,
N.K.51

FIG. 19.2. Title page of Andreas Divus' Latin translation (1539 printing)

1557   **Utrecht**
Aristophanis ... Nebulae
Latin translation of *Clouds* by Lambertus Hortensius.

*c.*1560   **France**
Le Plutus d'Aristophane
Translated into French by Jean-Antoine de Baïf (not printed, and now lost).[21]

1561   **Utrecht**
Aristophanis ... Equites
Latin translation of *Knights* by Lambertus Hortensius.

Utrecht
Aristophanis ... Ranae
Latin translation of *Frogs* by Lambertus Hortensius.

1575–77 **Pressburg [Bratislava]**
Annotated Latin translation of *Thesmophoriazusae* and *Lysistrata* by Nicasius Ellebodius, unpublished at the time of his death in 1577 and found in Ambrosian MSS.[22]

1577   **Spain**
Plutus translated into Spanish by Pedro Simón Abril.[23]

1579   **Paris**
Pierre Le Loyer writes *Néphélococugie*, a rehandling of *Birds*; it also imitates the style of Rabelais.[24]

1586   **Frankfurt**
Nicodemi Frischlini Aristophanes, veteris comoediae princeps; poeta longe facetissimus et eloquentissimus; repurgatus à mendis, et imitatione Plauti atque Terentii interpretatus, ita ut ferè carmen carmine, numerus numero, pes pedi, modus modo, Latinismus Graecismo respondeat
Latin translation in the style of Roman comedy by Nicodemus Frischlin; Greek and Latin on opposite pages; it contains *Plutus, Knights, Clouds, Frogs, Acharnians*. Reprinted 1597.

1588   **Cambridge**
Plutus performed in ancient Greek.

1589   **Paris**
Q. Septimi Florentis Christiani in Aristophanis Irenam vel Pacem commentaria glossemata ... cum latina graeci dramatis interpretatione latinorum comicorum stylum imitata et eodem genere versuum cum graecis conscripta
Peace translated into Latin in the style of Roman comedy by Florent Chrestien (1541–96; also known as Quintus Septimius Florens Christianus); Greek and Latin text on facing pages.

1593   **Naples**
Aristophanous Ploutos. Aristophanis Plutus
Translated by Orazio Salviani; Greek and Latin on facing pages.

1596   **Leiden**
Aristophanis comoediae quatuor, Plutus, Nebulae, Ranae, Equites; in usum scholarum
Anonymous Latin translation of *Plutus, Clouds, Frogs* and *Knights*.

*c.*1607   **Padua**
Cesare Cremonini, professor of philosophy at Padua, writes *Le Nubi* (*Clouds*), representing his colleague Giorgio Raguseo as a corrupter of young people.[25]

1607   **Geneva**
Aristophanis comoediae undecim
Edited by Edouard Bizet de Charlais and Aemilius Portus. Greek text and Latin translation in parallel columns; Greek notes; some prefatory matter in Latin, some in Greek. Commentator: Gilles Bourdin. Translators: Florent Chrestien (1541–96; also known as Quintus Septimius Florens Christianus), Andreas Divus, Nicodemus Frischlin.

1613   Strasburg
Performance of *Clouds* in ancient Greek at the Theatrum Academicum. Isaac Fröreisen publishes a very free German translation, under the title *Nubes*, to help those in the audience who do not know Greek.[26]

1624   Leiden
Aristophanis comoediae undecim, graecè & latinè
Text in Greek and Latin, edited by several hands led by Joseph Scaliger.

1651   London
Ploutophthalmia ploutogamia: A pleasant comedie, entituled Hey for honesty, down with knavery; translated out of Aristophanes his Plutus
An adaptation of *Plutus* in English (partly in verse) by Thomas Randolph and said to have been augmented by Francis Jaques (fl. 1642), who was also the publisher.[27]

1655   London
Thomas Stanley (1625–78) included a translation of sections of *Clouds* in his *History of Philosophy* (1655). There are several later editions.[28]

1659   London
The World's Idol, Plutus: A Comedy Written in Greek by Aristophanes
Translated by H.H.B., together with his notes, and a short discourse upon it.[29]

c.1659   Saumur
Tanaquili Fabri epistolae, quarum pleraeque ad emendationem scriptorium veterum pertinent. Pars altera. Additae sunt Aristophanis Ecclesiazusai cum interpretatione nova
Works by Tannegui Le Fèvre, including his Latin translation of *Ecclesiazusae*. This was reprinted in the Amsterdam edition of Aristophanes of 1670 (see below), and separately in 1665 and 1674.

1668   Paris
Les Plaideurs: comédie
Jean Racine's only comedy, a free imitation of *Wasps*, was performed in 1668.[30]

1670   Amsterdam
Aristophanis comoediae undecim, Graece et Latine ... ut et nova versio [Ekklesiazouson] à Tan. Fabro facta cum doctissimis eiusdem in eandem comoediam notis
Text in Greek, Latin translation on facing pages (divided into acts and scenes). *Plutus, Nubes, Ranae, Equites, Acharnenses* (translated by Nicodemus Frischlin); *Vespae, Pax, Lysistrata* (translated by Florent Chrestien (1541–96; also known as Quintus Septimius Florens Christianus); *Aves, Concionatrices, Cerealia celebrantes* (translated by Andreas Divus); contains the 1659 translation of *Ecclesiazusae* with notes and and emendations by Tannegui Le Fèvre.

1684   Paris
Le Plutus et les Nuées d'Aristophane. Comedies greques, traduites en françois. Avec des remarques & un examen de chaque piece selon les regles du theatre, par mademoiselle Le Fèvre
Plutus and *Clouds* translated into French prose by Anne Le Fèvre (Madame Dacier, daughter of Tannegui Le Fèvre).[31] Much reprinted.

1688   London?
An Edict in the Roman Law: In the 25. Book of the Digests, title 4. section 10. As concerning the visiting of a big-bellied woman, and the looking after what may be born by her
Anonymous (actually by Gilbert Burnet) text in Latin and English. Includes a translation of part of Aristophanes' *Thesmophoriazusae.*

1695   London
Aristophanous komoidiai duo Ploutos kai Nephelai = Aristophanis comoediae duae Plutus et Nubes
Edited by John Leng (bishop of Norwich) with his Latin translations of both plays.

1710   **Amsterdam**
         Aristophanis comoediae undecim, Graece et Latine, ex codd. mss. emendatae
         Edited by Ludolf Kuster. Greek and Latin text in parallel columns.

1715   **London**
         The Clouds: A Comedy, Translated from the Greek of Aristophanes
         Prose translation by Lewis Theobald.[32]
         London
         Plutus: or, The World's Idol. A Comedy
         Prose translation by Lewis Theobald.[33]

1729   **Paris**
         Œdipe tragédie de Sophocle, et Les oiseaux, comédie d'Aristophane
         Sophocles' *Oedipus* and Aristophanes' *Birds* translated into French by Jean Boivin the
         younger.

1742   **London**
         *Plutus, the God of Riches: A Comedy. Translated from the Original Greek of Aristophanes;
         with Large Notes Explanatory and Critical*
         Prose translation by Henry Fielding (1707–54) and the Revd. Mr William Young
         (d. 1757).[34]

1744   **Germany**
         Christlob Mylius, the cousin of Gotthold Ephraim Lessing, translates into German
         part of *Plutus* (ll. 1–252).

c.1750   **Italy**
         Aristophanes translated by Michelangelo Giacomelli into Italian (unpublished).

1751   **Florence**
         Il Pluto di Aristofane: commedia prima greco-italiana in versi con sue annotazioni
         Plutus translated into Italian verse by Giovanni Battista Terucci; edited with the help
         of Giuseppe Fabiani.

1752   **Venice**
         Il Pluto o sia Il dio della ricchezza, commedia di Aristofane
         Plutus translated into Italian by Michelangelo A. Carmeli.

1754   **Florence**
         Le Nuvole di Aristofane: commedia seconda greco-italiana in versi con sue annotazioni
         Clouds translated into Italian verse by Giovanni Batista Terucci; edited with the help
         of Giuseppe Fabiani. Greek and Italian text on facing pages, with notes in Italian.

1759   **London**
         *The Clouds: A Comedy. Written by Aristophanes, the wittiest man of his age, against Socrates
         ... translated, with the principal scholia, and notes*
         Edited and translated into English by James White.

1760   **Leiden**
         *Aristophanis comoediae undecim: graece et latine; ad fidem optimorum codicum mss. emendatae
         cum nova octo comoediarum interpretatione Latina ...*
         Edition of all eleven plays with notes and Latin translations (some of them new) by
         Stephan Bergler, Karl Andreas Duker, and Pieter Burman *et al.* Two volumes.

1767–68 **Germany**
         Christian August Clodius translates parts of some Aristophanic comedies.

1768   **Coburg**
         Chrestomathia Graeca poetica
         By Gottlieb Christoph Harles. It includes Aristophanes' *Plutus* in Greek, with parallel
         Latin translation by Stephan Bergler, and notes in Latin by Karl Andreas Duker.

1772   **Bamberg and Würzburg**
         Die Wolken. Eine Komödie, aus dem Griechischen des Aristophanes übersetzt
         Clouds translated into German by Johann Justus Herwig.

1776   Germany
Jakob Michael Reinhold Lenz writes a play about Christoph Martin Wieland based on *Clouds*, his *Vertheidigung des Herrn Wieland gegen die Wolken von dem Verfasser der Wolken*. Unpublished until 1902.[35]

1780   Weimar
Performance of *Die Vögel*, directed and adapted by Johann Wolfgang von Goethe; influenced by *Birds*. See under 1787.[36]

1781   Parma
Socrates: Fabula ex Aristophanis Nubibus ad usum Collegii nobilium Parmae. Versio Latina Coroliani Martirani … eiusdem latinae versionis paraphrasis italica Socrate: comedia tratta dale Nubi di Aristofane da rappresentarsi nel Collegio de' nobili di Parma
Published version of *Clouds* as presented at the Collegio de' nobili di Parma, with Latin translation by Coriolanus Martiranus (see under 1556 above) and Italian paraphrase by Count A. C. F. Bernieri Terrarossa.

Strasburg
Comoediae in latinum sermonem conversae
Aristophanes' comedies translated into Latin by Richard Franz P. Brunck. Three volumes. These translations were reprinted to accompany the Greek of several different editions, including *Aristophanis comoediam Plutum* edited by Johann Dieterich Albrecht Münter (Celle, 1784), the thirteen-volume edition by various hands including C. D. Beck and G. Dindorf published in Leipzig between 1794 and 1834, and the edition of Dindorf's text that E. P. M. Longueville published in Paris in 1860–62.

1783   Basel
Die Frösche: Ein Lustspiel aus dem Griechischen des Aristophanes
Translation by Johann Georg Schlosser (brother-in-law of Goethe). First German-language published version of *Frogs*.

1784   Halle
Die Wolken. Eine Komödie des Aristophanes
Translation of *Clouds* into German by the philologist Christian Gottfried Schütz published in *Literarische Spaziergänge*, April 1784. A second edition was published separately in Halle in 1798. This translation included stage-direction notes ('Regie-bemerkungen'), which was uncommon.[37] In 1770 Schütz had published (also at Halle) an edition of *Clouds* in Greek for the use of his students.

Paris
Théâtre d'Aristophane
Aristophanes translated into French, partly in verse, partly in prose, with the fragments of Menander and Philemon, by Louis Poinsinet de Sivry. Four volumes. Second edition in 1790.

1785   Oxford
The Frogs: A Comedy
English translation by Charles Dunster.

1787   Leipzig
Die Vögel. Nach dem Aristophanes. Von Goethe
Birds adapted into German by Johann Wolfgang von Goethe. 8th edition.

1788   Paris
Aristophane
Selections from the plays of Aristophanes, translated into French, as volume 10 of the series *Bibliothèque universelle des dames*.

Leipzig
Aristophanis Nubes, graece et latine
Clouds in Greek and Latin by Gottlieb Christoph Harles.

1792   Eton
Aristophanis Plutus, cum scholiis Graecis selectis, in usum studiosae juventutis
Greek text divided into acts and scenes with scholia, followed by an anonymous Latin
translation, which is also divided into acts and scenes.
London
Reform: A Farce, Modernised from Aristophanes
Adapted from *Plutus* by Francis Wrangham.

1794   **Germany**
Friedrich August Wiedeburg translates into German a part of the *Ecclesiazusae*.
Madrid
El Pluto, comedia de Aristófanes
Translated into Spanish by Pedro Estala.

1794–1806 **Germany**
Christoph Martin Wieland publishes German translations of *Knights, Birds, Acharnians*
and *Clouds* in the journal *Das Attische Museum*. *Knights* (1797) is subtitled *Die Demagogen*
and is explicitly aimed against Robespierre and the French revolution. Wieland's
translations were published separately in Vienna in 1813.

1795   **Germany**
Wilhelm von Humboldt translates into German the first act of *Lysistrata*.

1797   **Germany**
Gottfried Ernst Groddeck translates *Ecclesiazusae* into German for the first time. This
was never published.
London
The Clouds of Aristophanes
Translated into English by Richard Cumberland (1732–1811).
Paris
Athènes pacifiée
Three-act comedy in prose by Jean François de Cailhava, using material from all
eleven comedies of Aristophanes.

1802   **Paris**
*Lisistrata ou les Athéniennes: comédie en un acte et en prose, mêlée de vaudevilles, imitée
d'Aristophane; dont les représentations ont été suspendues par Ordre.*
Adaptation of *Lysistrata* by François-Benoît Hoffman.[38]

1804   **London and Florence**
Opere postume di Vittorio Alfieri
Alfieri's influential Italian translation of Aristophanes' *Frogs* is first published in this
collection.[39]

1806   **Cologne**
Lysistrata; ein Lustspiel des Aristophanes
First complete published translation of *Lysistrata* into German by August Christian
Borheck.

1807   **Cologne**
Der Friede; ein Lustspiel
Translation of *Peace* into German by August Christian Borheck.
Tübingen
Plutos; eine Komödie
Verse translation of *Plutus* into German by Karl Philipp Conz.

1808   **Zürich and Leipzig**
Die Frösche; eine Komödie
Verse translation of *Frogs* into German by Karl Philipp Conz.[40]

1810   **Giessen and Darmstadt**

Komödien von Aristophanes. Part 1: *Die Wolken*

Clouds translated by Friedrich Gottlieb Welcker.

1811   **Berlin**

Aristophanes Wolken: eine Komödie griechisch und deutsch

Clouds in Greek and German; edited and translated by Friedrich August Wolf.

1812   **Giessen and Darmstadt**

Komödien von Aristophanes. Part 2: *Die Frösche*

Frogs translated by Friedrich Gottlieb Welcker.

Berlin

Aus Aristophanes' Acharnern. Griechisch und deutsch mit einigen Scholien

Extracts from *Acharnians* edited and translated by Friedrich August Wolf. Bound with his *Clouds* of 1811.

1817   **Paris**

Les comices d'Athènes; où, Les femmes orateurs. Comédie vaudeville en un Acte, traduit du grec d' Aristophane

Comedy in one act, adapted from Aristophanes' *Ecclesiazusae* by Eugène Scribe and Antoine François Varner.[41]

London

The Frogs

A verse translation by John Hookham Frere of the first 837 lines of the play, printed on paper watermarked 1814 and 1815 but only privately circulated. See below under 1839.[42]

1820–22 **London**

The Comedies of Aristophanes

Translated by Thomas Mitchell and Richard Cumberland. Two volumes containing *Acharnians*, *Knights*, *Clouds*, and *Wasps*.

1821   **Braunschweig**

Aristofanes

The eleven comedies translated into German by Johann Heinrich Voss with notes by Heinrich Voss. Three volumes.

St Petersburg

Облака. Комедія Аристофана

Clouds translated in prose from Greek by I. M. Muravyov-Apostol. Published with the Greek original. First Russian translation of Aristophanes.

1822   **Oxford**

The Comedies of Plutus and The Frogs

Literally translated into English prose from the Greek of Aristophanes; with notes from the scholia and other commentaries.

1824   **London**

The Birds of Aristophanes

Translated with notes by Henry Francis Cary.

1825   **Odense**

Aristophanes' Komedier

Aristophanes' *Frogs*, *Clouds*, *Plutus* and *Acharnians* translated into Danish by Johan Krag.

London

Plutus, or, The God of Riches; A Comedy of Aristophanes

Translated by Edmund F. J. Carrington.

1826   **Stockholm**

Molnen; lustspel af Aristophanes

Clouds translated into Swedish by Johan Henrik Thomander.

Leipzig
Aristophanis comoediae, 13 vols. in 14
Edited by F. Invernizi; contains a Latin translation.

1828   **London**
Aristophanis comoediae cum scholiis et varietate lectionis; recensuit Immanuel Bekkerus. Accedunt versio latina …
Edited by Immanuel Bekker. Greek text with added Latin translation and notes in five volumes.

1829   **Stuttgart**
August von Platen publishes *Der romantische Oedipus*, a five-act comedy satirizing the works of Karl Immermann and Heinrich Heine, which imitates *Frogs*.

1830   **Oxford**
The Acharnians, Knights, Wasps, and Birds
Translated into English prose by 'a graduate of the University of Oxford' (actually John Wood Warter).

Paris
Comédies d'Aristophane
Complete plays translated into French by Nicolas-Louis-Marie Artaud. Two volumes. Subsequent editions published in 1841, 1879, 1894.

1832   **Leipzig**
Plutos: ein Lustspiel
Plutus translated into German verse by Emanuel Lindemann.

1833   **Oxford**
The Ecclesiazusae, or Female Parliament, translated from Aristophanes
Translated into English by Rowland Smith.

1834   **London**
Aristophanous Ploutos. The Plutus of Aristophanes, from the text of Dindorf; with critical and explanatory remarks, partly original, partly selected from the scholia and various commentators, … for the use of schools
By Henry Parker Cookesley.[43]

Uppsala
Demagogerna; Lustspel af Aristophanes
Knights translated into Swedish by Carl August Hagberg.

1835–38   **Berlin**
Des Aristophanes Werke
The comedies of Aristophanes translated into German by J. G. Droysen. Three volumes. Second edition 1869; reprinted 1881.

1836   **Stuttgart**
Weibervolksversammlung
German translation of *Ecclesiazusae* with notes and introductory material by Karl Friedrich Schnitzer (pseud.: Dr Glypheus). See also under 1842–54.

1837   **Oxford**
The Comedies of Aristophanes
Translated into blank verse by C. A. Wheelwright, with introductory materials. Two volumes.

London
The Comedies of Aristophanes
Translated into corresponding English metres by Benjamin Dann Walsh. It contains *Acharnians, Knights*, and *Clouds*. Reprinted 1848.

1839   **London**
The Frogs
Translated into English verse by John Hookham Frere: 'The greater part of this play … had been printed upwards of twenty years ago, having been intended for private distribution'.
Valetta
The Acharnians and *The Knights*
Verse translation by John Hookham Frere, privately printed in Malta. Reprinted with the addition of *Birds* in London in 1840, 1886, 1890, 1895, 1908 (with *Frogs* and *Peace*), 1911 and in various different collections of translations of Greek drama subsequently.
Valetta
The Birds
Verse translation by John Hookham Frere.

1840   **Oxford**
The Clouds, and Peace, of Aristophanes
Translated into English prose by 'a graduate of the University of Oxford' (actually Sir Edwin Arnold).

1841   **Athens**
Gynaikokratia
A five-act comedy in modern Greek by Dimitrios K. Vyzantios, imitating both *Lysistrata* and *Ecclesiazusae*.

1842   **London**
Aristophanous Nephelai
A literal translation of *Clouds*, with Greek text and English notes, by Charles P. Gerard. Privately printed.

1842–54 **Stuttgart**
Aristophanes Werke. Im alten Versmaass übersetzt
The eleven comedies translated by Karl Friedrich Schnitzer. Eleven volumes. Second edition published in 1875.

1843   **Paris**
Plutus
Translated into French with notes by D. Cattant. Reissued in Berlin (1877) and Paris (1897).

1843–46 **Leipzig**
Die Lustspiele des Aristophanes
The comedies translated by Hieronymus Müller. Three volumes. Second edition published in 1861.

1844   **Berlin**
Frösche
Rumoured performance of *Frogs* in an adaptation by August Kopisch.[44]

1844   **Dublin**
The Knights of Aristophanes
Literally translated into English prose by Frederick Henry Williams.
Leipzig
Der Reichthum von Aristophanes
Plutus in German by Gotthard Oswald Marbach.

1845   **St Petersburg**
Облака
Clouds translated from Greek by E. M. Karnovich.[45] Translation in verse, but not corresponding with the Greek metres. First Russian verse translation of this play.

1845–48 Frankfurt

Aristophanes translated into German by Ludwig Seeger, a Swabian democrat. Republished in Munich in 1913. Three volumes.

1846   London

The Birds of Aristophanes; a dramatic experiment in one act, being an humble attempt to adapt the said Birds to this climate by giving them new names, new feathers, new songs and new tales

By James Robinson Planché. First performed 13 April 1846.[46]

1847   London

The Plutus of Aristophanes

Translated into English verse, by Charles P. Gerard

1848   Oxford

The Frogs of Aristophanes Translated into English by Charles Cavendish Clifford.

1849   Paris

Plutus; ou La richesse, comédie d'Aristophane traduite du grec

Plutus translated into French verse by Eugène Fallex.

1850   Ahmedabad

Lakshmi

Plutus adapted into Gujarati by Dalpatram Dahyabhai; assisted by Alexander Kinloch Forbes.[47]

Turin

Commedie di Aristofane

The comedies translated into Italian by Coriolano di Bagnolo. Two volumes.

1852   Oxford

The Clouds of Aristophanes: The Greek Text with a Translation into Corresponding Metres, and Original Notes

By Benjamin Bickley Rogers. Reissued in 1916, 1919 and 1930.

1852–53 Turin

Commedie di Aristofane, i: *Commedie politiche*; ii: *Commedie fantastiche e di satira personale*

Aristophanes translated into Italian by Domenico Capellina. Two volumes.

1853   London

The Comedies of Aristophanes

A new literal translation, from the revised text of Dindorf, with notes and extracts from the best metrical versions by William James Hickie. Much reprinted in both Britain and the USA.

1854   London

The Knights of Aristophanes

Literally translated from the text of Thomas Mitchell by H. Wallace.

1855   Berlin

Die Ritter des Aristophanes. Deutsch und griechisch

Knights translated into German by E. Born.

1855–61 Stuttgart

Aristophanes Lustspiele

Complete comedies translated into German verse by Johannes Minckwitz. Three volumes. Reprinted 1881 and 1887.

1856   Constantinople

Acharnēs: kōmōdia eis tēn kathomiloumenēn paraphrastheisa

Acharnians translated into a moderate Greek Katharevousa by Ioannis Raptarchis.[48]

Copenhagen

Fuglene, Komedie af Aristophanes

Birds translated into Danish by Niels Vinding Dorph.

Leipzig

Die Frösche des Aristophanes. Griechisch und deutsch mit Einleitung und Commentar von Herbert Pernice

Frogs in Greek and German, with introduction and commentary by Herbert V. A. Pernice.

1857   **Copenhagen**

Ridderne, Komedie af Aristophanes

Knights translated into Danish by Niels Vinding Dorph.

Paris and Brussels

Les Nuées d'Aristophane, comédie en 5 actes

A verse translation of *Clouds* into French by A. J. Bécart.

1858   **Copenhagen**

Freden, Komedie af Aristophanes

Peace translated into Danish by Niels Vinding Dorph.

1859   **Paris**

Plutus, comédie

Plutus translated into French verse by J.-B. Bernot, with notes.

Paris

Scènes d'Aristophane

Selections from Aristophanes, translated into French verse by Eugène Fallex. Reprinted 1864.

1860   **Athens**

Aristofanous Nefelai, Eirini, Ornithes

Modern Greek Katharevousa translation of *Clouds*, *Peace* and *Birds* by Alexander Rizos Rangavis; published with his translation of Sophocles' *Antigone*.

Copenhagen

Aristofanes' Komedier

Niels Vinding Dorph's Danish translations of *Birds*, *Knights*, and *Peace* (first published in 1856, 1857, and 1858 respectively) are published together with *Hvepserne* (*Wasps*).

Paris

Aristophane

Complete plays of Aristophanes translated with introduction and notes by Constant Poyard, in one volume. Reprinted in at least 14 editions over several decades.

1861   **Athens**

Ploutos

Demotic prose adaptation of *Plutus* by Michail Chourmouzis of Constantinople, published anonymously in the Athenian newspaper *Merimna*, and staged by Sofoklis Karydis in 1868.[49]

1861–62 **Leipzig**

Die Lustspiele des Aristophanes

The comedies translated into German, using the original Greek metres, by Johann Jakob Christian Donner. Three volumes.

1862   **Leipzig and Vienna**

Die Verschworenen, oder Der häusliche Krieg. Komische Oper in einem Akt

Libretto by Ignaz Franz Castelli based on Aristophanes' *Lysistrata* and *Ecclesiazusae*: music composed in 1823 by Franz Schubert. Publication followed two performances in 1861.

Neisse [Nysa]

Die Vögel nach dem Aristophanes von Goethe

Philipp Bauer's edition of Goethe's 1780 adaptation of *Birds*.

Paris
Comédies d'Aristophane
Translated into French by Amédée Fleury. Three volumes.

1863 **Amiens**
Les Oiseaux; traduction nouvelle
Birds translated into French by Henri Dauphin.

1864 **Leipzig**
Die Acharner des Aristophanes
Edited and translated by Woldemar Ribbeck.

1866 **Leipzig**
Aus Friedrich Rückert's Nachlass, herausgegeben von Heinrich Rückert
This includes Friedrich Rückert's German translation of *Birds*.

London
The Peace of Aristophanes
The Greek text revised; with a translation into corresponding metres, and
original notes, by Benjamin Bickley Rogers. Reissued in 1867, 1913, and 1930.

Posen [Poznań]
Aristofanesa Chmury
Clouds translated into Polish by Marceli Motty.

1867 **Berlin**
Die Ritter des Aristophanes; griechisch und deutsch, mit kritischen und erklärenden Anmerkungen
Knights edited and translated by Woldemar Ribbeck.

London
Acharnians and *Knights* translated by William Charles Green.

London
Eight Comedies of Aristophanes, Translated into Rhymed Metres
Translation by Leonard-Hampson Rudd of *Acharnians, Knights, Clouds, Wasps, Peace, Birds, Frogs, Plutus* in a single volume.

1868 **Halle**
Die Acharner, in deutscher Übersetzung
Acharnians translated into German by Rudolf Westphal.

London
Clouds
Translated by William Charles Green.

London
Wasps
Translated by William Charles Green.

1869 **Florence**
Aristophanous Ploutos. Il Pluto di Aristophane. Greco e Italiano
Edited by Carlo Castellani. Greek and Italian text on facing pages.

Helsingborg
Aristophanes' lustspel Foglarne
Birds translated into Swedish by Hjalmar Säve.

Turin
Recitiamo Aristofane
Two-act comedy by Ottavio Boerio which adapts the first part of Aristophanes'
Plutus.

Zutphen
Nephelokokkygia, de Wolkenstad der Vogelen
Version of *Birds* in Dutch by Phantastikos (pseudonym).

1872   **Edinburgh**
        Aristophanes
        English translation by William Lucas Collins; published as volume 14 in the Ancient
        Classics for English Readers series.

1873   **London**
        The Peace of Aristophanes
        Translated by William Charles Green.
        Naples
        Le Nuvole d'Aristofane
        Clouds translated into Italian by Vincenzo Mannini.

1874   **Cambridge**
        The Birds of Aristophane
        Literally translated, with notes, by William Charles Green.
        Jena
        Die Gründer: eine griechische Komödie
        The Founders, an 'Aristophanic' political comedy in ancient Greek by Julius Richter.
        Never performed.
        London
        The Birds of Aristophanes
        Translated into English verse, with introduction, notes and appendices, by Benjamin
        Hall Kennedy.
        Paris
        Extraits d'Aristophane, accompagnés d'analyses et de remarques philologiques et historiques,
        traduction française
        Excerpts from *Clouds*, *Wasps*, *Frogs* and *Plutus* translated into French by J. Helleu.
        Warsaw
        Птицы
        Russian translation of *Birds* by M. Skvortsov.

1875   **Budapest**
        A Békák
        Frogs translated into Hungarian by Ignác Veress.
        London
        The Wasps of Aristophanes
        The Greek text revised, with a translation into corresponding metres and original
        notes, by Benjamin Bickley Rogers. Reissued 1876, 1919, 1920.
        Paris
        Extrait du Plutus, scène de la Pauvreté ...
        By Louis Humbert; with an analysis of the play, literary, and grammatical notes and
        extracts from *Timon* by Lucian.
        Vitoria
        Comedias escogidas de Aristófanes [*Selected Comedies of Aristophanes*]
        Translated into Spanish by D. Federico Baráibar y Zumárraga, with an introduction
        by Fermín Herrán (see also under 1880–81).

1878   **Leipzig**
        Die Acharner: Ein Lustspiel des Aristophanes
        Translated into German by Emil Schinck.
        London
        The Revolt of the Women: A Free Translation of the Lysistrata of Aristophanes
        By Benjamin Bickley Rogers. Reissued in 1911.

1879   **Cambridge**
        The Frogs of Aristophanes
        By William Charles Green.

Leipzig
Die Frösche. Ein Lustspiel des Aristophanes
Frogs translated into German by Emil Schinck.

1880   **Budapest**
Aristophanes Vigjátékai [Comedies]
Translated into Hungarian by János Arany. Three volumes.

Cambridge
The Clouds of Aristophanes
Literally translated, with notes, by William Charles Green. Reprinted 1889.

Leipzig
Die Vögel. Ein Lustspiel des Aristophanes
Translated into German by Emil Schinck.

London
Studies in Song
By Algernon Charles Swinburne; it includes his forty-line 'Grand Chorus of Birds from Aristophanes', reproduced in editions of his poems.[50]

London
The Wasps
Edited by William Charles Green. With this are bound English and French translations of *Wasps*.

1880–81 **Madrid**
Comedias de Aristófanes
Translated into Spanish by D. Federico Baráibar y Zumárraga, with an introductory essay on Aristophanes in Spain by M. Menéndez y Pelayo. Three volumes. See also under 1875.

1881   **Cambridge**
The Plutus of Aristophanes
Edited by William Charles Green; followed by English translation. Reissued 1887, 1901, 1913.

Florence
Le Nuvole di Aristofane
A verse translation of *Clouds* by Augusto Franchetti, with an introduction and notes by Domenico Comparetti.

Paris
Théâtre complet: Aristophane
French translation by André Charles Brotier; with an introduction and remarks on each play by Louis Humbert. Two volumes. Revised edition in 1882, 1889.

Stettin [= Szczecin]
Aristophanes: Lustspiele. Die Acharner; Die Ritter
Acharnians and *Knights* in German verse translation by A. F. W. Wissman.

1882   **London**
The Acharnians of Aristophanes
Translated into English verse by Charles James Billson.

Oxford
The Clouds
Edited by W. W. Merry (1835–1918), with introduction and notes. With this are bound: *Aristophanes: The Clouds*, literally translated by T. J. Arnold (see under 1885); also another English translation of the work, and a French one, both extracted from unidentified collections.

1883   **Cambridge**
The Birds of Aristophanes
The Greek text, as performed by members of the University at the Theatre Royal, Cambridge, November, 1883; with the English version of Benjamin Hall Kennedy.[51]
Cambridge
The Birds of Aristophanes
Translated by John Hookham Frere (1769–1846). The translation of the Parabasis, ll. 685–723, in anapaestic heptameters (corresponding to Greek tetrameters) by A. C. Swinburne. Edited by John Willis Clark. Reprinted: 1889 (edited by William Charles Green).
Dublin and London
The Acharnians of Aristophanes
Translated into English verse by Robert Yelverton Tyrrell (1844–1914). Reprinted: Dublin and London, 1890; Oxford and New York, 1914.
Oxford
A Literal Translation of Aristophanes' The Acharnians, Arranged for Interleaving with the Text of the Clarendon Press Edition
'By a first classman of Balliol College'. Reprinted 1898.
Oxford
A Literal Translation of Aristophanes' The Clouds
'By a first classman of Balliol College'.
Oxford
A Literal Translation of Aristophanes' The Frogs
'By a first classman of Balliol College'. From the text of Paley. Reprinted 1895 (revised by E. L. Hawkins).
Palermo
Le nuvole di Aristofane nel secolo XIX
Clouds in updated Italian adaptation by Giovanni Perez.
Uppsala
Molnen: lustspel
Clouds translated into Swedish by Alarik Hallstrøm.

1885   **Bologna**
Le Rane
A verse translation of *Frogs* into Italian, with introduction and notes, by Carlo Castellani (second edition published in 1886; third edition in 1891–92).
Cambridge
The Plutus of Aristophanes
Translated by Herbert Hailstone.
Leiden
Blijspelen van Aristophanes, stuk 1: *De Acharniërs*
Dutch translation by J. van Leeuwen, Jr. No more published.
London
The Music to The Birds of Aristophanes, as Performed at Cambridge, November 1883
Composed by Charles Hubert Hastings Parry (1848–1918); with an English version by A. W. Verrall (1851–1912). Reprinted in 1903: see below.
St Petersburg
Ахарняне. Комедія Аристофана
Verse translation of *Acharnians*, partly in original metres, by M. Georgievsky.[52]
Stuttgart
Aristophanes' Werke
Clouds and *Frogs* translated into German, with introduction and notes by Jakob Mähly.

1885/86   **St Petersburg**
Золотой дѣдъ: комедія в трехъ дѣйствіяхъ
The Golden Grandfather: comedy in three acts freely adapted from Aristophanes by
D. V. Averkiev.

1886   **Casale Monferrato**
Il Pluto di Aristophane
Plutus translated into Italian verse by Giulio Cesare Bernardi.
Città di Castello
Le Rane di Aristofane
Frogs translated into Italian verse by Augusto Franchetti, with introduction and notes
by Domenico Comparetti.
Philadelphia, Pennsylvania
*The Acharnians of Aristophanes: Performed by Undergraduates of the University of Pennsylvania,
in the Academy of Music, in Philadelphia, May 14th and 15th, 1886.* Parallel Greek text and
English translation.[53]

1887   **Oxford**
The Knights
Edited with an introduction and notes by W. W. Merry.
St Petersburg
Лягушки, комедія Аристофана
Russian prose translation of *Frogs*, with a commentary, by K. Neylisov.

1888   **Cambridge**
The Clouds of Aristophanes
Translated by Herbert Hailstone. Reissued 1892.
Kristiania [= Oslo]
Fuglene, en dramatisk Spøg efter Aristophanes
A Norwegian version of *Birds* by 'Mumle' (pseudonym for Kristian B.-R. Aars).
Paris
Mélanges grecs
Includes a scene from *Frogs* translated by Fernand Allègre.
Paris
Les Oiseaux
A new French translation of *Birds* by Félix Rabbe.

1889   **London**
The Plutus of Aristophanes
With an English translation, introduction, and notes by M. T. Quinn. University
Correspondence College Tutorial Series. Reprinted several times.
Paris
Comédies de Aristophane
A new translation, with introduction and notes, by Charles Marie Zévort; edited by
Jacques François Denis (see also under 1898 below).

1890   **London**
Odes from the Greek Dramatists: Translated into Lyric Metres by English Poets and Scholars
Edited by Alfred W. Pollard; it contains Oscar Wilde's versions of choral odes
from *Clouds*.[54]
Schaffhausen
Die Wespen
Wasps translated into German using the original metres by Robert Lang of the
Gymnasium in Schaffhausen.

1891   **Florence**
Pluto, Commedia di Aristofane
Plutus in Italian translation by Luigi Rasi, introduced by Augusto Franchetti.

1892   **Oxford and London**
        The Frogs of Aristophanes
        Greek text adapted for performance by the Oxford University Dramatic Society in
        1892, printed with an English version partly adapted from that of John Hookham
        Frere and partly written for the occasion by D. G. Hogarth and A. D. Godley.[55]
        St Petersburg
        Всадники
        Knights translated from the Greek by A. Stankevitch. Translation in verse, for the most
        part in the original metres.

1893   **Boston and New York**
        Greek Poets in English Verse, by Various Translators
        Edited with introduction and notes by William Hyde Appleton. It includes
        Aristophanes.
        Glasgow
        Aristophanes: Peace
        A literal translation, published in the Glasgow Translations of the Classics series.
        London
        Aristophanes' Vespae
        Translated by Francis Giffard Plaistowe. University Correspondence College Tutorial
        series.
        London
        Aristophanes' Vespae
        Wasps literally translated by J. A. Prout. Kelly's Keys to the Classics series.
        London
        Stories from the Greek Comedians: Aristophanes, Philemon, Diphilus, Menander,
        Apollodorus
        By Alfred John Church.
        Paris
        Lysistrata
        Maurice Donnay's four-act comedy in French prose based on *Lysistrata* (first performed
        in 1892). This work was much performed, reprinted, and translated: for example, into
        modern Greek in 1910 and English in 1919 (see below).
        St Petersburg
        Облака
        Prose translation of *Clouds* from the Greek by V. A. Alekseev.

1894   **Boston, Massachusetts**
        Stories from Plato and Other Classical Writers: Hesiod, Homer, Aristophanes, Ovid, Catullus,
        and Pliny
        By Mary E. Burt.
        Città di Castello
        Gli uccelli di Aristophane
        Birds translated into Italian verse by Augusto Franchetti, with an introduction and
        notes by Domenico Comparetti.
        Copenhagen
        Frøerne; Komedie
        Frogs translated into Danish by Peter Petersen.
        London and New York
        The Acharnians of Aristophanes
        Translated into English by W. H. Covington; with an introduction and memoir.

1896   **Cambridge**
        Aristophanes, Vespae
        Wasps translated into English by Herbert Hailstone.

Cambridge
The Wasps of Aristophanes
Literally translated, with notes and test papers, by John William Rundall.
Copenhagen
Skyerne: Komedie
Clouds translated into Danish by Johan B. Koch.
Eton
Plutus of Aristophanes up to date; or, Mammon Made Righteous
An imitation of Aristophanes' *Plutus* by Arthur C. James.
London
Aristophanes' Ranae
A close translation of *Frogs*, with test papers, by Francis Giffard Plaistowe. University Tutorial Series.
London
The Birds of Aristophanes, in English Rhyme for English Readers
Translated by George Samuel Hodges.
London
The Lysistrata of Aristophanes: Now First Wholly Translated into English and Illustrated with Eight Full-Page Drawings
The prose translation is 'notorious for its inclusion of comically grotesque and wildly indecent illustrations' by Aubrey Vincent Beardsley.[56] The translator was later identified as Samuel Smith.[57]
London
Ranae
Frogs literally translated by J. A. Prout. Kelly's Keys to the Classics series.
Lemberg [Lwów, now L'viv]
Lysistrata, czyli Wojna i Pokój [Lysistrata, or War and Peace]
A four-act prose translation into Polish, of Maurice Donnay's French adaptation of the Greek play, by Stanisław Koźmian.
New York
Library of the World's Best Literature: Ancient and Modern
Edited by C. D. Warner *et al.* This thirty-volume work contains Aristophanes.
Paris
Lysistratè, comédie d'Aristophane
By Robert Le Minihy de La Villehervé.
Paris
Plutus, adaptation d'Aristophane
By Paul Gavault.

1897   **Cambridge**
The Wasps of Aristophanes
As performed at Cambridge, 19–24 November 1897. With the verse translation by Benjamin Bickley Rogers. English and Greek on facing pages. Reprinted: 1909, 1916. American reprints: New York, 1916; New York, 1917.
Oxford
The Knights of Aristophanes
Adapted for performance by the Oxford University Dramatic Society, 1897, with an English version adapted from that of John Hookham Frere by L. E. Berman. Greek and English on opposite pages.
Paris
Aristophane
New translation into French by Eugène Talbot (1814–1894), with a preface by Sully Prudhomme. Two volumes.

St Petersburg
Комедіи Аристофана
First complete works of Aristophanes to be published in Russian; translated from the
French translations of Nicolas-Louis-Marie Artaud (see under 1830); in prose.
St Petersburg
Женщины на праздникѣ Өесмофорій
Thesmophoriazusae translated from the Greek by V. V. Trofimov. In iambic verse.

*c.*1897   Prague
Komedie Aristofanovy: Žáby; Plutos
Czech translations of *Frogs* and *Plutus* by Augustin Krejcí.

1898   Athens
The Acharnians; The Knights; The Clouds
Vol. 7 of *The Athenian Society's Publications*; the plays translated with introduction and
notes. Only 250 copies, privately printed for the Athenian Society.
Città di Castello
I Cavalieri
Knights translated into Italian verse by Augusto Franchetti, with introduction and
notes by Domenico Comparetti.
Città di Castello
Il Pluto di Aristofane
Translated by Augusto Franchetti, with notes by Domenico Comparetti, and
performed in Florence on 23 April 1898.[58] Reissued in 1900.

1901–03 Göteborg
Komedier af Aristophanes
Swedish translation by Johannes Paulson. Two volumes.
Paris
Lysistrata
Translated into French, with an introduction and notes, by Charles Marie Zévort
(see above under 1889). This separate edition of *Lysistrata* is decorated with more than
100 engravings ('gravures') by Notor, 'reproduites en couleurs d'après les documents
authentiques des musées d'Europe'.
Stockholm
Riddarne: Lustspel
Knights translated into Swedish by Johan Fredrik Håhl.

1899   England
The Frogs: Acting Edition, Prepared for Performance at Downside College
With a translation by Anthony Lawrence Kynaston. Privately printed.
Florence
Versione poetica degli Uccelli
A poetic version of *Birds* in Italian by Ettore Romagnoli, with preface by Augusto
Franchetti.
Leiden
Plutus: God van den rijkdom
Translation into Dutch by Johannes Benedictus Kan.
Rome
[Aristofane] Le concionatrici; saggio di traduzione poetica
Ecclesiazusae translated into Italian by D. Scenna.

1900   Amsterdam
Het Vrouwenparlement
Ecclesiazusae translated into Dutch by Abraham Halberstadt. Geritsen Women's
History, no. 95.

Budapest

Összes munkái

Contains translations of Shakespeare and Aristophanes into Hungarian by János Arany. Thirteen volumes.

Japan

Onna no heiwa: yonkei

Lysistrata translated into Japanese by H. Kozui and K. Chigiri.

Japan

Onna no heiwa matawa otoko no heiwa: arisutopanesu onna heiwa yori myūjikaru

Japanese adaptation of *Peace* by T. Fujita.

London

Aristophanes: The Eleven Comedies. Now for the first time literally and completely translated from the Greek tongue into English

With the translator's foreword, an introduction to each comedy and elucidatory notes. Printed for the Athenian Society. The Athenian Society Edition, in two volumes. Reissued in 1912.

London

The Frogs

Verse translation by E. W. Huntingford.

New York

Greek Dramas by Aeschylus, Sophocles, Euripides, and Aristophanes

Includes *Clouds* and *Plutus* translated by W. J. Hickie. Edited, with biographical notes and a critical introduction, by Bernadotte Perrin.

New York

Plays: by Greek, Spanish, French, German and English Dramatists

It contains *Knights*. By Albert Ellery Bergh.

Oxford

Frogs

Adapted for presentation at St Peter's College, Radley, with an English translation by L. James.

1901   **Athens**

Performance of *The Emancipation*, a comedy written by Georgios Ch. Souris, influenced by *Lysistrata* and *Ecclesiazusae*. Performed again in the 1909–10 season. It is not known whether this play was published.

Città di Castello

Le Donne a Parlamento

Ecclesiazusae translated into Italian verse by Augusto Franchetti, with introduction and notes by Domenico Comparetti.

London

Equites

Knights literally translated by J. A. Prout. Kelly's Keys to the Classics series.

London

Plutus

Literally translated by J. A. Prout. Kelly's Keys to the Classics series.

1902   **Boston and New York**

Masterpieces of Greek Literature

'The selections in this volume were made, and the biographical and other notes written, by Clara H. Seymour'; the editor was John Henry Wright (1852–1908). It includes Aristophanes.

London

The Ecclesiazusae of Aristophanes

The Greek text revised, with a translation into corresponding metres, introduction and commentary by Benjamin Bickley Rogers. Reissued in 1923.

London

Euripides: The Hippolytus and Bacchæ of Euripides, together with the Frogs of Aristophanes

Translated into English rhyming verse by Gilbert Murray. Reissued 1906. The *Frogs* translation was issued separately several times subsequently, including in 1908, 1912, 1915, and 1925.

London

The Frogs of Aristophanes

The Greek text revised, with a translation into corresponding metres, introduction and commentary by Benjamin Bickley Rogers. Reissued in 1919.

Milan

Gli Acarnesi

A poetic version of *Acharnians*, with introduction and notes by Ettore Romagnoli (1871–1938).

1903   **Berkeley, California**

Scenes from the Birds of Aristophanes

Translation by Isaac Flagg (1843–1931).

Cambridge

The Birds

The Greek text as performed by members of the University at the Theatre Royal, Cambridge, November 1883, and November 1903; with the English version of Benjamin Hall Kennedy.

Cambridge

The Music to The Birds of Aristophanes

Composed by Charles Hubert Hastings Parry (1848–1918), as performed at Cambridge, November 1883, and November 1903; with an English version by A. W. Verrall (1851–1912). First printed in 1885.

1904   **Athens**

Ekklisiazousai

Publication of a modern Greek verse translation of *Ecclesiazusae* by Polyvios T. Dimitrakopoulos. Performed this year in Athens by the Nea Skini company of Konstantinos Christomanos.[59]

Boston, Massachusetts

Selections from Aristophanes and Lucian

Translated by F. A. Paley.

Cambridge

The Bees, with Humblest Apologies to the Shade of Aristophanes

Adaptation of *Birds*, performed at Girton College, Cambridge, and privately printed (fig. 19.3).[60]

Edinburgh

Greek Lyrics

Translations (into English measures) of selected excerpts from Euripides, Sophocles and Aristophanes by D. T. Holmes.

London

Classic Curiosities of Dramatic Literature

Edited by Alfred Bates; it contains *Ecclesiazusae*.

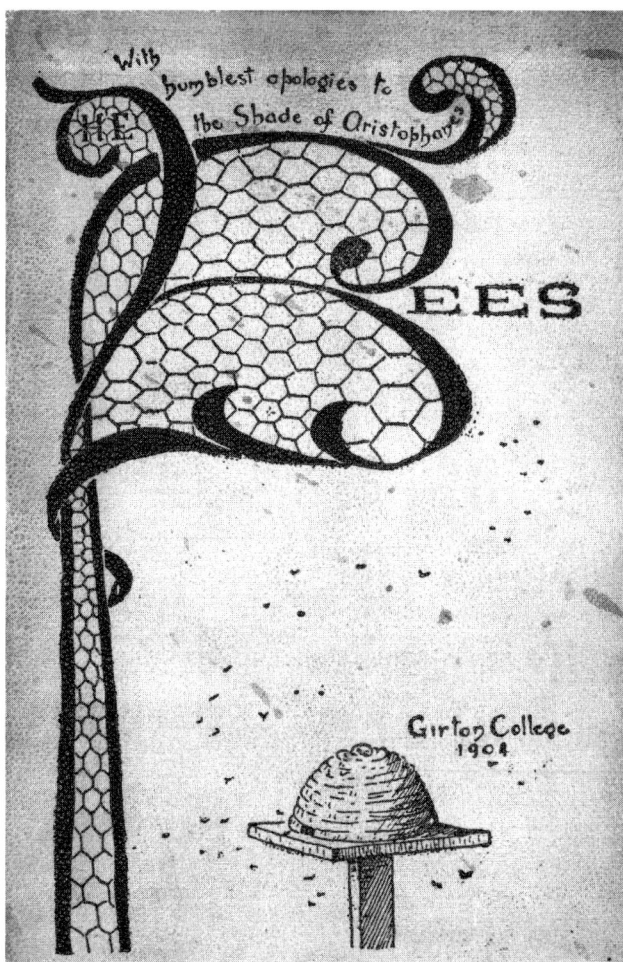

FIG. 19.3. Front cover of *The Bees* (adaptation of *Birds*), 1904

London
The Thesmophoriazusae of Aristophanes
The Greek text revised with a free translation into English verse, introduction
and commentary by Benjamin Bickley Rogers, with a preface by Gilbert Murray.
Reissued in 1911, 1912, and 1924.
Piacenza
Le Tesmoforiazuse
A poetic version in Italian of *Thesmophoriazusae*, with introduction and notes, by
Ettore Romagnoli.

1905   **Athens**
Ploutos Aristofanous
Publication of a verse translation of *Plutus* into modern Greek by Th. Solomos. The
text was performed in Athens the previous year under the direction of Thomas
Oikonomou.[61]

Città di Castello
Le donne alle Tesmoforie
Thesmophoriazusae translated into Italian verse by Augusto Franchetti, with introduction and notes by Domenico Comparetti.
Milan
Le nuvole; Le rane
Clouds translated into Italian by G. Terucci and *Frogs* by V. Alfieri.
Oxford
The Clouds
Adapted for performance by the Oxford University Dramatic Society, 1905, with an English version by A. D. Godley and C. Bailey.

1906   **France**
Sacha Guitry writes *Les Nuées* based on the Aristophanic *Clouds*.[62]
Kraków
Żaby
Frogs, translated into Polish by Edmund Żegota Cięglewicz.
London
The Birds of Aristophanes
The Greek text revised, with a translation into corresponding metres, introduction and commentary by Benjamin Bickley Rogers. Reissued in 1920 and 1930.
Paris
Aristophane: Scènes choisies
A new French translation of selected scenes, with an introduction and notes, by Louis Bodin and Paul Mazon.
Tarnów
Arystofanesa Żaby
Frogs, translated into Polish by Bogusław Butrymowicz.

1907   **Kraków**
Chmury; Komedya Arystofanesa
Clouds translated into Polish by Edmund Żegota Cięglewicz.
London
The Plutus of Aristophanes
The Greek text revised, with a translation into corresponding metres, introduction and commentary by Benjamin Bickley Rogers. A translation of Plautus' *Menaechmi* is added to this.

1908   **Berlin**
Lysistrata: Komödie frei nach Aristophanes
A free translation into German by Leo Greiner. Second edition: 1910. This translation was staged by Max Reinhardt in Berlin's Deutsches Theater in October 1908, with prologue by Hugo von Hofmannsthal.[63]
Paris
Les Nuées
'Comédie contemporaine en trois actes et en prose, imitée d'Aristophane', by Maurice Pujo. Part of the Théâtre d'Action française.
Kazan
Осы
Verse translation of *Wasps* by N. I. Kornilov, ed. F. G. Mishchenko.

1909   **Cambridge**
The Music to the Wasps of Aristophanes
Composed by R. Vaughan Williams (1872–1958); English translation by H. J. Edwards.

Cambridge

The Wasps of Aristophanes

As performed at Cambridge, 26 November–1 December 1909. Verse translation by Benjamin Bickley Rogers.

France

Les Oiseaux

Translated by Théodore Lascaris.

Liége

Les Guêpes: comédie

Wasps translated into French by Alphonse Willems.

London

The Acharnians of Aristophanes

With introduction, English prose translation, critical notes and commentary by W. J. M. Starkie (1860–1920). American reprint: New York, 1910.

St Petersburg

Лисистрата

Adapted for theatre by Leo Greiner (see above under 1908, Berlin); translated from German into Russian by A. I. Dolinov.

Turin

Le Commedie d'Aristofane

Complete works translated into Italian verse by Ettore Romagnoli, with introduction and notes. Two volumes. New edition: 1934.

Verona

Le Donne in Parlamento

Ecclesiazusae translated into the Veronese dialect by Giuseppe Fraccaroli.

1909–11 London

The Plays of Aristophanes

Vol. i with an introduction by John P. Maine (1909); vol. ii with an introduction by John Hookham Frere (1911). Everyman's Library.

1910   Athens

Aristofanous Lysistrati

Publication of a Demotic Greek translation of *Lysistrata* by Polyvios T. Dimitrakopoulos, in three acts and rhyming fifteen-syllable lines; published in 1910; but performed in 1905 at the Municipal Theatre in Athens.

Athens

Nefelai

Clouds translated into Demotic modern Greek by Georgios Ch. Souris, first published in 1910, but performed as early as 1900 in Athens.[64] Many critics compared Souris with Aristophanes.

Athens

Ornithes

Verse translation of *Birds* in Demotic Greek by Polyvios T. Dimitrakopoulos.

Athens

Vatrachoi

Verse translation of *Frogs* in Demotic Greek by Polyvios T. Dimitrakopoulos.

Athens

Translation into modern Greek of Maurice Donnay's *Lysistrata* (see under 1893, Paris) for a performance in Athens.[65] It is not known whether the performance text was published.

Jena
Die Vögel: eine Komödie in deutsche Reime gebracht
A rhyming verse translation of *Birds* into German by Dr Owlglaß (pseudonym for Hans Erich Blaich).

London
The Knights of Aristophanes
The Greek text revised, with a translation into corresponding metres, introduction, and commentary by Benjamin Bickley Rogers.

London
The Acharnians of Aristophanes
The Greek text revised, with a translation into corresponding metres, introduction and commentary by Benjamin Bickley Rogers.

1910–22 **Prague**
Komoedie Aristofanovy
The plays translated into Czech by Augustin Krejcí and published in seven volumes over a twelve-year period.

1911   **Athens**
Aristofanous Acharnis
Markos Augeris translates *Acharnians* into modern Greek.

Athens
Aristofanous Sfikes
Markos Augeris translates *Wasps* into modern Greek.

Athens
Eirini, Aristofanis
Markos Augeris translates *Peace* into modern Greek.

Città di Castello
La Lisistrata di Aristofane
Translated into Italian verse by Augusto Franchetti, with introduction and notes by Domenico Comparetti.

London
The Clouds of Aristophanes
With introduction, English prose translation, critical notes and commentary, including a new transcript of the scholia in the Codex Venetus Marcianus 474, by W. J. M. Starkie. American reprint: New York, 1911.

London
Lysistrata
A modern paraphrase in verse by Laurence Housman. Printed by The Woman's Press.[66]

Oxford and London
The Frogs
Translated 'into kindred metres' by Alfred Davies Cope.

Paris
Lysistrate
Translated into French by Lucien Dhuys. Original engravings by François Kupka.

Paris
Les Oiseaux
Two-act 'Fantaisie' inspired by *Birds*, written by Fernand Nozière using the translation of Théodore Lascaris (see under 1909 above).

*c.*1911   **Athens**
Ippeis
Markos Augeris translates *Knights* into modern Greek.

1912   **Athens**
Ploutos
Markos Augeris translates *Plutus* into modern Greek.
Brody
Rycerze
Knights in Polish by Bogusław Butrymowicz.
Cambridge
The Plutus of Aristophanes
Literally translated from the text in the Pitt Press Series by Cyril Henry Prichard.
London
The Plutus of Aristophanes
Translated into English verse with an introduction and notes by William Rann Kennedy.
Mt Kisco, New York
Lysistrata
Adapted into English by Martia Leonard.

1913   **Città di Castello**
Gli uccelli
Birds in Italian with notes by Silvio Pellini.
St Petersburg
Лягушки
Verse translation of *Frogs* from Greek in original metres by I. Tsvetkov.

1914   **Kazan**
Три комедии
Lysistrata, *Ecclesiazusae*, and *Frogs* translated from Greek by D. Shestakov. In verse; original metres.
Kazan
Женщины на праздник Θεσμοφορій
Thesmophoriazuae translated with comments by N. I. Kornilov; in verse, mostly in original metres.
London
The Acharnians
As played by the Oxford University Dramatic Society in February 1914; with a translation into English verse by Robert Yelverton Tyrrell (first published 1883: see above).[67]

1915   **New York**
Aristophanes' Lysistrata
Adapted and arranged by Winifred Ayres Hope.

*c.*1915   **Valencia**
Comedias, Aristófanes
Translated into Spanish by R. Martínez Lafuente. Three volumes.

1916   **Leiden**
De Kickers van Aristophanes
Part of *Frogs* translated into Dutch by Christian Deknatel.
St Petersburg
Женщины на праздник Θεσμοφορій
Thesmophoriazusae translated with comments by P. V. Nikitin; partly in verse, partly in prose and partly in original metres.

1917   **Amsterdam**
De Vogels
Birds translated into Dutch by Christian Deknatel.

1918   **Campobasso**
          Una Batracomiomachia macaronica
          By Enrico Donato Petrella. Partially an imitation of *Frogs* in Italian.
          Copenhagen and Kristiania [= Oslo]
          Frøerne, komedie af Aristofanes
          Frogs translated into Danish by Johan B. Koch.
          Copenhagen and Kristiania [= Oslo]
          Acharneerne: Komødie af Aristofanes
          Acharnians translated into Danish by M. Cl. Gertz.
          Munich
          Friede: ein burleskes Spiel nach den Acharnern und der Eirene des
          Aristophanes
          Peace, a burlesque drawing on both *Acharnians* and *Peace* by Lion Feuchtwanger.
          Paris
          Aristophane
          Complete plays translated into French with notes by Alphonse Willems; preface by
          L. Parmentier; biographical note by Ch. Lacomblé. Three volumes.
          Paris
          La Grève des Femmes
          'Comédie en 3 actes et 4 tableaux, imitée d'Aristophane', drawing on Aristophanes'
          'women' plays, by Jacques Richepin.
          Paris
          Lysistrata: Comedy in Four Acts
          English translation of Maurice Donnay's *Lysistrata* (see under 1893, Paris) by Helen
          Davenport Brown Gibbons.
1920   **Amsterdam**
          De vrede
          Peace, translated into Dutch by H. M. Wertheim.
          Vienna
          Die Vögel. Ein lyrisch-phantastisches Spiel nach Aristophanes
          Two-act opera adapted from *Birds*: music and vocal score in German with piano
          accompaniment, all by Walter Braunfels.
c.1920   **Volos**
          K. Kyros's troupe performs a free version of *Ecclesiazusae*, entitled *The Suffragettes*
          and Common Marriage.[68]

Notes to Chapter 19

1. Yarkho (2003).
2. S. D'Amico (1954–62), i. 859–78.
3. Van Steen (2000).
4. Werner (1975).
5. Solomos (1974), 244–76.
6. Flashar (1991).
7. Foster (1966), 21–26.
8. France (2000).
9. Bolgar (1954).
10. Solomos (1974), 254.
11. See Cecchini and Cecchini (1965); N. G. Wilson (1992), 30–31.
12. C. Lord (1979), 807.
13. Boas (1914), 16.
14. Ibid. See Garside (1966), 71–73 and the bibliography there. A reference to a 1551 performance,

identical in many particulars with this one, may perhaps be a mistake (see S. D'Amico (1954–62), vol. i, s.v. Aristofane).

15. See Van Kerchove (1974). *Plutus* was performed by Chilius' pupils on 7 and 8 Sept. 1533 at Bruges: see Van Kerchove (1974), 44.

16. Boas (1914), 17.

17. See Steggle, above, p. 54.

18. Süss (1911), 32.

19. See M. Smith (1986), who argues that Ronsard may well have translated the entire play and not just ll. 462–79, which were first published in Ronsard (1617). For the debate on the attribution of these lines to Ronsard, see the bibliography in Silver (1954), 154 at n. 23.

20. See e.g. Chasles (1862), 75; Darmesteter and Hatzfeld (1887), 155.

21. Beauchamps (1735), i. 438; Bolgar (1954), 508.

22. See Schreiber (1975).

23. Wickersham Crawford (1914), 172; Bolgar (1954), 509.

24. See Le Loyer (2004) for a recent edition, and Hall's Introduction, above, pp. 9–10.

25. For the text see Montanari (1990), with the discussion of Pellizzari (1998).

26. The text is published in Dähnhardt (1896–97).

27. See Hall, above, p. 67–68, and also Wyles, p. 96.

28. See Hall, above, p. 67.

29. See Wyles, above, ch. 5.

30. See further N. Gross (1965).

31. See Hall's Introduction, above, pp. 10–11.

32. See Hall, above, p. 72.

33. See Hall, above, p. 72.

34. See Hall, above, p. 74.

35. J. M. R. Lenz (1902).

36. See Hall's Introduction, above, pp. 11–14.

37. Werner (1975), 467.

38. See Orfanos above, Ch. 6.

39. Alfieri's comedy *La finestrina* has similarities with *Plutus* and *Frogs*.

40. Published in *Neues attisches Museum*, 2/2 (1808), 3–163.

41. See Hall, above, p. 66.

42. See Hall, above, p. 77–79.

43. See Vasunia, above, ch. 7.

44. See Hall above, p. 28 n. 54.

45. Published in Репертуаръ и пантеонъ, 9/1 (1845), 1–85.

46. See Hall, above, p. 79.

47. See Vasunia, above, ch. 7.

48. For discussion see Van Steen (2000), 63–65.

49. Ibid. 50–63, esp. n. 13.

50. See France (2000), 368–69.

51. See Hall, above, pp. 17–18.

52. Published in Журналъ Министерства Народнаго Просвѣщенія (*Journal of the Ministry of Education*), 242 (November–December 1885), 548–99.

53. See Hall, above, p. 86.

54. Reprinted in Poole and Maule (1995), 171–72.

55. See Wrigley, above, Ch. 8.

56. France (2000), p. 369.

57. See Hall, above, p. 91 n. 116.

58. 'Rappresentato al Politeama di Firenze il 23 aprile 1898, nelle onoranze italo-americane a Paolo Toscanelli e Amerigo Vespucci, per cura del Sotto comitato universitario della "Dante Alighieri"'. See Beta (2005), 188.

59. APGRD Database, Production ID 9510.

60. See Hall, above, p. 86.

61. APGRD Database, Production ID 9811.

62. *Les Nuées* was performed in Paris in 1906, but it is not known whether it was published before the *Théâtre complet* edition of Guitry's works (Guitry 1975).
63. See Seidensticker, above, p. 204. The prologue is published in Hofmannsthal (1908).
64. APGRD Database, Production ID 2288.
65. 'A carbon copy (in modern Greek translation) of . . . the *Lysistrata* of Maurice Donnay. . . . Since its 1892 première . . . Donnay's comedy had seen substantial reworking . . . in Paris and elsewhere in Europe' (Van Steen 2000, 110).
66. See Hall, above, p. 86–88.
67. See Wrigley, above, p. 149–50.
68. See Van Steen (2000), p. 106.

BIBLIOGRAPHY

❖

ADDERLEY, JAMES GRANVILLE (1888), *The Fight for the Drama at Oxford: Some Plain Facts Narrated*, with a preface by W. L. Courtney. Oxford: Blackwell

ADLER, THOMAS P. (2000), 'The Sung and the Said: Literary Value in the Musical Dramas of Stephen Sondheim', in Goodhart (2000, ed.), 37–60

ALBERT, MAURICE (1902), *Théâtres des Boulevards (1789–1848)*. Paris: Société française d'imprimerie et de librairie

ALBINI, UMBERTO (1991), *Nel nome di Dioniso: Vita teatrale nell'Atene classica*. Milan: Garzanti

—— (1998), *Testo e palcoscenico: Divagazioni sul teatro antico*. Bari: Levante Editore

ALLEN, W. SIDNEY (1987), *Vox Graeca: The Pronunciation of Ancient Greek*, 3rd edn. Cambridge: Cambridge University Press

ALS, HILTON (2004), 'Talkers and Togas: Revivals by Arthur Miller and Nathan Lane', *The New Yorker*, 9 August 2004, 97–99

AMOROSO, FILIPPO (1997), 'Les représentations d'Aristophane en Italie au XXᵉ siècle', in *Aristophane, la langue, la scène, la cité: Actes du colloque de Toulouse, 17–19 mars 1994*, ed. P. Thiercy and M. Mernu, 549–73. Bari

ANDERSEN, HANS CHRISTIAN (n.d.), *Eventyr og Historier*, 16 vols. Odense: Flensteds Forlag

ANDERSON, GRAHAM (1976a), *Lucian: Theme and Variation in the Second Sophistic* (*Mnemosyne*, Suppl. 41). Leiden: Brill

—— (1976b), *Studies in Lucian's Comic Fiction* (*Mnemosyne*, Suppl. 43). Leiden: Brill

ANDRIES, LISE (2000, ed.), *Le Rire* (= *Dix-Huitième Siècle*, 32), 1–320. Paris: Presses Universitaires de France

ANON. (1836a), *The Possums of Aristophanes, Recently Recovered*, in *Fraser's Magazine for Town and Country*, vol. xiv, no. 81 (September), 285–97

ANON. (1836b), 'St Paul's School', *The Times*, 6 May 1836, 3

ANON. (1881), 'The Classical Drama', *Frank Leslie's Popular Monthly*, 12/2, August 1881, 229–34

ANON. (1883a), 'Aristophane's [*sic*] *Birds* Acted: Cambridge Letter to the *London Standard*, Nov. 28', *New York Times*, 10 December 1883

ANON. (1883b), 'The *Birds* of Aristophanes', *The Times*, 23 November 1883, 4

ANON. (1892a), 'Charon at Oxford', *The Oxford Magazine*, 9 March 1892, 233–34

ANON. (1892b), 'Dr Parry's Music to *The Frogs*', *The Musical Times*, 1 April 1892, 215

ANON. (1892c), 'The *Frogs* at Oxford', *Black & White: A Weekly Illustrated Record and Review*, 3, no. 58, 12 March 1892, 348–49

ANON. (1892d), 'The *Frogs* at Oxford', *The Queen, The Lady's Newspaper*, 5 March 1892, 381

ANON. (1892e), 'The *Frogs* at Oxford', *Temple Bar*, 95, 238–40

ANON. (1892f), 'The *Frogs* at Oxford', *The Times*, 25 February 1892, 5

ANON. (1892g), 'The *Frogs* of Aristophanes at Oxford', *The Athenaeum*, 5 March 1892, 318

ANON. (1892h), 'The Libretto of the *Frogs*', *The Oxford Magazine*, 17 February 1892, 177

ANON. (1892i), 'The Music to *The Frogs*', *The Times*, 29 February 1892, 10

ANON. (1892j), 'OUDS. *The Frogs*', *The Oxford Magazine*, 2 March 1892, 206–07

ANON. (1895), *Fragments of the Rhopoperperethrades: A Comedy of Aristophanes*. Philadelphia, Pennsylvania

ANON. (1904), *The Bees, with Humblest Apologies to the Shade of Aristophanes. Girton College Second-Year Entertainment*. Cambridge: Metcalfe & Co

ANON. (1905), 'The Drama: Aristophanes Redivivus', *Times Literary Supplement*, 3 March 1905

ANON. (1914*a*), 'The Acharnians at Oxford', *The Musical Times*, 1 March 1914, 186–87

ANON. (1914*b*), 'The Acharnians at Oxford: Production by the OUDS', *The Times*, 19 February 1914, 9

ANON. (1914*c*), 'Oxford in the New Year', *The Times*, 22 January 1914, 10

ANON. (2002*a*), 'Ronconi: mi censurano', *La Stampa*, 20 May 2002, 32

ANON. (2002*b*), 'Berlusconi in New Censorship Row in Italy', *Agence France-Presse*, 20 May 2002

ANON. (2002*c*), 'Berlusconi Criticised for Censoring *Frogs*', *The Scotsman*, 21 May 2002

APGRD Database of Modern Performances of Ancient Drama, University of Oxford, edited by Amanda Wrigley, published online at http://www.apgrd.ox.ac.uk/database

ARBLASTER, ANTHONY (1992), *Viva la Libertà! Politics in Opera*. London: Verso

ARISTOPHANES (1607), *Comoediae Undecim cum Scholiis Antiquis,* ed. O. Bisetus. Geneva

ARMSTRONG, RICHARD H. (2002), review of Hall, Macintosh, and Taplin (2000), *American Journal of Philology*, 123/2, 289–93

ARNOLD, MATTHEW (1960–77), *The Complete Prose Works of Matthew Arnold*, ed. R. H. Super. 11 vols. Ann Arbor

ARROWSMITH, WILLIAM (1961, transl.), *The Birds by Aristophanes*. Ann Arbor: University of Michigan Press

—— (n.d.), '*Euripides Agonistes (Thesmophoriazousae)*', unpublished script

ASCHAM, ROGER (1570), *The Scholemaster*. London: John Daye. (Facs. Menston: Gregg Press, 1967)

ATKINS, STUART (1995), 'Goethe, Aristophanes, and the Classical Walpurgisnight', in id., *Essays on Goethe*, ed. Jane K. Brown and Thomas P. Saine (= *Goethe Yearbook*, special vol. 2), 243–58. Columbia, SC: Camden House

ATKINSON, BROOKS (1952*a*), 'At the Theatre', *The New York Times*, 20 November 1952

—— (1952*b*), 'First Night at the Theatre', *The New York Times*, 25 November 1952

AUSTIN, COLIN, and OLSON, S. DOUGLAS (2004, eds.), *Aristophanes: Thesmophoriazusae*. Oxford: Oxford University Press

AVLAMI, CHRYSSANTHI (2000), *L'Antiquité grecque à la française: Modes d'appropriation de la Grèce au XIXe siècle*. Lille: Septentrion

AYLMER, G. E. (1972, ed.), *The Interregnum: The Quest for Settlement, 1646–1660*. London: Macmillan

BACHMANN, INGEBORG, and HENZE, HANS WERNER (2004), *Briefe einer Freundschaft*, ed. Hans Höller. Munich: Piper

BAILY, LESLIE (1973), *Gilbert and Sullivan and their World*. London: Thames and Hudson

BALDWIN, T. W. (1944), *Shakspere's smalle Latine and lesse Greeke*, 2 vols. Urbana: Illinois University Press

BANFIELD, STEPHEN (1993), *Sondheim's Broadway Musicals*. Ann Arbor: University of Michigan Press

BARAKA, AMIRI, and BARAKA, AMINA (1987), *The Music: Reflections on Jazz and Blues*. New York: William Morrow

BARISH, JONAS (1981), *The Antitheatrical Prejudice*. Berkeley: University of California Press

BARLOW, SHIRLEY A. (1971), *The Imagery of Euripides: A Study in the Dramatic Use of Pictorial Language*. London: Methuen

BARNES, CLIVE (2004), 'No Great Leap in *The Frogs*', *New York Post*, 23 July 2004

BARRETT, DAVID (1964, transl.), *The Wasps; The Poet and the Women; The Frogs; Translated with an Introduction*. Penguin Classics series. Harmondsworth: Penguin

BEARDSLEY, AUBREY (1896), *The Lysistrata of Aristophanes: Now First Wholly Translated into English, and Illustrated with Eight Full-Page Drawings*. London: privately printed in a limited edn. by Leonard Smithers

BEAUCHAMPS, PIERRE-FRANÇOIS GODART DE (1735), *Recherches sur les theatres de France, depuis l'année onze cens soixante-un, jusques à présent*, 3 vols. Paris: Prault père

BEDNARZ, JAMES P. (2001), *Shakespeare and the Poets' War*. New York: Columbia University Press

BEHR, CHARLES A. (1981–86), *P. Aelius Aristides: The Complete Works, Translated into English*, 2 vols. Leiden: Brill

BELIN DE BALLU, JACQUES-NICOLAS (1783), *Hécube, première tragédie d'Euripide*. Paris: Knapen

BESSON, BENNO (1998*a*), *Benno Besson: Stationen seiner Theaterarbeit. Texte — Dokumente — Gespräche*, ed. Christa Neubert-Herwig. Berlin: Alexander Verlag

—— (1998*b*), *Benno Besson: Theater spielen in acht Ländern. Texte — Dokumente — Gespräche* (with a complete list of Besson's productions, 329–48), ed. Christa Neubert-Herwig. Berlin: Alexander Verlag

BETA, SIMONE (2001), 'Aristofane a Vienna: *Le congiurate* di Franz Schubert', *Quaderni Urbinati di Cultura Classica*, NS 67/1, 143–59

—— (2002), 'Aristofane a Berlino: la *Lysistrata* di Paul Lincke', *Quaderni Urbinati di Cultura Classica*, NS 72/3, 141–62

—— (2005), 'Aristofane e il musicalite molte facce del Lisistrata', *Dioniso* 4, 184–95

BETHE, ERICH (1900–37, ed.), *Pollucis Onomasticon*, 3 vols. Leipzig: Teubner

BEYE, CHARLES ROWAN (2004*a*), 'Buffoonery & Bathos: Aristophanes' *The Frogs*', *Lincoln Center Theater Review*, 38 (Summer), 7–8

—— (2004*b*), 'A Funny Thing Happened on the Way to the Agora', 23 August 2004, accessible online at http://www.greekworks.com/content/index.php/weblog/extended/a_funny_thing_happened_on_the_way_to_the_agora (accessed 3 October 2006)

BHATIA, NANDI (2004), *Acts of Authority/Acts of Resistance: Theater and Politics in Colonial and Postcolonial India*. Ann Arbor: University of Michigan Press

BIEBER, MARGARETE (1920), *Die Denkmäler zum Theaterwesen im Altertum*. Berlin

BILLINGTON, MICHAEL (2004), 'Terror of Modern Times Sets the Stage for Greek Tragedy: Theatrical Revivals Seen as Direct Reponse to Iraq War', *The Guardian*, 19 June 2004, 3

BLOCK, GEOFFREY (1997), *Enchanted Evenings: The Broadway Musical from Show Boat to Sondheim*. New York and Oxford: Oxford University Press

BOAS, FREDERICK S. (1914), *University Drama in the Tudor Age*. Oxford: Clarendon Press

BOIVIN, JEAN (1729), *Œdipe, tragédie de Sophocle, et Les oiseaux, comédie d'Aristophane*. Paris: Didot

BOLGAR, R. R. (1954), *The Classical Heritage and its Beneficiaries*. Cambridge: Cambridge University Press

BOLT, RANJIT (2005, trans.), *Lysistrata*. London: Oberon

BOLZONI, ATTILIO (2002*a*), 'Miccichè: "È vergognoso: lo denuncio per atti terroristici"', *La Repubblica*, 20 May 2002, 13

—— (2002*b*), '"Dal Cavaliere un atto di civiltà ma Miccichè cercava la rissa"', *La Repubblica*, 21 May 2002, 11

—— and FRANCO QUADRI (2002), 'Berlusconi non è un tiranno; levate la sua faccia dalla scena', *La Repubblica*, 20 May 2002, 13

BOMPAIRE, JACQUES (1958), *Lucien écrivain: imitation et création*. Paris: E. de Boccard

BONGI, MICAELA (2002), 'Tutte *le Rane* del Presidente', *Il Manifesto*, 21 May 2002, 2

BOSKER, MARGO RUTH (1994), *Sechs Stücke nach Stücken: Zu den Bearbeitungen von Peter Hacks*. New York: Lang

BOURDIEU, PIERRE (1993), *The Field of Cultural Production: Essays on Art and Literature*, ed. and introduced by Randal Johnson. New York: Columbia University Press

BOWERSOCK, GLEN WARREN (1994), *Fiction as History: Nero to Julian*. Berkeley, and London: University of California Press

BOWIE, A. M. (1993), *Aristophanes: Myth, Ritual and Comedy*. Cambridge: Cambridge University Press

BOWIE, EWEN L. (2002), 'The Chronology of the Earlier Greek Novels since B. E. Perry: Revisions and Precisions', *Ancient Narrative*, 2, 47–63

BOYLE, NICHOLAS (1991), *Goethe: The Poet and his Age*, i: *The Poetry of Desire (1749–1790)*. Oxford: Clarendon Press

BRANHAM, ROBERT BRACHT (1989), *Unruly Eloquence: Lucian and the Comedy of Traditions*. Cambridge, Massachusetts: Harvard University Press

BRANTLEY, BEN (2004), 'Gods, Greeks and Ancient Shtick', *The New York Times*, 23 July 2004

BRAUND, DAVID, and JOHN WILKINS (2000, eds.), *Athenaeus and his World: Reading Greek Culture in the Roman Empire*. Exeter: University of Exeter Press

BRECHT, BERTOLT (1965), *Die Antigone des Sophokles, Materialien zur Antigone*. Frankfurt am Main: Suhrkamp

BREYTENBACH, BREYTEN (1998), *Boklied: 'n Vermaaklikheid in drie bedrywe*. Cape Town: Human and Rousseau

BRIDGES, EMMA, HALL, EDITH, and RHODES, P. J. (2007, eds.), *Cultural Responses to the Persian Wars*. Oxford: Oxford University Press

BRINK, ANDRÉ P. (1971), *Die Hand vol vere*. Unpublished playscript obtainable from DALRO, (Dramatic, Artistic and Literary Rights Organisation), P.O. Box 31627, Braamfontein 2017, South Africa

BRISSON, PIERRE (1932), 'Feuilleton du Temps', *Chronique théâtrale*, 26 December 1932

BRISTED, CHARLES (1852), *Five Years in an English University*, 2nd edn. New York

BROCK, M. G., and CURTHOYS, M. C. (2000, eds.), *The History of the University of Oxford*, vol. 7: *Nineteenth-Century Oxford, Part 2*. Oxford: Oxford University Press

BROCKMANN, CHRISTIAN (2003), *Aristophanes und die Freiheit der Komödie: Untersuchungen zu den frühen Stücken unter besonderer Berücksichtigung der Acharner*. Munich: Saur

BROOKFIELD, ARTHUR MONTAGU (1884), *Simiocracy: A Fragment from Future History*. Edinburgh: Blackwood

BROWN, PETER (2001), 'Introduction' to *Menander: The Plays and Fragments*, trans. Maurice Balme, pp. ix–xxix. Oxford: Oxford University Press

—— (2006), '*The Eunuch* Castrated: Bowdlerization in the Text of the Westminster Latin Play', in P. Brown, T. Harrison, and S. Instone (eds.), *ΘΕΩΙ ΔΩΡΟΝ: Essays for Theo Zinn* (Leominster: Gracewing, 2006), 128–40

BROWNING, ROBERT (1875), *Aristophanes' Apology: Including a Transcript from Euripides, Being the Last Adventure of Balaustion*. London

BRUFORD, WALTER HORACE (1950), *Theatre, Drama and Audience in Goethe's Germany*. London: Routledge

—— (1962), *Culture and Society in Classical Weimar, 1775–1806*. Cambridge: Cambridge University Press

BRUMOY, PIERRE (1759), *The Greek Theatre of Father Brumoy, Translated by Mrs Charlotte Lennox*, 3 vols. London: printed for Millar, Vaillant, Baldwin, Crowder, Johnston, Dodsley, Wilson, and Durham

BRUSTEIN, ROBERT (2004), 'The Past Revisited', *The New Republic*, 30 August 2004

BUCKLE, RICHARD (1964), 'The Dancing *Birds*', *The Sunday Times*, 24 May 1964

BULWER, EDWARD LYTTON [later BULWER-LYTTON, FIRST BARON LYTTON] (1833), *England and the English*, 2 vols. London

BURIAN, PETER (1997), 'Tragedy Adapted for Stages and Screens: The Renaissance to the Present', in Easterling (ed.), 228–83

CAILHAVA, JEAN-FRANÇOIS DE (1791), *Les Ménechmes, grecs: Comédie en prose et en quatre actes précédés d'un prologue*. Paris: Boulard

—— (1796/7), *Athènes pacifiée: Comédie en trois actes et en prose tirée des onze pièces d'Aristophane*. Paris: Pougens

CAIN, TOM (1998), '"Satyres, that Girde and Fart at the Time": *Poetaster* and the Essex Rebellion', in Chedzgoy, Sanders, and Wiseman (1998, eds.), 48–70

CALANDRA, DALE, and COATES, DONALD (1990), *Lysistrata 2411 A.D.: Based on Aristophanes' Lysistrata*. Bookclub Edition. Garden City, New York: The Fireside Theatre

CAMPBELL, ISOBEL (2002), 'High-Flying Take on Democracy', *The Morning Star*, 1 August 2002, 9

CANNING, GEORGE (1825), *The Poetical Works of the Right Hon. George Canning, M.P.: Comprising the Whole of his Satires, Odes, Songs, and Other Poems*. Glasgow: printed by J. Starke

—— and FRERE, JOHN HOOKHAM (1991), *Poetry of the Anti-Jacobin 1799*. Facsimile reprint of the 1st edn. (1799), with new introduction by Jonathan Wordsworth. Oxford: Woodstock Books

CANNY, NICHOLAS (1976), *The Elizabethan Conquest of Ireland: A Pattern Established, 1565–76*. Hassocks: Harvester Press

—— (1996), 'The Attempted Anglicisation of Ireland', in Merritt (1996), 157–86

CAPES, WILLIAM WOLFE (1877), *University Life in Ancient Athens: Being the Substance of Four Oxford Lectures*. London: Longmans, Green, & Co

CARPENTER, HUMPHREY (1985), *OUDS: A Centenary History of the Oxford University Dramatic Society, 1885–1985*. Oxford: Oxford University Press

CARR, PHILIP (1898), 'The Greek Play, Oxford', in Elliot (ed.), 53–66

CARRINGTON, EDMUND F. J. (1825), *Plutus, or, The God of Riches; A Comedy of Aristophanes*. London: Wheatley and Adlard

CARTLEDGE, PAUL (1990), *Aristophanes and his Theatre of the Absurd*. Bristol: Bristol Classical Press

CARY, HENRY FRANCIS (1824), *The Birds of Aristophanes*. London: Taylor and Hessey

CASAUBON, ISAAC (1605), *De Satyrica Graecorum poesi, et Romanorum satira libri duo*. Paris

CAVE, TERENCE (1979), *The Cornucopian Text: Problems of Writing in the French Renaissance*. Oxford: Clarendon Press

CAVELL, STANLEY (1981), *Pursuits of Happiness: The Hollywood Comedy of Remarriage*. Cambridge, Massachusetts: Harvard University Press

CECCHINI, MARIA, and CECCHINI, ENZO (1965), *Versione del Pluto di Aristofane: (vv. 1–269), Leonardo Bruni. Introduzione e Testo Critico*. Florence: Sansoni

CHALLIS, DEBBIE (2005), 'Collecting Classics: The Acquisition and Reception of Classical Antiquities in Museums in England, 1830–1890', PhD thesis submitted to the University of London

CHAMFORT, SÉBASTIEN-ROCH-NICOLAS DE (1824), *Éloge de Molière*, in *Œuvres complètes*. Paris: Chaumerot

CHASLES, ÉMILE (1862), *La Comédie en France au seizième siècle*. Paris: Didier. Reprinted in 1969. Geneva: Slatkine Reprints

CHATTERJEE, PARTHA (1993), *The Nation and Its Fragments: Colonial and Postcolonial Histories*. Princeton: Princeton University Press

CHEDZGOY, KATE, SANDERS, JULIE, and WISEMAN, SUSAN (1998, eds.), *Refashioning Ben Jonson: Gender, Politics, and the Jonsonian Canon*. Basingstoke: Macmillan

CHOURMOUZIOS, AIMILIOS (1978), *To Archaio Drama: Meletemata [Ancient Drama: Essays]*. Athens: Ekdoseis ton Filon

CITRON, STEPHEN (2001), *Sondheim and Lloyd-Webber: The New Musical*. Oxford: Oxford University Press

CLARK, WILLIAM SMITH (1955), *The Early Irish Stage: The Beginnings to 1720*. Oxford: Clarendon Press

CLARKE, M. L. (1959), *Classical Education in Britain*. Cambridge: Cambridge University Press

COCKIN, KATHARINE (2001), *Women and Theatre in the Age of Suffrage: The Pioneer Players, 1911–1925*. Basingstoke: Palgrave

COHN, JOEL R. (1998), *Studies in the Comic Spirit in Modern Japanese Fiction*. Cambridge, Massachusetts: Harvard University Asia Center

COLAKIS, MARIANTHE (1993), *The Classics in the American Theater of the 1960s and Early 1970s*. Lanham, Maryland: University Press of America

COLEBROOK, CLAIRE (1997), *New Literary Histories: New Historicism and Contemporary Criticism*. Manchester: Manchester University Press

COLLINS, MORTIMER (1872), *The British Birds: A Communication from the Ghost of Aristophanes*. London: The Publishing Co

COLLINS, WILLIAM LUCAS (1872), *Aristophanes*. Ancient Classics for English Readers series. Edinburgh: Blackwood

CONDORCET, MARIE-JEAN-ANTOINE-NICOLAS DE CARITAT (2004), *Tableau historique des progrès de l'esprit humain: projets, esquisse, fragments et notes (1772–1794)*, ed. Jean-Pierre Schandeler and Pierre Crépel. Paris: Institut national d'études démographiques

CONRADIE, P. J. (1998), 'Aristophanes en die tweede bedryf van Breyten Breytenbach se *Boklied*: 'n Verkenning', *Akroterion*, 43, 15–22

COOK, ALBERT (1949), *The Dark Voyage and the Golden Mean. A Philosophy of Comedy*. Cambridge, Massachusetts: Harvard University Press

COOKESLEY, HENRY PARKER (1834), *Aristophanous Ploutos. The Plutus of Aristophanes, from the Text of Dindorf, with Critical and Explanatory Remarks [...] for the Use of Schools*. London: Richard Priestley

CORDE, FRANCO (2002), 'La commedia del potere e quelle cornici vuote piene di significato', *Corriere della Sera*, 20 May 2002, 1.5

CORNAZ, HENRI (1998, ed.), *Benno Besson: Jouer en apprenant le monde. En guise de lettre ouverte*. Yverdo: Edn de la Thièle

CORNFORD, FRANCIS (1993), *The Origin of Attic Comedy*, ed. with foreword and additional notes by Theodor H. Gaster; introduction by Jeffrey Henderson. Ann Arbor: Michigan University Press

COULON, VICTOR (1924, ed.), and Hilaire Van Daele (transl.), *Aristophane: texte établi par Victor Coulon et traduit par Hilaire Van Daele*, ii: *Les Guêpes; La Paix*. Paris: Les Belles Lettres

COURTNEY, W. P. (2004), 'Warter, John Wood (1806–1878)', rev. Triona Adams, *Oxford Dictionary of National Biography*. Oxford: Oxford University Press. Online at http://www.oxforddnb.com/view/article/28795 (accessed 10 April 2006)

CROCE, BENEDETTO (1922), *Aesthetic as Science of Expression and General Linguistic*, 2nd edn., trans. by Douglas Ainslie of 4th edn. of *Estetica come scienza dell'espressione e linguistica generale* (originally published 1909). London: Macmillan

CRONIN, MARI (1997), 'Sondheim: the Idealist', in Gordon (1997, ed.), 143–52

CROSS, WILBUR L. (1918), *The History of Henry Fielding*. New Haven, CT: Yale University Press

CSAPO, ERIC (2000), 'From Aristophanes to Menander? Genre Transformation in Greek Comedy', in Mary Depew and Dirk Obbink (2000, eds.), *Matrices of Genre: Authors, Canons, and Society*, 115–33. Cambridge, Massachusetts: Harvard University Press

—— (2004), 'Some Social and Economic Conditions behind the Rise of the Acting Profession in the Fifth and Fourth Centuries BC', in Christophe Hugoniot, Frédéric Hurlet, and Silvia Milanezi (eds.), *Le Statut de l'acteur dans l'Antiquité grecque et romaine* (Collection Perspectives Historiques, 9), 53–76. Tours: Maison des Sciences de l'Homme

—— and SLATER, WILLIAM J. (1994), *The Context of Ancient Drama*. Ann Arbor, Michigan: University of Michigan Press

CURTIUS, ERNST ROBERT (1990 [1953]), *European Literature and the Latin Middle Ages*, trans. Willard R. Trask. Princeton: Princeton University Press

DAIN, ALPHONSE (1954), *Le 'Philétaeros' attribué à Hérodien*. Paris: Les Belles Lettres

DÄHNHARDT, OSKAR (1896–97, ed.), *Griechische Dramen in deutschen Bearbeitungen von Wolfhart Spangenberg und Isaac Fröreisen* [*Alcestis, Hecuba*, and *Ajax* translated by Spangenberg; *Clouds* by Fröreisen]. *Nebst deutschen Argumenten* [to *Hecuba, Ajax, Clouds, Prometheus Vinctus, Medea*], 2 vols. Tübingen

DALE, MICHAEL (2004), '*The Frogs*: So What's the Problem?', review published online at http://www.broadwayworld.com/viewcolumn.cfm?colid=1084 (accessed 9 October 2006)

DALPATRAM DAHYABHAI (1850), *Lakshmi: A Comedy in the Guzrati Language*. Ahmedabad. Reprinted in Dalpatram Dahyabhai (1999*b*), ed. M. Parekh, 1–40. Gandhinagar

—— (1921), *Hunnarkhanni Chadhai*. 14th edn. Ahmedabad

—— (1999*a*), *Dalpat Granthavali, granth 1: Dalpat-kavya, bhag 1* [*Complete Works of Dalpatram, vol. 1: Poems by Dalpatram, part 1*], ed. C. Trivedi. Gandhinagar

—— (1999*b*), *Dalpat Granthavali, granth 4: Dalpat-gadya, bhag 1* [*Complete Works of Dalpatram, vol. 4: Prose Writings by Dalpatram, part 1*], ed. M. Parekh. Gandhinagar

—— (2000), *Dalpat Granthavali, granth 2: Dalpat-kavya, bhag 2* [*Complete Works of Dalpatram, vol. 2: Poems by Dalpatram, part 2*], ed. C. Trivedi. Gandhinagar

—— (2001), *Dalpat Granthavali, granth 3: Dalpat-kavya, bhag 3* [*Complete Works of Dalpatram, vol. 3: Poems by Dalpatram, part 3*], ed. C. Trivedi. Gandhinagar

DAMIANAKOU, VOULA (1960), 'The Battle of the *Birds*' [in Greek], in Rotas (ed.), 77–78

D'AMICO, MASOLINO (2002), 'Tra uomini e dèi, le rane', *La Stampa*, 22 May 2002, 30

D'AMICO, SILVIO (1954–62, ed.), *Enciclopedia dello spettacolo*, 9 vols. Roma: Le Maschere

DARMESTETER, ARSÈNE, and HATZFELD, ADOLPHE (1887), *Le Seizième Siècle en France*. 3rd edn. Paris

DAVENANT, WILLIAM (1657), *The First Days Entertainment at Rutland-House, By Declamations and Musick: After the Manner of the Ancients*. London: Printed by J. M. for H. Herringman

DAVIES, JOHN (1612), *A Discoverie of the True Causes why Ireland was Neuer Entirely Subdued*. London: for I. Iaggard

DAVIS, SHEILA (2006), 'No Rhyme before its Time: Sondheim's Lyrics are Repetitive Devices', *The Sondheim Review*, 13/1, 29–31

DAWSON, CARL, and JOHN PFORDRESHER (1979, eds), *Matthew Arnold, Prose Writings: The Critical Heritage*. London: Routledge

DEBIDOUR, VICTOR-HENRY (1965, trans.), *Aristophane. Théâtre complet*, i: *Les Acharniens, Les Cavaliers, Les Nuées, Les Guêpes, La Paix*. Paris: Gallimard

DELCOURT, MARIE (1934), *La Tradition des comiques anciens en France avant Molière*. Bibliothèque de la Faculté de Philosophie et Lettres de l'Université de Liége, 59. Paris

DE MARCHIS, GOFFREDO (2002), 'Su Aristofane la svolta del premier "Il muro contro muro non paga più"', *La Repubblica*, 21 May 2002, 10

DEMETZ, PETER (1973), *Die süße Anarchie: Skizzen zur deutschen Literatur seit 1945*. Frankfurt am Main: Ullstein

DIBBLE, JEREMY (2004), 'Parry, Sir (Charles) Hubert Hastings, baronet (1848–1918)', *Oxford*

Dictionary of National Biography. Oxford: Oxford University Press. Online at http://www. oxforddnb.com/view/article/35393 (accessed 19 August 2006)

DI BLASI, M. R. (1997*a*), 'Studi sulla tradizione manoscritta del *Pluto* di Aristofane. Parte I: I papiri e i codici *potiores*', *Maia*, 49, 69–86

—— (1997*b*), 'Studi sulla tradizione manoscritta del *Pluto* di Aristofane. Parte II: I codici *recentiores*', *Maia*, 49, 367–80

DICK, ALIFKI LAFKIDOU (1974), *Paideia through Laughter: Jonson's Aristophanic Appeal to Human Intelligence.* The Hague: Mouton

DIRCKS, PHYLLIS T. (2004), 'Foote, Samuel', *Oxford Dictionary of National Biography.* Oxford: Oxford University Press. Online at http://www.oxforddnb.com/view/article/9808 (accessed 10 April 2006)

DOODY, MARGARET ANNE (1996), *The True Story of the Novel.* New Brunswick, NJ: Rutgers University Press

DORAN, JOHN (1888), *Annals of the English Stage from Thomas Betterton to Edmund Kean,* rev. edn. by Robert W. Lowe. 3 vols. London: Nimmo

DOUGILL, JOHN (1998), *Oxford in English Literature: The Making, and Undoing, of 'The English Athens'.* Ann Arbor: University of Michigan Press

DOVER, KENNETH J. (1968), 'Greek Comedy', in *Fifty Years (and Twelve) of Classical Scholarship,* rev. edn. 123–58. Oxford: Blackwell

—— (1972), *Aristophanic Comedy.* London: Batsford

—— (1988), *The Greeks and their Legacy: Collected Papers,* ii: *Prose Literature, History, Society, Transmission, Influence.* Oxford: Blackwell

—— (1993, ed.), *Aristophanes, Frogs: Edited with Introduction and Commentary.* Oxford: Clarendon Press

DRAKE, LAURA (2001), '*The Women's Festival (Thesmophoriazusae 2001)*', unpublished script, freely adapted from Dudley Fitts's translation, for a musical comedy produced at Hunter College, Manhattan in 2001

DRANT, THOMAS (1567), *Horace his Arte of Poetrie, Pistles, and Satyrs Englished.* London: Thomas Marsh

DROMAZOS, STATHIS (1993), *Archaio Drama: Kritikē.* Athens: Kedros

DRYDEN, JOHN (1962), *Of Dramatic Poesy, And Other Critical Essays,* ed. George Watson, i. London: Dent

DUFFIN, ROSS W. (2004), *Shakespeare's Songbook,* with a foreword by Stephen Orgel. New York and London: Norton

DUNBAR, NAN (1994, ed.), *Aristophanes, Birds; Edited with Introduction and Commentary.* Oxford: Clarendon Press

DUNCAN, D. (1979), *Ben Jonson and the Lucianic Tradition.* Cambridge: Cambridge University Press

DUNN, FRANCIS M. (1996, ed.), *Sophocles' Electra in Performance (Drama: Beiträge zum antiken Drama und seiner Rezeption,* 4). Stuttgart: Metzlerschen and Pöschl

DUNSTER, CHARLES (1785), *The Frogs: A Comedy, Translated from the Greek of Aristophanes.* Oxford: Printed for J. and J. Fletcher

DURVYE, CATHERINE (2002), 'Le rire et la paix', in Rochefort-Guillouet (ed.), 75–85

EASTERLING, PAT (1997), 'From Repertoire to Canon', in id. (1997, ed.), 211–27

—— (1999), 'The Early Years of the Cambridge Greek Play', in Christopher Stray (ed.), *Classics in 19th and 20th Century Cambridge: Curriculum, Culture and Community (PCPS* suppl. 24), 27–47. Cambridge: Cambridge Philological Society

—— (1997, ed.), *The Cambridge Companion to Greek Tragedy.* Cambridge: Cambridge University Press

—— and EDITH HALL (2002, eds.), *Greek and Roman Actors: Aspects of an Ancient Profession.* Cambridge: Cambridge University Press

EDWARDS, H. J. (1909), 'Greek Plays Performed at Cambridge', in *Fasciculus Joanni Willis Clark dicatus*, 541–51. Cambridge: Cambridge University Press

EFFE, BERND (1979), 'Die Alterität der Aristophanischen Komödie: Der *Frieden* von und nach Aristophanes', *Der Deutschunterricht*, 31, 59–73

ELIOT, T. S. (1951), *Selected Essays*, 3rd edn. London: Faber

ELLIOT, W. G. (1898, ed.), *Amateur Clubs & Actors*. London: Arnold

EL-RAMLY, LENIN (2005), 'Comedy in the East and the Art of Cunning: A Testimony', in Kolk and Decreus (2005, eds.), 166–80

ENGEN, RODNEY (1983), *Laurence Housman*. Stroud, Gloucestershire: Catalpa Press

ENGLISH, MARY (2005), 'Aristophanes' *Frogs*: Brek-kek-kek-kek! on Broadway', *American Journal of Philology*, 126/1, 127–33

ERASMUS (1978), *The Collected Works of Erasmus: Literary and Educational Writings 2*, ed. & trans. by C. R. Thompson. Toronto: Toronto University Press

EUBEN, J. PETER (2001), 'Aristophanes in America', in id., *Platonic Noise: Essays on the Modernity of Classical Political Thought*, 64–84. Princeton: Princeton University Press

EVANS, LADY, *née* MARIA MILLINGTON LATHBURY (1893), *Chapters on Greek Dress*. London and New York: Macmillan

FABRICIUS, JOHANN ALBERT (1790–1809), *Bibliotheca Graeca, sive Notitia scriptorum veterum Graecorum quorumcumque monumenta integra aut fragmenta edita exstant tum plerorumque e MSS. ac deperditis*, rev. C. G. Harles, 12 vols. Hamburg and Leipzig

FARREN, ROBERT (1884), *The Birds of Aristophanes: A Series of Etchings to Illustrate the Birds of Aristophanes, as Represented at Cambridge by Members of the University, Nov. 27 to Dec. 1, 1883*. Cambridge: Macmillan and Bowes

FEINGOLD, MICHAEL (2004), 'The Illusion Fields', *The Village Voice*, 27 July 2004, review published online at http://www.villagevoice.com/issues/0430/feingold.php (accessed 3 October 2006)

FENTON, JAMES (1996), 'The Cherry Orchard Has to Come Down', *The New York Review of Books*, 4 April 1996, 16–17

FERREIRA, N. (1983), *Vrede*, Afrikaans translation for the theatre of Aristophanes' *Peace*. Unpublished playscript in the Archive of the Artscape Theatre, Cape Town

FESTING, GABRIELLE (1899), *John Hookham Frere and his Friends*. London: Nisbet

FIELDING, HENRY (1903), *The Author's Farce*, in *The Complete Works of Henry Fielding*, i: *Plays and Poems*, 193–263. London: Heinemann

—— and WILLIAM YOUNG (1742), *Plutus, the God of Riches: A Comedy, Translated from the Original Greek of Aristophanes, with Large Notes Explanatory and Critical*. London: Waller

FINKLE, DAVID (2004), 'The Frogs', review published online at http://www.theatermania.com/content/news.cfm?int_news_id=4945 (accessed 3 October 2006)

FISCHER-LICHTE, ERIKA (2004), 'Thinking about the Origins of Theatre in the 1970s', in Hall, Macintosh, and Wrigley (2004, eds.), 329–60

FISHER, JAMES (1997), 'Nixon's America and Follies: Reappraising a Musical Theater Classic', in Gordon (1997, ed.), 69–84

FIX, PETER (1970), 'Der *Frieden* des Aristophanes in der Bearbeitung von Peter Hacks: Dreizehn Inszenierungen und ihr Echo bei Publikum und Presse', Diplomarbeit Seminar für Klassische Philologie der Universität Leipzig [unpublished]

FLASHAR, HELLMUT (1991), *Inszenierung der Antike: Das griechische Drama auf der Bühne der Neuzeit, 1585–1990*. Munich: Beck

FLEEMING JENKIN, HENRY CHARLES (1887), *Papers Literary, Scientific, &c. by the Late Fleeming Jenkin, Professor of Engineering in the University of Edinburgh*, ed. Sidney Colvin and J. A. Ewing, with a memoir by Robert Louis Stevenson. 2 vols. London: Longmans, Green, & Co

FLETCHER, ALAN J. (2000), *Drama, Performance, and Polity in Pre-Cromwellian Ireland*. Toronto: University of Toronto Press

FOLEY, HELENE P. (1999), 'Modern Performance and Adaptation of Greek Tragedy', *Transactions of the American Philological Association*, 129, 1–12

—— (1999/2000), 'Twentieth-Century Performance and Adaptation of Euripides', in Martin Cropp, K. Lee, and David Sansone (eds.), *Euripides and Tragic Theatre in the Late Fifth Century*, 1–13. Illinois Classical Studies, special issue 24–25; Champaign: Stipes

FORBES, ALEXANDER KINLOCH (1856), *Ras Mala; or Hindoo Annals of the Province of Goozerat, in Western India*, 2 vols. London: Richardson

—— (1878), *Ras Mala; or Hindoo Annals of the Province of Goozerat, in Western India*, 2 vols, new edn. with an introduction by J. W. Watson and a memoir of the author by A. K. Nairne. London: Richardson

—— (1924), *Ras Mala; or Hindoo Annals of the Province of Goozerat, in Western India*, 2 vols, edited with historical notes and appendices by H. G. Rawlinson. London: Humphrey Milford

FOSTER, FINLAY MELVILLE KENDALL (1966), *English Translations from the Greek: A Bibliographical Survey*. New York: AMS Press

FOTOPOULOS, DIONYSIS (1980), *Maskes, Theatro*. Athens: Kastaniotis

—— (1986), *Endymatologia sto Elliniko Theatro*. Athens: Kastaniotis

—— (1989), interview by E. D. Hadjiioannou, *Ta Nea*, 3 July 1989, 25

FOWLER, HENRY WATSON, and FOWLER, FRANCIS GEORGE (1905), *Lucian. The Complete Works*. Oxford: Clarendon

FRANCE, PETER (2000, ed.), *The Oxford Guide to Literature in English Translation*. Oxford: Oxford University Press

FRANK, JOSEPH (1961), *The Beginnings of the English Newspaper, 1620–1660*. Cambridge, Mass.: Harvard University Press

FRANTZ, PIERRE (2000), 'Rire et théâtre carnavalesque pendant la Révolution', *Dix-Huitième Siècle*, 32, 291–306

FRASER, BARBARA MEANS (1997), 'Revisiting Greece: The Sondheim Chorus', in Gordon (ed.), 223–49

FRENCH, PETER J. (1972), *John Dee: The World of an Elizabethan Magus*. London: Routledge and Kegan Paul

FRERE, JOHN HOOKHAM (1867), *John Hookham Frere's National Poems*, edited and prefaced by Richard Herne Shepherd. London: Pickering

—— (1872), *The Works of John Hookham Frere in Verse and Prose, now First Collected with a Prefatory Memoir by his Nephews W. E. and Sir Bartle Frere*, 2 vols. London: Pickering

—— (1874), *The Works of the Right Honourable John Hookham Frere in Verse and Prose*, 3 vols, 2nd edn. London: Pickering

—— (1892), *The Frogs of Aristophanes: Adapted for Performance by the Oxford University Dramatic Society, 1892. With an English Version Partly Adapted from that of J. Hookham Frere and Partly Written for the Occasion by D. G. Hogarth and A. D. Godley*. Oxford

—— (1897), *The Knights of Aristophanes: Adapted for Performance by the Oxford University Dramatic Society, 1897. With an English Version Adapted from that of J. Hookham Frere by L. E. Berman*. Oxford

FRIEDLAND, PAUL (2003), *Political Actors: Representative Bodies and Theatricality in the Age of the French Revolution*. Ithaca: Cornell University Press

FRIEDLÄNDER, PAUL (1969), 'Aristophanes in Deutschland', in Paul Friedländer, *Studien zur antiken Literatur und Kunst*, 531–71. Berlin: De Gruyter

FRY, GÉRARD (1998), *Récits inédits sur la guerre de Troie*. Paris: Les Belles Lettres

FRYE, NORTHROP (1957), *Anatomy of Criticism: Four Essays*. Princeton: Princeton University Press

FULLEYLOVE, JOHN, and WARD, HUMPHRY (1888), *Pictures and Studies of Greek Landscape and Architecture: Athens; Ægina; Corinth; Delphi; Olympia; Ithome; Sparta; Argos; Nauplia; Mycenæ; Tiryns; &c; &c; with some Pencil Drawings of Oxford*. Oxford: Alden

FUMAROLI, MARC (2001), *La Querelle des anciens et des modernes: XVIIe–XVIIIe siècles*. Paris: Gallimard

FURIA, PHILIP (1990), *The Poets of Tin Pan Alley: A History of America's Great Lyricists*. New York and Oxford: Oxford University Press

GALLUZZO, MARCO (2002), 'Berlusconi: il mio governo non censura nessuno', *Corriere della Sera*, 21 May 2002, 5

GAMEL, MARY-KAY (1999, transl.), *Women on the Edge: Four Plays by Euripides. Alcestis, Medea, Helen, and Iphigenia at Aulis Edited and Translated by Ruby Blondell, Mary-Kay Gamel, Nancy Sorkin Rabinowitz, and Bella Zweig* (The New Classical Canon). New York: Routledge

—— (2000), *The Julie Thesmo Show (Thesmophoriazousai)*, unpublished script produced at the University of California, Santa Cruz (2000), Case Western Reserve University (2001), and the University of Durham (2006)

—— (2006), *The Buzzzz!!!! (Wasps)*, unpublished script produced at the University of California, Santa Cruz (2006)

—— (2002, ed.), *Performing/Transforming Aristophanes' Thesmophoriazousai*, special issue of *American Journal of Philology*, 123/2

GARDNER, ELYSA (2004), 'Musical *Frogs* Proves Less than Riveting', *USA Today*, 22 July 2004

GARDNER, PERCY (1883), 'The *Birds* at Cambridge', *The Academy*, 8 December 1883, 381–82

GARLAND, ROBERT (2004), *Surviving Greek Tragedy*. London: Duckworth

GARMA-BERMAN, ISABEL, and BIANCIOTTO, RAFAEL (2005), *Lysistrata (la grève du sexe), d'après Aristophane*. Paris: Les Cygnes

GARSIDE, CHARLES (1966), *Zwingli and the Arts*. New Haven: Yale University Press. Reprinted in 1981 by New York: Da Capo Press

GELBART, LARRY (2002), '*Lysistrata (Sex and the City-State)*', unpublished script commissioned by American Repertory Theatre

GEORGIADOU, ARISTOULA, and LARMOUR, DAVID H. J. (1998), *Lucian's Science Fiction Novel, True Histories: Interpretation and Commentary*. Leiden and Boston: Brill

GEORGOSOPOULOS, KOSTAS (1982), *Kleidia kai Kodices tou theatrou*, i: *Archaio Drama*. Athens: Estia

GERARD, CHARLES P. (1847), *The Plutus of Aristophanes: Translated into English Verse*. London: Robinson

GIANNOPOULOU, VASILIKI (forthcoming), *Tyche: Fortune and Chance in Fifth-Century Tragedy and Historiography*. Oxford: Oxford University Press

GILBERT, W. S. (1994), *The Savoy Operas*. Ware, Hertfordshire: Wordsworth Editions

GILLION, KENNETH L. (1968), *Ahmedabad: A Study in Indian Urban History*. Berkeley: University of California Press

GIVEN, JOHN P., III (2002), 'The Croaking Chorus of the *Frogs* of Aristophanes ... and Stephen Sondheim', unpublished manuscript, used by permission

—— (2004), 'Something Not So Familiar', *The Sondheim Review*, 11/2 (Fall)

GLORE, JOHN, WITH CULTURE CLASH (1998), '*The Birds*', unpublished script produced by South Coast Repertory Theatre and Berkeley Repertory Theatre

GLYTZOURIS, ANTONIS (2001), *I Skinothetiki Techni stin Ellada: I Anadisi kai i Edreosi tis Technis tou Skinotheti sto Neoellinikon Theatron [Stage Direction in Greece: The Rise and Consolidation of the Stage Director in Modern Greek Theatre]*, 2 vols. Athens: Ellinika Grammata

GOETHE, JOHANN WOLFGANG VON (1787), *Die Vögel nach dem Aristophanes*. Leipzig: Göschen

—— (1987), *Die Vögel nach dem Aristophanes*, in Hartmut Reinhardt (ed.), *Johann Wolfgang Goethe: Sämtliche Werke*, ii/1: *Erstes Weimarer Jahrzehnt, 1775–1786*, 313–37, 685–93. Munich: Hanser

GOLDHILL, SIMON (1991), *The Poet's Voice: Essays on Poetics and Greek Literature*. Cambridge: Cambridge University Press

GOLDMAN, HERBERT (1988), *Jolson: The Legend Comes to Life*. New York and Oxford: Oxford University Press

GOLDSMITH, ULRICH K. (1985), 'Aristophanes in East Germany: Peter Hacks' Adaptation of *Peace*', in William M. Calder *et al.*, *Hypatia: Essays in Classics, Comparative Literature, and Philosophy presented to Hazel E. Barnes on her 70th Birthday*, 105–23. Colorado: Colorado Associated University Press. Repr. in Hazel Barnes *et al.* (1989, eds.), *Studies in Comparison: Ulrich Goldsmith*, 351–70. New York: Lang

GOLDZINK, JEAN (1992), *Les Lumières et l'idée du comique*. Fontenay-aux-Roses: École normale supérieure Fontenay/Saint-Cloud

GOODHART, SANDOR (2000, ed.), *Reading Stephen Sondheim: A Collection of Critical Essays*. New York and London: Garland

GORDON, JOANNE (1990) *Art Isn't Easy: The Achievement of Stephen Sondheim*. Carbondale: Southern Illinois University Press

—— (1997, ed.), *Stephen Sondheim: A Casebook*. New York and London: Garland

GOSSON, STEPHEN (1974), *Markets of Bawdrie: The Dramatic Criticism of Stephen Gosson*, ed. Arthur Kinney. Salzburg: Salzburg University Press

GOTTFRIED, MARTIN (2000), *Sondheim*, rev. edn. New York: Abrams

GRACZYK, ANETTE (1989), 'Le théâtre de la Révolution française. Média de masse entre 1789 et 1794', *Dix-Huitième Siècle*, 21, 395–410

GRANVILLE-BARKER, HARLEY (1932), 'Exit Planché — Enter Gilbert', in John Drinkwater (ed.), *The Eighteen-Sixties: Essays by Fellows of the Royal Society of Literature*. Cambridge: Cambridge University Press

GREEN, AMY (n.d.), '*Lysistrata*', unpublished script

GREEN, JESSE (2004), 'A Funny Thing Happened on the Way to the Punch Line', *The New York Times*, 27 June 2004

GREEN, J. R. (1985), 'A Representation of the *Birds* of Aristophanes', in *Greek Vases in the J. Paul Getty Museum*, 2 (Occasional Papers on Antiquities, 3), 95–118. Malibu, California: J. Paul Getty Museum

—— (1989), 'Theatre Production: 1971–1986,' *Lustrum*, 31, 7–95

—— (1991), 'On Seeing and Depicting the Theatre in Classical Athens', *Greek Roman and Byzantine Studies*, 32, 15–50

—— (1994), *Theatre in Ancient Greek Society*. London: Routledge

—— (2002), 'Towards a Reconstruction of Performance Style', in Easterling and Hall (eds.), 93–126

GREINER, BERNHARD (1992), '"Zweiter Clown im kommunistischen Frühling": Peter Hacks' Komödien in der DDR', in id., *Die Komödie, eine theatralische Sendung: Grundlagen und Interpretationen*, 409–24. Tübingen: Uni-Taschenbücher

GRIFFIN, ERNEST G. (1959), 'The Dramatic Chorus in English Literary Theory and Practice', dissertation submitted to Columbia University

GRIMOND, JESSIE (2002), 'Why Ancient Greek *Frogs* Got Italian Leader's Goat', *The Independent*, 21 May 2002

GROSS, JOHN (2002), 'Beware Beaked Greeks', *Sunday Telegraph*, 4 August 2002, 8

GROSS, NATHAN (1965), 'Racine's Debt to Aristophanes', *Comparative Literature*, 17/3 (Summer 1965), 209–24

GRUBE, GEORGE M. A. (1965), *The Greek and Roman Critics*. London: Methuen

GRUMACH, ERNST (1949), *Goethe und die Antike: Eine Sammlung*, i. Berlin: de Gruyter

GRYPARIS, I. N. (1909, transl.), *The Tragedies of Sophocles*, i: *Antigone, Electra, Ajax, Women of Trachis* [in modern Greek]. Athens: Hestia-Kollaros

—— (1938, transl.), *The Tragedies of Aeschylus* [in modern Greek]. Athens: Hestia-Kollaros

GUARE, JOHN (2004), 'Savoring a Moment: A Conversation with Stephen Sondheim', *Lincoln Center Theater Review*, 38 (Summer), 9–10

GUARINI, RUGGERO (2002), 'Quell'inedito di Aristofane', *Il Giornale*, 21 May 2002, 12

GUERNSEY, OTIS L., JR. (1974, ed.), *Playwrights, Lyricists, Composers on Theater: The Inside Story of a Decade of Theater in Articles and Comments by its Authors, Selected from Their Own Publication, the Dramatists Guild Quarterly*. New York: Dodd, Mead

—— (1985, ed.), *Broadway Song and Story: Playwrights, Lyricists, Composers Discuss Their Hits*. New York: Dodd, Mead

GUITRY, SACHA (1975), *Théâtre complet*. Paris: Club de l'honnête homme

GUM, COBURN S. (1969), *The Aristophanic Comedies of Ben Jonson: A Comparative Study of Jonson and Aristophanes*. Studies in English Literature, 40. The Hague and Paris: Mouton

GURNEY, A. R. (2003), *The Fourth Wall*. New York: Dramatists Play Service

GYSI, BIRGID (1984), 'Zeitverständnis am Beginn der sechziger Jahre und die Inszenierung *Der Frieden*. Ein Erbeproblem', *Weimarer Beiträge*, 30, 172–93

HACKS, PETER (1956), 'Einige Gemeinplätze über das Stückeschreiben', *Neue Deutsche Literatur*, 4, fasc. 9, 119–26

—— (1963), '*Der Frieden* nach Aristophanes', in Peter Hacks, *Zwei Bearbeitungen*. Frankfurt am Main: Suhrkamp

—— (1977), *Die Maßgaben der Kunst: Gesammelte Aufsätze*. Düsseldorf: Claassen

—— (2006), *Der Frieden*, ed. by Wolfgang Matthias Schwiedrzik, Neckargmünd-Wien: Edition Mnemosyne (audio CD)

HADFIELD, ANDREW, and JOHN MCVEAGH (1994, eds), *Strangers to that Land: British Perceptions of Ireland from the Reformation to the Famine*. Gerrards Cross: Smythe

HADJIIOANNOU, ELENA (2004), 'Όλος ο Αριστοφάνης σε 120΄', *Ta Nea*, 1 April 2004

HALL, EDITH (1989), *Inventing the Barbarian: Greek Self-Definition through Tragedy*. Oxford: Clarendon Press

—— (1995), 'Epo popo popo popo! Aristophanes' *Birds* at the "Minor National Institution" of the Cambridge Greek Play', *Times Literary Supplement*, 4798, 17 March 1995, p. 16

—— (2002a), 'The Ancient Actor's Presence since the Renaissance', in Easterling and Hall (eds.), 419–34

—— (2002b), 'The Singing Actors of Antiquity', in Easterling and Hall (eds.), 3–38

—— (2004a), 'Aeschylus, Race, Class, and War', in Hall, Macintosh, and Wrigley (eds.), 169–97

—— (2004b), 'Towards a Theory of Performance Reception', *Arion*, 12/1 (Spring/Summer 2004), 51–89

—— (2004c), review of Holtermann (2004), *Bryn Mawr Classical Review* 2004.12.35

—— (2006), *The Theatrical Cast of Athens: Interactions between Ancient Greek Drama and Society*. Oxford: Oxford University Press

—— (forthcoming), 'Greek Tragedy 430–380 BCE', in Robin Osborne (ed.), *The Anatomy of Cultural Revolution*. Cambridge: Cambridge University Press

—— and MACINTOSH, FIONA (2005), *Greek Tragedy and the British Theatre, 1660–1914*. Oxford: Oxford University Press

—— —— and TAPLIN, OLIVER (2000, eds.), *Medea in Performance 1500–2000*. Oxford: Legenda

—— —— and WRIGLEY, AMANDA (2004, eds.), *Dionysus Since 69: Greek Tragedy at the Dawn of the Third Millennium*. Oxford: Oxford University Press

—— and WYLES, ROSIE (forthcoming, eds.), *New Directions in Ancient Pantomime*. Oxford: Oxford University Press

HALL, JOSEPH (1969), *The Poems of Joseph Hall*, ed. with introduction and commentary by Arnold Davenport. Liverpool: Liverpool University Press

HALLIWELL, STEPHEN (1991), 'Comic Satire and Freedom of Speech in Classical Athens', *Journal of Hellenic Studies* 111, 48–70

—— (1998, transl.), *Aristophanes: Birds, Lysistrata, Assembly-Women, Wealth*. Oxford: Oxford University Press

HALLSTRÖM, A. (1910), 'De aetate Antonii Diogenis', *Eranos*, 10, 200–01

HAMILTON, EDITH (1970 [1927]), 'W. S. Gilbert: A Mid-Victorian Aristophanes', in John Bush Jones (ed.), 111–33

HAMMOU, Malika (2002), 'Traduire pour la scène', in *La Paix!*, *L'Avant-scène / Théâtre*, 1110, 84–89

HARDWICK, LORNA (2003), *Reception Studies* (*Greece & Rome* New Surveys in the Classics, 33). Oxford: Oxford University Press

—— (2004), 'Greek Drama and Anti-Colonialism: Decolonizing Classics', in Hall, Macintosh, and Wrigley (eds.), 219–42

HARRISON, TONY (1992), *The Common Chorus: A Version of Aristophanes' Lysistrata*. London: Faber

HARTIGAN, KARELISA V. (1995), *Greek Tragedy on the American Stage: Ancient Drama in the Commercial Theater, 1882–1994*. Westport, Connecticut: Greenwood Press

HARVEY, DAVID, and JOHN WILKINS (2000), *The Rivals of Aristophanes: Studies in Athenian Old Comedy*, with a foreword by Kenneth Dover. London: Duckworth; Swansea: Classical Press of Wales

HAUPTFLEISCH, TEMPLE (1997), *Theatre and Society in South Africa: Some Reflections in a Fractured Mirror*. Hatfield, Pretoria: van Schaik

HAWKINS, JOHN (1787, ed.), *The Works of Samuel Johnson, LL.D.*, vol. 4. London: Buckland, Rivington and Sons

HAYNES, DOUGLAS E. (1991), *Rhetoric and Ritual in Colonial India: The Shaping of a Public Culture in Surat City, 1852–1928*. Berkeley: University of California Press

H.H.B. (1659), *The World's Idol; or, Plutus the God of Wealth, A Translation from Aristophanes by H. H. B.* London: Printed by W. G.

HENDERSON, JEFFREY (1991 [1975]), *The Maculate Muse: Obscene Language in Attic Comedy*, 2nd edn. New York and Oxford: Oxford University Press

—— (1995), 'Beyond Aristophanes', in Gregory W. Dobrov (ed.), *Beyond Aristophanes: Transition and Diversity in Greek Comedy*, 175–83. Atlanta, Georgia: Scholars Press

—— (1998), 'Attic Old Comedy, Frank Speech, and Democracy', in Deborah A. Boedeker and Kurt A. Raaflaub (eds.), *Democracy, Empire, and the Arts in Fifth-Century Athens*, 255–73. Cambridge, Massachusetts, and London: Harvard University Press

—— (1998–2002, ed.), *Aristophanes*, 4 vols. Loeb Classical Library. Cambridge, Massachusetts: Harvard University Press

—— (2002, ed. and transl.) *Aristophanes vol. 4: Frogs, Assemblywomen, Wealth*. Loeb Classical Library. Cambridge, Massachusetts: Harvard University Press

HENZE, HANS WERNER (1996), *Reiselieder mit böhmischen Quinten: autobiographische Mitteilungen, 1926–1995*. Frankfurt am Main: Fischer. English translation by Stewart Spencer, *Bohemian Fifths: An Autobiography* (published in 1998). London: Faber

HERBERT, TREVOR (1989), 'Sondheim's Technique', *Contemporary Music Review*, 5/1, 199–214

HERRICK, MARVIN (1950), *Comic Theory in the Sixteenth Century*. Urbana: University of Illinois Press

H.F. (1909), 'A Paean', *Varsity*, 8/11, 4 February, 432

HICKIE, WILLIAM JAMES (1853–74), *The Comedies of Aristophanes: A New and Literal Translation from the Text of Dindorf, with Notes and Extracts from the Best Metrical Versions* (Bohn's Classical Library), 2 vols. London: G. Bell

HIGHFILL, PHILIP, BURNIM, KALMAN, and LANGHANS, EDWARD (1991, eds.), 'Stoppelaer, Charles', in *A Biographical Dictionary of Actors, Actresses, Musicians, Dancers, Managers and Other Stage Personnel in London, 1660–1800*, xiv. 289–91. Carbondale: Southern Illinois University Press

HILLE, CURT (1907), *Die deutsche Komödie unter der Einwirkung des Aristophanes: Ein zur* (Breslauer Beiträge zur Literaturgeschichte, NF 2). Leipzig: Quelle and Meyer

HILSENBECK, FRITZ (1908), *Aristophanes und die deutsche Literatur des 18. Jahrhunderts*. Berlin: Eberling

HINES, SAMUEL PHILIP (1966), 'English Translations of Aristophanes' Comedies, 1655–1742', PhD thesis submitted to the University of North Carolina at Chapel Hill (UMI ProQuest Digital Dissertations, publication number AAT 6802196)

HIRZEL, RUDOLF (1895), *Der Dialog: Ein literarhistorischer Versuch*, 2 vols. Leipzig: Hirzel

HISCHAK, THOMAS S. (1991), *Word Crazy: Broadway Lyricists from Cohan to Sondheim*. New York: Praeger

HOFFMAN, FRANÇOIS-BENOÎT (1802), *Lisistrata ou les Athéniennes: comédie en un acte et en prose, mêlée de vaudevilles, imitée d'Aristophane; dont les représentations ont été suspendues par Ordre*. Paris

—— (1829), *Œuvres*, 10 vols. Paris: Lefebvre

HOFMANNSTHAL, HUGO VON (1908), *Vorspiele*. Leipzig: Insel

HOGARTH, D. G., and GODLEY, A. D. (1892, eds.), *Aristophanous Batrachoi. The Frogs of Aristophanes, Adapted for Performance by the Oxford University Dramatic Scoiety, 1892. With an English Version Partly Adapted from that of J. Hookham Frere and Partly Written for the Occasion by D. G. Hogarth and A. D. Godley*. Oxford: Printed by Horace Hart; London: Frowde

HOLE, WILLIAM (1884), *Quasi Cursores: Portraits of the High Officers and Professors of the University of Edinburgh at its Tercentenary Festival, Drawn and Etched by William Hole*. Edinburgh: Edinburgh University Press

HOLROYD, MICHAEL (2004), 'The Fearless Bernard Shaw', *Lincoln Center Theater Review*, 38 (Summer), 25–26

HOLTERMANN, MARTIN (2004), *Der deutsche Aristophanes: Die Rezeption eines politischen Dichters im 19. Jahrhundert*. Göttingen: Vandenhoeck und Ruprecht

HORN-MONVAL, MADELEINE (1958), *Traductions et adaptations du théâtre étranger du XVe siècle à nos jours*, i: *Théâtre grec antique*. Paris: CNRS

HOROWITZ, MARK EDEN (2003), *Sondheim on Music: Minor Details and Major Decisions*. Lanham, Maryland, and Oxford: Scarecrow

HORTON, ANDREW (2000), *Laughing Out Loud: Writing the Comedy-Centered Screenplay*. Berkeley, California, and London: University of California Press

HOUSMAN, LAURENCE (1937), *The Unexpected Years*. London: Cape

HOWARD, EDWARD (1671), *The Six Days Adventure; or, The New Utopia. A Comedy*. London: T. Dring

HUGHES, A. (1996), 'Comic Stages in Magna Graecia: The Evidence of the Vases', *Theatre Research International*, 21, 95–107

HUGHES, DEREK (1996), *English Drama, 1660–1700*. Oxford: Oxford University Press

HUBBARD, THOMAS K. (1991), *The Mask of Comedy: Aristophanes and the Intertextual Parabasis*. Ithaca: Cornell University Press

HUNTER, RICHARD L. (2000), 'The Politics of Plutarch's Comparison of Aristophanes and Menander', in Susanne Gödde and Theodor Heinze (eds.), *Skenika: Beiträge zum antiken Theater und seiner Rezeption*, 267–76. Darmstadt: Wissenschaftliche Buchgesellschaft

HURST, ISOBEL (2006), *Victorian Women Writers and the Classics: The Feminine of Homer*. Oxford: Oxford University Press

HYSLOP, BEATRICE F. (1945), 'The Theater during a Crisis: The Parisian Theater during the Reign of Terror', *The Journal of Modern History*, 17/4, 332–55

IADICICCO, ALESSANDRO (2002), 'Le rane di Ronconi gracidano contro Berlusconi, Fini e Bossi', *Il Giornale*, 20 May 2002, 19

INGRAM, WILLIAM HENRY (1966), 'Greek Drama and the Augustan Stage: Dennis, Theobald, Thomson', dissertation submitted to the University of Pennsylvania

INSKIP, DONALD (1972), *Forty Little Years: The Story of a Theatre*. Cape Town: Timmins

ISAKA, RIHO (1999), 'The Gujarati Literati and the Construction of a Regional Identity in the Late Nineteenth Century', unpublished PhD thesis submitted to the University of Cambridge

—— (2002), 'Lanugage and Dominance; The Debates over the Gujarati Language in the Late Nineteenth Century', *South Asia: Journal of South Asian Studies*, 25, 1–19

—— (no date), 'The Gujarati Elites and the Construction of a Regional Identity in the Late Nineteenth Century', unpublished paper given at the 16th European Conference on Modern South Asian Studies (Edinburgh, 6–9 September 2000), online at http://www.sociology.ed.ac.uk/sas/papers/panel45_Isaka.rtf (accessed 13 September 2006)

JACOB, P. L. (1843–45), *Bibliothèque dramatique de Monsieur de Soleinne, catalogue rédigé par P. L. Jacob, bibliophile* [pseud.], 7 vols. Paris: Administration de l'Alliance des arts

JÄGER, ANDREA (1986), *Der Dramatiker Peter Hacks: vom Produktionsstück zur Klassizität*. Marburg: Hitzeroth

JENKYNS, RICHARD (1980), *The Victorians and Ancient Greece*. Oxford: Basil Blackwell

JERKOV, BARBARA (2002), 'Ci attaccano coi nostri soldi', *La Repubblica*, 20 May 2002, 13

JHAVERI, KRISHNALAL MOHANLAL (1924), *Further Milestones in Gujarati Literature*. Bombay

—— (2003, ed.), *Gujarati Language and Literature*, v: *The Gujaratis: The People, Their History, and Culture*. Reprint. New Delhi: Cosmo

JOCELYN, H. D. (1993), 'The University's Contribution to Classical Studies', in John Prest (ed.), *The Illustrated History of Oxford University*, 160–95. Oxford: Oxford University Press

JONES, CHRISTOPHER P. (1993), 'Greek Drama in the Roman Empire', in Scodel (1993, ed.), 39–52

JONES, JOHN BUSH (1970, ed.), *W. S. Gilbert: A Century of Scholarship and Commentary*. New York: New York University Press

—— (2003), *Our Musicals, Ourselves: A Social History of the American Musical Theater*. Hanover, New Haven: Brandeis University Press

JONES, MERVYN (1999), *The Amazing Victorian: A Life of George Meredith*. London: Constable

JONES, RICHARD FOSTER (1919), *Lewis Theobald: His Contribution to English Scholarship, with Some Unpublished Letters*. New York: Columbia University Press

JONSON, BEN (1925–52), *Ben Jonson*, ed. C. H. Herford, P. Simpson, and E. Simpson, 11 vols. Oxford: Clarendon Press

—— (1995), *Poetaster*, ed. Tom Cain. Manchester: Manchester University Press

—— (2001), *Every Man Out of his Humour*, ed. Helen Ostovich. Manchester: Manchester University Press

JOSHI, SVATI (2004), 'Dalpatram and the Nature of Literary Shifts in Nineteenth-Century Ahmedabad', in Stuart Blackburn and Vasudha Dalmia (eds.), *India's Literary History: Essays on the Nineteenth Century*, 327–57. Delhi: Permanent Black

KALLERGES, LYKOURGOS (1999), 'Laike Skene: He Apheteria', *Kathemerine*, 14 February 1999, Sunday Supplement (on Karolos Koun)

KALOUSTIAN, DAVID (2004), 'Wrangham, Francis (1769–1842)', *Oxford Dictionary of National Biography*. Oxford: Oxford University Press. Online at http://www.oxforddnb.com/view/article/30009 (accessed 20 August 2006)

KANGELARI, DIO (2005), 'Classical and Classicizing' [in Greek], *I Kathimerini*, 5 June 2005 (special issue on fifty years of the Athens Festival), 4

KARNICK, KRISTINE BRUNOVSKA, and JENKINS, HENRY (1995), *Classical Hollywood Comedy.* New York and London: Routledge

KASSEL, RUDOLF, and COLIN AUSTIN (1983– , eds.), *Poetae comici Graeci,* 8 vols. Berlin: De Gruyter

KEIL, BRUNO (1898, ed.), *Aelii Aristidis Smyrnaei quae supersunt omnia,* ii. Berlin

KENNEDY, EMMET, NETTER, M.-L., McGREGOR, J. P., and OLSEN, M. V. (1996), *Theatre, Opera and Audiences in Revolutionary Paris: Analysis and Repertory.* Westport, CT, and London: Greenwood Press

KERR, JESSICA M. (1965), 'English Wedding Music', *The Musical Times,* 106, no. 1463 (January 1965), 53–55

KINGSTON, GERTRUDE (1937), *Curtsey While you're Thinking ...* London: Williams and Norgate

KIPPHARDT, HEINAR (1989), *Schreibt die Wahrheit. Essays, Briefe, Entwürfe,* i: *1949–64, Schreibt die Wahrheit* (Gesammelte Werke in Einzelausgaben). Reinbek bei Hamburg: Rowohlt

KISLAN, RICHARD (1980), *The Musical: A Look at the American Musical Theater.* Englewood Cliffs, NJ: Prentice-Hall

KISSEL, HOWARD (2004), 'Sondheim Shoulda Let Sleeping *Frogs* Lie', *Daily News (New York),* 23 July 2004

'K.L.' (1965), 'Drei Monate Zeit für Proben. Über die Arbeit des Deutsche Theaters in Ostberlin', *Die andere Zeitung* (Hamburg), 20 May 1965

KLEINKNECHT, HERMANN (1967), *Die Gebetsparodie in der Antike,* repr. from *Tübinger Beiträge zur Altertumswissenschaft,* 28 (1937). Hildesheim: Olms

KNUDSEN, HANS (1949), *Goethes Welt des Theaters: Ein Vierteljahrhundert Weimarer Bühnenleitung.* Berlin: Druckhaus Tempelhof

KOCK, THEODOR (1880–88, ed.), *Comicorum Atticorum Fragmenta.* Leipzig: Teubner

KOLK, MIEKE, and DECREUS, FREDDY (2005, eds.), *The Performance of the Comic in Arabic Theatre: Cultural Heritage, Western Models and Postcolonial Hybridity* (= *Documenta,* special issue 23/2)

KOLTSIDOPOULOU, ANNY TH. (1975), 'Epidaurus 1975' [in Greek], *Anti,* 2nd ser. 2/28, 20 September 1975, 50–51

KONSTAN, DAVID (1988), 'The Premises of Comedy', *Journal of Popular Film and Television,* 15, 180–90

—— and DILLON, MATTHEW (1981), 'The Ideology of Aristophanes' *Wealth'*, *American Journal of Philology,* 102, 371–94

KONTOGIORGI, ANASTASIA (2000), *The Stage Design of Greek Theatre, 1930–1960* [in Greek]. Thessaloniki: University Studio Press

KOTZAMANI, MARINA (1997), '*Lysistrata,* Playgirl of the Western World: Aristophanes on the Early Modern Stage', PhD dissertation submitted to the City University of New York

—— (2005), 'Performing Aristophanes' *Lysistrata* on the Arabic stage', in Kolk and Decreus (eds.), 235–43

KOUGIOUMTZIS, MIMIS (1989), 'Maske ston choro archaiou dramato', *II International Meeting on Ancient Greek Drama, Delphi, 15–20 June 1986,* 139–42. Athens: Proceedings of the European Cultural Centre of Delphi

KOUN, KAROLOS (1981), *Karolos Koun gia to theatro: keimena kai Synenteurei.* Athens: Ithaki

—— (1985), an interview by Vasilis Angelikopoulos, *Ta Nea,* 18 July 1985

—— (1997), *Kanoume theatro gia tin psychi mas,* 4th edn. Athens: Kastaniotes

KRAKOVITCH, ODILE (1982), *Les Pièces de théâtre soumises à la censure: 1800–1830.* Paris: Archives nationales

KUCKHOFF, ARMIN-GERD (1969), 'Rezeption antiker Dramen auf den Bühnen der DDR',

Das klassische Altertum in der sozialistischen Kultur, Wiss. Zeitschrift der Friedrich-Schiller-Universität Jena, 18, 61–66

—— (1973), 'Antike im Spannungsfeld der Zeit. Zur Rezeption antik-griechischer Dramatik im Theater', in *Die gesellschaftliche Bedeutung des antiken Dramas für seine und für unsere Zeit. Protokoll der Karl-Marx-Städter Fachtagung vom 24. bis 31.10. 1969.* Schriften zur Geschichte und Kultur der Antike, 6, 4–15

KUNERT, G. (2002), 'Von der Antike eingeholt', in Bernd Seidensticker and Martin Vöhler (eds.), 227–28

KUSCHNIA, MICHAEL (1986, ed.), *100 Jahre Deutsches Theater Berlin, 1883–1983*, 2nd edn. Berlin: Henschelverlag Kunst und Gesellschaft

KUSHNER, TONY (2003), 'Only We who Guard the Mystery Shall be Unhappy', *The Nation*, 24 March 2003. Online at http://www.thenation.com/doc/20030324/kushner (accessed 3 October 2006)

LA MATTINA, AMEDEO (2002), 'Berlusconi: il governo non censura nessuno', *La Stampa*, 21 May 2002, 11

LANE, NATHAN (2004*a*), '*The Frogs*', unpublished script, revised and edited from Shevelove (1975)

—— (2004*b*), 'A Leap of Fate', *Lincoln Center Theater Review*, 38 (Summer), 5–6

LANZA, DIEGO (1997), *La disciplina dell'emozione: Un'introduzione alla tragedia greca.* Milan: Il Saggiatore

LAUTER, PAUL (1964, ed.), *Theories of Comedy.* Garden City, New York: Anchor Books

LEAKE, WILLIAM R. M. *et al.* (1938), *Gilkes and Dulwich, 1885–1914: A Study of a Great Headmaster.* London: Alleyn Club

LEDERGERBER, P. ILDEPHONS (1905), *Lukian und der altattische Komödie.* Diss. Freiburg in der Schweitz. Einsiedeln: Benziger

LEEZENBERG, MICHIEL (2005), 'Comedy between Performativity and Polyphony: The Politics of Non-Serious Language', in Kolk and Decreus (eds.), 195–209

LE FÈVRE, ANNE [MADAME DACIER] (1684), *Le Plutus et Les nuées d'Aristophane: Comedies grecques, traduites en françois.* Paris: Denys Thierry

—— (1692), *Comedies grecques d'Aristophane, traduites en françois, avec des notes critiques, & un Examen de chaque Piece selon les regles du Theatre.* Paris: Denys

LE FÈVRE, TANNEGUI (1659), *Tanaquili Fabri epistolae, quarum pleraeque ad emendationem scriptorum veterum pertinent. Pars altera. Additae sunt Aristophanis Ecclesiazusae cum interpretatione nova.* Saumur

LEFKOWITZ, MARY R. (1981), *The Lives of the Greek Poets.* London: Duckworth

LE LOYER, PIERRE (2004), *La Néphélococugie, ou, La Nuée des cocus: Première adaptation des Oiseaux d'Aristophane en français*, ed. Miriam Doe and Keith Cameron. Geneva: Droz

LEMPRIÈRE, JOHN (1788), *Bibliotheca Classica; or, A Classical Dictionary, Containing a Full Account of All the Proper Names Mentioned in Antient Authors. To Which are Subjoined, Tables of Coins, Weights, and Measures, in Use among the Greeks and Romans.* Reading: A. M. Smart and T. Cowslade

LENIN, VLADIMIR ILYICH (1966), *Lenin Reader*, selected and edited by Stefan T. Possony. Chicago: Regnery

—— (1970), *Werke*, xxxi, 4th edn. of the German translation. Berlin: Dietz

LENZ, FRIEDRICH WALTHER, and BEHR, CHARLES ALLISON (1976, eds.), *P. Aelii Aristidis opera quae exstant omnia*, i: *Orationes 1–16.* Leiden: Brill

LENZ, JAKOB MICHAEL REINHOLD (1902), *Vertheidigung des Herrn Wieland gegen die Wolken, von dem Verfasser der Wolken (1776), von J. M. R. Lenz*, ed. Erich Schmidt. Deutsche Litteraturdenkmale des 18. und 19. Jahrhunderts, Nr. 121. Berlin: Behr

LESKY, ALBIN (1963), *Geschichte der griechischen Literatur*². Bern: Francke

LEVER, KATHERINE (1946), 'Greek Comedy on the Sixteenth Century English Stage', *Classical Journal*, 42, 169–73

LEVIN, HARRY (1987), *Playboys and Killjoys: An Essay on the Theory and Practice of Comedy*. New York: Oxford University Press

LEWES, G. H. (1867), *Female Characters of Goethe, from the Original Drawings by William Kaulbach, with Explanatory Text by G. H. Lewes*. London: n.p.

LINDNER, MARGRIT (1972), 'Antikenrezeption in der Dramatik der DDR', unpublished dissertation submitted to Universität Leipzig

LINDSAY, JACK (1956), *George Meredith: His Life and Work*. London: Bodley Head

LITTLEFIELD, DAVID J. (1968, ed.), *Twentieth Century Interpretations of the Frogs: A Collection of Critical Essays*. Englewood Cliffs, NJ: Prentice-Hall

LLOYD-JONES, HUGH, and PARSONS, PETER (1983, eds.), *Supplementum Hellenisticum*. Berlin and New York: de Gruyter

LOCRÉ, JEAN-GUILLAUME (1819), *Discussions sur la liberté de la presse, la censure, la propriété littéraire, l'imprimerie et la librairie qui ont eu lieu dans le Conseil d'État pendant les années 1808, 1809, 1810 et 1811*. Paris: Garnery

LONG, WILLIAM IVEY (2004), 'How High Should I Jump?', *Lincoln Center Theater Review*, 38 (Summer), 21–24

LORD, CARNES (1979), 'On Machiavelli's *Mandragola*', *The Journal of Politics*, 41/3 (August), 806–27

LORD, LOUIS E. (1925), *Aristophanes: His Plays and Influence*. London: Harrap. Boston, Massachusetts: Marshall Jones Company

LOTT, ERIC (1995), *Love and Theft: Blackface Minstrelsy and the American Working Class*. New York and Oxford: Oxford University Press

LUZI, GIANLUCA (2002), ' "Questo governo non censura" ', *La Repubblica*, 21 May 2002, 10

MAAZ, WOLFGANG. (2002), 'Berlin — Kunerts Antike', in Bernd Seidensticker and Martin Vöhler (eds.), 229–53

MACASDAR, PHILIPPE (1995), *Benno Besson, der fremde Freund. Wiedersehen mit dem faszinierenden Theatermann*, a film by Philippe Macasdar. Berlin: Unidoc Film & Video

MCCONICA, JAMES (2004), 'Erasmus, Desiderius (c.1467–1536)', in *Oxford Dictionary of National Biography*, ed. H. C. G. Matthew and Brian Harrison. Oxford: Oxford University Press. Online at http://www.oxforddnb.com/view/article/39358 (accessed 8 March 2006)

MCCUSKER, JANE A. (1984), 'Browning's "Aristophanes' Apology" and Matthew Arnold', *The Modern Language Review*, 29/4 (October), 783–96

MCDONALD, MARIANNE (1992), *Ancient Sun, Modern Light: Greek Drama on the Modern Stage*. New York: Columbia University Press

—— (2003), *The Living Art of Greek Tragedy*. Bloomington: Indiana University Press

MACDOWELL, DOUGLAS M. (1976), 'Bastards as Athenian Citizens', *Classical Quarterly*, NS 26/1, 88–91

—— (1993), 'Foreign Birth and Athenian Citizenship in Aristophanes', in Sommerstein *et al.* (eds.), 359–71

—— (1995), *Aristophanes and Athens: An Introduction to the Plays*. Oxford: Oxford University Press

MCGLEW, JAMES (1997), 'After Irony: Aristophanes' *Wealth* and its Modern Interpreters', *American Journal of Philology*, 118, 35–53

—— (2002), *Citizens on Stage: Comedy and Political Culture in the Athenian Democracy*. Ann Arbor: University of Michigan Press

MACINTOSH, FIONA (1997), 'Tragedy in Performance: Nineteenth- and Twentieth-Century Productions', in Easterling (ed.), 284–323

—— (1998), 'The Shavian Murray and the Euripidean Shaw: *Major Barbara* and the *Bacchae*', *Classics Ireland*, 5, 64–84

—— (2005), 'Viewing *Agamemnon* in Nineteenth-Century Britain', in Macintosh, Michelakis, Hall, and Taplin (eds.), 139–62

—— MICHELAKIS, PANTELIS, HALL, EDITH, and TAPLIN, OLIVER (2005, eds.), *Agamemnon in Performance, 458 BC–AD 2004*. Oxford: Oxford University Press

MACKINNON, ALAN (1910), *The Oxford Amateurs: A Short History of Theatricals at the University*, with a foreword by James Adderley. London: Chapman and Hall

MACLEOD, MALCOLM D. (1991), *Lucian. A Selection: Edited with an Introduction, Translation and Commentary*. Warminster: Aris and Phillips

McPHERSON, DAVID (1974), 'Jonson's Library and Marginalia: An Annotated Catalogue', *Studies in Philology*, 71/5, 1–106

MADAN, FALCONER (1885), 'The Day-Book of John Dorne', in C. R. L. Fletcher (ed.), *Collectanea*, i. 71–177. Oxford: Clarendon, printed for the Oxford Historical Society

MALTESE, CURZIO (2002), 'Il palcoscenico della signoria', *La Repubblica*, 21 May 2002, 1, 17

MALTHAN, PAUL (1970), 'Spiegelungen der Antike in der dramatischen Literatur der Gegenwart', *Gymnasium*, 77, 171–89

MALTHUS, THOMAS ROBERT (1798), *An Essay on the Principle of Population, as it Affects the Future Improvement of Society with Remarks on the Speculations of Mr Godwin, M. Condorcet, and Other Writers*. London: printed for J. Johnson

MANIAR, U. M. (1969), *The Influence of English on Gujarati Poetry*. Baroda: University of Baroda

MANSEL, HENRY LONGUEVILLE (1873), 'Scenes from an unfinished drama entitled *The Phrontisterion, or, Oxford in the 19th century*', in id., *Letters, Lectures and Reviews*, ed. Henry W. Chandler, 395–408. London: John Murray

MANZELLA, GIANNI (2002), 'La tragedia è quella politica', *Il Manifesto*, 21 May 2002, 2

MARÉCHAL, MARCEL (1969), 'Supplément au n°. 12 d'Approches, Journal de la Compagnie du Cothurne' (a copy of this document is held at the Bibliothèque de la Maison Jean Vilar, Avignon)

MARGRAFF, RUTH (2002), *Red Frogs: A Burlesque for the Summer Purgatorio*, published in *American Theater Magazine*, 19/9 (November), 45–60

MARKS, PETER (2004), '*The Frogs*: Nathan Lane Dives into Political Pond', *The Washington Post*, 23 July 2004

MARSHALL, C. W. (1996), 'Amphibian Ambiguities Answered', *Échos du Monde Classique/ Classical Views* 15, 251–65

MARSHALL, D. (1986), 'Rousseau and the State of Theatre', *Representations*, 13, 84–114

MARTINEAU, J. (1895), *The Life and Correspondence of Sir Bartle Frere*, 2 vols. London: Murray

MARTIN, JOHN (1952), 'The Dance: Approval', *The New York Times*, 30 November 1952

MAVROGENI, MARIA (2002), 'The Incorporation of Ancient Comedy in the Athens and Epidaurus Festivals — The Unsolvable Problem of Aristophanes' [in Greek], in Iosiph Vivilakis (ed.), *The Greek Theatre from the Seventeenth to the Twentieth Century* [in Greek], 345–55. Athens: Ergo

MEINECK, PETER (1991, transl.), *The Frogs Adapted and Directed by Fiona Laird*. Audiovisual recording. New York: Film Counselors

MELAS, SPYROS (1952, ed.), *Elliniki Dimiourgia*, 10, no. 115: special issue on Aristophanes

MENDELSOHN, DANIEL (2004), 'For the Birds', *The New York Review of Books*, 2 December 2004, 51–54

MEREDITH, GEORGE (1919), *An Essay on Comedy and the Uses of the Comic Spirit*. Standard edn. First published in *New Quarterly Magazine*, April 1877; 1st book edn. 1897. London: Constable

MERLO, FRANCESCO (2002), 'Le Rane e i buoi', *Corriere della Sera*, 21 May 2002, 1.5

MERRITT, J. F. (1996, ed.), *The Political World of Thomas Wentworth, Earl of Strafford, 1621–1641*. Cambridge: Cambridge University Press

MESSINA, SEBASTIANO (2002), 'I tiranni di Aristofane', *La Repubblica*, 20 May 2002, 1.14

MEZZABOTTA, MARGARET (1994), 'Frolicking Frogs Rap in Cape Town', *Didaskalia*, 1/3, published online at http://www.didaskalia.net/issues/vol1no3/mezzabotta.html (accessed 13 September 2006)

MICHELAKIS, PANTELIS (2002), 'Mise en scène de *La Paix* d'Aristophane', in Rochefort-Guillouet, 115–17

—— (2005), 'Introduction: *Agamemnons* in Performance', in Macintosh, Michelakis, Hall and Taplin (eds.), 1–20

MILLER, D. A. (1998), *Place for Us: Essay on the Broadway Musical*. Cambridge, Massachusetts: Harvard University Press

MILLER, JONATHAN (1986), *Subsequent Performances*. London and Boston: Faber and Faber

MILLER, SCOTT (1997), '*Assassins* and the Concept Musical', in Gordon (ed.), 187–204

MILTON, J. R. (2004), 'Locke, John (1632–1704)', *Oxford Dictionary of National Biography*. Oxford: Oxford University Press. Online at http://www.oxforddnb.com/view/article/16885 (accessed 6 August 2006)

MINTURNO, ANTONIO SEBASTIANO (1563), *L'arte poetica del sig. Antonio Minturno*. Venice

MIOLA, ROBERT S. (1994), *Shakespeare and Classical Comedy: The Influence of Plautus and Terence*. Oxford: Clarendon Press

MITCHELL, MICHAEL (1990), *Peter Hacks: Theatre for a Socialist Society*. Glasgow: Scottish Papers in Germanic Studies

MITCHELL, THOMAS (1839, ed.), *The Frogs of Aristophanes*. London

MITTENZWEI, WERNER (1978), 'Die Antikerezeption des DDR-Theaters: Zu den Antikestücken von Peter Hacks und Heiner Müller', in id., *Kampf der Richtungen: Strömungen und Tendenzen der internationalen Dramatik*, 524–56. Leipzig: Reclam

MIX, K. L. (1975), 'Laurence, Clemence and Votes for Women', *Housman Society Journal*, 2, 42–52

MOMIGLIANO, ARNALDO (1950), 'Ancient History and the Antiquarian', *Journal of the Warburg and Courtauld Institutes*, 13, 285–315; reprinted in id., *Studies in Historiography* (London, 1966), 3–30

MONTANARI, UGO (1990), 'L'opera letteraria di Cesare Cremonini', in *Centro Studi Girolamo Baruffaldi*, 125–247

MOORE, MICHAEL (2004). *Fahrenheit 9/11*, a film written and directed by Michael Moore. Columbia Tristar Films

MORANTE, ELSA (1968), *Il mondo salvato dai ragazzini*. Turin: Einaudi

MORASH, CHRISTOPHER (2002), *A History of Irish Theatre, 1601–2000*. Cambridge, New York, and Melbourne: Cambridge University Press

MORDDEN, ETHAN (1984), *Broadway Babies: The People Who Made the American Musical*. New York and Oxford: Oxford University Press

MORGAN, JOHN R. (1985), 'Lucian's *True Histories* and *The Wonders beyond Thule* of Antonios Diogenes', *Classical Quarterly*, NS 35, 475–90

MORRILL, JOHN (1992, ed.), *Revolution and Restoration: England in the 1650s*. London: Collins & Brown

MUKTA, PARITA (1999), 'The "Civilizing Mission": The Regulation and Control of Mourning in Colonial India', *Feminist Review* 63, 25–47

MULDOON, PAUL (1999), *The Birds*, translated by Paul Muldoon with Richard Martin. Loughcrew, County Meath: Gallery Press

MÜLLER, ANDRÉ (1967, ed.), *Der Regisseur Benno Besson: Gespräche, Notate, Aufführungsfotos*. Berlin: Henschelverlag Kunst u. Gesellschaft

MÜLLER, HEINER (1982), *Rotwelsch*. Berlin: Merve-Verlag

—— (1989), *The Battle: Plays, Prose, Poems*, ed. and transl. by Carl Weber. New York: Performing Arts Journal Publications

MURRAY, GILBERT (1902), *The Athenian Drama*, iii: *Hippolytus, Bacchae, Frogs*. London: G. Allen

—— (1933), *Aristophanes: A Study*. Oxford: Clarendon

MURRAY, MATTHEW (2004), 'The Frogs', review published online at http://www.talkinbroadway.com/world/Frogs.html (accessed 4 October 2006)

MYRSIADES, LINDA, and MYRSIADES, KOSTAS (1999), *Cultural Representation in Historical Resistance: Complexity and Construction in Greek Guerrilla Theater*. Lewisburg, Pennsylvania: Bucknell University Press

NAIRNE, ALEXANDER (1915), 'A Greek Prayer for Peace: To the Editor', *The Times*, 2 January 1915, 9

NAPOLÉON (1858–70), *Correspondance de Napoléon Ier, publiée par ordre de l'Empereur Napoléon III*. Paris: Plon-Dumaine

NASHE, THOMAS (1958), *The Works of Thomas Nashe*, ed. R. B. McKerrow, rev. F. P. Wilson, 5 vols. Oxford: Clarendon Press

NEHAMAS, ALEXANDER (1998), *The Art of Living: Socratic Reflections from Plato to Foucault*. Berkeley, California: University of California Press

NELSON, ALAN H. (1989, ed.), *Records of Early English Drama: Cambridge*, 2 vols. Toronto: Toronto University Press

NELSON, T. G. A. (1990), *Comedy. An Introduction to Comedy in Literature, Drama and Cinema*. Oxford: Oxford University Press

NISBET, GIDEON (2003), *Greek Epigram in the Roman Empire. Martial's Forgotten Rivals*. Oxford: Oxford University Press

NORDELL, ROBERT H. (2000), 'The Aristophanic Swift', PhD thesis submitted to the University of Nebraska-Lincoln

NORWOOD, GILBERT (1931), *Greek Comedy*. London: Methuen. Repr. 1964

—— (1968), 'Farce in the *Frogs*', an excerpt from Norwood (1931) reprinted in Littlefield (1968, ed.), 110

O'BRIEN, SEAN (1998), *The Deregulated Muse*. Newcastle upon Tyne: Bloodaxe

—— (1998b, ed.), *The Firebox: Poetry in Britain and Ireland after 1945*. London: Picador

—— (2002a), *The Birds by Aristophanes: A Verse Version*. London: Methuen

—— (2002b), *Cousin Coat: Selected Poems 1976–2001*. London: Picador

—— (2006), *Inferno: A Verse Version of Dante's Inferno*. London: Picador

OHLMEYER, JANE (1995, ed.), *Ireland from Independence to Occupation, 1641–1660*. Cambridge: Cambridge University Press

—— (1998), ' "Civilizinge of those Rude Partes": Colonization within Britain and Ireland, 1580s–1640s', in Nicholas Canny (ed.), *The Oxford History of the British Empire*, i: *The Origins of Empire*, 124–47. Oxford: Oxford University Press

—— (2000, ed.), *Political Thought in Seventeenth-Century Ireland: Kingdom or Colony*. Cambridge: Cambridge University Press

OLIVIER, CLAUDE (1961), 'Comment faire *La Paix*' (a debate between Jean Vilar, Hubert Gignoux, Michel Fontayne, and Antoine Vitez), *Les Lettres françaises*, 21 December 1961

OPIE, IONA, and OPIE, PETER (1951, eds.), *The Oxford Dictionary of Nursery Rhymes*. Oxford: Clarendon Press

ORFANOS, CHARALAMPOS (1998), introduction and notes to *Les Guêpes (The Wasps)*, ed. Victor Coulon and transl. by Hilaire Van Daele. Paris: Les Belles Lettres

—— (2002), 'Néphélococcygie et la jeunesse éternelle', *Cahiers du GITA*, 15, 137–71

—— (2003), 'Un tissu de mensonges. Essai sur le premier épisode du *Philoctète* de Sophocle', *Dioniso*, 2, 6–15

—— (2006), *Les Sauvageons d'Athènes ou la didactique du rire chez Aristophane*. Collection Histoire. Paris: Les Belles lettres

ORKIN, MARTIN (1991), *Drama and the South African State*. Manchester: Manchester University Press

ORMOND, LEONÉE (2004), 'Du Maurier, George Louis Palmella Busson (1834–1896)', *Oxford Dictionary of National Biography*. Oxford: Oxford University Press. Online at http://www. oxforddnb.com/view/article/8194 (accessed 17 September 2006)

PALMER-SIKELIANOS, EVA (1993), *Upward Panic: The Autobiography of Eva Palmer-Sikelianos*, ed. with introduction and notes by John P. Anton. Chur and Philadelphia: Harwood

PANOFKA, T. (1849), 'Komödienscenen auf Thongefäßen', *Archäologische Zeitung*, 7, 18–21, 34–44

PAREKH, H. T. (1935), *Gujarat Varnakyular Sosaitino Itihas*, 3 vols. Ahmedabad

PARKER, DOUGLASS (n.d.), '*Money*', unpublished script

PARKER, L. P. E. (1997), *The Songs of Aristophanes*. Oxford: Clarendon

PARRY, C. HUBERT H. (1892), *The Music to the Frogs of Aristophanes, Composed for Performance at Oxford in 1892 ... with an English Version by D. G. Hogarth and A. D. Godley*. Leipzig, Brussels, London, and New York: Breitkopf and Härtel

—— (1914), *The Music to The Acharnians of Aristophanes: As Written for Performance by the Oxford University Dramatic Society, 1914, with an English Version of the Choruses*. Leipzig, Brussels, London, and New York: Breitkopf and Härtel

PEARCY, LEE T. (2003), 'Aristophanes in Philadelphia: The *Acharnians* of 1886', *Classical World*, 96/3, 299–313

PEARSON, MIKE, and SHANKS, MICHAEL (2001), *Theatre/Archaeology*. London and New York: Routledge

PELLIZZARI, GIOVANNI (1998), 'Cesare Cremonini e Giorgio Raguseo', in *Atti e Memorie dell'Accademia Patavina di Scienze, Lettere ed Arti. Memorie della Classe di Scienze Morali, Lettere ed Arti*, 110, 17–37. Padova

PENNACCHI, GIANNI (2002), 'Berlusconi chiude il caso Ronconi: "Una commedia degli equivoci"', *Il Giornale*, 21 May 2002, 8

PERRET, DONALD (1992), *Old Comedy in the French Renaissance, 1576–1620*. Geneva: Droz

PERROTTA, GENNARO (1954), 'Aristofane', *Enciclopedia dello Spettacolo*, i. 859–78. Rome

PEYSER, JOAN (1987), *Leonard Bernstein*. London: Bantam

PHILLIPS, MARGARET MANN (1964), *The Adages of Erasmus: A Study with Translations*. Cambridge: Cambridge University Press

PICARAZZI, TERESA (1999, ed.), *Lus. The Light. Ermanna Montanari performs Nevio Spadoni*. West Lafayette: Bordighera Press

—— and FEINSTEIN, WILEY (1997, eds), *An African Harlequin in Milan: Martinelli performs Goldoni*. West Lafayette: Bordighera Press

PICKARD-CAMBRIDGE, ARTHUR (1953), *The Dramatic Festivals of Athens*. Oxford: Oxford University Press

PIETZSCH, INGEBORG (1966), *Der komische Held bei Peter Hacks, untersucht an der Figur des Moritz Tassow in einem Vergleich zum Trygaios in der Bearbeitung des Frieden*. Staatsexamensarbeit am Institut für Theaterwissenschaft an der Humboldt-Universität Berlin (unpublished)

—— (1969), 'Antike aus der Sicht von heute', *Theater der Zeit*, 9, 58–60

PINCUS, S. (1992), 'England and the World in the 1650s', in Morill (1992, ed.), 129–47, 153

PLANCHÉ, JAMES ROBINSON (1846), *The Birds of Aristophanes: A Dramatic Experiment in One Act*. London

—— (1872), *The Recollections and Reflections of J. R. Planché*, 2 vols. London

PLORITIS, MARIOS (1948), 'National Theatre and Ancient Drama: Theatre and Propaganda' [in Greek], *Eleutheria*, 17 June 1948

—— (1962), a review of *Birds* directed by Karolos Koun, *Eleutheria*, 20 June 1962

PÖHLMANN, EGERT, and WEST, MARTIN L. (2001), *Documents of Ancient Greek Music: The Extant Melodies and Fragments, Edited and Transcribed with Commentary*. Oxford: Oxford University Press

POIROT-DELPECH, BERTRAND (1961), an article in *Le Monde*, 20 December 1961

POLLARD, ALFRED WILLIAM, and REDGRAVE, GILBERT RICHARD (1976–91), *A Short-Title Catalogue of Books Printed in England, Scotland, and Ireland and of English Books Printed Abroad, 1475–1640*, 3 vols., 2nd edn. rev. and enlarged, begun by W. A. Jackson and F. S. Ferguson, completed by K. F. Pantzer. London: Bibliographical Society

POLLOCK, SHELDON (2001), 'The Death of Sanskrit', *Comparative Studies in Society and History*, 43, 392–426

To Pontiki, 19 August 1999 (special issue on Aristophanes' *Birds*)

POOLE, ADRIAN, and MAULE, JEREMY (1995, eds.), *The Oxford Book of Classical Verse*. Oxford: Oxford University Press

PORCHÉ, FRANÇOIS (1933), *La Paix, Adaptation libre en deux parties d'après Aristophane*. Paris: Fayard

PORDAGE, SAMUEL (1660), *Troades. A Tragedie writen in Latine by Lannaeus Seneca, Translated into English by S. P. with Comments Annexed*. London: Printed by W. G. for Henry Marsh [...] and Peter Dring

POSTIGLIONE, VENANZIO (2002*a*), 'Caricature in Scena, Forza Italia litiga con Ronconi', *Corriere della Sera*, 20 May 2002, 5

—— (2002*b*), '"Sarò stato brusco, ma se mi accusa lo porto in tribunale"', *Corriere della Sera*, 20 May 2002, 5

—— (2002*c*), 'Non rimetto i pannelli, ma il premier avrebbe riso', *Corriere della Sera*, 21 May 2002

—— (2002*d*), 'Micchichè e Prestigiacomo frenano: solo opinoni personali', *Corriere della Sera*, 21 May 2002, 5

PRINCIPE, IGOR (2004), '*Le Rane* di Aristofane nell'Atene del 2000', *Il Giornale*, 27 February 2004

PROVVEDINI, CLAUDIA (2004), '*Le Rane* di Ronconi: Dioniso parla romanesco e l'Ade diventa un garage', *Corriere della Sera*, 4 March 2004

PRUDHOE, JOHN (1973), *The Theatre of Goethe and Schiller*. Oxford: Blackwell

PRYNNE, WILLIAM (1633), *Histriomastix*. London: printed by E.A. and W.I. for Michael Sparke

QUADRI, FRANCO (2002*a*), 'Ronconi: "È una censura: dovrei lasciare questo paese"', *La Repubblica*, 20 May 2002, 13

—— (2002*b*), 'Invettiva contro la corruzione', *La Repubblica*, 21 May 2002, 11

QUÉRO, DOMINIQUE (2000), 'Les éclats de rire du public de théâtre', *Dix-Huitième Siècle* 32, 67–83

RADCLIFFE, PHILIP F. (1983), 'The Music', an article in 'A Hundred Years of the Cambridge Greek Play', a special programme to accompany the 1983 production of *The Women of Trachis* directed by David Raeburn

RANADE, REKHA (1990), *Sir Bartle Frere and His Times: A Study of His Bombay Years, 1862–1867*. New Delhi: Mittal Publications

RANDOLPH, THOMAS (1630), *Aristippus; or, The Iouiall Philosopher*. London: printed for Robert Allot

—— (1651), *Ploutophthalmia ploutogamia. A Pleasant Comedie entituled Hey for Honesty, Down with Knavery, translated out of Aristophanes his Plutus by Tho. Randolph; augmented and published by F.J.* London: Francis Jacques

—— (1652), *Poems. With the Muses Looking-Glasse*, 4th edn. London: F. Bowman

—— (1924), *The Drinking Academy; or, The Cheater's Holiday*, ed. Hyder E. Rollins. Baltimore: The Modern Language Association of America

—— (1930), *The Drinking Academy: A Play*, ed. Samuel A. Tannenbaum and Hyder E. Rollins. With facsimiles. Cambridge, Massachusetts: Harvard University Press

RANKIN, DEANA (2004), 'Burnell, Henry (*fl.* 1640–1654)', *Oxford Dictionary of National Biography.* Oxford: Oxford University Press. Online at http://www.oxforddnb.com/view/article/4054 (accessed 30 May 2006)

RASKOLNIKOFF, MOUZA (1990), 'Gaius Gracchus ou la Révolution introuvable (historiographie d'une révolution)', in id., *Des Anciens et des Modernes*, articles réunis par Ségolène Demougin, 117–34. Paris: Publications de la Sorbonne

—— (1992), *Histoire romaine et critique historique dans l'Europe des Lumières.* Rome: École Française de Rome

RAU, PETER (1967), *Paratragodia: Untersuchung einer komischen Form des Aristophanes.* Munich: Beck

RAVAL, R. L. (1987), *Socio-Religious Reform Movements in Gujarat during the Nineteenth Century.* New Dehi: Ess Ess Publications

RAYMOND, JOAD (1993, ed.), *Making the News: An Anthology of the Newsbooks of Revolutionary England, 1641–1660.* Moreton-in-Marsh: Windrush Press

RECHNER, LEO (1914), 'Aristophanes in England: eine literar-historische Untersuchung', a doctoral dissertation submitted to K. Ludwig-Maximilians-Universität, Munich

RECKFORD, KENNETH J. (1987), *Aristophanes' Old-and-New Comedy.* Chapel Hill: University of North Carolina Press

—— (2002), review of E. Segal (2001), *American Journal of Philology*, 123/4, 641–44

RENSBURG, J. P. J. VAN (1970, transl.), *Die Lusistrata* [*Lysistrata* translated into Afrikaans]. Cape Town: Human and Rousseau

REGIE INTERNATIONAL (1988), *Regie International: Akademie-Gespräche mit Claus Peymann, Ralf Langbacka, Patrice Chéreau und Benno Besson*, ed. Verband der Theaterschaffenden der DDR (Material zum Theater, 217: Reihe internationales Theater, 16). Berlin

RESTON, JAMES, JR. (1985), *Coming to Terms: American Plays and the Vietnam War.* New York: Theatre Communications Group

REVEL-MOUROZ, MARIANNE (2002), 'La puissance créatrice de la poésie de la paix', in Rochefort-Guillouet, 98–106

REVERMANN, MARTIN (1999/2000), 'Euripides, Tragedy and Macedon: Some Conditions of Reception', in M. Cropp, K. Lee, and D. Sansone, *Euripides and Tragic Theatre in the Late Fifth Century* (= *Illinois Classical Studies*, 24–25, 1999/2000), 451–67. Champaign, IL: Stipes Publishing

—— (2006), *Comic Business: Theatricality, Dramatic Technique, and Performance Contexts of Aristophanic Comedy.* Oxford: Oxford University Press

REYHL, KLAUS (1969), *Antonios Diogenes: Untersuchungen zu den Roman-Fragmenten der 'Wunder jenseits von Thule' and zu den 'Wahren Geschichten' des Lukian.* Dissertation: Tübingen

RIEDEL, VOLKER (1984), *Antikerezeption in der Deutschen Demokratischen Republik.* Berlin: Akademie der Künste der DDR

—— (2000), *Antikerezeption in der deutschen Literatur vom Renaissance-Humanismus bis zur Gegenwart: eine Einführung.* Stuttgart: Metzler

—— (2002), 'Utopien und Wirklichkeit. Soziale Entwürfe in den Antikestücken von Peter Hacks', *Gymnasium* 109, 49–68. Repr. in Volker Riedel (2002), *Der Beste der Griechen; Achill das Vieh. Aufsätze und Vorträge zur literarischen Antikerezeption II*, 195–209, 299–302. Jena: Bussert & Stadeler

RIEKS, RUDOLF (1993), 'Zum Aristophanesstreit zwischen A. v. Platen, K. Immermann und H. Heine', in Dieter Ingenschay and Gerd Stratmann (eds.), *Re-Collections: Grobe Tritte eines hinkenden Pegasus. Zu Reinhold Schiffers 60. Geburtstag*, 117–28. Trier

RILEY, KATHLEEN (2004), 'Heracles as Dr Strangelove and GI Joe: Male Heroism Deconstructed', in Hall, Macintosh, and Wrigley (eds.), 113–41

RISTINE, FRANK HUMPHREY (1963), *English Tragicomedy: Its Origin and History.* New York: Russell & Russell

RITTER, HEIDI (1976), 'Vom "aufklärerischen" zum "klassischen" Theater. Untersuchungen zum Traditionsverhältnis in den Dramen von Peter Hacks', PhD thesis submitted to Martin-Luther-Universität Halle-Wittenberg

ROBIC, GREG (1994, transl.), 'Clouds', unpublished script, staged at The Poor Alex Theatre, Toronto

ROBINSON, CHRISTOPHER (1979), Lucian and his Influence in Europe. London: Duckworth

ROCHEFORT-GUILLOUET, SOPHIE (2002, ed.), Analyses et réflexions sur Aristophane, La Paix. Paris: Ellipses

ROHDE, ERWIN (1876), Der griechische Roman und seine Vorläufer. Leipzig: Breitkopf & Härtel; 3rd edn. published in 1914; repr. Hildesheim: Georg Olms in 1960

ROILOU, IOANNA (1999), 'Performances of Ancient Greek Tragedy on the Greek Stage of the Twentieth Century: An Intercultural and Sociological Approach', in Savvas Patsalidis and Akis Sakellaridou (eds.), (Dis)Placing Classical Greek Theatre, 191–202. Thessaloniki: University Studio Press

RONSARD, PIERRE DE (1617), Les Œuvres de Pierre de Ronsard, 11 vols. Paris: Nicolas Buon

ROSENBERG, DEENA (1997), Fascinating Rhythm: The Collaboration of George and Ira Gershwin, rev. edn. Ann Arbor: University of Michigan Press

ROSSI, LUIGI ENRICO (1997), 'L'approccio non classicistico di Pasolini alla tragedia attica', in Lezioni su Pasolini, ed. Tullio De Mauro and Francesco Ferri, 123–31. Ripatransone: Sestante Edizioni

ROTAS, VASILIS (1960, transl.), Works of Aristophanes. Birds: Translation, Introduction, and Commentary [in Greek]. Athens: Hetairia Logotechnikon Ekdoseon

RUSKIN, JOHN (1856), Modern Painters, 3 vols. 5th edn. London: Smith, Elder & Co

RUSSO, CARLO FERDINANDO (1962), Aristofane, autore di teatro. Florence: Sansoni; rev. edn. 1984

—— (1994), Aristophanes: An Author for the Stage, translation of Russo (1962) by Kevin Wren. London: Routledge

RYALS, CLYDE DE L. (1976), '"Analyzing humanity back into its elements": Browning's "Aristophanes' Apology" and Carlyle', in John Clubbe (ed.), Carlyle and his Contemporaries: Essays in Honor of Charles Richard Sanders, 280–97. Durham, NC: Duke University Press

RYAN, DESMOND (2004a), 'Frogs has Few Fellows in War Talk', Philadelphia Inquirer, 25 July 2004

—— (2004b), 'Sondheim's Frogs Takes Erratic Leaps', Philadelphia Inquirer, 25 July 2004

RYMER, THOMAS (1693), A Short View of Tragedy: Its Original, Excellency, and Corruption. With Some Reflections on Shakespear, and Other Practitioners for the Stage. London

SALINGAR, LEO (1974), Shakespeare and The Traditions of Comedy. Cambridge: Cambridge University Press

SALSINI, PAUL (2004), 'A Revised Frogs will Leap on to Broadway', The Sondheim Review, 10/4 (Spring), 6–7

SANDERS, JULIE (1998), 'Print, Popular Culture, Consumption and Commodification in The Staple of News', in Chedzgoy, Sanders, and Wiseman (1998, eds.), 183–207

SARLÓS, ROBERT K. (1989), 'Performance Reconstruction: The Vital Link Between Past and Future', in Thomas Postlewait and Bruce A. McConachie (eds.), Interpreting the Theatrical Past, 198–229. Iowa City: University of Iowa Press

SAVIOLI, AGGEO (1976), 'Aristofane come sacciapensieri', Unità, 30 May 1976

SAXONHOUSE, ARLENE W. (2006), Free Speech and Democracy in Ancient Athens. Cambridge: Cambridge University Press

SCHECHTER, JOEL (1994), Satiric Impersonations: From Aristophanes to the Guerrilla Girls. Carbondale: Southern Illinois University Press

SCHECK, FRANK (2004), 'The Frogs', Reuters, 22 July 2004

SCHEID, JUDITH ROBERTA (1977), *"Enfant terrible" of Contemporary East German Drama: Peter Hacks in his Role as an Adaptor and Innovator.* (Studien zur Germanistik, Anglistik und Komparatistik, 65). Bonn: Bouvier

SCHLEGEL, FRIEDRICH (1794), 'Vom ästhetischen Wert der griechischen Komödie', in Ernst Behler (1958, ed.), *Kritische Friedrich-Schlegel-Ausgabe*, i/1, 19–33. Paderborn: Schöning

SCHMID, JOHANN CHRISTOPHER (1833), *Petit Théâtre de l'enfance.* Paris: Levrault

SCHMIDT, MARGOT (1960), *Der Dareiosmaler und sein Umkreis: Untersuchungen zur spätapulischen Vasenmalerei* (Orbis antiquus, 15). Münster: Aschendorffsche Verlagsbuchhandlung

—— (1998), 'Komische arme Teufel und andere Gesellen auf der griechischen Komödienbühne', *Antike Kunst*, 41, 17–32

SCHMITT, OLIVIER (1991), 'Aristophane dans l'actualité: le satiriste grec montrait déjà que la terre pue', *Le Monde*, 8 March 1991, p. 19

SCHMITZ, MICHAEL (1989), *Friedrich Dürrenmatts Aristophanes-Rezeption: Eine Studie zu den mutigen Menschen in den Dramen der 50er und 60er Jahre.* St Ottilien: EOS Verlag

SCHOLTZ, MERWE (1978, transl.), *Die Paddas* [*Frogs* translated into Afrikaans]. Johannesburg: Perskor

SCHREIBER, FRED (1975), 'Unpublished Renaissance Emendations of Aristophanes', *Transactions of the American Philological Association*, 105, 313–32

SCHÜTZE, PETER (1976), *Peter Hacks. Ein Beitrag zur Ästhetik des Dramas. Antike und Mythenaneignung* (Literatur im historischen Prozeß, 6). Kronberg/Taunus: Scriptor

SCODEL, RUTH (1993, ed.), *Theater and Society in the Classical World.* Ann Arbor: University of Michigan Press

SCOLNICOV, HANNA (1989), 'Mimesis, Mirror, Double', in Hanna Scolnicov and Peter Holland (eds.), *The Play out of Context: Transferring Plays from Culture to Culture*, 89–98. Cambridge: Cambridge University Press

SCOUTEN, ARTHUR H. (1961), *The London Stage, 1660–1800: A Calendar of Plays, Entertainments & Afterpieces.* Part 3: *1729–1747*, 2 vols. Carbondale: Southern Illinois University Press

SCRIBE, EUGÈNE (1817), *Les Comices d'Athènes, ou les femmes orateurs, comédie vaudeville en un acte, traduit du grec d'Aristophane.* Paris

SECREST, MERYLE (1998), *Stephen Sondheim: A Life.* New York: Knopf. London: Bloombury

SEDGWICK, A. C. (1952), 'Authentic Classics from Athens: The Greek National Theatre to Present Two of Sophocles' Dramas Here', *The New York Times*, 16 November 1952

SEFERIS, GIORGOS (1967), *On the Greek Style: Selected Essays in Poetry and Hellenism*, trans. Rex Warner and Th. D. Frangopoulos. London: The Bodley Head

SEGAL, CHARLES P. (1961), 'The Character and Cults of Dionysus and the Unity of the *Frogs*', *Harvard Studies in Classical Philology*, 65, 207–42

SEGAL, ERICH (1996, ed.), *Oxford Readings in Aristophanes.* Oxford: Oxford University Press

—— (2001), *The Death of Comedy.* Cambridge, Massachusetts: Harvard University Press

SEIDENSTICKER, BERND (1969), *Die Gesprächsverdichtung in den Tragödien Senecas.* Heidelberg: Winter

—— (1982), *Palintonos Harmonia: Studien zu komischen Elementen in der griechischen Tragödie.* Göttingen: Vandenhoeck and Ruprecht

—— (1999), 'DDR II: Literatur, Musik und Bildende Kunst', in *Der Neue Pauly: Enzyklopädie der Antike*, xiii: *Rezeptions- und Wissenschaftsgeschichte*, A–Fo: 689–99. Stuttgart: Metzler

—— (2003), *"Erinnern wird sich wohl mancher an uns ... ": Studien zur Antikerezeption nach 1945.* Auxilia, 52. Bamberg: Buchner

—— (2005), *Über das Vergnügen an tragischen Gegenständen. Studien zum antiken Drama.* Munich: Saur

—— KRUMEICH, RALF, and PECHSTEIN, NIKOLAUS (1999, eds.), *Das griechische Satyrspiel*. Darmstadt: Wissenschaftliche Buchgesellschaft

—— and VÖHLER, MARTIN (2002a, eds.), *Mythen in nachmythischer Zeit: Die Antike in der deutschsprachigen Literatur der Gegenwart*. Berlin: De Gruyter

—— —— (2002b, eds.), *Urgeschichten der Moderne: Die Antike im 20. Jahrhundert*. Stuttgart: Metzler

—— —— and EMMERICH, WOLFGANG (2005, eds.), *Mythenkorrekturen: Zu einer paradoxalen Form der Mythenrezeption*. Berlin and New York: De Gruyter

SGARBI, VITTORIO (2002), 'La messa in scena di Ronconi a Siracusa', *Il Giornale*, 22 May 2002, 1

SHASTRI, P. N., and P. LAL (1974), *The Writers Workshop Handbook of Gujarati Literature*, vol. I. Calcutta: Writers Workshop

SHAW, GEORGE BERNARD (1949), *A Puppet Play*. Private edn.; first rehearsal copy. Reprinted 1950. Stratford-upon-Avon: Lanchester

—— (1950), *Buoyant Billions: Farfetched Fables, & Shakes versus Shav*. London: Constable

SHERRY CHAND, SARVAR V., and KOTHARI, RITA (2003), 'Undisciplined History: The Case of *Ras Mala*', *Rethinking History*, 7/1, 69–87

SHETH, JAYANA (1979), *Munshi: Self-Sculptor*. Bombay: Bharatiya Vidya Bhavan

SHEVELOVE, BURT (1975), *The Frogs*. Chicago: Dramatic Publishing Company

SHIRLEY, JAMES (1634), *The Trivmph of Peace. A Masque, presented by the Foure Honourable Houses, or Innes of Court. Before the King and Queenes Majesties, in the Banquetting-house at White Hall, February the Third, 1633*. London: William Cooke

—— (1646), *Poems &c*. London: printed for Humphrey Moseley

SICHEL, WALTER (1970 [1911]), 'The English Aristophanes', in John Bush Jones (ed.), 69–109

SIDNELL, M. J. (1991, ed.), *Sources of Dramatic Theory*. Cambridge: Cambridge University Press

SIDWELL, KEITH (2000), 'Athenaeus, Lucian and Fifth-Century Comedy', in Braund and Wilkins (2000, eds.), 136–52

SIFAKIS, G. (1992), 'The Structure of Aristophanic Comedy', *Journal of Hellenic Studies*, 112, 123–42

SILK, MICHAEL S. (1980), 'Aristophanes as a Lyric Poet', *Yale Classical Studies*, 26, 99–151

—— (1988), 'Pathos in Aristophanes', *Bulletin of the Institute of Classical Studies*, 34, 78–111

—— (1993), 'Aristophanic Paratragedy', in Sommerstein *et al.* (eds.), 477–504

—— (1998), 'Putting on a Dionysus Show', review of L. P. E. Parker (1997), Block (1997), and Rosenberg (1997), *Times Literary Supplement*, 4978 (28 Aug. 1998), 18–19

—— (2000), *Aristophanes and the Definition of Comedy*. Oxford: Oxford University Press

—— (2002), *Aristophanes and the Definition of Comedy*, corr. edn. Oxford: Oxford University Press

—— (2004), *Homer, The Iliad*, 2nd edn. Cambridge: Cambridge University Press

—— and STERN, J. P. (1981), *Nietzsche on Tragedy*. Cambridge: Cambridge University Press

—— and ANTHONY HIRST (2004, eds.), *Alexandria, Real and Imagined*. Aldershot: Ashgate

SILVER, ISIDORE (1954), 'Ronsard Comparatist Studies: Achievements and Perspectives', *Comparative Literature*, 6/2 (Spring), 148–73

SINGER, BARRY (2004), *Ever After: The Last Years of Musical Theater and Beyond*. New York: Applause

SINGH, NAGENDRA K. (2000, ed.), *Encyclopaedia of the Indian Biography*, ii. New Delhi: APH

SINGH, R. (1990, ed.). *Parsi Theater*. Jodhpur

SLATER, NIALL W. (2002), *Spectator Politics: Metatheatre and Performance in Aristophanes*. Philadelphia, Pennsylvania: University of Pennsylvania Press

SMITH, BRUCE R. (1988), *Ancient Scripts & Modern Experience on the English Stage, 1500–1700*. Princeton: Princeton University Press

SMITH, CECIL (1881), 'Actors with Bird-Masks on Vases', *Journal of Hellenic Studies*, 2, 309–14

SMITH, DANE FARNSWORTH (1936), *Plays about the Theatre in England, from The Rehearsal in 1671 to the Licensing Act in 1737; or, The Self-Conscious Stage and Its Burlesque and Satirical Reflections in the Age of Criticism*. London: Oxford University Press

—— and LAWHON, M. L. (1979), *Plays about the Theatre in England, 1737–1800: or, The Self-Conscious Stage from Foote to Sheridan*. Lewisburg and London: Bucknell University Press

SMITH, G. G. (1904, ed.), *Elizabethan Critical Essays*, 2 vols. Oxford: Clarendon Press

SMITH, MALCOLM (1986), 'Lost Works by Ronsard', *The Library: The Transactions of the Bibliographical Society*, 6th ser. 8/2, 109–26

SMITH, RICHARD LANGHAM (2006), 'Bloch, André', in L. Macy (ed.), *Grove Music Online*, http://www.grovemusic.com (accessed 10 July 2006)

SMITH, THOMAS L. (1963–83), *Literary and Linguistic Works*, ed. Bror Danielsson, 2 vols. Stockholm: Almqvist & Wiksell

SMITH, WILLIAM (1842, ed.), *A Dictionary of Greek and Roman Antiquities*. London

SNUGGS, H. L. (1950), 'The Source of Jonson's Definition of Comedy', *Modern Language Notes* 65, 543–44

SOFER, ANDREW (2003), '*Lysistrata*', review of the 2002 production by the American Repertory Theatre (Cambridge, Mass.), *Theatre Journal*, 55, 137–38

SOLOMON, R. H. (1994), 'Culture, Imperialism, and Nationalist Resistance: Performance in Colonial India', *Theatre Journal*, 46, 323–47

SOLOMOS, ALEXIS (1961), *O Zontanos Aristophanes*. Athens: Diphros

—— (1974), *The Living Aristophanes*, trans. Alexis Solomos and Marvin Felheim. Ann Arbor: University of Michigan Press

SOMMERS, MICHAEL (2004), 'From Ancient Greece to N.Y. via Lane', *The Star-Ledger (New Jersey)*, 23 July 2004

SOMMERSTEIN, ALAN H. (1993), 'Kleophon and the Restaging of *Frogs*', in id. *et al.* (eds. 1993), 461–76

—— (1996, ed.), *Aristophanes, Frogs*. Warminster: Aris and Phillips

—— (2001, transl.), *Wealth*, edited with translation and commentary. Warminster: Aris and Phillips

——HALLIWELL, STEPHEN, HENDERSON, JEFFREY, and ZIMMERMANN, BERNHARD (1993, eds.), *Tragedy, Comedy and the Polis*. Bari: Levante Editori

SONDHEIM, STEPHEN (1991), 'Stephen Sondheim in a Q&A Session: Part I', *Dramatists Guild Quarterly*, 28/11, 8–15

—— (2001), *The Frogs/Evening Primrose (2001 Studio Cast)*. Audio recording. New York: Nonesuch Records

—— (2005), *The Frogs (2004 Broadway Cast)*. Audio recording. Bronxville, New York: P.S. Classics

SONDHEIM.COM's 'Finishing the Chat', online at http://www.sondheim.com/community (accessed 3 October 2006)

SREBRNY, STEFAN (1984). *Teatr Grecki i Polski*. Warsaw: Państwowe Wydawnictwo Naukowe

STAËL, MADAME DE (1991 [1800]), *De la littérature*, ed. Gérard Gengembre and Jean Goldzink. Paris: Flammarion

STAFFORD, EMMA (2000), *Worshipping Virtues: Personification and the Divine in Ancient Greece*. London: Duckworth; Swansea: The Classical Press of Wales

STANLEY, THOMAS (1655), *The History of Philosophy*, 3 vols. London

—— (1663), *Aischylou tragoidiai hepta, cum […] versione & commentario*. London

STEGGLE, MATTHEW (1998), *Wars of the Theatres: The Poetics of Personation in the Age of Jonson*. Victoria, BC: English Literary Studies

—— (1999), 'Charles Chester and Ben Jonson', *Studies in English Literature, 1500–1900*, 39, 313–26

—— (2004), *Richard Brome: Place and Politics on the Caroline Stage*. Manchester: Manchester University Press

STEINER, GEORGE (1984), *Antigones*. Oxford: Clarendon

STENGEL, ALBERT (1911), *De Luciani veris historiis*. Dissertation: Rostock. Berlin: Ebering

STEPHENS, SUSAN A., and WINKLER, JOHN J. (1995, eds.), *Ancient Greek Novels: The Fragments*. Princeton, New Jersey: Princeton University Press

STEYN, MARK (1999), *Broadway Babies Say Goodnight: Musicals Then and Now*. New York: Routledge

STUCKE, FRANK (2002), *Die Aristophanes-Bearbeitungen von Peter Hacks*. Berlin: Tenea

SÜSS, WILHELM (1911), *Aristophanes und die Nachwelt* (Das Erbe der Alten, 2–3). Leipzig: Dieterich

—— (1954), 'Scheinbare und wirkliche Inkongruenzen in den Dramen des Aristophanes', *Rheinisches Museum für Philologie*, NF 97, 115–59, 229–54, 289–316

SUVIN, DARKO (1979), *Metamorphoses of Science Fiction: On the Poetics and History of a Literary Genre*. New Haven: Yale University Press

SWAYNE, STEVE (2005), *How Sondheim Found His Sound*. Ann Arbor: University of Michigan Press

TAPLIN, OLIVER (1977), *The Stagecraft of Aeschylus: The Dramatic Use of Exits and Entrances in Greek Tragedy*. Oxford: Clarendon Press

—— (1987), 'Phallology, *Phlyakes*, Iconography and Aristophanes', *Proceedings of the Cambridge Philological Society*, 33, 92–104

—— (1993), *Comic Angels and Other Approaches to Greek Drama through Vase-Paintings*. Oxford: Clarendon

—— (2003), *Greek Tragedy in Action*, 2nd edn. London: Routledge. First edn. published by Methuen in 1978, and reprinted by Routledge in 1989

—— (2007), *Pots and Plays: Interactions between Tragedy and Greek Vase-Painting of the Fourth Century BC*. Los Angeles: Getty Publications

TARIN, RENÉ (1998), *Le Théâtre de la Constituante ou L'école du peuple*. Paris: Champion

TAYLOR, DON (n.d.), 'Women of Athens, or Thezmofrogistrata', unpublished script

TEACHOUT, TERRY (2004), 'Nathan Lane Plays God', *The Wall Street Journal*, 23 July 2004

THEOBALD, LEWIS (1715a), *The Clouds. A Comedy. Translated from the Greek of Aristophanes*. London: Jonas Brown

—— (1715b), *Plutus: or, the World's Idol. A Comedy. Translated from the Greek of Aristophanes*. London: Jonas Brown

—— (1731), *Orestes. A Dramatick Opera*. London: John Watts

THIERCY, PASCAL (1986), *Aristophane: fiction et dramaturgie*. Paris: Les Belles Lettres

THOMAS, EDWARD (1903), *Oxford, Painted by John Fulleylove, Described by Edward Thomas*. London: A. & C. Black

TRACHTMAN, PAUL (2006), 'Dada', *Smithsonian Magazine* (May), online at http://www.smithsonianmagazine.com/issues/2006/may/dada.php (accessed 4 October 2006)

TRAPP, MICHAEL (1994, ed.), *Maximus Tyrius: Dissertationes*. Stuttgart: Teubner

TRENTIN, SABRINA (2001), 'Seneca fonte di *Médée* di Luigi Cherubini', *Rivista italiana di musicologia*, 36, 25–65

TREU, MARTINA (1999), *Undici cori comici: Aggressività, derisione e tecniche drammatiche in Aristofane*. Genoa: Dipartimento di Archeologia, Filologia Classica e loro Tradizioni, Università di Genova

—— (2002), 'Aristofane imbalsamato', *Diario della Settimana*, 7/35–36, 13 September 2002, 88–91

—— (2003a), 'Attualizzare? È un classico!', *Hystrio*, 16/2, 34–36

—— (2003b), 'La "strana coppia" di Siracusa', in Delfino Ambaglio (ed.), *Sungraphé: Materiali e appunti per lo studio della storia e della letteratura antica* (Pubblicazione del Dipartimento di Storia Antica, Università di Pavia), 191–207. Como: New Press

—— (2005a), 'Ragazzi, salvate il mondo!', *Hystrio*, 18/4, 85

—— (2005b), *Cosmopolitico: Il teatro greco sulla scena italiana contemporanea*. Milano: Arcipelago Edizioni

TREVELYAN, GEORGE OTTO (1869), *The Ladies in Parliament and Other Pieces: Republished with Additions and Annotations*. Cambridge: Deighton, Bell, & Co

TREVELYAN, HUMPHRY (1941), *Goethe and the Greeks*. Cambridge

TRILSE, CHRISTOPH (1979), *Antike und Theater heute: Betrachtungen über Mythologie und Realismus, Tradition und Gegenwart, Funktion und Methode, Stücke und Inszenierungen*, 2nd edn. Berlin: Akademie-Verlag

—— (1981), *Peter Hacks: Das Werk*, 2nd edn. Berlin: Das Europäische Buch

TRIPATHI, GOVARDHANARAMA MADHAVARAMA (1958), *The Classical Poets of Gujarat and their Influence on Society and Morals*, 3rd edn. (first published in 1894). Bombay: Forbes Gujarati Sabha

TURNER, FRANK M. (1981), *The Greek Heritage in Victorian Britain*. New Haven and London: Yale University Press

TYLEE, CLAIRE M. (1998), '"A Better World for Both": Men, Cultural Transformation and the Suffragettes', in Maroula Joannou and June Purvis (eds.), *The Women's Suffrage Movement: New Feminist Perspectives*, 140–56. Manchester and New York: Manchester University Press

UPTON, JOHN (1749), *Remarks on Three Plays of Benjamin Jonson, viz: Volpone: Epicœne: and The Alchemist*. London

VALPY, ABRAHAM JOHN (1812, ed.), *Comedies of Aristophanes, Translated into English with Notes* [= *Clouds* by Richard Cumberland, *Plutus* by Henry Fielding and Revd. William Young, *Frogs* by Charles Dunster, and *Birds* by 'A member of one of the Universities']. London: Printed for A. J. Valpy

VAN KERCHOVE, DIRK (1974), 'The Latin Translation of Aristophanes's *Plutus* by Hadrianus Chilius, 1533', *Humanistica Lovaniensia*, 23, 42–127

VAN LENNEP, WILLIAM, AVERY, E. L., SCOUTEN, A. H., STONE, G. W, and HOGAN, C. B. (1965–68, eds.), *The London Stage, 1660–1800: A Calendar of Plays, Entertainments and Afterpieces together with Casts, Box-Receipts and Contemporary Comment Compiled from the Playbills, Newspapers and Theatrical Diaries of the Period*, 5 parts in 11 volumes. Carbondale: Southern Illinois University Press

VAN STEEN, GONDA A. H. (2000), *Venom in Verse: Aristophanes in Modern Greece*. Princeton: Princeton University Press

—— (2001), 'Playing by the Censors' Rules? Classical Drama Revived under the Greek Junta (1967–1974)', *Journal of the Hellenic Diaspora*, 27/1–2 (2001), 133–94

—— (2002), 'Trying (on) Gender: Modern Greek Productions of Aristophanes' *Thesmophoriazusae*', *American Journal of Philology*, 123/3, 407–27

—— (2007), 'Enacting History and Patriotic Myth: Aeschylus' *Persians* on the Eve of the Greek War of Independence' in Emma Bridges, Edith Hall and P. J. Rhodes (eds), *Cultural Responses to the Persian Wars: Antiquity to the Third Millennium*, 299–329. Oxford: Oxford University Press

VARAKIS, ANGELIKI (2003), 'The Use of Masks in the Modern Staging of Aristophanes in Greece', PhD thesis submitted to Royal Holloway, University of London

—— (2004), 'Research on the Ancient Mask', *Didaskalia*, 6/1, published online at http://www.didaskalia.net/issues/vol6no1/varakis.html (accessed 13 October 2006)

—— (2006), *Antigone*, with commentary and notes by Angeliki Varakis. Methuen Student Edition. London: Methuen

—— (2007, forthcoming), *Oedipus the King*, with commentary and notes by Angeliki Varakis. Methuen Student Edition. London: Methuen

—— (2007, forthcoming), 'Body and Mask in Performances of Classical Drama on the Modern Stage', in Lorna Hardwick and Christopher Stray (eds.), *A Companion to Classical Receptions*. Oxford: Blackwell

VAROD, GIL (2004). '*The Frogs*: A "Broadway Abridged" Script', published online at http://www.broadwayabridged.com/scripts/frogs.shtml (accessed 12 November 2006)

VAROPOULOU, ELENE (1977), 'Aristophane: *Eirene*', *I Avyi*, 29 July 1977

—— (1982), 'Anazetontas ton Aristophane gia Miso Aiona: He Symbole tou Karolou Koun', *He Mesemvrine*, 16 July 1982

VASSEUR-LEGANGNEUX, PATRICIA (2004), *Les Tragédies grecques sur la scène moderne: Une utopie théâtrale*. Villeneuve-d'Ascq: Presses Universitaires du Septentrion

VASUNIA, PHIROZE (2001), *The Gift of the Nile: Hellenizing Egypt from Aeschylus to Alexander*. Berkeley and London: University of California Press

—— (2005), 'Greek, Latin, and the Indian Civil Service', *Proceedings of the Cambridge Philological Society*, 51, 35–71

VECCHI, GIAN GUIDO (2002), 'Escobar: bene il premier, l'arte non si giudica come un comizio', *Corriere della Sera*, 21 May 2002, 5

VENEZIANI, MARCELLO (2002), 'Sceneggiata greca', *Il Giornale*, 21 May 2002, 1.8

VIALA, ALAIN (1997, ed.), *Le Théâtre français, des origines à nos jours*. Paris: Presses universitaires de France

VILAR, JEAN (1961), *La Paix: transposition moderne de Jean Vilar, d'après Aristophane*. Paris: Théâtre National Populaire

VITEZ, ANTOINE (1995), *La scène, 1954–1975*, ed. Nathalie Léger, with preface by Bernard Dort, Tome 2 of *Écrits sur le théâtre*. Paris, P.O.L

VITTI, MARIO (1989), *I Genia tou Trianta: Ideologia kai morfi*, 3rd edn. Athens: Ermis

VLACHOS, G. (1946), 'The National Theatre' [in Greek], *I Kathimerini*, 4 May 1946

—— (1948), 'A Parenthesis. The National Theatre' [in Greek], *I Kathimerini*, 13 June 1948

VORSTER, CHRIS (1996), 'Paradox (with Apology to Aristophanes)'. Unpublished playscript in the archive of the Centre for Theatre and Performance Studies, University of Stellenbosch, South Africa

WALTON, J. MICHAEL (1987), *Living Greek Theatre: A Handbook of Classical Performance and Modern Production*. New York and London: Greenwood Press

—— (2006), *Found in Translation: Greek Drama in English*. Cambridge: Cambridge University Press

WASE, CHRISTOPHER (1649). *The Electra of Sophocles. Presented to Her Highnesse the Lady Elizabeth; With an Epilogue Shewing the Parallell in Two Poems, The Return, and The Restauration*. The Hague: Sam Brown

WEIMANN, ROBERT (1970), 'Zur Tradition des Realismus und Humanismus: Kontinuität und Hauptentwicklungslinien des humanistischen und realistischen Kunsterbes', *Weimarer Beiträge*, 16/10, 31–119

WERNER, JÜRGEN (1975), 'Aristophanes-Übersetzung und Aristophanes-Bearbeitung in Deutschland', in Hans-Joachim Newiger (ed.), *Aristophanes und die Alte Komödie*, 459–85. Darmstadt: Wissenschaftliche Buchgesellschaft

WEST, MARTIN L. (1992), *Ancient Greek Music*. Oxford: Clarendon Press

WETMORE, KEVIN J. (2002), *The Athenian Sun in an African Sky*. Jefferson, North Carolina, and London: McFarland

WHITE, JOHN WILLIAMS (1906a), 'The Manuscripts of Aristophanes. I', *Classical Philology*, 1, 1–20

—— (1906b), 'The Manuscripts of Aristophanes. II', *Classical Philology*, 1, 255–78

WICKERSHAM CRAWFORD, J. P. (1914), 'The Influence of Seneca's Tragedies on Ferreira's *Castro* and Bermúdez' *Nise Lastimosa* and *Nise Laureada*', *Modern Philology*, 12/3, 171–86

WILAMOWITZ = WILAMOWITZ-MOELLENDORFF, ULRICH VON (1922), *Pindaros*. Berlin: Weidmann

WILES, DAVID (2000), *Greek Theatre Performance: An Introduction*. Cambridge: Cambridge University Press

—— (2004), 'The Use of Masks in Modern Performances of Greek Drama', in Hall, Macintosh, and Wrigley (eds.), 245–63

WILLIAMS, MAYNARD OWEN (1949), 'War-Torn Greece Looks Ahead', *The National Geographic Magazine*, 96/6, December 1949, 711–44

WILSON, H. F. (1892), 'The *Frogs* of Aristophanes at Oxford', *The Academy*, 1035, 5 March 1892, 237–38

WILSON, N. G. (1992), *From Byzantium to Italy: Greek Studies in the Italian Renaissance*. London: Duckworth

WINER, LINDA (2004), 'Rehatching of *The Frogs* Packs in the Sondheim and Silliness', *Newsday*, 23 July 2004

WINTER, JOHN GARRETT (1933), *Life and Letters in the Papyri*. Ann Arbor, Michigan: University of Michigan Press

WRANGHAM, FRANCIS (1792), *Reform: A Farce, Modernised from Aristophanes*. London: Printed for R. Edwards

WREN, CELIA (2004), 'Days of Our Lives: In a Season of Decision, Artists and Their Companies Grapple with the Issues', *American Theatre*, 21/7 (September 2004), 20–24, 88–90

WRIGLEY, AMANDA (2008), *Greek Drama in Oxford and on Tour with the Balliol Players*. Bristol: Bristol Phoenix Press

YAJNIK, R. K. (1933), *The Indian Theatre: Its Origins and Its Later Developments under European Influence with Special Reference to Western India*. London: George Allen and Unwin

YARKHO, V. N. (2003), 'Адриан Пиотровский — переводчик Аристофана' ['Adrian Piotrovsky, the Translator of Aristophanes'], in A. Piotrovsky (tr.), Аристофан. Комедии. Фрагменты, 936–59. Moscow

YASHASCHANDRA, SITANSU (1995), 'Towards Hind Svaraj: An Interpretation of the Rise of Prose in Nineteenth-Century Gujarati Literature', *Social Scientist*, 23/10–12, 41–55

'Y.T.O.' (1894), *Aristophanes at Oxford. O.W. By Y.T.O.* [= Leopold Charles M. S. Amery, F. W. Hirst, and H. A. A. Cruso]. Oxford: Vincent

ZADAN, CRAIG (1986), *Sondheim & Co.* New York: Harper & Row

ZIMMERMANN, BERNHARD (1987), *Untersuchungen zur Form und dramatischen Technik der Aristophanischen Komödien*, iii: *Metrische Analysen*. Frankfurt: Hain

—— (1996), 'The Parodoi of the Aristophanic Comedies', in E. Segal (1996, ed.), 182–93. Oxford: Oxford University Press

—— (1998), *Die griechische Komödie*. Dusseldorf: Artemis and Winkler

ZYL SMIT, BETINE VAN (2003), 'The Reception of Greek Tragedy in the "Old" and the "New" South Africa', *Akroterion*, 48, 3–20

—— (2006), '*Antigone* in South Africa', in John Davidson, Frances Muecke, and Peter Wilson (eds), *Greek Drama III: Studies in Honour of Kevin Lee*, 281–98. Supplementary volume of the *Bulletin of the Institute of Classical Studies*, 87; London

—— (forthcoming, 2007*a*), '*Medea* in Afrikaans', in J. Hilton and A. Gosling (eds.), *Alma Parens Originalis? The Reception of Classical Ideas in Africa, Europe, Cuba and the United States*. Frankfurt am Main: Lang

—— (forthcoming, 2007*b*), 'Multicultural Reception: Greek Drama in South Africa in the Late 20th and Early 21st Centuries', in Lorna Hardwick and Christopher Stray (eds.), *The Blackwell Companion to Classical Reception*. Oxford: Blackwell

Synopsis of *Peace* sketched by Clarice Holt, 2006

INDEX

❖